C Programming

Including
Numerical and
Statistical Methods

C Programming

Including Numerical and Statistical Methods

Madhumangal Pal

Alpha Science International Ltd.
Oxford, U.K.

C Programming
Including Numerical and Statistical Methods
630 pgs. | 51 figs. | 23 tbls.

Madhumangal Pal
Department of Applied Mathematics with
Oceanology and Computer Programming
Vidyasagar University
Midnapore

ALPHA SCIENCE INTERNATIONAL LTD.
7200 The Quorum, Oxford Business Park North
Garsington Road, Oxford OX4 2JZ, U.K.

www.alphasci.com

Printed from the camera-ready copy provided by the Author.

ISBN 978-1-84265-758-4

Printed in India

Preface

The aim of this book is to provide its reader with a deep insight and knowledge of C language and a clear concept of programming. It is mainly intended for the under graduate students of all branches of Engineering and Science. This book not only fulfils the requirements of the students mentioned above, but will also be useful for the post graduate students and research scholars. A variety of worked out examples are included to promote the readers grasp of programming and a graded set of problems are given to test the skill of the readers.

The version of C used in this book is ANSI C, standardized by the American National Standard Institution (ANSI). With the detailed description of C this book contains an overview of numerical and statistical methods. This book is essential for the beginners as well for the experts in C.

The organization of the book is as follows:

Chapter 1 is devoted to the fundamentals of computer. In this chapter, different components of computer, software and programming languages are discussed. A brief introduction of internet is provided. Definition of algorithm and the basic steps to develop an algorithm is presented in Chapter 2. A large number of algorithms and flow-charts are designed in this chapter. Chapters 3 to 14 contain an indepth presentation of C programming language. In Chapter 3, constants and variables are discussed along with declaration of symbolic constants. In Chapter 4, expressions, library functions, unary, binary, logical, assignment, conditional and comma operators are discussed. Different types of formatted and unformatted input/output functions are discussed in Chapter 5. Control statements such as if, goto, while, do-while, break, continue, switch and for loops are explained with suitable examples in Chapter 6. Chapter 7 is devoted to subscripted variables. Chapter 8 contains an exhaustive study on user defined functions, recursion and storage classes. In Chapter 9, the concept of pointers is introduced. Passing pointers to a function, arithmetic on pointers, dynamic memory allocation, array of pointers and function as pointers are discussed. Chapter 10 deals with literal data manipulation. String manipulation functions and operators are introduced here. A large number of programs are designed related to string manipulation. Chapter 11 discusses special types of data, viz. structure and union. User defined data type, structure and pointers, passing structure to function and linked list are discussed with suitable examples. The techniques to use a data file are described in Chapter 12. Different types of data handling features, such as writing to a file, reading from a file, searching a file, appending a file, merging two files, updating a file are discussed with appropriate examples. Binary files and file positioning functions are introduced in this chapter. The special feature of C programming language is macro and preprocessor. They are discussed in Chapter 13. Command line parameters, multifile programs and bitwise operations are extensively explained with examples in Chapter 14. Chapter 15 is mainly devoted to numerical methods.

A brief discussion along with program is presented for each of the following topics: Interpolation (Lagrange (one and two variables), Newton, Spline), integration (trapezoidal, Simpson's 1/3, Gaussian-Legendre, Double, Monte-Carlo), solution of algebraic and transcendental equations (bisection, Regula-falsi, iteration, Newton-Rapson, roots of a polynomial equation, Newton-Rapson method for two variables), evaluation of determinant and inverse of a matrix by partial pivoting method, solution of system of equations (Cramer's rule, matrix inverse, Gauss elimination, LU decomposition, solution of tri-diagonal system, Gauss-Seidal iteration), ordinary differential equation (Euler's, modified Euler's method, Runge-Kutta methods, Runge-Kutta method for a pair of equations, Predictor-Corrector methods, IVP, finite difference method for IVP and BVP), and eigenvalues and eigenvectors of a matrix. In Chapter 16, a large number of programs are designed to solve problems on statistical analysis. In this chapter, we have classified statistical data into four categories, viz., simple distribution, ungrouped and grouped frequency distribution and bivariate distribution. For these distributions, the programs are designed to solve the following statistical parameters: mean, quartiles, mode, mean deviation, quartile deviation, standard deviation, moments, skewness, kurtosis, Beta and Gamma coefficient, etc. Bivariate and multiple correlation and regression analysis are also presented here. Programs to fit linear, parabolic and geometric curves are available in this chapter. Generation of random numbers and its applications are discussed in this chapter. In Chapter 17, quick references of escape sequence, key words, different types of operators, data types, ASCII character set, control statement summary, header files, some C constants and library functions are provided.

At first I would like to thank E. Balagurusamy and B. Gottfried as from their books I learnt my first lesson in the subject. In writing this book I have taken help from several books and some websites mentioned in the bibliography. So, I acknowledge them gratefully.

This book could not have been complete without support of my wife Anita and my son Aniket. I feel great reverence for my parents, maternal uncle and aunty, sisters, sister-in-law Sumita, brother-in-law K.K. Pal and relatives for their blessings and being a constant source of inspiration.

I express my gratitude and appreciation to the former and present heads of the Department of Applied Mathematics with Oceanology and Computer Programming, Vidyasagar University, for providing me with excellent facilities in the department.

I express my sincerest gratitude to my teacher Professor G.P. Bhattacharjee, Indian Institute of Technology, Kharagpur for his continuous encouragement. I would like to thank all my colleagues, particularly Dr. Biswajit Sarkar, who provided a friendly environment and helped me directly or indirectly. I am also thankful to all the staff of the department for their kind help.

I would like to thank my former and present research scholars Dr. Monoranjan Bhowmik, Dr. Akul Rana, Dr. Sukumar Mondal, Dr. Prasun K. Nayak, Dr. Sk. Md. Abu Nayeem, Nasreen Khan, Amal K. Adak, Tapan Senapati, Sanjib Mondal, Rajkumar Pradhan, Sovan Samanta and Satyabrata Paul for typing and scrutinizing the manuscript.

I will be happy to receive constructive criticisms for the improvement of the book from the experts as well as the learners. They can directly send their suggestion to me at *mmpalvu@gmail.com*.

I thank the Narosa Publishing House for their sincere care in the publication of the book.

Madhumangal Pal

Contents

List of Programs

Chapter 1

Fundamentals of Computer

1.1 Introduction

Today life can't think without computers. Computers are used in every area of human, viz. structural analysis, weather forecasting, petroleum exploration, fusion energy research, artificial intelligence, remote sensing, medical diagnosis, expert system, aerodynamics simulation, automation, defence, genetic engineering, socio-economic, tele and satellite communication and several other scientific and engineering applications. Particularly, reservation of tickets in airlines and railways, payment of bills, deposit and withdrawal of money from bank, mobile communication, preparation and printing of documents are the outcome of the advancement of the computers.

A computer can perform arithmetic operations and take logical decisions. It can work at a very high speed and is very reliable. Computer is a machine which is capable of solving problems and manipulating data. It accepts data, processes it by doing some mathematical and logical operations and produces desired output. However, there are various limitations. Human beings do calculation on their own. But, computer is a dumb machine and needs instruction to carry out its calculation. For this we need to know how a computer works?

A computer can (i) accept data, (ii) store data, (iii) process data as per the requirement, (iv) retrieve the stored data as and when required, and (v) print the result in desired format.

1.2 Characteristics of Computer

The major characteristics of a computer are:- speed, accuracy, diligence, versatility and memory. As mentioned earlier a computer can work very fast. For computer it takes only a fraction of second for calculations whereas we take hours or days to compute. For example, the weather forecasting that we see everyday on television is the result of compilation and analysis of huge amount of data containing temperature, humidity, pressure, etc. of various places. It takes few minutes for a computer to process this huge amount of data and give the output.

Again, the degree of accuracy of computer is very high and every calculation is performed with the same accuracy. The accuracy level of a computer depends on the basis of design method of the computer. The errors generated by a computer are due to human inefficiency or inaccurate data.

It should be remembered that a computer is free from tiredness, lack of concentration, fatigue, etc. It can work for hours without any error. If thousands of calculations are performed simultaneously , a computer will perform every calculation with the same accuracy and using the same amount of time.

A computer is versatile, which means that it can do different types of works individually and simultaneously. For example, a computer can play music, print a document, compile a program, search web, etc. simultaneously.

A computer can store a huge amount of data or information. Any information can be stored for infinite time period and recall or retrieve it whenever necessary. Thus, one can say that retention power of a computer is very high.

It is very interesting to know that, a computer can perform very fast and accurately, but its dependent on the instruction from the user. A computer cannot take its own decision as we can.

It has no feelings, emotions, taste, knowledge and experience. Thus, it does not get tired even after working for long. A computer has an in-built memory where it can store a large amount of data.

1.3 History of Computer

It has a long history which started when man counted large numbers. Here some path-breaking inventions are discussed in brief.

The first calculating device called **ABACUS** was developed by the Egyptian and Chinese people. The ABACUS means a calculating board. It consists of sticks in horizontal positions on which different numbers of beads are inserted. In 1617 A.D., English mathematician John Napier built a mechanical device for the purpose of multiplication. This device was known as **Napier's bones**. In 16th century, another English mathematician Edmund Gunter developed the slide rule. This machine could perform addition, subtraction, multiplication and division. It was widely used in Europe. At the age of 19, Blaise Pascal designed a machine that could add and subtract. The machine consisted of wheels, gears and cylinders. In 1673, a German philosopher and mathematician Gottfried Leibniz built a mechanical device that could perform both multiplication and division. A significant development of computing machine was achieved in the year 1823. A famous English man Charles Babbage built a mechanical machine which could perform complex mathematical calculations. It was known as **difference engine**. Later he developed a calculating machine called **analytical engine** for general purpose.

In the beginning of 19th century the mechanical calculator was developed and it was used to perform all types of mathematical calculations. It was widely used till 1960s. Later the rotating parts of the mathematical calculator were replaced by electric motors and borned electrical calculator. The electronic calculator was designed by electron tubes, which was bulky and later it was replaced by **transistors**, which became another calculator with small size. This calculator could perform all kinds of mathematical computations, and store some data permanently. Some calculators also have in-built programs which can perform some complex calculations.

1.3.1 Generation of computers

The evolution of computer started from 16th century and resulted in the modern computer. Also, the present day computer has undergone a rapid change during the last few decades. In a computer, the use of certain components to perform logic functions, repetitive functions to store data and instructions, makes a lot of difference in the capacity of the computer. The advancement of electronic computer technology is generally classified in five categories called the 'generations of computers'.

First generation computers (1945-1955)

The first electronic computer was built in 1946 at the University of Pennsylvania, USA by John Eckert and John Mauchy. This computer called Electronic Numerical Integrator and Calculator (ENIAC) used high speed vacuum tube switching devices, commonly known as **valves**. The ENIAC was 30-50 feet long, weighed 30 tons, contained 17,000 vacuum tubes, 10,000 capacitors and required 1,50,000 watts of electricity. Thus, this computer consumed a great amount of electric power, generated a great amount of heat and was bulky and less reliable. It had a very small memory and was designed initially to calculate the trajectories of missiles. The computation speed was in the range of 3000-5000 additions per second.

A major change occurred in the logic design of computer when the concept of **stored program** was proposed by John Von Neumann in 1946. Using this concept Von Neumann designed an Electronic Discrete Variable Automatic Computer (EDVAC). The concept of storing data and instructions inside the computer was introduced here. The computation became fast since it had rapid access to both data and instructions. For this concept, the computer could do logical decision internally. Soon after wards, M.V.Wilkes of Cambridge University implemented the EDSAC (Electronic Delay Storage Automatic Computer), the *first operational stored memory computer.*

Using the stored program concept, Von Neumann alone designed a new, unique and feasible architecture called the 'Von Neumann Architecture'. Nearly all the modern computers still use this architecture. It consists of five basic elements–input, memory, control unit, arithmetic logic unit and output.

Commercial production of stored program electronic computers began in early 1950s. In 1951, Ecker and Mauchly produced a unique type of computer called UNIVAC-I which was built by Universal Accounting Computer.

Second generation computers (1955-1965)

The discovery of transistor in 1948 at the Bell Laboratories brought a great deal of changes in computer architecture. A **transistor** is a tiny semi-conductor device of size

1/50th that of a valve and can perform most of the functions of a vacuum tube but is much faster with only a fraction of energy consumption and generates small amount of heat. The use of transistors had reduced the size, manufacturing cost, and running cost and improved the reliability and processing power of computer. These computers has a calculating speed ranging from 2000 to 50,000 additions per second.

Another major invention during this period was **magnetic cores** for storage. These are the tiny rings and can be magnetized in either clockwise or anticlockwise direction. The memory capacity of second generation computer is about 100KB. Magnetic disk storage was also developed during this period. Due to the availability of large memory, the high level programming languages – FORTRAN, COBOL, Algol, and SNOBOL were also developed. The operating system (OS) was also developed during this period.

Most of the computers developed in this period were used in business and industry. Several application programs were designed to solve the problems in inventory control, marketing, planning, etc.

Some of the computers of this generation are IMB-7000 series, IBM-1620, IBM-1401.

Third generation computers (1965-1975)

In late 1950's, a large number of transistors were put together on a single thin chip of silicon. This is called **integrated circuit (IC)**, commonly known as chip. These chips can be as small as 1/16th of a square inch, weighs a small fraction of an ounce only, requires only a bit of power and its production cost is very low. A small chip is equivalent to 200 to 2000 transistors. Some chips were also developed to store data. These constitute the memory chips. Computers using the integrated circuits are called third generation computers. These computers were small in size and greater in capacity and performed as many as ten million additions per second.

These were major improvements in the field of magnetic core memories and magnetic disks. The capacity of main memory increased about 4MB. The time shearing operating system was designed during the period.

The high level languages were improved. FORTRAN IV, COBOL 68 were standardized by American National Standard Institute (ANSI). BASIC was developed during this period. PL/1 was a powerful programming language.

Some of the computers of this generation are IBM 360, IBM 370.

Fourth generation computers (1975-1990)

In fourth generation, the computers microprocessor was introduced. The advancement of chip technology had come to be known as Large and Very Large Scale Integration (VLSI), where millions of transistors were packed in a single chip. The size of the chip got shrunk and its components multiplied.

During this period the magnetic core memories were replaced by semi conductor memories. The capacity of semiconductor memory was 16MB.

Using microprocessor, IBM (International Business Machine Corporation) developed an extremely powerful personal computer (IBM PC). The cost of computer came down rapidly. At the same time, a new company Microsoft, developed a very small OS called MS-DOS (Microsoft Disk Operating System). Another OS, UNIX was also developed during this period. Networks of computers and distributed computer systems were also developed. Disk memories had become very large around 1000 MB.

Microprocessors such as Pentium, Power PC, etc. were used as the CPU of PC and portable laptop. The size of hard disk (100 GB) and optical storage became very large. New optical disks known as DVDROM with maximum storage capacity of around 17GB were developed.

Several programming languages, viz. C, C++, Java, PROLOG, etc. were developed and popularized during this period.

Fifth generation computers

The computers of 1990s are said to be computers of fifth generation. The speed is extremely high. Apart from this it can perform **parallel processing**. In a parallel computer, a huge number of processors are attached with a global memory. The concept of **artificial intelligence** has been introduced to the computer to take its own decision. It is still in a developmental stage. The initiative was taken by various countries like Japan followed by UK, Europe, USA and India. But, there was no revolutionary change in architecture.

The grid-computing, cloud-computing and utility computing are some important development in the recent years.

1.4 Logical Organization of Computer

The main five components of a computer are (i) input unit, (ii) arithmetic and logic unit (ALU), (iii) Control unit (CU), (iv) memory, and (v) output input.

The functional relationship among the components are shown in Figure 1.1.

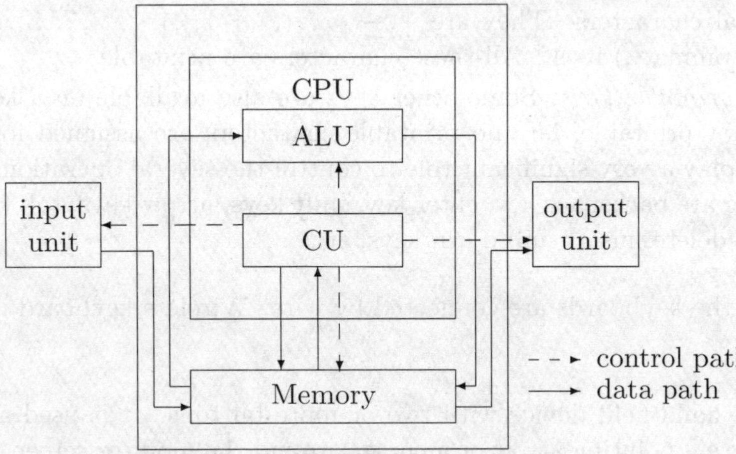

Figure 1.1: Functional relationship between the main components of a computer.

The communication between human and computer is done through the **input** and **output units**. The units through which the computer reads data or information are called input units. All the arithmetic and logical calculations are done in the arithmetic logic unit. The control unit acts as a supervisor in a computer. The information received from input unit is stored in the memory. The fundamental unit to measure capacity of memory is called byte, 1 byte is equal to 8 bits (0 and 1 are called bits). Other units are kilobyte (KB), (1KB = 1024bytes), Megabyte (MB) (1MB = 1024KB), Gigabyte (GB) (1GB = 1024MB), Terabyte (trillion TB) (1TB = 1024GB) and Petabyte (PB) (1PB = 1024TB).

All the results which are stored in the memory can be inscribed on an output unit. The ALU and CU together is called the Central Processing Unit (CPU) or simply a **processor**.

All these units are described in the subsequent sections.

1.5 Input Units

At present a variety of input units are used by computers. The most common input units are keyboard and mouse. The other input units are scanners, magnetic ink character readers, optical mouse readers, optical character readers, bar code readers, etc.

Keyboard

Every computer contains a keyboard as is the standard input unit and is used for entry of manual data. All the keys of a keyboard are categorised into five groups:-

- *Letter keys:* There are 26 keys allocated for 26 (upper and lower cases) English alphabets.
- *Digit keys:* Two sets of digit keys are available in a keyboard. For each set 10 keys are allocated for 10 numeric digits.
- *Special character keys:* The characters other than alphabets and digits are called special characters. They are +, −, ∗, /, (,), {, }, [,], <, >, ?,′, ”, ., !, @, #, $, %,^ , & and comma (,) itself. All these characters are printable.
- *Non-printable keys:* Some other keys are also available on a keyboard, but they are not printable, i.e. no printable characters are assigned for them, but these keys play a very significant role to control the several operations of the computer. These are backspace key, enter key, shift keys, arrow keys, tab key, ctrl keys, ALT keys, delete, insert, up, down keys, etc.

Most of the keyboards are connected by wire. Wireless keyboard is also available.

Mouse

Mouse is a hand-held device with two or more buttons. It is used as a locator and is used to move a pointing arrow or a cursor around the monitor screen to locate a desired point. An application program/command can be invoked by pressing appropriate mouse button at a proper position on the screen. Most of the mouse are connected by a wire with the computer. However, wireless mouse is also manufactured. Currently *optical mouse* is also available with the computer.

Video terminal (VDU)

The keyboard and the television screen together form a video terminal. When a key is pressed, the corresponding character (if it is printable) is displayed on the screen, and the cursor moves to the next position to display the next character. A cursor is an underline, a small arrow or a small rectangle which can move horizontally and vertically on the screen and indicates the position of a character.

Generally, a VDU is classified as an output unit, because the computed results are displayed on it, even though it is a part of an input device. When a character is pressed, it is immediately displayed on the screen, and one can verify whether the correct key has been pressed or not.

VDU uses cathode ray tube (CRT) for a long time, which is low priced, with a good colour resolution and is easy to view from any angle. It also has some disadvantages. It is long (around 20 cm), heavy, contains powerful magnets, needs more desk space, needs high voltage to accelerate the electron beam, CRT is not used in the laptop due to heavy weight and high power consumption. These drawbacks are removed in the flat screen displays.

Normally, in a screen 80 characters can be displayed along a horizontal line and 24 such lines exist. That is, a full screen is divided into $80 \times 24 = 1920$ locations, wherein each location is called a **pixel**. A character is displayed by a matrix of 5 pixels along the horizontal direction and 7 pixels in the vertical direction. Each character on the keyboard has a unique binary code. When a key is pressed, an appropriate coded series of electrical pulses are send to the memory and the corresponding character will be displayed on the screen.

Flat panel display

The laptop computers use flat panel display and is also gaining popularity for desktop PCs, due to its several advantages. It is light, consumes less power, does not require high voltage, screen is flat, thin (less than 3 inches depth) and hence occupies less desk space.

But, it is costly and has a narrower viewing angle, i.e. the display cannot be seen from side rather than straight.

Scanner

Through keyboard only text can be entered to the computer. It is not useful in case of entering a picture. Scanner is an optical device that can input any graphical image, which may be handwritten document, a typed, a printed document or a picture. A scanner reads an image, convert it into a set of 0's and 1's and stores them into memory. If the image is drawn over a pixel, then 0 is taken as an input for this pixel, otherwise it is taken as 1 (for black and white image). This representation is called the **bitmap** of the image.

Two major types of scanners are available – one is a hand-held scanner (MICR, OMR, OCR, Bar code reader) and other a flat bed scanner. The scanner can also store colour images. A 24-bit representation for each pixel is used to represent a maximum of $2^{24} = 4$ million colours. A bitmap image takes a huge amount of space to store it in the computer memory. But, before storing the image, it can be compressed by some softwares. Two popular formats for compressed bitmaps are **gif** (graphics interchange format) and **jpeg** (joint picture experts group). The compressed picture may be decompressed by using an appropriate software.

Magnetic Ink Character Recognition (MICR)

This device is widely used by banks to process large number of cheques and drafts. In this method, the characters are printed on documents (say cheques or drafts) using a special *magnetic ink*. In a cheque, cheque number and branch code are preprinted, using magnetic ink. These characters can be identified by a magnetic ink character reader. The amount may also be printed by magnetic ink. If a cheque enters into the reading unit it passes through the magnetic field which enables the read head to recognize the characters of the cheque.

Optical Mark Reader (OMR)

This technique is used when students have appeared in multiple choice test and they have to mark their answers by darkening a square or a circular space by pencil or ink. The main advantage of this method is that data is entered at its source and no further transcription is required, which also minimizes data entry errors. But, the response sheet should be entered into the device accurately.

Optical Character Recognition (OCR)

This technique is used to direct the reading of any printed or hand written characters. Suppose we have a sheet of paper containing hand written or printed characters and it is entered into the scanner. A character pattern is compared with a site of patterns stored inside the computer. Whichever pattern is matched it is called character read. Pattern that cannot be matched are rejected. OCRs are expensive particularly while identifying handwritten characters.

Bar Code Recognition

Bar code is the filled rectangular regions with varying thickness and spacing and it is generally printed on books, tags, badges, packets, etc. These bars are read by the optical readers and converted to the electrical pulses. The pattern of the bars is unique for a particular item, and these bars are read by a hand-held optical device and converted to bits. These devices are used in the retail stores, transaction of books in library, etc.

The other input devices are digital camera, web-camera, joystick, track ball, touch pad/screen, light pen, microphone, graphics tablets, blue tooth, biometric devices, etc.

1.6 Output Units

The most popular output device is Visual Display Unit (VDU) and other output devices are printer, plotter, etc. The VDU is discussed as an input device, it is also used as an output device. Printers, microfilm units are called **hard copy** devices as the data is printed on paper or microfilm and the printed document can read directly. There is another type of output device called **soft copy** devices (floppy disk, hard disk, CDROM, DVDROM, pen drives) which stores data as bit strings. To read the data stored in soft copy devices a computer is required.

Printers

It is an important output device which can be used to print a copy of the processed texts or results or graphics pictures on paper. Different types of printers are designed for different types of applications depending on their speed and approach of printing. Printers are classified as **impact** and **non-impact**. The impact printers use the familiar type writer approach of hammering a type face against the paper and ribbon. Dot-matrix printers are of this type. Non-impact printers do not hit or impact a ribbon to print. They use electro-static chemicals and ink-jet technologies. Laser printers and ink-jet printers are of this type.

Dot-matrix printers

These printers are also called *serial printers.* In a dot-matrix printer, the print head consists of an array of 24 pins arranged vertically. The printer head is moved horizontally. This printer prints 360×180 dots per inch. Dot-matrix printer can print text and graphics. The quality of colour is not good.

This printer receives a single (coded) character at a time from the memory and decodes it by the printer and activates the appropriate pins in the print head. These pins are moved forward and hit the ribbon in front of the paper to print the character. The printer head can move in both directions (bidirectional), i.e. left to right and from right to left.

The printing cost is very low and multiple copies can be taken by inserting carbon paper between two or more papers, hence these printers are very popular for the office use.

Ink-jet printers

This is one type of non-impact printer. The printer head of this printer contains a number of small holes or nozzles. The appropriate holes are heated very rapidly by an integrated circuit resistor. The ink near the heated resistor vaporizes and is ejected through the nozzle and makes a dot on the paper. A high resolution ink-jet printer can print 300 dots per inch. This printer has its own memory and can print 120 characters per second. Ink-jet printer also uses its print colour document and graphics. The printing cost is very high and multiple copies cannot be taken.

Laser printers

In dot-matrix and ink-jet printers the head of printer the moves on the paper. This mechanical movement is relatively slow. In laser printer, this mechanical movement is eliminated. In this printer, an electronically controlled laser beam is used to print a character on a photo conductive drum. The drum attracts an ink toner on the exposed areas and the image is transferred to the paper which is in contact with the drum. The printing quality (600 dots per inch) including graphics, is excellent, but the printing cost is high. Colour laser printer is also available but it is very expensive.

The cost of printing is highest for ink-jet, medium for laser and lowest for dot-matrix printers. But, the printing quality is highest for laser, medium for ink-jet and lowest for dot-matrix printers.

Plotters

It is used to draw a good quality graph. A plotter consists of a rotating drum and a pen. A paper is mounted on a rotating drum and a pen is mounted on a carriage which is perpendicular to the direction of drum rotation. The drum can move in clockwise and anticlockwise directions and the pen can move from left to right, right to left and up or down. The movements of the pen and drum are controlled by the graph plotting software.

The other output devices are projector, speaker, etc.

1.7 Memory

A memory unit or storage is an integral part of a computer system. Its primary function is to store all the information needed by the system. Generally, a memory unit holds programs and data. The performance of a computer largely depends on the organization, storage capacity and speed of operation of the memory system. In a broader sense, a computer memory can be logically divided into three groups – internal memory, main (primary) memory and secondary (auxiliary) memory.

The primary or internal storage section is made up of several small storage locations called **cells**. Each of these cells can store a fixed number of bits called *word length*. Each cell has a unique number assigned to it which is called the address of the cell and it is used to identify the cells. The address starts from 0 and goes up to the capacity of the memory and it is numbered as hexadecimal numbers. Thus, a memory location has two things – one is the address and other is the value stored in it.

1.7.1 Internal memory

It refers to the set of registers which constitutes the CPU. These registers hold temporary results when a computation is in progress. Since the registers and CPU are fabricated with the same technology, there is no speed disparities between them. But, the cost of internal memory is very high, therefore, few registers (usually 8 to 16) are included in the CPU.

1.7.2 Primary memory

Computer memory is used to stored two things – instructions to execute a program and data. When the computer performs any task, the data which is required for the task is stored in the primary memory. This data may come from an input device or from a secondary memory. The CPU can directly access the items are stored in the primary memory. Thus, all the programs and data must be stored in the primary memory to speed up the execution of program. Generally, MOS (Metal Oxide Semiconductor) technology is used to construct primary memory. Usually, the size of the primary memory is much larger than the internal memory, but its operating speed is slower than the processor registers speed.

RAM

If the time needed to access a memory location (cell) in a memory does not depend on the address of the cell, the memory is called **Random Access Memory** (RAM). This memory can randomly select and use any location of the memory directly to store and retrieve data. The main memory of a computer is called Random Access Memory. The RAM can be divided into two groups – read-write and read only. Normally, read-write random access memory is referred as RAM. It takes same time to access all memory locations. After getting an address, one can either read the stored contents from the memory location or write new contents in the memory location. The instructions and data stored in the RAM are temporary, which means that all the information stored in the RAM will disappear when the power to the computer is switched off. This type of memory is called **volatile** memory.

Semiconductor RAM

Semiconductor RAMs are of two types – static (SRAM) or dynamic (DRAM). The static RAM uses bipolar or MOS flip-flops (the fundamental device of memory, a flip-flop can store one bit of information), data is retained indefinitely as long as power is applied to the flip-flops. A dynamic RAM is designed as MOSFETs (Metal Oxide Semi-Conductor Field Effect Transistor) and capacitors that store data. The data stored in DRAM are refreshed every few milliseconds. Both the RAMs are volatile.

ROM

A Read Only Memory (ROM) is the simplest kind of memory. It is equivalent to a group of resisters, wherein each stores a data word permanently. The ROM stores some standard processing programs (such as tables of trigonometric functions, I/O programmes, small programs for special applications) during manufacturing. The ROM can only be read by the CPU, but it contents cannot be changed. The ROM is a non-volatile memory.

PROM

This is a particular type of ROM. We have seen that it is not possible to modify or erase programs stored in ROM, but is possible by a user to store his/her own special program in PROM (Programable Read Only Memory). Once a program is written in PROM, it cannot be changed and remains unchanged even if the power is off. This means that the information written in PROM or ROM cannot be modified or erased.

EPROM

EPROM (Erasable Programable Read Only Memory) is a special kind of ROM. The data stored in this type of ROM can be erased by passing a strong ultraviolet light through a window. All bits are erased and become 0. It can be reprogrammed using a special programming facility. When the EPROM is in use the information can only be read. This type of EPROM is known as UVEPROM.

The information stored in EPROM can also be erased by electrical pulses instead of ultraviolet light. This type of EPROM is called EEPROM (Electrically Erasable Programmable Read Only Memory).

Flash memory

It is a kind of EEPROM, but the technology used in it is different. It is designed by semiconductors and is non-volatile. Flash memory is of two types – NOR flash and NAND flash. NAND flash is widely used and is known as pen drive, memory stick and hard drive.

Cache memory

The speed of CPU is very high as compared to the access time of primary memory. Therefore, the performance of CPU decreases due to the slow speed of main memory. In such a situation, the system performance can be significantly improved by adding a small, expensive, but fast buffer memory between the CPU and the main memory. This memory is called cache memory. Accessed speed of cache memory is much more than RAM. It is used to store programs or data currently being executed or temporary data frequently used by the CPU. It is also very expensive to have a large cache memory and its size is normally small.

1.7.3 Secondary memory (storage)

As discussed in the previous section, the speed of primary memory or main memory should be very fast to increase the performance of CPU. But, the high speed memory is very expensive. Also, the storage capacity of main memory is limited, but the modern computer process a huge amount of data. To store such data, additional memory is required. This memory is called **secondary memory** or **auxiliary memory** or **storage**. The cost of secondary memory is low, the operating speed is slower than the main memory. It is non-volatile, can store huge amount of data and transferred to the primary memory as and when required.

The commonly used secondary memories are – magnetic tape, magnetic disk, floppy disk, hard disk, external hard disk, optical disk (CD-R, CD-RW, DVD-R, DVD-RW), pen drive, zip drive, memory cards, etc.

Magnetic tape

A magnetic tape consists of the electrical, mechanical and electronic components to provide the parts and control the mechanism for a magnetic tape. It is a strip of plastic coated with a magnetic recording medium. This device can stop, start to move forward or in reverse, and can also rewind. It is slow, inexpensive and non-volatile.

Magnetic disk

A magnetic disk is a circular metal plate coated on both sides with a thin film of magnetic material. Both sides of the disk are used and several disks are stacked on one spindle to make a disk pack. The disk pack is sealed and mounted on a disk drive. Each side which is called surface of the plate consists a read/write head. All disks rotates on its axis at a speed of around 7200 revolutions per minute. Bits are stored in the magnetized surface in spots along the concentric circles called **tracks**. The tracks are commonly divided into sections called **sectors** (see Figure 1.2).

In most systems the minimum quantity of information which can be transferred is a sector.

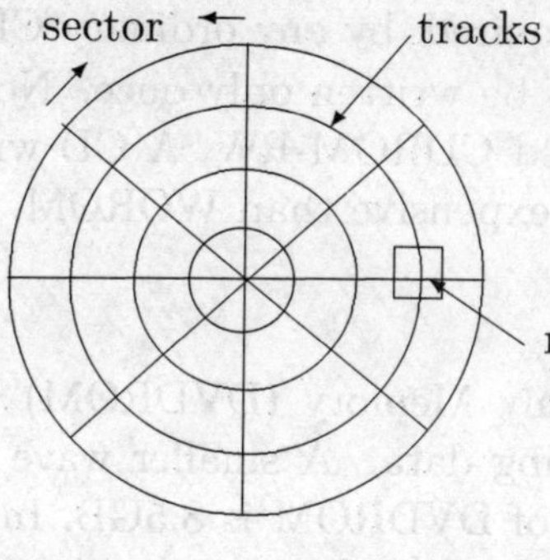

Figure 1.2: A surface of a plate

Read/write operations on a disk starts at sector boundaries. Assume b bytes are stored per second, s sectors are there per track, t tracks per surface and n plates ($2n$ surfaces). The capacity of the disk is then $b \times s \times t \times 2n$ bytes and if d is the diameter of the disk in inches, the density of the recording is $bs/(\pi d)$ bytes/inch.

Disk that are permanently attached to the unit assembly and cannot be removed by the occasional user are called **hard disks**. A disk drive with removable disk is called a **floppy disk**. There are two size of diameters, 5.25 and 3.5 inches. The 3.5 inches disk is smaller and can store 1.44MB data, whereas the capacity of 5.25 inches floppy is 360KB. It is a low cost device, but at present floppy disks are obsolete due to the emergence of flash memory.

Optical disk

The latest and the most popular high capacity secondary storage is known as Laser Disk Technology. Optical disks are of different types, as discussed below:

CDROM

Compact Disk Read Only Memory (CDROM) are made of reflective metals. CDROM is written by high power *laser beam* during the process of manufacturing. Its storage density is very high and can store more than 650MB of data, i.e. storage cost is very low. It is a shiny metal like disk whose diameter is 5.25 inches. The latest model of CDROM can read 7.8MB data per second. The disk speed of a CDROM is indicated by the notation nx, where n is an integer and indicates the factor by which the original nominal speed of 150KB/sec is to be multiplied. Thus, the reading speed of a 12x CDROM is 12×150 KB/sec $= 1800$ KB/sec.

As the CDROM can only be read, therefore we cannot write or make changes in the data contained.

Recordable CDROM or Write Once CDROM-WOROM

User cannot write anything on the CDROM. The WOROM allows the user to write data permanently on the disk. Once the data is written, it can never be erased. A laser beam is used to write data. A WOROM can store vast amount of data and the data can be read as many time as required, by any ordinary CDROM drive.

Old model of CDROM could be written only once. Now a days erasable-rewritable CDROM is available. It is called CDROM-RW. A CD writer can be used to write on this medium. This CD is more expensive than WOROM.

DVDROM

Digital Versatile Disk Read Only Memory (DVDROM) uses the same principle as a CDROM, for reading and writing data. A smaller wave length laser beam is used in DVDROM. The total capacity of DVDROM is 8.5GB. In double sided DVDROM two such disks are attached back to back and hence the size becomes 17GB. The 1x speed of DVDROM is 1.38MB/sec.

Writable DVDROMs called DVD-RW are also being introduced.

Solid state disks (Pen drives)

The hard disk (magnetic disk) takes more time to read data due to the mechanical rotation of the disk as compared to solid state disks. There are two types of solid state disks – DRAMs and flash memories. Flash memories are non-volatile, low cost, (DRAMs are volatile and higher cost), consume less power, have no rotating mechanical disk and the access time is very low. For these reasons flash memories, commonly known as **pen drives** are now being very popular. User can read and write data on these devices easily.

1.8 Central Processing Unit (CPU)

The arithmetic logic unit (ALU) and the control unit (CU) of a computer are jointly called the central processing unit. The CPU is referred as the brain of the computer.

Arithmetic Logic Unit (ALU)

The actual processing of the data and instruction (stored in primary memory) are performed by ALU. The major operations, viz. addition, subtraction, multiplication, division, logic and comparison are performed by the ALU. Data is transferred to ALU from primary memory when required. After processing, the output is send to the primary memory for further use.

Control Unit (CU)

The next component of CPU is control unit. This unit acts like a supervisor. The control unit determines the order in which computer programs and instructions are executed. CU also interprets the instructions and issue the necessary signals for other units of the computer to execute them. It also acts as a switch board operator when several users access the computer simultaneously. Therefore, it coordinates the activities of computers peripheral (the modem/Internet adapter, switch/hub, router, etc.) equipment as they perform the input/output. Thus CU is a manager of all operations.

1.9 Software and Programming Languages

In previous sections, we have discussed the different components of the computer. All the components of a computer can be divided into two major groups, viz. hardware and software (see Figure 1.3). **Hardware** is a machine itself which has various individual parts, viz. all mechanical, electronic and magnetic devices such as monitor, electronic circuit, floppy disk, hard disk, etc.

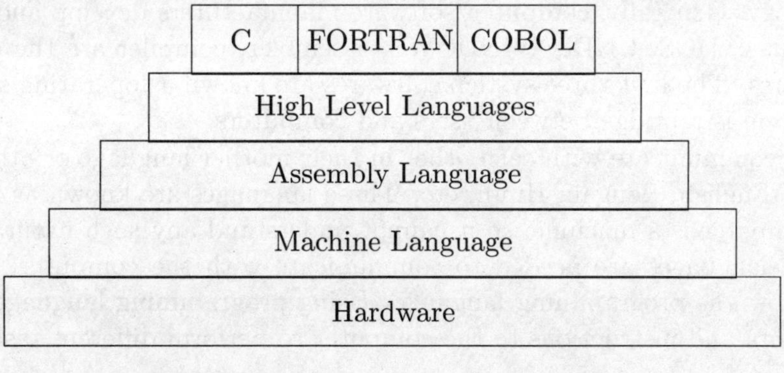

Figure 1.3: Layers of hardware and languages

Also, we know that computer cannot do any task without instructions from the user. To perform a specific task a user should supply a sequence of instructions to the computer. The sequence of instructions is called a **computer program**. **Software** is a set of computer programs. Also, we can say that it is a collection of programs, which increase the capabilities of the hardware. Software instructs the computer at every step where and when to start and stop during the execution of a particular task. The process of software development is known as **programming**.

Without the software a computer is a box of metal and without hardware components the software becomes meaningless. Thus software and hardware are complementary to each other. Hardware is one-time investment whereas software production is difficult, expensive and a continuous process.

1.9.1 Types of softwares

Computer software is normally classified into two broad categories, viz. application software and system software. **Application software** is a set of programs required to carry out different operations to solve a specific problem. Application softwares are useful for word processing, reservation (railways, airlines and others), billing system (electric bill, telephone bill, etc.), accounting, preparation of report, analysis of various data for research, weather forecasting, solution of a mathematical problem, preparation of merit list, etc. On the other hand, **system softwares** are general programs that are written for the system which creates an environment for writing of application softwares and for the operations of computer system as a whole. When a computer is on, the program written in ROM is executed which activates different units of the computer and makes it ready for the work. Thus, system software may be defined as a set of one or more programs designed to control the operations of computer system.

System software communicates with various hardware like printers, card readers, disks, ports, etc. It is also required to develop the application softwares. Note that it is not possible to run application software without system software. Design of system software is a very complicated task and it requires an extensive knowledge of the computer technology. Generally, computer/software manufacturers develop and supply the system softwares. DOS, UNIX, WINDOWS, assembler, compiler are the examples of system softwares. The first three system softwares are known as operating system. The operating system is a bridge between users and computers.

The people communicate with each other in their mother language or other common languages like English, Bengali, Hindi, etc. These languages are known as natural languages. A computer is a machine, so it cannot understand any such natural language. Thus, specific languages are needed to communicate with the computer. These languages are known as programming language. Using programming language a user can transfer the data and instructions to the computer to perform different tasks.

1.9.2 Programming languages

There are two major types of programming languages, viz. low level languages and high level languages. Further, low level languages are divided into machine language and assembly language. Low level languages are machine oriented and requires extensive knowledge of computer hardware and its organization.

Machine language

Machine language is directly understood by the computer. It does not require any conversion/translation. This language written in strings of 0's and 1's, i.e. all the instructions written in this language uses only 0 and 1. For example, an instruction written in machine language looks like 1100 1000. If an instruction is send to the computer, it recognizes the codes and converts it into electrical signals which are required to run it.

This language is considered as the first generation language. The only advantage of this language is that a program written in this language runs very fast because no translation is required for the CPU. But, this language is not suitable to write a program, because the programmer has to know the details of the hardware and has to remember a large number of codes to write a program. It is also difficult to debug the program.

Assembly language

The first step in developing the programming language is the introduction of the assembly language. It is considered as a second generation language. At this time the computer can handle numbers and alphabets. Therefore, some combination of numbers and alphabets (called mnemonics) are used to represent operation codes and addresses. That is, the binary codes used in machine language are replaced by mnemonics. The assembly language programs are written using a set of mnemonics and a translator program is required to translate the assembly language program to equivalent machine language program. There is a one-to-one correspondence between the assembly language program and the equivalent machine language program. This language is *machine dependent.* The program written in assembly language is called **source program**. This program is converted in to machine language program by a translator known as **assembler**. The translated program is called **object program** which is equivalent to machine language program. The assembler is a system program which is supplied by the computer manufacturer.

This language is better than machine language. The program written in assembly language has the same efficiency of execution as the machine level language, because there is one-to-one translation between these languages. From this machine language program one can get back the unique assembly language program. One of the major disadvantage of assembly language is that it is machine dependent. That is, if a program is written for one computer it may not run in the other computers.

High level languages

To write a program in machine language or assembly language, deep knowledge about the computer system is required. This difficulty has been removed in high level languages. Most of the computer programs are written in a language whose instruction set is more compatible with human languages and human thought process. The high level languages are like English and is easy to understand by any user. These languages are not machine dependent. A single instruction in a high level language is equivalent to several instructions in machine language. Programs written in high level languages can be run on any computer. High level languages have three significant advantages over the machine language, viz. simplicity, uniformity and portability, i.e. machine independence. A computer can directly understand the machine language but cannot understand assembly or high level languages.

Like assembly language program, the program written in high level languages can be converted to the equivalent machine language program. This conversion is done by **compiler** or **interpreter**. The program written in high level language is called **source program** and the translated program is known as **object program**. There is a one-to-one contact between the assembly language and machine language program, but it does not exist for high level language and machine language. Every high level language must have its own compiler or interpreter. Figure 1.4 shows the flow of the conversion from source program to object program.

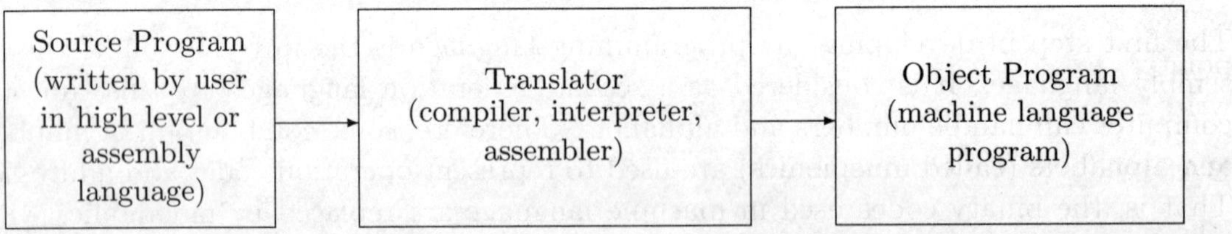

Figure 1.4: Conversion from source program to object program.

Compiler is a translator that translates the program written in high level language to machine level language. It compiles machine language instructions for every program instructions of high level language. The compiler is similar to assembler, but it is more sophisticated. It reads the entire program at a time and then translates it into machine language. After compilation one can execute the program. A compiler can translate only those source programs for which it is designed. For example, the compiler for C cannot compile the program written in FORTRAN.

Interpreter is another type of translator, which also translates a programme written in high level language to machine language. It considers one statement at a time, translates it into machine language and immediately executes it. Translation and execution are carried out statement-by-statement.

The interpreters are easy to write and do not require large memory space during the translation of the program. It eliminates the need for a separate compilation after modification of a statement. The disadvantage of an interpreter is that it is time consuming method, because each time a statement is translated and executed and same process is applied for next statement. Thus, compiled machine language program runs much faster than an interpreted program.

Now, some brief outlines are given for some commonly used programming languages.

FORTRAN

The first high level programming language developed was FORTRAN (FORmula TRANslation). It is still the most widely known programming language. It was developed at IBM by John Backus and his team (1954-1957) and was called FORTRAN I. FORTRAN was originally developed for manipulation of numerical data. Since then, FORTRAN has attracted wide attention and has undergone a number of changes and each new version is made, with a few changes in the basic statements and includes some additional features. The two major versions are FORTRAN II and FORTRAN IV. The FORTRAN was standardized in 1966 by the ANSI After standardization a FORTRAN program written for one computer could be run on another computer without any modification and then its applications evolved from strictly numerically oriented to move general applications involving character and file manipulations. A new FORTRAN standard (ANSI X3.9-1978) known as FORTRAN 77, was approved in 1977. Several new features were included in this version to make it more structured. FORTRAN is now a very popular language and is used by most engineers, mathematicians, statisticians, business analysts and other professionals.

The latest version of FORTRAN is known as FORTRAN 90. It includes recursion, pointers, modules, etc. Recently, FORTRAN 95 has been developed and it is useful to write a program for parallel computers.

BASIC

The expanded form of BASIC is Beginners' All purpose Symbolic Instruction Code. It was developed by John G. Kemeny and Thomas E. Kurtz at Dartmouth College, USA in 1963. This language is designed for the beginners as is very simple. The pictures can easily be drawn with the graphics feature of BASIC and the initialization of graphics is very simple. The BASIC programs are translated by interpreter. This language is commonly available with DOS operating system. BASIC language has not been standardized.

COBOL

The full form of COBOL is COmmon Business Oriented Language. The development of this language was started in 1959 under the leadership of Commander Grace Murray Hopper at Department of Defence, USA and it was first published in 1960 and revised in 1965. ANSI (American National Standards Institute) standardized it in 1968, 1974 and 1984. The object oriented features were introduced in 1997. This language was mainly used for business data processing, and is also used to write many legacy systems. It is a truly machine independent language and is quite close to English.

Pascal

This is a high level programming named after the French mathematician Blaise Pascal. This language was developed by Niklaus Wirth in 1971. It is a structure programming language, simple and logical. Pascal has been standardized by International Standards

Organisation (ISO) and ANSI. This language is useful to manipulate numerical data as well as a string of characters, sets, records, files, lists, vectors, matrices, etc. Pascal is an attractive language for professional computer scientists.

C

C language was developed by Dennis Ritchie at Bell Telephone Laboratories, USA in 1972. It is a general-purpose programming language with rich set of operators, modern flow control, data structures, and supports low level programming. It is not specialized to any particular area of application. C was mainly designed for and implemented on an operating system known as UNIX. The operating system, the C compiler and all essential UNIX applications programs are written in C. Many programs written for UNIX can be easily used by a C programmer to write application programs.

C becomes a powerful programming language because user can access the addresses (called pointer) in memory where the variables are stored. The access of pointers and the operations on it are the features of C language, and these are not available in any other high level language. C has been standardized by ANSI in 1983. The main disadvantage of C is extensive use of pointers, it is difficult to read a program and understanding of what it does.

C++

C++ is an Object Oriented Programming (OOP) language. It was developed by Bjarne Stroustrup at AT &T Bell Laboratories, USA in 1983. This language is the super set of C language. It includes all features of C and added new facilities. These are classes, derived classes, constructors and destructors, friend functions, virtual functions, data encapsulation and protection, inline functions, function and operator overloading, new libraries, etc. This language is extremely suitable to design a large software.

In languages such as C, FORTRAN, a problem is divided into some small problems and a routine (function or subroutine) is designed for each such problem and the solution of the original problem is obtained by combining them.

In OOP, the problem is solved based on the data called object. That is, in OOP the objects are identified and the operations are applied on them to solve the problem.

Java

This is another popular Object Oriented Programming language and widely used in computer Internet. Java achieved machine independence by defining a Java virtual machine for which the compiler is designed. It is a hypothetical machine which can be simulated by a software. A Java program compiled for the virtual machine is then executed on any machine by an interpreter which generates machine code.

Markup languages

A markup language is used to describe the content and structure of a document. In this language a symbol is added to a document which adds special meaning to the document.

It is used to design web pages for Internet applications and link to other documents. This language is standardized and is independent of computer hardware and operating system. HTML, XML are the examples of markup language.

Scripting languages

Scripting language is a high level language, which is used to combine several independent programs. The combined program finally solves a complex task. **Unix shell** programming is one of the old scripting language. Recently, Visual BASIC, PERL, etc. are widely used as scripting languages.

Publishing languages

These languages are used to prepare a document such as letter, report, book, etc. Word processor is the simplest publishing language. Another such language is LaTex. This language receives a set of commands and produced an output as .dvi file or .ps (postscript) file. Other popular publishing languages are page marker, TEX, etc.

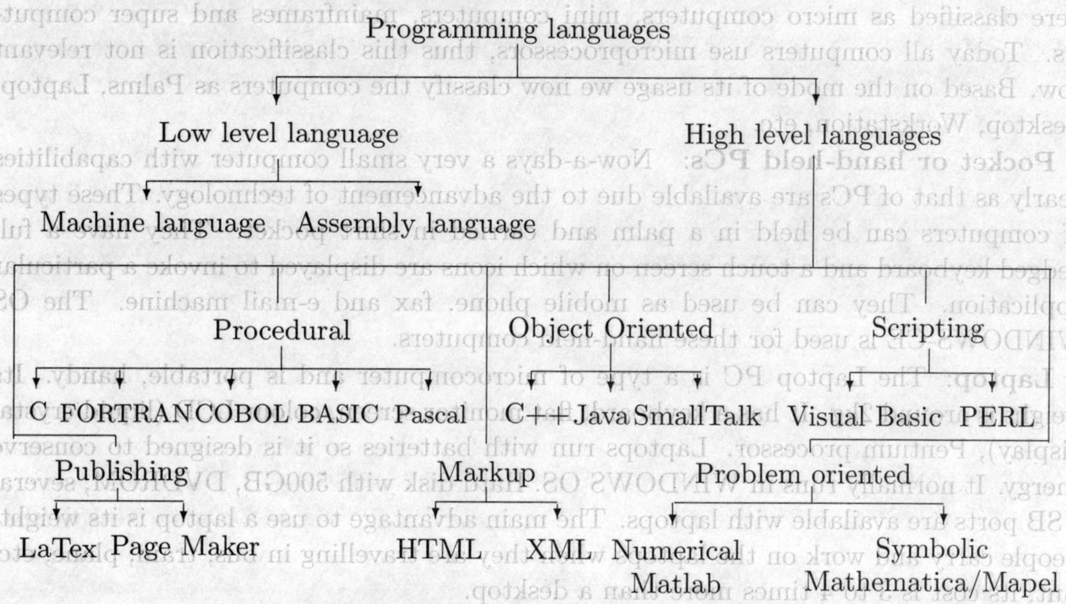

Figure 1.5: Classification of programming languages

1.10 Operating System

The operating system (OS) mainly performs resource management and human-to-machine translation functions. The resources are CPU, memory, I/O devices, etc. It is another computer program that instructs the computer what to do under a variety of conditions. Major OS functions include efficient sharing of the memory, I/O peripherals and CPU among several users. That is, an OS is:

(i) an interface between hardware and users,

(ii) a manager of system resources in accordance with system policy to achieve system objectives.

One of the old OS is DOS (Disk Operating System). A DOS called MS-DOS (Microsoft Disk Operating System) is widely used. The size of this OS is very small and it is not suitable for present day high powerful microprocessors. For these microprocessors the new OSs have been developed. These new operating systems are WINDOWS XP, WINDOWS 7, designed by Microsoft Corporation and UNIX.

The UNIX OS was developed by Ritchie and Thomson at the Bell Telephone Laboratories, USA in 1973. It is a multiuser, time sharing operating system and is written in C language. Different versions of UNIX are available today. The IBM version of UNIX is known as AIX, Hewlett Packard's version of UNIX is called HP-UX and Sun's version is known as SOLARIS. An open source version of UNIX is called LINUX.

1.11 Types of Computers

Depending on the size, efficiency, memory and number of users, initially the computers were classified as micro computers, mini computers, mainframes and super computers. Today all computers use microprocessors, thus this classification is not relevant now. Based on the mode of its usage we now classify the computers as Palms, Laptop, Desktop, Workstation, etc.

Pocket or hand-held PCs: Now-a-days a very small computer with capabilities nearly as that of PCs are available due to the advancement of technology. These types of computers can be held in a palm and carried in shirt pocket. They have a full fledged keyboard and a touch screen on which icons are displayed to invoke a particular application. They can be used as mobile phone, fax and e-mail machine. The OS WINDOWS-CE is used for these hand-held computers.

Laptop: The Laptop PC is a type of microcomputer and is portable, handy. Its weight is around 2kg. It has a keyboard, flat monitor screen, colour LCD (liquid crystal display), Pentium processor. Laptops run with batteries so it is designed to conserve energy. It normally runs in WINDOWS OS. Hard disk with 500GB, DVDROM, several USB ports are available with laptops. The main advantage to use a laptop is its weight. People carry and work on the laptops when they are travelling in bus, train, plane, etc. But, its cost is 3 to 4 times more than a desktop.

Desktop PCs: At present desktop PCs are most popular as most of the people use PCs. At present Intel Pentium core duo processor and WINDOWS-XP, WINDOWS 7, GNU/Linux OS are used in the PCs. A PC may have a large main memory (512MB to 6GB), a large hard disk (80 to 500GB), a flash ROM, CD/DVD ROM and several USB ports.

Workstations: These are also desktop PCs. But, they are more powerful and its processor speed is 10 times more than a PC. Generally, workstations have a large colour monitor, a large main memory (1GB to 6GB), a hard disk (80 to 500GB) and good graphics facilities. The common OS is UNIX. A workstation can execute multiple tasks at a time. The status of the process during their execution are displayed by a system called X Windows. The workstations can be connected to a Local Area Network (LAN).

Servers: Due to the advancement of processor, presently there is no difference between high end PCs and workstations. The workstations are generally used for interactive programming, whereas servers are used for special purpose such as high performance numerical computing, web page hosting, data base storage, e-mail server, printing, etc. Servers must have high performance processors with large main memory, a very large hard disk. Large monitor screens are not necessary. Servers are generally connected to a computer network along with several PCs.

Mainframe computers: These types of computers generally use 32-bit microprocessors. They operate at a very high speed, have very large storage capacity and can handle the work load of memory users. They are generally used in centralized databases. For example, bank process large number of transactions on-line. They require computers with very large disks to store a huge amount of data and transfer the data from disk to main memory at several hundred MB/sec. At present a very few companies are manufacturing mainframe computers and the number of mainframe users is going down.

Super computers: These computers are the fastest and most expensive machines. They have high processing speed as compared to other computers. These computers support multiprocessing technique. One of the ways in which supercomputers are designed is by interconnecting hundreds of microprocessors to achieve their speed. These are normally used to solve problems which require intensive numerical computations. Example of such problems are numerical weather prediction, designing supersonic aircraft, design of drugs and modelling complex molecules, etc. Examples of supercomputers are CRAY YMP, CRAY XMP, CRAY 2, NEC SX-3, and PARAM designed in India.

1.12 Computer Network

A **computer network** is an interconnection of various computer systems situated at different positions. In a computer network two or more computers are connected together with data communication devices for communication and sharing resources. In the network the individual computers are known as **nodes** or **workstations** or **terminals**. The computer which provides resources to the other computers is called **server**.

The computer network may be classified in two broad categories based on the geographical area. These are local area network (LAN) and wide area network (WAN).

1.12.1 Local Area Network

The network which is used to connect the computers in a single room, or rooms within a building or buildings on one site are called Local Area Network. Usually, LAN links within a limited geographical area because they must be connected by a cable. Wireless LAN is also available now. LAN transmits data with a speed of several megabits per second. A LAN gives the simultaneous access to some application softwares which are designed for multiple users. Also, the people on LAN can share a printer, a CDROM drive, a modem, a scanner, a fax machine, etc. Even if a LAN crashes, each person may continue working on his or her personal computer.

The following six operations can be performed with a LAN:

(i) **Share files:** If a file is stored in a server, that file can be accessed by several users on LAN simultaneously.

(ii) **Transfer files:** A LAN allows to copy files from machine to machine without using a floppy, CD, pen drive, etc. This is especially useful for large files which cannot fit on a single disk.

(iii) **Access information and files:** LAN users can access any software tools, application softwares from any computer which is connected with LAN.

(iv) **Share applications:** Same copy of any application software (such as Microsoft Word, Power Point, etc.) may be used simultaneously with different computers of a LAN, but two users cannot edit the same documents simultaneously.

(v) **Printer sharing:** One or more printers connected with LAN can be accessed from any computer of the same LAN.

(vi) **Electronic mail or e-mail:** LAN is used as a postoffice also. Through LAN one can send letters, reports, documents, etc. to other people. A LAN e-mail system can receive any message even when people are away from the computer.

Components of LAN

A LAN is constructed by computers, LAN cables, network adapter cards, network operating system software and LAN application software. Each workstation and file server contains a network adapter card and all workstations and file servers are connected by LAN cables or other media.

A LAN can use one of the several transmission media such as twisted-wire cable, coaxial cable, fiber-optic cable, radio waves, infrared waves, etc. The wireless LAN uses infrared or radio waves.

A special type of software called network operating system is required in a LAN. The popular network operating system softwares are NetWare, WINDOWS for Workgroups, WINDOWS 95, WINDOWS NT, WINDOWS XP, WINDOWS 7, OS/2, etc.

1.12.2 Wide Area Network (WAN)

A LAN works within a small area, whereas WAN is used to describe a computer network extending to a regional, national or global area. For example, the head office of the IGNOU (Indira Gandhi National Open University) is situated at New Delhi and the regional offices are situated in overall India. All the regional offices are connected to head quarters through WAN. The distance between computers on WAN is larger than LAN. So, the transmission medium used in WAN are generally telephone lines, microwaves and satellite links. The examples of WAN are Ethernet, Arpanet.

Difference between LAN and WAN

(i) LAN works within a small geographical area, whereas WAN covers a large region and operates nation wide and even world wide.

(ii) Computers and other peripheral devices in LAN are generally connected with wires and coaxial cables. In WAN, communication is done through telephone lines and satellite links.

(iii) Cost of data transfer in LAN is less, because the transmission is done through its own medium. But, in WAN the transmission cost is very high, because the transmission medium used is hired, through telephone lines or satellite links, and some cost have to be paid to the government.

(iv) The speed of transmission is much higher in LAN than a WAN.

(v) The communication errors in LAN is less than WAN.

1.12.3 Internet

An **Internet** is a network of computer networks (see Figure 1.6). A huge number of computers all over the world are connected through the Internet. Any person in the world can contact with another anywhere in the world through Internet. If a computer is connected to the Internet, then one can connect to millions of computers. Through Internet one can gather information and distribute his own information to the people across the world. Information in every field, viz. education, science, health, medicine, history, business, news, etc. can be obtained through Internet. Several softwares, programs, pictures, movies, etc. can also be downloaded from any where in the world.

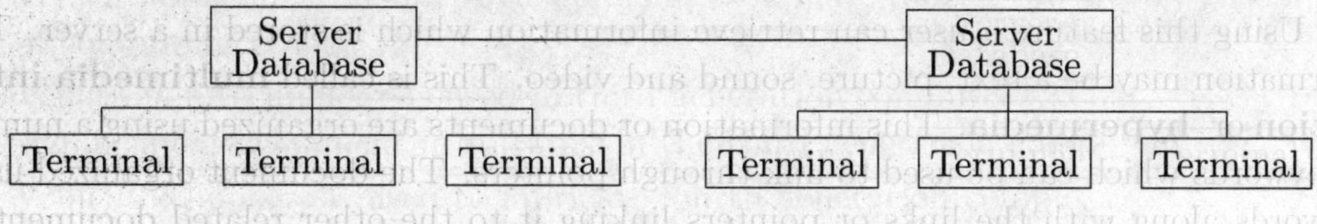

Figure 1.6: A network of networks

Origin of Internet

The first work on Internet was started by Advanced Research Projects Agency Network (ARPANET) by the Department of Defence, USA in 1969. The ARPANET started with a small network consisting of three computers. Later, several Universities and R&D organizations were to connected to the network. In a very short time, students linked their own campus networks into ARPANET, using a well-defined protocol called TCP/IP (Transmission Control Protocol/Internet Protocol). Around 1980, National Science Foundation Network (NSFNET) was created and ARPANET was handed over to it. Then NSFNET connected all regional networks. At present several millions host are connected to the Internet.

Internet services

Most of the Internet services are free of cost, but to connect the Internet, some money has to be paid to the Internet Service Provider (who provides the Internet service to the users).

The following are the common Internet services:

(i) **Electronic mail (e-mail):** Sending and receiving mails electronically. This is most widely and commonly used service of the Internet. The e-mail is similar to our conventional mails. But, in e-mail information/data is transmitted through Internet electronically (by sending a file), and hence any information/data can be transferred to any destination in the world within a few minutes.

If an e-mail address of a person is known, then anybody can send e-mail to that person at any time at any place of the world. An e-mail has two parts and they are separated by @ (the at sign). The first part before @ is the mailbox, which may be a personal name, and the part after @ is the domain name, usually the name of the computer. An e-mail address may look like `mmpalvu@gmail.com`

(ii) **File Transfer Protocol (FTP):** Transfer of files from one computer to another remote computer.

(iii) **Telnet:** Using this feature one can logon to a remote computer where the computer is attached directly to the network, wherein the user has a permission. By logging on to a remote computer, one can use its resources, such as softwares, lots of information, data, even some special devices like printer, scanner, camera, etc.

(iv) **World Wide Web (WWW):** This is another widely used service in the Internet. Using this feature a user can retrieve information which is stored in a server. This information may be a text, picture, sound and video. This is called **multimedia information** or **hypermedia**. This information or documents are organized using a number of keywords which can be used to link through pointers. The document organized using keywords along with the links or pointers linking it to the other related documents is called a **hypertext**. A particular rule is used to mark the keywords and links in hypertext and this rule is known as **hypertext mark up language (html)**. The world wide web is a hypertext based page that links a page to the other pages through out the global Internet. A **webpage** is simply a title, a collection of information, which serves as a pointer or hyperlink to other information. A computer of the Internet can store many webpages and this computer is called a **website**. Every webpage has a unique address called Universal Resource Locator (URL). To transfer files from one computer to another on the web, a special set of rules is used. This is called **hypertext transfer protocol (http)**. For example, the web address (URL) of Vidyasagar University is

`http://www.vidyasagar.ac.in`

To retrieve information from webpage a software called **search engine** is required. The information is retrieved by using appropriate keywords with the help of suitable search engine. At present the most popular search engine is **Google**.

Internet service provider

The Internet service provider is basically a server and it is directly connected to the Internet. The connection of a local computer to the Internet is done through a service provider. In India, Bharat Sanchar Nigam Limited (BSNL) is an Internet service provider and its services are available over the country. Other service providers are Airtel, Vodafone, Reliance, etc.

Exercise I

Review Questions

1. What are the main components of a computer system?
2. Draw a block diagram of a computer with its major components showing the transfer of data amongst themselves.
3. Write a short note on generations of computers.
4. Which technologies are used in different generations of computers?
5. Who designed the first electronic computer and when? What was it called?
6. Who invent the concept of stored program? What is the advantage of stored program?
7. Which type of memory is used in first generation computer? What languages were available in first generation computer?
8. What is the main difference between first and second generations of computers? Which type of operating system was used in second generation computer?
9. Which important software developments took place during the second generation of computers?
10. What main technology is used in third generation computer? What was the most significant development in software in the third generation computer?
11. Which technology is used to fabricate fourth generation computers?
12. What do you mean by input/output devices? Give some examples of commonly used input and output devices.
13. What is OCR? Where is it used?
14. Where is the use of MICR?
15. What is a bar code? Where is bar code used? What are the advantages of using a bar code?
16. What do you mean by hard copy and soft copy? Explain.
17. What is the difference between impact printer and non-impact printer? Which type of printers is better and why?
18. Compare inkjet printer and dot-matrix printer.
19. Compare inkjet printer and laser printer.
20. What is computer mouse? How is it used?

21. What is the purpose of the main memory of a computer? What do you mean by volatile and non-volatile memories? Give examples.
22. What is the fundamental (basic) unit to measure memory? Write the relations between bit, byte, KB, MB, GB, TB and PB.
23. Explain Random Access Memory. Compare it with Read Only Memory. Can a ROM be a RAM?
24. What are the differences between ROM and RAM?
25. What is a flash memory? What are its advantages?
26. What is a CDROM? Compare it with hard disk and floppy disk. How is data recorded on a CDROM?
27. What is a DVDROM? What are the differences between CDROM and DVDROM? What is the major application of the DVDROM?
28. Explain cache memory.
29. What do you mean by CPU, ALU and CU? Explain each of them in detail.
30. What is a CPU? Name the different components of the CPU and mention their functions.
31. What is the main purpose of control unit? How does the control unit work?
32. What do you mean by mainframe computers, microcomputers, personal computers, terminals/workstations, servers?
33. What do you mean by computer hardware and computer software?
34. What do you mean by system programs and application programs? Give examples of system programs and application programs.
35. (i) What are machine language, assembly language and high level langauge ?
    (ii) What are the differences between high level and low level languages?
36. (i) What are the differences between source program and object program?
    (ii) How a source program is converted into an object program? Explain with a diagram.
37. What do you mean by assembler, compiler and interpreter? Compare a compiler with an interpreter.
38. What is the difference between a program and a software? What do you mean by programming?
39. Write a brief note on each of the following languages:
    (a) FORTRAN, (b) BASIC, (c) COBOL, (d) Pascal, (e) C, (f) C++, (g) Java.
40. What are scripting languages and markup languages? What is their use?
41. What is an operating system? Why is it essential in a computer?
42. Explain the operating systems WINDOWS and UNIX. What is LINUX?
43. What do you understand by laptop, personal computer, minicomputer, mainframe computer and workstation?
44. What do you understand by super computer? What are the applications of the super computers?
45. What do you mean by LAN, WAN and Internet?

46. What services are provided by the Internet? Describe them briefly.
47. What are the advantages of the networks?
48. Write short notes on e-mail, FTP, Telnet, www.
49. Which services are available by a PC when it is connected to the Internet. Describe them.
50. What do you mean by Internet Service Provider? What is the role of it in the Internet?
51. Write short notes on workstation, server and LAN cables.
52. What is the world wide web? What is a web page? What are html and URL?

Chapter 2

Algorithms and Flowcharts

2.1 Algorithms

The central concept in computer science is algorithm. The word 'algorithm' originated from the Persian word 'algorism'. The meaning of algorithm is 'any special method of solving a certain kind of problem'.

An **algorithm** is a finite sequence of steps/instructions to solve a particular type of problem. For example, if an algorithm is designed to find the maximum among n numbers, then the algorithm finds the correct answer for any set of data. The possible steps are:

(a) Input

(b) Computation and decision

(i) assignment, (ii) decision, and (ii) iteration or repetition

(c) Output

An algorithm should follow the following criteria:

(i) *Input*: An algorithm has precise inputs which are externally supplied.

(ii) *Definiteness*: Each step must be clear, complete and unambiguous.

(iii) *Finiteness*: An algorithm should terminate after finite number of steps.

(iv) *Effectiveness*: All the steps specified in an algorithm should be executed in a finite amount of time.

(v) *Generality*:An algorithm should be designed in such a way that it can solve any particular type of problem for which it is designed.

(vi) *Output*: It has at least one output.

An algorithm can be described in many different ways. A natural language such as English may be used to design an algorithm but we must be careful that it is concise and satisfies all the conditions of the properties of algorithm and the code by which an algorithm is designed is known as **pseudo code**. There are no definite rules for describing algorithm but the main objective is that it should be easily understandable and the logic put in it should be able to solve the problem. It may be remembered that an algorithm is independent of any programming language.

In the following, two simple problems are considered and their algorithms are designed.

Example 2.1.1 Write an algorithm to find the area of a triangle whose three sides a, b, c are given.

Step 1: Read the sides as a, b, c.
Step 2: Compute $s = (a + b + c)/2$.
Step 3: Compute $area = \sqrt{s(s-a)(s-b)(s-c)}$.
Step 4: Print *area*.
Step 5: Stop.

Example 2.1.2 Write an algorithm to find the maximum among three numbers a, b, c.

Step 1: Read the numbers as a, b, c.
Step 2: Set $Big = a$.
Step 3: If $Big < b$ then set $Big = b$.
Step 4: If $Big < c$ then set $Big = c$.
Step 5: Print the maximum number *Big*.
Step 6: Stop.

The above two algorithms may also be written in other ways, but the logic must be same.

2.2 Main Steps to Solve Problems on Computer

The following steps should be followed sequentially to solve a problem on the computer.

(i) **Statement of the problem**: In the first step, to solve a problem on the computer, we must identify what are the inputs and outputs of the problem and what are the other information such as, working formula, termination condition, etc., available in it. If sufficient information is not available, then it is not possible to solve the problem by computer.

(ii) **Development of a model**: This is a very crucial and complicated step. Based on the problem, mathematical and logical formulae are developed to solve the problem. During the development of a model extreme care should be taken to design the correct model, because the solution of a problem depends on the mathematical/logical expressions.

There is no general rule to develop a model, it depends on the problem itself.

(ii) **Design of an algorithm**: This is a major step in solving a problem. If a method is known to solve the given problem then it is to be listed carefully as a sequence of statements. These sequence of statements will give the solution of the given problem. If a method is not known, then a suitable algorithm is required to be developed. Each algorithm should have the following features: (a) it should have a finite number of inputs, (b) it must terminate after a finite number of steps, (c) all the steps must be precise and unambiguous, (d) all statements are executed in a finite number of time, and (e) it must have at least one output.

(iv) **Correctness of the algorithm**: This is the most important step in designing an algorithm. After designing an algorithm it must be checked whether the algorithm will give correct answer for all possible inputs. This is a very difficult task. People generally think that, if the result obtained from the algorithm/program is same as the result obtained by hand calculation or known values, then the algorithm is correct. But, this is not always true. Because, it is not possible to test an algorithm/programm by entering all possible input values. There is no general rule to prove the correctness of an algorithm, but following guidelines may be followed:

Try to give justification for each step. It is better to establish a lemma/theorem (with proof) about the conditions involved in a step.

(v) **Construction of a flowchart**: Draw a flowchart of the algorithm. The flowchart is easy to understand (rather than the algorithm), and shows how the problem is solved by the computer.

(vi) **Writing a program (or coding):** Choose a programming language which is familiar to you and code the algorithm/flowchart into this programming language. The coding is the translation of algorithm/flowchart into the exact instructions of the programming language. At the time of coding the vocabulary and syntax rules of the language should be followed. Also, the programmer must be clear about the variables, their types, size of array (if there be any), need of linked list and subroutine/function. During coding, it is better to include comments/headings to improve the readability of the program. After writing a program, it must be entered in the computer through the keyboard with the help of an editor, which is usually available in the operating system. The particular coding can significantly affect both the memory requirements and the speed of the algorithm.

(vii) **Compilation and debugging**: After entering the program in the computer it is compiled by a compiler, (e.g. if the program is written in C language then it is to be compiled by the C compiler). The compiler will make an object program out of the source code, if there is no error or bugs in it. If there is any bug or error in the program then it is checked and made error free. This process is known as **debugging**. The errors which occur at the time of compilation are of two kinds: (i) syntax error and (ii) logical error (or execution error). If any statement violates the rules (syntax) of programming language in use, then the corresponding error is called a **syntax error**. But, even if the program is written maintaining and following all the rules of the programming language (i.e. compiles correctly), it may try to do something which is impossible or unintended (e.g. a loop is not terminated, gives an incorrect results etc.). Then **logical error** occurs. In this step the program should also be tested by some known input and output. After debugging, the program becomes error free and logically correct and so gives correct result.

(viii) **Analysis and complexity of the algorithm**: It is obvious that to solve a problem, different algorithms/programs may be designed by different programmers. One algorithm may be 'better' than other. To identify the 'better'/'best' algorithm we have to analyze the algorithms. Two parameters are generally estimated to analyze an algorithm, they are time and space complexities. Computation of space complexity is easy, because the space complexity determines the number of variables which are used in the algorithm. But, computation of time complexity is not easy. This depends on some assumptions. We assume that a random access machine is available which allows to access or store any element in a fixed amount of time. In an algorithm several different types of operations such as addition, subtraction, multiplication, division, comparison, etc. are involved. These operations take a fixed amount of time and we assume that their time is bounded by a constant. This is not true for all operations. For example, comparison of two strings (sequence of characters) depends on the comparison of two characters. The comparison of a character needs a fixed amount of time, so comparison of strings depends on their length. Even then we assume that to compare two strings takes a constant time.

For an algorithm/program two types of times can be determined. One is machine time (i.e. the time required to run a program) and other is theoretical bounds (a function which bounds the algorithm's computing time). Our aim is to determine the total time which the statement will spend during executing, with some initial statement of input data. This requires two information, the statements's *frequency count* (i.e. the number of time the statement will be executed) and the time for one execution. The product of these two numbers is the total time. The time per execution depends on the machine being used and the programming language together with its compiler, so the machine time is not unique and hence by computing the machine time one cannot compare two programs/algorithms. But, the frequency count of an algorithm is unique for an algorithm/program. This number can be determined directly from the algorithm, independent of the machine and the programming language. Thus, by using the bounds of frequency count one can compare two algorithms/programs. This method of analysis is free from any real machine and programming language.

By analyzing algorithms the weaker algorithm should be improved or discarded.

(ix) **Program testing:** Once a program has been written one can run it to get a result. In this step, the program is being tested for different types of data.

Sometimes it may happen that the algorithm/program is theoretically correct and also produces correct result for some sets of input, but gives incorrect result for other sets of input. For example a program to compute $n!$ will produce correct answer for low values of n, but it gives incorrect answer for large values of n. This type of serious mistake is generally identified during the testing of a program.

(x) **Documentation:** Sometimes it is hard to read a program, specially when it is written by other programmer. So, it is better to write some comments about the steps, particularly complicated steps. The most obvious reason for documentation is to enable individuals to understand a program which is not written by them. The best way to do this is to write code that is clear and self explaining.

The formal definition of time complexity is given below.

The **time complexity** of an algorithm is given by a function $T(n)$ which is the maximum over all input of size n, of the sum of the time required by each instruction executed. For a problem of size n, the maximum time required to solve the problem over all input sequences of that size is called the *worst case time complexity.* The minimum time taken by an algorithm to solve a problem for a particular set of input is called *best case time complexity.* Sometimes, it may happen that some algorithms take different amount of time for different sets of input. The average of time taken by the algorithm for all possible cases is called *average case time complexity.*

The space complexity of an algorithm is the number of memory units used. The space required by an algorithm is therefore, the maximum number of memory required at any time during the course of execution of the algorithm.

If $T(n)$ is a polynomial function of n then the algorithm is said to take a polynomial time (space). If $T(n)$ is a polynomial of degree one, then we say that the algorithm takes linear time (space). An algorithm is considered to be **efficient** if it takes a time which is a polynomial function of the problem size. The problems for which such algorithms exist, belong to the class P. Problems for which such algorithms do not seem to exist form the class of NP-complete problems. A problem which is NP-complete will have the property that it can be solved in polynomial time if and only if all other NP-complete problems can also be solved in polynomial time. If a NP-hard problem can be solved in polynomial time then all NP-complete problems can be solved in polynomial time. That is, all NP-complete problems are NP-hard but all NP-hard problems are not NP-complete.

Several notations are used to analyse an algorithm, among them O (big-oh) notation is frequently used. To represent the asymptotic upper bound this notation is used. For a given function $g(n)$, we denote by $O(g(n))$, the set of functions

$$O(g(n)) = \{f(n) : \text{there exist positive constants } c \text{ and } n_0 \text{ such that } 0 \le f(n) \le cg(n) \text{ for all } n \ge n_0\}.$$

In other words, $f(n) = O(g(n))$ if and only if

$$\lim_{n\to\infty} \frac{f(n)}{g(n)} = c, \text{ where } c \text{ is a non-zero constant.}$$

For example, if $f(n) = 5n^3 + 100n^2 - 500n$, then $f(n) = O(n^3)$

$$\lim_{n\to\infty} \frac{f(n)}{g(n)} = \lim_{n\to\infty} \frac{5n^3 + 100n^2 - 500n}{n^3} = \lim_{n\to\infty} \left(5 + \frac{100}{n} - \frac{500}{n^2}\right) = 5,$$

a non-zero constant.

Some properties of O-notation

(i) If $A(n) = a_k n^k + \cdots + a_1 n + a_0$, then $A(n) = O(n^k)$, k is independent of n.

(ii) $O(f(n)) + O(g(n)) = O(\max_n\{f(n), g(n)\})$.

(iii) $O(f_1(n)) + O(f_2(n)) + \cdots + O(f_k(n)) = O(\max_n\{f_1(n), f_2(n), \ldots, f_k(n)\})$, k is independent of n.

(iv) $c\,O(f(n)) = O(f(n))$, c is independent of n.

(v) $O(f(n)) \times O(g(n)) = O(f(n) \times g(n))$.

(vi) $n^k \times O(f(n)) = O(n^k f(n))$, k is independent of n.

(vii) $O(n^k) \times O(n^l) = O(n^{k+l})$, k and l are independent of n.

2.3 Flowchart

The pictorial representation of an algorithm is called a **flowchart**. In a flowchart each processing step is placed in a box and the arrows are used to indicate the next step. Boxes of different shapes are used to indicate different operations.

There are many symbols used while drawing a flowchart, but many of them are not useful. We have illustrated some of them, which are adequate to draw the flowchart of any algorithm.

1. **Start/Stop box:** This is flat-oval or elliptic in shape and is used to indicate the beginning or ending of an algorithm. One of the following words BEGIN, START, STOP, EXIT, END, RETURN, etc., is written within the box (see Figure 2.1).

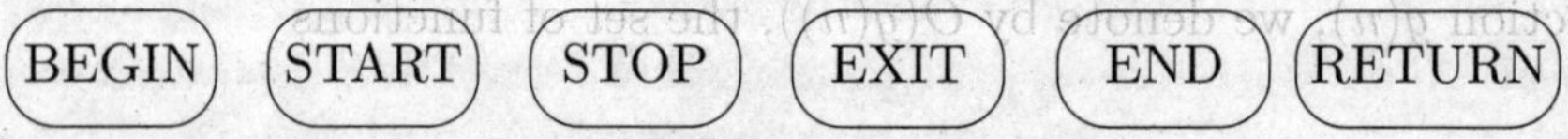

Figure 2.1: Start/Stop box

2. **Input/Output box:** Usually a parallelogram is used to indicate the input or output of an algorithm (see Figure 2.2).

Figure 2.2: Input/Output box

3. **Assignment/Computation box:** Generally, a rectangle is used to indicate the assignment of a new value or the value or result of some previous computation (see Figure 2.3).

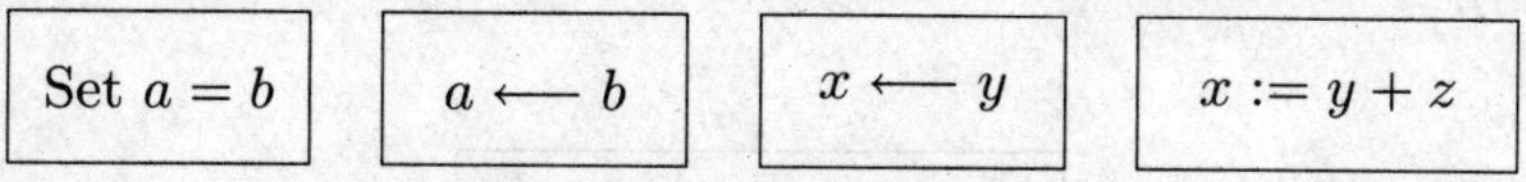

Figure 2.3: Assignment box

4. **Flow indicator:** The arrow is used to indicate the flow/order in which the steps of the algorithm are to be proceeded (see Figure 2.4).

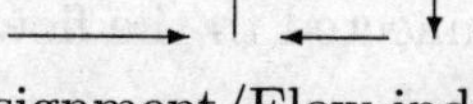

Figure 2.4: Assignment/Flow indicator symbol

5. **Decision box:** A diamond shaped box is used to indicate a decision position. A logical expression is written within the diamond box. Depending on its value the direction of the flow is considered and is indicated by an arrow (see Figure 2.5).

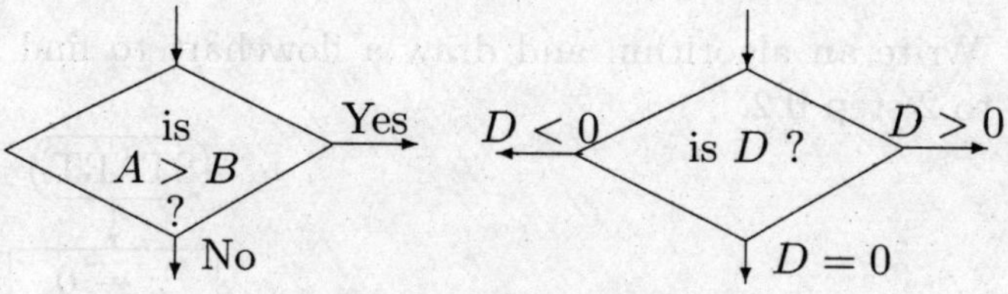

Figure 2.5: Decision box

6. **Loop representation box:** A hexagonal box is used to indicate the beginning of a loop (see Figure 2.6).

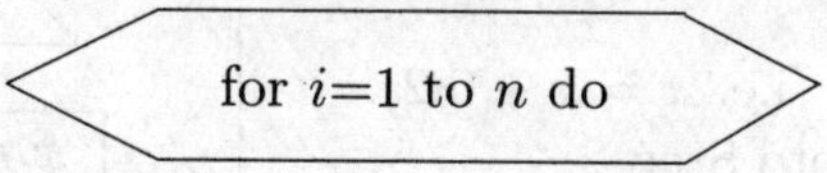

Figure 2.6: Loop representation box

7. **Connection box:** A circle is used as a connection box. When it is inconvenient or impossible to draw a flow chart within a single page, e.g. when a flow chart is so large that it requires more than one page to draw, then this symbol is used. The numbers are written within the circles which corresponds the continuation of flow (see Figure 2.7).

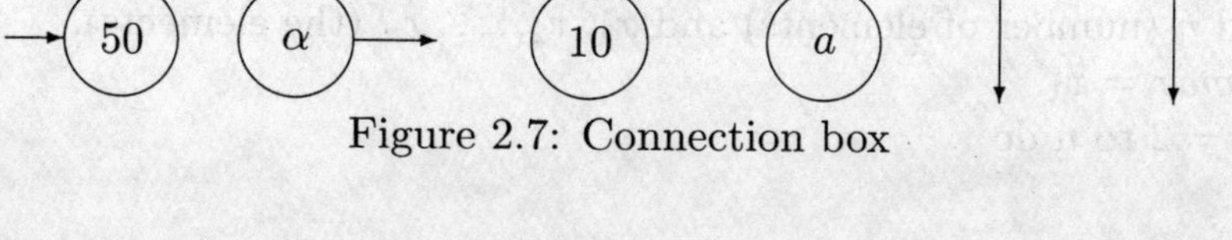

Figure 2.7: Connection box

8. **Sub-procedure/function box:** A sub-procedure or a function is represented in a flowchart by a double lined rectangle. The name of sub-procedure or function is written within the box and the details of this sub-procedure or function are specified elsewhere (see Figure 2.8).

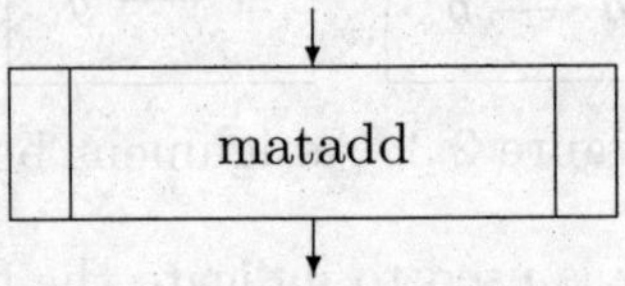

Figure 2.8: Sub-procedure/function box, 'matadd' is sub-procedure/function.

9. **Annotation box:** It is used to add a comment in a flowchart. It is symbolised by an open-sided rectangle and is connected to the flow chart by a dotted line (see Figure 2.9).

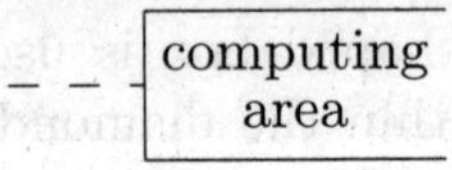

Figure 2.9: Annotation box

Example 2.3.1 Write an algorithm and draw a flowchart to find the values of $y = e^x + x^2$ for $x = 0$ to 2 step 0.2.

Algorithm:
Step 1: Set $x = 0$.
Step 2: Compute $y = e^x + x^2$.
Step 3: Print y.
Step 4: Add 0.2 with x (i.e. $x = x + 0.2$).
Step 5: If $x \leq 2$ then goto Step 2.
Step 6: Stop.

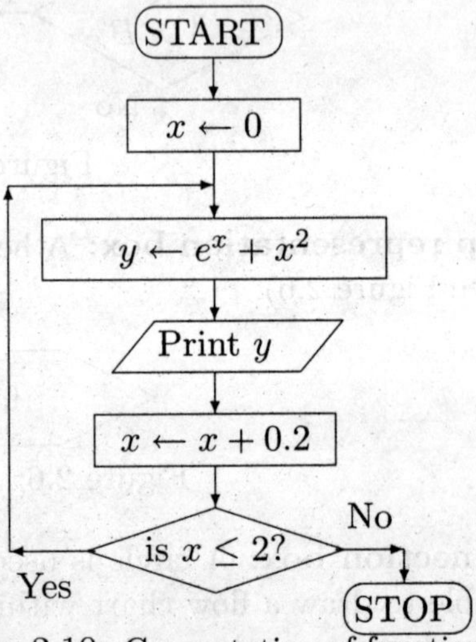

Figure 2.10: Computation of function

In the following, two algorithms MAXA and MAXB are designed for the same problem, viz. to find the maximum among n numbers and the better one is noted.

Algorithm MAXA
Step 1: Read n (number of elements) and $x_1, x_2, \ldots, x_n$ (the elements).
Step 2: Set $max = x_1$.
Step 3: for $i = 2$ to n do

if $max < x_i$ then $max = x_i$ endif;
endfor;
Step 4: Print max.
Step 5: Stop.

Algorithm MAXB
Step 1: Read n (number of elements).
Step 2: Read x.
Step 3: Set $max = x$.
Step 4: for $i = 2$ to n do
read x;
if $max < x$ then $max = x$ endif;
endfor;
Step 5: Print max.
Step 6: Stop.

The variables used in algorithm MAXA are n, $x_1, x_2, \ldots, x_n, max, i$, i.e. the total number of variables is $n+3$ while the variables used in algorithm MAXB are n, x, max, i, i.e. only four variables. Thus, algorithm MAXB is better than algorithm MAXA with respect to space complexity.

2.4 Worked Out Examples

Example 2.4.1 Write an algorithm to read three lengths a, b, c and check whether a, b, c forms a triangle. If they form a triangle, then check whether it is
(i) equilateral triangle, (ii) isosceles triangle, (ii) right angled triangle, (iv) scalene triangle.

Algorithm **Triangle-test.**
Step 1: Read a, b, c
Step 2: Arrange a, b, c such that $a \geq b \geq c$ as
(i) if $a < b$ then swap(a, b)
(ii) if $a < c$ then swap(a, c)
(ii) if $b < c$ then swap(b, c)
/* swap(a, b) interchanges the values between a and b */
Step 3: If $b + c > a$ then
(i) Print 'The sides a, b, c form a triangle';
else
(i) Print 'The sides a, b, c do not form a triangle';
(ii) Stop;
endif;
Step 4: If $a = b = c$ then
(i) Print 'The triangle is equilateral';
(ii) Stop;
endif;

Step 5: If $a \neq b$ and $b \neq c$ and $a \neq c$ then
(i) Print 'The triangle is scalene';
endif;
Step 6: If $a = b$ or $b = c$ or $c = a$ then
(i) Print 'The triangle is isosceles';
endif;
Step 7: If $a^2 = b^2 + c^2$ then
(i) Print 'The triangle is right angled';
(ii) Stop;
endif;
Step 8: End.

Note 2.4.1 Comments or headings may be put within /* */. Also, a comment may be initiated with the symbol //.

Example 2.4.2 The Fibonacci sequence is defined as follows:
The first and second terms of the sequence are 0 and 1. The third and subsequent terms of the sequence is the sum of the two terms just preceding it, i.e. $t_0 = 0, t_1 = 1, t_n = t_{n-1} + t_{n-2}, n \geq 2$. Write an algorithm and draw a flowchart to obtain all the numbers in the Fibonacci sequence less than a fixed number, say 300.

Algorithm **Fibonacci.**
Step 1: Set $F0 = 0$ and $F1 = 1$.
Step 2: Compute $F2 = F0 + F1$.
Step 3: If $F2 < 300$ then
(i) Print $F2$;
(ii) Set $F0 = F1$, $F1 = F2$;
(ii) Goto Step 2;
endif;
Step 4: End.

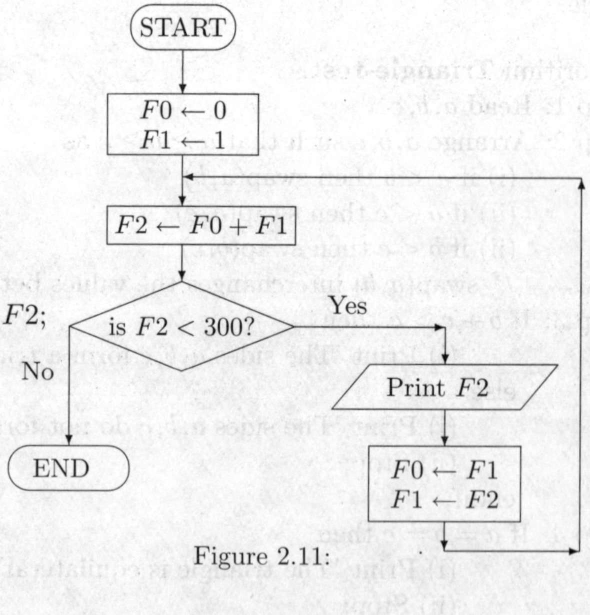

Figure 2.11:

Example 2.4.3 Write an algorithm and draw a flowchart to find the value of ${}^nC_r$.

By definition of ${}^nC_r$,

$$\begin{aligned} {}^nC_r &= \frac{n!}{r!(n-r)!} = \frac{n(n-1)(n-2)\cdots(n-\overline{r-1})(n-r)!}{r!(n-r)!} \\ &= \frac{n(n-1)\cdots(n-\overline{r-1})}{r(r-1)\cdots 2.1} \\ &= \prod_{k=0}^{r-1}\left(\frac{n-k}{r-k}\right). \end{aligned}$$

The value of ${}^nC_r$ may be computed by finding the factorial of n, r and $(n-r)$. But, the factorial of an integer is very large, it can even be around 10. Thus, there is a chance of integer overflow (exceeds the upper limit of integer value).

Algorithm **NCR**
Step 1: Read N, R.
Step 2: Set $P = 1$ (initial value of NCR);
Step 3: For $k = 0$ to $R-1$ do
$P = P \times (\frac{N-k}{R-k})$;
endfor;
Step 4: Print P.
Step 5: End.

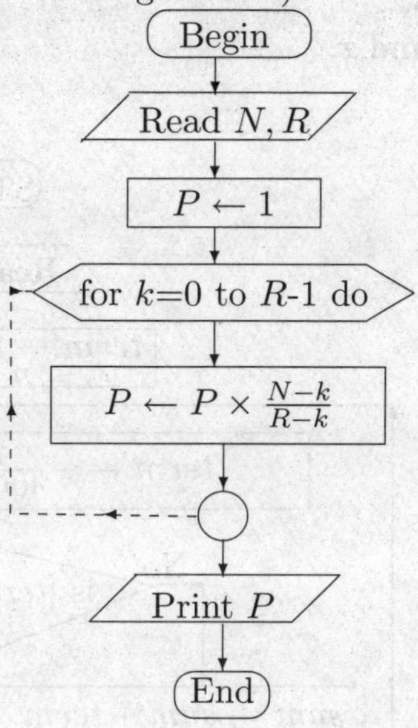

Figure 2.12:

Example 2.4.4 Write an algorithm and draw a flowchart to find the sum of the following series (zero-th order Bessel function):

$$J_0(x) = 1 - \frac{x^2}{2^2.1!.1!} + \frac{x^4}{2^4.2!.2!} - \frac{x^6}{2^6.3!.3!} + \cdots\cdots$$

To calculate the sum of an infinite series, calculate a term for a given x and check whether it is less than a specified small number ε (called the error tolerance). If the value of the term is not small, then add it with the sum and calculate the next term. Repeat this process until the term is smaller than ε.

The nth and $(n+1)$th terms of the series are respectively

$$t_n = (-1)^n \frac{x^{2n}}{2^{2n}.n!n!}, \quad t_{n+1} = (-1)^{n+1} \frac{x^{2n+2}}{2^{2n+2}.(n+1)!(n+1)!}$$

$$\frac{t_{n+1}}{t_n} = -\frac{x^2}{4(n+1)^2} \quad \text{or,} \quad t_{n+1} = -\frac{x^2}{4(n+1)^2} t_n, \; n \geq 1 \text{ and } t_0 = 1.$$

That is, the next term$=-\frac{x^2}{4(n+1)^2}\times$ the current term.

Algorithm **J0X**
Step 1: Read x and error tolerance ε.
Step 2: Set $term = 1$, $sum = 1$ and $n = 0$ (the initial term and sum).
Step 3: Compute $term = -\frac{x^2}{4(n+1)^2} \times term$.
Step 4: If $|term| < \varepsilon$ then goto Step 7.
Step 5: Compute (i) $sum = sum + term$;
(ii) $n = n + 1$;
Step 6: Goto Step 3.
Step 7: Print *sum* and x.
Step 8: End.

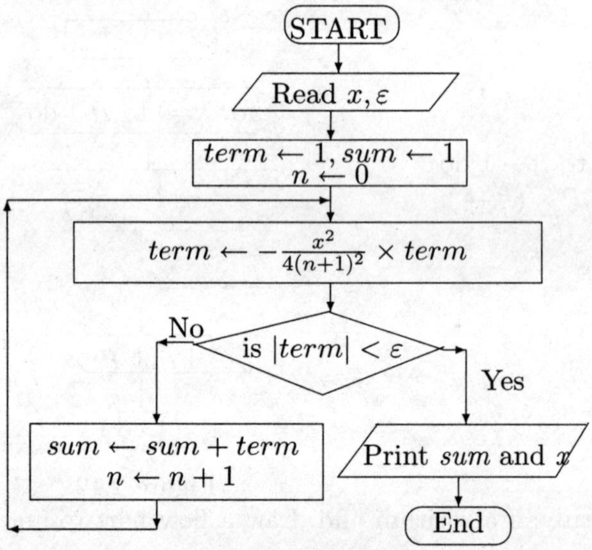

Figure 2.13:

Example 2.4.5 Write an algorithm and draw a flowchart to find the roots of a quadratic equation.

Let $ax^2 + bx + c = 0$ be a quadratic equation, where $a \neq 0$. The roots of this equation are

$$x = \frac{-b \pm \sqrt{b^2 - 4ac}}{2a} = \frac{-b}{2a} \pm \frac{\sqrt{b^2 - 4ac}}{2a}.$$

Let $d = b^2 - 4ac$, $p = \dfrac{-b}{2a}$ and $q = \dfrac{\sqrt{|d|}}{2a}$.

If $d > 0$, then the roots are $p + q$ and $p - q$, if $d = 0$ then the roots are p, p and if $d < 0$ then the roots are $p + iq$ and $p - iq$.

Algorithm **Quadratic**
Step 1: Read the coefficients as a, b, c.
Step 2: Calculate $d = b^2 - 4ac$.
Step 3: Calculate $p = -b/(2a)$ and $q = \sqrt{|d|}/(2a)$.
Step 4: If $d > 0$ then,
    Print 'The roots are real and distinct and they are', $p + q, p - q$;
  elseif $d = 0$ then
    Print 'The roots are real and equal and they are', p, p;
  else
    Print 'The roots are imaginary and they are', $p + iq, p - iq$;
  endif;
Step 5: End.

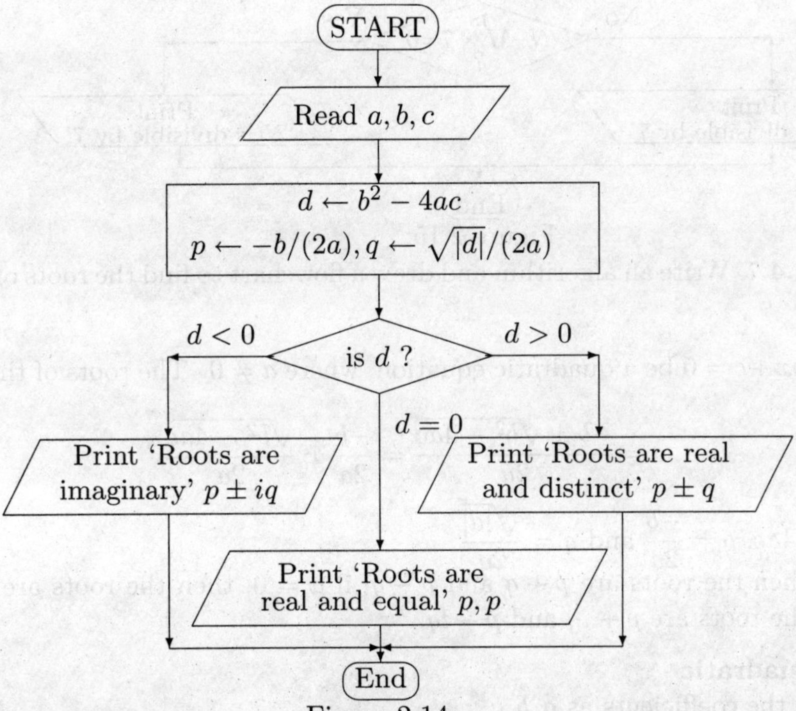

Figure 2.14:

Example 2.4.6 Write an algorithm and draw a flowchart to test whether an integer is divisible by 7.

To check whether N is divisible by 7, find the remainder (R) of $N/7$. If the remainder is zero, then the number is divisible by 7, otherwise it is not divisible by 7. The remainder R may be calculated as $R = N - 7\times$ (integer part of $N/7$).

Algorithm **Divisibility_by 7**
Step 1: Read the number as N.
Step 2: Calculate M=integer part of $(N/7)$.
Step 3: If $(N - 7 \times M = 0)$ then
    Print 'The number is divisible by 7';
  else
    Print 'The number is not divisible by 7';
  endif;
Step 3: End.

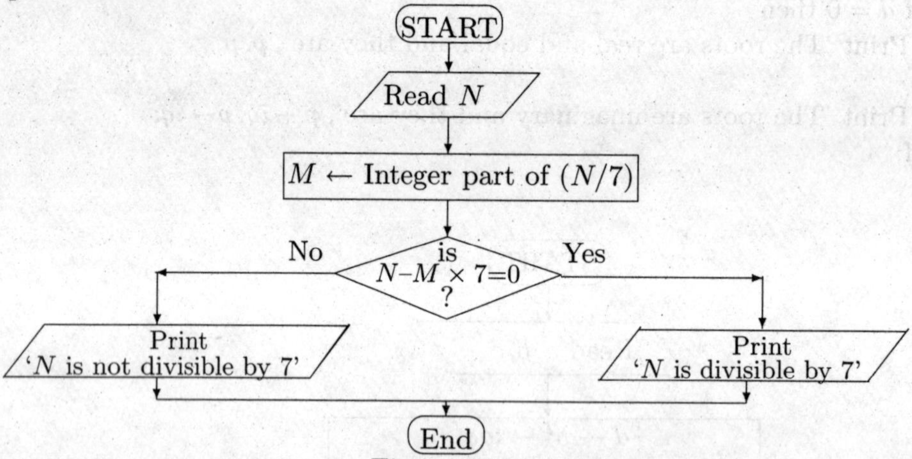

Figure 2.15:

Example 2.4.7 Write an algorithm and draw a flowchart to find the roots of a quadratic equation.

Let $ax^2 + bx + c = 0$ be a quadratic equation, where $a \neq 0$. The roots of this equation are

$$x = \frac{-b \pm \sqrt{b^2 - 4ac}}{2a} = \frac{-b}{2a} \pm \frac{\sqrt{b^2 - 4ac}}{2a}.$$

Let $d = b^2 - 4ac$, $p = \dfrac{-b}{2a}$ and $q = \dfrac{\sqrt{|d|}}{2a}$.

If $d > 0$, then the roots are $p + q$ and $p - q$, if $d = 0$, then the roots are p, p and if $d < 0$, then the roots are $p + iq$ and $p - iq$.

Algorithm **Quadratic**
Step 1: Read the coefficients as a, b, c.
Step 2: Calculate $d = b^2 - 4ac$.
Step 3: Calculate $p = -b/(2a)$ and $q = \sqrt{|d|}/(2a)$.
Step 4: If $d > 0$ then
    Print 'The roots are real and distinct and they are', $p + q, p - q$;
  elseif $d = 0$ then
    Print 'The roots are real and equal and they are', p, p;
  else

Print 'The roots are imaginary and they are', $p + iq, p - iq$;

endif;

Step 5: End.

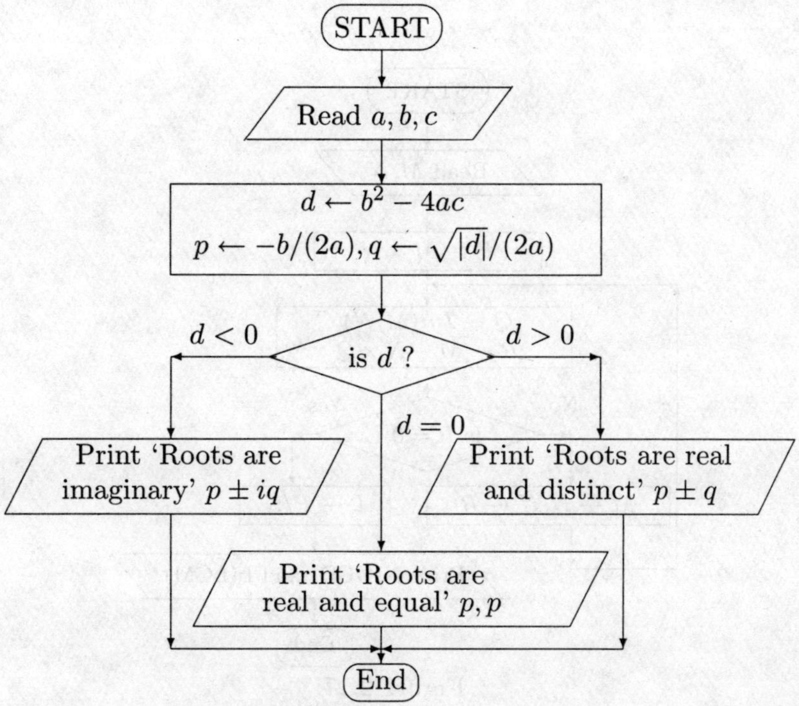

Figure 2.16:

Example 2.4.8 Write an algorithm and draw a flowchart to compute G.C.D and L.C.M of two given integers.

Quotient-division method is used to find the L.C.M. and G.C.D. Let $M > N$. If M is divisible by N, then N is the G.C.D., if it is not, then let R be the remainder. Now, divide N by R, if the remainder is zero then R is the G.C.D. If N is not divisible by R, then let $N = R$ and R be the new remainder. Repeat this process until remainder becomes zero.

Algorithm **GCD-LCM**

Step 1: Read the numbers as M and N.

Step 2: Calculate the product $P = M \times N$.

Step 3: Compute Q (quotient) = integer part of (M/N).

Step 4: Compute R (remainder) $=M - N \times Q$.

Step 5: If $R = 0$ then

goto Step 6;

else

(i) Set $M = N$;

and $N = R$;

(ii) goto Step 3;

endif;

Step 6: Compute L (the L.C.M) $=P/N$.

Step 7: Print N (the G.C.D) and L (the L.C.M).

Step 8: End.

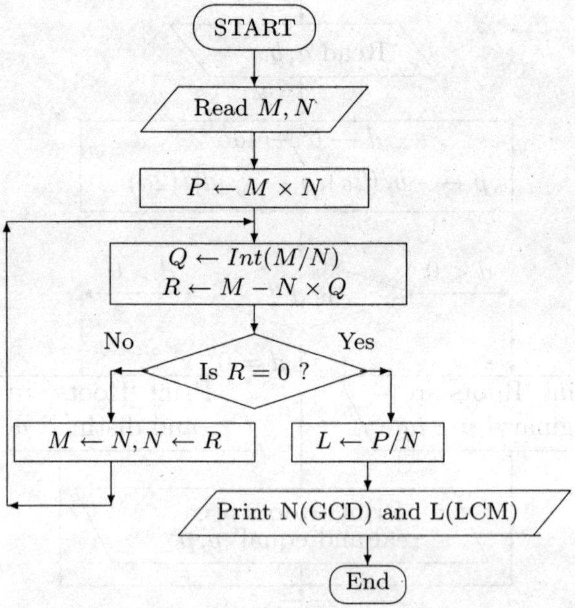

Figure 2.17:

Example 2.4.9 Write an algorithm and draw a flowchart to convert a decimal number (integer and fraction) to its binary equivalent.

In the following algorithm convert a decimal number (whose integer part is M and fraction part is N) to its binary equivalent. Step 2 to Step 6 converts M to its binary equivalent while Step 7 to Step 10 converts N to its binary equivalent.

Algorithm **B2D**

Step 1: Read integer part as M and fraction part as N.

Step 2: Set $i = 1$.

Step 3: Divide M by 2. Let Q and R be the quotient and remainder, i.e. Q=integer part of $(M/2)$ and $R = M - Q \times 2$.

Step 4: Set $b_i = R$ and $i = i + 1$, (b_1 is the least significant digit)

Step 5: If $Q = 0$ then

goto Step 6;

else

(i) Set $M = Q$;

(ii) goto Step 3;

endif;

Step 6: Set $l = i$; (l is the total number of bits in the integer part)

Step 7: Set $i = 1$

Step 8: Multiply N by 2. Let I, R be the integer and fraction parts of this product, i.e. I=integer part of $(N \times 2)$ and $R = N \times 2 - I$.

Step 9: Set $f_i = I; i = i + 1;$

Step 10: If $R = 0$ then
  goto Step 11
 else
  (i) Set $N = R$;
  (ii) goto Step 8;
 endif;

Step 11: Print $b_i, i = l, l-1, \ldots, 1$ and $f_j, j = 1, 2, \ldots, i$.
(the binary equivalent is $b_l b_{l-1} \cdots b_2 b_1 . f_1 f_2 \cdots f_i$)

Step 12: End.

Exercise II

Review Questions

1. Define algorithm. State its important characteristics.
2. Describe the steps to solve a problem using computer.
3. Define time and space complexities. What do you mean by an efficient algorithm?
4. Define O notation and state some of its important properties.
5. Define a flowchart. Draw the basic symbols to draw a flowchart of a problem.
6. Write short notes on: input/output box, decision box and flow indication symbols.

Problems

1. Write an algorithm and draw a flowchart to find the largest among four given numbers.
2. Write an algorithm and draw a flowchart to find the minimum among n given numbers.
3. Draw a flow-chart to find the largest amongst N given real numbers.
4. Write an algorithm and draw a flowchart to find the maximum and minimum among n given numbers.
5. Given a set of n integers. Write an algorithm and draw a flowchart to find
(i) total number of even integers.
(ii) total number of odd integers.
(ii) sum and product of the even integers.
(iv) sum and product of the odd integers.
(v) the maximum and minimum among the even integers.
(vi) the maximum and minimum among the odd integers.

6. The Fibonacci sequence is defined as follows: The first and second terms of the sequence are 0 and 1. The third and subsequent terms of the sequence are the sum of the two terms preceding it, i.e. $t_0 = 0, t_1 = 1$, and $t_n = t_{n-1} + t_{n-2}$, $n \geq 2$. Write an algorithm and draw a flowchart to obtain all numbers of the Fibonacci sequence between two specified numbers, say, a and b.
7. Write an algorithm and draw a flowchart to read n (=50) points in a plane and find the number of points in each of the four quadrants of the plane. [The point (a, b) lies on the first quadrant, if $a, b > 0$, second quadrant, if $a < 0, b > 0$, third quadrant if $a, b < 0$ and fourth quadrant if $a > 0, b < 0$].
8. Write an algorithm and draw a flowchart to read 50 pairs of length and breadth of rectangles, and find (i) the area and perimeter of each rectangle, (ii) all the rectangles whose area is greater than its perimeter, (ii) the average area of the rectangles.
9. Write an algorithm and draw a flowchart to read 100 sets of three numbers (a, b, c) and check whether each set a, b, c form a triangle. If the sides a, b, c form a triangle, then print its area.
10. Write an algorithm and draw a flowchart to read two sides of a triangle and the angle between them and find the area of the triangle.
11. Given three points $A(x_1, y_1), B(x_2, y_2)$ and $C(x_3, y_3)$, write an algorithm and draw a flowchart to find the area of the triangle ABC. [Area $= \frac{1}{2}\{x_1(y_2 - y_3) + x_2(y_3 - y_1) + x_3(y_1 - y_2)\}$]
12. Given three points $A(x_1, y_1), B(x_2, y_2)$ and $C(x_3, y_3)$, write an algorithm and draw a flowchart to check if they are collinear. [A, B, C will be collinear if the area of the triangle ABC is zero.]
13. Given a sequence of n numbers, write an algorithm and draw a flowchart to check if it is strictly ascending or descending. [A sequence $(x_1, x_2, \ldots, x_n)$ is strictly ascending (descending) if $x_i < x_{i+1} (x_i > x_{i+1})$ for all i.]
14. Write an algorithm and draw a flowchart to read the radii of 50 circles and find the area and circumference of each.
15. Write algorithms and draw flowcharts to find the sum of the following series, correct upto six decimal places.

$$(i) \quad \sum_{r=1}^{100} x^r, \ |x| \leq 1$$

$$(ii) \quad x - \frac{x^2}{2!} + \frac{x^3}{3!} - \frac{x^4}{4!} + \cdots$$

$$(ii) \quad x - \frac{x^2}{2} + \frac{x^3}{3} - \frac{x^4}{4} + \cdots$$

$$(iv) \quad 1 + x + \frac{x^2}{2!} + \frac{x^3}{3!} + \frac{x^4}{4!} + \cdots$$

$$(v)\quad x - \frac{x^3}{3!} + \frac{x^5}{5!} - \frac{x^7}{7!} + \cdots$$

$$(vi)\quad 1 - \frac{x^2}{2!} + \frac{x^4}{4!} - \frac{x^6}{6!} + \cdots$$

16. Write an algorithm and draw a flowchart to generate all prime numbers between two given integers.
17. Write an algorithm and draw a flowchart to test whether an integer is (i) prime, (ii) perfect square, (ii) even or odd, and (iv) divisible by 5. [In each case separate algorithm and flowchart should be made.]
18. Write an algorithm and draw a flowchart to compute the value of $n!$.
19. Write an algorithm and draw a flowchart to split a number into digits.
20. Write an algorithm and draw a flowchart to find the value of ${}^nP_r$.
21. Write an algorithm and draw a flowchart to list all three digit numbers which are equal to the sum of the cubes of the digits. [Such numbers are called Armstrong numbers]
22. Given ten values of x, say, $x_1, x_2, \ldots, x_{10}$, write an algorithm and draw a flowchart to compute the values of y, $2 - y^2, y + y^6$, where

$$y(x) = 1 - \frac{x^2}{2} + \frac{x^4}{24.6} - \frac{x^6}{120.8}.$$

23. Write an algorithm and draw a flowchart to
(i) read cartesian coordinates (x, y) and find its polar transformation (r, θ), $[r = \sqrt{x^2 + y^2}$ and $\theta = \tan^{-1}(y/x)]$
(ii) read polar coordinates (r, θ) and convert it to cartesian coordinates (x, y). $[x = r\cos\theta, y = r\sin\theta]$.
24. Write an algorithm to convert a binary number to its decimal equivalent.
25. Write an algorithm and draw a flowchart to find the value of $(x+1)/(2x+1)^{1/3}$, where x varies from 0 to 2, at steps of 0.2.
26. Write an algorithm and draw a flowchart to read the values of a, b, c, compute $d = b^2 - 4ac$ and then print the value of y defined by

$$y = \begin{cases} (-b + \sqrt{d})/2a, & \text{if } d \geq 0 \\ (-b + \sqrt{-d})/2a, & \text{if } d < 0. \end{cases}$$

27. Write an algorithm and draw a flowchart to solve the following equations $a_1x + b_1y = c_1, a_2x + b_2y = c_2$.
28. Write an algorithm and draw a flowchart to compute the value of y for a given x, where

$$y = \begin{cases} x - 1, & \text{for } x < 1 \\ 1 - x, & \text{for } 1 \leq x < 2 \\ 2 - x^2, & \text{for } x \geq 2. \end{cases}$$

29. Write an algorithm and draw a flowchart to compute the value of the function

$$f(x) = \begin{cases} x^3 e^x, & \text{if } x \le 1 \\ x \cos x & \text{if } x > 1 \end{cases}$$

for $x = 0.1, 0.2, \ldots, 1.5$.

30. Write an algorithm and draw a flowchart to compute the values of

$$f(x) = \frac{\sqrt{x^2+3}}{\sqrt{x+2}}$$

for $x = 0$ to $x = 2$ with a spacing of 0.1.

31. Write an algorithm and draw a flowchart to compute the function $y(x)$ defined as

$$y(x) = \begin{cases} 15x + 7.4, & \text{when } x \le 6.5 \\ 17x, & \text{when } x > 6.5 \end{cases}$$

for a given value of x.

32. Write an algorithm and draw a flowchart to compute the value of

$$y = \sum_{x=0}^{13} \frac{x^2 - x + 2}{x+3}.$$

33. Write algorithms and draw flowchart to compute the sum of two series (i) $S = 1^2 + 2^2 + \cdots + 100^2$, (ii) $S = 1^3 + 2^3 + \cdots + N^3$ (where N is a given integer).

34. A function $f(x)$ is defined as follows:

$$f(x) = \begin{cases} ax^3 - bx^2 + cx - d, & \text{if } x > 1 \\ 1, & \text{if } x = 1 \\ ax^2 + bx + c, & \text{if } x < 1. \end{cases}$$

Write an algorithm and draw a flowchart to read the values of a, b, c, d and x, and print out the value of $f(x)$.

35. Write an algorithm and draw a flowchart to compute the average of the largest numbers from several set of numbers.

36. Write an algorithm and draw a flowchart to obtain the scalar product of two vectors $X = (x_1, x_2, \ldots, x_n)$ and $Y = (y_1, y_2, \ldots, y_n)$ given by

$$\text{scalar product} = \sum_{i=1}^{n} x_i y_i.$$

37. Write an algorithm and draw a flowchart to generate all triplets (a, b, c), such that $a^2 + b^2 = c^2$, where a, b, c are positive integers, $a < b < c$, and $a, b \le 50$.

38. Write an algorithm and draw a flowchart to calculate the values of x and y, where $x = a \sin\theta - b\cos\theta, y = a\cos\theta + b\sin\theta$, a and b are fixed numbers (say $a = 10, b = 15.5$) and θ varies from 0 to 360°.

Chapter 3

Constants and Variables

To solve a problem by computer, the programmer should supply the program and data to the computer. This data may be numeric type or alphabetic type. The numeric data is also of different types, such as, whole number or fraction. These supplied data are stored at various locations of the memory and these stored values are referred by names of variables. The value of a variable at any instant, during the execution of a program, is the value stored at the location identified by the variable name. The variables are of different types. In this chapter, different types of constants and variables are discussed.

3.1 Character Set

A computer key board contains many symbols (characters), some of them are used to write a program in C.

The C character set is shown in Table 3.1.

Some characters which produce blank space (horizontal or vertical) during printing are called *whitespace*. In C they are *blank space, horizontal tab, vertical tab, carriage return, new line, form feed.*

The digits combined with the letters are called **alphanumeric characters**, and the remaining symbols are termed as **special characters**. In C language, *upper case letters and lower case letters are different*, e.g. N and n are different. That is, *C is a case sensitive language.* A program in C must be written using only the defined set of characters.

3.2 Constant Data

Any entry which remains unchanged during the execution of a program is defined as a **constant**. It may be numeric, character or logical type. Like other programming languages, C also supports several different types of constants. Each of them is represented differently, in terms of the computer memory allocation. Mainly four basic data types are available in C, viz. integer (`int`), floating point (`float`), character (`char`) and

A-Z	Alphabets (Upper case)	a-z	Alphabets (Lower case)
0-9	Digits	b̸	blank space
,	comma	.	period
;	semicolon	:	colon
?	question mark	'	single quotation
"	double quotation	!	exclamation mark
|	vertical bar	/	slash
\	backslash	~	tilde
_	underscore	$	dollar
%	percent sign	&	ampersand
^	caret	*	asterisk
−	minus sign	+	plus sign
>	greater than sign	<	less than sign
(	left parenthesis	)	right parenthesis
[	left bracket	]	right bracket
{	left brace	}	right brace
#	hash sign	=	equal sign

Table 3.1: The C characters set

double precision (`double`) (see Table 3.2). These data types also have some extended forms.

Data type	Description	Typical memory requirement
`int`	integer quantity	2 bytes
`char`	single character	1 byte
`float`	floating point number	4 bytes
`double`	double-precision floating point number (store more significant figures)	8 bytes

Table 3.2: Basic data type

The memory requirement for each data type may vary from C compiler to compiler.

The memory requirement of each numerical constant determines the permissible range of values it can take. The memory requirement of different types of constants in different computers.

3.2.1 Numeric type

Any string of digits preceded by a single algebraic sign (+ or −) is called a **numeric constant**, which may also contain a decimal point.

Numeric type constants are further subdivided as integer and floating point.

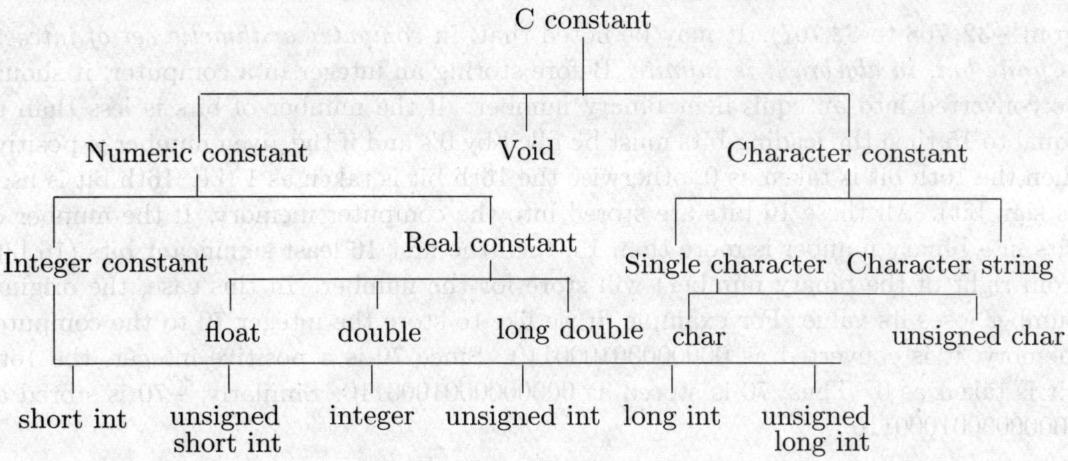

Figure 3.1: Types of constants

Integer constant

An **integer constant** is a whole number which is written as a string of decimal digits without a decimal point or an exponent symbol. It can either be positive or negative. It is also called a fixed point constant. The integer constant is of three types – `short int`, `int` and `long int`, in both signed and unsigned forms. The `long` and `unsigned` integers are used to increase the range of values.

Some valid integer constants:

`45  2  -66  +34223`

Some invalid integer constants:

–43.0, –4.5 (contains a decimal point)
432+ (sign following the constant is not allowed)
–3,674 (comma is not allowed)
3456122000 (too large, not a valid integer constant)
32E4 (E is not allowed in an integer constant)
$346 (currency symbol is not allowed)
+ –356 (consecutive two signs are not allowed)

Note 3.2.1 For a positive integer '+' sign is optional. The range of the integer constants vary from computer to computer.

C language also supports octal and hexadecimal integers. An octal constant begins with zero (0) and a hexadecimal constant begins with 0x or 0X. For example, the decimal integer 15 is written in octal system in the form 017 and in hexadecimal system it is of the form 0xf or 0XF.

The valid range of integer depends on the word-length of the computer. For a 16-bit word-length computer, the allowable range of integer constant is -2^{15} to $2^{15}-1$ (i.e.

from $-32,768$ to 32,767). It may be noted that, in *computer arithmetic set of integers is finite but, in algebra it is infinite.* Before storing an integer in a computer, it should be converted into an equivalent binary number. If the number of bits is less than or equal to 15 then the leading bits must be filled by 0's and if the given number is positive then the 16th bit is taken as 0, otherwise the 16th bit is taken as 1 (i.e. 16th bit is used as sign bit). All these 16 bits are stored into the computer memory. If the number of bits in a binary number is more than 15, then the first 16 least significant bits (16 bits from right of the binary number) will store for the number. In this case, the original number loses its value. For example, if we like to store the integer 70 to the computer memory, it is converted as 000000001000110. Since 70 is a positive integer, the 16th bit is taken as 0. Thus, 70 is stored as 0000000001000110. Similarly, -70 is stored as 1000000001000110.

Unsigned and long integer constants

C also supports other types of integers called short integer, long integer, unsigned integer, etc. The qualifiers `u, l` and `ul` (or `U, L, UL`) are used to represent unsigned integer, long integer and unsigned long integer. For example, `3458U, −98308766L, 89288339UL` represent unsigned decimal integer, long integer and unsigned long integer respectively. The numbers `04734506L, 057456321U, OX5AB69U, OXFECD58UL` represent octal long, octal unsigned, hexadecimal unsigned and hexadecimal unsigned long integers respectively.

In unsigned integer, all 16 bits are used to store the magnitude of the number. Thus for a 16-bit computer the range of unsigned integer is 0 to $2^{16} - 1$. A long integer constant uses 32-bit to store its value and the range of the values is -2^{31} to $2^{31} - 1$, i.e. from -2147483648 to 2147483647. However, the range of unsigned long integer is from 0 to $2^{32} - 1$, i.e. from 0 to 4294967295, and needs 32 bits to store it. On the other hand, short integer takes only 16 bits to store its value and its range is -2^{15} to $2^{15} - 1$, which is same as `int`, but some machine takes 8 bits to store `short int`.

Note 3.2.2 All the ranges of values for different types of integers depends on the computer/compiler.

Floating point constant

A signed or an unsigned whole number containing a decimal point or an exponent or both, is called a **floating point** or **floating point constant**. The extended form of floating point constant is `double`. Floating point constants are of two forms (i) fixed point form, and (ii) exponent form. In many mathematical calculations, high accuracy is required, in this case floating point data is not sufficient, the `double` type constant can do this task efficiently. A `double` type constant uses 8 bytes as a storage space. This type of constant is known as **double precision** constant. Double and floating point constants are similar, but double precision constant gives more precision. Double precision numbers may also be defined as `long float`.

(i) *Floating point constant of fixed point form*

A floating point constant of fixed point form is a constant with a decimal point and may have a fractional part.

Some valid floating point constants:

`3.432, 0.34, -0.678, 0.000023, .324, 2.`

Some invalid floating point constants:

2,133.3 (comma is not allowed)
127 (does not have a decimal point)
−4/5 (special character is not allowed)
.123256734234234234 (fractional part is too large)
45 ƀ 43.24 (blank (ƀ) space is not allowed)

(ii) *Floating point constant of exponent form*

Often very large or very small numbers are involved in scientific computations. It is not possible to represent these numbers using fixed point form. These numbers can be represented by a form known as exponent form. A floating point constant of the exponent form have a format containing a mantissa and an exponent. The mantissa must have at least one digit and a decimal point. It may have a sign. The mantissa is followed by the letter E and an exponent. The exponent must be an integer and must have at least one digit. A sign of the exponent is optional.

Some examples of floating point constants of exponent form are given below:

Scientific form	*C floating point form*
6.23×10^{23}	`6.23E23` or `6.23E+23`
$.000345 = .345 \times 10^{-3}$	`.345E-3`
10^{-14}	`1.0E-14`
-561.3452	`-561.3452E0` or `-.5613452E+3`
25×10^{12}	`25.0E12`

Some valid floating point constants :

`344.e02, 456.0E3, 678.e+5, 456.E+06, 34.1E4, 3467.E5,`
`-.210E-4, 678.234E+14, .02341E03.`

Some invalid floating point constants :

231*E2 (special character '*' is not allowed)
+345.3E (exponent part does not contain any digit)
-123.4E1.3 (exponent cannot be a fraction)
456,321.14E-5 (comma is not allowed in mantissa)
E34 (mantissa do not have any digit)
12 ƀ24.E01 (blank (ƀ) is not allowed)
2.67E-50 (too small)
24E{-50} (the characters '{' and '}' are not allowed).

Note 3.2.3 The actual number of digits in the mantissa and in the exponent depends on the computer being used.

The Table 3.3 shows the size and range of constants of different types, for the computers having 16-bits as word length.

The memory requirement of each numerical constant determines the permissible range of values it can take. The memory requirements of different types of constants vary according to different computers. The readers are requested to check the valid range of data in their computer.

Types of constants	Number of bytes used	Range of values	
`character`	1		-128 to 127
`short int`	2	-2^{16-1} to $2^{16-1}-1$	-32768 to 32767
`unsigned short`	2	0 to $2^{16}-1$	0 to 65535
`int`	2	-2^{16-1} to $2^{16-1}-1$	-32768 to 32767
`unsigned int`	2	0 to $2^{16}-1$	0 to 65535
`long int`	4	-2^{32-1} to $2^{32-1}-1$	$-2,147,483,648$ to 2,147,483,647
`unsigned long int`	4	0 to $2^{32}-1$	0 to 42949672965
`float`	4		8.43×10^{-37} to 3.37×10^{38}
`double or` `long float`	8		2.225074×10^{-308} to 1.797693×10^{308}
`long double`	10		3.4E$-$4932 to 1.1E+4932

Table 3.3: Memory allocation for constants

The range of a numeric number is not specified in the ANSI standard. Thus, different compilers may provide different range for floating point numbers. The actual range of the values of the constants that a compiler supports can be determined by some predefined constants, which are available in the header files `limits.h`, `float.h`, `values.h`.

3.2.2 Character constant

A character constant is a single character written within single quotations (apostrophes). For example, `'a'` `'z'` `'6'` `'$'` `' '`, etc. are the valid character constants. But, `'12'` (more than two characters), `"a"` (double quotations) are not valid character constants. Each character constant has unique integer value for a given computer. This code may vary from one computer to another. The integer value corresponding to a character is called ASCII (American Standard Code for Information Interchange) code (most of the computer uses ASCII character set). In ASCII code, each character is coded using 7 bits, and hence $2^7 = 128$ different characters can be coded using ASCII code. It may be noted that one byte space is required to store a character type constant. Table 3.4 shows the ASCII codes (in decimal) for the characters normally used in a computer.

Since each character has a unique integer value, it is possible to perform arithmetic operations on character set. For example, the ASCII values of `'3'` and `'z'` are respectively 51 and 122. The the value of the expression `'3'`−`'z'`= 51 − 122 = −71. The value of `'3'`−2= 51 − 2 = 49.

Some computers use EBCDIC (Extended Binary Coded Decimal Information Code) character set. In this character set each character is encoded into 8-bit binary number.

3.2.3 String constant

A string constant is a string of characters (alphabets, digits or special characters) enclosed in double quotation marks.

The following are valid string constants:

```
"X=12"  "INDIA"   "B.Sc"   "C=A+B"
"VIDYASAGAR"   "Final Examination"   "Sum="
```

It should be remembered that the constants `"A"` and `'A'` are different. `'A'` represents a character constant, it has an integer value 65 and it occupies one byte of space, while `"A"` represents a string constant, it does not have any value and needs two bytes of space, one for the ASCII code of `A` and another for the null character with value 0.

3.2.4 Escape sequences

C provides some more characters other than character constants and string constants, which are normally used during printing of output. These non-printable characters are called **escape sequences** or **backslash characters**. An escape sequence always begins with a backslash and is followed by one or more special characters. For example, a line feed (LF, ASCII code 10) is used as a *newline*, which is denoted as `\n`. Escape sequence represents a single character, even though it is written as a combination of two or more characters.

Some commonly used escape sequences are listed in Table 3.5.

The null character `\0` has a particular use. This character is used to indicate the end of a *string* and it may be noted that the null character `\0` is not equivalent to the character constant '0'.

Usually, a C function returns a value, but, sometimes it may happen that the function does not return any value. In this case, the return type of the function is referred as `void`.

In any C program, every word is either classified as an identifier or a keyword. Every keyword has a predefined meaning and it cannot be changed by the user. A list of keywords is given in Table 3.6. The identifiers required to identify or name variables, symbolic constants, functions, etc. The rules regarding the name of an identifier are discussed below.

ASCII value	Character	ASCII value	Character	ASCII value	Character	ASCII value	Character
000	NUL	032	blank	064	@	096	`
001	SOH	033	!	065	A	097	a
002	STX	034	”	066	B	098	b
003	ETX	035	#	067	C	099	c
004	EOT	036	$	068	D	100	d
005	ENQ	037	%	069	E	101	e
006	ACK	038	&	070	F	102	f
007	BEL	039	’	071	G	103	g
008	BS	040	(	072	H	104	h
009	HT	041	)	073	I	105	i
010	LF	042	*	074	J	106	j
011	VT	043	+	075	K	107	k
012	FF	044	,	076	L	108	l
013	CR	045	-	077	M	109	m
014	SO	046	.	078	N	110	n
015	SI	047	/	079	O	111	o
016	DLE	048	0	080	P	112	p
017	DC1	049	1	081	Q	113	q
018	DC2	050	2	082	R	114	r
019	DC3	051	3	083	S	115	s
020	DC4	052	4	084	T	116	t
021	NAK	053	5	085	U	117	u
022	SYN	054	6	086	V	118	v
023	ETB	055	7	087	W	119	w
024	CAN	056	8	088	X	120	x
025	EM	057	9	089	Y	121	y
026	SUB	058	:	090	Z	122	z
027	ESC	059	;	091	[	123	{
028	FS	060	<	092	\	124	|
029	GS	061	=	093	]	125	}
030	RS	062	>	094	↑	126	~
031	US	063	?	095	—	127	DEL

Table 3.4: The ASCII character set

Escape sequence	Character/use	ASCII value
`\a`	bell (alert)	007
`\b`	backspace	008
`\t`	horizontal tab	009
`\n`	newline (line feed)	010
`\v`	vertical tab	011
`\f`	form feed (new page)	012
`\r`	carriage return	013
`\"`	double quotation	034
`\'`	single quotation	039
`\?`	question mark	063
`\\`	backslash	092
`\0`	null	000

Table 3.5: Escape sequences

3.3 C Variables

A quantity that varies during the program execution is called a **variable**. Each C variable has a specific storage location in memory where its value is stored. The following rules must be followed by every C variable.

(i) The first character must be an alphabet. However, some systems allow underscore (_) as the first character.

(ii) The variable name can have at most 31 characters, in ANSI C. If a variable name contains more than 31 characters, the first 31 characters are to be recognized by the compiler and the remaining characters will be ignored. Some compilers recognize only the first 8 characters and some other compilers support arbitrary number of characters.

(iii) The variable name should not contain any special character other than underscore (_). Blank spaces are not allowed as valid characters in variable name.

(iv) No C keywords (which have some standard, predefined meaning/action in C, these keywords can be used only for their intended purpose) are allowed as variable name. A list of keywords are given in Table 3.6.

(v) Both upper case and lower case alphabets are used as variable name. But, they are used for naming two different variable names. For example, N and n are two different names. Similarly, `PNB`, `pnb`, `Pnb`, `pNB`, `pnB`, etc. are all distinct variable names.

Some compilers may also support the following keywords.

`ada` `far` `near` `asm` `fortran` `pascal` `entry` `huge`

auto	break	case	char
const	continue	default	do
double	else	enum	extern
float	for	goto	if
int	long	registrar	return
short	signed	sizeof	static
struct	switch	typedef	union
unsigned	void	volatile	while

Table 3.6: C keywords

The C language provides different types of variables like constants, viz. (a) integer, (b) floating point, (c) character, and (iv) string.

Some valid variable names:
`INCOME, India, cats5, ISRO, apple, p100xy, I, K, m1, theta, degree24, B, X1, stop, OUTPUT, READ, WRITE, -p25`

Some invalid variable names :
2ND (first character is invalid, it should be an alphabet)
M32,6 (special character comma is not allowed)
M.Sc (special character dot (.) is not valid)
L(4)X (special character parentheses are not allowed)
X-RAY (special character '-' is not allowed)
int, if (they are keywords)
A,12 (special character comma (,) is not allowed)
A+B (special character + is not allowed)

3.3.1 Array

Sometimes, it is necessary to represent a group of values by a common variable name. For example, the roll number of 100 students of a class may be represented by a variable, say `roll` and the variables `roll[0]`, `roll[1]`, ..., `roll[99]` represent the rolls of first student, second student, ..., 100th student. A set of data with similar properties and which are stored in consecutive memory locations under a common variable name is called an **array** or a **subscripted variable**. Here `roll` is an array, it is also called the subscripted variable with a subscript. Each element of an array is identified by using subscript (or subscripts) within square brackets after the common variable name (i.e. by the array name). The individual items are called the array elements. For example, `roll[4]` is the fifth element of the array `roll`. An array is known by the array name.

There are several types of arrays such as integer array, floating point array, character array, and also one-dimensional array, two-dimensional array, etc. The one-dimensional character array is known as **string**. Here we concentrate only on string, i.e. on one-dimensional character array. The details about array are discussed in Chapter 7.

If an array contains n elements, the subscript will be an integer quantity whose values are $0, 1, \ldots, n-1$. But, an n-character string contains $(n+1)$ elements, because of the null character (\0) which is automatically placed at the end of the string.

To explain the behaviours of string, let us consider the string "`India`". Suppose this string is stored into a one-dimensional array `x`. The string "`India`" contains 5 characters, so the size of the array `x` is 6. The value of each array element of `x` is shown below.

Element no.	Subscript	Array element	String character
1	0	`x[0]`	`I`
2	1	`x[1]`	`n`
3	2	`x[2]`	`d`
4	3	`x[3]`	`i`
5	4	`x[4]`	`a`
6	5	`x[5]`	`\0`

Thus, the third element of the character string `x` is the alphabet `d`.

3.4 Variable Declarations

It is required to declare the type of the variable before it is used in a program. All variables must be declared before the first executable statement. It is better to declare all the variables at the beginning of each function/program.

A declaration consists of a data type followed by one or more variable names (separated by comma(s), if there are more than one variables) and terminates by a semicolon (;). The array variable must be followed by a pair of square brackets, and within the bracket there is a positive integer mentioning the size of the array. The syntax for declaration $a_1, a_2, \ldots, a_n$ as variables is

$$\texttt{data\_type} \quad \mathtt{a_1, a_2, \ldots, a_n;}$$

Suppose, we consider two variables roll and marks. If they are integer variables, then the declaration statement is

```
int roll, marks;
```

or it can also be declared as

```
int roll;
int marks;
```

or as

```
int roll; int marks;
```

It may be noted that, comma (,) represents the separation between the variables and semicolon (;) represents the end of the declaration.

If roll is an integer variable and marks is a floating point variable, then the declaration statement may be of the following form.

```
int roll; float marks;
```

or

```
int roll;
float marks;
```

Suppose `name` is an array which represents the name of a country and assumed that the maximum number of characters required to name the country is 25, then the appropriate declaration is

```
char name[26];
```

Thus, the variable `name` can take 26 characters at a time as its value. But, if we declare

```
char name;
```

then the variable `name` will take only one character as its value.

Different types of data and the corresponding keywords are shown in Table 3.7.

Data type	Keywords
Character (or signed character)	`char` (or `signed char`)
Unsigned character	`unsigned char`
Integer or signed character	`int` (or `signed int`)
Unsigned integer	`unsigned int` (or `unsigned`)
Signed short integer	`signed short int` (or `short int` or `short`)
Unsigned short integer	`unsigned short int` (or `unsigned short`)
Signed long integer	`signed long int` (or `long int` or `long`)
Unsigned long integer	`unsigned long int` (or `unsigned long`)
Floating point	`float`
Double-precision floating point	`double`
Extended double-precision floating point	`long double`

Table 3.7: Different types of data and their keywords

3.4.1 Initialization of variable during declaration

The initial values of the variables can also be assigned during type declaration. This declaration must contain a data type, followed by a variable name, an equal sign and an appropriate constant value. The syntax of this declaration is

```
data_type   variable_name = constant;
```

The following are the valid declarations.

```
int    i=0;
float  x=10.5, y=2.5, p=8.54;
char   n='x';
char   country[]="India";
```

Note that the declaration `char country[]="India"`. In this declaration, `country` is a character array/string containing 6 elements. The first 5 elements represent the alphabet of the word "`India`" and the 6th element represents the null character (\0).

Noted that the size of the array is not mentioned here, computer will automatically determine the size of the array. If we would like to mention the size of the array, then it must be accurate, otherwise the array will store incorrect information.

For example, the declaration `char country[3]="India";` gives error; whereas the declaration `char country[10]="India";` will store the word "India" and the null character into the first 6 array elements `country[0]` to `country[5]`, the remaining elements may be assigned zeros or they may be filled by some other arbitrary characters.

3.5 typedef Statement

A user defined data type can be created using `typedef` statement. For example,

```
typedef char string[25];
```

declares `string` as a new data type which contains 25 characters. The statement

```
string name, address;
```

declares `name` and `address` are two variables of types `string` and each variable can store up to 25 characters against them.

3.6 Enumerations

An enumeration is a user defined data type. A finite set of identifiers called enumeration constants and they have signed integer values. The general form is

```
enum tag{member1, member2, ..., memberm};
```

where `enum` is the keyword, `tag` is user defined identifiers and `member1, member2, ..., memberm` represent the individual identifiers. All these members are distinct.

If the enumeration is defined, the corresponding variables can be declared as

```
enum tag variable1, variable2, ..., variablen;
```

where `variable1, variable2, ..., variablen` are the enumeration variables of type `tag`. The value of a variable of `enum` type is one of the enumeration constants.

Enumeration constants are automatically assigned consecutive integer values starting with 0. Therefore, `member1` will be assigned the value 0, `member2` will be assigned 1, and so on.

For example,

```
enum colour {white, red, green, blue, black};
```

defines `colour` as a new data type and enumeration constant will represents the following integer values.

Identifier	Value
white	0
red	1
green	2
blue	3
black	4

The value of the enumeration constants may be assigned as per users choice. For example, the declaration

```
enum colour{white=0, red=5, green, blue, black=15};
```

assigns the values of `white, red, green, blue` and `black` as 0, 5, 6, 7 and 15 respectively. Note that the value of `red` is 5 and the values of `green` and `blue` are not specified, but, they take next highest integers for `green` and `blue`.

The variables of type `colour` can be declared as

```
colour a, b=blue;
```

where `a` and `b` are declared as variables of type `colour` and the value of `b` is initialized as `blue`. The possible values of `a` and `b` are `white, red, green, blue` and `black`. The following declaration

```
colour b=yellow;
```

is invalid because `yellow` is not a valid value of `b` of type `colour`.

A variable of type enumeration can be declared during its definition as follows.

```
enum colour{white,red,green,blue,black} a, b;
```

Here `a, b` are two variables of type `colour`.

In a program several enumerations can be defined, but the enumeration constants must be distinct. That is,

```
enum colour1{white,yellow,red};
enum colour2{yellow,blue,black};
```

are not valid declarations because the values of `yellow` in two declarations are different, 1 in `colour1` and 0 in `colour2`.

3.7 Symbolic Constants

Sometimes it happened that a constant, say π, may be used in many places within a program. The value of π is an irrational number and its value correct up to 5 decimal places is 3.14159; and correct up to 8 decimal places is 3.14159265. Suppose we calculated the value of some expressions (used in the program) using $\pi = 3.14159$. Later we observed that we need more accurate values of the expression and we consider $\pi = 3.14159265$. If π occurs in many places in the program, then we have to update the value of π in all these places, but this process takes time and there is a chance to overlook one or more positions of π. In this situation, we may use a symbolic name for π, say PI. A **symbolic constant** is a name that substitutes a sequence of characters. The characters may be a numeric constant, a character constant or a string of characters. During compilation of the program, all the symbolic names are replaced by the corresponding character sequence. The symbolic constants are generally defined at the beginning of a program.

The syntax of this declaration is

```
#define   symbolic_name   value_of_constant
```

`symbolic_name` represents a symbolic name, which follow the rules of a variable name, and is usually written in upper case letters, to distinguish between symbolic constant and identifier. `value_of_constant` represents the sequence of characters for the `symbolic_name`. Symbolic names are also known as *constant identifiers*.

Some valid symbolic constants are:

```
#define  PI         3.14159
#define  f(x)       x*x+3*x+5.2
#define  TRUE       1
#define  COUNTRY    "India"
```

The following points are kept in mind during declaration of a symbolic constant.

- No blank space between the sign # and the keyword `define` is allowed.
- The first character of the line must be #.
- Blank spaces are required in between `#define` and `symbolic_name` and in between the `symbolic_name` and the `value_of_constant`.
- The declaration must not end with a semicolon, because during compilation, the symbolic name is replaced by the constant and the semicolon will appear in the wrong position. For example, if N is declared as

  ```
  #define    N    10;
  ```

  and the statement `M=N+5;` is in the program, then this statement becomes `M=10;+5;` and it is obviously incorrect.
- The value of the symbolic constant cannot be altered. For example, if the value of the symbolic constant TRUE is defined as 1 then the assignment TRUE=2 and TRUE=2*TRUE, etc. are illegal.
- No separate declaration for data type is required, its data type depends on the value assigned to the symbolic name.
- `#define` statements may appear in any place of the program, but usually it is placed at the beginning of the program.

Some illegal `#define` statements are given below.

`#define A=10`	[= sign is not allowed]
`#define N 5.3;`	[; at the end is not allowed]
`# define N 10`	[no blank space between # and `define`]
`#define N 5, m 10`	[multiple declarations are not allowed]
`#Define B 5`	[first character must be a lower case letter]

Note 3.7.1 It may be noted that the value of a variable can be changed, but the value of a symbolic name cannot be changed. The symbolic name is the representative of some constant, character, string or an expression. During compilation the value of the symbolic name is replaced by its value. But, variable always store a single value.

`#define` statement is a **preprocessor** (it is a program that provides the first step during conversion of a C program into machine language), compiler directive and has several features. The other features are discussed in detailed later.

3.8 `const` Qualifier

Several scientific constants are used in mathematical computation. For example, π, e and many others. The values of these quantities remain the same. If the values of these quantities are changed by mistake or any other way, then the result obtained from an expression containing these quantities, must be incorrect. To overcome these unexpected situation, C provides a feature called `const` declaration. For example, the value of π correct up to five decimal places can be declared as

```
const float PI=3.14159;
```

This means that `PI` is a floating point identifier whose value cannot be changed within the program.

Exercise III

Review Questions

1. Write all characters that are used to write a program in C.
2. Name and describe the four basic data types in C.
3. What do you mean by constant? Describe the four basic types of constants used in C.
4. What is unsigned and signed integer constants? What is the advantage of unsigned integer constant?
5. Which special rules are applied on integer constants?
6. How decimal constants, octal constants and hexadecimal constants can be distinguished from one another?
7. What are the uses of the qualifiers U, L and UL?
8. What are unsigned integer constants? What are long integer constants? How these constants differ from ordinary integer constants? How can they be written and identified?
9. Describe two ways to write floating point constants.
10. What is character constants? How a character constant is different from numeric constant? Do character constants represent numerical values?
11. What is an escape sequence? What is its purpose?
12. Write a brief note on escape sequences.
13. Can escape sequences be included in a string constant?
14. What is a variable? How can variables be characterized?
15. What are the rules for naming a C identifier? Are upper case and lower case letters equivalent? Are digits and special characters allowed in identifiers name?
16. How many characters are allowed in an identifier name? Are all these characters equally important?
17. What are keywords in C? Can keyword be used as an identifier? What restrictions apply to their use?

18. What do you mean by initialization of a variable? What is meant by value of a variable?
19. How do variables and symbolic name differ?
20. What are the differences between the declaration of a variable and definition of symbolic name?
21. What is the enumeration variable? How are they declared? What is the advantage of enumeration in a program?
22. What is the use of the qualifiers `const`?
23. What is the purpose of a type declaration? What does a type declaration consist of?
24. How an initial value can be assigned to a variable within type declaration? How are strings assigned to one-dimensional character array?
25. What is the difference between 'E' and "E"?
26. Which of the followings are not acceptable as an integer constant and why?
(i) 625 (ii) -4683 (iii) 0 (iv) 0.0 (v) 0. (vi) 15.0 (vii) −420. (viii) 13,50 (ix) 5/4
(x) $65 - 8 + 20$ (xi) $+ -$ 378 (xii) 15E3 (xiii) '101' (xiv) 010 (xv) +005 (xvi) 1D5
(xvii) FIVE (xviii) 5844334512 (xix) *532 (xx) $25 (xxi) Rs 124 (xxii) (2,3)
27. Which of the followings are not acceptable as floating point constant and why ?
(i) 40.0 (ii) 40 (iii) 40. (iv) 40,358 (v) 35,538.59 (vi) 48.0+36.0 (vii) −4250.83
(viii) 48E02 (ix) 420E3.5 (x) −.085E−6 (xi) 40/2.5 (xii) + *38.0 (xiii) 38.34.5
(xiv) THIRTY FIVE.THREE (xv) 37 $\not b$ 85.0 (xvi) 1.0D0 (xvii) (2.5,3)
(xviii) 90XE-12 (xix) −1.5E+128 (xx) 1.8×10^{-12} (xxi) 3×4 (xxii) 10^5
(xxiii) 5000$
28. Represent the following numbers as acceptable exponential forms.
(i) 6.023×10^{23} (ii) 42×10^5 (iii) .00000050 (iv) 105300000 (v) -325.029×10^{-15}
(vi) 150 (vii) -10^{18} (viii) 2/10,000,000
29. Which of the followings are not acceptable as a string constant and why ?
(i) "madam" (ii) theta (iii) "*****" (iv) "0000" (v) "its" (vi) 'its'
(vii) "vidyasagar university"
30. Which of the followings are not valid variable names in C ? State reasons.
(i) total−a (ii) end (iii) d.a. (iv) 5number (v) x5 (vi) x+y (vii) `int` (viii) `for` (ix) `char` (x) `enum`
31. Which of the followings are not acceptable type declaration statements and why?
(i) float ser, mass, hota.
(ii) int calcutta, kat, 50.5
(iii) double, x1, x2
(iv) long int a5, mass
(v) float a+b, 5star
32. Write the type declaration statements to declare
(i) roll, marks, subcode as integer variables.
(ii) name, add as string variables each of length 30 characters.

(iii) found, valid, x2 as double variables.

(iv) opt, menu, sub as character variables of length 1, 50 and 10 characters respectively.

Chapter 4

Operators and Expressions

In C, an **expression** is a combination of variables, constants, operators and functions (to be discussed later). An algebraic expression can not be entered to the computer directly. Before entering an algebraic expression in the computer it should be converted to a C expression. The algebraic and C expressions differ only in their syntax. Any algebraic expression can be converted to a C expression by using certain specific rules. At the time of execution of an expression the values of the variables (stored in memory) are used, to perform necessary operations. C provides different types of operators according to their use. They are classified as (i) arithmetic operators, (ii) unary operators, (iii) relational operators, (iv) logical operators, (v) assignment operators, (vi) conditional operators, and (vii) comma operator.

Other operators may also be available in C which are discussed later. C provides three major types of expressions namely (i) arithmetic expression, (ii) logical expression and (iii) character/string expression.

In this chapter, we will discuss about arithmetic and logical expressions. The character/string expression is discussed in Chapter 10.

4.1 Arithmetic Operators

The symbols for binary operators in C corresponding to different arithmetic operators are given in Table 4.1.

The operator % gives the remainder when an integer is divided by another integer. The remainder operator (%) requires that both the operands must be integers and second operand is nonzero. Similarly, in division (/) the second operand should be nonzero. The division of an integer by another integer is called **integer division** and the result of this division is an integer.

It may be noted that like FORTRAN, BASIC, etc., C does not provide any operator for exponentiation. However, the library function (`pow`) is used to carry out exponentiation.

Arithmetic operators	C operators
Addition (+)	+
Subtraction (–)	–
Multiplication (×)	*
Division (÷)	/
Modulo division	%

Table 4.1: Arithmetic operators

4.2 Arithmetic Expressions

Three types of arithmetic expressions are defined in C namely (i) integer expression, (ii) floating point expression, and (iii) mixed mode expression.

4.2.1 Integer expression

The mathematical expression obtained by combining integer variables and integer constants with the help of arithmetic operators, is known as integer expression.

Rules for writing an integer expression:

(i) A signed or unsigned integer variable or an integer constant is an integer expression.
e.g. `i, -k, -4, +4, 5`

(ii) An integer expression connected by an arithmetic operator to an unsigned integer constant is an integer expression.
e.g. `-ia*ib, -ia*ib+ic, -ia*ib+ic/j`

(iii) An integer expression enclosed in parentheses is an integer expression.
e.g. `(-k*i+j), (kat*mat/nat)`

(iv) Two integer expressions connected by an arithmetic operator is an integer expression.

(v) Two arithmetic operators should not occur in succession in an integer expression.

Some invalid integer expression:

`ia ib` (operator missing, correct expression may be `ia*ib` or `ia+ib` etc.)
`l.m` (dot(.) is not a valid arithmetic operator)
`(ix*(ly+j)` (mismatch in the parentheses, correct expression may be `(ix*(ly+j))`
`ia/-k` (consecutive two operators are not allowed)

Note on integer division

When an integer is divided by an another integer then the result may contain a fractional part. But in C, the fractional part is discarded during calculation, e.g. the value of 5/4 is 1 and not 1.25, 4/5 is 0 and not .8.

The value of the expression `32/5*5+8/9` is calculated as follows:
`32/5*5+8/9=6*5+0=30+0=30`

4.2.2 Floating point expression

The mathematical expression obtained by combining floating point constants and variables with the help of arithmetic operators, is known as floating point expression.

Rules for writing a floating point expression:

(i) A signed or unsigned floating point variable or a floating point constant is a floating point expression.
e.g. `abe, -ab, -4.5, 2.0, .5e-5`

(ii) A floating point expression connected by an arithmetic operator to an unsigned floating point variable name or an unsigned floating point constant is a floating point expression.
e.g. `-a+bat+ball+a*b`

(iii) A floating point expression enclosed in parentheses is a floating point expression.
e.g. `(bat+4.5), (a+all)`

(iv) Two floating point expressions connected by an arithmetic operator is a floating point expression.
e.g. `a*all+pal+doll, (are*al)/(ball*am)`

(v) Two arithmetic operators should not occur in succession in a floating point expression.

(vi) A floating point expression may be exponentiated by an integer expression to form a floating point expression.

Some invalid expressions:
B*A+6.53– (operator – at the end of the expression is not allowed)
z–r/–s (consecutive two operators)
z/(x–x) (division by zero).

The expression is scanned from left to right, to complete the execution of all divisions and multiplications in the order of their appearance. Finally, all additions and subtractions are performed again from the left of the expression. If there is any parentheses within the expression then the expression within the parentheses is evaluated first, using the above rules. The following expression is evaluated according to the above rules.

e.g. `4.0*a-b/(c+6.7)`
$= 4.0 * a - b/e_1$ where $e_1 = c + 6.7$
$= e_2 - e_3$ where $e_2 = 4.0 * a$ and $e_3 = b/e_1$
$= e_4$ where $e_4 = e_2 - e_3$.

At first the value of `c+6.7` (within parentheses) is evaluated and stored in e_1. In second step all multiplications and divisions are done from left to right. The values of $4.0 * a$ and b/e_1 are stored in e_2 and e_3 respectively. Finally, addition and subtraction are performed from left to right.

4.2.3 Mixed mode expression and implicit conversion

An expression, formed by an integer, floating point or character constants or variables is called a **mixed mode expression**. Modern computers execute mixed mode expressions. Suppose we have to compute the value of `A/B`. If `A` is an integer variable and `B` is floating point variable then before the division `A` must be converted to floating point and then `A` is divided by `B`. Finally, the result is stored as a floating point number.

Figure 4.1 shows the execution of the mixed mode expression

$$f = a * b + c/(l + m) - l * (m/5),$$

where a, b, c are floating point variables and l, m are integer variables.

During evaluation of mixed mode expression, the types of the operands are automatically converted in appropriate data type so that the expression can be evaluated without losing any significance. This automatic conversion is known as **implicit type conversion**. During conversion the 'lower' type operands are converted to 'higher' type operands and the result is of the higher type.

The sequence of higher to lower data types are shown in Table 4.2.

`long double`	higher
`double`	
`float`	
`unsigned long int`	↓
`long int`	
`unsigned int`	
`int`	
`char, short`	lower

Table 4.2: Conversion hierarchy

If one of the operands is `double` (higher type) and other is `float` (lower type), then the operand of type `float` is converted first to `double` type and the result will be double. Similarly, if one operand is `float` and other is `int`, then the `int` operand is converted to `float` type and the result will be of type `float`, and so on.

The final result of an expression is converted to the type of the variable of the left hand side of the expression. It may be noted that during

(i) `float` to `int` conversion, the fractional part is truncated,

(ii) `double` to `float` conversion, the fractional part is rounded,

(iii) `long int` to `int` conversion, the higher order bits are dropped.

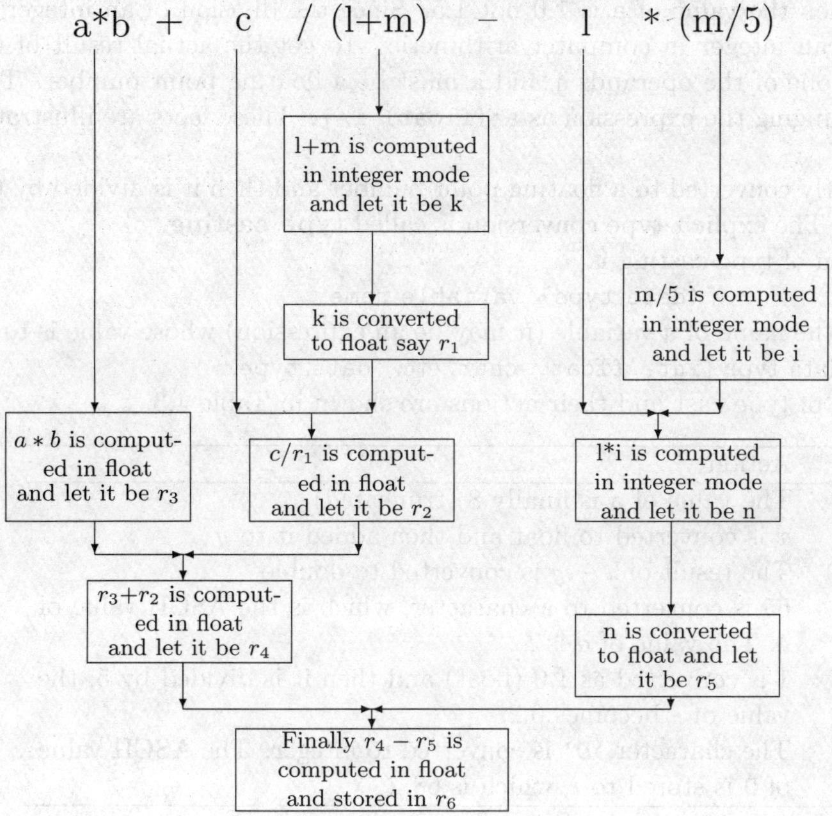

Figure 4.1: Steps to compute a mixed mode expression

Examples on arithmetic expression
1. $\frac{a+b}{x-y^2}$. A translation of this expression into C is `(a+b)/(x-y*y)`.
2. $23.9 \times 10^{-2}mv^2 + fg/4d$.
In C it becomes `23.9E-2*m*v*v+f*g/(4.*d)`

Mode of arithmetic expression and type casting

A floating point variable may be set equal to an integer expression and vice-versa.

If an integer variable or expression is set equal to a floating point expression, then the value of the floating point expression is 'truncated' and stored as an integer variable. If `l=3./2.` and `l` is an integer variable, then `l=1`, and if `l=2.0/4.0`, then the value of `l` is `0`.

If a floating point variable is set equal to an integer expression then the value of the integer expression is converted to floating point mode before it is stored as a floating point variable.

For example, let `j, k` be two integer variables and `a` be a floating point variable. If `j=4, k=2` and `a=j/k`, then the value of `a` is 2.0, which takes four bytes to store its value. If `j=3` and `k=2`, then the value of `a` is 1.0 not 1.5. Since the division of an integer by another integer is an integer in computer arithmetic. To get the actual result of the expression `a=j/k`, one of the operands `j` and `k` must be a floating point number. This can be done by changing the expression as `a=(float) i/j`. These facts are illustrated in Figure 4.1.

Here `i` is explicitly converted to a floating point number and then it is divided by the integer variable `j`. The explicit type conversion is called **type casting**.

The general form of type casting is

```
(data_type) variable_name
```

`variable_name` is the name of a variable (it may be an expression) whose value is to be changed into the data type (`int, float, char`, etc.) `data_type`.

Some more uses of type cast and their actions are shown in Table 4.3.

Expression	Action
`a=(int)8.75`	The value of `a` is finally 8 (truncated)
`b=(float)x+y`	x is converted to float and then added it to y
`c=(double)(x+y)`	The result of $x + y$ is converted to double
`d=(char)65`	65 is converted to a character, which is the ASCII value of `A`. The value of d is `A`.
`e=(float)1/5`	1 is converted as 1.0 (float) and then it is divided by 5; the value of e becomes 0.2.
`i=(int)'D'`	The character `'D'` is converted to integer. The ASCII value of `D` is stored to i, which is 68.

Table 4.3: Some uses of type cast operators

4.2.4 Hierarchy of arithmetic operators

In general, an arithmetic expression contains numeric constants, numeric variables (integer, floating point and character), arithmetic operators (addition, subtraction, multiplication, division and modulo division) and parentheses. At the time of execution of an expression only one arithmetic operation is executed at a time.

The hierarchy of operators is the order in which the arithmetic operations are executed. The hierarchy of arithmetic operators is shown in Table 4.4.

Example 4.2.1 Evaluate the following arithmetic expression, if `a=2.5, b=7.2, c=2.4, i=5, j=2`

Operator	Hierarchy
multiplication (*), division (/) and modulo division (%)	first
addition (+) and subtraction (−)	second

Table 4.4: Hierarchy of arithmetic operators

(i) `a*b+c/j*i`, (ii) `i/j+b*c+i*a`
where `i`, `j` are integer and `a`, `b`, `c` are floating point variables.

Solution.
(i) `a*b+c/j*i=2.5*7.2+2.4/2*5`
```
=18.0+2.4/2*5=18.0+1.2*5=18.0+6.0
=24.0
```
(ii) `i/j+b*c+i*a`
```
=5/2+7.2*2.4+5*2.5=2+7.2*2.4+5*2.5
=2+17.28+5*2.5=2+17.28+12.5
=2.0+17.28+12.5=19.28+12.5
=31.78
```

Example 4.2.2 Suppose `a`, `b` are floating point variables having values `a=2.7`, `b=3.5` and `j` and `k` are integer variables with values `j=3`, `k=-2`. Find the values of `x` and `l` after each pair of statements are executed:
(i) `x=a+j*pow(k,2)+b`, `l=a+j*pow(k,2)+b`
(ii) `x=k/3*a/2`, `l=k/3*a/2`, where `x` and `l` are floating point and integer variables respectively.

Solution. (i) `x=a+j*pow(k,2)+b`
```
=2.7+3*pow(--2,2)+3.5=2.7+3*4+3.5
=2.7+12+3.5=2.7+12.0+3.5=14.7+3.5
=18.2
```
`l=a+j*pow(k,2)+b=18.2` (computed using previous technique)
therefore, `l=18` (as `l` is an integer variable)
(ii) `x=k/3*a/2=-2/3*2.7/2 = 0*2.7/2 = 0.0*2.7/2 = 0.0/2 = 0.0/2.0 = 0.0`
`l=k/3*a/2=0.0` (same as above)
Therefore, `l=0`

Example 4.2.3 Evaluate the following expressions for $i = 4, j = 5, k = 3, l = 2, c = 0.8$
(i) `v=0.123e02+34.5e-01+pow(4,0.5)+c`
(ii) `m=j+l*i/3+j/i-pow(k,i)/l`. Here `i, j, k, l` are integer variables and `c` is a floating point variable.

Solution. (i) `v=0.123e02+34.5e-01+pow(4,0.5)+0.8`
`=0.123e02+34.5e-01+2.0+0.8`

= 15.75+2.0+0.8 = 17.75+0.8 =18.55
(ii) m=j+l*i/3+j/i-pow(k,i)/l
= 5+2*4/3+5/4-pow(3,4)/2 = 5+2*4/3+5/4-81/2 = 5+8/3+5/4-81/2
= 5+2+1-40 = 7+1-40 = 8-40 =-32

Example 4.2.4 Find the values of a1 and aj:
(i) a1 = pow(i,k)/2 + k/8 + i * k/2 - i/4 * k + int(a) where i = 2, k = 4, a=-2.05
(ii) aj =2*b/2-l*(m/2) + c/pow(2,1e01/2)-log(j/pow(2,l)) where j= 4, l = 2, m = 3, c = 4.0, b = 12.5.

Here i, j, k, l, m are integers and a, a1, aj, b, c are floating point variables.

Solution. (i) a1 = pow(2,4)/2 +4/8 + 2*4/2 - 2/4 * 4 + int(-2.05)
= 16/2 + 4/8 + 8/2 - 2/4 *4 - 2
= 8 + 0 +4 - 0*4 - 2 = 8 + 0 + 4 - 0 - 2 = 10
therefore, a1 = 10.0
(ii) aj = 2 * 12.5/2 - 2 * (3/2) + 4.0/ pow(2,1e01/2) -log(4/pow(2,2))
= 25.0/2 - 2 *1 + 4.0 / pow(2, 5.0) - log(4/4)
= 12.5 - 2 + 4.0/32.0 - log(1)
= 12.5 - 2 + .125 - 0.0
= 10.625

4.3 Library Functions

There are certain mathematical functions such as trigonometric, exponential, logarithmic, etc. which are frequently used in programs, especially to solve scientific problems. These functions are generally referred as **library functions**, or **built-in functions** or **intrinsic functions**. The general form of these functions is

function_name (arguments)

The argument of a function can be a valid variable name or an expression. It can also be a floating point number, an integer or a character. The argument should be written within parentheses. If a function has more than one argument then they are separated by a comma.

A library function is used simply by writing the function name followed by necessary arguments, which is the input of the function. The parentheses must be present after the function name, even if there are no arguments. A function generally returns a value. This is called the output of the function. If there is no output of the function, then the word void is used to indicate that it does not give any output.

To use the library function in a program, certain specific information is included in the program. The information is generally stored in some special files, which are available with the C compiler. Such file names are included in the beginning of each program using the following preprocessor statement.

```
#include <filename>
```

Mathematical function	C equivalent	Mode of input	Mode of output
Power (a^b)	`pow(a,b)`	double,double	double
Power (10^a)	`pow10(a)`	double	double
Exponential (e^x)	`exp(x)`	double	double
Logarithm ($\log_e x$)	`log(x)`	double ($x > 0$)	double
($\log_{10} x$)	`log10(x)`	double (x >0)	double
Square root ($\sqrt{x}$)	`sqrt(x)`	double (x >0)	double
Sine ($\sin x$)	`sin(x)`	double (x in radian)	double
Cosine ($\cos x$)	`cos(x)`	double (x in radian)	double
Tangent ($\tan x$)	`tan(x)`	double (x in radian)	double
Hyperbolic sine ($\sinh x$)	`sinh(x)`	double	double
Hyperbolic cosine ($\cosh x$)	`cosh(x)`	double	double
Hyperbolic tangent ($\tanh x$)	`tanh(x)`	double	double
Arc sine ($\sin^{-1} x$)	`asin(x)`	double ($-1 \leq x \leq 1$)	double
Arc cosine ($\cos^{-1} x$)	`acos(x)`	double ($-1 \leq x \leq 1$)	double
Arc tangent ($\tan^{-1} x$)	`atan(x)`	double	double
Absolute value ($\|x\|$)	`abs(x)`	int	int
	`fabs(x)`	double	double
Integer to double conversion	`float(n)` or `(float)n`	integer	double
Double to integer conversion	`int(x)` or `(int)x`	double	integer
Round up to next integer value	`ceil(x)`	double	double
Round down to the next integer values	`floor(x)`	double	double
Return remainder	`fmod(x1,x2)`	double, double	double

Table 4.5: Some library functions

where **`filename`** represents the actual name of a specific file. Several such files are available in any C compiler.

Some commonly used files are **`stdio.h`**, **`math.h`**, **`stdlib.h`**, **`string.h`**, etc. The file extension 'h' is designated as a 'header' file. Some frequently used library functions are given in Table 4.5.

The details about the header files are available in Chapter 17.

Note 4.3.1 (i) The square root function `sqrt` gives only the positive root.

(ii) In the hierarchy of operators the library function operation gets precedence over all other operators.

(iii) The argument of a function can also be some other functions, i.e. one may have function of functions.

Some unacceptable expressions:
`w=x/0.0` (division by 0 (zero)).
`w=sqrt(64)` (argument of the function `sqrt` should be floating point).
`p=sqrt(-64.0)` (argument can never be negative).

Note 4.3.2 A straight forward translation of the expression $x^{\frac{2}{3}} - y^{-2}$ in C is `pow(x,2/3)-pow(y,-2)`.

But this expression is incorrect since the term `pow(x,2/3)`, the division 2/3 is an integer division of 2 by 3. In integer expression evaluation the result can only be an integer. Thus 2/3 gives an integer value 0 (zero). The correct translation of the expression is `pow(x,2.0/3.0)-pow(y,-2)` or `pow(x,2.0/3.0)-1./(y*y)`

The following three header files with their functions are frequently used in several programs.

`stdio.h` (standard I/O header file)

Function name	Use
`gets`	Reads a string
`puts`	Prints a string
`getchar`	Reads a character
`putchar`	Prints a character
`scanf`	Reads multiple variables of different types
`printf`	Prints multiple variables of different types

`string.h` (string manipulation header file)

Function name	Use
`strcat`	Concatenates of two strings
`strcmp`	Compares two strings
`strcpy`	Copies a string to another string
`strlen`	Determines the length of the string

`ctype.h` (character type header file)

Function name	Use
`toascii`	Returns the ASCII code of a character
`tolower`	Converts a character into lower case character
`toupper`	Converts a character into upper case character

Example 4.3.1 Write the following expressions in C equivalent:

(i) $\frac{\alpha}{\sqrt{\alpha^2+\omega^2}} \cos(\omega t+\phi)+\sin^{-1}(a+b)$

(ii) $\log_e \sqrt{\frac{x}{yz}} + \log_{10}|x|$

(iii) $\dfrac{1 - e^{-\alpha\sqrt{x}}}{1 + xe^{-|x|}} + \eta \cos\theta$

(iv) $a\cos x + b\cos^2 x + c\cos^3 x$

(v) $2.5\log_{10} x + \cos 32^o + |x^2 - y^2| + \sqrt{2xy}$

(vi) $kappa = \sqrt{\sin(a^2) + \cos(\sqrt{b}\log c)}$

(vii) $y = (a + b^2 + ab)^5/\sqrt{a + b + 1}$

(viii) $power = 2.9 \times 10^{-2}\left(1.0 + \dfrac{.7454LD^2}{v}\right)LD^2R$

(ix) $R = \sqrt{2\pi}e^{-n}n^{n+1/2}$

(x) $\dfrac{a + b}{c - d}$

(xi) $r = \sqrt{a^2 + b^2 - 2ab\cos\theta} + |x^{1/3} - y^{1/2}|$

(xii) $\sqrt{1 - .162\sin^2\phi} + \sqrt{\dfrac{3x + 2}{3}}$

(xiii) $x =$(fraction part of a) $\times \sqrt{|a - b|\sin^{-1} a + \dfrac{\log_{10} c}{e^d}}$

(xiv) $n =$(integer part of x) $\times \tan hy + a^5 \log_e y$

(xv) $g = 32.17 \times 10^{23}\left(\dfrac{a}{a + h}\right)^2 + \sin a \sin b - |g - a|$

(xvi) $A = \dfrac{1 - \cos\theta}{1 + \cos\theta} + \dfrac{e^{\beta^2}\sin\theta}{\sqrt{2\alpha x + \gamma}} \cdot \dfrac{ab^2}{c}$

(xvii) $x + \tan^{-1}(\sqrt{x + y}) - \dfrac{\log_e(p + |q|)}{2r}$

(xviii) Absolute value of the product of a and b – $e^{-2x^2} - \sin\left(\dfrac{n^2\cos hx}{1 - xy\sec x}\right)$

(xix) $p = \sec x + \log_e(|\cos^{-1} x + \tan^{-1} y|)$

(xx) $x = \sqrt{a^2 + b^2}\tan(b/a) + \dfrac{8}{2\sqrt{3}}\log_{10} c$

(xxi) $v = A\log_{10}(\cos p) - B\sqrt{\cos^{-1}(\sqrt{B^2 + T^2} + |c|)}$

(xxii) $a = \dfrac{x^3\sqrt{\sin(x + \sqrt{x})}}{1 + \pi x^3 \log x}$

(xxiii) $x =$ (decimal part of a) $\times \sqrt{|a-b|\sin^{-1} a}$

(xxiv) $x_{n+1} = \frac{1}{k}\left[x_n + \frac{a}{x_n^{k-1}}\right]$

Solution.

(i) `alpha* cos(omega*t+phi)/sqrt(alpha*alpha + omega*omega) + asin(a+b)`
(ii) `log(sqrt(x/(y*z))) + log10(fabs(x))`
(iii) `(1.0-exp(-alpha*sqrt(x)))/ (1.0+x*exp(-fabs(x)))+ eta* cos(theta)`
(iv) `a*cos(x)+b*pow(cos(x),2)+c*pow(cos(x),3)`
(v) `2.5*log10(x)+cos(3.14159*32.0/180.0)+ fabs(x*x-y*y) + sqrt(2.0*x*y)`
(vi) `kappa=sqrt(sin(a*a)+cos(sqrt(b)*log(c)))`
(vii) `y=pow((a+b*b+a*b),5)/sqrt(a+b+1.0)`
(viii) `power=2.9e-2*(1.0+.7454*l*d*d/v)*l*d*d*r`
(ix) `r=sqrt(2.*3.14159)*exp(-n)*pow(n,n+0.5)`
(x) `(a+b)/(c-d)`
(xi) `r=sqrt(a*a+b*b-2*a*b*cos(theta)) + fabs(pow(x,(1.0/3.0)) -sqrt(y))`
(xii) `sqrt(1.0-0.162*sin(phi)*sin(phi))+sqrt((3.*x+2.)/3.)`
(xiii) `x=(a-(int)a)*(sqrt(fabs(a-b)*asin(a)))+ log10(c) /exp(d)`
(xiv) `n=(int)x*tanh(y)+pow(a,5)*log(y)`
(xv) `g=32.17e23*pow((a/(a+h)),2)+ sin(a)* sin(b)-fabs(g-a)`
(xvi) `a=(1.-cos(theta))/ (1.+cos(theta)) + (exp(beta*beta)`
`* sin(theta) *a*b*b)/ (sqrt(2.*alpha*x+gamma)*c)`
(xvii) `x+atan(sqrt(x+y))-(log(p+fabs(q)))/(2.*r)`
(xviii) `fabs(a*b)-exp(-2.0*x*x)- sin((n*n*cosh(x)) / (1.0-x*y/cos(x)))`
(xix) `p=1./cos(x)+log(fabs(acos(x)+atan(y)))`
(xx) `x=sqrt(a*a+b*b)*tan(b/a)+8.*log10(c)/(2.0*sqrt(3.0)`
(xxi) `v=a*log10(cos(p))-b*sqrt(acos(sqrt(b*b+t*t+fabs(c))))`
(xxii) `a=x*x*x*sqrt(sin(x+sqrt(x)))/(1.0+3.1415*x*x*x*log(x))`
(xxiii) `x=(a-(int)a)*sqrt(fabs(a-b)*asin(a))`
(xxiv) `x=(x+a/pow(x,(k-1)))/k`

4.4 Unary Operators

C supports different types of unary operators. The negative operator (−) is the most common operator, which is used both as binary and unary operator. Other unary operators are `+`, `++`, `--`, etc. In unary operation, only one operand is required.

Generally, unary operators precede their operands, but some unary operators are written after their operands. C provides two new unary operators called **increment** (`++`) and **decrement** (`--`) operators.

The increment operator increases the value of the operand by 1, whereas decrement operator decreases the value of the operand by 1.

Suppose the value of the variables `x` and `i` are respectively `5.234` and 4. The expressions `++x` and `++i` are equivalent to `x=x+1` and `i=i+1`. After execution of these expressions the values of `x` and `i` become `6.234` and `5` respectively. Similarly, if `x=5.234` and `i=4`, then after execution of the expressions `--x` and `--i` the values of `x` and `i` change to `4.234` and `3` respectively.

The increment and decrement operators can also be used in other ways. These operators may be used after the operand (postfix form). The use of the forms `++i` and `i++` have the same effect. In both cases, the value of `i` is increased by 1. But, if we use these expressions in another way, the prefix (`++i`) and postfix (`i++`) operators give different results. For example, we consider `j=++i` and `k=i++`, and the value of `i` is 5. The value of `i` in both cases is equal to 6. After execution of `j=++i`, the values of `j` and `i` are 6 and 6. Again, if `i=5`, then after execution of `k=i++`, the values of `k` and `i` are `k=5` and `i=6`. In the expression `j=++i`, the operator `++` is applied on `i` first and then assigns the incremented value of `i` to `j`. In this case, the values of `i` and `j` are same. Whereas in the expression `k=i++`, the value of `i` is assigns to `k` first and then the value of `i` is incremented by 1. In this case, the value of `k` is 1 less than `i`.

4.4.1 sizeof operator

Another unary operator available in C is `sizeof`. This operator gives the size of its operand in bytes. The operand may be a variable or an expression or cast (the data type).

To illustrate the use of `sizeof` operator, the following declarations are considered.

```
short int i;
int j;
long int k;
float a;
double b;
long double c;
```

The values of the expression `sizeof i; sizeof j; sizeof k; sizeof a; sizeof b; sizeof c;` are 2, 2, 4, 4, 8, 10 respectively.

This operator is also used to find out the number of characters in a string. For example, we consider the following string declaration

```
char a[]="India";
```

The value of the variable n in the statement `n=sizeof a` is 5.

The statement `sizeof (int); sizeof (float); sizeof (char)` gives the output 2, 4, 1 respectively.

It is very important to note that the *precedence of unary operator is higher than the binary operators. The associativity of unary operator is right-to-left.*

There are some other unary operators available in C, which will be discussed later.

4.5 Relational and Logical Operators

Often we need the comparison of two numerical numbers or expressions.

These types of operators which are not arithmetical are called **relational operators**. The relational operators and their C equivalent are given below.

Algebraic form	$a > b$	$a \geq b$	$a < b$	$a \leq b$	$a = b$	$a \neq b$
C form	a > b	a >= b	a < b	a <= b	a == b	a =!b

The operators < . <=, >, >= fall in the same precedence group whereas == and =! fall in another precedence group called **equality operators**. The associativity of these operators is left-to-right.

The precedence of relational operators is lower than unary and arithmetic (binary) operators. Again, the precedence of equality operators is lower than the relational operators. An expression containing these six operators, operands and their combination is called **relational expressions**. For example, a > y, x >= 4.5 are the relational expressions. The value of the relational expression is either *true* or *false*. The resulting expression is of type integer, since *true* and *false* are represented by integer value 1 and 0 respectively.

Examples:

Let a and b be numeric constants.

(i) `(5/2 > 3.5*2-7)` (value of this expression is *true*)

(ii) `!(a > b)`

(iii) `c=(a>b)<=(b>=5.2)`

4.5.1 Logical operators

Two or more relational expressions can be combined by two or more operators *and* and *or*. Also, the negation of a relational expression is done by another operator called *not*. These operators are called **logical operators**. The symbols for logical *and*, *or* and *not* operators are &&, || and ! respectively.

Logical and (&&)

The syntax of this operator is

```
a && b
```

where a and b are two relational variables/expressions. The value of the entire expression `c=a && b` is obtained according to the rule given below.

a	b	logical value of c	integer value of c
true	true	true	1
true	false	false	0
false	true	false	0
false	false	false	0

Logical `or` (||)

The syntax of this operator is

`a || b`

where `a` and `b` are two relational variables/expressions. If both the values of `a` and `b` are false then the value of this expression is false, otherwise it is equal to true. The value of the expression `c=a || b` is obtained as per the following rule.

a	b	logical value of c	integer value of c
true	true	true	1
true	false	true	1
false	true	true	1
false	false	false	0

Logical `not` (!)

If `a` is a logical variable, then the expression

`!a`

gives the opposite (negation) value of `a`. That is, if `a` is *true*, then `!a` is *false* and if `a` is *false* `!a` is *true*. It may be noted that the logical not operator is a unary operator.

The precedence of logical operators are !, &&, ||.

Let us consider the following logical expression
`!(c=='x'||p>=5)&&(i<5&&v!=5)`, and the values of `p`, `i`, `v` and `c` are respectively 6, 4, 5 and `'x'`.

The above expression is evaluated as follows:
`!(true||true)&&(true&&false)`

[since the priority of the relational operator is higher than logical operator]

`=!true&&false`
`= false&&false` [since priority of unary operator (!) is higher]
`= false.`

4.6 Assignment Operators

The assignment operator is essential in every program. This operator assigns a new value to a variable. Its general form is

`variable=exp;`

where `variable` is a variable and `exp` may be a constant, another variable or an expression to which a value has been assigned previously or a formula which can be evaluated by the computer.

Both `variable` and `exp` should be of same type, i.e. both should be either numeric or character, etc. This statement assigns the value of `exp` to `variable`. The new value replaces the earlier value, if any, associated with `variable`.

Some arithmetic assignment statements are `x=5.9,  z=a,  z=a+b*c`.

In algebra, the equations `x=2` and `2=x` both are same, but in C, `2=x` is an invalid statement, because the value of `x` can not be stored in 2 as it is a constant quantity.

Similarly, the assignment `b+c=a` is also invalid because the value of `a` can not be stored in an expression.

Some invalid assignment statements:
(i) `1.2=y` (variable should be on the left hand side)
(ii) `s=a*b+c/3+pow(-6.5,3.0)` (floating point exponent is not allowed for negative base)
(iii) `v=a(b+c)-d/5` (operator missing after the variable a)
(iv) `r=a/2+b*5-log(-3)` (argument of the function `log` should be positive and floating point number)

It may be noted that the assignment operator = and the equality operator == are two different operators. The assignment operator, assigns a value to a variable, whereas the equality operator is used to check whether two expressions have the same value. The entire expression containing variable, assignment operator and righthand side expression is also known as **assignment statement**.

If two operators in an assignment statement are of different data types, then the value of the right hand side expression will automatically be converted to the type of the left hand variable. For example, if `i` is an integer variable and the assignment statement is `i=4.5;` then 4 is assigned as the value of `i`.

The following points are to be noted during automatic type conversion.

- A floating point value may be truncated if it is assigned to an integer variable.
- A double precision value may be truncated if it is assigned to a floating point (single precision) variable.

Multiple assignments are also permissible in C. That is

```
a=b=x=z=2.5;
```

is a valid statement in C. For this statement the value of the variables `a, b, x` and `z` become 2.5.

The associativity of multiple assignment is right-to-left. This means, in above example, 2.5 is assigned to `z` first, then the value of `z` is assigned to `x`, then the value of `x` is assigned to `b`, and so on. One interesting situation is illustrated below.

Suppose `i` and `a` are integers and floating point variables respectively. The multiple assignment statement

```
i=a=3.4;
```

assigns the value 3.4 to `a` and the truncated value of `a`, which is 3 assigned to `i`, i.e. `a=3.400000` and `i=3` are the final values of `a` and `i`, whereas the assignment statement `a=i=3.4`, assigns the truncated value 3.4, i.e. 3 to `i` and then the value of `i` is assigned to `a`, i.e. `i=3` and `a=3.000000`.

It is very interesting that C supports five more assignment operators, viz. `+=`, `-=`, `*=`, `/=` and `%=`. These operators are basically shortened form of the operators `+`, `-`, `*`, `/` and `%`.

The assignment expression

`a+=b;`

is equivalent to

`a=a+b;`

Similarly, the expression

`a*=b;`

is equivalent to

`a=a*b;`

Generally, `a` is a variable or an array element.

The use of these operators are shown in Table 4.6.

Expression	Equivalent expression
`i+=6`	`i=i+6`
`i-=5`	`i=i-5`
`i*=4`	`i=i*4`
`i/=7`	`i=i/7`
`i%=8`	`i=i%8`

Table 4.6: Arithmetic expression

The precedence of these operators is
`=, +=, -=, *=, /=, %=` and the *associativity is right-to-left.* The precedence of these operators among all the operators discussed so far is the lowest.

4.7 Conditional Operator

The only **ternary operator** (needs three operands) in C is `?:`, combination of a question mark and a colon. The general syntax of this operator is

`expression1 ?  expression2 :  expression3;`

At the time of execution of this expression, the value of `expression1` is evaluated first. If the value of `expression1` is true, then `expression2` is performed, otherwise `expression3` is performed. The evaluated value is the final value of the conditional expression. It may be noted that exactly one expression, either `expression2` or `expression3` is performed during the execution of this statement.

Suppose `i` and `j` are two integer variables and `j=5`. We consider the following conditional expression

`k=(i > 5) ?  j++:  j--;`

If the condition `i>5` is true then `j` is assigned to `k` and then `j` is incremented by 1, i.e. the value of `k` and `j` are respectively `k=5, j=6`. Otherwise, the value of `j` is assigned to `k` (`k=5`) and then `j` is decremented by 1.

The following conditional statement is also valid in C.

`sign = (d > 0) ? '+' :  '−';`

In this case, if `d` is greater than `0`, then the value of `sign` is '+', otherwise the value of `sign` is '-'.

4.8 Comma Operator

A set of expressions written within parentheses and separated by commas can be assigned to a variable. For example, let `i, j` and `k` be integer variables and consider the following declaration

```
int i,j,k=5;
```

Let us consider the following statement

```
i=(j=10,j=j*k,++j);
```

Note that three expressions `j=10, j=j*5` and `++j` are written within the parentheses and they are separated by commas. The expression within parentheses are evaluated *left to right* and the value of *last expression* is the final value of the variable `i`. In the first expression 10 is assigned to `j`, then the value of `j*k` ($= 10 \times 5 = 50$) is assigned to `j`, finally the incremented value of `j` ($= 51$) is assigned to `i`. Thus the final value of `i` is 51.

Example 4.8.1 Let `i, j, k, l` be integer variables and `i=10, j=25`. Find the values of `k` and `l` from the following.
(i) `k=(i % j) + (i++) *5;`
(ii) `l=(++i)+(j % i)-sizeof(j);`

Solution.
```
(i)  k  =(10%25)+(i++)*5
        =10+10*5
        =60
(ii) l  =11+(25%11)-2
        =11+3-2
        =12
```

Example 4.8.2 Let `i=5, j=12, k, l` be the integers variables. Find the values of the following variables/expressions.
(i) `k=(i>2) ? j++ : 10` (iv) `i+=j+(int)5.6`
(ii) `l=(i++,j+i)` (v) `(i/j)+(float)i/j`
(iii) `l=(j=10,j+5,j+i)`

Solution. (i) Here `i=5`, so `i>2` is true. Thus the value of `k` is equal to `j++`, which is 13.

(ii) The value of `i` after increment becomes 6. The value of `j+i` is then 18, this value is assigned to the variable `l`. Thus the final value of `l` is 18.

(iii) In this case, the value of `j` is assigned as 10. The value of the expression `j+5` is 15, but it does not store to any variable, as it is not the last expression. The value of `j+i` which is `10+5=15`, is assigned to `l`. Thus the final value of `l` is 15.

(iv) The value of `(int) 5.6` is 5. The value of right side is `j+5=12+5=17`. This value is added to the previous value of `i`. Thus the final value of `i` is `5+17=22`.

(v) The value of `i/j=5/12=0`. But, the value of `(float) i/j` is equivalent to `5.0/12` and its value is `0.416667`. Thus the final value of the expression is `0+0.416667=0.416667`.

The precedence of all operators are listed in Table 4.7.

Operator	Description	Precedence	Associativity
( )	Function call	1	$L \rightarrow R$ (left to right)
[ ]	Array element reference		
+	Unary plus	2	$R \rightarrow L$
−	Unary minus		
++	Increment		
−−	Decrement		
!	Logical negation		
*	Pointer reference		
&	Address		
`sizeof`	Size of an object		
(type)	Type cast		
*	Multiplication	3	$L \rightarrow R$
/	Division		
%	Modulus		
+	Addition	4	$L \rightarrow R$
−	Substraction		
<	Less than	5	$L \rightarrow R$
<=	Less than or equal to		
>	Greater than		
>=	Greater than or equal to		
==	Equality	6	$L \rightarrow R$
!=	Inequality		
&&	Logical AND	7	$L \rightarrow R$
||	Logical OR	8	$L \rightarrow R$
? :	Conditional expression	9	$R \rightarrow L$
=,*=,/=,%= +=, −=	Assignment operators	10	$R \rightarrow L$
,	Comma operator	11	$L \rightarrow R$

Table 4.7: Precedence and associativity of operators

Important Points

1. Take care to use increment and decrement operators, particularly postfix and

prefix operators. Avoid these operators on floating point numbers. Apply these operators only on the variable identifier.

2. Put a semicolon at the end of each expression.
3. Avoid division by zero or very small number and subtraction between two small numbers.
4. Care should be taken of the precedence and associativity of operators while writing an expression. To avoid the confusion about the precedence and associativity of operators, use parentheses in appropriate places.
5. The modulo operator % is applicable only on integer operands.
6. Do not use a variable in an expression whose value is not assigned earlier. Otherwise, garbage value will be assigned to the variable causes incorrect result.
7. Integer division always gives integer part only, the fractional part is truncated. Use it carefully. Use casting, if required.
8. Remember that == and = are two different operators. First one is a relational operator and second one is the assignment operator.

Exercise IV

Review Questions

1. What do you mean by operator? Describe different types of operators that are used in C?
2. What is an operand? What is the relationship between operators and operands?
3. Explain five arithmetic operators in C.
4. What do you mean by expression? What are its components?
5. What is integer arithmetic? How integer arithmetic differs from floating point arithmetic.
6. Describe the evaluation method of mixed mode expression.
7. How can the value of an expression be converted to other data type? Explain implicit and explicit conversion of data. What do you understand by type casting? Why is it necessary?
8. What are unary operators? Explain them. How many operands are associated with a unary operator?
9. What do you mean by prefix and postfix operations?
10. What is meant by hierarchy (precedence) of operator? Write down the hierarchy of unary, arithmetic, relational, logical and assignment operators.
11. What do you mean by associativity? What is the associativity of arithmetic operators?
12. Explain the use of `sizeof` operator. Is it unary operator? What is the value of the expression `sizeof(double)`?

13. Explain the four relational operators included in C. Mention different types of operands where can they be used? What are the possible values of a relational expression?
14. What are the logical operators in C? Explain them.
15. How can multiple assignments be written in C? In what order will the assignments be carried out?
16. Explain conditional operator? How many operands are required in this operator?
17. How are library functions accessed? How is an information passed to a library function from the access point?
18. Write short notes on (i) assignment operator, (ii) logical operator, (iii) relational operators, (iv) ternary operator, (v) unary operators, (vi) library function.
19. What do you mean by (i) integer, (ii) floating point, and (iii) mixed mode expressions.
20. What are the differences between algebraic expression and C expression.

Problems

1. Write the assignment statements in C for the following algebraic statements. (i) Assign the value of $\sqrt{x^2+3}$ to y. (ii) Assign the area of a triangle of base a and height h to AREA. (iii) Assign the area of a triangle of sides a and b and angle between them is θ. (iv) Assign the sum of x, y to z. (v) Assign k times $A+B$ to V. (vi) Assign average of a, b, c to mean. (vii) Assign square root of sum of squares of x, y, z to DIST.
2. Express the following algebraic expressions into their equivalent C expressions.
   (a) area $= \frac{1}{2}ab\sin\theta$
   (b) $\frac{p^x}{q} + xy$
   (c) $(\frac{\sin x + 1.2}{1234d})^{3/2}$
   (d) $\frac{p+q}{x+y}$
   (e) $a + 2b - \frac{c}{1+\frac{x}{y}}$
   (f) $T = 1 + \frac{P}{V+|\frac{X}{C}|}$
   (g) $R = \sqrt{2\pi}e^{-n}n^{n+1/2}$
   (h) $z = |\frac{x}{y}|\log_e z$
   (i) $(a+b)/(|a|+|b|)$
   (j) $\sin(x+2y) - e^{-x+y}$
   (k) $\frac{x^3}{\sin(a+b)} + \sqrt{x^2-y^2} + e^{xy+y^3}$
   (l) $\frac{a^{2/3}+\sqrt{a^3}}{\sqrt{a+\sqrt{x+\sqrt{x}}}}$

(m) $\sqrt{(ab^2+ba^2)(x+y-\frac{ab}{a^3-b^3})}$
(n) $(\frac{a+b}{c+d})^2+\frac{ab+bc+ac}{\frac{x+y+z}{abc}}$
(o) $\sqrt{|\cos(a-\sqrt{|\log_e x|})|}$
(p) $A=\log_e\sqrt{a^2+b^2}\sin[\cos^{-1}(b/a)]$
(q) $r=\sqrt{a^2+b^2-2ab\cos\theta}+|x^{1/3}-y^{1/2}|$
(r) $\frac{pe^q}{2q}+\log p+\frac{|x|}{\sin y^3}$
(s) $d=\frac{(a+b)(x-y)^{3/2}}{v(s+cosec\sqrt{c})}$
(t) $1+\frac{x}{\sqrt{1+x^2}}-\frac{x}{|1+x|}+a(4+|y|)^{3/2}$
(u) $\sqrt{1-.162\sin^2\phi+\frac{\sqrt{3x+2}}{3}}$
(v) $\beta=[((a+b)^2+(c+d)^2)/((a+b)^2-(c+d)^2)]^{3/2}$
(w) $\frac{1}{1+e^x}+\frac{x^2+y^2}{|x-y|}+\frac{a}{c.d}$
(x) $\frac{1}{k}[(k-1)x\frac{a}{x^{k-1}}]$
(y) $a=\frac{x^3\sqrt{\sin(x+\sqrt{x})}}{1+\pi x^3\log x}$
(z) $b=2^x\sqrt{1+\tan x}+e^{-x}x^2$

3. Express the following algebraic expressions into their equivalent C expressions.
(a) $p=\sec x+\log_e|\cos^{-1}x+\tan^{-1}y|+\tan^{-1}y$
(b) $g=32.17(\frac{a}{a+h})^2+\sin a\sin b-|g-a|$
(c) $\frac{1}{\sigma\sqrt{2\pi}}e^{-\frac{1}{2}(\frac{x-m}{\sigma})^2}$
(d) $g=32.17(\frac{4390}{4390+h})^2+32.17(1+\frac{h}{4390})$
(e) $(x+1)(2x+1)^{1/3}$
(f) $x=\sqrt{a^2+b^2}\tan(b/a)+\frac{8}{2\sqrt{3}}\log_{10}c+\log_a b$
(g) $y=(a+b^2+ab)^5/(\sqrt{a}+b+1)$
(h) $p=a\log_{10}(\sin v)-b\sqrt{\cos^{-1}(abx)}$
(i) $Y=\frac{\tan\sqrt{x^2+3}}{\sqrt{x+2}}+\sin(\tan^{-1}\frac{\sqrt{a^2+b^2}}{c})$
(j) $Z=e^{\cos(y+1)}+\sqrt{|x+y|}+x|x|$
(k) $Z=|r|^{1/n}[\cos(\frac{\theta+2\pi(k-1)}{n})+\sin(\frac{\theta+2\pi(k-1)}{n})]$
(l) $X=1.23\times10^{-5}-\frac{y}{\frac{a+b}{c}+\frac{d}{a}}+z^{5/4}$

(m) $V = \frac{-1}{\sqrt{|x^2-y^2|}} + be^{\sqrt{(x/3d)t^2}}$

(n) $E = \frac{a+b}{z} - v^{a+b+c} + \sqrt{|\sin x| + |\tan^{-1} a|e^{-\alpha x^2}}$

(o) $A = \frac{1-\cos\theta}{1+\cos\theta} + \frac{e^{\beta^2}\sin\theta}{\sqrt{2\alpha x+\gamma}}.\frac{ab^2}{c}$

(p) $T = r\cos x\sin y + \cot y + \log_e(|\cos x + \tan hy|)$

(q) $F = \frac{a}{b+\frac{c}{d+\frac{e}{f+g}}}$

(r) $R = [\frac{n}{y}\cos(\frac{32^o}{n}) + (\sin\frac{35^o}{n})^2]^{1/3}$

(s) $y = \frac{x-\beta e^{-\alpha\sqrt{|x|}}}{x+\gamma e^{\gamma\log|x+y|}}$

(t) Absolute value of the product of a and $b - e^{-2x^2} - \sin(\frac{n^2\cos hx}{1-xy\sec x})$

(u) $\frac{1}{\sqrt{1+x^2+x^4}} + x^{3/2}e^{2x/a} + x^{1/3}$

(v) $x =$(fraction part of a) $\times \sqrt{|a-b|\sin^{-1}a} + \frac{\log_{10}c}{e^d}$

(w) $n =$(integer part of x) $\times \tan hy + a^5\log_e y$

(x) (i) $A = \pi R^k - R\log_{10}(\tan^{-1}x) - \frac{pq}{2t}$ (ii) $\frac{a}{2b} + \frac{b-c}{d}(\frac{r^5}{f}) + \log x^2$

4. Indicate whether the following statements are valid in C and if not, why ?
(i) `v=a(b+c)-d/5+b/-3`, (ii) `r=-a/2+b*5-sqrt(-3)+pow(x,-2)`,
(iii) `x/y=z`, (iv) `i=12,500+5*3`, (v) `k=5/i+pow(10,2)` (if `i=0`),
(vi) `x+2=x`, (vii) `v=(a-b)(c+d)`, (viii) `x=a-b/(c+d)`, (ix) `+y = p+ q-r`,
(x) `y=SQRT(x)+a%b`, (xi) `x=b/(a-a)`, (xii) `y= log(-5) * b/-c`,
(xiii) `a = 4(b+pow(c,-.5))`, (xiv) `s = a*b + c/3+pow(-6.5,3)`

5. Find the value of the following relational/logical expressions.
(a) `log10(100.0) >= pow(3,2)`, (b) `(5*8-2) == (58-28/2)`, (c) `sqrt(64.) > 10/8`, (d) `(5/2) > fabs(-3)`, (e) `sin(3.14159/2.0) != cos(3.14159)`,
(f) `!(a || b) && (!a)` (if `a=true, b=false`)

6. Write the following relational expressions as C relational/logical expressions:
(a) $1 \le x < 2.5$, (b) $|t|+|y| > v$, (c) $a/b+c/d > i*n$, (d) $\sqrt{r} < 10$ or $\sqrt{k}+5l > 10$, (e) $\sqrt{x}\log_e y < 1/2$ and $\cos y < 1/2$, (f) not $(a > 12)$, (g) $\sqrt{x} < 2.5$ and $\log_e y > 10$ but not $\sin^{-1}x > 0.5$, (h) $a/b > c/d$ and $x \ne 5$.

7. Find the values of `i` and `a` where
(i) `i=3/pow(2,2)*2+3/8*3+pow(3,2)/2`,
(ii) `a=3e02/pow(4.0,0.5)* 2.0+c/ 8.0*3.0+ pow(3.0,2)/2` (where `c=0.8`)

8. If `a=2.7, b=3.5, j=3` and `k=-2` find the values of `l` and `x`
(i) `l=fabs(a-j*b)/5+7/4`, (ii) `x=5*j/4*k`, where `j, k, l` are integers and `a, b, x` are floating point variables.

9. Assume `j=3, k=4, x=3.0, y=4.0`, find the values of the following
(i) `x=j/2*k/3-j/5.0+pow(k,2)/4.0`,
(ii) `i=2.0*pow((k/3),0.3)/y*6.0- y/3.0 +pow(3.0,y)/2.0`, where `i, j, k` are integers and `x, y` are floating point variables.

10. Suppose a, b, j and k contain the following values:
    `a=2.7, b=3.5, j=3, k=-2`
    Find the values of x and l after execution of each pair of the statements.
    (i) `x=a+j*pow(k,2)+b, l=a+j*pow(k,2)+b`
    (ii) `x=k/3*a/2, l=k/3*a/2`, where k, l are integers variables and other variables are floating point.
11. Find the values of the following expressions.
    (i) `r=2/4+7.5`, (ii) `l=2.0/4+7.5`, (iii) `(1.0/2.0)*20+5.5`,
    (iv) `l=10/3*(4/6)+7-2*5`, where l is the integer variable and r is the floating point variable.
12. Find the value of n calculated from the following statements:
    (i) `n=pow(j,2)+k*2/5-pow(j,3)/8+(j++)` (if `j=2, k=5`)
    (ii) `n=1/2.0+5/a+3*a-b` (if `a=4.0, b=2.5`)
    (iii) `n=m/2*2-m` (for any even (or odd) number m)
    (iv) `n=3*4/5*2-4%5`,
    where j, k, l, m, n are integers and a, b are floating point variables.
13. Find the values of ai and aj:
    (i) `ai=pow(i,k)/2+k/8+i*k/2-i/4*k+int(a)` where `i=2, k=4, a=-2.05`
    (ii) `aj=2*b/2-l*(m/2)+c/(pow(2,1e01/2))-log(j/pow(2,l))` where `j=4, l=2, m=3, c=4.0, b=12.5`, where i, j, k, l, m are integers and a, ai, aj, b, c are floating point variables.
14. Find the value of k for the following program segment.
    ```
    a=2.5;
    i=3;
    b=5.0;
    a-=b*i;
    k=a+b+i;
    ```
    , where i, k are integers and a, b are floating point variables.
15. Find the value of c for the following statements.
    ```
    a=10.0;
    c=2.0;
    i=5;
    c*=a+5*i;
    ```
16. Suppose c1, c2 and c3 are character type data with values A, C, b. Determine the values of the following expressions.
    (a) `c1-c2+c3` (b) `c1% c3` (c) `c1-2`
    (d) `c1-'2'` (e) `c2*5` (f) `'5'*c2`

Chapter 5

Input and Output Statements

Every program should take at least one input and must produce at least one output. To solve any problem, it is necessary to transfer the data from the input device to the memory of the computer. This task is performed by the input statement. There are several input devices available with a computer. In this chapter, we assume that the data is entered to the computer through the standard input device, such as keyboard.

Using the output statement, the results of the computation are transferred from the memory of the computer to the output device.

Several input/output (I/O) functions are available in C language, viz. `getchar`, `putchar`, `scanf`, `printf`, etc. All these I/O functions are available in the header file `stdio.h`.

In general, the input values of the variables are separated by blank spaces.

5.1 Reading a Character

The function `getchar` reads a single character from the standard input device followed by a carriage return. This function is a part of standard I/O library.

The syntax of this function is

```
char_variable=getchar();
```

where `char_variable` is a pre-defined character type variable. Note that this function does not take any argument, though a pair of parentheses must be given with the function.

The function `getchar` reads only one character at a time, but using it repeatedly, one can read a string of characters. Though this function reads a single character, even then we have to press an additional character return key.

This additional character (carriage return) is not required in the function `getche`. This function also reads a single character, but after entering the input character there is no need to press the return key. Suppose we would like to enter five characters by repeated call of this function. When exactly five characters are entered, the execution of the function stops automatically.

Another variation of getchar function is also available in C language. The function getche will read a single character from keyboard and there is no need to press the return key. The character which is entered through the function getche will be displayed on the screen. The function getch do the same task like getche, but the input character will *not be displayed on the screen.* A summary of these three functions are given in Table 5.1.

Function	Needs return key	Character displayed on the screen
getchar	Yes	Yes
getche	No	Yes
getch	No	No

Table 5.1: Character input functions

5.2 Output a Single Character

The putchar function is used to print a single character on the screen. This function is also a part of standard C I/O library. This function must need an argument enclosed within parentheses. The value of this argument will display on the screen.

The syntax of this function is

```
putchar(char_variable);
```

where char_variable is some pre-defined character variable.

The function putchar('\n') will print a carriage return, i.e. cursor moves to the beginning of the next line.

Let us consider the following statements

```
char ch;
ch=getchar();
putchar(ch);
```

The first statement declares ch as a character variable. The second statement reads a character from the keyboard and stores it to the variable ch. The last statement will print the character ch on the monitor screen.

5.3 Input/Output of String

The function getchar and putchar are used to read and print a single character. The functions gets and puts are used to read and print a string of characters including whitespace, tab, etc. The general form of gets function is

```
gets(string_name);
```

and that of puts is

```
puts(string_name);
```

where `string_name` is a variable of type string (an array of characters). This function reads all the characters from keyboard until a newline character is encountered. At the end, the function `gets` adds a null character (`'\0'`) to the end of the string. Note that the newline character is not added to the string.

The `puts` function will display the string `string_name` on the screen as it is stored in the memory.

Note that the use of `getchar` and `gets` functions. The function `getchar` does not take any argument, it reads a character and returns a character, which can be assigned to a variable. The function `gets` takes an argument (of type string), reads a string and assigns to the argument.

Let us consider the following example.

```
char name[30];
gets(name);
puts(name);
```

The first line declares `name` as a string of 30 characters. Second line reads a string as `name` and third line prints the value of `name`.

The input/output of this program is shown below.

<u>Anil Kumar Pal</u>
`Anil Kumar Pal`

The functions `getchar, getche, getch, putchar, gets` and `puts` are used only to read and write either a single character or a string of characters. To read and write other types of variables, including character and string variables, the functions `scanf` and `printf` are used. These functions are used for all types of variables. They are discussed in the following.

5.4 The General Input (scanf function)

The most powerful input statement of C language is `scanf`. This function is used to read any type of data, viz. integer, character, float, string, etc.

The syntax of `scanf` function is

```
scanf("control_string", arg1, arg2, ..., argn);
```

where the `control_string` specifies a string containing some formatting information and `arg1, arg2, ..., argn` represent the address of locations of individual data items. It may be noted that the control string and arguments are separated by comma.

The control string is a complicated group of characters. For each argument there is one group of characters of the form

`%wp`

It has three parts, the conversion character %, data type (or type specifier) character p and w, represents the width of the input value, which is optional.

The character groups in control sting may be continuous or they are separated by blank spaces, tabs, newline characters or any specified characters. If these characters are used in the control string, they are read by the computer but ignored. The commonly used type specifiers are given in Table 5.2.

Format specifier	Meaning
`%c`	Read a single character
`%d` or `%D`	Read a decimal integer
`%f`	Read a floating-point number
`%e` or `%E`	Read a floating-point number of exponent form
`%g` or `%G`	Read a floating-point number
`%h`	Read a short integer
`%i` or `%I`	Read a decimal, hexadecimal or octal integer
`%o` or `%O`	Read an octal integer
`%s`	Read a string of characters
`%u` or `%U`	Read an unsigned decimal integer
`%x` or `%X`	Read a hexadecimal integer
`%[...]`	Read a string of characters or words

Table 5.2: Format specifiers for input

It is very important to note that the variables or arrays should match with the corresponding character group in control string. Each character group must begin with the symbol %. Each argument is the combination of ampersand (&) sign and the variable name. That is, the arguments are basically pointers which represent the addresses of the computer where the values of the variables are stored.

Suppose `a,b` and `x` are integer, floating point and character variables. Then, the values of these variables can be read using the following input statement.

```
scanf("%d%f%c",&a,&b,&x);
```

In this statement, `%d%f%c` is the control string or called format specifiers, it contains three character groups. The first group `%d` indicates that a variable is to be read which is an decimal integer, the second character group `%f` indicates the type of the variable must be floating-point and the third group `%c` indicates that this format will read a character.

It may be noted that the data items should correspond to the arguments in the `scanf` function in number, in type and in order with the control string. The values to be assigned to the variables (for the above example they are `a, b` and `x`) are typed in a succession in a line starting from any position. The leading blank spaces are skipped. The values are typed in the same order as in the list and they are separated by blank spaces (other non-standard separators are also available in C, which are discussed later). If some values are not typed on a line, then they may be typed on the next line. Note that *a single value should not be typed in two or more lines.*

If the values of the variables `a,b` and `x` are respectively 58, 67.253 and M, and the statement being

```
scanf("%d%f%c",&a,&b,&x);
```

then they should be typed as

58 67.253 M

If the values of all the variables are not found on a single line then the lines following it are read until the values are assigned to all the variables.

The `scanf` function is a versatile input function. It contains several facilities through which we can specify the rules to read the data. The `scanf` function, during its execution, scans a series of input fields, one character at a time, then converts each field according to the format specifier, which is supplied within control string. The format specifiers direct the `scanf` function to read and convert characters from the input field into specific types of values. This converted input is stored in an address passed as argument. It may be remembered that, there must be one format specifier and address for each input field.

Some invalid input statements

Here we assume that `a,b` are floating point variables, `i,j,k` are integer variables and `p` is a character variable.

`scanf("%d%d",&i,&j)`	(; missing at the end)
`scanf("%d",&(i+j));`	(expression is not allowed)
`scanf("%d%d%d",&i,&j,5);`	(constant 5 is not allowed)
`scanf("%d%d%d",i,j,k);`	(missing address operators (&))
`scanf(%d%f%f,&i,&a,&b);`	(quotations missing in control string)
`scanf('%d%f%d',&i,&a,&j);`	(control string must be enclosed by double quotations)
`scanf("%d%d%f,&i,&j,&a");`	(arguments must not be written within control string)
`scanf("%d%c",&i,&'p');`	('p' a character constant, is not allowed)
`scanf(&a,&b);`	(control string missing)
`scanf("%d%d",&a,&b);`	(data type mismatched)
`scanf("%d%d",&a &b);`	(comma missing between the arguments)
`scanf("%d%d\n",&i,&j);`	(white space is not allowed)
`scanf("A=%fB=%f",&a,&b);`	(only format specifier are allowed within control string)

5.5 The General Output (`printf` function)

The most powerful output statement in C is `printf` function. This function is used to print any type of data, such as numeric, single character and string. The `printf` function will display the values of the variable to the standard output device such as monitor screen.

The general form of `printf` function is

```
printf("control_string",arg1, arg2, ..., argn);
```

where `control_string` is a string that contains formatting information and `arg1, arg2, ..., argn` are n variables, constants, array names or expressions. The function call may also be allowed. It may be noted that the arguments of `printf` function do not represent memory addresses and hence no ampersand signs are required.

The control string contains three types of information.

(i) Format specifications for the arguments.

(ii) The characters (other than format specifiers) which will be displayed as they appear as output.

(iii) The escape sequence characters such as `\n`, `\t`, etc.

These three types of items may not be present together within a control string, and even arguments may be omitted. The simplest form of control string contains only format specifiers, i.e. it consists of individual group of characters, with one character group for each argument. Each character group begins with % (similar to `scanf` function).

Let us consider the following example. Suppose $a = 58$ and $b = 25.652$ and the output statement is

```
printf("a=%d b=%f\n",a,b);
```

Here `%d` and `%f` are format specifier `a=` and `b=` are the other characters, they will display the same is and '`\n`' is the escape sequence.

The output of this statement is

```
a=58 b=25.652000
```

Here the characters `a=` and `b=` are printed as they appear within the control string. The value of `a` is printed in place of `%d`. One blank space is inserted in between `%d` and `b` within the control string, so one blank space is printed after the value of `a`. The value of `b` (=25.652) is printed as `25.652000`, because the default precision is 6 (every floating point variable will print its decimal part with 6 decimal places, if it is not mentioned).

After printing this output, the cursor moves to the first column of the next line, due to the escape sequence '\n'.

It may be remembered that the `printf` function does not encounter `newline` automatically. Therefore, if no newline ('`\n`') character is included to any `printf` function, among multiple `printf` functions, then all the outputs will displayed in a single line.

The commonly used format specifiers for `printf` are listed in Table 5.3.

To print the short integer, long integer and long double the character conversion characters `h`, `l` and `L` are used with the above conversion characters.

Note 5.5.1 (i) The infinite floating point members are printed as `+INF` and `−INF`.

(ii) The Not_A_Number is printed as `+NAN` or `−NAN`.

Now, from the ongoing discussions we have sufficient resources to write a complete program in C.

Format specifier	Meaning
`%c`	Print a single character
`%d` or `%D`	Print a decimal integer
`%f`	Print a floating-point number without exponent
`%e` or `%E`	Print a floating-point number of exponent form
`%g` or `%G`	Print a floating-point number either in `e`-format or in `f`-format conversion, depending on the magnitude of the value
`%i` or `%I`	Print a signed decimal integer
`%o` or `%O`	Print an octal integer, without leading to zero
`%s`	Print a string of characters
`%u` or `%U`	Print an unsigned decimal integer
`%x` or `%X`	Print a hexadecimal integer, without leading `0x`

Table 5.3: Format specifiers for output

Format specifier	Meaning
`%ld` or `%li`	Print a decimal long integer
`%lu`	Print a decimal unsigned long integer
`%hd` or `%hi`	Print a decimal short integer
`%hu`	Print a decimal unsigned short integer
`%le` or `%lf` or `%lg`	Print a signed, double
`%Le` or `%Lf` or `%Lg`	Print a signed, long double
`%lo`	Print an octal long integer
`%lx`	Print a hexadecimal long integer

Table 5.4: The format specifiers for short, long and long double

5.6 Complete Programs

A C program (the main function) has four parts, viz. inclusion of header files, beginning of main function, declaration of variables and body of the program/main function. The following example illustrates these parts.

Example 5.6.1 (Fahrenheit to Centigrade) Write a program to find Fahrenheit temperature from the corresponding Centigrade temperature.

Solution. The relation between Fahrenheit (f) and Centigrade (c) temperature is

$$\frac{c}{5} = \frac{f-32}{9} \qquad \text{or} \qquad f = \frac{9c + 5 \times 32}{5}.$$

Program 5.1

Inclusion of header file	`#include<stdio.h>`
beginning of main	`void main()`
opening of main	`{`
declaration of variables	`int c,f;`

body of main	`printf("Enter the value of C");`
	`scdanf("%f",c);`
	`f=(9*c+160.0)/5.0;`
	`printf("c=%f f=%f",c,f);`

end of main	`}`

A sample of input/output:

```
39
c=39.000000 f=102.200000
```

Every C program contains the function `main`. The execution of program begins from this function. The other functions may also be allowed in a C program. It may be noted that all the statements including declaration of variables must be written within the opening ({) and closing (}) braces.

This entire portion constitutes the function `main`.

Example 5.6.2 (Area and circumference of circle) Write a program to find the area and circumference of a circle whose radius is r respectively.

Solution. The area and circumference of a circle whose radius r are πr^2 and πr.

Program 5.2

```
/* Program to find the area and circumference of a circle */
#include<stdio.h>
main()
 {
   float r,area,peri;
   scanf("%f",&r);
   area=3.14159*r*r;
   peri=2.0*3.14159*r;
   printf("The area is %f\n",area);
   printf("The circumference is %f\n",peri);
}
```

A sample of input/output:

```
2.5
The area is 36.316784
The circumference is 21.362812
```

Look at the first line. This line begins with '/*' and ends with '*/', which contains some information. The entire line is called the **comment**. The comment lines are used to identify or explain the various parts of a large program. A comment may be written in any place and in any number of lines within the program, but it must begin with '/*' and end with '*/'. The comment lines are not compiled to produce object code. Thus, we can write any thing as comment. It is optional.

5.7 More About Format Specifiers for Input

The very simplest form of `scanf` function has been discussed in the previous section. Now, details and variations of different format specifications are discussed here. All format specifiers used in a C program are classified into seven categories, listed below.

(i) Single character (`%c`)
(ii) Character array (`%wc`)
(iii) String (`%s`)
(iv) Floating-point (`%f`)
(v) Floating-point with exponent (`%e, %g`)
(vi) Unsigned (`%d, %i`, etc.)
(vii) Search sets (`%[...]%[^...]`)

The consecutive non-white space characters form a **field**. Two fields are separated by white space.

Now, we will discuss all these format specifications one by one.

5.7.1 %c format specifier

This format specification reads a single character from the keyboard. If the control string contains more than one character groups, without white space characters, then c-type conversion gives different results.

To explain this, let us consider the following program segment.

```
char a, b, c;
scanf("%c %c %c",&a,&b,&c);
```

If the input is

```
x y z
```

then `x, y` and `z` are assigned as `a=x, b=y` and `c=z`.

In this case, the blank spaces are used as separator between the characters.

For the `scanf` statement,

```
scanf("%c%c%c",&a,&b,&c);
```

with the same input string, the values are assigned as `a=x, b=b̸, c=y`.

The blank space between x and y in the input data is taken as the value of b. Since no blank separators are used within the control string, the consecutive characters are taken as input characters.

The other form of %c is %wc, where w indicates the length of the input string. That is, using this specifier a string of characters can be read at most w characters including blank space. The reading will terminate when a newline character is encountered.

Let us consider the statements,

```
char a,b,c,p[10];
scanf("%c%c%c%10c",&a,&b,&c,p);
```

and the input string,

```
xyzMy India
```

The value of the variables are assigned as a=x, b=y, c=z and p=My India

For the input statement,

```
scanf("%c%c%c%4c",&a,&b,&c,p);
```

with the same input, the values of the variables are assigned as a=x, b=y, c=z, p=My I. Note that only first four characters (including blank space) are assigned to p.

5.7.2 %s format specifier

This specifier is used to read a string. The general form of this specifier is

%ws

where w represents the length of the string. But, this specification *terminates reading at the encounter of a blank space* or *newline*, whereas %wc will not terminate when a blank space is encountered.

Let us consider the following example.

```
char s1[20],s2[20];
scanf("%20s",s1);
scanf("%20s",s2);
```

The input strings are

```
My India is great
My_India_is_great
```

The value stored at s1 and s2 are

s1=My and s2=My_India_is_great.

The first scanf terminates at the first blank space (after My). Thus, only My is stored to s1. In the second string no blank space is included, so the entire string is assigned to s2.

But, the %20c format specifier reads two strings completely.

5.7.3 %d format specifier

This format specification is used to read a decimal integer data. The general form of this specification is

%wd

where w represents the field width of the data item. Using this specification one can read an integer data at most w digits. The data item may contain fewer than w digits, but it cannot exceed w digits.

If any white space character is encountered in the input, then it terminates the reading for that variable and even its length is less than w.

Let us consider the following statements

```
int i,j,k;
scanf("%4d %3d %2d",&i,&j,&k);
```

with the input data,

123 45 31

The values of i, j and k are i=123, j=45 and k=31

Note that the reading of values of i and j are terminated at the blank spaces. These blank spaces are used as separators of the data item.

For the input statement,

```
scanf("%4d%3d%2d",&i,&j,&k);
```

with input data,

12456783456

the values of i, j and k are stored as i=1245, j=678 and k=34.

Note that the last two digits 5 and 6 are ignored.

For the input data

123 45 90123

the values are i=123, j=45 and k=90.

Here the blank spaces separate the data items.

Separators in input data

In C, the standard separator is blank spaces. But, other separators may also be used. These separators are specified within the control string.

Let us consider the following example.

```
int i,j,k;
scanf("%d,%d,%d",&i,&j,&k);
```

Suppose the input data is

123,45,875

then i, j, k are stored as i=123, j=45 and k=875.

When separators are used in control string, then the input data must be separated by the same separators, otherwise incorrect assignment will be encountered.

If the input data is

```
123 45 875
```

then i,j,k will store incorrect values as i=123, j=478, k=2965 (these values may be changed for other run of the program).

That is, once separators are used then the same separators must be used in the input data, otherwise the variables will store incorrect values.

Like blank space separator, in other separators also, the width of data item may be used. Similar to blank space separator, the value of a variable will terminate (even its width does not match) while the separator character is encountered. But, if the number of digits in input data is more than the specified width, then the first variable reads correctly and the values of other variables is incorrect.

For example, if the input statement is

```
scanf("%3d,%4d,%2d",&i,&j,&k);
```

and the input data is,

```
2345,8907,89
```

then the values of i, j, k are i=234, j=480, k=2965 (garbage values), the values of j and k are incorrect.

Thus, the use of separators is not suggested, as in this situation special attention is required while entering data.

But, it is useful in some particular cases. For example, if we would like to enter a data with a specific format, say, dd:mm:yyyy or dd-mm-yyyy, then the use of format specification is highly suggested.

Consider the following program segment

```
int date,month,year;
printf("Enter date dd:mm:yyyy\n");
scanf("%d:%d:%d",&date,&month,&year);
printf("date=%d month=%d year=%d",date,month,year);
```

The I/O of this program segment is

```
Enter date dd:mm:yyyy
22:11:2010
date=22 month=11 year=2010
```

Another interesting feature called **assignment suppression** is discussed below.

Assignment suppression

In C, there is a scope to skip over a data item, using a special type of format specifier %*p, where p is a standard format specifier such as d,f,c, etc. When this format specification execute the corresponding data, field will skip without assigning any variable.

Suppose the input statement is

```
int a,b,c;
scanf("%d %*d %d %d",&a,&b,&c);
```

and input data is

125 78 390 49

Then the values of a, b and c are 125, 390 and 49 respectively. 78 will not be assigned to any variable due to the presence of the format specification %*d, even it is read by the computer, along with other data items. This specification is useful when the data is written in a file in a tabular form, to skip a particular column for a specific application.

5.7.4 %f format specifier

This format specification is used to read floating point data. Its general form is

%wf

where w represents the width of the data (including sign and decimal point). The w characters are read from input data and it is converted as floating point data before storing it in the memory.

For example, the input statement,

```
float a,b,c;
scanf("%5f%3f%4f",&a,&b,&c);
```

reads the values of a, b, c from the input data

12.345.678.9

asa=12.34, b=5.6, c=78.9.

If the input data is

123458903

then a=12345, b=890, c=3
and if it is,

12345890357837

then a=12345, b=890, c=3578 and the digits 3 and 7 are ignored.

If the input data is

2.3e45.678.3

then $a = 2.3e4 = 2.3 \times 10^4, b = 5.6$ and $c = 78.3$.

Note that the constant 2.3e4 is written using e specification, though it is entered using f specification.

The double type data, can be read using %lf specification instead of %f specification.

For example, the statements

```
long int i;
double x;
scanf("%ld %lf",&i,&x);
```

read the long int and double variables i and x.

A data may be skipped using the %*f specification.

The format specifiers %e, %E, %g and %G all are used to read floating point values. These formats are specially significant in case of output statement.

Reading mixed data

It is mentioned earlier that by using `scanf` function one can read mixed mode data, i.e. using a single `scanf` function different types of data can be read. Extreme care should be taken to specify format specifications and order of variable names. If the value of a variable does not match with its expected format specification (which is supplied through the control string), the `scanf` function does not read further.

The statements,

```
int i;
char name[15];
scanf("%3d%15c",&i,name);
```

read the data,

```
125Aniket Pal
```

correctly as `i=125` and `name=Aniket Pal`

The statements,

```
int i;
float a;
char s[10];
scanf("%2d%5f%10s",&i,&a,s);
```

read the data,

```
5628.51My India
```

as `i=56, a=28.51` and `s=My`

The characters after blank space (before `India`) are not encountered by `%s` specification.

For the same input data, the `scanf` function

```
scanf("%2f%5d%10s",&a,&i,s);
```

read `a` correctly (`a=56`), but does not read `i` and `s` correctly, because, the next 5 input characters are 28.51, and it can not be converted as an integer.

5.7.5 `%[...]` and `%[^...]` format specifiers

C provides a very flexible method to read a string. The format specification `%[...]` is used to read a string which is defined in a particular domain. Suppose, we would like to read a string which contains only lower case alphabets, then the appropriate input statement is

```
scanf("%[a-z]",s);
```

The reading will terminate at the first occurrence of the other characters (other than lower case alphabets mentioned as `a-z`).

If the string,

```
my india
```

is entered as input for the above input statement, then only `my` is store at `s`, since the blank space is not included within the format specification `%[a-z]`. If we enter the string `My India`, then no character will store `s`, because the first character (M) is an upper case alphabet, which is not included within the format specification. To read lower and upper case alphabets, digits and blank space, the following specification is required.

```
%[a-zA-Z0-9' ']
```

This specification is also used to read a specific group of characters. For example,

```
char ch;
printf("Do you want to continue (Y/N)?");
scanf("%[YN]",ch);
```

In this program segment, if the input data is 'Y' or ('N'), then `ch` stores `Y` (or `N`), otherwise, no characters are stored to `ch`. The set of characters written within [...] is called **search set**.

The other format specification is `%[^...]`.

One or more characters may be written after circumflex (i.e. ^). When the program is executed, successive characters are read from the keyboard as long as each input character does not match one of the characters written within the square brackets.

Thus, the specification `[^...]` works opposite to `[...]` specification. Also, using this specification one can read multiline input and input will terminate when an input character will match with any one of the characters written in `[^...]`. If the format `[^\n]` is used to read a string, it reads all the characters until a newline character is encountered.

The set of characters written within `[^...]` is called **inverted search set**.

The statements,

```
char name[30];
int roll;
scanf("%3d%[^\n]",&roll,name);
```

will read the input,

```
250A. K. Sarma
```

correctly as `roll=250` and `name=A. K. Sarma`.

Using the following program segment one can enter multiline data.

```
char st[50];
printf("Enter the data, at end type $\n");
sacnf("%[^$]",st);
printf("%s",st);
```

If the input of this program segment is

C is a very good
programming language.
Its incremented form is

C++$

then the output (the value of `st`) is

```
C is a very good
programming language.
Its incremented form is
C++
```

Rules for ranges of search set

(i) The character prior to the minus sign (−) must be lexically less than the other, i.e. `a-z` is valid but `z-a` is not valid.

(ii) If minus sign is the first or last character in the set, then it is considered the character (−) itself and not a range definer.

(iii) The characters on both sides of − sign indicate the boundaries of the range and not a part of some other range.

5.8 Detection of Errors in Input

It is mentioned earlier that `scanf` and `printf` are library functions, they return integer constant.

Suppose a `scanf` function is used to read 5 arguments and all the arguments are successfully read. In this case, the `scanf` function will return 5.

Actually, this function returns the value of number of items that are successfully entered.

Suppose the input data is

```
50 80.2 Diwali
```

and consider the following two input statements,

```
float b;
char s[20];
int a,u,v;
u=scanf("%d %f %s",&a,&b,s);
v=scanf("%d %s %f",&a,s,&b);
```

when execute these statements, the value of `u` becomes 3 (as the first `scanf` function correctly reads three arguments) and that of `v` be 2 because first and second variables are read properly.

Using this technique one can test whether an input is correctly entered or not.

5.8.1 %o and %x format specifiers

The octal and hexadecimal numbers are read using these formats. Every octal and hexadecimal number begins with `0` (zero) and `0x` respectively. These prefixes indicate that the integers are either octal or hexadecimal. An octal and hexadecimal number can be printed directly in other types of numbers, such as decimal, hexadecimal and octal. The general form of %o specifier is

```
%wo
```

where w represents length of the octal integer including leading 0 (zero).

The scanf function

```
int i;
scanf("%o",&i);
```

reads the input data,

```
0123
```

as octal integer (i=123) and its equivalent decimal integer is 83. It may be noted that 0123 is not a decimal integer.

The general form of hexadecimal number is

```
%wx
```

where w represents the length of the input data including 0x. The following scanf function

```
int r;
scanf("%x",&r);
```

reads r=25a from the input line 0x25a whose decimal equivalent is 346.

Look at the following statements

```
int a,b;
scanf("%3o%4x",&a,&b);
printf("a=%3o a=%3x a=%3d\n",a,a,a);
printf("b=%4o b=%4x b=%4d\n",b,b,b);
```

Suppose the input line is 0250xa5

The output of this program segment is,

```
a=25 a=15 a=21
b=245 b=a5 b=165
```

This program segment shows that C automatically converts one type of integer to another type of integer.

5.9 Format Specifiers for Output

All most all format specifiers are used to print output. But, output format specifiers are more useful than the input format specifiers.

5.9.1 %d format specifier

This specifier is used to pass the values of integer variables from the computer to the output field. The general form is

`%wd`

where `w` is the width of the integer number including sign. If the number of digits of an integer is more than `w`, then the full integer will print out, overridden with the specification. If the number of digits are less than `w`, then blank spaces are to be added at the beginning to make `w` width. The leading blank spaces may also be filled up by 0. Normally, the numeric numbers are printed in right justified form. But, left justification is also be possible by using flags.

The behaviour of `%d` is illustrated in the following examples. Suppose $i = 185$.

Print statement	Output					Remark
`printf("%d",i)`	1	8	5			
`printf("%5d",i)`			1	8	5	right justified
`printf("%2d",i)`	1	8	5			overridden format specifier
`printf("%-5d",i)`	1	8	5			force to left justified due to the flag −
`printf("%05d",i)`	0	0	1	8	5	leading blanks filled by 0
`printf("%+5d",i)`		+	1	8	5	+ flag is used to print the sign of `i`
`printf("%+5d",-i)`		−	1	8	5	+ flag is used

In the above examples, three additional characters minus (−), plus (+) and zero (0) are used, they are known as **flags**.

To print long integer and short integer the format specifiers `%ld` and `%hd` are used.

5.9.2 %w.pf format specifier

This format specifier is used to print floating point number without an exponent. If the number is very large this specification cannot print the number correctly. The general form of this format is

`%w.pf`

where `w` is the field width indicating the total number of characters in the field including sign and decimal point, and `p` is the number of digits to the right of decimal point called precision.

It should be noted that the width (`w`) must exceed the number of decimal places by at least three, to make room for a sign and for at least one digit to the left of the decimal point. The output is right justified. `p` digits are printed to the right of the decimal point. If the number of digits in the fractional part is less than `p`, then the remaining positions to the right are filled will zeros. If the fractional part has more than `p` digits then the number rounded off. Considering the fractional part in this manner, if we see that the format specification `%w.pf` cannot provide enough number of columns for the number, then the full number is printed, overridden with format specification. The default precision is 6. The value of `w` may be 0. In this case, the number is printed in left justified form with an appropriate width. The leading blanks may be replaced by 0 and printing with left justification is also possible by using minus (−) flag. To demonstrate the feature of `%w.pf` specification, we assume `a=167.2358` and `b=-785.3854`.

Print statement	Output	Remark
`printf("%8.4f",a)`	167.2358	
`printf("%8.2f",a)`	167.24	right justified and rounded off
`printf("%-8.2f",a)`	167.24	left justified
`printf("%4.4f",a)`	167.2358	overridden width
`printf("%08.2f",a)`	00167.24	filled by 0
`printf("%6.1f",b)`	−785.4	
`printf("%8.0f",a)`	167	no decimal part
`printf("%0.3f",a)`	167.236	note that w is 0

The width and precision can also be specified dynamically. The syntax to use such facility is

```
printf("%*.*f",width,precision,argument);
```

where `width` and `precision` are integer, constant, variable and expression of the printable argument. The flags 0 and minus sign may also be used here.

For example, let `a=347.7567, i=8, j=2`. The statements

```
int i=8,j=2;
float a=347.7567;
printf("%*.*f",i,j,a);
```

print the value of `a` as, 347.76

and for the statement,

```
printf("%0*.*f",i+2,j,a);
```

the output is, 0000347.76

5.9.3 %e or %E format specifier

This format specification is used to print a large number like 6.23×10^{23}. This type of number is called floating point number with exponent form. The number 6.23×10^{23} is represented in computer as $6.23E+23$. It has two parts: the left hand side of E is called mantissa and the right hand side of E is called an exponent. The mantissa, in general, is a floating point constant and exponent is an integer constant. The general form of this format is

`%w.pe` or `%w.pE`

where `w` is the field width that indicates the total number of characters in the field, indicating sign, decimal point and the exponent symbol. `p` represents the number of digits after the decimal point in the mantissa.

These two formats are same. If `e` (or `E`) is used in the format specification, then `e` (respectively `E`) is printed in the output.

During printing, `p` significant digits are printed to the right of the decimal point and if the number contains more than `p` digits, then the fraction part is rounded off. It should be noted that width `w` must exceeds the number of decimal places `p` by at least seven to make room for a sign, at least one digit to the left of the decimal point, the decimal point, the exponent symbol, sign of exponent and the two digits exponent.

Let `a=6.2346`$\times 10^{30}$`=6.2346E+30`.

Print statement	Output												
`printf("%10.4e",a)`	6	.	2	3	4	6	e	+	3	0			
`printf("%10.4E",a)`	6	.	2	3	4	6	E	+	3	0			
`printf("%E",a)`	6	.	2	3	4	6	0	0	E	+	3	0	default specification
`printf("%10.2e",a)`			6	.	2	3	e	+	3	0			fraction part rounded
`printf("%-10.2e",a)`	6	.	2	3	e	+	3	0					left justified due to – flag
`printf("%010.0e",a)`	0	0	0	0	0	6	e	+	3	0			filled by 0
`printf("a=%8.2e",a)`	a	=	6	.	2	3	e	+	3	0			

The `%f` format specifier cannot print the above number properly. But, `%e` specifier can print non-exponent number appropriately. In scientific computation, it is not always possible to predict the magnitude of a value.

Thus, to print all floating point values `%e` specification can be used. But, if the value is small in magnitude, then the result with `e`-specification is not good in appearance. For example, if $a = 123.56$ the print statement

```
printf("a=%6.2e",a);
```

gives the output,

```
a=1.24e+02
```

Obviously, $a = 123.56$ is a good representation than $a = 1.24e{+}02$, also it is rounded. This problem is removed by using `%g` or `%G` specifier, as discussed below.

5.9.4 %g or %G format specifier

Both are same. The general form is

`%w.dg` or `%w.dG`

where `w` is the total width and `d` represents the first `d` digits of the number. This specification prints the value either in `%f` or in `%e` specification depending on the magnitude and the values of `w` and `d`.

Let `a=123.5698`. Read carefully the following print statements and output.

Print statement	Output							
`printf("%G",a)`	1	2	3	.	5	6	9	8
`printf("%8.3G",a)`						1	2	4
`printf("%8.4G",a)`				1	2	3	.	6
`printf("%8.5G",a)`			1	2	3	.	5	7
`printf("%8.7G",a)`	1	2	3	.	5	6	9	8
`printf("%8.2g",a)`		1	.	2	e	+	0	2
`printf("%08.3g",a)`	0	0	0	0	0	1	2	4

5.9.5 `%c` format specifier

This format is used to print a single character. The general form is

`%wc`

where `w` represents the width of the display field. The character displayed is rightly justified. The left justification can also be done by using minus (−) flag.

5.9.6 `%s` format specifier

The general form of this format specification is

`%w.ds`

This format first prints `d` characters of the string in a display field of length `w` characters. The default justification is right. The minus (−) flag is used to print left justified data.

Here `d` is optional. If `d` is not present in the specifier, then the whole string is printed within `w` field width. If `w` is less than the length of the entire string, then also the full string is displayed as left justified form.

To explain the different forms of this format, let us consider the string "Vidyasagar University".

Format specification	Output																								
`%s`	V	i	d	y	a	s	a	g	a	r		U	n	i	v	e	r	s	i	t	y				
`%21s`	V	i	d	y	a	s	a	g	a	r		U	n	i	v	e	r	s	i	t	y				
`%25s`					V	i	d	y	a	s	a	g	a	r		U	n	i	v	e	r	s	i	t	y
`%25.8s`																		V	i	d	y	a	s	a	g
`%.10s`	V	i	d	y	a	s	a	g	a	r															
`%10s`	V	i	d	y	a	s	a	g	a	r		U	n	i	v	e	r	s	i	t	y				

Normally, the octal and hexadecimal numbers are printed without leading `0` or `0x`. To get the leading `0` (for octal) and `0x` (for hexadecimal) the flag # is used.

For example, let `i=125` and `j=2382`, both be decimal integers. Let us consider the following print statements.

```
printf("i=%o j=%x\n",i,j);
printf("i=%#o j=%#x\n",i,j);
```

The output of these statements is shown below.

```
i=175   j=94e
i=0175   j=0x94e
```

A list of flags commonly used in output statements is given in Table 5.5.

Flag	Meaning
−	Output is left justified, the leading fields are filled by blank spaces, if there are any.
+	The sign (+ or −) of the number appears in the output.
0	The leading blanks are filled by 0.
# (o or x)	The octal and hexadecimal numbers are printed with the prefixes 0 and 0x respectively.
# (e,f or g)	Decimal point must placed to print a floating point number, even if it is a whole number. Also, it prevents the truncation of trailing zeros in g format.

Table 5.5: Flags used in printf function

We have discussed earlier how different types of values are printed on the output device. The output can also be printed with more readable form using appropriate number of blank spaces, newline ('\n') and tab ('\t') characters. Also, some string of characters may be included within control string for a clear understanding of the output.

The following example is used to illustrate the use of other features of printf function.

Example 5.9.1 (Surface area and volume of rectangular parallelepiped) Write a program to find the surface area and volume of a rectangular parallelepiped. The length of its sides are a, b and c.

Solution. The surface area and volume of a rectangular parallelepiped are respectively $2(ab + bc + ca)$ and abc.

Program 5.3

```
/* Computation of volume and surface area
   of a rectangular parallelepiped */
 #include<stdio.h>
 main()
 {
  float a,b,c;
```

```
  float surface,vol;
  printf("Enter three sides\n");
  scanf("%f%f%f",&a,&b,&c);
  surface=2.*(a*b+b*c+c*a);
  vol=a*b*c;
  printf("Surface area is %8.4f and\nVolume is %8.4f", surface,vol);
}
```

A sample of input/output:

```
Enter three sides
2.3 4.5 7.6

 Surface area is 124.0600 and
Volume is  78.6600
```

Note 5.9.1 In C, all most all library functions and user defined functions have fixed number of arguments except `scanf` and `printf` functions. These two functions can take any number of arguments, viz. control string and the arguments. This feature (a function with variable number of arguments) is called *function polymorphism.*

Important Points

1. It is better to avoid format specification in `scanf` function.
2. Avoid use of separators in `scanf` function.
3. The address operator (&) must be used with ordinary variables in `scanf` function.
4. The address operator (&) should not be used with variables in `printf` function.
5. Insert blank spaces or suitable separators between two fields on output.
6. The control string must be written within double quotes.
7. Control string and arguments must be separated by commas.
8. Do not use any white-space at the end of `scanf` function.
9. The format specifications and data type must be compatible, otherwise incorrect conversion will occur during running of the program.
10. Character string should be enclosed with double quotes.
11. A single character should be enclosed with single quotes.

12. Include `stdio.h` header file to every program to access input/output functions.

13. Include `ctype.h` header file to handle character related functions.

14. The `scanf` function terminates abnormally in the following situations.

    (a) The next character in the input filed does not match with the corresponding format string.

    (b) The next character in the input filed is EOF.

    (c) The format string specification is insufficient for the list of variables.

    (d) If a character sequence which is not a part of format specifier occurs in the format string.

5.10 Worked Out Examples

Example 5.10.1 Describe the line of output produced by the statement

```
printf("%3d  %6.2f  %4d %6.3f",m,x,n,y);
```

where $m = -1234, x = 34.45, n = 104, y = 1.4565$.

Solution. The values of the variables according to the given format specification are `m=-1234, x=b̸34.45, n=b̸104, y=1.456`. The output is

Col. no.	1	2	3	4	5	6	7	8	9	0	1	2	3	4	5	6	7	8	9	0	1	2	3	4	5	6	7
	−	1	2	3	4					3	4	.	4	5					1	0	4		1	.	4	5	6

Example 5.10.2 Indicate the printed form of the output of the following statement.

```
printf("%8.2f\n\n\n%10.2e%10.2E\n%8.4f\n%4d",x,y,z,p,i);
```

where $x = 23.2, y = 10.02, z = -0.01, p = 0.81, i = -50$.

Solution. The output is

Col. no.	1	2	3	4	5	6	7	8	9	0	1	2	3	4	5	6	7	8	9	0
Line no. 1				2	3	.	2	0												
Line no. 2																				
Line no. 3																				
Line no. 4			1	.	0	0	e	+	0	1		−	1	.	0	0	E	−	0	2
Line no. 5			0	.	8	1	0	0												
Line no. 6		−	5	0																

The value of `x` is printed in the first line as b̸ b̸ b̸`23.20` since its format specification is `%8.2f`. For the first newline character ('`\n`'), the cursor goes to the second line, for the second '`\n`' the cursor goes to the third line and for the third '`\n`' the cursor moves to the fourth line. The printing begins here. The values of `y` and `z` are printed in this line according to the format specifications `%10.2e` and `%10.2E`. For the next '`\n`' character the cursor moves to the fifth line and the value of p is printed here according to the format specification %8.4f. Again, the cursor moves to the sixth line due to the presence of '\n'. Finally, the value of i is printed in this line as per the format specification %4d.

Example 5.10.3 Write a program to find the area of a triangle whose coordinates of vertices are $(x_1, y_1), (x_2, y_2), (x_3, y_3)$.

Solution. The area of a triangle is given as $\frac{1}{2}[x_1(y_2 - y_3) + x_2(y_3 - y_1) + x_3(y_1 - y_2)]$.

Program 5.4

```
/* The area of a triangle whose vertices are given */
#include<stdio.h>
main()
{
  float x1,y1,x2,y2,x3,y3;
  float area;
  printf("Enter three coordinates\n");
  scanf("%f%f%f%f%f%f",&x1,&y1,&x2,&y2,&x3,&y3);
  area=(x1*(y2-y3)+x2*(y3-y1)+x3*(y1-y2))/2.0;
  printf("The area is %8.3f",area);
}
```

A sample of input/output:

```
Enter three coordinates
2.3,4.5,6.7,3.2,1.2,6.8

The area is    4.345
```

Example 5.10.4 Assuming $a_1b_2 \neq a_2b_1$, the solution of the linear equations $a_1x + b_1y = c_1$, $a_2x + b_2y = c_2$ is given by

$$x = \frac{b_2c_1 - b_1c_2}{a_1b_2 - a_2b_1}, \qquad y = \frac{a_1c_2 - a_2c_1}{a_1b_2 - a_2b_1}.$$

Write a program to read the values of a_1, b_1, c_1 and a_2, b_2, c_2 and to print the values of x and y.

Program 5.5

```
/* Solution of a pair of equations containing two variables */
#include<stdio.h>
main()
{
```

```
  float a1,b1,c1,a2,b2,c2,x,y;
  printf("Enter the coefficients of the first equation\n");
  scanf("%f%f%f",&a1,&b1,&c1);
  printf("Enter the coefficients of the second equation\n");
  scanf("%f%f%f",&a2,&b2,&c2);
  x=(b2*c1-b1*c2)/(a1*b2-a2*b1);
  y=(a1*c2-a2*c1)/(a1*b2-a2*b1);
  printf("The solution is x=%6.3f, y=%6.3f",x,y);
}
```

A sample of input/output:

```
Enter the coefficients of the first equation
2 3 4
Enter the coefficients of the second equation
4 3 2
The solution is x=-1.000, y= 2.000
```

Example 5.10.5 Write a program to read the Basic Pay (BP) of an employee and calculate his/her D.A. (DA), H.R.A. (HRA), Tax, Gross Pay (GP) and Net Pay (NP) and print them, where DA = 43% of BP, HRA = 15% of BP, Tax = 20% of BP, GP = BP + DA + HRA, NP = GP – Tax.

Program 5.6

```
/* Program to calculate payment of an employee */
#include<stdio.h>
main()
{
  float np,bp,da,hra,tax,gp;
  printf("Enter basic pay\n");
  scanf("%f",&bp);
  da=bp*0.43;
  hra=bp*0.15;
  tax=bp*0.20;
  gp=bp+da+hra;
  np=gp-tax;
  printf("Basic pay=%6.0f\nD.A.=%6.0f\nH.R.A.=%8.2f\n",bp,da,hra);
  printf("Tax deducted=%8.2f\nGross Pay=%6.0f\nNet Pay=%6.0f",tax,gp,np);
}
```

A sample of input/output:

```
Enter basic pay 50890
```

```
Basic pay= 50890
D.A.= 21883
H.R.A.= 7633.50
Tax deducted=10178.00
Gross Pay= 80406
Net Pay=70228
```

Example 5.10.6 Write a program to find the slope and midpoint of a straight line whose two end points are (x_1, y_1) and (x_2, y_2).

Solution. The slope of a straight line whose end points (x_1, y_1) and (x_2, y_2) is $\frac{y_2 - y_1}{x_2 - x_1}$ and the coordinates of midpoint is $\left(\frac{x_1 + x_2}{2}, \frac{y_1 + y_2}{2}\right)$.

Program 5.7

```
/* Program to compute slope and midpoint of a line segment */
#include<stdio.h>
main()
{
  float x1,y1,x2,y2,slope,x,y;
  printf("Enter two points (x1,y1) and (x2,y2)\n");
  scanf("%f%f%f%f",&x1,&y1,&x2,&y2);
  slope=(y2-y1)/(x2-x1);
  x=(x1+x2)/2.;
  y=(y1+y2)/2.;
  printf("Slope is %6.2f\n",slope);
  printf("Midpoint is (%-6.2f,%6.2f)",x,y);
}
```

A sample of input/output:

```
Enter two points (x1,y1) and (x2,y2)
5.4 3 7.8 3.9

Slope is   0.38
Midpoint is (6.60  ,  3.45)
```

Example 5.10.7 The formula to compute the yearly depreciation of an item is given by

$$\text{Depreciation} = \frac{\text{Purchase price} - \text{Salvage value}}{\text{Years of service}}.$$

Write a program to determine the salvage value of an item when the purchase price, years of service, and the annual depreciation are given.

Solution. Here the inputs are purchase price (`p_price`), depreciation (`dep`) and years of service (`service_length`). The output is salvage value (`sal_value`). The formula to compute salvage value is

$$\text{salvage value} = \text{purchase price} - \text{depreciation} \times \text{years of service}.$$

The program is listed below.

Program 5.8

```
/* Program to calculate salvage value of an item */
#include<stdio.h>
void main()
{
 float p_price,dep,sal_value;
 int service_length;
 printf("Enter the value of purchase price\n");
 scanf("%f",&p_price);
 printf("Enter the value of depreciation per year\n");
 scanf("%f",&dep);
 printf("Enter service length\n");
 scanf("%d",&service_length);
 sal_value=p_price-dep*service_length;
 printf("The salvage value of the item is %6.2f\n",sal_value);
}
```

A sample of input/output:

```
Enter the value of purchase price
2000
Enter the value of depreciation per year
20
Enter service length
7
The salvage value of the item is 1860.00
```

Example 5.10.8 In inventory management, the Economic Order Quantity (EOQ) for a single item is given by

$$EOQ = \sqrt{\frac{2 \times D \times C_s}{C_h}}$$

where D is the demand rate, C_s is the setup cost and C_h is the holding cost per item per unit time.

Write a program to compute EOQ, given demand rate (items per unit time), setup cost (per order), and the holding cost (per item per unit time).

Solution. Here the inputs are D, C_s and C_h and the output is EOQ. The program is listed below.

Program 5.9

```
/* Program to compute Economic Order Quantity for a single item */
#include<stdio.h>
#include<math.h>
void main()
{
 float d,cs,ch,EOQ;
 printf("Enter demand rate\n");
 scanf("%f",&d);
 printf("Enter setup cost\n");
 scanf("%f",&cs);
 printf("Enter holding cost\n");
 scanf("%f",&ch);
 EOQ=sqrt(2*d*cs/ch);
 printf("EOQ is %6.3f\n",EOQ);
}
```

A sample of input/output:

```
Enter demand rate
50
Enter setup cost
105.5
Enter holding cost
130.0
EOQ is 9.008
```

Exercise V

Review Questions

1. Write short notes on `scanf` and `printf` functions.
2. Explain the format specifiers `c,d,e,f,g,o,s,x` and [...], [^...].
3. What is the purpose of the `putchar` function? How is it used within a C program? Compare it with `getchar` function.
4. Compare the character input functions `getchar`, `getche` and `getch`.
5. What is the purpose of the `scanf` function? How is it used within a C program? Compare with the `getchar` function.
6. What is the purpose of the control string in a `scanf` function? What type of information does it convey?

7. If a control string within a `scanf` function contains multiple character groups, how are the character groups separated? Are the whitespace characters required?
8. Normally blank spaces are used to separate the input data. How other characters, such as comma, is used as a field separator?
9. Write a brief note on the commonly used conversion characters within the control string of a `scanf` function.
10. Why & symbol is required with the variable in the `scanf` function?
11. While entering data through `scanf` function, what relationship should exist between the data items and the corresponding arguments? How are multiple data items separated from one another?
12. How octal and hexadecimal data are entered via `scanf` function?
13. Explain `scanf` function to read a string using `%s` format specification.
14. What happens if an input data item contains more characters than the maximum allowable field width? What happens if the data item contains few characters?
15. What is the rule to indicate short integer, long integer and double-precision arguments within the control string of a `scanf` function?
16. How can the assignment of an input data item to its corresponding argument be suppressed?
17. What is the purpose of `printf` function? How is it used within a C program?
18. Compare `printf` and `putchar` functions to print a character.
19. If the control string within a `printf` function contains multiple character groups, how are the character groups separated? How are the separators interpreted?
20. Summarize the meaning of the more commonly used conversion characters within the control string of a `printf` function. Compare it with the conversion characters which are used in a `scanf` function.
21. What is the difference between the format specifications `f, e, g` to read a floating point data using `printf` function?
22. How a string containing whitespace characters can be entered through the keyboard?
23. How can the minimum field width for a data item be specified within the `printf` function?
24. What happens if an output data item contains more characters than the minimum field width? What if the data item contains fewer characters?
25. What is meant by the precision of an output data? How can the precision be specified within a `printf` function?
26. How are uppercase conversion characters interpreted differently than the corresponding lowercase conversion characters in a `printf` function? This feature apply to which kind of conversion?
27. Write a note about different types of flags that are commonly used in the `printf` function.
28. Explain the use of the format specifications `%0.2f` and `%6.2f`.

29. Explain the main four parts of a C program.

Problems

1. Write C statements to perform the following:
(i) Read the values for X, Y, Z from keyboard.
(ii) Print the value of VALUE followed by the words VALUE IS:
(iii) Read the values of A, B, C, I, K from a line and print the values of A, B, C in the first line and I, K in the second line, using single `printf` function.
2. If the input line is

20.5 10

then determine the output of the following program segments

```
(i)  scanf("%f%d",&a,&m);
     printf("M= %d A=%f",m,a);
     n=m*m+2;
     x=a*a;
     printf("%f %d",x,n);

(ii) scanf("%f%d",&a, &m);
     printf("%f %d %f",a,m,a+m);
```

3. Identify the errors, if any, in the following program segments.

```
(i)   int b; float a;
      scanf("%f%d",a,b);
      printf("%f %f %f",A,B,A+B);
      printf("%f",a*n);

(ii)  int a, b,c
      scanf(a);
      b=a*2;
      printf(%d %d %d,a,b,c);

(iii) float x,y;
      scanf("%f",&x);
      y/4=x*x+5;
      printf("%f %d",x,y);

(iv)  float a,b;
      scanf("%f %d",&a,5);
      b=a+5;
      printf("a= b=",a,b);
```

```
(v)   float a; int m;
      scanf("%f %d" &a,&m);
      printf("a=%f m=%f",a,m);
      printf("%f",m+1);

(vi)  float A,B,C;
      S=A+B+C;
      AREA=SQRT(S*(S-A)*(S-B)*(S-C));
      printf("%f %f",S, AREA);
```

4. A C program contains the following declaration:
`int i, j, k;`
Write an appropriate `scanf` function to enter numerical values for `i, j` and `k`, where
(a) The values of `i, j` and `k` are decimal integers
(b) The value of `i` is a decimal integer, `j` is an octal integer and `k` is a hexadecimal integer.
(c) The values for `i` and `j` are hexadecimal integers and `k` is an octal integer.
5. Suppose `i, j, k` are integer variables. Write an appropriate `scanf` function to enter the values of `i, j` and `k` as per following specifications.
(a) The values of `i, j` and `k` are decimal integers not exceeding six characters each.
(b) The value of `i` is a decimal integer, `j` is an octal integer and `k` is a hexadecimal integer, with each quantity not exceeding 8 characters.
(c) The values of `i` and `j` are hexadecimal integers and `k` is an octal integer. Each quantity will be 7 or fewer characters.
6. Let `x, y, z` be floating point variables. Write a `printf` function for each of the following groups of variables or expressions.
(a) `x, y` and `z`
(b) `x*y, x/y`
7. Let us consider the following declaration.
`int i=3456, j=0x34bc, k=073245`
Write the output resulting from each of the following `printf` statements.
(a) `printf("%d %x %o",i,j,k);`
(b) `printf("%4d %4x %4o",i,j,k);`
(c) `printf("%-7d %-7x %-7o",i,j,k);`
8. Let us consider the following declaration.
`float int i=3.456, j=0.0004, k=3456`
Write the output resulting from each of the following `printf` statements.
(a) `printf("%7.4f %7.4f %7.3f",i,j,k);`
(b) `printf("%7.3f %7.3f %7.3f",i,j,k);`
(c) `printf("%8.3e %8.4E %9.4e",i,j,k);`
(d) `printf("%-8f %-8f %+8.4f",i,j,k);`

Programming Problems

1. Write a program to find the,
   (a) area, perimeter and diagonal of a rectangle whose two adjacent sides are a and b.
   (b) area and diagonal of a square whose each side is a.
   (c) area of a triangle whose sides are a, b and c.
   (d) area of a triangle whose two sides are a, b and the angle between them is θ (area $= \frac{1}{2}ab\sin\theta$).
   (e) area and circumference of a circle of radius r.
   (f) volume of a cylinder.
   (g) volume of a cone.
   (h) volume of a sphere.

2. Write a program to find the
   (a) distance between two points (x_1, y_1, z_1) and (x_2, y_2, z_2). [dist=$\sqrt{(x_1-x_2)^2+(y_1-y_2)^2+(z_1-z_2)^2}$]
   (b) distance from the point (x_1, y_1, z_1) to the plane $ax+by+cz+d=0$. [distance=$|\frac{ax_1+by_1+cz_1+d}{\sqrt{a^2+b^2+c^2}}|$]
   (c) angle between the straight lines $y = m_1x + c_1$ and $y = m_2x + c_2$. [angle $\theta = \tan^{-1}\frac{m_1-m_2}{1+m_1m_2}$]
   (d) angle between the planes $a_1x+b_1y+c_1z+d_1=0, a_2x+b_2y+c_2z+d_2=0$.
   $$\left[\text{angle } \theta = \cos^{-1}\frac{a_1a_2+b_1b_2+c_1c_2}{\sqrt{a_1^2+b_1^2+c_1^2}\sqrt{a_2^2+b_2^2+c_2^2}}\right]$$

3. If the equation of a sphere is $x^2+y^2+z^2+2ux+2vy+2wz+d=0$, then the centre and radius of it are respectively $(-u,-v,-w)$ and $\sqrt{u^2+v^2+w^2-d}$. Write a program to read the values of u, v, w and d and find the center and radius of the sphere, assuming that $u^2+v^2+w^2-d>0$.

4. Write a program to solve each of the following programs.
   (a) Find the volume and surface area of a sphere of radius r. [volume=$\frac{4}{3}\pi r^3$, surface area $= 4\pi r^2$]
   (b) Find the volume and surface area of a right circular cylinder of radius r and height h. [volume=$\pi r^2 h$ and surface area=$2\pi rh$]
   (c) Find the volume of a right circular cone of height h and radius of the base is r. [volume=$\frac{1}{3}\pi r^3 h$].

5. Write a program to read two vectors $\bar{a} = (a_1, a_2, a_3)$ and $\bar{b} = (b_1, b_2, b_3)$.
   (a) Find the scalar product $(\bar{a}.\bar{b})$ and vector product $(\bar{a}\times\bar{b})$. [$\bar{a}.\bar{b} = a_1b_1+a_2b_2+a_3b_3$, $\bar{a}\times\bar{b} = (a_2b_3-a_3b_2, b_1a_3-a_1b_3, a_1b_2-a_2b_1)$)].
   (b) the magnitude $|\bar{a}|$ and $|\bar{b}|$, where $|\bar{a}| = \sqrt{a_1^2+a_2^2+a_3^2}$.
   (c) the angle between them. [angle $\theta = \cos^{-1}\frac{\bar{a}.\bar{b}}{|\bar{a}||\bar{b}|}$]

6. Assuming $a_1b_2 \neq a_2b_1$, the solution of the linear equations $a_1x+b_1y=c_1, a_2x+b_2y=c_2$ is given by $x = \frac{b_2c_1-b_1c_2}{a_1b_2-a_2b_1}$, $y = \frac{a_1c_2-a_2c_1}{a_1b_2-a_2b_1}$. Write a program to read the values of a_1, b_1, c_1 and a_2, b_2, c_2 in two lines and to print the values of x and y.

7. Write a program to read the value of a variable A in feet and convert it into (i) yard, (ii) inches, (iii) centimeter, (iv) meter, (v) kilometer and (vi) mile. [1 yard=3 feet, 1 foot=12 inches, 1 inch=2.54 c.m., 1 meter=100 c.m., 1 K.M.=1000 meter, 1 mile =1760 yard].
8. Write a program to read the values of (i) x and y and print the values of r and θ, where $r = \sqrt{x^2 + y^2}, \theta = \tan^{-1}(y/x)$, (ii) r and θ and print x, y, where $x = r \cos\theta, y = r \sin\theta$.
9. (i) A person deposits Rs. P in a bank. The rate of interest (simple) is @Rs. R% per annum. Write a program to determine the total interest (I) and amount (A) at the end of T years. [I=PRT/100, A=P+I]
(ii) A person deposits Rs. P in a bank. The bank gives compound interest @Rs. r% compounded n times in a year. Write a program to determine the amount (A) at the end of t years. [$A = P(1 + \frac{r}{100n})^{nt}$].
10. Write a program to convert Fahrenheit (Centigrade) temperature to Centigrade (Fahrenheit).
11. Write a program to read three numbers a, b, c, compute their sum, average and print them.
12. Write a program to interchange the values between the variables a and b (i) using a third variable and (ii) without using a third variable.
13. Write a program to interchange the values of a, b, c so that a gets b's value, b gets c's value and c gets a's value.
14. Write a program to read the Basic Pay (BP) of an employee and calculate his/her D.A (DA), H.R.A (HRA), Tax, Gross Pay (GP) and Net Pay (NP) and print them, where DA=32% of BP, HRA=15% of BP, Tax=20% of BP, GP=BP+DA+HRA, NP=GP-Tax.
15. Write a program to read the vertices $A(x_1, y_1), B(x_2, y_2)$ and $C(x_3, y_3)$ of a triangle and find its area.
16. Write a program to read the value of x and find the value of $y = 1 - \frac{x^2}{2} + \frac{x^3}{6} - \frac{x^4}{24}$.

Chapter 6

Control Statements

Normally, the statements in a C program are executed in the order in which they appear in the program and this is known as normal flow of control. But, to solve a problem sometimes, the sequence of execution of statements are changed under certain conditions. To obtain a solution to problem decisions, repetitions, branching, etc. are performed sometimes. The statements which control the sequence of execution of statements are called **control statements**. If the transfer of control depends on some conditions, then the transfer is called **conditional transfer** and if the transfer of control does not depend on any condition, then the transfer is called **unconditional transfer**. C supports several control statements such as `goto`, `while`, `do-while`, `switch`, `for`, etc. The statements `if`, `if-else`, `switch` are called decision making statements and `for`, `while`, `do-while` are called loop construct. In this chapter, all these statements are discussed.

6.1 The if Statement

This statement is very powerful and essential in any programming language. It is of four types, (i) `if`, (ii) block `if` or `if-else`, (iii) nested `if`, and (iv) multi-alternative `if`.

6.1.1 The simple if statement

Its general form is

```
if (logical_expression)
{
    statements;
}
```

where `logical_expression` is a logical expression and `statements` are executable C statements. This statement is also known as logical `if` statement.

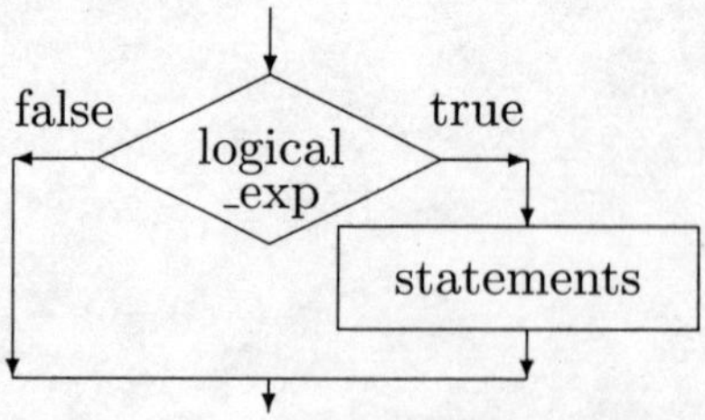

Figure 6.1: Flowchart of `if` statement

If the logical expression `logical_expression` is true (value 1), then the `statements` are executed and control goes to the next statement of this `if` statement. But, if the expression is false (value 0), then the `statements` are skipped and the statement just after the `if` statement is executed. The flowchart of the `if` statement is shown in Figure 6.1.

If the number of statements in `statements` is one, then there is no need of opening ({) and closing (}) braces.

Example 6.1.1 The value of y is given by

$$y = \begin{cases} 2x + 3.5 & \text{if } x \leq 2.5 \\ 2x^2 - 1.5 & \text{if } x > 2.5. \end{cases}$$

The `if` statements to determine y for a given x are

```
if(x <= 2.5) y=2.0*x+3.5;
if(x > 2.5) y=2.0*x*x-1.5;
```

Now, if the problem is to find the value of y and print it for a given x, then the above statements are changed to

```
if(x <= 2.5)
     {
         y=2.0*x+3.5;
         printf("y=%f",y);
     }
if(x > 2.5)
     {
         y=2.0*x*x-1.5;
         printf("y=%f",y);
     }
```

Here two logical `if` statements are used to determine the value of y, but it can be done by using only one `if` statement called block `if` statement as discussed below.

6.1.2 `if-else` or block `if` statement

The general form of this statement is

```
if(logical_expression)
    {
        statement_1;
    }
else
    {
        statement_2;
    }
```

where `statement_1` and `statement_2` are any valid C statements. The statements `statement_1` and `statement_2` are called *if block* and *else block* respectively. If the value of `logical_expression` is true, then `statement_1` will be executed and else block will be skipped. If `logical_expression` is false, then if block will be skipped and `statement_2` of the else block will be executed. If there is no statement in the else block, then the keyword `else` is not required and in this case block `if` statement becomes a simple `if` statement. The flow chart of block `if` statement is shown in Figure 6.2. If there is only one statement in any block, then the braces are not required.

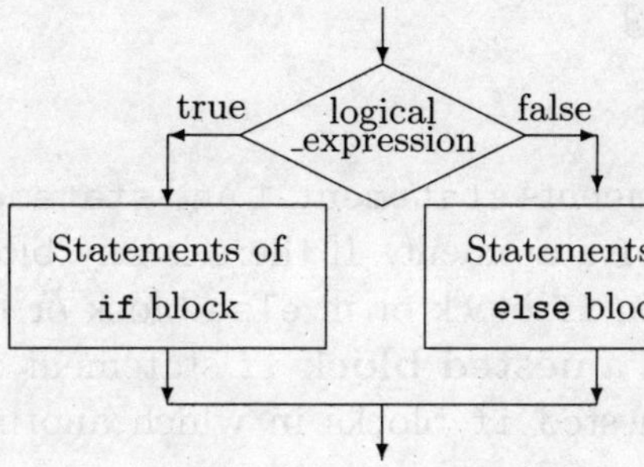

Figure 6.2: Flowchart of block `if` statement

Example 6.1.2 The block `if` statement to compute y, where

$$y = \begin{cases} 2x + 3.5, & \text{if } x \leq 2.5 \\ 2x^2 - 1.5, & \text{if } x > 2.5 \end{cases}$$

is written below.

```
if(x <= 2.5)
    {
        y=2*x+3.5;
    }
else
    {
        y=2*x*x-1.5;
    }
```

This statement can also be written as

```
if(x <= 2.5)
    y=2*x+3.5;
else
    y=2*x*x-1.5;
```

Example 6.1.3 The perimeter and area of a circle are $2\pi a$ and πa^2 respectively and that of rectangle are $2(a+b)$ and ab. Write block if statement to evaluate the perimeter and area, when the object code (c for circle and r for rectangle) is given.

```
if(object == 'c')
    {
    perimeter=2*3.14159*a;
    area=3.14159*a*a;
    }
else
    {
    perimeter=2*(a+b);
    area=a*b;
    }
```

6.1.3 Nested `if` statement

In block `if` statement, the statements `statement_1` and `statement_2` can be some other block `if` statement or simple `if` statement. If there is any block `if` statement within the initial block `if` statement in `if` block or in `else` block or in both the blocks, then the resulting structure is called a **nested block** `if` statement or structure.

We illustrate the usage of nested `if` blocks in which another `if` statement occurs within the initial `if` block.

Suppose the value of z and $z1$ are defined as follows:

$$z = x + y; z1 = x/y \quad \text{if } x > 5, y > 1$$
$$z = x * y; z1 = 0 \quad \text{if } x > 5, y \leq 1$$
$$z = x - 5; z1 = 0 \quad \text{if } x < 5$$

The flow chart of the above problem is given in Figure 6.3.

The following program segment compute the values of z and $z1$ using nested `if` statement.

```
if(x > 5)
   {
     if(y > 1.)
     {
        z=x+y;
        z1=x/y;
     }
```

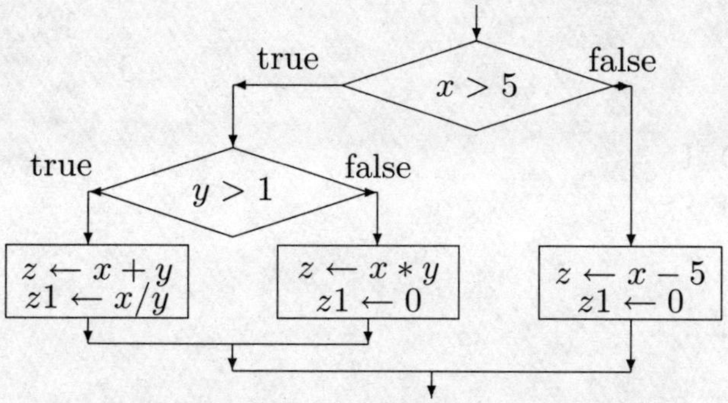

Figure 6.3: Flowchart of nested if

```
        else
        {
            z=x*y;
            z1=0;
        }
      }
    else
      {
        z=x-5;
        z1=0;
      }
```

Some other valid nested block if structures are given below, where *expl*1 and *expl*2 are logical expressions.

```
(i) if(expl1)  {
      if(expl2)
        {
          . . . . . .
        }
      else{
          . . . . . .
        }
      }
    else{
        if(expl3) {
          . . . . . .
          }
        else
          {
          . . . . . .
        }
```

```
(ii) if(expl1) {
          . . . . . .
        }
      else{
        if(expl2) {
            . . . . . .
          }
        else{
          . . . . . .
        }
      }
(iii)  if(expl1) {
          if(expl2) {
              . . . . . .
            }
          else{
              . . . . . .
```

```
    }                                                    }
                                                      }

(iv) if(expl1) {
        if(expl2) {
            . . . . . .
          }
        else{
            . . . . . .
      }
     }
    else {
        . . . . . .
      }
```

Multi-alternative if statement

In block `if` statement there are only two alternatives, one is `if` block (to be executed when the `logical_expression` is true) and other is else block (to be executed when `logical_expression` is false). Thus, the function $f(x)$ defined by

$$f(x) = \begin{cases} x^2 + 5, & \text{if } x < 0 \\ 2x, & \text{if } 0 \le x < 1 \\ x - 1, & \text{if } x \ge 1 \end{cases}$$

can not be easily implemented using block `if` statement. A modification of this block `if` statement is necessary for the implementation of this type of function. This modified `if` statement is known as **multi-alternative `if` statement** and is of the form

```
if(expl1) {
      S1
   }
else if(expl2) {
      S2
   }
else if(expl3) {
      S3
   }
.........
else if(expln-1) {
      Sn-1
   }
else
   {
      Sn
   }
```

where $expl_1, expl_2, \ldots, expl_{n-1}$ are logical expressions and $S_1, S_2, \ldots, S_n$ are blocks of C statements.

Here all `else if` are part of `if` block. The above function $f(x)$ is implemented using multi-alternative `if` statement as follows:

```
if(x<0.0)
    fx=x*x+5.;
else if((0.0 ≤ x) && (x<1.0))
    fx=2.0*x;
else
    fx=x-1.0;
```

Example 6.1.4 (Income tax calculation) The rates of income tax for individual tax payee is given below.

Particulars	Tax
1. Standard deduction. For male employee is Rs. 1,80,000 and for female employee is Rs. 1,90,000	Nil
2. For male (female) employee, the total income exceeds Rs. 1,80,000 (Rs. 1,90,000) but does not exceed Rs. 5,00,000	10% of the amount by which total income exceeds Rs. 1,80,000 (Rs. 1,90,000 for female employee)
3. The total income exceeds Rs. 5,00,000 but does not exceed Rs. 8,00,000.	Rs. 32,000 (for male), Rs. 31,000 (for female) plus 20% of the amount by which the total income exceeds Rs. 5,00,000.
4. The total income exceeds Rs. 8,00,000.	Rs. 92,000 (for male), Rs. 91,000 (for female) plus 30% of the amount by which the total income exceeds Rs. 8,00,000.

Write a program to read the total income of an employee with his/her sex and compute the total tax.

Program 6.1

```
/* Calculation of income tax */
#include<stdio.h>
void main()
 {
   float income,tax;
   char sex;
   printf("Enter total income and sex(m/f) of an employee\n");
```

```
  scanf("%f %c",&income,&sex);
  if(sex=='m')
    {
      if(income<=180000) tax=0;
      else if(income>180000 && income<=500000)
       tax=(income-180000)*0.10;
      else if (income>500000 && income <=800000)
       tax=32000+(income-500000)*0.20;
      else if(income>800000) tax=92000+(income-800000)*0.30;
    }
    else /* female */
    {
      if(income<=190000) tax=0;
      else if(income>190000 && income<=500000)
       tax=(income-190000)*0.10;
      else if (income>500000 && income <=800000)
       tax=31000+(income-500000)*0.20;
      else if(income>800000) tax=91000+(income-800000)*0.30;
    }
 printf("Income = %0.2f Tax=%0.2f",income,tax);
}
```

A sample of input/output:

```
Enter total income and sex(m/f) of an employee
840000 m
Income = 840000.00 Tax=104000.00
```

6.2 The goto Statement

The `goto` statement is used for jumping from one position to other place within `main` or within some other function. The general form of this statement is

```
goto label;
```

where `label` is a valid C identifier and is the statement label of an executable statement (called target statement) in the same function (function will be discussed in Chapter 8) to which the control is transferred and from that label normal sequential execution continues.

The general form of target statement is

```
label : statement;
```

Note that a colon must be given after label. A label can be used against only one statement, i.e. no two statements can have the same label.

Example 6.2.1 Write a program to compute and print the value of $(x+1)(2x+1)^{1/3}$ for x varying from $x = 0$ to 2 at steps of 0.2.

Program 6.2

```
/* Program to find the value of a function for different
  values of x */
#include<stdio.h>
main()
{
  float x, y;
  x=0;
  nexty: y=(x+1.)*pow((2.0*x+1.0),1./3.);
  printf("x=%f  y=%f",x,y);
  x+=0.2;
  if(x<=2.0) goto nexty;
}
```

Most of the programming languages support `goto` statement, though the use of this statement is discouraging. The `goto` statement is mainly used in:

(i) Branching from a statement or a group of statements under certain conditions;

(ii) Jumping to the end of a loop under certain conditions;

(iii) Jumping out from a loop under certain conditions.

Since C is a structured language, all these situations can be solved by using other statements, without using `goto` statement. The situations (i), (ii) and (iii) can be accomplished with the block `if` statement, `continue` statement and `break` statement respectively. The last two statements will be discussed later. The structured features in C suggests that the program should be written in an order, sequential manner and thus the use of `goto` statement should generally be avoided in a C program.

6.3 The `while` Statement

Using `if` statement, repeated execution of a group of statements can be performed. Another useful statement which used to perform such type of execution is `while` statement. It is a structured statement. The repetition of the loop is defined only on a logical expression. The general form is

```
while (logical_expression)
    {
        statements;
    }
```

where logical_expression (test-condition) is a logical expression. If the logical expression logical_expression is true, then the statements between braces will execute.

The loop is continued when logical_expression is true. If logical_expression is false, then the control goes to the next statement of the while loop.

The logical_expression must depend on a variable, this variable is known as control variable of the while loop. The value of this variable must be updated to satisfy logical_expression. If the control variable is not updated within the loop, the loop never terminates.

The flowchart of this statement is drawn in Figure 6.4, where *l_exp* is a logical expression.

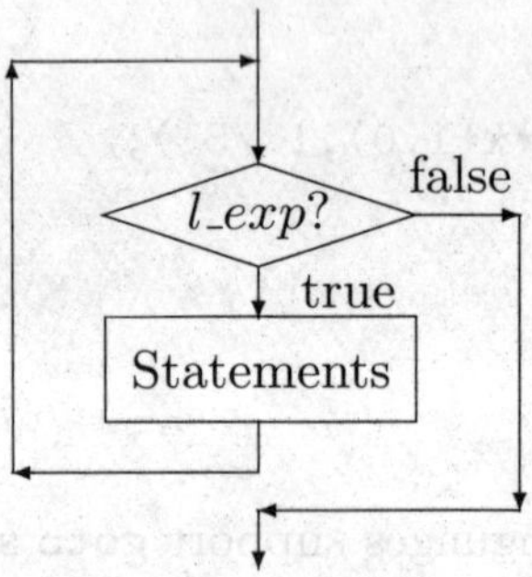

Figure 6.4: Flowchart of while loop

The following statements are valid but they have some special meaning.

(i) `while(i++);` This is a loop without any body.

(ii) `while(1) printf("I never stop\n");` In this case, the condition remains true and hence the loop never terminates.

Example 6.3.1 Write a program to evaluate x^n, where n is a positive integer and x is any real number.

Program 6.3

```
/* Program to find x^n for different n */
#include<stdio.h>
main()
 {
   int n,i=1;
   float prod=1.0,x;
   scanf("%f%d",&x,&n);
   while(i<=n)
     {
       prod*=x;
       i++;
```

```
    }
   printf("x=%f  n=%d Value=%f\n",x,n,prod);
 }
```

A sample of input/output:
2 10

```
x=2.000000  n=10 Value=1024.000000
```

Example 6.3.2 (Palindrome testing) Write a program to test whether a given integer is a palindrome or not, by reversing the digits of the number.

Solution. An integer is said to be a palindrome if it is same with its reverse integer, i.e. first digit is equal to the last digit, second digit equals the last but one digit and so on. For example, the integer 1234321 is a palindrome but 1234561 is not a palindrome. The following program tests whether an integer is a palindrome or not and also prints its reverse integer.

Program 6.4

```
/* Checking of palindrome of an integer */
#include<stdio.h>
main()
 {
   long int n,m,revers;
   printf("Enter an integer\n");
   scanf("%d",&n);
   m=n;
   revers=0;
   while(n!=0)
     {
       revers=10*revers+n%10;
       n=(int)n/10; /* integer part after division by 10 */
     }
   printf("The reserve number is %d\n ",revers);
   if(m==revers)
     printf("%d is a palindrom\n ",m);
   else
     printf("%d is not a palindrom\n",m);
 }
```

A sample of input/output:

```
Enter an integer 23432
```

```
The reserve number is 23432
 23432 is a palindrome

Enter an integer 23451

The reserve number is 15432
 23451 is not a palindrome
```

6.4 The do-while Statement

Another type of loop is available in C, which is known as `do-while` statement. This statement is similar to `while` statement, but one difference is that the logical condition which appears in this statement is tested at the end of the loop. For this reason this loop must be executed at least once.

The general form of this statement is

```
do
   {
        statements;
   }
while(logical_expression);
```

where `logical_expression` is a logical expression.

The loop will repeat when `logical_expression` (the test-condition) is true. The loop will terminate when `logical_expression` is false (this is used as termination condition).

A variable (called control variable) must be used in the `logical_expression`. The value of the control variable must be updated within the loop to reach the termination condition. When the `logical_expression` becomes false, then the loop terminates.

The flowchart of this statement is shown in Figure 6.5.

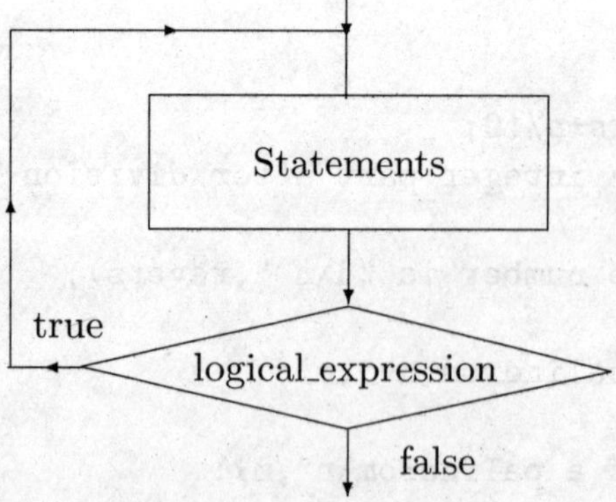

Figure 6.5: Flowchart of `do-while` loop

Example 6.4.1 Write a program to find the sum of some integers until sum of the integers is just greater than or equal to 500.

Program 6.5

```
/* Sum of integers */
#include<stdio.h>
main()
 {
   int sum=0,count=0,m;
   do
     {
       scanf("%d",&m);
       sum+=m;
       count++;
     } while(sum<500);
   printf("Sum=%d count=%d",sum,count);
 }
```

A sample of input/output:

100
250
100
120

```
Sum=570 count=4
```

It may be noted that the logical condition is tested at the end of the loop. The execution is terminated when the logical expression is false and the loop is repeated when the condition is true. Also, this loop is executed for at least one time since the condition is tested at the end of the loop. But, in `do-while` loop, the condition is tested at the beginning of the loop, and if the condition is false for the first time, then the loop terminates without entering into the loop.

6.5 The `break` Statement

This statement is used to terminate the loops. It is generally used in `while`, `do-while`, `for` and `switch` statements.

The general form is

```
break;
```

It may be noted that no condition is required to execute this statement. This statement is frequently used in `switch` statement; and when the `break` statement is executed within a `switch` statement, then control goes out of the switch statement. This statement is also used to exit from a loop such as `do-while, while` and `for`.

The flowchart for `break` statement is shown in Figure 6.6.

The `break` statement is illustrated in the following program.

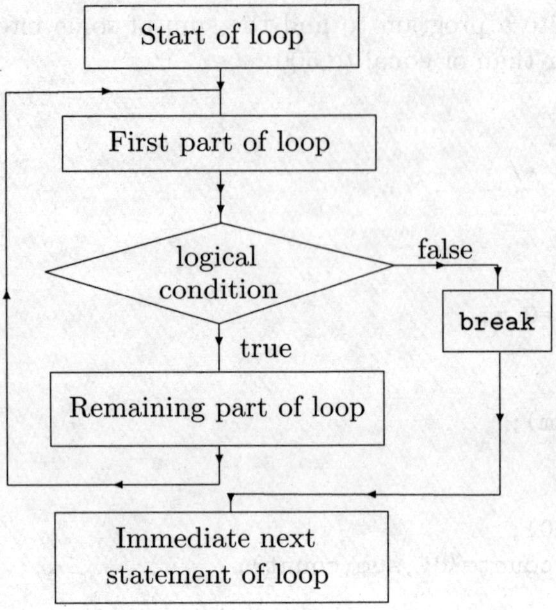

Figure 6.6: Flow chart of `break` statement

Example 6.5.1 (Use of `break` statement) Write a program to read a sequence of at most 100 integers and count the number of positive integers up to the first occurrence of negative integer.

Solution. The corresponding program is written below.

Program 6.6

```
/* Use of break statement */
#include<stdio.h>
main()
 {
   int count=0,x;
   do
    {
      scanf("%d",&x);
      if(x<0) break;
      count++;
    }
   while(count<100);
   printf("Number of positive integers entered is %d",count);
 }
```

The `do-while` loop repeats 100 times, if all the integers are positive or zero, but if there are any negative integer, then the loop terminates and the value of `count` is printed.

6.6 The `continue` Statement

The `continue` statement is generally used within a loop (`while, do-while, for, switch`, etc) to bypass a portion of the loop. The `continue` statement causes the loop to be continued with the next iteration after skipping any statement in between. Recall that, when `break` statement is encountered within a loop, the control goes outside the loop.

The general form of the `continue` statement is

```
continue;
```

The flow chart of this statement is shown in Figure 6.7.

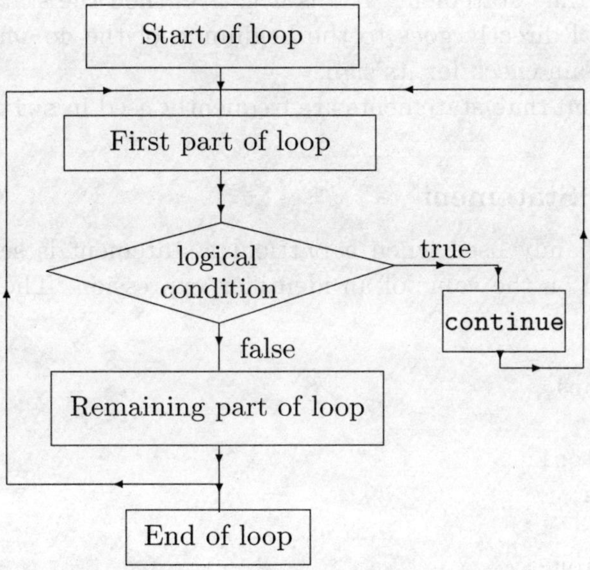

Figure 6.7: Flow chart of `continue` statement

The following example is considered to illustrate the `continue` statement.

Example 6.6.1 (Use of `continue` statement) Given a set of n real numbers. Find the sum of only positive numbers.

Program 6.7

```
/* Use of continue statement */
#include<stdio.h>
```

```
main()
 {
   int n, i=0;
   float x, sum=0;
   printf("Enter  the value of n ");
   scanf("%d",&n);
   do{
     scanf("%f",&x);
     i++;
     if(x<0) continue; /* read next number */
     sum+=x;
   }while(i<n);
   printf("The sum of positive numbers is %f",sum);
 }
```

Look at the `continue` statement. If x is negative, then the statement `sum+=x` is not executed, the control directly goes to the beginning of the `do-while` loop. Read the next number and again check for its sign.

The `break` and `continue` statements are frequently used in `switch` statement, which is discussed below.

6.7 The `switch` Statement

This statement is mainly used when a particular statement is selected from a group of statements, based on the value of an identifier/expression. The general form of this statement is

```
switch (expression)
  {
    case expression1:
       statements;
       break;
    case expression2:
       statements;
       break;
       .
       .
       .
    case expression:
       statements;
       break;
    default:
       statements;
   }
```

The expression1, expression2, ..., expressionn are generally integer or character constants. Here expression is an integer variable or integer expression. It may be noted that all these expressions can also be of character type, as each individual character has an equivalent integer value.

The values of expression1, expression2, ..., expressionn all are distinct (i.e. deferent alternatives) and they are referred as *case labels.* These case labels identify different groups of statements and they are unique within a switch statement. The default label is optional. The switch statement is executed as follows:
At first the value of expression is determined. If the value of it is equal to expression1, then the control goes to the case expression1. The statements following it are executed and then the control goes outside the switch statement (due to the presence of break statement). If the value of expression is equal to expression2, then the control directly goes to the case expression2, execute the statement(s) of this group (i.e. the statements between first and third cases) and the control goes outside the switch statement and so on. If the value of expression does not match with any one of expression1, expression2, ..., expressionn, then the statements under default label will be executed, if it is there. If default label is absent and the value of expression does not match with any one of expression1, expression2, ..., expressionn, then the switch statement does nothing.

Here we consider an example where the switch statement is appropriately used.

Example 6.7.1 (Evaluation of Legendre polynomials) Write a program to compute the value of the Legendre polynomials $P_1(x), P_2(x), P_3(x)$ and $P_4(x)$ defined by

$P_1(x) = x$
$P_2(x) = \frac{1}{2}(3x^2 - 1)$
$P_3(x) = \frac{1}{2}(5x^3 - 3x)$
$P_4(x) = \frac{1}{8}(35x^4 - 30x^2 + 3)$ for given $n(= 1, 2, 3, 4)$ and x.

Program 6.8

```
/* Program to compute the value of the Legendre polynomials */
#include<stdio.h>
main()
{
   int n;
   float x,p;
   printf("Enter the value of n and x ");
   scanf("%d%f",&n,&x);
   switch (n)
   {
     case 1:
       p=x;
       break;
```

```
  case 2:
     p=(3.0*x*x-1.0)/2.0;
     break;
  case 3:
     p=(5.0*x*x*x-3.0*x)/2.0;
     break;
  case 4:
     p=(35*pow(x,4)-30*x*x+3.0)/8.0;
     break;
  default:
     printf("The value of n other than 1, 2, 3, 4\n");
 }
 printf("\nP=%f for x=%f",p,x);
}
```

A sample of input/output:

```
Enter the value of n and x 3 .5

P=-0.437500 for x=0.500000
```

If the value of n is 3, then the control directly goes to the label `case 3` and the value of p is evaluated from the expression $P_3(x)$ (from the block of `case 3`) and then exit from the `switch` statement. Finally, the value of `p` is printed by the `printf` statement.

6.8 The for Loop

The most useful loop is `for` loop, it is very powerful statement in C. One or more variables are used to control the loop. These variables are called the control variables. The simple form of `for` loop is

```
for(exp1; exp2; exp3) /* heading of the for loop */
  {
    statements; /* body of the for loop */
  }
```

where `exp1` assigns the initial value of the control variable, `exp2` generally represents test condition. If this condition is true, then the statements within the `for` loop executed. `exp3` is used to update the value of the control variable. Generally, `exp1` is an assignment statement, `exp2` is a logical expression and `exp3` is a unary expression or an assignment statement. Notice that `exp1`, `exp2` and `exp3` are separated by semicolons, which means they are three different statements/expressions. `exp1`, `exp2` and `exp3` have different meanings and uses. They are discussed later.

During the execution of `for` loop, the value of control variable initialize its value by executing `exp1`. Then `exp2` is evaluated and checks `exp2` if it is true or false. If `exp2` is true, then all the statement(s) within the `for` loop are executed, otherwise the control goes outside the for loop. After execution of all statements of for loop (this is called one pass of the loop) the exp3 is evaluated. exp3 updates the value of control variable and then executes exp2 to check its validity. This process is repeated until exp2 is true.

The for loop can also be implemented with the help of while loop, as shown below.

```
exp1;
while (exp2)
  {
    statements;
    exp3;
  }
```

If the number of statements within for loop is one, then there is no need to use braces.

The flow chart of for loop is shown in Figure 6.8.

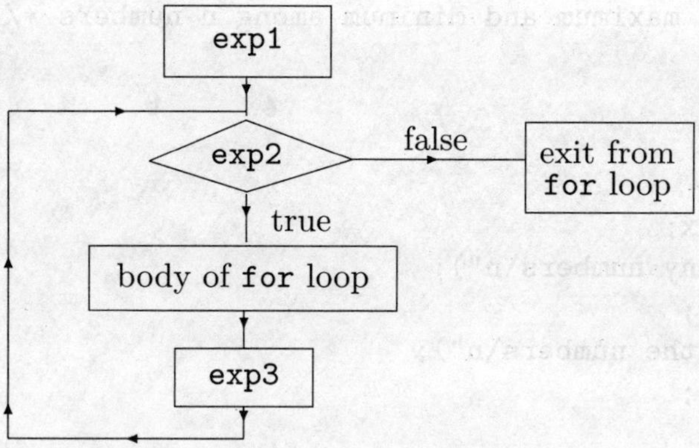

Figure 6.8: Flow chart of for loop

Now, we consider an example, where for loop is used. Let us determine the sum of 10 numbers using for loop.

```
main()
{
  float sum=0, x;
  int i;
  for(i=1;i<=10;i++)
    {
      scanf("%f ",&x);
      sum+=x;
    }
  printf("Sum of 10 numbers is %f",sum);
}
```

Here `i` is the control variable which is initialized as `1` (since `exp1` is `i=1`). The `exp2` is `i<=10`, a logical expression. The value of `i` is known (`i=1`). Thus, the expression `i<=10` is true. Then, the `for` loop reads a number as `x`. Add it to the variable `sum`. Then, the value of `i` is incremented by 1, since `exp3` is `i++` (a unary operator). Therefore, the value of `i` now becomes 2. This value satisfies the condition `i<=10`. The loop repeats until the condition `i<=10` remains true.

It is easy to observe that the loop is repeated 10 times. It may be noted that there is no semicolon (;) at the end of heading of `for` loop. If there is a semicolon, then this is also a valid `for` statement and this loop repeats until `exp2` is true, but it does not execute any statement.

Example 6.8.1 (Maximum and minimum evaluation) Write a program to find the maximum and minimum among N numbers.

Program 6.9

```
/* Computation of maximum and minimum among n numbers */
#include<stdio.h>
main()
 {
   int n,i;
   float max,min,x;
   printf("How many numbers\n");
   scanf("%d",&n);
   printf("Enter the numbers\n");
   scanf("%f",&x);
   max=x;
   min=x;
   for(i=2;i<=n;i++)
     {
       scanf("%f",&x);
       if(max<x) max=x;
       if(min>x) min=x;
     }
   printf("Maximum=%f, Minimum=%f\n",max,min);
 }
```

A sample of input/output:

```
How many numbers
5
Enter the numbers
-23 89 56 12 34

Maximum=89.000000, Minimum=-23.000000
```

In this program the first number is read as x and it is stored in max and min. Since one number is given as input so n is reduced by one, hence the for loop is repeated for n-1 times. Each time the loop reads a number as x, it is compared with max and min. If it is greater than max (less than min), then we set max=x (min=x) and control passes to the statement at the end of for loop. If x is not greater than max, then the statement max=x is not executed.

Example 6.8.2 (Evaluation of factorial) An approximate formula to find $n!$ is $n! = \sqrt{2\pi n}.n^n e^{-n}$ (Stirling's formula). Write a program to compute $n!$ exactly and by Stirling formula for $n = 1, 2, \ldots, 10$ and estimate the percentage of error in each case.

Program 6.10

```
/* Computation of factorial using direct method
   and using Stirling's formula */
#include<stdio.h>
#include<math.h>
main()
 {
   long int factd;
   float facts,error;
   int i,n;
   printf("========================================\n");
   printf("n      Exact    by Stirling     Percent\n");
   printf("       value    formula         error\n");
   printf("========================================\n");
   for(n=1;n<=10;n++)
     {
       /* factorial by direct method */
       factd=1;
       for(i=1;i<=n;i++)
          factd*=i;
       /* factorial by Stirling's formula */
       facts=sqrt(2*3.141592653*n)*pow(n,n)*exp(-n);
       error=fabs(factd-facts)*100.0/(float)factd;
       printf("%d\t%ld\t%-9.2f\t%f\n",n,factd,facts,error);
     }
   printf("========================================\n");
 }
```

Output:

```
=============================================
n    Exact     by Stirling    Percent
     value     formula        error
=============================================
1    1         0.92           7.786298
2    2         1.92           4.049784
3    6         5.84           2.729837
4    24        23.51          2.057600
5    120       118.02         1.650696
6    720       710.08         1.378030
7    5040      4980.40        1.182619
8    40320     39902.39       1.035728
9    362880    359536.88      0.921276
10   3628800   3598695.50     0.829599
=============================================
```

The `getchar` function with `for` loop may be used to read a multi-character string. For example, the program segment,

```
for(i=0;(c[i]=getchar()) != '\n';i++);
or for(i=0;(c[i++]=getchar()) != '\n';);
```

reads a string of characters while the newline character is entered. The function `getchar` reads a character from the key board, assigns it to the string `c`, and if the entered character is not a newline, then reads the next character. The loop terminates when the newline character is entered.

We observe that three expressions/statements are written in the heading of `for` loop. But, these three quantities are not compulsory while using `for` loop. It should be remembered that termination condition must be present as `exp2`, otherwise loop never terminates. Here, we discuss some special cases of `for` loops.

In general, `exp3` represents an expression that updates the control variable. `exp3` may be used as another C statement which is illustrated below. The following statements

```
for(i=1;i++<=5;)
        printf("Hallow India\n");
```

print the string `Hallow India` for five times. Note that two semicolons are present in the heading of the `for` loop and nothing is written for `exp3`. But, the role of `exp3` is performed in `i++<=5` (`exp2`). In this expression, the control variable `i` is incremented, as well as the test-condition is checked. These statements can also be written as

```
for(i=1;i++<=5;printf("Hallow India\n"));
```

Note that in this case `exp3` is a C statement, not an updating expression. The output of this single statement is same as the above two statements.

Like `exp3`, `exp1` can also be utilized by another way. For example,

```
int i=1;
for(; i++<=5; )
    printf("Hallow India\n");
```

Note that in the heading of the for loop, exp1 and exp3 both are missing. But, they are utilized as i=1 and i++<=5.

The sum of first seven natural numbers can be computed as

```
int i=1; sum=0;
for(; i<=7; )
    sum+=i++;
```

Note that the control variable i is initialized during declaration and it is incremented in the statement sum+=i++;

The following program calculates the values of $f(x)$ for different values of x with spacing 0.5.

```
#include<stdio.h>
#define f(x) (x)*(x)-(x)+2.0
void main()
  {
    float x=0;
    for(; (x+=0.5)<=10; printf("%f%f\n",x,f(x));
  }
```

This program listing the values of x and $f(x)$ for $x = 0, 0.5, 1.0, 1.5, 2.0, \ldots, 10.0$.

Some other special cases of for loops are discussed below.

(i) Let us consider the statement

```
for(;; i++)
```

In this case initialization (exp1) and test-condition (exp2) are missing. This loop never stop, if there is no break or exit statement within the body of the loop. For example,

```
int i=1;
for(; ; i++){
    printf("i=%d\n",i);
    if(i==5) break;
  }
```

The loop repeats for five times and it is terminated when the statement if(i==5) break; is executed.

Let us consider the following modified program segment,

```
int i=1;
for(; ; ){
    printf("i=%d\n",i++);
    if(i==5) break;
  }
```

In this case, the `for` loop repeats four times. Note that none of `exp1, exp2` and `exp3` are written in the heading of `for` loop. But, they are incorporated by other ways.

(ii) The statement

```
for(i=1;i<=5;i++); /* ; at the end of for loop */
```

is a valid `for` loop. Note that ; is at the end of `for` loop. That is, there is no body of the loop. In this loop, the value of control variable `i` is assigned to 1, checks the validity of the statement `i<5` and increments the value of `i`, and this is repeated five times.

(iii) The statements

```
for( ; ; );     for(; ; i++);     for(i=1; ;i++);
```

all are valid `for` loops, but these loops never terminate, because the test-condition (`exp2`) is missing in all cases. So, these statements can be used to create infinite loop.

Thus, `exp1, exp2` and `exp3` may or may not be used in the heading of the `for` loop, but these three expressions/statements must be associated with the loop. Otherwise loop will not work properly. If `exp2` is missing, then the loop becomes infinite.

Though the above forms of `for` loop are available, even then, it is better to avoid them. The use of simplest form is suggested.

6.9 Nested `for` Statement

A `for` loop (outer `for` loop) may contain one or more `for` loops (inner loops) within its range. `for` loops occurring in this fashion are called nested `for` loops.

When one `for` loop is nested inside the another, the inner `for` loop must be entirely contained within the range of the outer `for` loop. There must be no over-lapping of the statements and each loop must have its own unique control variable. However, the loops may have the same terminal statement. The following are valid nested `for` loops.

(i) A `for` loop may contain completely within another `for` loop.

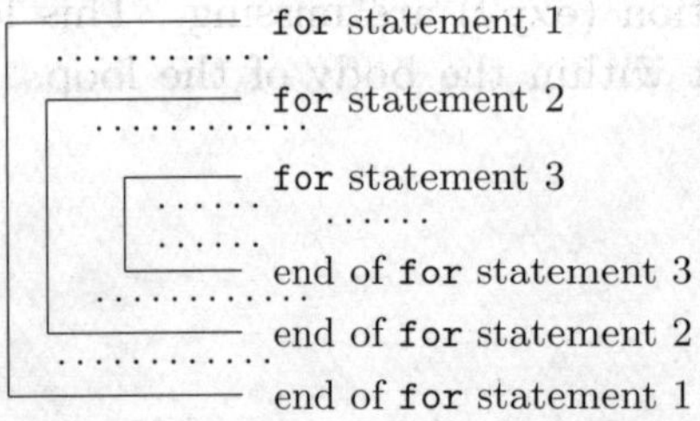

This is the complete nesting of loops.

(ii) Two or more `for` loops may contain within another `for` loop.

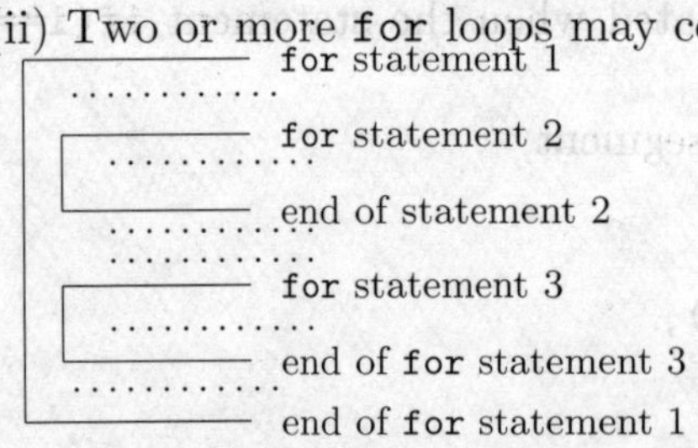

(iii) Two or more for loops starting at different positions may end at the same position.

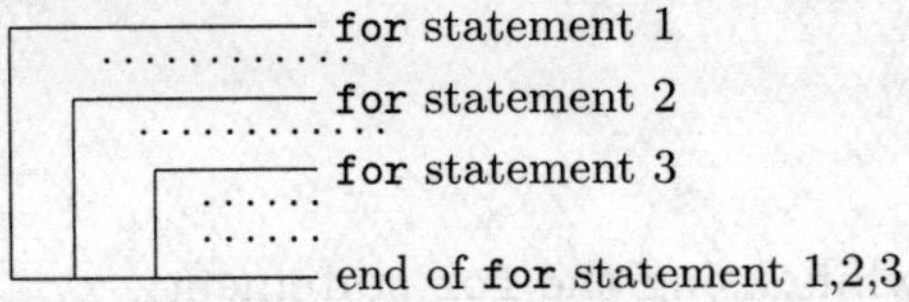

(iv) Transfer of control from any position within for loops inside and outside of its domain are allowed.

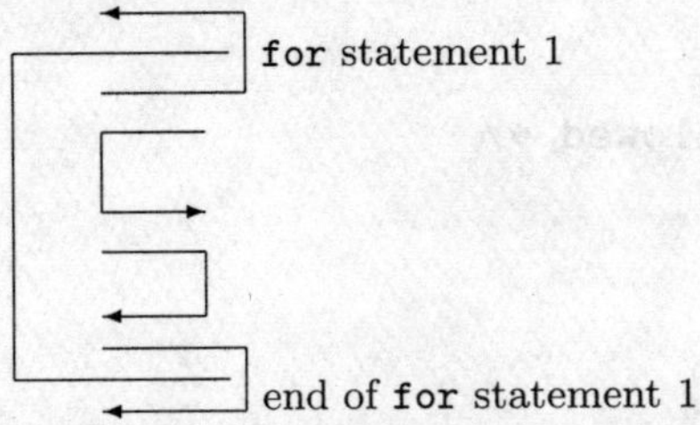

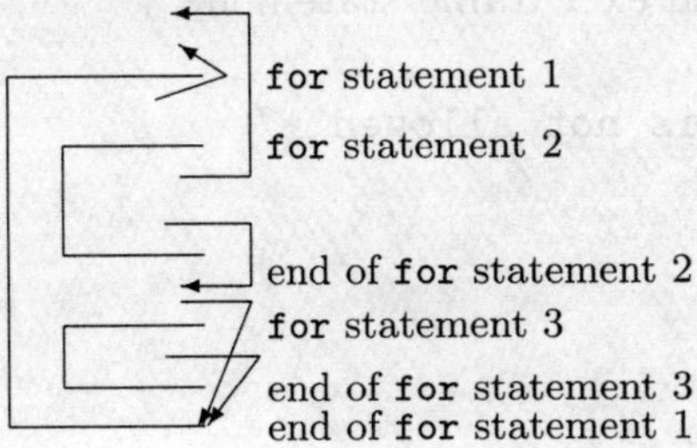

Some examples of invalid for loops

(i) The domain of one for loop must not intersect the domain of another for loop.

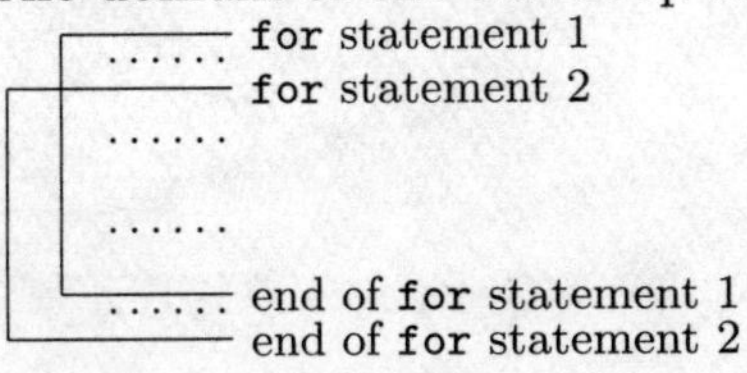

(ii) A transfer of control from outside to within the domain of a for loop is not allowed.

(iii) The transfer of control from one for loop to another for loop is not valid.

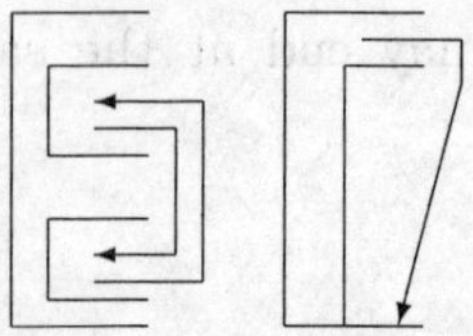

The following points should be remembered while using the `for` statement.

(i) `exp1, exp2, exp3` should not be redefined by statements within the domain of that `for` loop. For example, the following program segment is **invalid**.

```
/* FOLLOWING IS NOT VALID */
        for(i=j; i<=k; i+=2)
        {
            k=k*2; /* k is redefined, not allowed */
            ..................
            ..................
        }
```

(ii) The first statement in a `for` loop should be an executable statement.

```
/* FOLLOWING IS NOT VALID */
        for(i=i; i<=n;i++) /* declaration is not allowed */
        {
            int roll,mark;
            ..................
            ..................
        }
```

(iii) The terminal statement of a `for` loop must be an executable statement, but should not be a control statement, i.e. `goto`, `if` another `for` statements, etc. must not be the last statement in the domain of a `for` loop.

```
/* FOLLOWING IS NOT VALID */
        for(i=i;i<=n;i++)
        {
next:       ..................
            ..................
          goto next;
        }
```

If these situations occur, then do not use any of the above mentioned disallowed statements. In these cases the `continue` statement may be used.

6.9.1 The `comma` operator

We have mentioned that `exp1, exp2` and `exp3` each of these expressions/statements contains single expression/statement. But, in general, each of them may contain more than one statement/expression and they are separated by the comma operator (,). For example,

```
for(i=0,j=10; i<=10, j>=5; i++,j--)
   {
      statement1;
      statement2;
      .
      .
      .
      statementn;
   }
```

This statement initialize `i = 0` and `j = 10`. Then, check the validity of the expressions `i <= 10` and `j >= 5`. If both are valid, then execute all the statements `statement1, statement2, ..., statementn`. Then, the values of `i` (increment) and `j` (decrement) are updated.

It may be noted that the `for` loop repeats when all the conditions under `exp2` are true. If at least one condition is false, then the `for` loop terminates. In the above example, the loop repeats for 6 times, because the condition `j>=5` becomes false after 6 times, though `i <= 10` remains true.

The rules of execution of the `for` loop are given below.

(i) The number of executions (M) is given by $M = \frac{p_t - p_s}{p_i} + 1$ where p_t, p_s and p_i denote initial, terminal and increment value of the control variable.

If the computed value of M is a floating point number, it is truncated to the nearest integer. For example, if the value of M is 7.8, then M becomes 7.

(ii) If $M < 0$ or $= 0$, then the body of the `for` loop is not executed. The execution continues from the statement immediately following the `for` loop.

(iii) If $M > 0$, the initial value of the `for` control variable is set to p_s.

(iv) For the execution of `for` loop, the steps (v) and (vi) are repeated for M times.

(v) All the statements within the loop are executed.

(vi) The value of the control variable is to be set as the sum of the current value of the control variable and the value of the parameter p_i.

(vii) After the execution of `for` loop, the execution is to be continued from the statement immediately following the `for` loop.

6.10 Jumping and Skipping

During execution of loop (`while, do-while, for`) the control can move outside the loop. This can be done using the statements `goto` and `break`. When a `break` statement is encountered inside a loop, then the loop immediately exits and the execution of the program continues with the statement immediately following the loop. The `break` statement exits from only one loop, i.e. if there are nested loops in a program, the `break` would only exit from the loop containing it.

Again, the `goto` statement is used to transfer the control from one position to another within the same function. This statement can also be used to exit from multiple nested loops by single calling of it. Note that a single `break` statement can exit from a single loop. Some examples of jumping are shown in Figure 6.9.

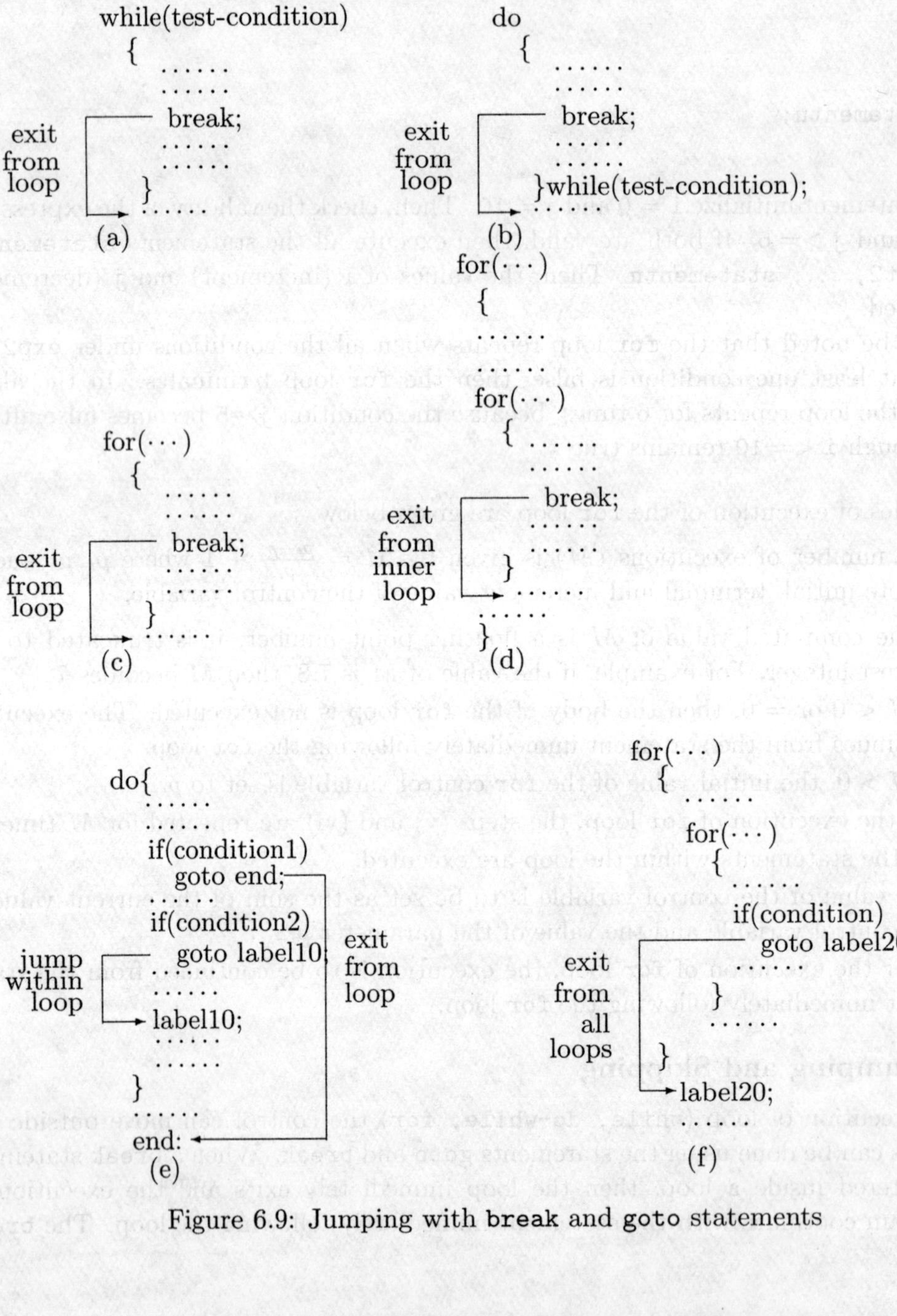

Figure 6.9: Jumping with `break` and `goto` statements

Some valid and invalid jumps within a `for` loop are discussed in Section 6.9.

In the above examples we have seen the jump of a loop using the `break` and `goto` statements. Also, we can jump out of a program by using the library function `exit()` (this function is available in the header file `stdio.h`). The use of this function is shown below.

```
. . . . . .
if(condition) exit(0);
. . . . . .
```

when the `condition` is true, then it terminates the execution of the program and returns to the operating system. The argument of the function `exit` is an integer, generally 0 is used to indicate the normal termination of the program.

In `while` and `do-while` loops when `continue` statement is encountered, the control goes directly to the test-condition of the loop and then to continue the repetitions. In case of `for` loop, the `exp3` (increment/decrement) of the loop is executed before the test-condition (`exp2`) is evaluated. Skipping of loops using `continue` statement are shown in Figure 6.10.

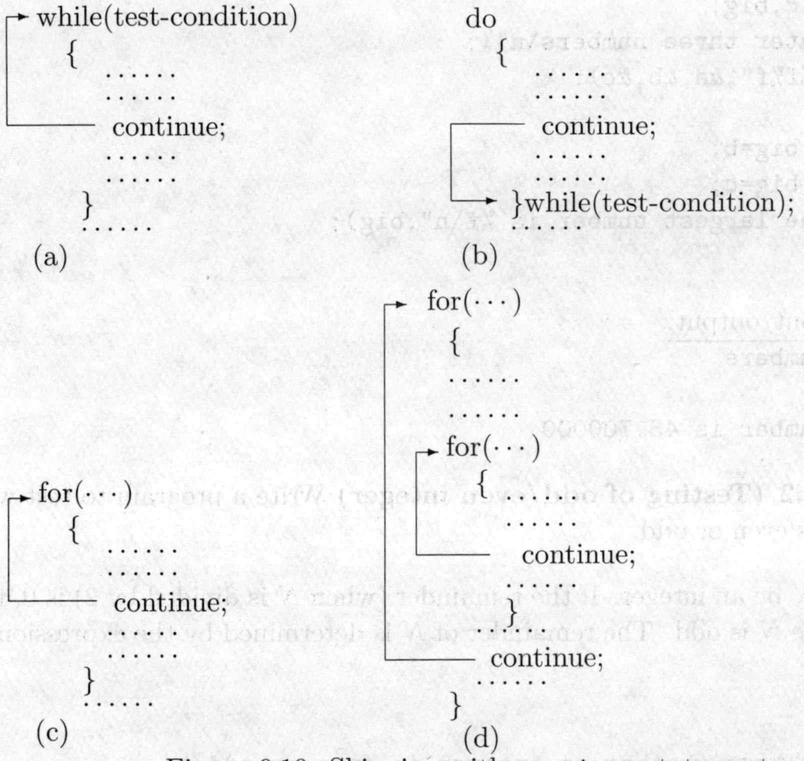

Figure 6.10: Skipping with `continue` statement

Avoid `goto` statement

When the `goto` statement is used, many compilers generate a less efficient code and the use of this statement makes a complicated program logical and makes the program unreadable. Thus, it is good practice to avoid the use of `goto` statement. This can be done with the proper use of `while` and `do-while` loops.

6.11 Worked Out Examples

Example 6.11.1 (Maximum among three numbers) Write a program to find the maximum among three numbers.

Solution. The following program is designed to find the maximum among three numbers using `if` statements.

Program 6.11

```
/* Program to find the maximum among 3 numbers */
#include<stdio.h>
main()
 {
    float a,b,c,big;
    printf("Enter three numbers\n");
    scanf("%f%f%f",&a,&b,&c);
    big=a;
    if(big<b) big=b;
    if(big<c) big=c;
    printf("The largest number is %f\n",big);
 }
```

A sample of input/output:

```
Enter three numbers
23.08 45.7 12.8
The largest number is 45.700000
```

Example 6.11.2 (Testing of odd/even integer) Write a program to test whether a given integer is even or odd.

Solution. Let N be an integer. If the remainder (when N is divided by 2) is 0, then N is even, otherwise N is odd. The remainder of N is determined by the expression $N\%2$.

Program 6.12

```
/*  Program to test whether an integer is even or odd */
#include<stdio.h>
main()
 {
   int n;
   printf("Enter an integer\n");
```

```
  scanf("%d",&n);
  if(n%2==0)
    printf("%d is even\n",n);
  else
    printf("%d is odd\n",n);
 }
```

A sample of input/output:

```
Enter an integer
567
567 is odd
```

Example 6.11.3 (Testing of divisibility) Write a program to test if a given integer is divisible by 7.

Solution. Let N be an integer and it will be divisible by 7 when the remainder (when N is divided by 7) is 0. Otherwise it is not divisible by 7.

Program 6.13

```
/* Program to test whether an integer is divisible by 7 or not */
#include<stdio.h>
main()
 {
  int n;
  printf("Enter an integer\n");
  scanf("%d",&n);
  if(n%7==0)
    printf("%d is divisible by 7\n",n);
  else
    printf("%d is not divisible by 7\n",n);
 }
```

A sample of input/output:

```
Enter an integer
2341
2341 is not divisible by 7
```

Example 6.11.4 (Testing of Armstrong number) Write a program to test whether an integer is Armstrong number.

Solution. An integer N is said to be an Armstrong number, if the sum of cube of its digits is equal to the number itself. For example, the number 153 is an Armstrong number as $1^3 + 5^3 + 3^3 = 153$.

Program 6.14

```
 /* Program to test whether an integer is an Armstrong number */
#include<stdio.h>
#include<math.h>
main()
 {
   int n,m,rem,sum=0;
   printf("Enter an integer\n");
   scanf("%d",&n);
   m=n;
/* Finding sum of cube of the digits */
   while(n!=0)
    {
     rem=n%10; /* finding remainder */
     sum+=pow(rem,3); /* sum of cube of digits */
     n=n/10;
    }
   if(m==sum)
     printf("The integer %d is an Armstrong number",m);
   else
     printf("The integer %d is not an Armstrong number",m);
 }
```

A sample of input/output:

```
Enter an integer
225
The integer 225 is not an armstrong number
```

Example 6.11.5 Write a program that reads the values of x and y, and computes and prints the value of $F(x)$ defined by

$$F(x) = \begin{cases} 1 + \frac{x}{\sqrt{1+x^2}}, & \text{if } |x| < 3 \\ 0, & \text{if } 3 \leq |x| < a \\ 1 - \frac{x}{\sqrt{1+x^2}}, & \text{if } |x| \geq a \end{cases}$$

where $a = (4 + |y|)^{\frac{3}{2}}$.

```
/* Evaluation of function */
#include<stdio.h>
#include<math.h>
main()
 {
```

```
  float x,y,a,fx=0.;
  printf("Enter the values of x and y\n");
  scanf("%f%f",&x,&y);
  a=pow(4.0+fabs(y),1.5);
  if(fabs(x)<3.0)
    fx=1.0+x/sqrt(1+x*x);
  else if (fabs(x)>=a)
    fx=1.0-x/sqrt(1.0+x*x);
  /* note when (3<=fabs(x)<a) fx=0 */
  printf("fx=%f  x=%f  y=%f\n",fx,x,y);
}
```

A sample of input/output:

```
Enter the values of x and y
1.2 -3.4
fx=1.768221 x=1.200000 y=-3.400000
```

Example 6.11.6 (Quadratic equation) Write a program to identify only the nature of the roots of a quadratic equation.

Solution. The discriminant d of the equation $ax^2 + bx + c = 0$ is $b^2 - 4ac$. If $d < 0$, then the roots are complex; if $d = 0$, then the roots are real and equal; and if $d > 0$, then the roots are real and distinct.

Program 6.15

```
/* Program to find the nature of the roots of a quadratic equation */
#include<stdio.h
#include<math.h>
main()
 {
   float a,b,c,d;
   printf("Enter the values of a, b, c\n");
   scanf("%f%f%f",&a,&b,&c);
   d=b*b-4*a*c;
   if(d<0)
     printf("Roots are complex\n");
   else if (d==0)
     printf("Roots are real and equal\n");
   else
     printf("Roots are real and unequal\n");
 }
```

A sample of input/output:

```
Enter the values of a, b, c
1 7 12
Roots are real and unequal
```

Example 6.11.7 (Roots of a quadratic equation). Write a program to find the roots of a quadratic equation.

Solution. Let the quadratic equation be $ax^2+bx+c=0$. Its roots are $x = \dfrac{-b \pm \sqrt{b^2-4ac}}{2a}$. Let $d = b^2 - 4ac$ and $p = -\dfrac{b}{2a}$, $q = \dfrac{\sqrt{|d|}}{2a}$. If $d < 0$, then the roots are $p \pm iq$, if $d = 0$, then the roots are p, p and if $d > 0$, then the roots are $p \pm q$. The complex roots $p \pm iq$ are written as $(p, q), (p, -q)$.

Program 6.16

```
/* Program to find the roots of a quadratic equation */
#include<stdio.h>
#include<math.h>
main()
 {
   float a,b,c,d,p,q;
   printf("Enter the values of a, b, c\n");
   scanf("%f%f%f",&a,&b,&c);
   d=b*b-4*a*c;
   p=-b/(a+a);
   q=sqrt(fabs(d))/(a+a);
   if(d<0)
     printf("Roots are (%f,%f) and (%f,%f)\n",p,q,p,-q);
   else if (d==0)
     printf("Roots are %f and %f\n",p,p);
   else
     printf("Roots are %f and %f\n",p+q,p-q);
 }
```

A sample of input/output:

```
Enter the values of a, b, c
1 2 3

Roots are (-1.000000,1.414214) and (-1.000000,-1.414214)
```

Example 6.11.8 Write a program that reads N integers and find the sum of even and odd integers separately. Also find the sum of all integers.

Program 6.17

```
/* Program to find the sum of even and odd integers among n integers */
#include<stdio.h>
#include<math.h>
main()
 {
   int sumodd=0,sumeven=0,n,m,count=0;
   printf("Enter the value of n\n");
   scanf("%d",&n);
   do
    {
      scanf("%d",&m);
      count++;
      if(m%2 == 0)
         sumeven+=m;
      else
         sumodd+=m;
    }while(count<n);
  printf("Sum of odd integers is %d\n",sumodd);
  printf("Sum of even integers is %d\n",sumeven);
  printf("Sum of all integers is %d\n",sumodd+sumeven);
 }
```

A sample of input/output:

```
5
12
25
34
78
55

Sum of odd integers is 80
Sum of even integers is 124
Sum of all integers is 204
```

Example 6.11.9 (Solution of system of 2 unknowns) The system of equations $ax + by = c$, $dx + ey = f$ has,
(i) no solution, if $ae - bd = 0$ but $af - cd \neq 0$, or, $bf - ce \neq 0$
(ii) a unique solution, if $ae - bd \neq 0$
(iii) an infinite set of solutions, if $ae - bd = af - cd = bf - ce = 0$.

Write a program that reads the values of a, b, c, d, e and f and outputs the values of x and y, if they exist, otherwise print the appropriate message like 'No solution', 'Infinite set of solutions'.

Solution. The solution of the equations $ax + by = c$ and $dx + ey = f$ is

$$x = \frac{ce - bf}{ae - bd} = \frac{v}{q} \text{ and } y = \frac{af - cd}{ae - bd} = \frac{u}{q}$$

where $q = ae - bd$, $v = ce - bf$ and $u = af - cd$.

Program 6.18

```
/*  Program to solve a pair of linear equations */
#include<stdio.h>
#include<math.h>
main()
 {
   float a,b,c,d,e,f,u,v,q;
   printf("Enter the coefficients a,b,c,d,e,f\n");
   scanf("%f%f%f%f%f%f",&a,&b,&c,&d,&e,&f);
   u=a*f-c*d;
   v=c*e-b*f;
   q=a*e-b*d;
   if((q==0) && ((u!=0) ||(v !=0)))
     {
       printf("No solutions\n");
       exit(0);
     }
   if(q !=0)
     {
       printf("Solution is %f and %f\n",v/q,u/q);
       exit(0);
     }
   if((q==0) && (u==0) && (v==0))
       printf("Infinite set of solutions\n");
 }
```

A sample of input/output:

```
Enter the coefficients a,b,c,d,e,f
3 4 2
8 7 2
Solution is -0.545455 and 0.909091
```

Example 6.11.10 Write a program to read N real numbers and count the negative, zero and positive numbers among them.

Program 6.19

Program 6.19

```
/* Counting of positive, negative and zero */
#include<stdio.h>
main()
 {
  int n, i,neg=0,pos=0,zero=0;
  float a;
  printf("Enter number of numbers\n");
  scanf("%d",&n);
  printf("Enter the numbers\n");
  for(i=1;i<=n;i++)
     {
       scanf("%f",&a);
       if(a<0) neg++;
       else if (a>0) pos++;
       else zero++;
     }
   printf("Negative no.=%d, Positive no.=%d, Zero=%d\n",neg,pos,zero);
 }
```

A sample of input/output:

```
Enter number of numbers
7
Enter the numbers
12 -89 0 23 -12 0 -27
Negative no.=3, Positive no.=2, Zero=2
```

Example 6.11.11 For a particular electrical circuit with an inductance L and resistance R, the damped natural frequency is given by

$$\text{frequency} = \sqrt{\frac{1}{LC} - \frac{R^2}{4C^2}}$$

It is desired to study the variation of this frequency with capacitance. Write a program to calculate the frequency for different values of C, L and R in a tabular form.

Program 6.20

```
/* Calculation of frequency */
#include<stdio.h>
#include<math.h>
void main()
{
  float C,R,L,Freq;
  printf("  L     R     C      Freq\n");
```

```
  for(C=0.01;C<=0.03;C+=0.01)
    for(L=0.1;L<=0.3;L+=0.1)
      for(R=0.1;R<=0.2;R+=0.1)
      if(4*C>L*R*R)
        {
          Freq=sqrt(1.0/(L*C)-R*R/(4*C*C));
          printf("%0.3f %0.3f %0.3f %0.3f\n",L,R,C,Freq);
        }
}
```

Output

```
  L     R     C     Freq
0.100 0.100 0.010 31.225
0.100 0.200 0.010 30.000
0.200 0.100 0.010 21.794
0.200 0.200 0.010 20.000
0.100 0.100 0.020 22.220
0.100 0.200 0.020 21.794
0.200 0.100 0.020 15.612
0.200 0.200 0.020 15.000
0.100 0.100 0.030 18.181
0.100 0.200 0.030 17.951
0.200 0.100 0.030 12.802
0.200 0.200 0.030 12.472
```

Example 6.11.12 (Sum of finite series) Write a program to find the sum of the series

$$1 + x + \frac{x^2}{2!} + \frac{x^3}{3!} + \cdots + \frac{x^n}{n!}$$

for given x and n.

Solution. Here $t_n = \dfrac{x^n}{n!}$ and $t_{n+1} = \dfrac{x^{n+1}}{(n+1)!}$.

Therefore, $\dfrac{t_{n+1}}{t_n} = \dfrac{x^{n+1}}{(n+1)!} \times \dfrac{n!}{x^n} = \dfrac{x}{n+1}$.

Thus, $t_{n+1} = \dfrac{x}{n+1} \times t_n$.

Program 6.21

```
/* Program to find the sum of a finite series */
#include<stdio.h>
#include<math.h>
```

```
main()
 {
  int n, i;
  float x,sum=1,term=1;
  printf("Enter the values of x and n\n");
  scanf("%f%d",&x,&n);
  for(i=1;i<=n;i++)
     {
       term*=x/i;
       sum+=term;
     }
     printf("Sum of the series = %f at x=%5.2f and n=%d\n",sum,x,n);
 }
```

A sample of input/output:

```
Enter the values of x and n
1.2 20
Sum of the series = 3.320117 at x= 1.20 and n=20
```

Example 6.11.13 (Sum of infinite series, 0th order Bessel's function) Write a program to compute

$$J_0(x) = 1 - \frac{x^2}{2^2 1!1!} + \frac{x^4}{2^4 2!2!} - \frac{x^6}{2^6 3!3!} + \cdots$$

for a given x by direct summation of successive terms up to and including the first term that has a magnitude greater than 10^{-8}.

Solution. Here the nth term of the series is

$$t_n = (-1)^n \frac{x^{2n}}{2^{2n}(n!)^2}, n = 0, 1, 2, \ldots.$$

Therefore,

$$t_{n+1} = (-1)^{n+1} \frac{x^{2n+2}}{2^{2n+2}\{(n+1)!\}^2}.$$

Now,

$$\frac{t_{n+1}}{t_n} = -\frac{x^2}{4(n+1)^2} \text{ or } t_{n+1} = -\frac{x^2}{4(n+1)^2} t_n.$$

That is, if a term is known, then the next term of the series is obtained by

$$-\frac{x^2}{4(n+1)^2} \times term,$$

where *term* means nth term.

Program 6.22

```
/* Program to evaluate 0th order Bessel's function */
#include<stdio.h>
#include<math.h>
main()
 {
   float x,sum,term,eps=1.0e-8;
   int n,m;
   printf("Enter the value of x\n");
   scanf("%f",&x);
   /* initialization of sum, term, n */
   term=1.0;
   sum=1.0;
   n=0;
   while (fabs(term)>eps)
     {
       term=-x*x*term/(4.*(n+1.)*(n+1.));
       sum+=term;
       n++;
     }
   printf("J0(%5.3f)= %f\n",x,sum);
 }
```

A sample of input/output:

```
Enter the value of x
.526
J0(0.526)= 0.932018
```

Example 6.11.14 (GCD and LCM) Write a program to compute Greatest Common Divisor (GCD) and Lowest Common Multiple (LCM) of two given integers.

The method to calculate GCD and LCM is described in Chapter 2.

Program 6.23

```
/* Program to determine GCD and LCM of two integers
   prod, rem represent respectively product and remainder */
#include<stdio.h>
main()
 {
   int n,m,prod,rem,gcd,lcm;
   printf("Enter two positive integers\n");
   scanf("%d%d",&m,&n);
```

```
  printf("m=%d  n=%d\n",m,n);
  prod=m*n;
  while(n!=0)
    {
      rem=m % n;
      if(rem==0) break;
      m=n;
      n=rem;
    }
  lcm=prod/n;
  gcd=n;
  printf("LCM= %d and  GCD= %d\n",lcm,gcd);
}
```

A sample of input/output:

```
Enter two positive integers
8 60

 m=8  n=60
LCM= 120 and  GCD= 4
```

Example 6.11.15 (Fibonacci sequence) Write a program to generate first N terms of the Fibonacci sequence.

Solution. The Fibonacci sequence is 0, 1, 1, 2, 3, 5, 8, 13, ... It may be noted that the sum of two preceding terms is the next term. Mathematically, $F_{n+2} = F_{n+1} + F_n$, where $F_0 = 0, F_1 = 1$. F_n is the nth term of the sequence. The following program generates first N terms of this sequence for a given N.

Program 6.24

```
/* Generation of Fibonacci sequence */
#include<stdio.h>
main()
 {
  int f0=0,f1=1,f,n,i;
  printf("How many numbers\n");
  scanf("%d",&n);
  printf("The Fibonacci sequence is\n");
  printf("0  1 ");
  for(i=2;i<n;i++)
    {
      f=f0+f1;
      f0=f1;
```

```
      f1=f;
      printf("%4d",f);
    }
 }
```

A sample of input/output:

```
How many numbers
12

The Fibonacci sequence is
 0  1    1   2   3   5   8  13  21  34  55 89
```

Example 6.11.16 (Evaluation of function) Write a program to print a table of values of x and $f(x) = \sqrt{x}\cos(2x+5)$ for $x = 0$ to $x = 1$ with spacing 0.1.

Program 6.25

```
/* Evaluation of function using for loop */
#include<stdio.h>
#include<math.h>
main()
 {
  float x,fx;
  printf("  x\t  f(x)\n");
  for(x=0.0;x<=1.0;x+=0.1)
     {
      fx=sqrt(x)*cos(2*x+5.0);
      printf("%5.2f\t%f\n",x,fx);
     }
 }
```

Output

```
  x         f(x)
 0.00     0.000000
 0.10     0.148158
 0.20     0.283843
 0.30     0.424795
 0.40     0.560052
 0.50     0.678943
 0.60     0.771918
 0.70     0.830958
 0.80     0.849914
 0.90     0.824783
 1.00     0.753902
```

Example 6.11.17 (Testing of prime) Write a program to test whether an integer is prime or not.

Solution. A positive integer N is said to be prime, if it is only divisible by 1 and N and not by any other positive integer. It is shown that if N is not divisible by an integer less than or equal to $\sqrt{N}$, then N is not divisible by the integer greater than $\sqrt{N}$. So to test, whether N is prime or not, it is required to divide N by 2, 3, ..., $\sqrt{N}$. If N is not divisible by these numbers, then N is a prime. But, if N is divisible by at least one of these integers, then N is not prime. Here, we assume that 1 is a prime number.

Program 6.26

```
/* Program to test whether a given number is prime or not*/
#include<stdio.h>
#include<math.h>
main()
 {
  int n,i,m,flag=1;
  printf("Enter an integer\n");
  scanf("%d",&n);
  if(n<=0)
    {
      printf("The no. is negative or 0\n");
      exit(0);
    }
  if((n==1)||(n==2)) flag=1;
  m=(int)sqrt(n);
  for(i=2;i<=m;i++)
     {
       if((n%i)==0)
         {
           flag=0;
           break;
         }
     }
 if (flag==1)
    printf("%d is prime\n",n);
 else
    printf("%d is not prime\n",n);
 }
```

A sample of input/output:

```
Enter an integer
```

```
17
17 is prime
```

Example 6.11.18 (Prime numbers between two integers) Write a program to find the prime numbers between two given integers.

Program 6.27

```
/* Program to generate prime numbers between two given integers */
#include<stdio.h>
#include<math.h>
main()
 {
  int i,j,k,n,m,flag=1;
  printf("Enter two positive integers m and n (m<n)\n");
  scanf("%d%d",&m,&n);
  for(i=m;i<=n;i++)
    {
      flag=1;
      k=(int)sqrt(i);
      /* checking i for prime */
      for(j=2;j<=k;j++)
        {
          if((i%j)==0){
              flag=0;  break;
            }
        }
      if(flag==1) /* i is prime */
     printf("%4d ",i);
    }
 }
```

A sample of input/output:

```
Enter two positive integers m and n (m<n)
40 80

   41   43   47   53   59   61   67   71   73   79
```

Example 6.11.19 (Testing of perfect number) Write a program to test whether an integer is perfect or not.

Solution. An integer is called perfect, if the sum of the factors of the integer is equal to the integer itself. For example, 28 is a perfect number, because sum of its factors 1, 2, 4, 7, 14 is equal to 28.

Program 6.28

```
/* Testing of perfect number */
#include<stdio.h>
void main()
{
  int i,n,sum=0;
  printf("Enter an integer\n");
  scanf("%d",&n);
  for(i=1;i<=n/2;i++)
    if(n%i==0) /* i is a factor */
       sum+=i;
  if(sum==n)
    printf("%d is a perfect number",n);
  else
    printf("%d is not a perfect number",n);
}
```

A sample of input/output:

```
Enter an integer
496
496 is a perfect number
```

Example 6.11.20 (Generation of Pascal triangle) Write a program to generate Pascal triangle.

Solution. In a Pascal triangle, the binomial coefficients are written in a triangular form.

The binomial expansion of $(1+x)^n$ is

$$(1+x)^n = 1 +^n C_1 x +^n C_2 x^2 +^n C_3 x^3 + \cdots +^n C_r x^r +^n C_{r+1} x^{r+1} + \cdots + x^n.$$

Let $t_r =^n C_r$ and $t_{r+1} =^n C_{r+1}$. Now,

$$\frac{t_{r+1}}{t_r} = {}^nC_{r+1}/{}^nC_r = \frac{n-r}{r+1}, \text{i.e. } t_{r+1} = \frac{n-r}{r+1} t_r$$

for $r = 0, 1, 2, \ldots, n-1$ where $t_0 = 1$.

For a given n, the binomial coefficients are $t_0(=1), t_1, t_2, \ldots, t_n(=1)$. When $n = 0$, the only binomial coefficient is taken as 1. The value of n varies from 1 to L (L represents the number of rows of the Pascal triangle).

Program 6.29

```
/* Printing of Pascal triangle */
#include<stdio.h>
#include<math.h>
void main()
{
  int t,n,L,i,r;
  printf("How many rows\n");
  scanf("%d",&L);
  for(i=45;i>0;i--) printf(" "); printf("1\n");
  for(n=1;n<=L;n++)
    {
      /* printing of leading blank */
      for(i=40-3*n;i>0;--i) printf(" ");
      t=1;
      printf("%6d",t);
      for(r=0;r<n;r++)
        {
          t=t*(n-r)/(r+1);
          printf("%6d",t);
        }
      printf("\n");
    } /* for */
}
```

A sample of input/output:

```
How many rows
6

                   1
                1     1
             1     2     1
          1     3     3     1
       1     4     6     4     1
    1     5    10    10     5     1
 1     6    15    20    15     6     1
```

Example 6.11.21 (Graph plotting) Write a program to draw the curve sin(x) for a given range of x.

Solution. Here, the curve sin(x) is plotted for $x = -4$ to 4 radian with space 0.2 radian. The values of sin(x) are evaluated at these points and all these values are multiplied by 20 to magnify them and is added by 20 to make all the values positive.

Program 6.30

```
/* Program to draw sine curve */
#include<stdio.h>
#include<math.h>
#define s 20 /* scale factor */
void main()
 {
   float x;
   int y,z;
  clrscr();
  /* printing of head of x-axis */
  for(z=0;z<s;z++) printf(" "); printf("x\n");
  for(z=0;z<s;z++) printf(" "); printf("%c\n",94);/* uparrow */
  /* plotting of the curve */
  for(x=-4;x<=4;x+=.2)
   {
    y=(int)(s*sin(x)+s+.5); /* .5 is used for round off */
    if(y<s)
      {
        /* printing of graph point */
        for(z=0;z<y;z++) printf(" "); printf("*");
        /* printing of vertical bar for x-axis */
        for(z=y+1;z<s;z++) printf(" "); printf("|"); printf("\n");
      }
    if(y==s)
      {
       for(z=0;z<=2*s;z++) printf("-"); /* drawing of y-axis */
       printf(">y\n");
      }
    if(y>s)
      {
        /* printing of vertical bar for x-axis */
        for(z=0;z<s;z++) printf(" "); printf("|");
        /* printing of graph point */
        for(z=s+1;z<y;z++) printf(" "); printf("*\n");
      }
   }
 }
```

Output:

```
                    x
                    ^
                    |              *
                    |           *
                    |        *
                    |    *
                    |*
                 *  |
             *      |
          *         |
      *             |
    *               |
  *                 |
 *                  |
*                   |
*                   |
 *                  |
   *                |
      *             |
         *          |
            *       |
                *   |
---------------------------------------->y
                    |   *
                    |       *
                    |          *
                    |             *
                    |                *
                    |                  *
                    |                   *
                    |                   *
                    |                 *
                    |               *
                    |             *
                    |         *
                    |      *
                    |  *
                   *|
               *    |
           *        |
        *           |
```

Example 6.11.22 (Calculation of loan interest) Suppose that Rs. P has borrowed from a bank, with the understanding that Rs. E will be repaid each month until the entire loan has been repaid. A part of monthly instalment will be interest and other part will be the unpaid balance. The rate of interest is R. Write a program that will determine the following information for 12 months.

(i) The amount of interest and amount of principal paid each month.
(ii) The cumulative amount of interest that has been paid at the end of each month.
(iii) The amount of the loan that is still unpaid at the end of each month.
(iv) The number of monthly payments required to repay the entire loan.

Solution. Let P, R, E represent respectively the amount of loan, yearly rate of interest and monthly instalments. The interest (I) per month is calculated as

$$I = P \times R \times \frac{1}{1200}.$$

Rs. I and Rs. $(E - I)$ are deducted as interest and loan amount. Thus, total unpaid loan at the end of each month is obtained from $P - (E - I)$.

Program 6.31

```
/* Calculation of interest at each month of the loan */
#include<stdio.h>
void main()
{
  float R,P,POld,E,I,CI=0;
  int i;
  printf("Enter loan amount and monthly instalment\n");
  scanf("%f%f",&P,&E);
  POld=P;
  printf("Enter yearly rate of interest\n");
  scanf("%f",&R);
  printf("Month Loan       Interest Loan  Unpaid  Cumulative\n");
  printf("      unpaid     paid     paid  loan    interest\n");
  printf("-----------------------------------------------------\n");
  /* computation of remaining time to repaid the full loan */
  for(i=1;i<=12;i++)
   {
     I=P*R/1200;  /* monthly interest */
     CI+=I;
     printf("%2d   %7.0f %7.0f  %7.0f %7.0f %7.0f\n",i,P,I,E-I,P-E+I,CI);
     P=P-(E-I);
     if(P<=0) break; /* loan is repay before 12 month */
   }
```

```
 printf("-------------------------------------------\n");
 i=0; P=POld; /* initial principal */
 do{
   I=P*R/1200; /* monthly interest */
   P=P-E+I;    /* remaining loan */
   i++;        /* increment of month */
 }while(P>0);
 printf("The loan will be repaid after %d months",i);
}
```

A sample of input/output:

```
Enter loan amount and monthly instalment
1000000 10000
Enter yearly rate of interest
8
Month Loan      Interest Loan  Unpaid Cumulative
      unpaid    paid     paid  loan    interest
-------------------------------------------------
  1   1000000   6667     3333  996667   6667
  2    996667   6644     3356  993311  13311
  3    993311   6622     3378  989933  19933
  4    989933   6600     3400  986533  26533
  5    986533   6577     3423  983110  33110
  6    983110   6554     3446  979664  39664
  7    979664   6531     3469  976195  46195
  8    976195   6508     3492  972703  52703
  9    972703   6485     3515  969187  59187
 10    969187   6461     3539  965649  65649
 11    965649   6438     3562  962086  72086
 12    962086   6414     3586  958500  78500
-------------------------------------------------
The loan will be repaid after 166 months
```

Important Points

1. Use semicolon appropriately in the `while`, `do-while` and `for` loops.
2. Do not forget to update the control variable in the body of the `while` and `do-while` loops.
3. Do not change the value of control variable in the body of `for` loop.
4. Do not forget to initialize the control variable in the loops.

5. The initialization, termination and updation of `for` loop may be done outside the heading of a `for` loop, but avoid them.
6. Floating point variable may be used as a control variable in `for` loop, but it is better to avoid them due to round off and truncation errors during updating of control variable.
7. Do not compare floating point values for equality.
8. Try to eliminate the use of `break` and `continue` statements in any loop to jump from one place to another.
9. Avoid the use of `goto` statement.
10. Remember that when `break` statement is executed the control goes outside the loop, but the execution of the function `exit` terminates the execution of the program.

Exercise VI

Review Questions

1. Write short notes on (i) `goto` statement, (ii) `if` statement, (iii) block `if` statement, (iv) nested `if` statement, (v) multi-alternative `if` statement.
2. Draw flowcharts of (i) `goto` statement, (ii) `if` statement, (iii) block `if` statement, (iv) nested `if` statement, (v) multi-alternative `if` statement.
3. What is meant by looping? Describe two different types of loops.
4. What are the use of `if` and `if-else` statement? Explain them using flowcharts.
5. Compare the statement `if-else` with the operator `?:`. Express the operator `?:` using `if-else` statement.
6. Explain nested `if` and multi-alternative `if` statements.
7. Write short notes on (i) `for` loop, (ii) `while` loop, (iii) `do-while` loop, (iv) `continue` statement, (v) `break` statement.
8. What is the use of `while` loop? Explain this loop with the help of a flowchart. When will this loop terminate? What is the minimum number of times that a `while` loop can be executed?
9. What is the use of `do-while` loop? Explain this loop with the help of flowchart. When will this loop terminate? What is the minimum number of times that a `do-while` loop can be executed?
10. What are the differences between `while` and `do-while` loops?
11. What is the purpose of `for` loop? How does it differ from `while` and `do-while` loops?
12. Can `while` loop replace the `for` loop? Explain with an example.
13. Write `for` loop with the help of `while` loop. Is it possible to express `for` loop with the help of `do-while` loop? Explain.

14. How many times a `for` loop can be executed? What is the difference between a comma and semicolon used in the heading of the `for` loop?
15. Can any of the three expressions in the `for` statement be omitted? If so, what are the consequences of each omission? How an infinite loop can be constructed using `for` loop?
16. Can loops be nested within `if-else` statements? Can `if-else` statements be nested within loops? Explain.
17. Explain `switch` statement. Can the task of `switch` statement be implemented by multi-alternative `if` statement? Explain. Which is more convenient?
18. Why `break` statement is necessary with `switch` statement? Is it compulsory?
19. What happens when the value of the expression in the `switch` statement matches the value of one of the case labels? What happens when the value of this expression does not match any one of the case labels?
20. What are the use of `break` and `continue` statements?
21. What is the purpose of `break` statement? Within which control statements can the `break` statement be included?
22. Compare `continue` and `break` statements.
23. What is the purpose of the comma operator? Within which control statement does the comma operator usually appear?
24. How can the `getchar` function be used to read a multi-character string?

Problems

1. Indicate the errors, if any in the following C statements.

(i) `goto next`

(ii) `goto p1;`

(iii) `go to 156`

(iv) `if(x+y) y=5`

(v) `if(x<=y) max==y;`

(vi) `if(x<y) z=x+y;`

(vii) `if(x<y) then z=x+y;`

(viii)
```
if(x<=y)
    z=x+y
else
    z=x-y;
```

(ix)
```
if(x<y)
    z=x+y;
  else
    z=x-y
```

(x)
```
if(x<y)
    z=x+y;
```

```
    else if
      z=x-y;
    else
      z=0;
```

(xi)
```
count=0;
      do{
      count=count+1;
      printf("%d",count);}
      while(count=1)
```

(xii)
```
for(x=10;x>0;);
      x=x-1;
      printf("%f",x);
```

(xiii)
```
sum=0; x=0;
      do
       sum+=x;
       scanf("%d",&x);
      while(x>0);
```

(xiv)
```
while(x != 0);
       {
       scanf("%d",&x);
       sum+=x;
       }
```

2. Assume that, at the beginning of each of the following program segment $m = 5$ and $n = 15$. What will be the final values of n and m after the execution of each segment ?

(i)
```
if(m<n) n=n+5;
n+=3;
```

(ii)
```
     if(2*m ==n) goto 150;
     n++;
     goto 120;
150: n=m;
120: n+=5;
```

(iii)
```
if((m-n)*3 ==n) {
    m=n-m;
    n=m-n;
}
else {
    m=1;
    n=2;
}
```

3. Explain the meaning of the following statement.

```
max=y;
if(x>y) max=x;
```

4. Express the following as C statements.
   (i) If $I = K$ and $I > K$, assign $R = |a + b|$ otherwise $R = |a|$.
   (ii) If $B \leq A^2 \leq B + C$, then $F = x \tan^{-1} x$, otherwise $F = x^2 + 2$.
5. Indicate the errors, if any, in the following `for` statements.
   (i) `for(i=1,i<=5,++i);`
   (ii) `for(i=0;i=5;++i);`
   (iii) `for(i=0;i<=10);`
   (iv) `for(i=1;i<=5;i+=2)`
   (v) `for(j=i;j<=10;i++);`
   (vi) `for(x=0.0;x>=10.5;x++);`
   (vii) `for(x=0;x<5;x++;x=x+0.5);`
   (viii) `for(k=-5;k<5;k);`
   (ix) `for(i=1,j=2;i<5,j>-5;i++);`
   (x) `for(i=0,j=2;i<5;i++,j++);`
   (xi) `for(i=0,j=12,k=3;i<10,j>0;i++,j--,k++);`

6. Write the following segment using `for` loop.

```
        count=0;
        i=1;
next:   scanf("%f",&a);
        if(a>0) count++;
        i++;
        if(i<=250) goto next;
```

7. Rewrite the following program segment without using `for` loops.

```
for(i=1;i<=4;i++)
  for(j=1;j<=20;j++)
    printf("%d%d",&i,&j);
```

8. Find the output of each of the following program segments:

(i)

```
i=2;
j=5;
for(k=1;k<=5;k++)
  {
    j++;
```

```
    i=j*2;
    j+=k;
  }
printf("%d %d %d",i,j,k);
```

(ii)

```
m=100;
n=0;
i=0;
count=0;
for(j=1;j<=5;j++)
  for(k=4;k>=0;k-=2)
    {
      i+=2;
      for(l=1;l<=2;l++)
        {
          n+=2;
          m--;
        }
      count++;
    }
printf("%d %d %d",m,n,count);
```

(iii)

```
for(i=1;i<=10;i++)
  for(j=i+1;j<=11;j++)
    {
      k=i+j;
      if(k/2*2==k) printf("%d",k);
    }
```

(iv)

```
s=0.0;
for(k=1;k<=3;k++)
  for(j=5;j>=1;j--)
    s+=j;
printf("%f",s);
```

(v)

```
osum=0.0;
esum=0.0;
for(i=1;i<=100;i++)
```

```
      {
        if(i%2==0)
          esum++;
        else
          osum++;
      }
    printf("%f %f",osum,esum);
```

(vi)

```
i=5;
for(j=1;j<=i;j++)
  {
    printf("%d %d",j,i);
    i--;
  }
```

(viii)

```
for(; scanf("%d",&m) !=-1 ;)
 {
   printf("%d",m);
 }
```

9. At the completion of the following program loops, what will be the values of k, l and m ?

```
m=0;
for(i=1;i<=10;i++)
  {
    k=i;
    for(j=1;j<=5;j++)
      {
        l=j;
        m++;
      }
  }
```

10. Find the values of the variables a and m at the completion of the following program.

```
a=1.5;
for(i=1;i<=5;i++)
  {
    a+=i;
```

```
        for(j=1;j<=5;j++)
          m=i+j;
      }
```

11. Write the following for loops using while and do-while loops.

(i)
(ii)

```
for(; scanf("%d",&m) !=-1 ;)        for(i=1;i<10;i++)
   printf("%d",m);                     printf("%d\n",i);
```

12. What is the use of the loop

```
for( ; ; );
```

Programming Problems

1. Write a program to find only the real and unequal roots, if any, of a quadratic equation, with appropriate message.
2. Write a program to check the nature (real and equal, real and distinct or imaginary) of the roots of the quadratic equation $ax^2 + bx + c = 0$.
3. Write a program to find the roots of the equation $ax^2+bx+c = 0$ for five different sets of values of a, b, c in tabular form.
4. Write a program to find the sum of the following series, correct up to 5 significant digits.
   (a) $\sin x = x - \frac{x^3}{3!} + \frac{x^5}{5!} - \frac{x^7}{7!} + \cdots\cdots$ (when x given in degree/radian).
   (b) $\cos x = 1 - \frac{x^2}{2!} + \frac{x^4}{4!} - \frac{x^6}{6!} + \cdots\cdots$ (when x given in degree/radian).
   (c) $e^x = 1 + x + \frac{x^2}{2!} + \frac{x^3}{3!} + \frac{x^4}{4!} + \cdots\cdots$ (for any x).
   (d) $\log_e(1+x) = x - \frac{x^2}{2} + \frac{x^3}{3} - \frac{x^4}{4} + \cdots\cdots$ (for $-1 < x \leq 1$).
   (e) $J_0(x) = 1 - \frac{x^2}{2^2.1.1} + \frac{x^4}{2^4.2!.2!} - \frac{x^6}{2^6.3!.3!} + \cdots\cdots$ (for any $-1 \leq x \leq 1$).
   (f) $\tan x = x + \frac{1}{3}x^3 + \frac{9}{15}x^5 + \cdots\cdots$ (for $0 \leq x < \pi/2$).
   (g) $\log_e \sec x = \frac{1}{2}x^2 + \frac{1}{12}x^4 + \frac{1}{45}x^6 + \cdots\cdots$ and hence find the value of $\sec x$.
   (h) $\sin^{-1} x = x + \frac{1}{2}\frac{x^3}{3} + \frac{1}{2}\frac{3}{4}\frac{x^5}{5} + \frac{1}{2}\frac{3}{4}\frac{5}{6}\frac{x^7}{7} + \cdots\cdots$.
   (i) $\tan^{-1} x = \sum_{r=1}^{\infty}(-1)^{r+1}\frac{1}{2r-1}x^{2r-1}; |x| \leq 1$.
   (j) $\log x = (x-1) - \frac{1}{2}(x-1)^2 + \frac{1}{3}(x-1)^3 - \cdots\cdots ; 0 < x \leq 2$.
5. Write a program to read N real numbers and count the negative, zero and positive numbers among them.

6. Write a program to test whether an integer is (i) divisible by 2, (ii) divisible by 3, (iii) divisible by 7 and (iv) divisible by 5.
7. A university gives first class degree, if the average marks in an examination are 60% or above, second class if the marks are 40% or above and the candidate fails if his marks are below 40%. Write a program to find the grade of N (=10 say) students.
8. Write a program that reads the values of x and y and computes and prints the value of $F(x)$ defined by

$$F(x) = \begin{cases} 1 + \frac{x}{\sqrt{1+x^2}}, & \text{if } |x| < 3 \\ 0, & \text{if } 3 \le |x| < a \\ 1 - \frac{x}{\sqrt{1+x^2}}, & \text{if } |x| \ge a \end{cases}$$

where $a = (4 + |y|)^{3/2}$.
9. Write a program to calculate and print the product of even numbers between 1 and 10.
10. A nationalised bank has a fixed deposit scheme and the rate of interest for different periods are given below:

duration	rate of interest
3 yrs or more	10%
2 yrs to less than 3 yrs	9%
1 yr to less than 2 yrs	8.5%
less than 1 yr	7.5%

The interest is compounded quarterly. Write a program to find the total amount to be returned by the bank, on a fixed capital, at the end of a fixed period.
[total return $A = P(1 + \frac{r}{4\times100)})^{4t}$]
11. The commission of a salesman on total SALES is as follows:

Total SALES	Commission
Rs. 100	0%
Rs. 100 < SALES ≤ Rs. 2000	5% of SALES
Rs. 2000 < SALES ≤ Rs. 10,000	Rs. 100 + 7.5% of SALES

Write a program that reads total SALES and print out the salesman's commission.

12. The rate of income tax (IT) for a financial year is given below:

total income	rate of IT
upto Rs. 50,000	nil
above Rs. 50,000 to Rs. 60,000	10%
above Rs. 60,000 to Rs. 1,00,000	Rs. 6000 + 20% of excess of Rs. 60,000
above Rs. 1,00,000	Rs. 9000 + 25% of excess of Rs. 1,00,000

Write a program that reads the total income of an employee and prints the total income tax payable by the employee.

13. Write a C program to print a table of values of x and $f(x) = \frac{\tan\sqrt{x^2+3}}{\sqrt{x+2}}$ for $x = 0$ to $x = 2$ with a spacing of 0.5.

14. Write programs to find
(i) minimum among n numbers.
(ii) maximum among n numbers.
(iii) maximum and minimum among n numbers.
(iv) largest number among four numbers.

15. Given a set of n integers. Write programs to find the
(i) total number of even integers.
(ii) total number of odd integers.
(iii) sum and product of even integers.
(iv) sum and product of odd integers.
(v) the maximum/minimum among even integers.
(vi) the maximum/minimum among odd integers.

16. The Fibonacci sequence is defined as follows: The first and second terms of the sequence are 0 and 1. The third and subsequent terms of the sequence are the sum of just preceding two terms. That is, $t_0 = 0, t_1 = 1$, and $t_n = t_{n-1} + t_{n-2}$, $n \geq 2$. Write a program to find the first N (=100, say) numbers of the sequence.

17. Write a program to read n points in a plane and find the number of points in each of the four quadrants in a plane. [The point (a, b) lies on the first quadrant, if $a, b > 0$, second quadrant, if $a < 0, b > 0$, third quadrant, if $a, b < 0$ and fourth quadrant, if $a > 0, b < 0$].

18. Write a program to read N (=50, say) pair of length and breadth of rectangles and find (i) the area and perimeter of each rectangle.
(ii) all the rectangles whose area is greater than its perimeter.
(iii) the average area of the rectangles.

19. Write a program to read N (=100, say) sets of three numbers (a, b, c) and check whether each of the set $\{a, b, c\}$ forms a triangle. If the sides a, b, c forms a triangle, then print its area.

20. Write a program to read the radius of N (=50, say) circles and find the area and circumferences of all the circles.

21. Write a program to print the negative integers between -1 and -200 and their cubes.

22. Write a program to read 50 numbers and if it is positive print the square root of it.

23. Write a program to print (a) squares of even integers between 2 and 100.
(b) the sum of the cubes of odd integers between 11 and 75.

24. Write programs to find the values of the following finite series:

(i) $S = \sum_{r=1}^{100} x^r$ for $-1 \le x \le 1$.

(ii) $S = \sum_{x=0}^{20} \frac{x^2-5x+3}{2x+7}$.

(iii) $S = 1 + 2 + 3 + \cdots + N$ (sum of first N natural numbers).

(iv) $S = 1^2 + 2^2 + 3^2 + \cdots + N^2$ (sum of square of first N natural numbers).

(v) $S = 1^3 + 2^3 + 3^3 + \cdots + N^3$ (sum of cube of first N natural numbers).

(vi) $\frac{1}{10^3} + \frac{1}{11^3} + \frac{1}{12^3} + \cdots + \frac{1}{20^3}$.

(vii) $\frac{1}{51^2} + \frac{1}{53^2} + \frac{1}{55^2} + \cdots + \frac{1}{99^2}$.

25. Write a program to read x and y and calculate $y = \sum_{i=1}^{n} (x^i + y^i)$ for a given n.

26. Write programs to test whether an integer is (i) prime, (ii) perfect square, (iii) even or odd, (iv) divisible by 5 and 7.

27. Write a program to generate all prime numbers lying between two given integers.

28. Write the programs to find the values of (i) $n!$, (ii) ${}^nP_r$, (iii) ${}^nC_r$.

[The value of ${}^nC_r$ may be calculated as follows:

$${}^nC_r = \frac{n!}{(n-r)!r!} = \frac{n(n-1)\cdots(n-r-1)(n-r)!}{(n-r)!r!} = \frac{n(n-1)\cdots(n-r-1)}{r(r-1)\cdots(r-r-1)} = \prod_{i=0}^{r-1}\left(\frac{n-i}{r-i}\right)]$$

29. Write a program to list all three-digit numbers which are equal to the sum of the cubes of the digits.

30. Given ten values of x, say, $x_1, x_2, \ldots, x_{10}$. Write a program to compute the value of $y, 2-y^2, y+y^6$ for each x, where

$$y(x) = 1 - \frac{x^2}{2} + \frac{x^4}{24.6} - \frac{x^6}{120.8}.$$

31. Write programs to find the value of y in each of the following cases.

(i) $y = (x+1)/(2x+1)^{1/3}$ for $x = 0$ to 2 at step of 0.2.

(ii)

$$y = \begin{cases} x-1, & \text{for } x < 1 \\ 1-x, & \text{for } 1 \le x < 2 \\ 2-x^2, & \text{for } x \ge 2 \end{cases}$$

for $x = 0$ to 3 in steps of 0.1.

(iii)

$$y = \begin{cases} x^3 e^x, & \text{for } x \le 1 \\ x \cos x, & \text{for } x > 1 \end{cases}$$

for $x = 0.1, 0.2, \ldots, 1.5$.

(iv)

$$y = \begin{cases} 4x^3 + 1, & \text{for } 0 \leq x < 0.5 \\ 4x^3 - 1, & \text{for } 0.5 \leq x \leq 1.0 \end{cases}$$

for $x = 0.1$ to 1.0 with spacing h =0.1.

(v) $y = \sqrt{\frac{x^2+3}{x+2}}$ for $x = 0$ to 2 with spacing of 0.1.

32. Write a program to find the sum and average of n numbers.
33. Write a program to generate all triplets (a, b, c), where a, b, c are positive integers and $a < b < c$, such that $a^2 + b^2 = c^2$ and $a, b \leq 50$.
34. Write a program to calculate the values of x and y where $x = a \sin\theta - b\cos\theta$, $y = a\cos\theta + b\sin\theta$; a, b are fixed numbers (say, $a = 10, b = 15.5$) and θ varies from 0° to 360°.
35. Write a program segment to find the sum of the numbers which are the multiples of 3 and lies within [0,N] (both inclusive), where N is a given integer.
36. Write a program to read the name and age of 500 people and then to list all the persons whose age is 18 years and above as voters.
37. Write a program to tabulate the function

$$f(x, y) = \frac{x^3 + y^3}{x - y}$$

for the following set of values

x	0	2	4	6	8	10
y	-9	-6	-3	0	3	6

38. The nth order Legendre polynomial $P_n(x)$ follows the following recurrence relation $(n+1)P_{n+1}(x) = (2n+1)P_n(x) - nP_{n-1}(x)$, with $P_0(x) = 1$ and $P_1(x) = x$. Write a program to find $P_n(x)$ for given n and x.
39. The shape of a rotor in a Wankel engine depends on x, θ, B and m. They are connected by the equation

$$P_f = [\sqrt{x + \theta} - e^{-2.4m} \log B] \sin\theta.$$

The best design of the rotor is obtained when P_f is the maximum. Find the values of x, θ, B and m for which the design is best (i.e. P_f is maximum), when x varies from 0 to 8, B varies from 1 to 8, θ varies from 0° to 360° and m varies from 7 to 10.5.

40. If a projectile with initial velocity u (m/sec) is fired at an angle θ (with the horizontal), then the horizontal range (R) is given by $R = \frac{u^2 \sin 2\theta}{g}$ where $g = 9.81 m/sec^2$. Write a program to compute the value of R for each of the following values of u and θ.

u	θ
20	0° to 90° in step of 10°
200	20° to 60° in step of 5°

41. Write a program to compute the value of the following integral

$$\int_0^{\phi} \frac{x \sin x \, dx}{1 - 2y \cos x + y^2} = \begin{cases} \frac{\phi}{|y|} \log_e(1 + |y|), & y < 1 \\ \phi \log_e(1 + 1/y), & y > 1 \end{cases}$$

for y=0.1 to 2.0 in step of 0.05 and for a given value of ϕ.

42. The approximate value of the factorial of a large integer n is given by the Stirling's formula as $n! = \sqrt{2\pi n} n^n e^{-n}$. Write a program to compute the exact value of $n!$ and compare this value with the approximate value obtained by Stirling's formula, for $n = 1, 2, \ldots$.
43. The mean arrival rate of a queue is λ and the mean service rate is μ. If it is assumed that the arrival and the service process follow the Poisson distribution, then the mean number of persons waiting for service in a queue is given by $n = \frac{\lambda/\mu}{1-\lambda/\mu}$, if $\lambda/\mu < 1$ and the probability that there are n persons waiting in the queue is $P_n = (\lambda/\mu)^n(1 - \lambda/\mu)$, if $\lambda/\mu < 1$. Write a program to do the following:
(i) For $\mu = 20$ compute the number of persons waiting in the queue for $\lambda = 0, 1, 2, \ldots, 19$.
(ii) For $\mu = 20$ and $\lambda = 4, 8, 12, 16$ compute P_n for $n = 0, 1, 2, \ldots, 20$.
44. Consider a particle falling down freely under the gravity with initial velocity u. The displacement s at any time t is given by $s = ut + \frac{1}{2}gt^2$ where $g = 9.8$ m/sec^2. Write a program to calculate s for the values of u from 1 m to 10 m increment 2 m and for values of t from 0 sec to 2 sec increment 0.5 sec.
45. Write a program to print the following triangle of numbers:

```
1
1 2
1 2 3
1 2 3 4
1 2 3 4 5
1 2 3 4 5 6
```

46. Write a program to print the following triangle of numbers:

```
5
4 5
3 4 5
2 3 4 5
1 2 3 4 5
0 1 2 3 4 5
```

Chapter 7

Arrays

Sometimes, it is necessary to represent a group of values by a common variable name. For example, the marks obtained by 200 students in an examination may be represented by a variable, say `MARK`, and the variables `MARK[1]`, `MARK[2]`, ..., `MARK[200]` represent the marks of the first student, second student, ..., 200*th* student respectively. A method should be used for numbering the students. A set of data with similar properties (homogeneous) and which are stored in consecutive memory locations under a common variable name is called an **array** or **subscripted variable**. Here MARK is an array. It is also called the subscripted variable with one subscript. An individual item is called the **element of the array**. Each element of an array is identified by using subscript (or subscripts) within square brackets after the common variable name (i.e. by the array name). An array is called by the name of the variable part. In C, an array can have one, two or three subscripts. If there is only one subscript, the array is called **one dimensional**. If there occurs two (three) subscripts, then the array is called two (three) dimensional. Some computers allow even more than three subscripts.

7.1 Subscript

The general form of a subscripted variable or array is

`name[i], name[i][j]`

where `name` is a valid C variable and `i, j` are subscripts. The use of an appropriate type declaration, a variable name can be declared as floating point, integer, character, etc. The following rules should be followed while using a subscript.

(i) A subscript may be a valid integer (constant or variable or expression).

(ii) The value of a subscript may be zero or positive.

(iii) A subscript must not be a subscripted variable.

(iv) If a variable is used to represent an array, it should not be used as an ordinary variable, i.e. if `x` denotes an array, then `x` can not be used as an ordinary variable.

The following are valid subscripts (assuming i, j, k, m, mk are `int`):
$7, i+2, i+k, i*j+5, 4*m-5, 2*mk, j*j$
The following are *invalid* subscripts (assuming x, y, a, k are `float`):
$x+y, m[5], 2.0, a, k.2$
A subscripted variable should be declared prior to its use.

7.2 Declaration of One Dimensional Array

In C, an array is declared in the same way as an ordinary variable. Only new thing is that the size of the array must be specified within the square brackets after the array's name. The general form of declaration of one-dimensional array is

```
data_type array_name[exp];
```

where `data_type` is the type of data (i.e. `int, float`, etc.), `array_name` is the valid variable name in C, and `exp` is a positive integer constant or variable, which represents the size of the array.

Some one-dimensional array declaration is shown below.

```
int x[20];
float a[10];
char name[20];
```

In the first declaration, the array name is `x` and its size is 20. For this declaration, a memory is allocated for `x` to store 20 integers, i.e. `x` can store only 20 integer values, and these values will store to the variables `x[0], x[1], x[2]`, ..., `x[19]`.

Similarly, in second declaration, `a` is an array of size 10 and it can store only ten values to the variables `a[0], a[1], a[2]`, ..., `a[9]`, whereas third declaration indicates that `name` is an array of size 20. It may be noted that the *memory is allocated for an array during its declaration.*

The array size may also be defined by a symbolic name rather than a fixed integer constant. This makes easier to change the array size in future. By changing the value of the symbolic constant, the size of the array can be changed. The value of symbolic constant may be defined by using `#defined` statement as follows.

```
#define MAX 10
```

The following declaration

```
int x[MAX];
```

declares an integer array of size `MAX`, i.e. of size 10. The constant `MAX` may be used within the program but its value remains 10.

7.2.1 Initialization of one dimensional array

The values of the array elements can be entered in two stages – at compile time and at run time.

Compile time initialization

Like ordinary variable, an array can also be initialized during its declaration. The general form is,

```
data_type array_name[exp]={value1, value2, ..., valuen};
```

where data_type, array_name and exp are same as in previous declaration. The value1 is the value of the first element, value2 is the second element of the array and so on. exp is optional in this declaration.

Example 7.2.1 The following declarations initialize the three arrays roll, vowel and weight.

```
int roll[6]={10,20,15,20,60,30};
char vowel[5]={'e','i','o','a','u'};
float weight[3]={40.5,50.8,30.9};
```

These declarations initialize three arrays roll, vowel and weight. The value of individual elements are shown below.

```
roll[0]=10  vowel[0]=e  weight[0]=40.5
roll[1]=20  vowel[1]=i  weight[1]=50.8
roll[2]=15  vowel[2]=o  weight[2]=30.9
roll[3]=20  vowel[3]=a
roll[4]=60  vowel[4]=u
roll[5]=30
```

A variation of this declaration is also available in C. If the values of some array elements are not specified within braces, then the initial values of these elements are automatically assigned to 0. Consider the following declarations.

```
int roll[6]={10,15,20};
float weight[3]={40.5,2.0};
```

For these declarations the values of the individual elements are assigned as follows.

```
roll[0]=10  weight[0]=40.5
roll[1]=15  weight[1]=2.0
roll[2]=20  weight[2]=0.0
roll[3]=0
roll[4]=0
roll[5]=0
```

Thus, to initialize all elements of an array to 0, the following statement may be used

```
float a[10]={0};
```

In this declaration, 0 is assigned explicitly to the first element a[0]. Since the values of the other elements are not mentioned explicitly, the default values of the other elements are taken as zero.

Another facility is also available in initialization. The array size need not be specified explicitly during initialization. For numerical array, the array size is automatically determined by the number of elements supplied within braces. Consider the following declarations.

```
int roll[]={10,20,15,20,60,30};
float vowel[]={'e','i','o','a','u'};
```

These declarations determine `roll` and `vowel` are two arrays of size 6 and 5 respectively. The individual elements are

```
roll[0]=10  vowel[0]=e
roll[1]=20  vowel[1]=i
roll[2]=15  vowel[2]=o
roll[3]=20  vowel[3]=a
roll[4]=60  vowel[4]=u
roll[5]=30
```

In case of string initialization, the process is something different. Consider the following two string declarations.

```
char country[]="India";
char country[5]="India";
```

These two declarations have different meanings. The first declaration defines the following assignment.

```
country[0]=I
country[1]=n
country[2]=d
country[3]=i
country[4]=a
country[5]=\0
```

whereas the second statement is assigned as

```
country[0]=I
country[1]=n
country[2]=d
country[3]=i
country[4]=a
```

This shows that the second statement is not correct; since null character `'\0'` is not included at the end of the array. The correct declaration is

```
char country[6]="India";
```

Run time initialization

An array can be initialized during the execution of the program in two different ways: (i) by using assignment statement and (ii) using input statement, such as **scanf**, **getchar**, etc. For example,

```
for(i=1;i<=10;i++)
    a[i]=1.0;
```

When these statements are executed (at run time), the values of all elements of the array a are set to 1.0, with the help of assignment statement.

The same task can be performed by the following input statement

```
for(i=1;i<=10;i++)
    scanf("%f",&a[i]);
```

In this case, the values of the elements are entered through a keyboard.

Comparison, assignment, etc. operations between two similar arrays can not be done with a single statement. These operations are performed element wise with the help of a loop statement such as `for` loop. For example, array `a` can be assigned to array `b` by the following statement

```
for(i=0; i<n; i++)
    b[i]=a[i];
```

C does not check the validity of the subscript during the compile time. For example,

```
int a[10];
a[12]=15;
```

In this case, `a` is declared as an array of size 10 and 15 is assigned to the twelfth element of `a`. No errors will be generated at compile time and the program will compile successfully. But, during run time, it gives unpredictable results. Thus, proper care must be taken while using an array.

7.2.2 Input/Output of one-dimensional array

There is no single statement to read an array in C. But, loops (`for, while`, etc.) are used to read/write an array. Usually the `scanf`/`printf` functions are used to read/write an array.

Suppose `a` is a floating point array of size 50. This array can be read by the following statements.

```
for(i=0; i<50; i++)
    scanf("%f",&a[i]);
```

Similarly, this array can be printed by the following statements.

```
for(i=0; i<50; i++)
    printf("%f",a[i]);
```

Let `name` be an array of characters containing 20 characters. This array can be read as follows:

```
for(i=0; i<20; i++)
   name[i]=getchar();
```

or this array may be read as

```
k=0;
do
 {
   name[k]=getchar();
   k++;
 }while(k<20);
```

To print the array of characters, putchar function instead of getchar function is used.

Example 7.2.2 (Sum and average of numbers) Write a program to find the sum and average of N numbers using an array.

Solution. Let $a_i, i = 1, 2, \ldots, n$, be an array of size n. The sum $\sum_{i=1}^{n} a_i$ is computed in the following program.

Program 7.1

```
/* Computation of the sum and average of n numbers */
#include<stdio.h>
main()
 {
    float a[50],sum=0,ave;
    int n,i;
    printf("Enter the value of n\n");
    scanf("%d",&n);
    printf("Enter the numbers\n");
    for(i=1;i<=n;i++){
       scanf("%f",&a[i]);
       sum+=a[i];
      }
    ave=sum/n;
    printf("Sum=%f  Average=%f\n",sum,ave);
 }
```

A sample of input/output:

```
Enter the value of n
6
Enter the numbers
100.45 345.32 879.23 89.45 76.20 78.4

Sum=1569.049927 Average=261.508331
```

7.3 Multidimensional Arrays

In multidimensional arrays, the number of subscripts is more than one. For example, a_{ij} is a two-dimensional array containing two subscripts i and j, usually used to handle matrices. Similarly, a_{ijk} is a three-dimensional array with three indices i, j and k. The declaration of two or more dimensional arrays is similar to one-dimensional array, except that a pair of square brackets is needed for each subscript. That is, for k-dimensional array, k pairs of square brackets are needed. The general form of declaration of multidimensional array is

```
data_type array_name[exp1][exp2]···[expk];
```

where `exp1, exp2, ..., expk` are k positive valued integer constants or variables, which indicate the number of elements associated to each subscript.

The following statement

```
float x[4][5];
```

declares that `x` is a two-dimensional array with the first subscript ranging from 0 through 3 and second subscript ranging from 0 through 4, i.e. it declares the following elements.

```
x[0][0] x[0][1] x[0][2] x[0][3] x[0][4]
x[1][0] x[1][1] x[1][2] x[1][3] x[1][4]
x[2][0] x[2][1] x[2][2] x[2][3] x[2][4]
x[3][0] x[3][1] x[3][2] x[3][3] x[3][4]
```

Thus, the size of this array is 20. It may be noted that the elements of a two-dimensional array are stored in the memory, according to the order (row wise) above.

In a two-dimensional array, first and second subscripts are generally referred as row and column respectively.

A three-dimensional array can be declared as

```
float a[10][5][4];
double records[T][R][C];
```

The first declaration defines a three-dimensional array `a` whose first subscript ranges from 0 to 9, second subscript ranged from 0 to 4 and the third one ranges from 0 to 3. That is, the array `a` can store $10 \times 5 \times 4 = 200$ elements. Similarly, in second declaration, the array `records` can store $T \times R \times C$ elements, where T, R and C are symbolic constants.

7.3.1 Initialization of multidimensional array

Like one-dimensional array, the multidimensional array can also be initialized. A two-dimensional array is initialized row wise. For example, the array `a[3][4]` is initialized in the following order.

```
a[0][0] a[0][1] a[0][2] a[0][3]
a[1][0] a[1][1] a[1][2] a[1][3]
a[2][0] a[2][1] a[2][2] a[2][3]
```

That is, keeping the first subscript fixed, the second subscript varies from 0 to the last value, then it increases the value of the first subscript by one, and repeat all the values of second subscript, and so on. Consider the following initialization.

```
int mark[2][3]={50,20,30,40,60,80};
```

The values of all elements of the array `mark` for this initialization is shown below.

```
mark[0][0]=50     mark[0][1]=20     mark[0][2]=30
mark[1][0]=40     mark[1][1]=60     mark[1][2]=80
```

If the number of elements within the braces is less than the array size, then the remaining elements are set to zero. For example, the declaration,

```
int mark[2][3]={50,20,30,40};
```

initializes the elements as

```
mark[0][0]=50     mark[0][1]=20     mark[0][2]=30
mark[1][0]=40     mark[1][1]=0      mark[1][2]=0
```

A two-dimensional array can also be initialized as a group of elements. The above array `mark` is initialized as follows.

```
int mark[2][3]={
                {50,20,30},
                {40,60,80}
               };
          or
int mark[2][3]={{50,20,30},{40,60,80}};
```

Note the positions of commas and semicolon.

In this initialization, the numbers of the set {`50,20,30`} are assigned to the elements `mark[0][j]` for $j = 0, 1, 2$ and the numbers of the second set $\{40, 60, 80\}$ are assigned to the elements `mark[1][j]` for $j = 0, 1, 2$.

If the number of values within braces are less than the number of elements of the array, then the remaining elements are set to zero. For example,

```
int mark[2][3]={
                {50,20},
                {40}
               };
```

assigns the values of the elements as follows:

```
mark[0][0]=50     mark[0][1]=20     mark[0][2]=0
mark[1][0]=40     mark[1][1]=0      mark[1][2]=0
```

The declaration

```
int mark[2][3]={
                         {50,20,30}
                         };
```

assigns the values to the elements of the array mark as follows.

```
mark[0][0]=50    mark[0][1]=20    mark[0][2]=30
mark[1][0]=0     mark[1][1]=0     mark[1][2]=0
```

If the number of values within the braces is more than the number of array elements, then this will result in a compilation error. The following declaration gives compilation error.

```
int mark[2][3]={
                         {50,20,30,10},
                         {20,40,60,5}
                         };
```

The initialization of a three-dimensional array is similar to a two-dimensional array. For example,

```
int x[2][3][4]={
            {    /* for first subscript 0 */
              {1,2,3,4}, /* for second subscript 0 */
              {5,6,7,8}, /* for second subscript 1 */
              {0,1,4,5}, /* for second subscript 2 */
            },
            {    /* for first subscript 1 */
              {10,20,30,40}, /* for second subscript 0 */
              {50,60,70,80}, /* for second subscript 1 */
              {90,100,101,102}, /* for second subscript 2 */
            }   /* end of first subscript */
        }; /* end of declaration */
```

The element wise assignment is shown below.

```
x[0][0][0]=1    x[0][0][1]=2     x[0][0][2]=3     x[0][0][3]=4
x[0][1][0]=5    x[0][1][1]=6     x[0][1][2]=7     x[0][1][3]=8
x[0][2][0]=0    x[0][2][1]=1     x[0][2][2]=4     x[0][2][3]=5
x[1][0][0]=10   x[1][0][1]=20    x[1][0][2]=30    x[1][0][3]=40
x[1][1][0]=50   x[1][1][1]=60    x[1][1][2]=70    x[1][1][3]=80
x[1][2][0]=90   x[1][2][1]=100   x[1][2][2]=101   x[1][2][3]=102
```

The assignment, comparison, etc. operations between two arrays are performed element-by-element.

The input/output statements for multidimensional arrays are similar to one-dimensional array. For example, the input statement to read the floating point array a[i][j], where $i = 1, 2, \ldots, m$ and $j = 1, 2, \ldots, n$ is

```
for(i=0;i<m;i++)
    for(j=0;j<n;j++)
        scanf("%f",&a[i][j]);
```

Similarly, its output statement is

```
for(i=0;i<m;i++)
    for(j=0;j<n;j++)
        printf("%f ",a[i][j]);
```

To print this array, row wise, the following statements are used.

```
for(i=0;i<m;i++)
  {
    for(j=0;j<n;j++)
        printf("%f ",a[i][j]);
        printf("\n"); /* for new line */
  }
```

An example of a two-dimensional array is given below.

Example 7.3.1 (Transpose of matrix) Write a program to find the transpose of a matrix of order $m \times n$.

Solution. Let $A = [a_{ij}]_{m \times n}$ be a matrix and its transpose be $B = [b_{ij}]_{n \times m}$, where $b_{ji} = a_{ij}$ for $i = 1, 2, \ldots, m; j = 1, 2, \ldots, n$.

Program 7.2

```
/* Program to find transpose of a matrix */
#include<stdio.h>
main()
 {
   int i,j,m,n;
   float a[10][10], b[10][10];
   printf("Enter the order of the matrix a\n");
   scanf("%d%d",&m,&n);
   printf("Enter the elements of the matrix a\n");
   for(i=0;i<m;i++)
      for(j=0;j<n;j++)
         scanf("%f",&a[i][j]);
   /* computation of transposed matrix b*/
   for(i=0;i<m;i++)
      for(j=0;j<n;j++)
           b[j][i]=a[i][j];
```

```
   printf("The transpose of a is \n");
   for(i=0;i<n;i++){
      for(j=0;j<m;j++)
         printf("%5.2f ",b[i][j]);
         printf("\n");
   }
}
```

A sample of input/output:

```
Enter the order of the matrix a
3 4
Enter the elements of the matrix a
2 3 4 6
7 8 9 0
1 2 3 4

The transpose of a is
 2.00  7.00  1.00
 3.00  8.00  2.00
 4.00  9.00  3.00
 6.00  0.00  4.00
```

7.4 More About Arrays

In every C program, all the arrays must be declared with a specific size. Thus, the arrays are created at the compile time with fixed size. Therefore, the size of the array cannot be modified at the run time. This process of allocation of memory at compile time is known as **Static memory allocation** and the arrays are called **static arrays**. There is no problem in using an array if the requirement of data is known in advance. We observed that, if the size of an array is 10, then at most 10 elements can be stored to the array, and without modification of the source code, it is not possible to access more than 10 elements with this array. This drawback is removed in C language with the help of **dynamic memory allocation** techniques. Using this feature an array can be created at run time. The dynamic memory allocation is not as simple as static memory allocation. The dynamic memory allocation can be done by using the concept of **pointer variables** and some memory management functions, which are discussed later.

Other use of arrays are discussed in the subsequent chapters.

7.5 Worked Out Examples

Example 7.5.1 (Sine series) Write a program to compute

$$x - \frac{x^3}{3!} + \frac{x^5}{5!} - \frac{x^7}{7!} + \cdots\cdots$$

to three significant digits for $x = 30^o, 50^o$ and 73° by direct summation of successive terms and print the values of x, number of terms used in the series to obtain the accuracy and value of the series in tabular form as

x No. of terms Value of the series

Solution. Here the series is the sine series and the nth term of it is,
$t_n = (-1)^{n-1}\frac{x^{2n-1}}{(2n-1)!}, n = 1, 2, \ldots$
Therefore $t_{n+1} = (-1)^n \frac{x^{2n+1}}{(2n+1)!}$.
Now,

$$\frac{t_{n+1}}{t_n} = -\frac{x^2}{(2n+1)(2n)}, \text{ or, } t_{n+1} = -\frac{x^2}{2n(2n+1)} t_n, n = 1, 2, \cdots\cdots$$

That is, the *newterm*$=-\frac{x^2}{2n(2n+1)}\times$ *oldterm*, where initially *oldterm=first term=x*.

Program 7.3

```
/* Program to find the sum of the sine series */
#include<stdio.h>
#include<math.h>
main()
 {
   float x,term,sum,a[4],eps=1.0e-5;
   int n,i;
   printf("Enter three values in degree\n");
   scanf("%f%f%f",&a[1],&a[2],&a[3]);
   printf("x(in deg)  No. of  Value of \n");
   printf("           terms   the series\n");
   for(i=1;i<=3;i++)
     {
       x=a[i]*3.14159/180.; /* change to radian */
       term=x;
       sum=x;
       n=1;
       do
         {
           term=-x*x*term/((2.*n)*(2*n+1));
           sum+=term;
           n++;
         }while(fabs(term)>eps);
       printf("%5.2f\t%5d\t%9.3f\n",a[i],n,sum);
     }
 }
```

A sample of input/output:

```
Enter three values in degree
30 50 73

x(in deg)  No. of   Value of
           terms    the series
30.00        4       0.500
50.00        5       0.766
73.00        6       0.956
```

Example 7.5.2 (Horner method to polynomial evaluation) Write a program to find the value of a polynomial by Horner's method.

Solution. Let the polynomial of degree n be

$$a_n x^n + a_{n-1}x^{n-1} + a_{n-2}x^{n-2} + \cdots + a_1 x + a_0.$$

This can be written as

$$\begin{aligned}(a_n x + a_{n-1})x^{n-1} &+ a_{n-2}x^{n-2} + \cdots + a_1 x + a_0\\ &= ((a_n x + a_{n-1})x + a_{n-2})x^{n-2} + \cdots + a_1 x + a_0\\ &= \cdots\cdots = (((\cdots((a_n x + a_{n-1})x + a_{n-2})x + \cdots + a_1)x + a_0.\end{aligned}$$

The computation begins from the inner parentheses, i.e. from $(a_n x + a_{n-1})x$, and terminates when $n = 1$. It may be noted that to find the value of each inner loop, one addition and one multiplication is required. So, to compute the value of a polynomial of degree n we have to compute only n additions and n multiplications.

Program 7.4

```
/* COMPUTATION OF POLYNOMIAL USING HORNER METHOD */
#include<stdio.h>
main()
{
   float a[20],sum=0.,x;
   int i,n;
   printf("Enter the degree of the polynomial ");
   scanf("%d",&n);
   printf("Enter the coeffn. from highest degree\n");
   for(i=n;i>=0;i--)
      scanf("%f",&a[i]);
   printf("Coefficients of the polynomial are\n");
   for(i=n;i>=0;i--)
      printf("%6.3f ",a[i]);
   printf("\nEnter the value of x ");
      scanf("%f",&x);
   /* Evaluation of polynomial */
   for(i=n;i>=1;i--)
```

```
      sum=(sum+a[i])*x;
    sum+=a[0];
    printf("\nVALUE OF THE POLYNOMIAL AT %6.3f IS %9.4f",x,sum);
  }
```

A sample of input/output:

```
Enter the degree of the polynomial
4
Enter the coeffn.  from highest degree
1.2 3.4 5.6 8.1 5
Coefficients of the polynomial are
1.200 3.400 5.600 8.100 5.000
Enter the value of x
1.5
VALUE OF THE POLYNOMIAL AT   1.500 IS 47.3000
```

Example 7.5.3 (Split a number) Write a program to split a number into digits and find the
(i) sum of the digits,
(ii) product of the digits,
(iii) the largest digit in the number with its position of occurrence and print the digits in reverse order with single spacing.

Solution. Let N be the given number. First of all we divide N by 10. Then, the remainder is the right most digit of the given number. Let it be D[1]. The quotient is taken as N. Again we divide N by 10. The remainder is taken as D[2] and the quotient as N. This process is repeated until the remainder becomes 0. Let k be the total number of digits of the given number. Then D[k], D[$k-1$], ..., D[1] are the digits of the given number in succession. Next, from the array D we compute the largest digit with its position and the sum of the digits. The digits in reverse order are obtained by printing the array D as D[1], D[2], ..., D[k].

Program 7.5

```
/* Program to split a number into digits and to find
   the sum, the product of digits, maximum digit within the
   number with position and printing of digits in reverse order.
*/
#include<stdio.h>
main()
 {
   int d[10], n,m,k=0,i,sum=0,prod=1,max,pos;
   printf("Enter an integer ");
```

```
  scanf("%d",&n);
  do
   {
     m=n/10;
     k++;
     d[k]=n%10; /* remainder */
     n=m;
   }while(n!=0);
  printf("The digits are \n");
  for(i=k;i>=1;i--)
     printf("%3d",d[i]);
/* Sum and product of digits */
  for(i=1;i<=k;i++)
     {
       sum+=d[i];
       prod*=d[i];
     }
  printf("\nSum of the digits = %4d and product=%5d\n",sum,prod);
/* Computation of maximum digit with position */
  max=d[1];
  pos=1;
  for(i=2;i<=k;i++)
     if(d[i]>max){
     pos=i;
     max=d[i];
   }
  printf("Maximum digits is %d at position %2d\n",max,k-pos+1);
  printf("Digits in reverse order\n");
  for(i=1;i<=k;i++)
     printf("%2d",d[i]);
  return;
 }
```

A sample of input/output:

```
Enter an integer
2873

The digits are
  2  8  7  3
Sum of the digits =   20 and product=  336
Maximum digits is 8 at position  2
Digits in reverse order
 3 7 8 2
```

Example 7.5.4 (Decimal to binary conversion) Write a program to convert a decimal number to its equivalent binary number.

Solution. The decimal number N (given) is repeatedly divided by 2 and the remainder is noted. The remainders in reverse order give the required binary number. The necessary algorithm is presented in Chapter 2.

Program 7.6

```
/* Decimal to binary conversion */
#include<stdio.h>
main()
 {
   int d[25],k=0,i;
   long int n,nold;
   printf("Enter the decimal number\n");
   scanf("%ld",&n);
   nold=n;
   do
   {
     k++;
     d[k]=n%2;
     n=n/2;
   }while(n!=0);
   printf("Binary equivalent of %ld is \n",nold);
   for(i=k;i>=1;i--)
     printf("%1d",d[i]);
 }
```

A sample of input/output:

```
Enter the decimal number
23451
Binary equivalent of 23451 is
101101110011011
```

Example 7.5.5 (Trace of a matrix) Write a program to find the trace of a square matrix of order $n \times n$.

Solution. The trace of a square matrix is the sum of its diagonal elements, i.e. if $A = [a_{ij}]_{n\times n}$, then trace is $\sum_{i=1}^{n} a_{ii}$.

Program 7.7

```
/* Program to find the trace of a matrix */
#include<stdio.h>
main()
 {
   int i,j,n;
   float a[10][10],sum=0;
   printf("Enter the order of the square matrix \n");
   scanf("%d",&n);
   printf("Enter the elements of the matrix \n");
   for(i=0;i<n;i++)
      for(j=0;j<n;j++)
         scanf("%f",&a[i][j]);
   for(i=0;i<n;i++)
         sum+=a[i][i];
   printf("The trace of the matrix is %f6.2\n",sum);
 }
```

A sample of input/output:

```
Enter the order of the square matrix
4
Enter the elements of the matrix
3 4 5 6
8 9 01
-4 -5 -6 -7
9 0 1 2

The trace of the matrix is
        8.00
```

Example 7.5.6 (Maximum element of a matrix) Write a program to find the maximum element with the position among all the elements of a matrix of order $m \times n$.

Program 7.8

```
/* Program to find the maximum among all elements of a matrix */
#include<stdio.h>
main()
 {
   int i,j,m,n,k,l;
   float a[10][10],big;
   printf("Enter the order of the matrix\n");
   scanf("%d%d",&m,&n);
   printf("Enter the elements of the matrix\n");
```

```
   for(i=0;i<m;i++)
      for(j=0;j<n;j++)
         scanf("%f",&a[i][j]);
   big=a[0][0];
   k=0; l=0; /* k,l represent position */
   for(i=0;i<m;i++)
      for(j=0;j<n;j++)
         if(a[i][j]>big) {
            big=a[i][j];
            k=i; l=j;
         }
   printf("Maximum element is %6.3f \n",big);
   printf("at position (%2d,%2d)\n",k+1,l+1);
   return;
 }
```

A sample of input/output:

```
Enter the order of the matrix
3 4
Enter the elements of the matrix
-3 4 5 6
100 2 3 4
230 -9 3 4

Maximum element is 230.000
at position ( 3, 1)
```

Example 7.5.7 (Sum of matrices) Write a program to find the sum of two matrices of order $m \times n$.

Solution. We know that the addition between two matrices is possible, if they are of same order. Let $A = [a_{ij}]$ and $B = [b_{ij}]$ be two matrices of order $m \times n$. Let $C = [c_{ij}]$ be the sum of A and B, where $c_{ij} = a_{ij} + b_{ij}, i = 1, 2, \ldots, m; j = 1, 2, \ldots, n$.

Program 7.9

```
/* Program to find the sum of two matrices */
#include<stdio.h>
main()
 {
   int i,j,m,n,p,q;
   float a[10][10], b[10][10],c[10][10];
   printf("Enter the order of the matrix A\n");
   scanf("%d%d",&m,&n);
```

```
   printf("Enter the elements of the matrix A\n");
   for(i=0;i<m;i++)
      for(j=0;j<n;j++)
     scanf("%f",&a[i][j]);
   printf("Enter the order of the matrix B\n");
   scanf("%d%d",&p,&q);
   if((m!=p) || (n!=q)) {
      printf("Order is not compatible! Addition is not possible\n");
      exit(0);
    }
   printf("Enter the elements of the matrix B\n");
   for(i=0;i<m;i++)
      for(j=0;j<n;j++)
      scanf("%f",&b[i][j]);
   /* finding sum */
   for(i=0;i<m;i++)
      for(j=0;j<n;j++)
         c[i][j]=a[i][j]+b[i][j];
   /* printing of matrix */
   for(i=0;i<m;i++){
      for(j=0;j<n;j++)
         printf("%6.3f ",c[i][j]);
         printf("\n");
      }
 return;
 }
```

A sample of input/output:

```
Enter the order of the matrix A
2 3
Enter the elements of the matrix A
4 5 6
7 6 9.5
Enter the order of the matrix B
2 3
Enter the elements of the matrix B
4.5 6.7 8
2 1 -3

 8.500 11.700 14.000
 9.000  7.000  6.500
```

Example 7.5.8 (Product of matrices) Write a program to find the product of two matrices of order $m \times n$ and $n \times l$.

Solution. The product AB of two matrices A and B is possible, if the number of columns of A is equal to the number of rows of B. Let $A = [a_{ij}]_{m\times n}$ and $B = [b_{ij}]_{n\times l}$ be two given matrices. If the product AB is equal to C, then $c_{ij} = \sum_{k=1}^{n} a_{ik}b_{kj}$, $i = 1, 2, \ldots, m; j = 1, 2, \ldots, l$.

Program 7.10

```
/* Program to find the product of two matrices */
#include<stdio.h>
main()
 {
   int i,j,k,m,n,p,q;
   float a[10][10], b[10][10],c[10][10];
   printf("Enter the order of the matrix A\n");
   scanf("%d%d",&m,&n);
   printf("Enter the elements of the matrix A\n");
   for(i=0;i<m;i++)
      for(j=0;j<n;j++)
         scanf("%f",&a[i][j]);
   printf("Enter the order of the matrix B\n");
   scanf("%d%d",&p,&q);
   if(n!=p) {
      printf("Matrix product is not possible\n");
      exit(0);
    }
   printf("Enter the elements of the matrix B\n");
   for(i=0;i<p;i++)
      for(j=0;j<q;j++)
         scanf("%f",&b[i][j]);
   /* finding product */
   for(i=0;i<m;i++)
      for(j=0;j<q;j++)
         {
           c[i][j]=0.0;
           for(k=0;k<n;k++)
              c[i][j]+=a[i][k]*b[k][j];
         }
   printf("Product of the matrices\n");
   for(i=0;i<m;i++){
      for(j=0;j<q;j++)
         printf("%6.3f ",c[i][j]);
         printf("\n");
```

```
    }
return;
}
```

A sample of input/output:

```
Enter the order of the matrix A
2 3
Enter the elements of the matrix A
2 3 4
5 4 3
Enter the order of the matrix B
3 3
Enter the elements of the matrix B
4 5 -1
2 3 1
2 0 1
Product of the matrices
22.000 19.000  5.000
34.000 37.000  2.000
```

Important Points

1. An array is referred by its name, and each element is accessed by the name of an array and subscript.
2. The subscripts of an array are $0, 1, 2, \ldots, n-1$, where n is the size of the array. That is, if `a` is an array of size 5, only the valid variables are `a[0]`, `a[1]`, `a[3]` and `a[4]`.
3. Take care about the validity of subscript.
4. The array elements must be initialized, otherwise they will store garbage.
5. When expression is used as subscript, the value of the expression must not be less than 0 and not more than $n-1$, where n is the size of the array.
6. During initializing character array, enough space must be provided for terminating null character.

Exercise VII

Review Questions

1. What is an array? Explain how an array variable is different from an ordinary variable?

2. How the individual array elements are identified?
3. Explain the salient features of an array and its uses.
4. What do you mean by subscript? How are they written? What restrictions apply to the values that can be assigned to subscript?
5. State the rules used to declare one-dimensional array.
6. What advantage is there in defining an array size in terms of a symbolic constant rather than a fixed integer quantity?
7. How are initial values written in a one-dimensional array definition? Do you think the entire array must be initialized? What value is automatically assigned to the array elements that are not explicitly initialized?
8. How are the individual elements accessed and processed in an array?
9. Describe the method to initialize a string constant to a one-dimensional character array. When a one-dimensional character array of unspecified length is assigned an initial value, what extra character is automatically added to the end of the string?
10. What is a multidimensional array and how is it different from an one-dimensional array ?
11. How can we read to and print from an array in C. Describe.
12. Write short notes on (i) subscripted variable, (ii) array declaration.
13. Suppose an array a is declared as `float a[100]`. What will happen if we want to store (i) 40 elements, (ii) 150 elements in a.
14. Discuss how initial values can be assigned to a multidimensional array.

Problems

1. Describe the array that is defined in each of the following statements. Indicate what values are assigned to the individual array elements.
   (a) `int a[4]={2,3,4,5};`
   (b) `int a[5]={6,7};`
   (c) `int b[10]={0};`
   (d) `int b[7]={1,4,0};`
   (e) `float c[2][3]={1.5,4.2,0.5,6.6,5.9,7.2};`
   (f)
```
int c[2][3]={
              {1,4,5},
              {6,5,7}
            };
```
   (g)
```
int c[2][3]={
              {4,5},
              {6}
            };
```

2. What is the difference between the declarations

```
char point[]="South";      and
char point[]={'S','o','u','t','h'};
```

3. Which of the following declarations is correct to declare a matrix containing 4 rows and 3 columns?

```
int matrix[4][3];
int matrix[4],[3];
int matrix[4,3];
int matrix[2+2][2+1];
int matrix[3][2];
int matrix[3][4];
```

4. Which of the following initializations are correct and why?

```
char str[]="India";
char str[5]="India";
char str[6]="India";
char str[4]="India";
```

5. Supply the missing details in the following program for adding the numbers $x[i]$, $i = 1, 2, \ldots, 100$.

```
#include<stdio.h>
main()
  {
   float x[100];
   int n;
   scanf("%d",&n);
   for(i=1;i<=n;i++) scanf("%f",a[i]);
   sum=
   for(i=1;i<=n;)
     sum=sum
   printf("%f",sum);
  }
```

6. What is the output of the following program segment?

```
int sum=0;
int x[10]={3,4,5,6,8};
for(i=1;i<10;i++){
    printf("%d \n",x[i]);
```

```
        sum+=x[i];
    }
    printf("Sum=%d",sum);
```

7. Let D be a matrix of size 4×2 with the following initialization.

```
int D[4][2]={3,4,5,8,9,0,-2,3};
```

Write the necessary statements to print this two-dimensional array as matrix form (row wise).

8. Suppose a is an array of size 1000. Describe a method to initialize first 1000 natural numbers to this array.

Programming Problems

1. Write a program to read an integer array $x_i, i = 1, 2, \ldots, n$, and find the sum of even and odd integers in it separately.
2. Write a program to read n integers $M_i, i = 1, 2, \ldots, n$, and find the product of the even integers only.
3. Let $x_i, y_i, i = 1, 2, \ldots, n$, be two vectors each of size n. Write a program to find the

   (i) scalar product between x and y, defined as $x.y = \sum_{i=1}^{n} x_i y_i$.

   (ii) norm of x and y, where norm $(||x||) = \sqrt{\sum_{i=1}^{n} x_i^2}$.

   (iii) angle (θ) between x and y, defined as

$$\theta = \cos^{-1} \frac{x.y}{||x||\ ||y||}.$$

4. Let x_i and $y_i, i = 1, 2, \ldots, n$, be two arrays. Write a program to find the values of, (i) $S1 = \sum_{i=1}^{n} x_i$, (ii) $S2 = \sum_{i=1}^{n} x_i^2$, (iii) $S3 = \sum_{i=1}^{n} x_i^3$, (ii) $S = \sum_{i=1}^{n} x_i y_i$.
5. Write a program to find the value of $S = \frac{h}{2}[y_0 + 4(y_2 + y_4 + \cdots + y_{n-2}) + 2(y_1 + y_3 + \cdots + y_{n-1}) + y_n]$, where h and $y_i, i = 0, 1, 2, \ldots, n$, are given.
6. Write a program to arrange n real (or integer) numbers in descending/ascending order.
7. Write a program to read an array of n elements $A_i, i = 1, 2, \ldots, n$, and another number k and check whether the element k is in the array A_i.
8. Write a program to read an array $P_i, i = 1, 2, \ldots, n$, which contains negative, zero and positive numbers, and find the minimum (maximum) among the positive (negative) numbers.

9. Write a program to read the name and age of 500 people of a locality and then to list the name and age of voters among them whose age is above 18 years.
10. Write a program to find the sum and difference of two matrices of equal size.
11. Write a program to find the product AB of the matrices A and B, where the order of A is $m \times n$ and that of B is $n \times 1$.
12. Write a program to find the product of two matrices of order $m \times n$ and $n \times l$.
13. Write a program to find the transpose of a matrix of order $m \times n$.
14. Write a program to find the maximum (minimum) among all the elements of a matrix of order $m \times n$.
15. Write a program to find the maximum (minimum) element of each row (column) of a matrix of order $m \times n$.
16. Write a program to find the trace of a square matrix of order $n \times n$. (Trace of a square matrix $A = [a_{ij}]_{n \times n}$ is $\sum_{i=1}^{n} a_{ii}$).
17. Write a program to find the norm of a square matrix of order $n \times n$. [Norm ($||A||$) of a square matrix $A = [a_{ij}]_{n \times n}$ is $||A|| = \sqrt{\sum_{i=1}^{n}\sum_{j=1}^{n} a_{ij}^2}$.]
18. Write a program to find the sum of squares of the diagonal elements of a square matrix of order $n \times n$.
19. Write a program to test whether a square matrix is symmetric. [A square matrix is symmetric, if $a_{ij} = a_{ji}$ for all $i, j = 1, 2, \ldots, n$.]
20. Write a program to test whether a square matrix is skew-symmetric. [A square matrix is skew-symmetric, if $a_{ij} = -a_{ji}$ for all $i, j = 1, 2, \ldots, n$.]
21. Write a program to test whether a square matrix is orthogonal. [A square matrix A of order $n \times n$ is said to be orthogonal if $AA^t = I$, where A^t is the transpose of A and I is the unit matrix of order $n \times n$.]
22. Let $A = [a_{ij}]_{n \times n}$ be a square matrix. Write a program to find the upper bound, ρ, on the eigen values of the matrix A, where
$$\rho = max\left(\sum_{k=1}^{n} |a_{1k}|, \sum_{k=1}^{n} |a_{2k}|, \ldots, \sum_{k=1}^{n} |a_{nk}|\right).$$
23. Write a program to find the value of a determinant of order 3.
24. Write a program to find the minimum (maximum) among the elements of a specified row (or column) of a matrix of order $m \times n$.
25. Write a program to arrange the elements of each row of a matrix in increasing order. e.g. if
$$A = \begin{bmatrix} 18 & 3 & 21 \\ 0 & -5 & 3 \\ 21 & 81 & -9 \end{bmatrix}$$

after arrangement, A becomes

$$A = \begin{bmatrix} 3 & 18 & 21 \\ -5 & 0 & 3 \\ -9 & 21 & 81 \end{bmatrix}.$$

26. A square matrix $A = [a_{ij}]_{n \times n}$ is called a diagonal matrix if $a_{ij} = 0$ for $i \neq j, i, j = 1, 2, \ldots, n$. A is called upper triangular, if all the elements below the diagonal are zero, i.e. $a_{ij} = 0$ for $i < j, i, j = 1, 2, \ldots, n$, and lower triangular, if all the elements above the diagonal are zero, i.e. $a_{ij} = 0$ for $i > j, i, j = 1, 2, \ldots, n$. Write a program that reads a matrix and determines, if it is one of the above types.
27. The daily maximum temperature recorded in 5 cities during the month of May (for 31 days) have been tabulated as follows:

	City				
Day	1	2	3	4	5
1					
2					
⋮					
31					

Write a program to read the elements of the table into a two-dimensional array temperature, and to find the city and day corresponding to
(a) the highest temperature, and
(b) the lowest temperature.
28. Pascal's triangle is a set of numbers having the following properties. Each row begins and ends with 1's and each number between two 1's is the sum of the numbers on either side of it in the above row. The first six rows of Pascal's triangle is shown below.

```
          1
        1   1
      1   2   1
    1   3   3   1
  1   4   6   4   1
1   5  10  10   5   1
```

Write a program to compute and print the first 15 rows of this triangle.
29. Write a program to read a number N and print out digit by digit, expressing it in words. For example, the number 5208, should be printed as "Five Two Zero Eight".

30. Write a program to read an array of n numbers and print the contents of it in reverse order.
31. Every book published by International Publishers should carry an International Standard Book Number (ISBN). It is a 10 character 4 part number shown as $d_0 - d_1d_2 - d_3d_4d_5d_6d_7d_8 - d_9$

    The first part (d_0) denotes the region, the second (d_1d_2) represents the publisher code, the third ($d_3d_4d_5d_6d_7d_8$) identifies the book and the fourth (d_9) is the error checking digit. The check digit is computed as follows:

$$\text{sum} = \sum_{i=1}^{9} i \times d_i.$$

    Check digit is the remainder when sum is divided by 11 and if the remainder is 10, then the checked digit is denoted by X. Write a program that reads a given ISBN number and checks whether it represents a valid ISBN.
32. Write a program to read n numbers and find the average of the non-negative and negative integers separately.
33. Write a program to read a set of numbers $x_1, x_2, \ldots, x_n$, and a number k, and check whether the number k is present in the array. If it is in the array print out, then how many times the number k is repeated in the array?
34. Write a program to read a set of numbers to store it in an one dimensional array, A. Copy the elements in another array B in the reverse order. Find the sum of the individual elements of the arrays A and B and store them in another array C. Also display all the three arrays.
35. Write a program to read a two dimensional array and find the sum of the elements in each row and column separately and display them.
36. Write a program to generate a magic square A, where the sum of the elements in each row and column are the same.
37. Write a program to read two numbers and store them into two arrays, digit wise. Find the sum of the numbers by adding these two arrays.
    For example, let $M = 153$ and $N = 567$ be two numbers and we stored them in the arrays A and B as $A_1 = 1, A_2 = 5, A_3 = 3$; $B_1 = 5, B_2 = 6, B_3 = 7$ and the sum of M and N is stored in the array C as $C_1 = 7, C_2 = 2, C_3 = 0$.

Chapter 8

Functions

In C, every problem is decomposed into functions. The concept of function is the most powerful and convenient way to solve a large problem. A programmer can divide a large problem into several smaller subprograms, which when reassembles, constitutes the complete C program. A function is a self-contained program segment and it can be developed and tested separately. The use of function reduces the complexity and the size of source code of the main program significantly. Also, the same variable names can be used in several functions. Every C program contains one or more functions. One such function has a special name `main`. The execution of a C program begins from this function. The other functions are called from `main` function or another function. A function can be called from any position of the main function or from another function.

The functions in C are broadly of two types – library functions or built-in functions and user-defined functions. The library functions such as `abs, sqrt, sin,` etc. are already mentioned. In this chapter, only user defined functions are discussed.

8.1 The Function `main`

The function `main` is a user defined function except that the name of the function. Every program must have a `main` function and the execution of program begins from `main`. The statements of the function `main` are written by the programmer, therefore `main` is a user defined function. The entire program can be written within the `main` function, but it is not suitable for the complicated problem. In this case, the program becomes too large and hence debugging, testing and maintaining the program becomes difficult. If a program is divided into small parts, then each part may be coded separately and combine them to obtain a single program. These small parts are called *subprograms* known as **function** in C.

The functions are used in a program due to the following advantages.

(i) The length of the source code becomes less.

(ii) Easy to debug and test.

(iii) Easy to identify a faulty function.

(iv) It facilitates top-down modular approach.
(v) A function may be used by several other programs.

The use of library function is simple. If we need the value of square root of 5, it is obtained by simply calling the function `sqrt(5.0)`. Only the associated header file `math.h` is to be included. But, the use of user-defined function is not this much easy. To use a user-defined function, we have to establish the following three elements.
(i) Function definition
(ii) Function declaration, and
(iii) Function call.

8.2 Definition of Function

The task of the function is implemented here. All the formulae, logical expressions, etc. related to the function are defined here. A *function definition*, also known as *function implementation* has two main parts, viz.
(i) function header, and
(ii) function body.

Again, the function header has three elements:
(i) function name,
(ii) return type of function, and
(iii) list of parameters,
while the function body has the following three elements:
(i) local variables,
(ii) statements, and
(iii) return statement.

The general structure of a function definition in C is

```
data_type function_name(arg1, arg2,..., argn)
  {
     declaration of local variables;
     body of the function;
     return (expression);
  }
```

The first line is the header of the function.

`data_type` represents the type of the value which is returned by the function. The `data_type` may be omitted if the function returns an integer or a character (a character value is represented as an integer) value. If the function does not return any value, then the keyword `void` is written as `data_type`.

The `function_name` is any valid C identifier and therefore must follow the rules of formation of C variables. It is better to use the appropriate name of the function which is relevant to the task of the function. However, avoid the use of library function names and OS commands.

`arg1, arg2,..., argn` are called the `formal arguments` or `formal parameters`.

Formal arguments

Only the variables are used as formal arguments. The formal arguments allow information to be transferred from the calling portion of the program to the function. The variables used as formal arguments are 'local' in the sense that they are not identified outside the function, i.e. these variables may be used as other variables outside the function. It may be noted that the formal arguments are separated by commas and enclosed by a pairs of parentheses. If the function does not require any arguments, then only a pair of parentheses or `void` enclosed by the parentheses must be written after the function name.

The formal arguments are separated by commas and each formal argument has separate data type. For example,

```
int sum(int a, int b)          float sqr(float x)
  {                               {
    . . .                           . . .
  }                               }
```

Note that there is no semicolon after the closing brace. Data types of formal arguments cannot be combined together. That is, `int sum(int a,b)` is not valid, a separate variable declaration is required for `b`.

Let us consider a function which computes the area of a rectangle whose sides are `a` and `b`.

```
float area(float a, float b)
  {
    float r;
    r=a*b;
    return r;
  }
```

In this function, the first line `float area(float a, float b)` is the header, the function name is `area`, this function returns a `float` value. The formal arguments are `a` and `b`, and the type of both the arguments are `float`.

The function header varies from compiler to compiler. The older compilers require the following form of function definition.

```
float area(a, b)
float a, b;
  {
    float r;
    r=a*b;
    return r;
  }
```

Here, only the names of the parameters are mentioned within the parentheses following the function name. The data types of the parameters are given after the parentheses and before the opening brace. This is an old style to define a function. ANSI C accept both old and new-style declarations.

8.2.1 Body of the function

The main part of a function is known as **body** of the function. It contains the declarations and statements necessary for performing task for the function. The body of the function is written within a pair of braces. It has three parts listed below.
(i) Declaration of local variables,
(ii) C statements that require to perform the task,
(iii) Return statement.

The arguments with the header of a function are the local variables. If more variables are needed to execute the task of the function, it can be declared at the beginning of the function body. In the above function `area`, the local variable (other than formal arguments) is `r`. This variable is local to the function `area`, which means the variable `r` can be used only within the function `area`, and this variable cannot be accessed by other function, even `main`. If `main` contains the variable `r`, then these two `r` are treated as two different variables and the spaces allocated for them are different.

The statements of the function are the necessary C statements that perform the task for which the function is defined. The formal arguments are used in these statements. It can access other functions. Also, it can access the function itself (this process is known as **recursion**, to be discussed later).

In the function `area` the only statement is `r=a*b;` Note that `r` is the local variable and `a, b` are the formal arguments. The values of `a` and `b` are passed at the time of calling the function `area`.

8.2.2 Return value

The value obtained in a function is transferred to the calling program using the `return` statement. The `return` statement also causes control to be returned to the point from which the function was called. The general form is

```
return;      or  return exp;   or  return(exp);
```

The `exp` may be constant, variable or any expression. If `exp` represents an expression, then `exp` must be written within a pair of parentheses. The value of `exp` is returned to the calling function. The `exp` is optional, i.e. `return` statement may be written without it. Its role is the closing brace of the function. If `exp` is absent, then the function does not return any value to the calling function, the control goes to return back to the calling function. Only one `exp` can be included in the `return` statement. Thus, a function returns only one value to the calling function. But, `return` statement may be written in different positions with different expressions, if the function contains multiple branches. For example,

```
if(error)
```

```
            return 0;
        else
            return 1;
```

Normally, all functions return `int` type data. Also, other typed of data can be returned by the function by using *type specifier* in the header of the function.

The flow between the calling function and a function is shown in Figure 8.1.

```
/* main function or calling function */
{
.........
v=sum(a,b); /* jump to the function sum */
..........  /* return from function */
.........
}
/* function definition */
float sum(float x,float y) /* jump from calling function */
{
.........
exp=.....
return exp; /* return back to the calling function */
}
```

Figure 8.1: The flow between the function and calling function.

Suppose a function `sum` is called from the `main` function, then a portion of memory is allocated to store all the identifiers and the necessary stack, etc. used in the function `main`. After completion of execution of the function (`sum`), the necessary value is returned to the calling function (`main`) and the memory allocated for the function (`sum`) becomes free.

8.3 Function Calls

Once a function is defined, it can be used in several times within a program. It is *called* or *accessed* by specifying its name, followed by a list of actual arguments enclosed in parentheses. The arguments must be separated by commas. If a function does not require any arguments, a pair of empty parentheses must be included after the function name. The actual arguments may be constants, variables or expressions. Each actual argument must be of same data type as its corresponding formal argument.

When a single value is passed to a function through an actual argument, the value of actual argument is *copied* into the corresponding formal argument for the function. Therefore, the value of the formal argument can be changed within the function, but the value of actual arguments remains same within the calling function. This procedure for passing the value of an argument to a function is known as **passing by value**.

For example,

```
float area(float, float); /* function declaration */
main()
  {
    float A;
    A=area(10.0,25.5); /* function call */
    printf("Area is %f",A);
  }
float area(float a, float b) /* function definition */
  {
    float c;
    c=a*b;
    return c; /* function returns a value */
  }
```

In the above program, the function `area` is called by the statement

`A=area(10.0,25.5);`

Here 10.0 and 25.5 are the actual arguments and these values are sent to the function `area`. 10.0 and 25.5 are copied to the formal arguments `a` and `b` respectively.

When a function is called, the control goes to the beginning of the function. Then all the statements of the function are executed in the sequence and a value is returned by the `return` statement. The value obtained by evaluating the function `area` is assigned to `A`.

A function can be called in many ways. For example,

```
area(10.0,20.5);      area(5.3,x);      area(x,y);
area(5.0,area(2.0,5.2));      area(x+y,a+b);
```

A user-defined function can also be used within an expression like other variables and library functions. The following are the valid statements

```
printf("Area is %f", area(20.0,15.25));
if(area(a,b)>area(x,y)) printf("a*b is more than x*y");
x=area(5.2,8.3)*area(a,b);
```

But, no value can be assigned to a function because no memory is allocated for a function. For example, `area(a,b)=25.5` is invalid.

A function may not return any value. If the function does not return any value, it is not used in expression, but it must be called to perform the tasks specified in the function.

Position of functions

In C, the function can be placed in any position within the program, before or after the `main` function. But, if the program is large and contains many functions, then it is suggested that the function `main` be placed at the beginning of the program. But, in this case, the compiler don't know about the functions used in `main`. To avoid it, each function is declared (its name, return type and parameters) prior to `main` itself.

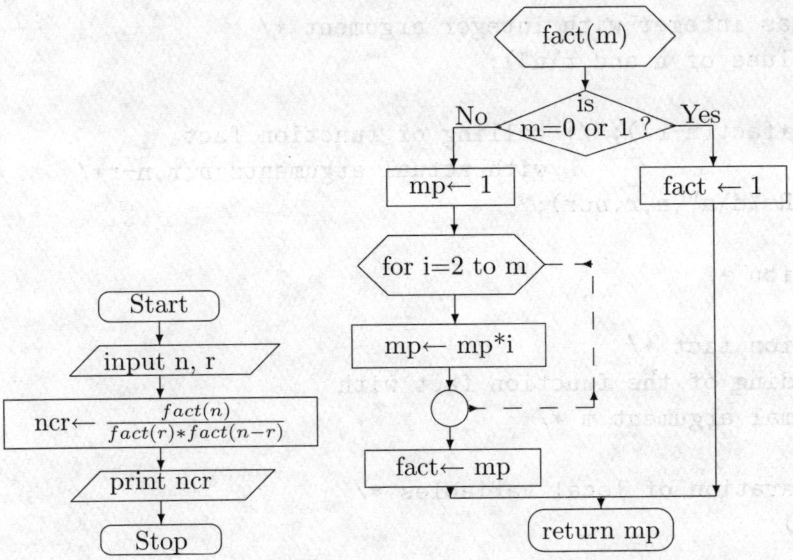

Figure 8.2: Flow chart to compute ${}^nC_r$.

The following program computes the value of ${}^nC_r$ by calling a function `fact` (which determines factorial) for three times.

Example 8.3.1 (Computation of ${}^nC_r$) Write a program to find the value of ${}^nC_r$ for given n and r using function.

Solution. The value of ${}^nC_r$ is

$$\frac{n!}{r!(n-r)!}$$

where $0! = 1$ and $n! = n.(n-1)(n-2)\ldots 2.1$, n and r are positive integers. To compute the value of ${}^nC_r$, we have to compute the values of $n!$, $r!$ and $(n-r)!$, i.e. same computations are required for different values, such as n, r and $n-r$. Thus, use of function is appropriate to compute the value of ${}^nC_r$. A function `fact(m)` is written with argument m and it is called three times for $m = n, r$ and $n - r$.

Program 8.1

```
/* Computation of n-c-r using function */
#include<stdio.h>
main()
 {
  int n,r,ncr;
  int fact(int m); /* declaration of function fact
```

```
                           as integer with integer argument */
  printf("Enter the values of n and r\n");
  scanf("%d%d",&n,&r);
  ncr=fact(n)/(fact(r)*fact(n-r)); /* calling of function fact
                                     with actual arguments n,r,n-r*/
  printf("N=%d R=%d NCR=%d\n",n,r,ncr);
  return;
 }/* end of main function */

/* definition of function fact */
int fact(int m) /* heading of the function fact with
                        formal argument m */
 {
   int i,mp=1; /* declaration of local variables */
   if((m==0) || (m==1))
     mp=1;
   else
     for(i=2;i<=m;i++)
       mp*=i;
   return mp;
 }/* end of function fact */
```

A sample of input/output:

```
Enter the values of n and r
7 3

N=7 R=3 NCR=35
```

In this program, the value of `ncr` is obtained by calling the function `fact` for first time with the actual argument n. The function is executed by taking $m = n$ and return the value of `mp` (the value of $n!$) to the main function. Again, the function `fact` is called for the argument r. The function is evaluated for $m = r$ and returns its value to the main function. Lastly, the function `fact` is called for the argument $n - r$. Thus, the same function `fact` is called for three times with three different arguments and the value of `ncr` is evaluated using the expression `fact(n)/(fact(r)*fact(n-r));`.

8.4 Function Prototypes

All the functions used in a program must be declared before their use. The general form of **function declaration**, also known as **function prototype**, is

```
data_type function_name(list of arguments);
```

It has four parts – return type (`data_type`) of the function, function name (`function_name` list of arguments and semicolon at the end.

This is similar to function header except the end semicolon. The function `area` may be declared as

```
        float area(float a, float b);   /* function prototype */
    or, float area(float,float);
```

The declaration of functions may be placed outside any function (including `main`) or inside a function (`main` function or any other functions).

If the functions are declared outside all functions, the prototype is called **global prototype** and these functions can be accessed from any function. If the functions are declared within a function, the prototype is called **local prototype**. In this case, the functions are mainly used by the function containing them.

It is good practice to declare prototypes in the global declaration section before `main`. The following is the example of global prototype.

```
int sum(int,int); /* global function prototype */
main()
  {
    int b;
    b=sum(5,6); /* function call */
  }
int sum(int x, int y) /* function definition */
  {
    return(x+y);
  }
```

while the following is the example of local prototype

```
main()
int sum(int,int); /* local function prototype */
  {
    int b;
    b=sum(5,6); /* function call */
  }
int sum(int x, int y) /* function definition */
  {
    return(x+y);
  }
```

Note that prototype declaration is not mandatory. But, if the function prototype is not declared before its use, the compiler will assume that they all are available during linking. Since prototype is not declared, C will assume that the return type of the function is integer and the types of parameters match the formal definition. If any one of these assumptions is wrong, an error message will produced by linker.

Another situation may occurs. The function declaration `int area();` causes some C compilers to assume that `area` is a function that accepts any number of arguments. No type checking is done at the compile time. Some compilers assumes that the function `area` accepts no parameter.

Thus, it is suggested to use function prototype.

The following points are kept in mind during the declaration of function and function definition.

(i) The arguments must be separated by commas.

(ii) The argument names may be different in prototype declaration and function definition.

(iii) The argument names in the declaration is optional.

(iv) If the arguments list is empty, write `void` as argument list.

(v) The arguments number, order and type must be same in prototype declaration and function definition.

(vi) The return type is optional, if the function returns an integer value.

(vii) If the function does not return any value, then the return type is `void`.

8.5 Category of the Functions

Based on the return type of the function and number of arguments, the functions are categorized as follows:

1. no arguments and no return values,
2. arguments and no return values,
3. arguments and one return value,
4. no arguments and one return value,
5. with or without arguments and multiple return values.

Below, all these types of functions are discussed with examples.

No arguments and no return values

For these types of functions no data is transfered between the calling function and the called function.

```
#include<stdio.h>
main()
  {
    void sum(void);
    printf("The sum is ");
    sum(); /* function call, not assigned to a variable */
  }
void sum(void)
  {
    int a,b;
    scanf("%d%d",&a,&b);
    printf("%d",a+b);
  } /* no return statement, automatically returns to main */
```

Note, that the function `sum` is called from `main`. The function `sum` reads two values for `a` and `b`. The value of `a+b` is printed using the `printf` function. The output of this program is

```
The sum is 10
```

if the values of `a` and `b` are 3 and 7.

Note that there is no return statement in the function `sum`, the closing brace acts as `return` statement. The statement `return;` may be used at the end of the body of `sum`.

Arguments and no return values

In this type of function, the arguments are passed to the calling function, but the function does not return any value. The example of this type of function is given below.

```
#include<stdio.h>
main()
  {
    void sum(int,int);
    int a,b;
    scanf("%d%d",&a,&b);
    printf("The sum is ");
    sum(a,b); /* function call, not assigned to a variable */
  }
void sum(int a, int b)
  {
    printf("%d",a+b);
    return; /* it is optional */
  }
```

Here, the values of two arguments are read in `main` and they are passed to the function. The function computes the values of `a+b` and print it within the function `sum`.

Arguments with one return value

This type of function is frequently used in C programs. Here, the data is transferred from calling function to called function and vice-versa.

```
#include<stdio.h>
main()
  {
    void sum(int,int);
    int a,b,c;
    scanf("%d%d",&a,&b);
    c=sum(a,b); /* function call, assigned it to the variable c */
    printf("The sum is %d",c);
  }
void sum(int x, int y)
```

```
{
  return(x+y); /* this statement is compulsory */
}
```

Here, the values of a and b are transferred to the function sum and they are copied as x and y. It returns the value of $x + y$ to the main function and this value is assigned to the variable c and it is printed by printf statement.

No arguments and one return value

This type of function does not transfer any arguments from calling function, but returns a value. Example of such function is given below.

```
#include<stdio.h>
main()
  {
    int sum(void);
    int c;
    c=sum(); /* calling of function */
    printf("The sum is %d",c);
  }
void sum(void)/* no arguments are passed */
  {
    int a,b;
    scanf("%d%d",&a,&b);
    return(a+b); /* returns a value */
  }
```

In this program, the values of a and b are read within the function sum. The value of a+b is returned to the function main. The sum a+b is stored in c and then it is printed.

Normally, a C function returns a single value, but multiple values may be returned using the concept of structure, array and pointer which are discussed later.

8.6 Passing Arrays to a Function

Like ordinary variables, arrays can also be passed to a function. To pass arrays to a function, it is sufficient to list the name of arrays *without any subscripts* or *brackets* as actual arguments. The corresponding formal arguments must be written in the same order and then be declared as array within the formal argument declarations. During declaration of array as a formal argument, the array name is written with a pair of empty square brackets. The size of the array *is not specified* within the square bracket in the formal argument declaration.

Suppose x is an integer array of size 50. If we calculate the maximum among n integers using a function, the declaration of function and array in main function is as follows.

```
main()
 {
   int n; /* declaration of variable */
   float max; /* declaration of variable */
   int x[50]; /* declaration of array */
   int maximum(int[],int); /* declaration of function */
   . . . . . . . . . . . . . . . . . . . . . . . . .
   . . . . . . . . . . . . . . . . . . . . . . . . .
   max=maximum(x,n); /* calling of function with actual arguments */
   . . . . . . . . . . . . . . . . . . . . . . . . .
   . . . . . . . . . . . . . . . . . . . . . . . . .
 }
```

The definition of the function maximum is shown below.

```
int maximum(y,m) /* function definition */
int m;           /* declaration of formal argument */
int y[];         /* declaration of formal argument (array) */
 {
   . . . . . .
   . . . . . .
 }
```

From the main function the function maximum is called with two actual arguments x and n. Observe that x appears as an ordinary variable. In the definition of function, it is observed that two formal arguments y and m are used. The formal arguments y and m are declared as integer array and integer variable. Thus, there is a correspondence between the formal and actual arguments.

The formal arguments can also be declared in the header of the function definition. For the function maximum, the header may be written as

```
int maximum(int y[], int m)
```

It is mentioned earlier that the arguments are passed to a function by *value*, when the formal arguments are ordinary variables. But, when an array is passed to a function, the values of the array elements *are not* passed to the function directly.

In this case, the *address* of the first array element is passed to the corresponding formal argument. That is, rather than passing the actual values of the array elements, a reference (called *pointer*) is passed to the function. Passing of argument in this way is called **passed by reference** rather than by value.

When the pointer of an array is passed to the function, the values of all elements of the array can be accessed by some memory management procedure.

Example 8.6.1 (Maximum and minimum) Write a program to find the maximum and minimum values among n numbers.

Solution. Let x be a floating point array and n be the number of elements from which the maximum and minimum are to be determined. Two functions maximum and minimum are defined to find the maximum and minimum values of the array x.

Program 8.2

```
/* Computation of maximum and minimum from the elements of an array */
#include<stdio.h>
main()
 {
  int i,n;
  float x[100],max,min; /* declaration of array and variables */
  float maximum(float[],int); /* declaration of function
                                     with type of arguments */
  float minimum(float[],int);
  printf("Enter array size\n");
  scanf("%d",&n);
  printf("Enter the elements of the array\n");
  for(i=0;i<n;i++) scanf("%f",&x[i]);
  max=maximum(x,n); /* calling of function */
  min=minimum(x,n); /* calling of function */
  printf("The maximum is %f\n",max);
  printf("The minimum is %f\n",min);
  return;
 }/* end of main function */

/* definition of the function maximum */
float maximum(float a[], int m) /* definition of function
                                      with two formal arguments */
 {
   int i; /* declaration of local variable */
   float max;
   max=a[0];
   for(i=1;i<m;i++)
      if(max<a[i]) max=a[i];
   return max;
 }/* end of the function maximum */

/* definition of the function minimum */
float minimum(float a[], int m)
 {
   int i; /* declaration of local variable */
   float min;
```

```
  min=a[0];
  for(i=1;i<m;i++)
     if(min>a[i]) min=a[i];
  return min;
 }/* end of the function minimum */
```

A sample of input/output:

```
Enter array size
7
Enter the elements of the array
-90 12 34 56 78 892 73
The maximum is 892.000000
The minimum is -90.000000
```

8.7 Recursion

We have seen that a function is called the main function and also mentions that from any function, one can call another function. Now, if a function is called from the same function, then the procedure is called **recursion**. A few high level languages support this facility. In recursion, a function calls *itself* repeatedly, until some termination condition has been satisfied.

This process reduces the effort to write a program to solve a problem. But, two criteria must be fulfilled to solve a problem using recursion.

(i) The problem must be expressed as a recursive form.

(ii) There must be a termination condition of repeated calls.

The very common example to illustrate the recursion is determination of $n!$. Normally, the value of $n!$ is determined by $n \times (n-1) \times \cdots \times 2 \times 1$. But, its recursive form is $n \times (n-1)!$. That is, the value of $n!$ depends on the value of $(n-1)!$, and the value of $(n-1)!$ depends on $(n-2)!$ and so on. That is, when the value of $(n-1)!$ is known, then one can calculate the value of $n!$. Also, we know that $1! = 1$. This is the termination condition for this problem.

The following program computes the value of $n!$ for a given n.

Example 8.7.1 ($n!$ using recursion) Calculate factorial of a positive integer n using recursion.

Program 8.3

```
/* Computation of n! using recursion */
#include<stdio.h>
main()
 {
  int n;
```

```
  long int fact(int n); /* function declaration */
  printf("Enter an integer ");
  scanf("%d",&n);
  printf("n!=%ld\n",fact(n)); /* calling of function fact from printf */
}
/* function definition */
long int fact(int n)
  {
     long int f;
     if(n<=1)
       return 1;
     else
       f=n*fact(n-1); /* function fact is called with argument n-1*/
  }
```

A sample of input/output:

```
Enter an integer
10
n!=3628800
```

Here, the function `fact` is declared as `long int`, because the value of factorial is large even for small value of n.

It is observed that the function `fact` is called `main` for a single time and it is called for $(n-1)$ times from itself. In each call, the value of actual argument of the function `fact` is reduced by 1. The repetition terminates, when the argument becomes 1. The body of the function is not simple like other functions. To illustrate the mechanism of this function, we assume that $n = 4$.

Since $n \neq 1$, the statement `f=n*fact(n-1)` will be executed with $n = 4$. That is, the value of `f` is

`f=4*fact(3);`

and `f` depends on the value of `fact(3)`. The value of `fact(3)` is evaluated using the formula

`f=3*fact(2);`

Here, also `fact(2)` is not known. Again, the function `fact` is called for $n = 2$. In this case,

`f=2*fact(1);`

Again, the function `fact` is called for $n = 1$. In this case, termination condition has been satisfied and `fact` returns 1. All the intermediate values of $n(= 3, 2, 1)$ are stored on a data structure called *stack*[1] until the termination condition has been satisfied. After reaching the termination condition, the actual value is returned according to the following reverse order.

[1]The **stack** is an order list of data structure in which all insertion and deletion are made in one end called top.

```
fact(1)=1
fact(2)=2*fact(1)=2×1=2
fact(3)=3*fact(2)=3×2=6
fact(4)=4*fact(3)=4×6=24
```

If a recursive function contains one or more local variables (the variables declared within the recursive function), then in each call a different set of local variables is created. The names of the local variables remain same (as they are declared) within the function, but their values form different set in each call. Each set of values are stored on the stack and they are used in appropriate reversed call.

Example 8.7.2 (Reverse an integer using recursion) Write a program that reads an integer from the keyboard and then calls a recursive function to print it out in reverse. For example, if the user enters 4762, it prints as 2674.

Solution. Let the number be N. Divide this number by 10. Print the remainder and reset N as $N/10$. Repeat this process until N becomes 0. The program is shown below.

Program 8.4

```
/* Program to reverse an integer using recursion */
#include<stdio.h>
void main()
 {
   int n;
   int rev(int);
   printf("Enter an integer ");
   scanf("%d",&n);
   printf("The reverse integer is ");
   rev(n);
 }
/* Function to reverse an integer */
int rev(int n)
 {
   int r;
   r=n%10; /* r is the remainder */
   printf("%d",r);
   n=n/10;
   if(n==0) return(0);
   rev(n);
 }
```

A sample of input/output:

```
Enter an integer
```

```
6543
The reverse integer is 3456
```

Example 8.7.3 (Computation of GCD) Write a recursive program to find the greatest common divisor (GCD) between two unsigned integers.

Solution. The detailed procedure to find GCD is given in Chapter 2. Here only the program is listed.

Program 8.5

```
/* Computation of GCD using recursion */
#include<stdio.h>
void main()
 {
   unsigned a,b;
   unsigned gcd(unsigned,unsigned);
   printf("Enter two positive integers\n");
   scanf("%u%u",&a,&b);
   printf("The GCD between %u and %u is %u",a,b,gcd(a,b));
 }
unsigned gcd(unsigned m, unsigned n)
 {
   unsigned r;
   r=m%n;
   if(r==0)
     return n;
   else
     gcd(n,r);
 }
```

A sample of input/output:

```
Enter two positive integers
500 356
The GCD between 500 and 356 is 4
```

The variables used in a C program are broadly categorized, depending on the place of their declaration, as **local** (or **internal**) and **global** (or **external**). The local variables are those which are declared within a particular function, while external variables are declared outside any function. The local variables are accessed within the function only where it is declared, where as the global variables can be accessed from any function within the program.

The use of local and global variables are illustrated in the following program.

Example 8.7.4 Write a program to find the sum and average of n numbers, without passing the array to the function.

Program 8.6

```
/* Computation of sum and average using global variable */
#include<stdio.h>
float x[100]; /* declaration of global array, before main() */
float sum(int); /* declaration of global function */
main()
 {
  int i,n;

  float average(int); /* declaration of local function */
  printf("Enter array size\n");
  scanf("%d",&n);
  printf("Enter the elements of the array\n");
  for(i=0;i<n;i++) scanf("%f",&x[i]);
  printf("The sum of the elements is %f\n",sum(n));
  printf("The average is %f\n",average(n));
  return;
 }/* end of main function */

/* definition of the function sum */
float sum(int n)
 {
   int i;
   float s=0; /* i,s are local variables */
   for(i=0;i<n;i++)
     s+=x[i]; /* use of global variable */
   return s;
 }/* end of the function sum */

/* definition of the function average */
float average(int n)
 {
   float ave;
   ave=sum(n)/n; /* calling of global function sum */
   return ave;
 }/* end of the function average */
```

A sample of input/output:

```
Enter array size
```

```
7
Enter the elements of the array
10 23.5 67.4 90.2 -87.3 45 23


The sum of the elements is 171.800003
The average is 24.542858
```

8.8 Storage Classes

Recall, when a function is called from `main` or any other functions, the space is allocated for the variables declared within the function. The values of the variables are stored within the allocated space for this function and when the function returns a value to the `main` or other calling functions, then the allocated space becomes free and as a result, all the variables declared within the function lose their values. But, the values of the variables of `main` (or other calling function) do not alter during execution of the called function. Thus, we observed that some variables are active and some are not. This leads to the concept of `scope` and `longevity` of the variables, while using function in a program. The scope of variable means, for what portion of the program a variable is available for its use, i.e. the variable is active. The longevity or lifetime means the period for which a variable retains its value during execution of a program, i.e. the variable is alive. To indicate the scope and longevity of variable, we have to mention the **storage class** of it. Thus, each C variable has a **data type** and a **storage class**.

There are four different storage classes in C. They are **automatic, external, static** and **register**. They are mentioned by the keywords `auto, extern, static` and `register` respectively.

Some variable declarations with storage class are shown below.

```
auto int x,y;
static int z;
extern char c;
register float a, b;
```

8.8.1 Global and local variables

All the C variables are broadly classified into two categories depending on their place of declaration. These are **local** (*internal*) and **global** (*external*).

The local variables are created and used in a particular function and they are useful only within the function where they are defined. Whereas global variables are created outside any function and they can be used by any function within the program. The values of global variables can be changed from any place of the program, but, the values of local variables can only be altered within the function, where it is defined.

The diagrammatic representation of global and local variables is shown in Figure 8.3.

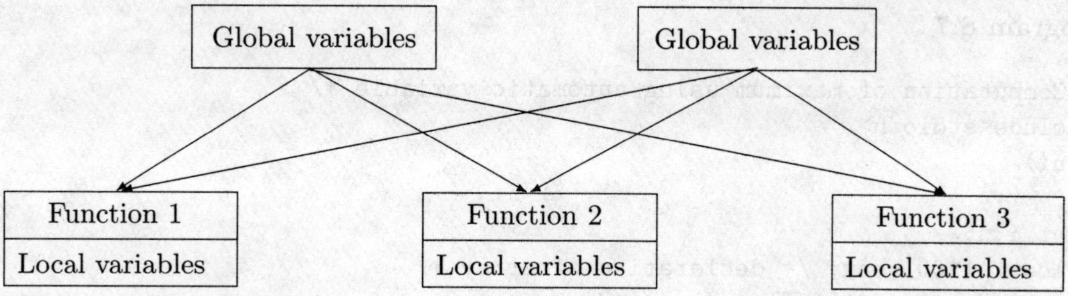

Figure 8.3: Use of global and local variables

8.8.2 Automatic variables

The automatic variables are local. They are created during function call and destroyed automatically when the execution of function is finished. This suggests the name. A variable declared within a function is recognized as an automatic variable unless a different storage class specification is mentioned. Thus, if a variable is used as automatic, the keyword `auto` is not required at the beginning of each variable.

For example, the variables x, y are automatic in the following functions

```
void sum()
  {
    int x, y;
    . . .
    . . .
  }
void sum()
  {
    auto int x, y;
    . . .
    . . .
  }
void sum()
  {
    auto int x;
    int y;
    . . .
    . . .
  }
```

The variables x, y are automatic in all these functions.

Example 8.8.1 (Use of auto variable) Write a program to find the maximum among n numbers. Use the concept of automatic variable.

Program 8.7

```
/* Computation of maximum using automatic variable */
#include<stdio.h>
main()
 {
  int i,n;
  float a[100],max; /* declaration of array */
  float maximum(float[],int); /* declaration of function
                              with type of arguments */
  printf("Enter array size\n");
  scanf("%d",&n);
  printf("Enter the elements of the array\n");
  for(i=0;i<n;i++) scanf("%f",&a[i]);
  max=maximum(a,n); /* calling of function */
  printf("The maximum is %f\n",max);
  return;
 }
/* definition of the function maximum */
float maximum(float a[], int m)
/* definition of function with two formal arguments */
 {
   auto int i; /* declaration of local variable */
   auto float max;
   max=a[0];
   for(i=1;i<m;i++)
     if(max<a[i]) max=a[i];
   return max;
 }
```

A sample of input/output:

```
Enter array size
7
Enter the elements of the array
10 140 311 334 -123 54 23
The maximum is 334.000000
```

Within the function maximum, the variables max and i are declared explicitly as automatic variables. By the declaration

```
float max;
int i;
```

the variables max and i, by default, are automatic variables. It may be remembered that the variable max declared in both the function main and maximum is not same though the name is same. When main starts its execution, a space for max (variable of main) is allocated. When the function maximum begins its execution, another space for max (variable of maximum) is allocated. In this time duration both max are active and occupies two different memory locations. When the function maximum exits, the memory allocated for max (variable of maximum) becomes free and then this max becomes inactive. But, the max declared in main is still alive and its allocated space remains unaffected. This variable becomes inactive, when the execution of main is finished. Similar fact is also true for the array a.

From this explanation one can conclude that the value assigned to automatic variable within a function will be lost, once the function is exited. Thus, in every call of a function, the initial values of all automatic variables are to be assigned or new values are to be stored. The automatic variables can assign initial values by including appropriate expressions.

8.8.3 External variables

The external variables are global, they are both active and alive during the execution of the whole program. Since external variables are global they can be accessed from any function within the program. Thus, if a value is assigned to an external variable within a function, or the value is changed by some expressions, then the new value can be used by another function, i.e. the value of an external variable is changed globally. The external variables are declared outside a function.

We know that a C function returns a single value only, two or more values can not be returned by a function. But, this can be done with the help of external variables.

The values of external variables are assigned in same way as internal variables.

Example 8.8.2 (Swapping) Write a program to interchange two values using function call.

Solution. Let x and y be two numbers. We have to interchange their values, i.e. x gets y value, and y gets x value. A third variable temp is used to do this. The basic idea is that the variable temp is to store the value of x and x copies the value of y and finally the value of temp is assigned to y.

Program 8.8

```
/* Program to interchange two values */
#include<stdio.h>
float x,y; /* global declaration */
main()
 {
   void swap(); /* the function does not return any value */
   printf("Enter two numbers \n");
   scanf("%f%f",&x,&y);
```

```
   printf("Before call x=%f  y=%f\n",x,y);
   swap();
   printf("After call x=%f  y=%f\n",x,y);
   return;
 }
void swap()
{
  float temp; /* x and y are changed globally */
  temp=x;
  x=y;
  y=temp;
}
```

A sample of input/output:

```
Enter two numbers
6785 984

Before call x=6785.000000  y=984.000000
After call x=984.000000 y=6785.000000
```

The swap interchanges two values and it returns two values implicitly with the help of global variables.

An array can also be declared as an external variable. The programmer should take care about the use of external/global variables, because the values of these variables can be modified from any place.

If a variable is declared as a global variable, that variable can also be used as a local variable. If a global variable, say x is redeclared within a function, then this variable becomes local within that function only and if the value of x is change within the function, it does not change the value of global x. For instance, let us consider the following example.

Program 8.9

```
/* Illustration of global and local variables */
#include<stdio.h>
int x; /* global x*/
main()
 {
   void funct();
   int y=5;
   x=y; /* global x changes its value */
   printf("First print from main x=%d\n",x);
   funct();
```

```
  printf("Second print from main x=%d\n",x);
}
void funct()
  {
    int x;   /* local declaration of x */
    x=10;    /* local change of x */
    printf("Print from the function x=%d\n",x);
  }
```

The output of this program is

```
First print from main x=5
Print from the function x=10
Second print from main x=5
```

Observe that the execution of the function `funct` does not change the value of global variable.

If the function `funct` is redefined as

```
 void funct()
  {
    x=10; /* global change of x */
    printf("Print from the function x=%d\n",x);
  }
```

then the output will be

```
First print from main x=5
Print from the function x=10
Second print from main x=10
```

8.8.4 Static variables

To solve a simple problem (the beginners are doing this) the entire program is generally written in a single file. This program is called **single-file** program. But, to solve a complex problem, the program is written in multiple files. These multifiles are combined later to make a single program (details about multifiles program discussed in Chapter 13). This type of program is called **multifiles** program. The role of static variables are different for single-file and multifile programs.

Now, we discuss static storage class for the single-file program. The static variables can be declared as local (automatic) variable as well as global (external) variable. If a static variable is declared within a function, then it has same scope as automatic variable, except the static variable retains its value throughout the life of the **program**. This means, if a function exits and reenters further, then the value of the static variable defined within the function retains its previous value.

The declaration, initialization and use of static variable are same as automatic variable. The keyword **static** must be used to declares a static variable. The following program illustrates the use of local static and local automatic variables.

Example 8.8.3 Write a program to illustrate local static and local automatic variables. Also, count the number of function calls.

Program 8.10

```
/*  Illustration of local static and local automatic variables */
#include<stdio.h>
main()
 {
   int i;
   void funct1();
   for(i=0;i<=4;i++)
      funct1();
 }

void funct1()
  {
    int x=0;                /* automatic variable */
    static int y=0;         /* static variable */
    static int count=0; /* static variable */
    x+=5;
    y+=2;
    count++;
    printf("%d %d %d \n",x,y,count);
  }
```

The values of `x`, `y` and `count` for each call of `funct1` are shown below. Here `x` is automatic variable whereas `y` and `count` are static variables.

i	x	y	count
0	5	2	1
1	5	4	2
2	5	6	3
3	5	8	4
4	5	10	5

Notice that at each call the value of `x` is initialized to 0 and by the execution of the statement `x+=5`, the value of `x` is changed to 5. But, for the first call of the function, the value of `y` and `count` are assigned to 0 and by the execution of the statements `y+=2` and `count++` the values of `y` and `count` become 2 and 1 respectively. In the second call, the initial values of y and count are taken as 2 and 1 respectively (not 0) and at the end they change to 4 and 2. In the third call, the starting value of y and count are 4 and 2 respectively, and at the end of this call, the values are changed to 6 and 3. It may be noted that the variable count determines the number of calls of the function funct1.

Example 8.8.4 (Fibonacci sequence) Write a program to generate Fibonacci sequence using function. The static variable may be used in the program.

Solution. The terms of Fibonacci sequence are defined as

$$f_0 = 1, f_1 = 1 \text{ and } f_n = f_{n-1} + f_{n-2} \text{ for } n \geq 2.$$

That is, the sum of two consecutive terms of Fibonacci sequence is the next term. Let f_1 and f_2 be two terms at any instant. Then, the next term of sequence is evaluated as $f = f_1 + f_2$, where initial values of f_1 and f_2 are 0 and 1 respectively. After finding f, reset $f_1 = f_2$ and $f_2 = f$. The program is shown below.

Program 8.11

```
/* Generation of Fibonacci sequence using static variable */
#include<stdio.h>
main()
 {
  int i,n;
  unsigned long int fibonacci(int);
  printf("How many Fibonacci numbers do you want ?\n");
  scanf("%d",&n);
  for(i=1;i<=n;i++)
     printf("F(%d)=%ld\n",i,fibonacci(i));
 }

/* function to calculate a Fibonacci number */
unsigned long int fibonacci(int i)
  {
   static unsigned long int f1=0,f2=1;
   unsigned long int f;
   if(i<3)
      f=1;
   else
      f=f1+f2;
   f2=f1;
   f1=f;
   return f;
  }
```

A sample of input/output:

```
How many Fibonacci numbers do you want
12

F(1)=0
F(2)=1
F(3)=1
F(4)=2
F(5)=3
F(6)=5
F(7)=8
F(8)=13
F(9)=21
F(10)=34
F(11)=55
F(12)=89
```

The `unsigned long int` is used to generate a large number members of Fibonacci sequence. Note on the static declaration. In the second and successive call of the function the values of `f1` and `f2` are taken as the values of previous call.

An external static variable is declared like external variable, i.e. it is declared outside any function including `main` function. This variable can also be accessed from any place. The static external variable is available only within the program file where it is defined. On the other hand, the simple external variable can be accessed by other program files (for multifiles program) also.

8.8.5 Register variables

Normally, the values of the variables used in a program are stored in the main memory of the computer during execution of the program. Another storing device is also available with a computer which is called `register`. Registers are special storage devices which are available with computer's CPU. Some registers are automatically used by computer during execution of a program to store different addresses, data, etc. However, user can use a very few number of registers to store the values of some variables.

The exact number of available registers depends on a particular computer and the C compiler. Generally, only *integer variables are stored in the register.* However, some compilers allow the register storage class with other types of variables having same word size.

A register variable can be declared as

```
register int list_of_variables;
```

For example,

```
register int a,b,x;
```

This statement declares that `a, b` and `x` are integer variables and their storage class is `register`. Hence, the values of `a, b` and `x` are stored in three registers rather than main memory.

Since the number of registers in a CPU is limited, any number of variables can not be accommodated in the registers. Moreover, if three variables are declared as register variables, but only two registers are available at this moment, then only two variables are stored in the registers and the value of the third variable will automatically store within the main memory of the computer. Thus, declaration of register variables does not guarantee that they are actually stored in registers. If the sufficient number of registers are not available at any instant, the remaining variables will be treated as the storage class automatic.

The scope of automatic and register variables are same. Like automatic variables, the register variables are also local, if they are declared within a function. The use of automatic and register variables are same except that the address operator (&) is not applicable for the register variable.

The advantage to use register variable is that the execution speed becomes higher than the use of non-register variable. Because, to read (write) a value from (to) register needs less time than to read (write) from (to) main memory.

The pointer declaration may also be permitted with storage class register. For example, the following declaration are allowed.

```
register int x;   /* variable declaration */
register int *pv; /* pointer declaration */
```

8.9 Worked Out Examples

Example 8.9.1 (Evaluation of function) Write a function to compute the value of $f(x)$ defined as

$$f(x) = \begin{cases} e^x, & x < 0 \\ \sin x, & 0 \leq x < 1 \\ \log_e x, & x \geq 1. \end{cases}$$

Then, use this function in the main segment to compute and print $f(x)$ for $x = -1$ to 2 with spacing 0.5 in tabular form.

Program 8.12

```
/* Evaluation of a function using function */
#include<stdio.h>
#include<math.h>
main()
 {
   float x;
   float f(float x);
   printf("~~~~~~~~~~~~~~~~~~\n");
   printf("  x          f(x)\n");
```

```
   printf("~~~~~~~~~~~~~~~~~\n");
   for(x=-1.0;x<=2.0;x+=0.5)
      printf(" %4.1f   %8.3f\n",x,f(x));
   printf("~~~~~~~~~~~~~~~~~\n");
 }
/* Definition of the function f(x) */
   float f(float x)
     {
       float fx;
       if(x<0)
          fx=exp(x);
       else if((0<=x) && (x<1))
          fx=sin(x);
       else
          fx=log(x);
       return fx;
     }
```

Output:

```
~~~~~~~~~~~~~~~~~
  x         f(x)
~~~~~~~~~~~~~~~~~
-1.0       0.368
 -0.5      0.607
  0.0      0.000
  0.5      0.479
  1.0      0.000
  1.5      0.405
  2.0      0.693
~~~~~~~~~~~~~~~~~
```

Example 8.9.2 Write a function to find the sum of three numbers and use it to compute the sum of nine numbers.

Solution. Let `SUM3(x,y,z)` compute the sum of the numbers x, y, z. Using it four times, we can compute the sum of nine numbers.

Program 8.13

```
/* Sum of nine numbers using function */
#include<stdio.h>
main()
```

```
{
  float a1,a2,a3,a4,a5,a6,a7,a8,a9;
  float u,v,w;
  float sum3(float,float,float);
  printf("Enter nine values\n");
  scanf("%f%f%f%f%f%f%f%f%f",&a1,&a2,&a3,&a4,&a5,&a6,&a7,&a8,&a9);
  u=sum3(a1,a2,a3);
  v=sum3(a4,a5,a6);
  w=sum3(a7,a8,a9);
  printf("Sum=%f\n",sum3(u,v,w));
}

/* Definition of the function sum3() */
  float sum3(float x, float y, float z)
    {
      return (x+y+z);
    }
```

A sample of input/output:

```
Enter nine values
3 5 10 30 15 -10 4 8 13

Sum=78.000000
```

Example 8.9.3 (Evaluation of determinant) Write a function to compute the value of a determinant of order 2 and use it to find the value of a determinant of order 3.

Solution. Let the determinant be

$$D = \begin{vmatrix} a_1 & b_1 & c_1 \\ a_2 & b_2 & c_2 \\ a_3 & b_3 & c_3 \end{vmatrix}.$$

Its value is

$$\begin{aligned} D &= a_1 \begin{vmatrix} b_2 & c_2 \\ b_3 & c_3 \end{vmatrix} - b_1 \begin{vmatrix} a_2 & c_2 \\ a_3 & c_3 \end{vmatrix} + c_1 \begin{vmatrix} a_2 & b_2 \\ a_3 & b_3 \end{vmatrix} \\ &= a_1.DET2(b_2, c_2, b_3, c_3) - b_1.DET2(a_2, c_2, a_3, c_3) \\ &\quad +c_1.DET2(a_2, b_2, a_3, b_3) \end{aligned}$$

where

$$DET2(a, b, c, d) = \begin{vmatrix} a & b \\ c & d \end{vmatrix} = a.d - b.c.$$

Program 8.14

```
/* Evaluation of determinant of order 3 using function */
#include<stdio.h>
 main()
 {
   float a1,b1,c1,a2,b2,c2,a3,b3,c3,det3;
   float det2(float,float,float,float);
   printf("ENTER THE ELEMENTS OF THE DETERMINANT ROW WISE\n");
   scanf("%f%f%f%f%f%f%f%f%f",&a1,&b1,&c1,&a2,&b2,&c2,&a3,&b3,&c3);
   det3=a1*det2(b2,c2,b3,c3)-b1*det2(a2,c2,a3,c3)+c1*det2(a2,b2,a3,b3);
   printf("The value of the determinant = %f\n",det3);
 }
 float det2(float a, float b, float c, float d)
   {
     return(a*d-b*c);
   }
```

A sample of input/output:

```
Enter the elements of the determinant row wise
3 4 5 8 9 1.4 9 -3 -4

The value of the determinant = -442.000000
```

Example 8.9.4 (Testing of unit matrix) Write a logical function to test whether a square matrix A is a unit matrix. Complete the program with appropriate output message.

Solution. A square matrix $A = [a_{ij}]_{n\times n}$ is a unit matrix, if $a_{ii} = 1$ and $a_{ij} = 0$ for $i \neq j, i, j = 1, 2, \ldots, n$. Initially, we subtract 1 from the diagonal elements, i.e. from $a_{ii}, i = 1, 2, \ldots, n$. Now, if all the elements are 0, then the matrix is a unit matrix.

Program 8.15

```
/* Testing of unity of a square matrix */
#include<stdio.h>
#define TRUE 1
#define FALSE 0
main()
 {
   float a[10][10];
   int n,i,j;
   int unit(float a[10][10],int n);
   printf("Enter the order and the elements of the matrix\n");
```

```
   scanf("%d",&n);
   for(i=0;i<n;i++)
      for(j=0;j<n;j++)
         scanf("%f",&a[i][j]);
   if(unit(a,n))
      printf("The matrix is unit\n");
   else
      printf("The matrix is not unit\n");
 }

/* Function to test unity of a square matrix */
int unit(float a[10][10],int n)
  {
    int i,j,flag;
    flag=1;
    for(i=0;i<n;i++)
       a[i][i]=a[i][i]-1.; /* subtract 1 from diagonal */
    for(i=0;i<n;i++)
       for(j=0;j<n;j++)
          if(a[i][j]!=0){
             flag=0;
             break;
       }
    return flag;
  }
```

A sample of input/output:

```
Enter the order and the elements of the matrix
3
2 22 12 23 11 10 20 22 21
The matrix is not unit
```

Example 8.9.5 (Formation of matrix) Write a function to generate a matrix A whose elements are given by

$$a_{ij} = \frac{5}{2^i + 3^j}; \qquad i = 1, 2, \ldots, m; \qquad j = 1, 2, \ldots, n.$$

Program 8.16

```
/* Generation of a specific matrix */
#include<stdio.h>
#include<math.h>
float a[10][10]; /* global declaration of the matrix */
```

```
/* function to generate matrix */
void matgen(int m, int n)
  {
    int i,j;
    for(i=1;i<=m;i++)
       for(j=1;j<=n;j++)
          a[i][j]=5.0/(pow(2,i)+pow(3,j));
  }

/* Main function */
main()
 {
   int m,n,i,j;
   printf("Enter the size of the matrix\n");
   scanf("%d%d",&m,&n);
   matgen(m,n);
   for(i=1;i<=m;i++)
      {
       for(j=1;j<=n;j++)
          printf("%6.3f ",a[i][j]);
       printf("\n");
      }
  return;
 }
```

A sample of input/output:

```
Enter the size of the matrix
6 4

 1.000  0.455  0.172  0.060
 0.714  0.385  0.161  0.059
 0.455  0.294  0.143  0.056
 0.263  0.200  0.116  0.052
 0.143  0.122  0.085  0.044
 0.075  0.068  0.055  0.034
```

Example 8.9.6 (Gamma function) Write a program to find $\Gamma(x)$ for any given x, $x > 0$.

Solution. The gamma function is generally denoted by $\Gamma(x)$ and is defined as

$$\Gamma(x) = \int_0^\infty e^{-t} t^{x-1}\, dx, \;\; x > 0.$$

The recurrence relation of this function is $\Gamma(x+1) = x\,\Gamma(x)$. (1)

The approximate value of $\Gamma(x)$ is obtained by computing the following finite series.

$$\Gamma(x) = 1 + c_1(x-1) + c_2(x-1)^2 + \cdots + c_8(x-1)^8, \quad 1 \le x \le 2 \qquad (2)$$

where

$$\begin{aligned} c_1 &= -0.577191652, & c_2 &= 0.988205891, \\ c_3 &= -0.897056937, & c_4 &= 0.918206857, \\ c_5 &= -0.756704078, & c_6 &= 0.482199394, \\ c_7 &= -0.193527818, & c_8 &= 0.035868343. \end{aligned}$$

When x lies between 1 and 2, then $\Gamma(x)$ is computed directly from (2). If $0 < x < 1$, then $\Gamma(x)$ may be computed by the relation

$$\Gamma(x) = \frac{\Gamma(x+1)}{x}. \qquad (3)$$

When x lies between 0 and 1, then $x+1$ lies between 1 and 2. In this case, $\Gamma(x)$ is computed using the relations (3) and (2).

When $x > 2$, then use (1) repeatedly until the argument of the function becomes less than 2 and then use (2) to compute $\Gamma(x)$. e.g.

$$\Gamma(5.2) = 4.2 \times 3.2 \times 2.2 \times 1.2 \times \Gamma(1.2)$$

and use (2) to compute $\Gamma(1.2)$.

The following program computes $\Gamma(x)$ for any $x > 0$.

Program 8.17

```
/* Program to evaluate gamma function for different values of x */
#include<stdio.h>
#include<math.h>
void main()
 {
   float x;
   float gamma(float); /* declaration of gamma function */
   printf("     x       Gamma(x)\n");
   for(x=0.5;x<=6.0;x+=0.5)
      printf("   %4.2f      %8.5f\n",x,gamma(x));
 }
/* Function to determine gamma(x) for any x */
float gamma(float x)
 {
   float gx,tx,rx,y;
   float gamma12(float x);
   if(x<=0) return (-1);
   if((0<x) && (x<1))
     gx=gamma12(x+1)/x;
   else if((1<=x) && (x<=2))
```

```
     gx=gamma12(x);
   else
     {
       rx=x-(int)x+1;
       tx=1.0;
       for(y=(x-1);y>=rx;y--)
          tx=tx*y;
       gx=tx*gamma12(rx);
     }
   return (gx);
 }
/* The function gamma12 which evaluates gamma(x)
   when x lies between 1 and 2, including 1, 2 */
float gamma12(float x)
  {
    float c[9],gx;
    int i;
    c[1]=-0.577191652;
    c[2]=0.988205891;
    c[3]=-0.897056937;
    c[4]=0.918206857;
    c[5]=-0.756704078;
    c[6]=0.482199394;
    c[7]=-0.193527818;
    c[8]=0.035868343;
    gx=1.0;
    for(i=1;i<=8;i++)
       gx+=c[i]*pow((x-1),i);
    return (gx);
  }
```

Output:

```
     x        Gamma(x)
   0.50        1.77245
   1.00        1.00000
   1.50        0.88623
   2.00        1.00000
   2.50        1.32934
   3.00        2.00000
   3.50        3.32335
   4.00        6.00000
   4.50       11.63173
```

```
5.00      24.00000
5.50      52.34278
6.00      120.00000
```

Example 8.9.7 (Reverse of a string) Write a recursive program to read a string of characters and display the characters in reverse order.

Program 8.18

```
/* Printing a string in reverse order using recursion */
#include<stdio.h>
void reverse(void); /* function prototype */
main()
 {
   printf("Enter a string\n");
   reverse(); /* call of function */
 }
void reverse(void)
 {
   char c;
   if((c=getchar()) !='\n')
        reverse(); /* recursive call of function */
   putchar(c);
 }
```

A sample of input/output:

```
Enter a string
```
Aniket's dob is 06.07.2001

```
  1002.70.60 si bod s'tekinA
```

Important Points

1. A function may or may not return a value. If it returns a value, then it can return only one value. The `void` function does not return any value.
2. Return type of the function in prototype declaration and function definition should be same otherwise a syntax error will be reported.
3. The number of arguments, their type and order in the calling function and function definition/declaration must be the same, otherwise syntax error will be reported.
4. The name of formal arguments and local variables must be different.

5. The return statement may return a constant or the value of a variable or an expression.
6. If the function is expected to return a value, the return statement must be used with a value. The statement `return;` is not acceptable.
7. If the return type of a function is `void`, trying to return a value is invalid.
8. A function cannot return any value without the use of return statement. If a function is declared as `void`, then it does not return any value and hence no return statement is required for this function.
9. Without `return` statement a function cannot return any value.
10. All the variables in the arguments list must be declared separately.
11. If a function has no arguments, the argument list must be declared as `void` or empty.
12. Do not put a semicolon at the end of the header of a function. It is not a syntax error.
13. Definition of function within the body of another function is not allowed.
14. The default return type of a function is an integer.
15. A user-defined function, which returns a value, can be used within a C expression.
16. If a function does not return any value, it cannot be assigned to any variable. It is used only as a stand-alone statement, conversely if a function returns a value, it cannot be used as a stand-alone statement.
17. A function may contain more than one `return` statements, and they can be placed any where in the program.
18. A function may be written any where within the program. Also, the functions may be written in any arbitrary order. However, it is suggested that the function `main` be placed at the beginning of the program. It is an user defined function, and the execution of the program begins from the `main` function.
19. The value of a global variable assigned/modified in a function remains unchanged, even if it has exited from the function. On the other hand, the value of the local variable is destroyed when it is exited from the function.
20. A local variable declared `static` retains its value even after the function is exited.
21. A global variable is visible only from the position of its declaration to the end of the program.
22. The global variables can be accessed from any where of the program and it is alive up to the end of the execution of the program.
23. The initial values are assigned to the static variables at the beginning of the program execution. Static variables are initialized at compile time only. The variables retain these values until the end of execution of the program, unless different values are assigned during the execution.
24. The default initial value of a static variable is 0. This is not allowed for other types of variables.

Exercise VIII

Review Questions

1. What is a function? List out the advantages and disadvantages of using a function.
2. The `main` is a user-defined function. How does it differ from other user-defined functions?
3. How function is declared within a program?
4. What do you mean by arguments of function (actual and formal arguments)? What is the relationship between the formal and actual arguments?
5. Can the names of the formal arguments within a function coincide with the names of other variables defined outside the function? Explain.
6. What are the main components of a function definition?
7. What is the purpose of the keyword `void`? Where is it used?
8. In C, can a function be called from more than one place within a program?
9. What do you mean by function prototype? Why is it necessary?
10. What are the differences between built-in function and user-defined function?
11. What do you mean by function call? What is their purpose? List the rules that apply to a function call.
12. What are the rules that govern the passing of arrays to function?
13. What is the purpose of the `return` statement?
14. Can an array be passed from a function to the calling portion of the program via a `return` statement?
15. When a multidimensional array is passed to a function, how are the formal argument declarations written?
16. Describe two methods of passing parameters to functions. Explain when they are suitable?
17. When passing an array to a function, how should the array argument be written? How is the corresponding formal arguments written?
18. How is an array name interpreted when it is passed to a function?
19. When passing an argument to a function, what is the difference between passing by value and passing by reference? To what types of arguments does each apply?
20. What are the differences between passing an array to a function and passing a single-valued data item to a function?
21. What is recursion? What are the advantages and disadvantages to use it?
22. When a program containing recursive function calls is executed, how are the local variables within the recursive function interpreted?

23. Distinguish between the following:
    (a) Actual and formal arguments.
    (b) `main` function and other user-defined functions
    (c) Library functions and user-defined fnctions
    (d) Global and local variables.
    (e) Automatic and static variables
    (f) Scope and longevity of variables.
24. How a global variable is declared in C?
25. What is meant by the storage class of a variable? Name the four storage class specification available in C.
26. What do you mean by scope of a variable within a program?
27. What is the use of an automatic variable? What is its scope? How is it defined and initialized?
28. Does an automatic variable retain its value, once control is transferred out of its defining function?
29. What is the use of an external variable? What is its scope? How is an external variable defined and initialized? What happens if an external variable definition does not include the assignment of an initial value?
30. What do you mean by static variable? What is the purpose of static variable and its scope?
31. What is the scope of static external variable?

Problems

1. Which of the following prototype declarations are invalid and why?
   (a) `void sum(int a, int &b);`
   (b) `float sum(float, float)`
   (c) `float sum(a,b,c);`
   (d) `float sum(float a,b,c);`
   (e) `sum(float a,float b,float c);`
   (f) `float sum(void,void);`
2. Which of the following header of a function is invalid and why?
   (a) `void sum(int a, int &b)`
   (b) `float sum(float, float)`
   (c) `float sum(a,b,c)`
   (d) `float sum(float a,b,c)`
   (e) `sum(float a,float b,float c);`
   (f) `float sum(void,void)`
   (g) `float sum(int a; int b)`
3. Each of the following is the header of a function definition. Explain the meaning of each.
   (a) `float S(float a, float b)` (b) `void f(void)`
   (c) `void S(float a, float b)` (d) `void f(int a, int b)`

4. Find error, if any, in the following functions definitions:

(a)

```
void g(int a, int b)
  {
    int x;
    x=a+b;
    return x;
  }
```

(b)

```
int g(int a, int b)
  {
    int x;
    x=a+b;
  }
```

(c)

```
int g(int a, int b)
  {
    float x;
    x=a+b;
    return x;
  }
```

(d)

```
void g(int a, int b)
  {
    x=a+b;
    return void;
  }
```

5. Determine the output of the following programs:

(a)

```
int diff(int,int);
main()
  {
    int c;
    c=diff(10,diff(20,30));
    printf("C=%d",c);
  }
int diff(int a, int b)
    {
      return (a-b);
    }
```

(b)

```
int mul(int a,int b);
main()
  {
    int c=10, d=20,p;
    p=mul(c,d)-mul(d,c);
    printf("p=%d",p);
  }
int mul(int a, int b)
    {
      return (a*b-1);
    }
```

(c)

```
int mul(int a, int b);
main()
 {
   int c=10, d=20,x;
```

(d)

```
int f(int);
main()
  {
    int a,x;
```

```
    x=(int)(sqrt(mul(c,c)+mul(d,d)));
    printf("x=%d",x);
  }
int mul(int a, int b)
  {
    return (a*b);
  }
```

```
  for(x=1;x<=5;x++){
     a=f(x);
     printf("a=%d",a);
  }
}
int f(int a)
   {
     int b=0;
     b+=a;
     return(b);
   }
```

(e)

```
int f(int);
main()
 {
   int a,x;
   for(x=1;x<=5;x++){
   a=f(x);
   printf("a=%d",a);
  }
 }
int f(int a)
{
  static int b=0;
  b+=a;
  return(b);
}
```

Programming Problems

1. Write a function to find the product of two square matrices of order $n \times n$ and use this to compute
(i) the matrix function

$$e^A = I + A + \frac{A^2}{2!} + \frac{A^3}{3!} + \cdots + \frac{A^n}{n!} + \cdots$$

by summing the first 50 terms of the series.
(ii) the matrix polynomial

$$R = 5I + 8A - 2A^2 + 8A^3 + 5A^4$$

where I is a unit matrix of order $n \times n$.

2. Write a function to find the product $\sum_{i=1}^{n} A(i)B(i)$ of two vectors $A(i)$ and $B(i)$, $i = 1, 2, \ldots, n$, and use it to find the value of

$$R = \sum_{i=1}^{n} [A(i)B(i) + B(i)C(i) + C(i)A(i)].$$

3. Write a function to test whether a square matrix A is orthogonal. [A square matrix A is said to be orthogonal, if $AA^T = I$, where A^T represents the transpose of A and I is a unit matrix.]
4. Write a function to find the sum (product) of four numbers and use it to find the sum (product) of sixteen numbers.
5. Write a function to find the maximum (minimum) among three numbers and use it to find the maximum (minimum) among nine numbers.
6. Write a function to test whether a matrix is null (symmetric). If it is null (symmetric), then the value of the function will be 1, otherwise, the value will be 0. Complete the program to test the matrix.
7. Write a function `sump` to find the value of the expression $\sum_{i=1}^{n} x_i^p$ with the array x_i and p (a positive integer) as dummy arguments. Use it to find the value of

   (i) $S1 = \sum_{i=1}^{n} x_i$, (ii) $\bar{x} = \frac{1}{n}\sum_{i=1}^{n} x_i$, (iii) $S2 = \sum_{i=1}^{n} x_i^2$,

   (iv) $S3 = \sum_{i=1}^{n} x_i^3$ and (v) $S = \frac{1}{n}\sum_{i=1}^{n} (x_i - \bar{x})^2$.
8. Write a function to compute the gamma function from the approximation $\Gamma(x + 1) = 1 - 0.574865x + 0.95123x^2 - 0.699859x^3 + 0.42455x^4 - 0.101068x^5$, for $0 \le x \le 1$. Use this function to find the value of $\Gamma(x)$ for any x (>0). [The relation $\Gamma(x + 1) = x\Gamma(x)$ may be used]
9. Write a function to generate a matrix A whose elements are given by

   (i) $a_{ij} = 2^{i+j}; i, j = 1, 2, \ldots, n$

   (ii) $a_{ij} = \dfrac{4}{2^i + 3^j}; i = 1, 2, \ldots, m; j = 1, 2, \ldots, n.$
10. Write a function `norm` to find the norm of a vector $x_i, i = 1, 2, \ldots, n$ (the norm ($||x||$) of a vector x is $||x|| = \sqrt{\left(\sum_{i=1}^{n} x_i^2\right)}$. Write a complete program to read two vectors x_i and y_i, $i = 1, 2, \ldots, n$, and verify the relation $||x + y|| \le ||x|| + ||y||$.
11. Write a function defining $div(x, y) = \frac{x^2 - y^2}{x^2 + y^2}$ and use this function to compute (i) $\alpha = \frac{1-a^2}{1+a^2}$, (ii) $\beta = 3\sin^{-1}\left(\log\frac{(a+b)^2 - c^2}{(a+b)^2 + c^2}\right)$.

12. Write a function to find the value of $\sin x = x - \frac{x^3}{3!} + \frac{x^5}{5!} - \cdots$, for a given x (in degree). Use this function to find the value of $\sin x$ for $x = -90^o$ to 90°, with spacing of 10°, and print the result in a tabular form.
13. Let $A = [a_{ij}]_{n\times n}$ be a two dimensional array. Write two functions, one of which will compute the sum $\displaystyle\sum_{k=1}^{n} a_{ik}$, $i = 1, 2, \ldots, n$, and the other will compute the sum of product $\displaystyle\sum_{k=1}^{n} a_{ik}a_{jk}; i, j = 1, 2, \ldots, n$. Use them to compute

$$\theta_{ij} = \cos^{-1} \frac{\sum_{k=1}^{n} a_{ik}a_{jk}}{\sqrt{\sum_{k=1}^{n} a_{ik}}\sqrt{\sum_{k=1}^{n} a_{jk}}}; i, j = 1, 2, \ldots, n.$$

14. Write a function that computes the expression $a^x + b^y$, and use it to compute the following expressions:
(i) $dist = (\sqrt{x+5} + \sqrt{y-3})^2$
(ii) $a = \frac{p^r+q^s}{q^r+p^s} + \frac{x^2+y^2}{x^3-y^3}$
(iii) $t = \sin(x^a) + (1 + x^a)$.
15. Write a function GCD(i, j) to find the greatest common divisor of two integers i, j. Use this function to find the G.C.D among a finite set of integers (say 50). [The following relation may be used: if n =GCD$(m_1, m_2, \ldots, m_k)$, then GCD$(m_1, m_2, \ldots, m_k, m_{k+1})$
= GCD(n, m_{k+1}).]
16. Write a function to calculate the inner product $a_1b_1 + a_2b_2 + \cdots + a_nb_n$ of two vectors a_i and $b_i, i = 1, 2, \ldots, n$. Use this function to compute the value of

$$\frac{\sqrt{x_1^2 + x_2^2 + \cdots + x_n^2}\sqrt{y_1^2 + y_2^2 + \cdots + y_n^2}}{\sqrt{x_1y_1 + x_2y_2 + \cdots + x_ny_n}}.$$

17. Write a function to calculate $\sqrt{x^2 + y^2 + z^2}$ and use it to compute the values of $p = \sqrt{(u-1)^2 + (v-2)^2 + (w-3)^2}$, $q = \frac{1}{\sqrt{u^2+v^2+w^2}}$, $r = \sqrt{u^4 + 9v^2 + 16w^2}$, $s = \sqrt{5u^2}\sqrt{3v^2}\sqrt{7w^2}$,
$t = \sqrt{x^2 + y^2 + \sqrt{1 + u^2 + v^2}}$.
18. Write a recursive program to read a string and reverse it.
19. The Legendre polynomials are defined by $P_0 = 1, P_1 = x$, and

$$P_n = \frac{2n-1}{n} x P_{n-1} - \frac{n-1}{n} P_{n-2}$$

where $n = 2, 3, 4, \ldots$ and x is a floating-point number which lies between -1 and 1. Write a recursive program to generate n Legendre polynomials for given n and x.

Chapter 9

Pointers

It is well known that every variable occupies one or more memory locations (cells) to store its value. A single cell can store one byte of information. A single character needs one byte space, so it can store in a single memory cell. An integer needs two bytes space, to store it two contiguous memory cells are required. A floating point number needs four contiguous cells. Each memory cell is recognized by a number associated with it, called **address** of the memory cell. The addresses of cells are usually done by hexadecimal numbers starting from 0. The compiler assigns the memory cells for all variables used in the program, without knowledge of the user and forms a table containing variable names and their address, called hash table. Thus, during the execution of a program computer determines the address of a variable from hash table and then finds the value of the variable from the located address. Therefore, with each variable two quantities are associated – one is the value of the variable and other is the address of the memory cell where the value is stored. If a variable needs more than one cell to store it, then the address of the variable means the address of the first cell. The value stored in a cell is called its **content**.

The use of pointers in a program has a lot of advantages as discussed below.

(i) Using pointer one can return multiple values from a function.

(ii) The pointer variables, arrays, structures, etc. can be destroyed after their use. The space occupied by them becomes free and can be reused.

(iii) A function can be passed to another function with the help of pointer.

(iv) Use of pointers in character strings saves the storage space in memory.

(v) C supports dynamic memory allocation and it is possible with the help of pointers.

(vi) The data structures, viz. structures, stacks, queues, linked lists, trees, etc. are implemented using pointers.

(vii) Use of pointers in a program increases the execution time and hence reduces the running time.

In C, one can easily determine the address of a variable. The technique and related topics regarding the address of a variable are discussed in the next section.

9.1 Address Operator

Suppose v is a variable. The address of this variable is obtained by the expression,

$$\&v$$

where & is a unary operator, called the **address operator** and read as **address of**. The address of a variable can store to another variable. For example, the statement

$$pv = \&v;$$

stores the address of the variable `v` to the variable `pv`. This variable `pv` is called a **pointer** to `v`, as it points to the location where `v` is stored. The variable `pv` is called **pointer variable**, that is, a pointer variable is a variable whose value is the address of another variable. It may be noted that `pv` stores the address of `v` and not its value. A pointer `points` to another variable. The content of a memory cell, i.e. the value (of `v`) stored in a memory cell is obtained by the expression

$$*pv$$

where $*$ is a unary operator, called the **indirection operation**. Thus, we have seen two pointer operators `&` and `*`. `&` gives the address of a variable and `*` retrieves the value pointed to by the pointer.

Thus, three elements are associated with a pointer variable, they are
(i) pointer variable,
(ii) value of the variable, and
(iii) address of the variable.

The following program illustrates the use of address operator.

```
#include<stdio.h>
void main()
 {
     int i=100;
     float a=7.5;
     char c='b';
     printf("Address of i=%x and its value =%d\n",&i,i);
     printf("Address of a=%x and its value =%f\n",&a,a);
     printf("Address of c=%x and its value =%c\n",&c,c);
 }
```

The output of this program is

```
Address of i=fff4 and its value =100
Address of a=fff0 and its value =7.500000
Address of c=ffef and its value =b
```

Note that the addresses of the variables `i`, `a` and `c` may be changed for other computer or different runs, since the addresses printed above are available for a particular moment for a particular computer. The free addresses depend on many factors, such as, size of operating system, other programs stored in the memory, the data and program sizes of current program, etc. The values 100, 7.500000, b are the contents of the memory address `fff4`, `fff0`, `ffef` respectively. The addressing of memory cells is done by using hexadecimal integers. But, it is not an integer type data, it is a completely separate data type. The contents and addresses are shown in Figure 9.1.

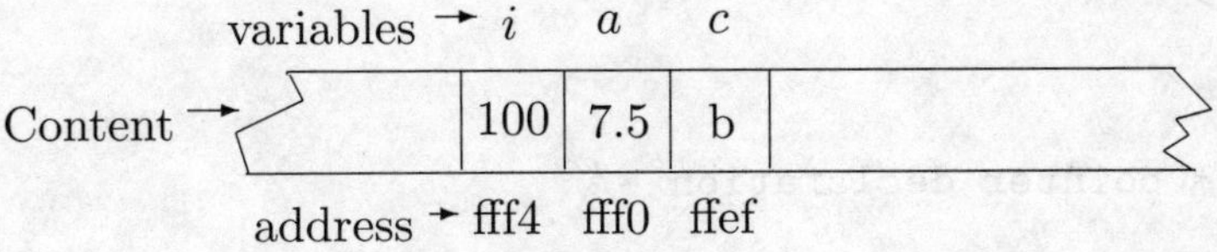

Figure 9.1: Addresses and contents of variables.

9.2 Pointer Declaration

Like other variables, each pointer variable must be declared before its use. The rules for declaration of a pointer variable are similar to that of an ordinary variable. The difference is that, when a pointer variable is declared, the variable name must be preceded by an asterisk (*). The asterisk makes a difference between the ordinary variable and the pointer variable. The general form of pointer declaration is

`data_type *ptvar;`

where `ptvar` is the name of the pointer variable and `data_type` is any one of the C data types like `int`, `long`, `char`, `float`, etc. Note that `ptvar` is the pointer, its value is the address of certain memory location and it is a hexadecimal number. Whereas `*ptvar` is the value stored at the address `ptvar`. So, the value of `*ptvar` is either an `int` or `long` or `char` and so on, which is same as `data_type`.

The pointer operator * has two meanings, explained in the following example.

```
int a, b, *pa;  /* here * say "pointer to" */
pa=&a;          /* address of a is stored to pa */
b=*pa;    /* here * say "value at" or "value pointed to by" */
```

Note that the last two statements are equivalent to `b=a;`

During declaration of pointer variables, the unary operator * can appear in any position between the data type and the pointer variable name. Following declarations are all valid.

```
int *v;
int* v;
int * v;
```

The pointer variables and ordinary variables can be declared together, i.e. the following statements are valid.

```
int a, b, *pv, *pu;
float *a, *b, x, y;
```

The first type declaration is popular and is convenient for multiple declarations.

Let us consider the following program to illustrate the use of a pointer variable.

Program 9.1

```
/* Illustration of pointer variable */
#include<stdio.h>
main()
 {
   int *ptvar; /* pointer declaration */
   int u, v;
   u=10;
   v=50;
   printf("Value of ptvar=%X\n",ptvar);
   ptvar=&u; /* address of u is assigned to the pointer ptvar */
   printf("Value of ptvar=%X and its content=%d\n",ptvar,*ptvar);
   ptvar=&v; /* address of v is assigned to the pointer ptvar */
   printf("Value of ptvar=%X and its content=%d\n",ptvar,*ptvar);
   *ptvar=500;  /* 500 is assigned as content of ptvar */
   printf("Value of ptvar=%X and its content=%d\n",ptvar,*ptvar);
 }
```

The output of this program is

```
Value of ptvar=3C2
Value of ptvar=FFF4 and its content=10
Value of ptvar=FFF2 and its content=50
Value of ptvar=FFF2 and its content=500
```

Initially, the values of `u` and `v` are 10 and 50 respectively and the values of `u` and `v` are stored in some memory locations. The value of `ptvar` is 3C2 (in the current execution, it may be changed in another execution). The statement `ptvar=&u` copied the address of `u` to the pointer variable `ptvar` and it is changed to FFF4. And the subsequent `printf` function prints the content of the address FFF4, i.e. the value of `u`. The statement `ptvar=&v` assigns the address of `v` to the pointer variable `ptvar` and hence the `printf` function prints the contents of `ptvar` (FFF2) which is 50. The statement `*ptvar=500` assigns the numeric value 500 to the content of `ptvar`, does not change the value of `ptvar`. The value of `ptvar` remains the same (FFF2), see the last print statement.

Note that the initialization of pointer is a very sensitive task. Arbitrary initialization may cause a serious error in the program, as the value of a pointer variable is unpredictable, it depends on computer, execution instant, etc. However, we can assign null pointer as

```
#define NULL 0
float *ptvar=NULL;
```

The variable ptvar is initially assigned a value 0 to indicate some special task.

9.3 Pointer Expressions

Like ordinary variables, the pointer variables are also used in the arithmetic and logical expressions. The followings are the examples of pointer variables in arithmetic expression. Besides, pointers can also be compared using the relational operators. The expressions pu>pv, pu==pv, pu!=pv where pu and pv are pointer variables, are allowed. But, comparison of pointers that refer to different and unrelated variables makes no sense. Also, division and multiplication of a pointer by another pointer or an integer are not allowed, i.e. pu*pv, pu/pv, pu/5, pu*5 are *not valid.*

```
int *pv, v=10, u=5;
pv=&v; /* address of v is assigned to pv,
          thus the value of *pv becomes 10 */
*pv+=2; /* the value of *pv changed to 10+2=12 */
v=u* *pv; /* the value of v=5*12=60 */
v=*pv * 8; /* v=480 */
```

The value of *pv after second line becomes 10 (=v). In third line, the content of pv, i.e. the value of *pv is changed to 12. The value of v (in the fourth line) is $5 * 12 = 60$. That is, the content of &v is also changed to 60. Thus, the content of pv is changed to 60. That is, the value of *pv is now 60 (not 12). Therefore, the statement v=*pv*8 changes the value of v to 480.

9.4 Void Pointer

It is seen that a pointer variable can hold the address of same type of data. That is, an integer pointer variable can hold only the address of an integer variable, it does not hold the address of any other types of variables. This fact is illustrated in the following.

```
int *ipv;
float x;
ipv=&x; /* illegal assignment */
```

The assignment ipv=&x is not valid as ipv is an integer pointer variable, whereas x is a floating point variable. To store the value of x needs four bytes space, while two bytes space is allocated for ipv.

The void pointer eliminates this restriction. If a pointer variable is declared as void, then any type of pointer assignment can be done with this variable. For example,

```
void *vptr;
int i;
char c;
float f;
vptr=&i;
vptr=&c;
vptr=&f;
```

All these assignments are valid. But, when arithmetic operations are done on the contents of pointer variables, it must be suitably type cast to the required data type.

9.5 Passing Pointers to a Function

Like ordinary variables, pointers can also be passed to a function as arguments, i.e. an address is passed as arguments. This process is referred as passing arguments by **reference** or by **address**. When an argument is passed by value to a function, then the actual argument is copied to the formal argument. If the values of this formal argument is changed within the function, it does not alter the value of the actual argument as formal arguments are local within the function. But, when an argument is passed by reference, then the address of the variable is passed to the function. Since the address of a memory location is unique, therefore the content of the passing address can be accessed from any place (from the function and also from the calling function). Thus, any change in the content of an address can be identified from any place, i.e. the content of a data item are changed globally.

In formal pointer arguments declaration, each argument must be preceded by an asterisk. It is obvious that the actual arguments are the addresses of the variables.

The following example illustrates the use of transfer of arguments by reference.

Example 9.5.1 (Swapping) Write a program to interchange the values of two variables using pointers.

Solution. A function in C can not return more than one value. But, to interchange the values of two variables using function we have to return two values, it is not possible by passing values. This can be done by passing reference as shown below.

Program 9.2

```
/* Program to interchange two values using pointer */
#include<stdio.h>
main()
 {
   float a,b;
   void swap(float *, float*); /* declaration of function */
   printf("Enter two values\n");
   scanf("%f%f",&a,&b);
```

```
  printf("The given values are a=%f b=%f\n",a,b);
  swap(&a,&b);
  printf("The changed values are a=%f b=%f\n",a,b);
  return;
 }
/* u and v are declared as pointer variables */
 void swap(float *u, float *v)
  {
    float *temp;
    *temp=*u;
    *u=*v;
    *v=*temp;
  }
```

The input/output of this program is shown below.

```
Enter two values
89.44999 456.32

The given values are a=89.449990 b=456.320000
The changed values are a=456.320000 b=89.449990
```

In the function swap all the variables u, v and temp are pointers. The addresses of a and b are passed to swap and they are copied as u and v respectively. Then, the contents of u and v are interchanged and hence the values of a and b are interchanged.

9.5.1 Returning pointer from functions

A function normally returns a single value. The multiple values are also returned through pointer parameters. A function can also return a pointer to the calling function rather than its value. The following program (determines maximum among three elements) illustrates the use of this feature.

Program 9.3

```
/* Determines maximum among three integers using pointers */
#include<stdio.h>
void main()
 {
  int *max(int *,int *, int *); /* function passes integer pointers
                                   and returns integer pointer */
  int a=30,b=60,c=10,*big;
  big=max(&a,&b,&c); /* function call, passing addresses
                         of a,b,c; big is a pointer */
  printf("Max. is %d",*big); /* max. stored at the address of big */
 }
```

```
int *max(int *x,int *y,int *z) /* receive pointers */
 {
   int *largest;
   *largest=*x; /* assigns value of a */
   if(*largest<*y) *largest=*y; /* assigns value of b */
   if(*largest<*z) *largest=*z;/* assigns value of c */
   return(largest); /* returns address of the largest value,
                          either address of a, b or c */
 }
```

The following function (max) can also be used to find maximum.

```
int *max(int *x,int *y,int *z) /* receive pointers */
 {
  int *largest;
  largest=x; /* assigns address of a */
  if(*largest<*y) *largest=*y; /* assigns address of b */
  if(*largest<*z) *largest=*z;/* assigns address of c */
  return(largest); /* returns address of the largest value,
                         either address of a, b or c */
 }
```

The function max receives the addresses of the variables a, b and c and store them to the pointers x, y and z. The function max determines the maximum among the values *x, *y, *z stored in the addresses x, y and z and return the address (as largest) of the maximum value, and not the value itself.

9.5.2 Passing array to a function

It is already discussed how an array can be transferred to a function. Since the array name of an array is itself a pointer, the array's name is sufficient to use as an actual argument, no ampersand sign is required preceding array name. Thus, if a is an array of size n, then this array can be transferred to the function sum by the statement

```
sum(a);
```

In this call the address of the base element, i.e. address of the element a[0] is passed as reference to the function, and the entire array is passed to the function. The first line of the function definition must be of the form

```
float sum(float *x)
```

Also, one can pass a portion of an array, rather entire array to a function by passing the address of an appropriate array element. Suppose a is an array of size 50 and if we pass a[20] to a[49] (last element) to the function sum, then the following call is necessary.

```
sum(&a[20]);
```

In this call, the elements a[20] to a[49] are available for the function sum. Here it is noted that the address of the element a[20] is passed to the function.

A function can also return a pointer. This can be done by appropriate function declaration.

9.6 Arithmetic on Pointer Variables

The arithmetic operations, such as addition (+), subtraction (-), increment (++) and decrement (--) can be performed on pointer variables under some restrictions. The values of these operations on pointer variables depend on the size of the data type of the pointer variable. Normally, the memory requirement for character, integer, floating point and double type variables are 1 byte, 2 bytes, 4 bytes and 8 bytes respectively. An integer can be added to (or subtracted from) a pointer variable. But, *the operations addition, subtraction, division, multiplication can not be performed between pointer variables.* The increment and decrement operations are valid on pointer variables. The increment and decrement operators give some interesting values. For example, let us consider the declaration.

```
float *v;
int *a;
```

Now, the operation `a++` increases the address of `a` by *two*, not *one* and `v++` increases the address of `v` by *four*, not *one*. If the value of `v` is 8F80FFF2, then value of `v+5` is 8F800006. The value of the expression is 20 bytes (4 bytes for float × 5 for addition of 5) more than the value of `v`. Similarly, the value of `a-3` is 6 (2 bytes for int × 3) units less than `a`. That is, if the value of `a` is 8F80FFF0, then the value of `a-3` is 8F80FFEA.

The following program illustrates the pointer arithmetic.

Program 9.4

```
/* Illustration of pointer arithmetic */
#include<stdio.h>
void main()
{
  int *i1,*i2;
  float *f1,*f2;
  clrscr();
  printf("Before increment: i1=%X, f1=%X\n",i1,f1);
  i1++; f1++;
  printf("After  increment: i1=%X, f1=%X\n",i1,f1);
  i1=i2+2; f1=f2-3;
  printf("i1=%X, i2=%X\n",i1,i2);
  printf("i1-i2=%d\n",i1-i2);
  printf("f1=%X, f2=%X\n",f1,f2);
  printf("f1-f2=%d\n",f1-f2);
  printf("(i1-i2)=%d bytes\n",(char*)i1-(char*)i2);
  printf("(f1-f2)=%d bytes\n",(char*)f1-(char*)f2);
}
```

Output:

```
Before increment: i1=754, f1=766
After  increment: i1=756, f1=76A
i1=14D1, i2=14CD
i1-i2=2
f1=3BA, f2=3C6
f1-f2=-3
(i1-i2)=4 bytes
(f1-f2)=-12 bytes
```

Here the values of `i1` and `f1` are incremented by 2 bytes and 4 bytes as explained before. 2 is added to `i2` and stored in `i1` and 3 is subtracted from `f2` and the result is stored in `f1`. These are valid pointer arithmetics. The result is in units of the size of the data type is being pointed to. That is, the value of `i1` is increased by 2 units (1 unit = size of (`int`)) and that of `f1` is decreased by 3 units (here 1 unit = size of (`float`)). The value of `i1-i2` is 2 (units) and `f1-f2` is −3 (units), not actual bytes. Note that the values of `i1-i2` and `f1-f2` are printed, but the subtraction between pointers is not allowed. This mean the assignment `i3=i1-i2` (`i3` points to an integer) is not valid. To get the difference `i1-i2` and `f1-f2` in bytes, type cast operators are used to the pointers, into `char` pointers. Thus, the expressions `(char*) i1-(char*) i2` and `(char*) f1-(char*) f2` give the difference of `i1-i2` and `f1-f2` in bytes.

The pointer arithmetic cannot be performed on `void` pointers, as they have no data type associated with them.

Some valid and invalid pointer arithmetics are given below.

`int *u, *v, c;`	
`u=v-c;`	valid
`v=v+c;`	valid
`u=u-v;`	non-portable pointer conversion
`u=(int*)(u-v);`	valid
`v=u+v`	invalid pointer addition
`u=(int*)(u+v);`	invalid pointer addition
`u=u-v-c;`	non-portable pointer conversion
`u=(int*)(u-v)+c;`	valid
`u=-v;`	illegal use of pointer
`u>>1;`	illegal use of pointer
`u=u*v;`	illegal use of pointer
`u=u*c;`	illegal use of pointer
`u=u/v;`	illegal use of pointer
`u=u/c;`	illegal use of pointer
`u=c/u;`	illegal use of pointer

9.7 Pointers and One-Dimensional Array

Now, we extended the idea of arithmetic on pointers to array. Recall that the address of the first element of an array is the address of the entire array. Thus, if a is an integer array (one-dimension), then the address of the first element is given by either &a[0] or by simply a.

The address of a[0] is called the base address of the array. That is, the array name (without a subscript) is a pointer value. Here a is a pointer constant and always contains the address of the first element (a[0]). For example,

```
int *pa;
pa=&a[0];
pa=a;
```

The last two lines assign the same address.

The address of the second element is obtained by &a[1] or by a+1. In general, the address of the $(i+1)$th element of the array a can be determined either from the expression &a[i] or from the expression a+i, where i is called the **offset**.

One important point is that the array elements are always stored in contiguous memory locations irrespective of the size of the array. That is, if the address of a[0] (a is an integer array) is FFF0, then the address of the element a[1] is FFF2, that of a[2] is FFF4, and so on. In general, a pointer when incremented, always points to a location after skipping the number of bytes required for the data type pointed by it. That is, address of

a[i]= address of a[0] + i $\times$ size of (data type of a).

If a is an integer array, then address of a[5]= address of a[0] $+5\times2 = 500+10 = 510$, assumed that address of a[0] is 500.

The following program illustrates the above fact.

```
#include<stdio.h>
main()
 {
   int a[]={10,12,8,5};
   int i, *pa;
   pa=&a[0]; /* address of the array is assigned to pa */
   for(i=0;i<4;i++)
      {
        printf("%X  %d  %X \n",pa,*pa,a+i);
        pa++;  /* pointer incremented */
      }
 }
```

The output of this program is

```
FFEE   10   FFEE
```

```
FFF0    12    FFF0
FFF2    8     FFF2
FFF4    5     FFF4
```

Note the output. The first and third columns are identical. This means, the address of an array element can be obtained by incrementing pointer variable and also by simple addition of the position (i.e. subscript) of the array element with array name. The status of the memory, its contents and array elements are shown in Figure 9.2.

Address		FFEE	FFF0	FFF2	FFF4	
Content	......	10	12	8	5	......
Variable		a[0]	a[1]	a[2]	a[3]	

Figure 9.2: The array elements, corresponding address and the contents.

It is very interesting that, if the address of the first element of the array `a` is FFF0 (say), then the value of the expression `a+2` is not necessarily FFF2, it may be FFF4 or FFF8 or something else depending on the data type of the array `a`. The value of the expression `a+i` will automatically be determined by the C compiler, without the knowledge of user regarding the number of memory cells required for different data types.

Thus `&a[i]` and `(a+i)` both represent the same memory address for the $(i+1)$th element of the array `a`, and `a[i]` and `*(a+i)` both represent the contents (i.e. the value of the $(i+1)$th element) of the same address. These two terms are interchangeable. It may be noted that the pointer accessing method is much faster than array indexing.

The following program illustrates the relationship between the array elements and their address.

Program 9.5

```
/* Illustration of relationship between array elements
   and their address */
#include<stdio.h>
main()
 {
    int a[5]={10,12,20,25,30};
    int i;
    for(i=0;i<5;i++)
       {
         /* printing of values */
         printf("a[%d]=%d  *(a+%d)=%d",i,a[i],i,*(a+i));
         /* printing of address */
         printf("&a[%d]=%X  (a+%d)=%X\n",i,&a[i],i,(a+i));
```

```
        pa++;  /* pointer incremented */
    }
}
```

The output of the above program is shown below.

```
a[0]=10  *(a+0)=10  &a[0]=FFEC  (a+0)=FFEC
a[1]=12  *(a+1)=12  &a[1]=FFEE  (a+1)=FFEE
a[2]=20  *(a+2)=20  &a[2]=FFE0  (a+2)=FFE0
a[3]=25  *(a+3)=25  &a[3]=FFE2  (a+3)=FFE2
a[4]=30  *(a+4)=30  &a[4]=FFE4  (a+4)=FFE4
```

From this output, it is observed that `a[i]` and `&a[i]` are different, first one represents the value and second one represents the address of the $(i+1)$th element. Similarly, `*(a+i)` and `(a+i)` are also different, `*(a+i)` represents the value and `a+i` represents the address of the $(i+1)$th element. Thus, `a[i]` and `*(a+i)` are same and `&a[i]` and `(a+i)` are same.

It is sometimes necessary to assign an address to a variable, but, it is not possible to assign an arbitrary address to an array name or to an array element. Also, the address of one array element cannot be assigned to some other array element, i.e. the statement `&a[2]=&a[1]` is not valid.

Example 9.7.1 (Sum of two arrays using pointer) Write a program to add the elements of two arrays using a pointer.

Solution. Let `a` and `b` be two arrays of size 10. We add these two arrays and store it to the array `c`, `c[i]=a[i]+b[i]`.

Program 9.6

```
/* Addition of two arrays using pointers */
#include<stdio.h>
void main()
 {
   int a[10],b[10],c[10];
   int i,n;
   void sum(int*,int*,int*,int);
   printf("Enter array size\n");
   scanf("%d",&n);
   printf("Enter elements of the first array\n");
   for(i=0;i<n;i++) scanf("%d",&a[i]);
   printf("Enter elements of the second array\n");
   for(i=0;i<n;i++) scanf("%d",&b[i]);
   sum(a,b,c,n);
```

```
    printf("The sum of two arrays\n");
    for(i=0;i<n;i++) printf("%d  ",c[i]);
  }
void sum(int *a,int *b,int *c, int n)
  {
    int i;
    for(i=0;i<n;i++)
         *(c+i)=*(a+i)+ *(b+i);  /* addition of pointers */
  }
```

A sample of input/output:

```
Enter array size
5
Enter elements of the first array
3 7 9 12 6
Enter elements of the second array
-4 2 6 -2 9
The sum of two arrays -1 9 15 10 15
```

In the function sum, no formal array subscript is used to find the sum of two elements. The contents of the addresses of the elements are added.

9.8 Dynamic Memory Allocation

In conventional array declaration, the size of an array must be mentioned. For this declaration a fixed amount of memory is reserved for array. For example, for the declaration

```
int a[10];
```

total ($10 \times 2 =$) 20 bytes memory space is reserved for the array a. Also, at most 10 values can be stored against a. Suppose in a program the array size is declared as large enough say 100 and only 40 elements are used in an execution. In this case, the space for remaining ($100 - 40 =$) 60 elements is unnecessarily occupied. This is the wastage of memory.

These two draw backs to use array are removed in dynamic memory allocation. In dynamic allocation an array is defined as a pointer variable. When an array is defined as a pointer variable, then the space for the array is not fixed, it can be changed as per the requirement. A special declaration is required to allocate the space for the array. This is called **dynamic memory allocation**. The library function malloc is generally used for this purpose.

Suppose a is a one-dimensional integer array containing 15 elements. The conventional method to define a as an array is

```
int a[15];
```

But, a can be defined as a pointer variable as

```
int *a;
```

This type of declaration does not mean a is an array, it look likes an ordinary integer pointer variable. Therefore, this statement does not allocate a memory block for 15 elements. To assign appropriate memory for a, the following statement is necessary.

```
a=(int *) malloc (15*sizeof(int));
```

The function malloc allocates a block of memory for 15 integers and the allocated space is $(15 \times 2 =)$ 30 bytes (if the size of an integer is 2). This function returns a pointer which points to the first element of the array a (i.e. the address of a[0]). The cast operator (int *) is required, because this pointer points to an integer array.

If a is a floating point array, then the above statement must be of the following form.

```
a=(float *) malloc (15*sizeof(float));
```

If the malloc function returns 0, i.e. NULL pointer, then memory allocation is failed. This happens when the sufficient amount of space is not available in the memory.

If an initialization is required for an array, then the array must be defined as an ordinary array rather than a pointer variable.

Example 9.8.1 Write a program to read a string of characters (only alphabets and blank spaces) and count the number of blank spaces, vowels and consonants in the string.

Solution. Suppose x is an array containing n characters. The array is defined as a pointer variable. The space for this character array is allocated by the function malloc.

Program 9.7

```
/* Use of pointer in a string of characters */
#include<stdio.h>
void main()
 {
   char *x,c;
   int n,i,vcount=0,bcount=0,ccount=0;
   printf("Enter string size\n");
   scanf("%d",&n);
   x=(char *) malloc (n*sizeof(char)); /* allocation of memory */
   printf("Enter the string\n");
   for(i=0;i<=n;i++)
      *(x+i)=getchar();
   printf("Given string is\n");
   for(i=1;i<=n;i++) printf("%c",*(x+i));
   for(i=1;i<=n;i++)
      {
       c=toupper(*(x+i)); /* converted to upper case */
       if(c==' ') bcount++;
       if(c=='A'||c=='E'||c=='O'||c=='U'||c=='I') vcount++;
```

```
  }
  ccount=n-vcount-bcount;
  printf("\nBlank space=%d Vowel=%d Consonent=%d\n",
                               bcount,vcount,ccount);
}
```

A sample of input/output:

```
Enter string size
18
Enter the string
I read in class iv

Given string is
I read in class iv
Blank space=4 Vowel=6 Consonent=8
```

The space for the array x of size n is allocated by

```
x=(char *) malloc (n*sizeof(char));
```

A character is read by `getchar()` and it stores at the address `(x+i)`. To check the type of a character, first it is converted to the upper case letter by the function `toupper`. Then, this character is checked for vowel and blank space.

Another function `calloc` is available for dynamic allocation of memory. The general form of this function is

```
*calloc(n,size);
```

where `n` is an integer, which indicates the number of items to be allocated and `size` specifies the size of each item. For example, to allocate 15 integers, the following statement may be used

$$\texttt{a} = (\texttt{int}*)\texttt{calloc}(\texttt{n}, \texttt{sizeof}(\texttt{int}));$$

This statement allocates a block of memory of size $n \times size$. Note that this function needs two parameters while `malloc` takes only one parameter. Also, `calloc` initializes all bytes in the allocated block to zero, but `malloc` does not.

The memory allocated for a pointer array can be destroyed (if it is not required in future) by the function `free`. The occupied memory becomes free and this free space may be used within the same program, if needed. Let `x` be a pointer array. The following statement will free the space occupied for the array `x`.

```
free(x);
```

9.9 Multidimensional Arrays

The concept of one-dimensional pointer array can be extended to multidimensional arrays. A two-dimensional array is basically a collection of one-dimensional arrays. Thus, a two-dimensional array is defined as a pointer to a group of contiguous one-dimensional arrays. A two-dimensional array is declared as

```
date_type (*array_name)[array_size2];
```

whereas the conventional declaration is

```
date_type array_name[array_size1][array_size2];
```

A three-dimensional array can be declared as

```
date_type (*array_name)[array_size2][array_size3];
```

rather than

```
date_type array_name[array_size1][array_size2][array_size3];
```

In general, an n-dimensional array can be defined as

```
date_type (*array_name)[array_size2][array_size3]··· [array_sizen];
```

The `data_type` is the type of data of the array, `*array_name` is the name of array and it represents the name of the pointer variable, and `array_size1, array_size2, ..., array_sizen` are the non-negative integer constants or variables that indicate the maximum number of array elements allowed to this array.

The parentheses enclose the asterisk and `array_name` must be present, otherwise we would define an array of pointers rather than a pointer to a group of arrays.

Suppose `a` is a two-dimensional integer array with 10 rows and 15 columns. The conventional way to declare this array is `int a[10][15]`. Using pointer variable we can declare `a` as

```
int (*a)[15];
```

In this declaration, `a` is defined to be a pointer to a group of contiguous one-dimensional array and the size of each one-dimensional array is 15.

Now, `a` is the address of the first one-dimensional array (of size 15), `a+1` is the address of the second one-dimensional array (of size 15), and so on. In general, `a+i` is the address of the $(i+1)$th one-dimensional array, which is actually row i of the original two-dimensional array as illustrated in Figure 9.3.

Thus, `a+i` is the address of the $(i+1)$th one-dimensional array, i.e. it points to the first element of the $(i+1)$th array (row i).

The address of the other element of the two-dimensional array can be accessed by the repeated use of the indirection operation. But, this method is not straight forward.

An individual array element, say a_{34}, can be accessed by $a[3][4]$ in conventional method, but by using pointer variable this element can be accessed by writing

```
*(*(a+3)+4);
```

The expression `a+3` is the pointer of the 4th one-dimensional array, and the object of this pointer (`*(a+3)`) refers to the entire row. Since each row is a one-dimensional array, `*(a+3)` is a pointer to the first element of row 3, i.e. it is the pointer of the element $a[3][0]$, not content of $a[3][0]$. Now, `*(a+3)+4` represents a pointer which points to the element $a[3][4]$. The content of this pointer, i.e. the value of the element $a[3][4]$ is obtained from the expression `*(*(a+3)+4)`.

A three-dimensional integer array can be declared as

```
int (*x)[10][20];
```

Here `x` is defined as a pointer to a group of contiguous two-dimensional 10×20 integer arrays. Therefore, `x` points to the first two-dimensional array of size 10×20, `x+1` points

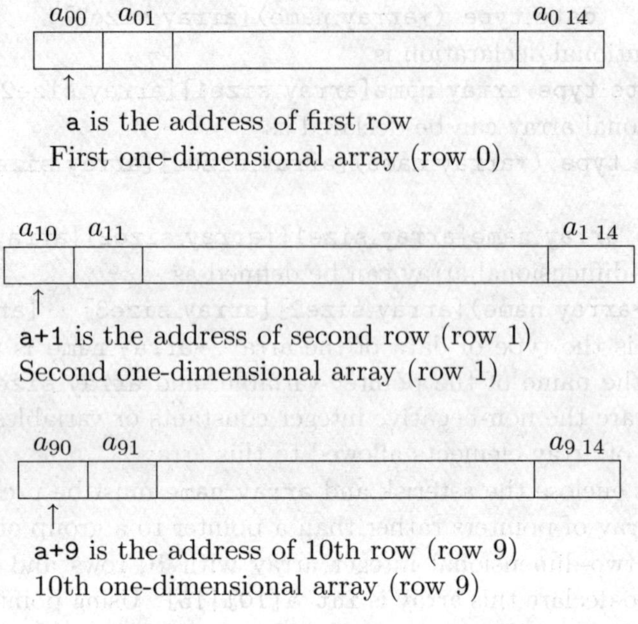

Figure 9.3: Group of one-dimensional arrays

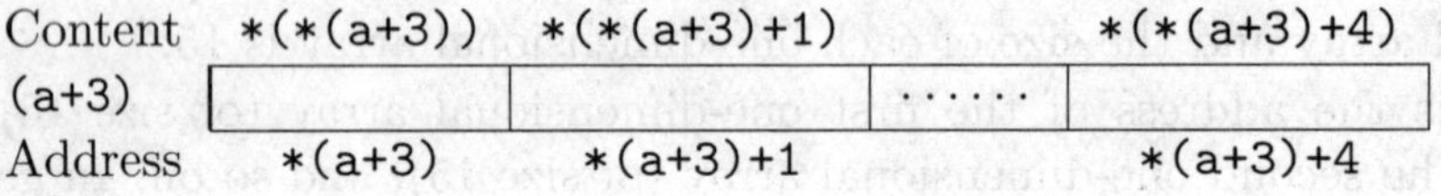

Figure 9.4: Address and content of the element $a[3][4]$.

to the second two-dimensional array of same size, and so on.

9.10 Pointer Constants

It is mentioned that the array name holds the address of the array. Specifically, it holds the address of the 0th element of the array. The address of the $(i+1)$th element is obtained from the expression `a+i`. Thus, the address of the second element (`a[1]`) of a is obtained by `a+1` and it is equivalent to `a++`. But, `a++` is not a valid expression (if a is an array name), because no memory is allocated for the array name unlike a pointer variable which has a memory location. The address of the array has been placed in the code directly by the compiler, and hence it makes the array name constant. Since the array name is a constant, like 10, therefore the expressions `a++` and `10++` behave alike and both are meaningless. The array name can be assigned to a pointer variable, and increment operator can be applied on it. Let us consider the following program segment to illustrate this concept.

```
int a[]={10,20,50,-20};
```

```
int *pa,i;
pa=a;
for(i=0;i<4;i++)
    printf("%d",*pa++);
```

The output of this program segment is

```
10 20 50 -20
```

The address of the array a is stored in the pointer variable pa. The value of *pa is the value of the array element a[0] which is 10. This value is printed and then increments the variable pa (by pa++). Note that the expression *pa++ is the combination of two expressions *pa and pa++.

Remember that when a pointer variable is declared, a memory location is allocated, but not initialized. Before using the pointer variable, it should be assigned a valid address.

9.11 Pointers to Pointers

In C, pointer is a special data type. Thus, variables of type pointer can also be used in C. The general form to declare pointer type data is

```
data_type **x;
```

where, the variable x is a pointer pointing to a data of type data_type. Note that two asterisks (**) written together are used to indicate this type of declaration. Pointers to pointers are very flexible to handle arrays, passing pointer variables to functions, etc. This concept is illustrated in the following program segment.

```
int *x;      /* pointer to an integer */
int **px;    /* pointer to int pointer */
int a;
x=&a;        /* x points to a */
px=&x;       /* px points to x */
*x=50;       /* set 50 as content of x, same as a=50 */
printf("a=%d\n",a);
**px=75;
printf("a=%d\n",a);
```

The output of this program segment is

```
50
75
```

The following example, illustrates the use of pointer notation to handle a two-dimensional array. However, this program may be written in many different forms.

Example 9.11.1 (Product of matrices using pointer) Write a program to find the product of two matrices $a_{m\times n}$ and $b_{n\times p}$ using the concept of pointer array.

Program 9.8

```
/* Program to find the product of two matrices using pointers */
#include<stdio.h>
#define maxrow 10
void readmatrix(int **a, int m, int n);
void matrixmul(int **a, int **b,int **c,int m, int n, int p);
void printmatrix(int **a, int m, int n);

void main()
 {
 int m,n,n1,p,i;
 /* a, b, c are three matrices of sizes mxn, nxp and mxp*/
 int **a, **b, **c; /* declaration of pointers of pointers */
 printf("Enter the size of the first matrix ");
 scanf("%d%d",&m,&n);
 /* allocation of memory for a */
 a=(int **) malloc (m*sizeof(int));
 for(i=0;i<m;i++)
   a[i]=(int*)malloc(n*sizeof(int));
 readmatrix(a,m,n); /* input matrix a */
 printf("Enter the size of the second matrix ");
 scanf("%d%d",&n1,&p);
 if(n!=n1){
     printf("Matrix multiplication is not possible !");
     exit(0);
   }
 /* allocation of memory for b */
 b=(int **) malloc(n*sizeof(int));
 for(i=0;i<n;i++)
   b[i]=(int*)malloc(p*sizeof(int));
 readmatrix(b,n,p); /* input matrix b */
 /* allocation of memory for c */
  c=(int **) malloc(m*sizeof(int));
  for(i=0;i<m;i++)
    c[i]=(int*)malloc(p*sizeof(int));

 matrixmul(a,b,c,m,n,p); /* calling of matrixmul */
 printmatrix(c,m,p); /* calling of printmatrix */
}
/* Function to read a matrix */
 void readmatrix(int **a, int m, int n)
 {
   int i,j;
```

```
   printf("Enter the elements\n");
   for(i=0;i<m;i++) for(j=0;j<n;j++)
     scanf("%d",(*(a+i)+j));
 }
/* Function to find the product of two matrices */
void matrixmul(int **a,int **b,int **c,int m,int n,int p)
 {
  int i,j,k;
  for(i=0;i<m;i++)
  for(j=0;j<p;j++)
   {
     *(*(c+i)+j)=0.0;
     for(k=0;k<n;k++)
      *(*(c+i)+j)+=*(*(a+i)+k)* *(*(b+k)+j);
      /* equivalent to c[i][j]+=a[i][k]*b[k][j] */
   }
 }
/* Function to print a matrix */
 void printmatrix(int **c, int m, int p)
 {
   int i,j;
   printf("Product matrix is\n");
   for(i=0;i<m;i++)
   {
     for(j=0;j<p;j++) printf("%-3d ",*(*(c+i)+j));
     printf("\n");
   }
 }
```

A sample of input/output:

```
Enter the size of the first matrix
3 3
Enter the elements Enter
3 4 5
1 2 3
0 1 2
Enter the size of the second matrix
3 4
Enter the elements 2 0 1 1
3 4 5 9
2 9 0 0

 Product matrix is
```

28 61 23 39 14 35 11 19 7 22 5 9

Since a, b, c are defined as pointers, initial memory allocation is required for them. For each row of the matrices a, b, c, the necessary amount of memory is allocated. For example, the memory for the row i of the matrix a is allocated by the following statement.

```
*a[i]=(int *) malloc (n*sizeof(int));
```

The value of ijth element of the matrix a is read by the statement

```
scanf("%d",(*(a+i)+j));
```

this can also be done using the conventional technique

```
scanf("%d",&a[i][j]);
```

Similarly, to find the ijth element of the matrix c, the following expression is used

```
*(*(c+i)+j)+=*(*(a+i)+k)* *(*(b+k)+j);
```

This expression can also be written as

```
c[i][j]+=a[i][k]*b[k][j];
```

9.12 Array of Pointers

A two or more dimensional array can be expressed in terms of an array of pointers rather than as a pointer to a group of contiguous arrays. In this case, the array will have one less dimension than the original multidimensional array. Each pointer will indicate the beginning of a separate $(n-1)$-dimensional array.

A two-dimensional array can be defined as a one-dimensional array of pointers by the declaration

```
data_type *array_name[array_size1];
```

rather than the conventional definition.

```
data_type array_name[array_size1][array_size2];
```

Note that the array name and the asterisk are *not enclosed in parentheses*. The asterisk establishes that the array contains pointers. Also, note that the last (array_size2) expression is omitted during declaration of array of pointers (compare to the declaration in preceding section).

Suppose a is a two-dimensional array having 15 rows and 25 columns. We define a as a one-dimensional array of pointers by the declaration

```
int *a[15];
```

In this case, a[0] points to the beginning of the first row, a[1] points to the beginning of the second row and so on. Notice that the *number of elements within each row is not explicitly specified.*

The array element $a[3][4]$ can be accessed by the expression *(a[3]+5), whereas a[3]+5 represents the address of this element.

These types of arrays are appropriately used in handling of string. Because, for a set of strings, the length of the strings are different. These types of strings can be stored by making pointers to strings of varying lengths. Suppose we would like to store the name of three students "Aniket Pal", "Raman" and "Prativa". These three strings can be stored using the following declaration `char *student_name[3]={"Aniket Pal", "Raman", "Prativa"};`

In the above declaration `student_name` declares as an array of three pointers to characters, each pointer points to a particular name as shown below.

```
student_name[0]   Aniket Pal
student_name[1]   Raman
student_name[2]   Prativa
```

They stored in the memory as per the following form

A	n	i	k	e	t		P	a	l	\0
R	a	m	a	n	\0					
P	r	a	t	i	v	a	\0			

and needs only 25 bytes to store these three strings. But, if these strings are stored by the following declaration

`char student_name[3][11]={"Aniket Pal", "Raman", "Prativa"};`

then 33 bytes are required to store them.

Thus, the declaration using arrays of pointers save the substantial amount of space.

The jth character of the ith `student_name` can be accessed by `*(student_name[i]+j)`.

The arrays with the rows of varying length are called **ragged** arrays and are better handled by pointers.

Note that the difference between the notations `*a[10]` and `(*a)[10]`. Since the precedence of $*$ is less than the precedence of [ ], `*a[10]` declares `a` as an array of 10 elements, while `(*a)[10]` declares `a` as a pointer to an array of ten elements.

9.13 Function as Pointers

Sometimes it may happen that a function is to be passed to another function, like an ordinary variable, array, etc. This passing is possible, because like a variable, a function has an address in the memory. Thus, by the declaration of a pointer to a function, it (function) can be used as an argument in another function. A pointer to a function is declared as

`data_type (*function_name)();`

where `data_type` represents the data type which is returned by the function. `function_name` is the name of the function and it is a pointer to the function. The parentheses rounding `*function_name` are necessary, because `function_name` is a function. The necessary arguments are to be written within the parentheses. This function can be accessed by the means of indirection operator. The indirection operator must precede the function name (i.e. the formal argument).

Now, we explain the use of function as pointer in the following program.

Example 9.13.1 (Use of function as pointer) Write a program to find the area and perimeter of a rectangle whose length and breadth are respectively a and b.

We define two functions area(a,b) and perimeter(a,b) to calculate the area and perimeter of a rectangle. The function perform is used to call the functions area and perimeter.

Program 9.9

```
/* Use of function pointer */
#include<stdio.h>
main()
 {
   float area(), perimeter(), perform();
   float a,b,ar,pe;
   printf("Enter the values of a, b\n");
   scanf("%f%f",&a,&b);
   ar=perform(area,a,b); /* called 'perform' by
                            passing the function area */
   printf("The area is %f\n",ar);
   pe=perform(perimeter,a,b); /* called 'perform' by
                                 passing the function perimeter */
   printf("The perimeter is %f\n",pe);
 return;
 }
/* definition of function perform */
float perform(funct,a,b)
float (*funct)(); /* formal argument declaration
                     as a pointer to a function */
float a, b;
  {
   float ans;
   ans=(*funct)(a,b); /* the passing function is
                         executed with argument a, b  */
   return(ans);
  }
/* definition of function area */
float area(a,b)
float a,b;
  {
   return(a*b);
  }
/* definition of function perimeter */
float perimeter(a,b)
float a,b;
  {
```

```
    return(2*(a+b));
  }
```

A sample of input/output:

```
Enter the values of a, b
30.45 25.87

The area is 787.741516
The perimeter is 112.639999
```

When the function **perform** is called for **ar** from **main** with argument **area, a, b**, then the value of the pointer **funct** (for ans) becomes **area** and the expression for **ans** returns to the following form

`ans=area(a,b);`

and the final value of **ans** is obtained by calling the function **area** for the argument **a,b**.

Similarly, when **perform** is called for second time for **pe** with argument **perimeter, a, b**, then the value of **funct** becomes **perimeter** and then the equivalent expression for **ans** becomes

`ans=perimeter(a,b);`

The final value of **ans** is obtained by calling the function **perimeter**.

The data type of the argument can also be included within the function declaration. With this inclusion the above program is now written below.

Program 9.10

```
/* Alternative form of above program */
#include<stdio.h>
main()
 {
   float area(float,float), perimeter(float,float);
   /* function declaration with type */
   float perform(float(*)(float,float),float,float);
   float a,b,ar,pe;
   printf("Enter the values of a, b\n");
   scanf("%f%f",&a,&b);
   ar=perform(area,a,b);
   printf("The area is %7.4f\n",ar);
   pe=perform(perimeter,a,b);
   printf("The perimeter is %7.4f\n",pe);
 return;
 }
/* definition of function perform */
float perform(float(*funct)(float a,float b),float a,float b)
  {
```

```
    float ans;
    ans=(*funct)(a,b); /* the passing function is
                            executed with argument a, b  */
    return(ans);
  }
/* definition of function area */
float area(float a,float b)
  {
    return(a*b);
  }
/* definition of function perimeter */
float perimeter(float a,float b)
  {
    return(2*(a+b));
  }
```

A sample of input/output:

```
Enter the values of a, b
34.5 67.8
The area is 2339.1001
The perimeter is 204.6000
```

In the above program, the argument names and their data types are mentioned. Now, we summarize the declaration of different types of pointers in the following.

Declaration	Description
`int *a;`	a is a pointer, points to an integer
`int *a[50];`	a is a 50-element array of pointers to integers
`int (*a)[50];`	a is a pointer to a 50-element integer array
`int *a();`	a is a function, returns a pointer to an integer
`int a(char *b);`	a is a function whose argument is a pointer to a character, returns an integer
`int *a(char *b);`	a is a function whose argument is a pointer to a character and returns a pointer to an integer
`int (*a)(char *b);`	a is a pointer to a function whose argument is a pointer to a character and returns an integer
`int a(char *b[]);`	a is a function whose argument is an array of pointer to characters, returns an integer
`int a(char (*b)[]);`	a is a function, whose argument is a pointer to a character array and returns an integer
`int *a(char b[]);`	a is a function whose argument is a character array and returns a pointer to an integer
`int *a(char *b[]);`	a is a function whose argument is an array of pointers to characters and returns a pointer to an integer

Example 9.13.2 (Use of external function) Write a complete program, using pointer notation, that will generate a table counting, following three columns

$$t \qquad 4\cos t \qquad e^{-2t}\cos 3t.$$

Organize the program in the following manner. Write functions `funct1` and `funct2`, where `funct1` evaluates the quantity $4\cos t$ and `funct2` evaluates $e^{2t}\cos 3t$. The `main` function will call the function `table` which will generate the actual table. Pass `funct1` and `funct2` to `table` as arguments. Generate the table for $t = 0.0, 0.5, 1.0, 1.5, \ldots, 5.0$.

Program 9.11

```
/* Computation of functions using external function call */
#include<stdio.h>
#include<math.h>
void main()
 {
   void table(float(*f)(float a), float s, float t, float i);
   float funct1(float t);
   float funct2(float t);
   printf("Table of 4 cos t\n");
   table(funct1, 0,5.0,0.5);
   printf("\nTable of exp(-2t)cos3t\n");
   table(funct2,0,5.0,0.5);
 }
/* definition of function table */
void table(float(*f)(float a), float s, float t, float i)
 {
   float x,value;
   for(x=s;x<=t;x+=i)
     {
       value=(*f)(x);
       printf("%4.2f\t %7.4f\n",x,value);
     }
 }
/* definition of function funct1 */
float funct1(float t)
 {
   return(4*cos(t));
 }
/* definition of function funct2 */
float funct2(float t)
 {
```

```
  return(exp(-2*t)*cos(3*t));
}
```

A sample of input/output:

```
Table of 4 cos t
0.00      4.0000
0.50      3.5103
1.00      2.1612
1.50      0.2829
2.00     -1.6646
2.50     -3.2046
3.00     -3.9600
3.50     -3.7458
4.00     -2.6146
4.50     -0.8432
5.00      1.1346

Table of exp(-2t)cos3t
0.00      1.0000
0.50      0.0260
1.00     -0.1340
1.50     -0.0105
2.00      0.0176
2.50      0.0023
3.00     -0.0023
3.50     -0.0004
4.00      0.0003
4.50      0.0001
5.00     -0.0000
```

Important Points

1. A pointer variable can store only the address of the variable where the value of the variable is stored.
2. The type of pointer variables must be the same while one pointer variable is assigned to another pointer variable.
3. It is not possible to assign a pointer of one type to a pointer of another type without cast.
4. Let `pv` be a pointer variable. `pv` stores the address of the variable and `*pv` represents the value (content) stored at the address `pv`.

5. The value of a variable cannot be assigned to a pointer variable.
6. Pointer variables must be initialized before its use, otherwise they store garbage.
7. When a pointer variable is declared, a memory is allocated only for the pointer variable, not for the variable to which it is pointing.
8. If the value of a variable is passed to a function by address, then the corresponding formal argument must be a pointer variable.
9. Assignment of a numerical value or variable to a pointer variable is not possible. Similarly, a pointer variable cannot be assigned to an ordinary variable.
10. Care should be taken of the precedence and associativity rules in pointer variables.
11. Be careful about the use of address operator (&) and the indirection operator (*).
12. When an array is passed to a function, the address (pointer) of an element of the array is passed as an argument, not the values of all the elements of the array. This mechanism saves the time of passing of values from calling function to called function.

Exercise IX

Review Questions

1. What is meant by the address of a memory cell? How are addresses usually numbered?
2. How is the address of a variable determined?
3. What is a pointer? What type of information is stored by a pointer variable?
4. What is the relation between the address of a variable and the corresponding pointer variable?
5. What is the relation between the data represented by a variable and the corresponding pointer variable?
6. What is the difference between `v`, `&v` and `*v` for the declaration `int *v`?
7. How a pointer variable declared? What is the purpose of the data type included in the declaration?
8. How initial value can be assigned to a pointer variable during its declaration?
9. How a function is passed to another function? Explain.
10. What is the relationship between an array name and a pointer? How is an array name interpreted when it appears as an argument to a function?
11. If an array is a formal argument of a function, how can the array be declared within the function?
12. How can a portion of an array be passed to a function? What is the difference between to pass `a[5]` and `&a[5]` to a function?
13. What is the difference between `(*a)[5]` and `*a[5]`?

14. How can a function return a pointer to its calling function?
15. Suppose an integer is added or subtracted from a pointer variable. How can the sum or difference be interpreted?
16. What are the arithmetic operators that are permitted on pointers?
17. What is the relationship between function name and the function?
18. How can a one-dimensional array of pointers be used to represent a collection of strings? If several strings are stored within one-dimensional array of pointers, how can an individual sting be accessed?
19. What do you understand by a pointer to a pointer? Can this be extended to any level?
20. Explain the difference between an array and a pointer.
21. Explain the difference between an array of characters and two dimensional array.
22. Explain the difference between a pointer to a constant and a constant pointer with an example.
23. What is the use of the function `malloc`? Distinguish between the functions `malloc` and `calloc`.
24. Suppose `a` is one dimensional array. What is the difference between `*(a+i)` and `a[i]`? Which is better and why?

Problems

1. If `pv` is a pointer to a user defined type or basic type, by how many bytes is `pv` incremented when the statement `pv++` is executed?
2. What is the difference between the following declarations:
   (a) `void sum(int a[]);`
   (b) `void sum(int *a);`
3. Find the error, if any, in each of the following cases.
   (a) `int a=50;`
   (b) `int *b=300;`
   (c) `int &b=300;`
   (d) `int a, *b=&a;`
4. What are the values of `u` and `v` at the end of the execution of the following program segment?

```
int *pu, *pv, u, v
pu=&a; pv=&b;
*pu=100; *pv=140;
*pv=(*pu)++ -(*pv);
```

5. What are the output of the following program segment?

```
int a=1021;
int *pa=&a;
int **paa=&pa;
printf("%d  %d",*pa,**paa);
```

6. Let us consider the following declaration.

   `int a[6]=4,5,6,7,9,12;`

   (a) What is the meaning of a?

   (b) What is the meaning of (a+2)?

   (c) What is the value of *a?

   (b) What is the value of (*a+3)?

   (b) What is the value of *(a+3)?

7. Write the output obtained by the following statements:

```
int a[5];
int *x=&a;
a[0]=10; a[1]=20;
printf("%d %d %d",*x; ++*x; *x+5);
```

8. What is the output of the following program?

```
#include<stdio.h>
int funct(int *);
void main()
  {
    int a[7]={3,4,5,2,-1,8,9};
    printf("%d ",funct(a+2));
  }
int funct(int *c)
  {
    int i,sum=0;
    for(i=2;i<=6;i++)
      sum+=*(c+i);
    return sum;
  }
```

Programming Problems

1. Suppose three numbers x, y, z are passed to a function. Implement this function to assign the values of y to x, z to y and x to z and return these three changed values to `main`. Use pointer.
2. Write a program to read a string and print the address of its starting location.
3. Write a function that reads two integers by reference and performs a swap.

4. Write a function using pointers to add two matrices and to return the resultant matrix to the calling function.
5. Write a program using pointers to read in an array of integers and print its elements in reverse order.
6. Write a program using pointer to read an array of integers and find the maximum among them.
7. Write a program using pointer to find the sum of each row of a matrix and print them sequentially.
8. Write a program to read three integers and print their sum. These integers are transferred to the function `sum` by reference, the function `sum` finds the sum of them and returns it to the main function.

Chapter 10

String Manipulation

Manipulation of strings is a very common problem in any programming language. Using the functions of strings one can design different types of softwares related to text manipulation, viz. text editor, which is commonly used by the users. Different techniques and functions are used in manipulation of strings in C. C has a very rich library to manipulate strings.

10.1 Strings Constants and Variables

The character constant is a single character enclosed within single quotes. For example, 'A', 'a', '2', are character constants. Each character constant has a numerical value known as ASCII value. The ASCII values of all characters are given in Table 3.4.

Since each character has a numerical value, so arithmetic calculations can be done among them. For example, if `x='a'; y='c'`, then `x+y` is a valid expression and its value is 196, sum of ASCII values of 'a' (97) and 'c' (99). The ASCII value of 'a' is 97 and 'A' is 65. That is, if i is the ASCII code of an upper case alphabet, then the ASCII code of corresponding lower case is $i + 32$. Using this arithmetic operation one can generate all upper case and lower case alphabets, as shown in the following program.

Program 10.1

```
/* Generation of all upper case and lower case alphabets and
   their ASCII values */
#include<stdio.h>
#include<string.h>
void main()
 {
   int i;
   for(i=65;i<65+26;i++)
     {
```

```
    printf("%d %c %c| ",i,i,i+32); /* printing of ASCII code, upper
                                      and lower case alphabets */
    if((i-2)%8==0) printf("\n");
  }
}
```

The output of the above program.

```
65 A a| 66 B b|
67 C c| 68 D d| 69 E e| 70 F f| 71 G g| 72 H h| 73 I i| 74 J j|
75 K k| 76 L l| 77 M m| 78 N n| 79 O o| 80 P p| 81 Q q| 82 R r|
83 S s| 84 T t| 85 U u| 86 V v| 87 W w| 88 X x| 89 Y y| 90 Z z|
```

Look at the print statement `printf("%d %c %c| ",i,i,i+32);`. Here `i` is an integer variable and its value is printed by `%d` and `%c` format specifiers. The value of first `i` is printed as integer and second `i` as character and produce integer value 65 (for $i = 65$) and the character `A`. The value of the expression `i+32` when printed using `%c` format specifier gives `a`, as the ASCII value of `a` is 97 (65+32).

A sequence of characters form a string and it is written within double quotes. For example, "I love my India" is an example of a string.

A character variable is declared by the type specifier `char`. For example, the statement

`char a, s;`

declares `a` and `s` as character variables whereas the statement

`char st[30], name[20];`

declares `st` and `name` as two character strings of size 30 and 20 respectively.

The I/O statements for strings are discussed in Chapter 3. In the following example, a string is printed with different lengths.

Program 10.2

```
/* Printing of string in different length */
#include<stdio.h>
void main()
 {
   int i;
   char st[]="Vidyasagar";
   for(i=0;i<=9;i++)
     printf("%10.*s\n",i+1,st);
   for(i=9;i>=0;i--)
     printf("%10.*s\n",i+1,st);
}
```

The output of the above program is shown below.

```
         V
        Vi
       Vid
      Vidy
     Vidya
    Vidyas
   Vidyasa
  Vidyasag
 Vidyasaga
Vidyasagar
Vidyasagar
 Vidyasaga
  Vidyasag
   Vidyasa
    Vidyas
     Vidya
      Vidy
       Vid
        Vi
         V
```

10.2 String Handling Functions

The common string manipulation functions are listed in Table 10.1.

Function	Action
`strlen(str1)`	determines the length of the string `str1`
`strcat(str1,str2)`	concatenates (joins) two strings `str1` and `str2`
`strcmp(str1,str2)`	compares two strings `str1` and `str2`
`strcpy(str1,str2)`	copies the string `str2` over the string `str1`

Table 10.1: String manipulation functions

The details of the string manipulation functions are explained below.

`strlen()`

This function determines the length of a string, i.e. counts the number of characters present in the string excluding null character. The general form of this function is

`strlen(str1);`

where `str1` is a string constant or a string variable. This function returns a non-negative integer. For example, let `str1="Good"` and `str2="Good "`. Then, the output of the execution of the functions strlen(str1) and strlen(str2) are respectively 4 and 5.

strcat()

This function concatenates two strings. The general form of this function is

```
strcat(str1,str2);
```

where str1 and str2 are two strings. This function joins the string str2 to the end of the string str1. This function removes the null character from the end of the string str1 and str2 is added to str1 from this point. The string str2 remains unchanged. To illustrate the use of this function, consider the following strings

```
str1="Good"
str2="Day"
str3="Good "
```

The strings after execution of the function

```
strcat(str1,str2);
```

are str1="GoodDay" and str2="Day" and the strings after execution of the function

```
strcat(str3,str2);
```

are str3="Good Day" and str2="Day".

It must be remembered that the length of the first string of the function strcat is large enough to store both the strings.

strcmp()

This function compares two strings and returns an integer value. If the two strings are identical it returns 0, otherwise returns a non-zero integer value. Its general form is

```
strcmp(str1,str2);
```

where str1 and str2 are two string variables or constants.

Two strings are compared with respect to the ASCII values of the individual character of the strings. Since the ASCII values of upper case and lower case alphabets are different, therefore the strings str1="aBc" and str2=abc" are different. The ASCII value of a is 97 and that of B and b are 66 and 98 respectively. For these strings, the ASCII codes of first characters, viz. a are same, but the ASCII codes of second characters are 66 and 98. Then "aBc" comes before "abc" in the dictionary order. It may be noted that the value of the function strcmp("aBc","abc") is $66 - 98 = -32$. Thus, the negative value of the function strcmp(str1,str2) indicates that the string str1 comes before str2 with respect to the dictionary order.

strcpy()

This function is used to assign a string (constant or variable or expression) to another string. Its general form is

```
strcpy(str1,str2);
```

where str1 is a string variable and str2 is a string constant, variable or an expression. The value of str2 is assigned to the string str1. Note that the length of the variable str1 must be at least the length of str2.

That is, if str1 and str2 are "Ram" and "India" respectively, then the execution of the function

```
strcpy(str1,str2);
```

results str1="India" and str2="India". It may be noted that str1=India is not a valid assignment statement. If any string constant or variable or expression is required to assign to another string variable, then the function strcpy must be used.

The following program illustrates the use of the functions strcmp and strcpy.

Example 10.2.1 (Sorting of names) Write a program to arrange the names of some students in alphabetic order.

Program 10.3

```
/* Sorting of names in alphabetic order */
#include<stdio.h>
#include<string.h>
void main()
 {
   char name[10][25], temp[25];
   int i,j,n;
   printf("Enter number of students\n");
   scanf("%d",&n);
   printf("Enter names line by line \n");
   for(i=1;i<=n;i++) /* reading of names */
      scanf("%[^\n]",name[i]);
   /* sorting begins */
   for(i=1;i<=n-1;i++)
     for(j=i+1;j<=n;j++)
       {
         if(strcmp(name[i],name[j])>0) /* name[i]>name[j] */
           { /* interchange between the strings */
             strcpy(temp,name[i]);
             strcpy(name[i],name[j]);
             strcpy(name[j],temp);
           }
       } /* end of sorting */
  printf("\nSorting list is\n");
  for(i=1;i<=n;i++)
     printf("%s\n",name[i]);
 }
```

A sample of input/output:

```
Enter number of students
6
Enter names line by line
Raja
Aniket
Pratik
Kajal
Rani
Moni

Sorting list is
Aniket
Kajal
Moni
Pratik
Raja
Rani
```

`strrev()`

The general form of this function is

`strrev(str1);`

This build in function revert a string `str1` and return the reversed string as output. For example, if `str1="Aniket"` and `str2=strrev(str1)`, then `str2` becomes `tekinA`.

10.3 More String Functions

The string functions `strlen, strcpy, strcat` and `strcmp` are discussed in previous section and all these functions are available in <string.h>. Some more string manipulation functions are also available in C. They are discussed below.

Function	Action
`strncat(str1,str2,n)`	concatenate `n` characters of `str2` to end of `str1`
`strncmp(str1,str2,n)`	same as `strcmp`, but only first `n` characters of `str1` compares with `str2`
`strncpy(str1,str2,n)`	copy at most n characters of `str2` over the string `str1`
`strstr(str1,str2)`	return the pointer of first occurrence of the string `str2` in the string `str1`
`strchr(str1,c)`	return the pointer of first occurrence of the character `c` in the string `str1`
`strrchr(str1,c)`	return the pointer of last occurrence of the character `c` in the string `str1`

These functions are also found in the header file <string.h>.

`strncat()`

This function is similar to the function `strcat()`. The general form of this function is

`strncat(str1,str2,n);`

where `str1` and `str2` are two strings and `n` is an integer. This function concatenates the first n characters of `str2` to the end of the string `str1`. For example, if `str1="My "` and `str2="India is great"`, then after execution of the statement `strncat(str1,str2,5);` the string `str1` becomes `"My India"`. If the length of the string `str2` is less than n, then garbage will be added at the end of the string `str2`. It must be ensured that the target string (`str1`) has enough space to hold the source string (`str2`). If this condition is not fulfilled then no error message will be produced.

`strncmp()`

This function is a also similar to the function `strcmp`. The general form of this function is

`strncmp(str1,str2,n);`

The function `strcmp(str1,str2)` compares two strings `str1` and `str2`, whereas the function `strncmp(str1,str2,n)` compares first n characters of the string `str1` with the string `str2`. This function returns an integer value. If the first n characters of `str1` are same as the first n characters of `str2`, then the function returns 0. If the number of characters (say m) of `str2` is less than n and these characters are equal to the first m characters of `str1`, then the function gives a positive value, otherwise it returns a negative value.

For example, let `st1="India is great"`, `st2="India"` and `st3="Ind"`. The function `strncmp(st1,st2,5)` returns 0 and the function `strncmp(st1,st3,5)` returns a positive value.

`strncpy()`

The general form of this function is

`strncpy(str1,str2,n);`

Like `strcpy`, this function also copies first n characters of the string `str2` over the string `str1`. If the number of characters of the string `str2` is more than n, then a null character must be added at the end of the string `str1`.

For example, let `st2="India"`. The function `strncpy(st1,st2,3)` copies the first 3 characters `"Ind"` to the string `st1`. Since the last character of the string `st1` is not a null character, it to be added explicitly at the end (4th position) of `st1`, using the statement `st1[4]='\0'`.

`strstr()`, `strchr()`, `strrchr()`

The function `strstr(str1,str2)` determines the occurrence of the string `str2` as a substring of the string `str1` and it returns a pointer of first occurrence of the string `str2` within the string `str1`. If the string `str2` is not present within the string `str1`, then it returns the `NULL` pointer. This function may be used as follows.

```
        if(strstr(str1,str2)==NULL)
           printf("%s is not within the string %s ",str2,str1);
        else
           printf("%s is a substring of %s ",str2,str1);
```

A variation of this function is strchr(str1,c). This function determines the first occurrence of the character c in the string str1 and returns a pointer.

Another variation of this function is strrchr(str1,c). This function determines the last occurrence of the character c in the string str1 and returns a pointer.

These three functions are illustrated in the following program.

Program 10.4

```
/* Finding the position of last occurrence of a character in a string */
#include<stdio.h>
#include<string.h>
#include<ctype.h>
void main()
{
  char *i;
  char st1[]="This is a test code !!!",
  st2[]="is";
  clrscr();
  printf("Given string is: %s",st1);
  i=strstr(st1,st2);
  printf("%s \n",i);
  i=strchr(st1,'s');
  printf("First occurrence of s: %s\n",i);
  i=strrchr(st1,'s');
  printf("Last occurrence of s: %s\n",i);
}
```

The output of this program is

```
Given string is: This is a test code !!!
is is a test code !!!
First occurrence of s: s is a test code !!!
Last occurrence of s: st code !!!
```

10.4 Functions to Test Type of Character

Some special functions are available to test the type (such as uppercase, lowercase, digits, etc) of a character. The functions are found in the header file <ctype.h>. For each function, the argument is either a character or an integer, and the returned value is an integer. The functions return non-zero (true) if the argument c satisfies the condition described, and zero if not. A list of such functions and their uses are described in Table 10.2.

Function	Action
isalnum(c)	true, if c is an alphabet or digit
isalpha(c)	true, if c is an alphabet either uppercase or lowercase
iscntrl(c)	true, if c is a control character
isdigit(c)	true, if c is a decimal digit
isgraph(c)	true, if c is a printable character except space
islower(c)	true, if c is a lower-case alphabet
isprint(c)	true, if c is a printable character including space
ispunct(c)	true, if c is a printable character except space, alphabet and digit (punctuation symbols)
isspace(c)	true, if c is a space, formfeed, newline, carriage return, tab, vertical tab
isupper(c)	true, if c is an upper-case alphabet
isxdigit(c)	true, if c is a hexadecimal digit

Table 10.2: Some character testing functions

The following program illustrates the use of these functions.

Program 10.5

```
/* Determines the number of alphanumeric characters, alphabets,
   digits, upper case and lower case letters and
   punctuation symbols. */
#include<stdio.h>
#include<string.h>
#include<ctype.h>
void main()
 {
  int i;
  char st[50],c;
  int alnum=0,alpha=0,digit=0,upper=0,lower=0,space=0,punct=0,L;
  printf("Enter a string\n");
  gets(st);
  L=strlen(st);
  for(i=0;i<L;i++)
    {
     c=st[i];
     if(isalnum(c)) alnum++;
```

```
    if(isalpha(c)) alpha++;
    if(isdigit(c)) digit++;
    if(islower(c)) lower++;
    if(isupper(c)) upper++;
    if(ispunct(c)) punct++;
    if(isspace(c)) space++;
  }
  printf("Given string\n");
  printf("%s\n",st);
  printf("No. of \n");
  printf("Alphanumeric characters %d\n",alnum);
  printf("Alphabets               %d\n",alpha);
  printf("Digits                  %d\n",digit);
  printf("Lower case characters   %d\n",lower);
  printf("Upper case characters   %d\n",upper);
  printf("Punctuation symbols     %d\n",punct);
  printf("Space                   %d\n",space);
}
```

A sample of input/output:

```
Enter a string
```

My son is Aniket. His age is 9 yrs 8 months.

```
Given string
My son is Aniket. His age is 9 yrs 8 months.
No. of
Alphanumeric characters 32
Alphabets               30
Digits                  2
Lower case characters   27
Upper case characters   3
Punctuation symbols     2
Space                   10
```

Example 10.4.1 (Sum of digits of floating number) Write a program to read a floating point number and find the sum of the digits of the numbers.

Solution. The function `atoi()`, found in <`stdlib`>, is used to convert a string (not a single character) of digits to numeric digits. If the string contains non-digit characters (including decimal point), then only the left-hand character-digits converts to numeric digits. For example, the functions `atoi("1234.578")` and `atoi("23nk")` returns `1234` and `23` respectively.

In this example, a single character is taken from a string of characters (`st1`) (may contain any characters) and it saved as a string `c[1]`. Then, this single character is converted to numeric digit using the function atoi. The checking of non-digit characters and occurrence of multiple decimal points are incorporated in this program.

Program 10.6

```
/* Sum of all digits of a floating point number.
   This program also tests whether a given number is a valid
   floating point number or not */
#include<stdio.h>
#include<string.h>
#include<stdlib.h>
void main()
 {
   int i,sum=0,error=0,dotcount=0;
   char st1[15],c[1];
   printf("Enter an unsigned number\n");
   scanf("%s",st1);
   printf("Given number is\n%s\n",st1);
   for(i=0;i<strlen(st1);i++)
    {
      c[0]=st1[i];
      if(isdigit(st1[i]))
         sum+=atoi(c);
      else if(st1[i]=='.')
        {
          dotcount++; continue;
        }
      else
        {
          error=1; break;
        }
    }
   if(error==1||dotcount>1)
      printf("Invalid numeric number\n");
   else
      printf("Sum of the digits is %d\n",sum);
 }
```

A sample of input/output:

```
Enter an unsigned number
347598765634.34

Given number is
```

```
347598765634.34
Sum of the digits is 74
```

10.5 Examples on String Manipulation

Counting the number of words and lines in a string

The following program reads a string of characters as st and counts the number of words in it. A word is a sequence of consecutive characters (containing alphabets, digits or any special character) without blank space.

Program 10.7

```
/* Counts the number of words, the words beginning
   with vowel and number of characters */
#include<stdio.h>
#include<string.h>
void main()
 {
   char *st;
   int i,count=0,wordcount=1,line=1,L;
   int vowel(char);
   printf("Enter a string end with $\n");
   scanf("%[^$]",st); /* reads a string */
   L=strlen(st);
   if((st[L]=='\n') && (st[L-1]=='\n'))
     L--;
   /* counting word */
   for(i=0;i<L;i++)
     if(((st[i]==' ') && (st[i+1]!=' '))||(st[i]=='\n'))
       wordcount++;
   /* counting words starting with vowel */
   if(vowel(st[0])) count++;
   for(i=1;i<L;i++)
     if(((st[i]==' ')&&(vowel(st[i+1])))||(st[i]=='\n'&&vowel(st[i+1])))
       count++;
   /* counting lines */
   for(i=0;i<L;i++)
     if(st[i]=='\n')
       line++;
   if(line>1) wordcount--;
   printf("Total no. of words is %d\n",wordcount);
   printf("The no. of words beginning with a vowel is %d\n",count);
   printf("No. of lines is %d\n",line);
```

```
 }
/* Checking whether a character is  vowel or not */
int vowel(char c)
 {
  char C;
  C=toupper(c);
  if(C=='A'||C=='O'||C=='U'||C=='E'||C=='I')
    return(1);
  else
    return(0);
 }
```

A sample of input/output:

```
Enter a string end with $
```

An owl is sitting on a tree
A fox is standing under the tree$

```
Total no.  of words is 14
The no.  of words beginning with a vowel is 8
No.  of lines is 2
```

Counting the occurrence of a character in a string

Let st be a string and ch be a single character. The following program counts the frequency of ch in the string st.

Program 10.8

```
/*  Number of occurrence of a character in a given string */
#include<stdio.h>
#include<string.h>
void main()
  {
    char *st, ch;
    int i,count=0;
    printf("Enter the string \n");
    gets(st);
    printf("Enter the character ");
    ch=getchar();
    printf("Given string is\n%s\n",st);
    for(i=0;i<=strlen(st);i++)
       if(st[i]==ch) count++;
    printf("%c occurs %d times",ch,count);
  }
```

A sample of input/output:

```
Enter the string
The C language is versatile
Enter the character e

Given string is
The C language is versatile
e occurs 4 times
```

Printing a string in reverse order

Let `st1` be an input string and this string is to be stored into another string `st2` (output string) in reverse order. For example, if `st1="I love my India"`, then the output that will be stored in `st2` is `"aidnI ym evol I"`.

Program 10.9

```
/* Program to print a string in reverse order,
   using and without using library functions */
#include<stdio.h>
#include<string.h>
void main()
  {
    char st1[80],st2[80];
    int L,i;
    printf("Enter the string\n");
    gets(st1);
    printf("The given string is\n%s",st1);
    L=strlen(st1);
    L--;  /* to avoid newline character */
    for(i=0;i<=L;i++)
       st2[i]=st1[L-i];
    printf("\nReverse of string without library function\n");
    puts(st2);
    printf("\nReverse of string using library function\n%s",strrev(st1));
  }
```

A sample of input/output:

```
Enter the string
C Program

The given string is
C Program
Reverse of string without library function
 margorP C
```

```
Reverse of string using library function
margorP C
```

Replacing a specified character by another character

The following program replaces every occurrence of the character `olett` (old character) in a given string by the character `nlett` (new character).

Program 10.10

```
/* Replace every occurrence of a character 'olett' in a
   given string by 'nlett' */
#include<stdio.h>
#include<string.h>
void main()
  {
    char st[80],olett,nlett;
    int i;
    printf("Enter the string\n");
    gets(st);
    printf("Enter the old and new characters\n");
    scanf("%c %c",&olett,&nlett);
    printf("The given string is\n");
    puts(st);
    printf("Old character : %c New character : %c\n",olett,nlett);
    for(i=0;i<strlen(st);i++)
      if(st[i]==olett) st[i]=nlett; /* assignment of character */
    printf("The new string is \n");
    puts(st);
  }
```

A sample of input/output:

```
Enter the string
vidyasagar university
Enter the old and new characters
v b
Old character :  v New character :  b
The new string is
bidyasagar unibersity
```

Palindrome checking

A palindrome is a string of characters which represents the same string when read from either direction, i.e. either from backward or forward. For example, MADAM, MALAYALAM, 34543, etc. are palindromes. That is, a string A of L characters is a palindrome, if $A[0] = A[L]$, $A[1] = A[L-1]$, $\cdots$, $A[i] = A[L-i]$, for all $i = 1, 2, \ldots, L/2$. The following program determines whether a string is a palindrome or not.

Program 10.11

```
/* Program to check whether a string is palindrome or not */
#include<stdio.h>
#include<string.h>
void main()
  {
    char st1[80],st2[80];
    int i,L,flag=1;
    printf("Enter a string\n");
    gets(st1);
    printf("The given string is\n%s\n",st1);
    L=strlen(st1);
    L--;  /* to avoid newline character */
    for(i=0;i<=L;i++)
       if(st1[i]!=st1[L-i])
         {
           flag=0; break; /* fails to palindrome */
         }
    if(flag==1)
       printf("String is palindrome\n");
    else
       printf("String is not palindrome\n");
  }
```

A sample of input/output:

```
Enter a string
123madam321
The given string is
123madam321
String is palindrome
```

Searching a substring among a set of strings

Let us consider the following problem of string searching.
Read the titles from a list of books and print the titles which contains a given substring. The following program reads the titles of up to 100 books (each title containing at most 40 characters) as BOOKS, and prints the titles containing the substring SWORD.

Program 10.12

```
/* Program to read a list of titles of books and prints the titles
   containing a given substring */
#include<stdio.h>
#include<string.h>
#include<stdlib.h>
void main()
 {
   typedef char string[50];
   string books[80]; /* string is a user defined data type */
   char sword[20];
   int nbooks,i;
   printf("Enter number of books\n");
   scanf("%d",&nbooks);
   printf("Enter the name of the books\n");
   for(i=0;i<nbooks;i++)
      gets(books[i]);
   printf("Enter search word\n");
   gets(sword);
   printf("The list of the books\n");
   for(i=0;i<nbooks;i++)
     if(strstr(books[i],sword) != NULL)
    printf("%s \n",books[i]);
 }
```

A sample of input/output:

```
Enter number of books
4
Enter the name of the books
Mathematical Analysis
FORTRAN Programming
Computer Fundamentals
Programming in C
Enter search word
Program
List of the books
FORTRAN Programming
Programming in C
```

Rewrite the name in short form

The following program reads the full name (up to 50 characters) of a person in the usual form (i.e. in the form GURU PRASANNA BHATTACHARJEE) and rewrite it in its short form (i.e. in the form G.P.BHATTACHARJEE).

Program 10.13

```
/* Writing of name in short form */
#include<stdio.h>
#include<string.h>
void main()
{
 char st[50], t[40]; /* st is the given string, t is the short form */
 int k=0,i,l,m=0;
 printf("Enter the string\n");
 gets(st);
 l=strlen(st);
 t[0]=st[0]; /* first character puts to t*/
 for(i=1;i<=l;i++)  /* finds other blank position */
    if(st[i-1]==' ' && st[i] !=' ')
      {
       k+=2;
       t[k-1]='.';
       t[k]=st[i];
       m=i; /* m is the last blank position within the string */
      }
 /* finds surname */
 if(m==0) k=0;
 for(i=m+1;i<=l;i++)
     t[++k]=st[i];
  printf("The short name is\n");
  puts(t);
}
```

A sample of input/output:

```
Enter the string
Guru Prasanna Bhattacharjee
The short name is
G.P.Bhattacharjee
```

Rewrite the name with their surname first

The following program reads the name of a person (e.g. Debabrata Pal) and then prints its surname first and the other parts of the name at the end, i.e. in the form Pal Debabrata.

Program 10.14

```
/* Write name with surname first */
```

```
#include<stdio.h>
#include<string.h>
void main()
{
 char st[50];
 int k=0,i,l;
 printf("Enter name\n");
 gets(st);
 l=strlen(st);
 /* determines last blank position */
 for(i=1;i<=l;i++)
    if(st[i-1]==' ' && st[i] !=' ') k=i;
 printf("The change name is\n");
 if(k==0)
    printf("%s",st);
 else
    {
      for(i=k;i<=l;i++) printf("%c",st[i]); /* prints surname */
      for(i=0;i<k;i++) printf("%c",st[i]); /* prints other parts */
    }
}
```

A sample of input/output:

```
Enter name
Debabrata Pal
The change name is
Pal Debabrata
```

Decimal (integer) to hexadecimal conversion

Let N be a decimal integer. We divide N by 16 and store the quotient as N and the remainder as the least significant (right most) digit of hexadecimal number. Again we divide N by 16 and store the remainder as second least significant digit and quotient as N. This process is repeated until $N = 0$. Note that if the remainders are 10, 11, 12, ..., 15, then the corresponding digits in hexadecimal number are respectively A, B, C, D, E and F, i.e. if $10 \leq$ remainder ≤ 15, then the hexadecimal number is the character whose ASCII code is (55+remainder). The ASCII code of A, B, C, D, E, F are respectively 65, 66, 67, 68, 69, 70 and that of 0, 1, 2, ..., 9 are respectively 48, 49, 50, ..., 57.

Program 10.15

```
/* Decimal to hexadecimal conversion */
#include<stdio.h>
#include<string.h>
```

```
void main()
  {
    char st[15];
    long int n,nold;
    int k=0,i,r;
    printf("Enter a decimal integer\n");
    scanf("%ld",&n);
    nold=n;
    do
     {
      r=n%16;
      n=n/16;
      if(r<=9)
        st[k++]=(char)(r+48);
      else
        st[k++]=(char)(r+55);
     }while(n>0);
    printf("Hexadecimal equivalent of %ld is ",nold);
    for(i=k-1;i>=0;i--) printf("%c",st[i]);
  }
```

A sample of input/output:

```
Enter a decimal integer
465773
Hexadecimal equivalent of 465773 is 71B6D
```

Sum of two long integers

Here a program is written to find the sum of two very long integers. The integers are read as two strings of length at most 40. Let the integers be $x = x_0x_1x_2x_3 \cdots x_{n-1}x_n$ and $y = y_0y_1y_2y_3 \cdots y_{k-1}y_k$, assume that $k \leq n$. Since the integers are read as strings, all x's and y's are numeric characters. To find the sum of two numeric characters, we have to convert them into digits and it is done by using the function `atoi()`. Then, the sum of three digits x_i, y_j and carry (from previous sum) is determined column wise. For example, we consider two integers $x_0x_1x_2x_3x_4x_5x_6$ and $y_0y_1y_2y_3$. The column wise sum is performed according to the following conventional method.

c_1	c_2	c_3	c_4	c_5	c_6	0	← carry from previous step
x_0	x_1	x_2	x_3	x_4	x_5	x_6	
			y_0	y_1	y_2	y_3	
c_0s_0	s_1	s_2	s_3	s_4	s_5	s_6	← sum
c_0	c_1	c_2	c_3	c_4	c_5	c_6	← carry

s's and c's are the sum and carry. The final sum of two integers is $c_0s_0s_1s_2s_3s_4s_5s_6$. In the program the sum is performed in two steps. In first step, the sum of the integers

$x_3x_4x_5x_6$ and $y_0y_1y_2y_3$ is performed. The carry obtained in this step is passed to the second step where the sum of this carry and the remaining part $x_0x_1x_2$ of x is performed. Each s's is converted to a character to get the final sum.

Program 10.16

```
/* Program to find the sum of two positive integers
   containing up to 40 digits */
#include<stdio.h>
#include<string.h>
#include<stdlib.h>
void main()
 {
   char x[40],y[40],c1[1],c2[1],temp[40];
   int x1,y1,carry=0,sum,Lx,Ly,i,k;
   char ans[41];
   printf("Enter two positive integers\n");
   scanf("%s%s",x,y);
   printf("Given integers are \n%s and %s\n",x,y);
 /* To make x be the larger number */
   if(strlen(x)<strlen(y)){
      strcpy(temp,x);
      strcpy(x,y);
      strcpy(y,temp);
    }
   Lx=strlen(x);  /* x is the larger number */
   Ly=strlen(y);
   k=Lx;
 /* Sum of Ly number of digits */
   for(i=Ly-1;i>=0;i--)
    {
       c1[0]=(char)x[i+Lx-Ly];
       c2[0]=(char)y[i];
       x1=atoi(c1); /* convert to integer */
       y1=atoi(c2);
       sum=x1+y1+carry; /* sum of a column */
       carry=(int)sum/10; /* carry for next column */
       sum=sum%10; /* final sum of a column */
       ans[k--]=(char)(48+sum); /* digit is converted to a character */
    }
 /* Sum of remaining part of x */
  for(i=Lx-Ly-1;i>=0;i--)
   {
```

```
    c1[0]=(char)x[i];
    x1=atoi(c1);
    sum=x1+carry;
    carry=(int)sum/10;
    sum=sum%10;
    ans[k--]=(char)(48+sum);
   }
  if(carry!=0) /* carry is set to first digit */
    ans[0]=(char)(48+carry); else ans[0]=' ';
  printf("Sum of the integers\n");
  for(i=0;i<=Lx;i++) printf("%c",ans[i]);
 }
```

A sample of input/output:

```
Enter two positive integers
847593573957395735379
845353535353535
Given integers are
847593573957395735379 and 845353535353535
Sum of the integers
847594419310931088914
```

Here, to store two such integers $40 + 40 = 80$ bytes space is used. But, these integers can be stored using 20 bytes by partitioning each integer into 10 parts (each part is an integer of 4 digits). The reader can try to determine the sum of two long integers using this technique.

Example 10.5.1 (Numeric number to word number) Write a program to convert a numeric number to a word number, i.e. write the numeric number 23067 as 'twentythree thousand sixtyseven'.

Solution. A long int is taken as input and it splits the integer into digits. If the number of digits is less than 9, then the left most digits are taken as 0 to make it a nine digits integer. Then the whole number is grouped into five groups for crore, lakh, thousand, hundred and tens-ones. The integer (at most two digits) for each group is now converted in the word form.

Program 10.17

```
 /* Conversion of a numeric number to words number */
#include<stdio.h>
#include<stdlib.h>
#include<string.h>
char c_number[100];
```

```
void main()
{
  int i=0,digit[10];
  long int number,N;
  char unit[5][10]={""," crore"," lakh"," thousand"," hundred"};
  void num2str(int,int);
  printf("Enter an (at most 9 digits) integer\n");
  scanf("%ld",&number);
  N=number;
  while(N>0) /* split in digits */
   {
     digit[++i]=N%10;
     N=N/10;
   }
  while(i<9) /* leading digits filled by zero */
    {
     digit[++i]=0;
    }
 /* formation of the string */
 /* crore, lakh and thousand places */
for(i=1;i<=6;i+=2)
 {
   N=10*digit[10-i]+digit[9-i];
   if(N!=0) {
     num2str(digit[10-i],digit[9-i]);
     strcat(c_number,unit[(i+1)/2]);
   }
 }
 N=digit[3]; /* hundredth place */
 if(N!=0) {
   num2str(0,digit[3]);
   strcat(c_number,unit[4]);
  }
 /* unit and tenth places */
 N=10*digit[2]+digit[1];
 if(N!=0) {
   num2str(digit[2],digit[1]);
  }
 printf("The given number is %ld\n",number);
 printf("Number in words\n%s",c_number);
}
```

```
void num2str(int n1,int n2)
 {
  char digit2c[][10]={"","one","two","three","four","five","six",
        "seven","eight","nine","ten","eleven","twelve","thirteen",
        "fourteen","fifteen","sixteen","seventeen","eighteen",
        "nineteen"};
  char digitc[10][8]={"","","twenty","thirty","forty","fifty",
        "sixty","seventy","eighty","ninety"};
  if(n1>=2)
    { /* number between 20 and 99 */
      strcat(c_number," "); strcat(c_number,digitc[n1]);
      if(n1>0) strcat(c_number,digit2c[n2]);
    }
  else
    { /* number between 1 and 19 */
      strcat(c_number," ");
      strcat(c_number,digit2c[n1*10+n2]);
    }
 }
```

A sample of input/output:

```
Enter an (at most 9 digits) integer
267503
The given number is 267503
Number in words
   two lakh sixtyseven thousand five hundred three
```

Important Points

1. The character constants are written within single quotes while string constants are written in double quotes. If it is required to print a double quote within a string constant, place a \ with the double quote.
2. The header file <string.h> must be included during handling of string manipulation functions.
3. The header file <ctype.h> must be included during handling of character manipulation functions.
4. The header file <stdlib.h> is required to use general utility functions.
5. The header file <stdio.h> is required for standard I/O functions.
6. Sufficient memory must be allocated for a string to hold a null character.
7. The address operator (&) is not required during reading of a string variable, but it is required for a single character variable.

8. A string cannot be assigned to a string variable, as no string assignment operator is available in C. The appropriate string functions must be used.
9. Care should be taken to add null character at the end of a string.
10. During copying and concatenation of strings, make sure that the target string has enough space to store the final string.

Exercise X

Review Questions

1. Compare the functions `getchar`, `getche`, `getch` to read a single character.
2. Describe the limitations of the functions `getchar` and `scanf` to read a string.
3. Describe all the functions which are used to read a string in C.
4. The value of a string variable can be assigned as follows:
   (a) During type declaration `char st[]="....";`
   (b) Reading using `scanf` function `scanf("%s",st);`
   (c) Reading using `gets` function `gets(st);`
   (d) Using `strcpy` function `strcpy(st,"....");`

   Compare all these situations where one is superior than the other.
5. Describe all the techniques used to assign a string to a string variable.
6. Compare the following functions:
   (a) `strcpy` and `strncpy`;
   (b) `strcat` and `strncat`;
   (c) `strcmp` and `strncmp`.
7. Write a short note on the built-in functions used for string manipulation.
8. Discuss the different ways to read the character variables.
9. What do you mean by a substring? Explain with an example.
10. Write short notes on the following functions
    `strlen(), strcat(), strcpy(), strcmp(), strncat(), strncpy(), strncmp(), strrev(), strstr(), strchr(), strrchr().`
11. Write short notes on the functions
    `isalnum(), isalpha(), iscntrl(), isdigit(), isgraph(), islower(), isprint(), ispunct(), isspace(), isupper().`
12. Suppose the string variable `str1` contains the value "I love my India." and `str2` is a string variable of length 16. Write the output of the following statements/program segments.
    (a) `printf("%s",str1);`
    (b) `printf("%s",str1[0]);`
    (c) `puts(str1);`
    (d) `for(i=0;str1[i]!=".";i++) printf("%c",str1[i]);`
    (e) `for(i=0;str1[i]!="\0";i++) printf("%d",str1[i]);`

(f) `strcpy(str2,str1); printf("%s",str2);`
(g) `strncpy(str2,str1,6); printf("%s",str2);`
(f) `printf("%d",strlen(str1));`

13. What will be the output of the following program segments?

(a)
```
char st1[]="Kolkata";
char st2[]="Kolapur";
printf("%s",strncmp(st1,st2,2));
```
(b)
```
char st1[]="Kolkata";
char st2[]="Jitpur";
strcpy(st1,st2);
printf("st1=%s st2=%s",st1,st2);
```
(c)
```
char st1[]="Kolkata";
char st2[]="Jitpur";
strncpy(st1,st2,3);
printf("st1=%s st2=%s",st1,st2);
```
(d)
```
char st[]="Kharagpur";
printf("%s",strrev(st));
```

Programming Problems

1. Write a program to do the following.
   (a) To output the question "What is your name?".
   (b) To read the name.
   (c) To print out "Thanks".
2. Suppose `char st[]="123456789";`

   Write a program to display the following output from this string.

```
    1
   232
  34543
 4567654
567898765
```

3. Write a program to read the cost of an item in the form *rrrrrrrr.pp* (where *rrrrrrrr* and *pp* represent rupees and paise respectively) and convert this numerical price into words. For example, if the price is 1234.56, the output will be RUPEES ONE THOUSAND TWO HUNDRED THIRTY FOUR AND PAISE FIFTY SIX.
4. Write a program to convert a hexadecimal (or binary or octal) number to its decimal equivalent.
5. Write a program to read a string and delete all occurrences of a given word from the string.

6. Write a program to find the frequency of all the characters of a given string.
7. Write a program to read a string of characters and encrypt it by replacing a letter by the next letter in a collating sequence. Thus, A is replaced by B, B by C, and so on and finally Z is replaced by A.
8. Write a program to read a string of characters and compute the number of different words of the string.
9. Write a program to delete all the vowels from a string of characters.
10. Write a program to read a word of 4 characters and generate all possible combinations of it.
11. Write a program to count the occurrence of a specified alphabet in a given string of characters.
12. Write a program to read a string of 80 characters and convert all the characters into upper case.
13. Write a program to read a string and print it in reverse order.
14. Write a program to read a string and replace all the occurrences of 'v' by 'b'.
15. Write a program to check whether a string is a palindrome.
16. Write a program to read the name of 10 students of a class and search for a specified name from this list of names.
17. Write a program to read 100 names and sort them in alphabetical order.
18. Write a program to read the complete name of a person and rewrite it into short form.
19. Write a program to read the name Krishna Keshab Pal and print it in the form Pal Krishna Keshab. (i.e. surname first, first name in middle and middle name at last).
20. Write a program to read a string and count the occurrence of a specified word.
21. Write a program to read a string and replace all occurrences of a specified word by another specified word.
22. Write a program to read a string and sort the words of the string in alphabetic order. Then, count the frequency of the words and the total number of different words in the string.
23. Write a program to read a numeric number 23587 as characters and print it in the form 2 $\not{b}$3 $\not{b}$5 $\not{b}$8 $\not{b}$7.
24. Write a program to insert a string IST within the string ST at a specified position.
25. Write a program to find all the positions of occurrence of a specified letter within a string.
26. Write a program to find the first occurrence of a specified letter in a string, using built-in function and without using built-in function.
27. Write a program to read a line of characters and squeeze out all blanks from it. Print the line without blank spaces.

28. Write a program to generate all symbols whose ASCII codes lie between 32 and 125.
29. Write a program to find the ASCII code of a specified letter or a digit.
30. Consider the following list of countries and their capitals.

Country	Capital
Bangladesh	Dhaka
Canada	Ottawa
China	Beijing
England	London
France	Paris
Germany	Bonn
India	New Delhi
Italy	Rome
Japan	Tokyo
Pakistan	Islamabad
United States	Washington D.C.

Write an interactive C program that will read the name of a country as input and display the corresponding capital, and vice-versa. Design the program so that it executes repeatedly, until the word `End` is encountered.

Chapter 11

Structures and Unions

The structure is a very important and useful topic in C language. A group of data binds together to form a single data with the help of structure. A single structure may contain different types of data, viz. `int, float, char`, etc. Other types of data such as array, pointer and even other structure can also be included in a single structure. With the help of a structure, one can define a new type of data and their associated functions. The individual elements are called **members** of the structure.

The `union` also contains multiple members and it is closely associated with the structure. The members of union share the same memory location, even if they are different by type. The advantage of union is that it can store different data items in same portion of the memory in different instances.

11.1 Definition of Structure

Several data items of different types are grouped into a structure. The general form to define a structure is

```
struct struct_name
  {
    data_type member1;
    data_type member2;
    . . . . . . . .
    data_type membern;
  };
```

Here `struct` is the keyword to declare a structure, `struct_name` is the name of the structure called the **tag** (this is user defined), `member1, member2, ..., membern` are n different members (variables) called **members** or **structure elements** of the `struct_name`.

It may be remembered that definition and declaration of a structure are same. Note that the semicolon (;) after closing brace (}).

The members of a structure may be ordinary variables (of type `int, char, float,` etc.) arrays, pointers and also other structures. But, storage class can not be assigned to an individual member and no member can be initialized within a structure. If a structure includes another structure, its name must be distinct, but member name may be the same.

Note that the above definition does not declare any variables. It simply describes its members and their data type, and it is called **structure template.**

Suppose a class contains 100 students and an institute would like to process the student records. For simplicity, we assume that the institute will store only roll number, name, sex and height of each student for their record. A structure for these fields can be defined as

```
struct student
  {
    int roll_no;    /* integer variable */
    char name[30]; /* an array of char */
    char sex;       /* a character variable /*
    float height    /* a floating point variable */
  }
```

Here, the structure name is `student` and the members are `roll_no, name` (30-element array), `sex` and `height`. The diagrammatic representation is shown in Fig. 11.1.

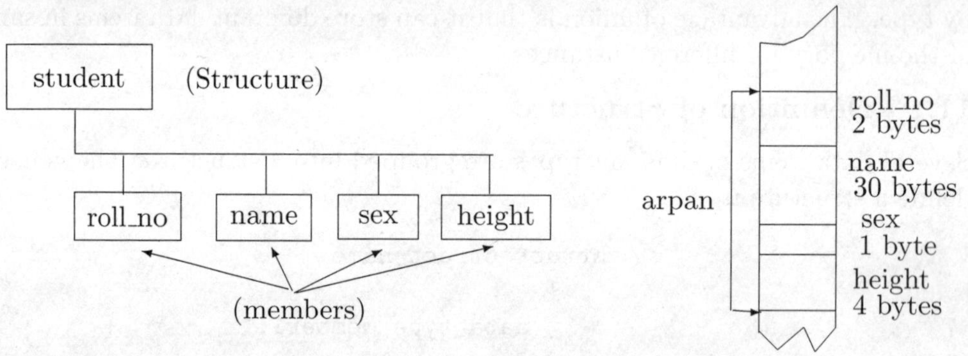

Figure 11.1: Memory allocation for structure variable

By this declaration, the structure `student` becomes a new type of data and one can define variables of type `student`. The following statement declares two variables `rajesh` and `arpan` of type `student`.

```
struct student rajesh, arpan;
```

Note that the keyword `struct` must be present during the declaration and `rajesh` and `arpan` become two structure type variables.

The general form to declare structure type variables is

```
storage_class struct struct_name var1,var2, ..., varn;
```

where `storage_class` represents storage class specifier and it is optional, `struct` is a keyword, `var1, var2, ..., varn` are n variables of type `struct_name`.

The declaration of structure type variables and the definition of structure are written together as

```
storege_class  struct  struct_name
  {
    data_type  member1;
    data_type  member2;
    . . . . . . . . . .
    data_type  membern;
  } var1,var2,...,varm;
```

In this declaration, the m variables `var1, var2, ..., varm` are declared together and their type is `struct_name`, i.e. each variable contains n data items `member1, member2, ..., membern`. The m variables are separated by commas and the declaration ends with a semicolon. The `storage_class` is optional. Also, `struct_name` is optional for this type of declaration.

Thus, the variables `rajesh` and `arpan` can be declared as

```
struct  student
  {
    int roll_no;
    char name[30];
    char sex;
    float height;
  } rajesh,arpan;
```

When a structure variable declares, a portion of memory is allocated for it and its size is equal to the sum of the bytes needed for all members of the variable. For example, 37 bytes (2 bytes for `roll_no`, 30 bytes for `name`, 1 byte for `sex` and 4 bytes for `height`) memory space is allocated for the variable `arpan` and another 37 bytes is also allocated for `rajesh`.

Note that a structure contains different types of data, so a structure is called a *heterogeneous* data type.

Difference between arrays and structures

The arrays and structures are classified as similar data types as their mechanisms are same. But, they are different in many ways.

(i) An array is a collection of elements of same data type, whereas a structure is a collection of elements of heterogeneous data type.

(ii) An array is a derived data type, but a structure is a user-defined data type.

(iii) An array is a built-in data type (`int`, `float`, `char`, etc.) An array can directly be declared and used. But, it is not possible for a structure. Firstly, a structure must be defined and then a variable of that type can be declared and used.

11.2 Accessing a Structure

Though a structure groups a number of data together, even then an individual element can be accessed separately, i.e. an individual element can be read, write, update, etc. separately. An individual member of a structure is accessed by

`variable.member`

where `variable` is a structure type variable (not structure name) and `member` is a member which is defined within the structure. The dot(.) separates the variable name and the member name. This is *an operator in C, its precedence is high and associativity is left-to-right.*

Now, consider the previous structure `student`. The member `roll_no` of the variable `arpan` is written as `arpan.roll_no`.

Similarly, `arpan.name` represents the name of `arpan`, etc. The input and output of a structure variable can be done by reading and writing all members individually. For example, the following program segment is used to read the (structure) variable `arpan`.

```
scanf(%d%s%c%f",&arpan.roll_no, arpan.name,&arpan.sex,&arpan.height);
```

Similarly, the necessary output statements to print the (structure) variable `arpan` are

```
printf("The record for arpan \n");
printf("Roll No. is: \%d\n ",arpan.roll_no);
printf("Name is     : \%s\n ",arpan.name);
printf("Sex is      : \%c\n ",arpan.sex);
printf("Height is   : \%6.2f\n ",arpan.height);
```

Notice that the expressions `&arpan.roll_no` and `&(arpan.roll_no)` are identical. Because, the precedence of dot(.) is higher as compared to the unary operators and arithmetic, relational, logical and assignment operators. Thus, the value of the expressions `++arpan.roll_no` and `++(arpan.roll_no)` are same. First the value of `arpan.roll_no` is determined and then it is incremented. This is a meaningful expression. Obviously, `++arpan` does not give any value as `arpan`, which is a group of data and it is an erroneous expression. A particular element, say fifth, of the member `name` (it is an array) can be accessed as `arpan.name[5]`. It gives the fifth character of the member `name` of the structure variable `arpan`.

11.3 Copying and Logical Operations on Structure Variables

A structure type variable can be assigned to another structure type variable of same type, like ordinary variables. If `a, b, c` are three structure type variables of same type then the statements

```
a=b;
b=c;
```

are valid.

But, two structure type variables can not be compared. For example, `a==b` or `a !=` `b` or `a>b` are not valid. Two structure type variables of similar type are equal, if the individual elements are same. If any two individual members of two structure variables are different (either their types or values), then they are different (structure) variables.

11.4 Nested Structure

A structure can be defined within another structure. This process is called **nesting of structure**.

Now, we add the date of birth of the students to the structure `student`. A date has three parts – day, month and year, and a structure for it can be defined as

```
struct date
    {
      int day;
      int month;
      int year;
    };
```

Now, we include this structure to the structure `student`. The necessary declaration is

```
struct student
    {
      int roll_no;
      char name[30];
      char sex;
      float height;
      struct date date_of_birth;
    };
```

Here the structure `date` is nested within the structure `student`. The structure `student` contains another structure `date` and this new structure contains more information than the old one.

If `arpan` is a variable of this new structure `student`, then the three individual members of `date_of_birth` can be accessed by writing,
`arpan.date_of_birth.day,arpan.date_of_birth.month,arpan.date_of_birth.year`

These members behave as ordinary variables and one can apply any unary, binary or any other operations as required. The memory allocation for the structure variable `arpan` is shown in Fig. 11.2.

In general, a member of nested structure can be accessed as

`variable.outer_memebr.inner_member`

where `variable` is a structure type variable, `outer_member` is the direct member of the structure and `inner_member` is the member of the structure defined within the structure.

The above nested structure can also be defined as

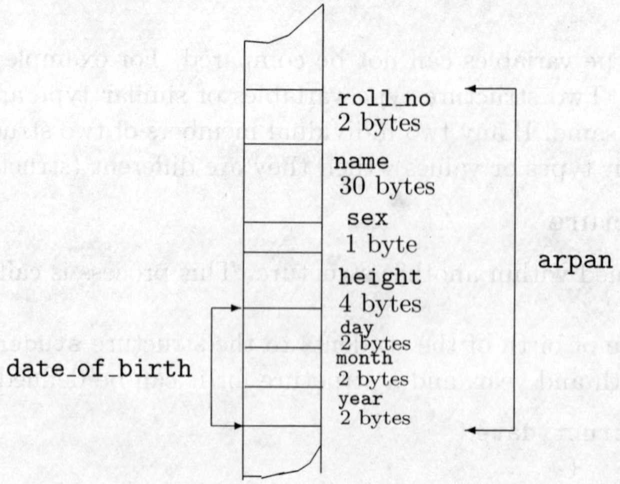

Figure 11.2: Memory allocation for the variable arpan.

```
struct student
        {
            int roll_no;
            char name[30];
            char sex;
            struct date
                {
                    int day;
                    int month;
                    int year;
                } dob;
        };
```

An illustration of a structure variable is given below.

Example 11.4.1 In a two-dimensional Cartesian coordinates system, a point has two components namely (abscissa, ordinate). A line is an object connecting two such points. Using C structures how do you represent a point, and a line.

Write a function in C that accepts a line structure and returns

1, if the line is horizontal,

2, if the line is vertical,

3, if the line is oblique.

Program 11.1

```
/* This program defines a line (2-D) using structure and tests the
```

```
   orientation (vertical, horizontal, oblique) of the line. */
#include<stdio.h>
/* Global declaration of structure */
struct point /* declaration of point */
   {
     float x,y;
   };
struct line  /* declaration of line */
   {
     struct point p,q;
   };
void main()
 {
  int i;
  struct line a;   /* a is declared as a line */
  int line_type(struct line);
  printf("Enter first end point of the line\n");
  scanf("%f%f",&a.p.x,&a.p.y);
  printf("Enter second end point of the line\n");
  scanf("%f%f",&a.q.x,&a.q.y);
  i=line_type(a);  /* function passes a structure a of type line */
  switch (i)
    {
     case 1: printf("Line is horizontal "); break;
     case 2: printf("The line is vertical ");break;
     case 3: printf("The line is oblique "); break;
    }
 }
/* Function to determine the type of a line */
int line_type(struct line a)
 {
   float slope_num,slope_den;
   slope_num=a.p.x-a.q.x;
   slope_den=a.p.y-a.q.y;
   if(slope_den==0)
    return(1);
  else
    if(slope_num==0)
     return(2);
    else
     return(3);
}
```

A sample of input/output:

```
Enter first end point of the line
3 7
Enter second end point of the line
3.4 6.7
The line is oblique
```

In this program, a point is defined in terms of two floating point values. A line is formed with the help of two points. The end points of the line are supplied using `scanf` function. The numerator and denominator of the slope are computed and based on these values, the orientation of the line is determined.

11.5 Initialization of Structure Variable

Like ordinary variables, the members of a structure variable can also be initialized. The general form is

```
storege_class struct struct_name
                  variable={value1, value2, . . ., valuen};
```

where `variable` is a variable of type `struct_name`. The quantities `value1, value2, . . ., valuen` are the values of the first, second, and so on members of the `variable`. The initial values of (`value1, value2, . . ., valuen`) must appear in the order in which they are declared within the structure. A structure variable can be initialized only if its storage class is either `external` or `static`.

Suppose `arpan` is a variable of the modified structure `student` (containing the structure variable `data_of_birth`). The assignment of initial value can be done by the statement

```
static struct student arpan={777,"Arpan Pal",'m',48,6,7,2001};
```

This declaration initializes the members as follows.

```
arpan.roll_no=777;
arpan.name="Arpan Pal";
arpan.sex='m';
arpan.height=48;
arpan.date_of_birth.day=6;
arpan.date_of_birth.month=7;
arpan.date_of_birth.year=2001;
```

It means the date of birth is 6 July 2001. The above statements can also be used to initialize the variable `arpan`.

Rules of initializing structure variables

The following rules must be followed during the initialisation of structures.

(i) Individual member cannot be initialized inside the structure definition.

(ii) The order of values within braces must match the order of members defined in a structure.

(iii) Partial initialization is also possible. In this case, only first few members can be initialized and the remaining members remain blank.

(iv) The uninitialized members assign default values. The integer and floating point members set to 0 and characters and strings are assigned to '\0'.

11.6 Array of Structure

Since structure variable is a new type (user define) of data, like integer array one can define array of a structure variable. Each element of the array is a structure. The general form to declare such array is

```
struct student cs_student[50];
```

In this declaration `cs_student` is an array of 50 elements and each element is a structure of type `student`. This array can also be defined as

```
struct date                    struct student
   {                              {
     int day;                       int roll_no;
     int month;                     char name[30];
     int year;                      char sex;
   };                               float height;
                                    struct date date_of_birth;
                                 }cs_student[50];
```

The date of $(i+1)$th `cs_student` can be accessed as

```
cs_student[i].roll_no,
cs_student[i].name,
cs_student[i].sex,
cs_student[i].height,
cs_student[i].date_of_birth.day,
cs_student[i].date_of_birth.month,
cs_student[i].date_of_birth.year,
```

These represent respectively the `roll_no`, `name`, `sex`, `height` and date of birth (`day`, `month`, `year`). A particular character, say 5th, of the member `name` of the 10th student is obtained from the expression

```
cs_student[9].name[4];
```

11.6.1 Initialization of array of structure

An array of structures can be initialized in the same way as a single structure. The process is very simple and illustrated by the following example.

```
struct date                     struct student
{                               {
  int day;                        int roll_no;
  int month;                      char name[30];
  int year;                       char sex;
};                                float height;
                                  struct date dob;
                                }cs_student[50];
```

The following statement initializes the record of 5 students.

```
struct student cs_student[5]=
  {
     777,"Aniket Pal",'m',48,6,7,2001,
     555,"Amal Adak",'m',50,7,2,2002,
     333,"Tapan Senapati",'m',58,15,3,2001,
     333,"Nasreen Khan",'f',78,12,12,2003,
     222,"Akul Rana",'m',57,10,5,2002
  };
```

Here `cs_student` is an array of 5 elements of data type student. `cs_student[0]` will be assigned the first set of values, `cs_student[1]` the second set of values and so on. Here, the 5 sets of data are written in five different lines for clear understanding, but, these values can be written in a single line also. Again, values for a member can be enclosed within braces. This representation is far better than the other forms. That is, the above initialization can be rewritten as

```
struct student cs_student[5]=
  {
     {777,"Aniket Pal",'m',48,6,7,2001},
     {555,"Amal Adak",'m',50,7,2,2002},
     {333,"Tapan Senapati",'m',58,15,3,2001},
     {333,"Nasreen Khan",'f',78,12,12,2003},
     {222,"Akul Rana",'m',57,10,5,2002}
  };
```

Now, we consider an example to explain the advantage of structure data.

Example 11.6.1 (Sorting of record) Suppose the roll number, name and total marks of some students are known. Write a program to read the roll number, name and marks of all students and prepare a merit list for them (i.e. sort the records in descending order of marks).

Program 11.2

```
/* Sorting of record in descending order with respect to marks */
#include<stdio.h>
void main()
 {
   struct student
     {
       int roll_no;
       char name[15];
       int mark;
     };
 struct student cs_student[40], temp;
 int i,j,n;
 printf("How many students \n");
 scanf("%d",&n);
 /* reading of records */
 printf("Enter the records\n");
 for(i=0;i<n;i++)
     {
      scanf("%d",&cs_student[i].roll_no);
      scanf("%s",cs_student[i].name);
      scanf("%d",&cs_student[i].mark);
     }
 /* sorting of records */
  for(i=0;i<=n-2;i++)
    for(j=i+1;j<=n-1;j++)
     {
      if(cs_student[i].mark<cs_student[j].mark)
        {
           /* interchange between two records */
           temp=cs_student[i];
           cs_student[i]=cs_student[j];
           cs_student[j]=temp;
        }
     }
 /* printing of records */
printf("Sorted record is\n");
for(i=0;i<n;i++)
  printf("%4d %-15s %5d\n",cs_student[i].roll_no,
           cs_student[i].name,cs_student[i].mark);
}
```

A sample of input/output:

```
How many students
```

```
6
Enter the records
11 Aniket 90
22 Rahul 34
33 Sanjib 50
44 Tapan 60
55 Kalyani 35
66 Monoranjan 47

Sorted record is
  11 Aniket          90
  44 Tapan           60
  33 Sanjib          50
  66 Monoranjan      47
  55 Kalyani         35
  22 Rahul           34
```

A structure named **student** is defined having three data members, roll number, name and marks. An array `cs_student` of size 40 is declared whose type is `student`. The records for all students are read by `scanf` functions. The sorting of records with respect to mark is done by exchange sorting technique. The new thing is that the interchange between two records. The statement `cs_student[i]=cs_student[j]` copies all the members of the $(j+1)$th element of the array `cs_student` to the corresponding members of the $(i+1)$th element of the same array, i.e. entire structure is copied by this single statement. This statement is equivalent to the following three statements

```
cs_student[i].roll_no=cs_student[j].roll_no;
cs_student[i].name=cs_student[j].name;
cs_student[i].maek=cs_student[j].mark;
```

Instead of these three statements, only one statement is used to copy a structure and this is a major advantage to use structure.

11.7 User Defined Data Types

Using the concept of structure we have seen that a new data type can be defined in C. But, to declare a variable of structure type the keyword `struct` is written before the structure name. This can be removed by using the keyword `typedef`. Using this keyword a new data type can be defined that is equivalent to the standard data type. Once a new data type is defined, the ordinary variables, arrays, pointers, etc. can be declared like standard data type.

The general form to define new data type is

```
typedef data_type new_data_type;
```

where `data_type` is either a standard data type or other user defined data type, `new_data_type` is the name of new data type and `typedef` is the required keyword.

For example,

```
typedef int mark;
```

defines a new data type `mark` which is basically an integer. Now, one can declare the variables of type `mark` as follows:

```
mark phy_mark, chem_mark;
```

Thus like integer (or any other standard) variable one can define variables of type `mark`. Here `phy_mark` and `chem_mark` are two variables of type `mark`, these are actually of type integer because type of `mark` is `int`.

The following declaration is interesting.

```
typedef char string[50];
string name, address;
```

The first line defines a data type `string` which is a 50-element array. The second line declares two variables `name` and `address` of type `string`. Since `string` is a 50-element array of type `char`, therefore `name` and `address` are also arrays of length 50 of type `char`. These types of data are useful in some particular applications.

The above definition is equivalent to the following one.

```
typedef char string;
string name[50], address[50];
```

The feature of `typedef` is significant when it is used in structure. A new data type which contains multiple members can be defined with the help of `typedef` and structure.

The following syntax is used to define a new data type whose base is a structure

```
typedef struct
{
    . . . . . .
    . . . . . .
} new_data_type;
```

where `new_data_type` (this is supplied by user) is the user defined data type. Remember that this is not the name of the variable.

Now, the variable of `new_data_type` is declared as same as standard data type.

Let us consider the following structure.

```
typedef struct
{
    int roll_no;
    char name[30];
    char sex;
    float height;
} student;
```

The variables of type `student` is declared as

```
student cs_student, me_student,ee_student[4];
```

Note that the keyword `struct` is not required to declared a variable, but the keyword `typedef` is used to define structure.

The more complicated data type can be defined by repeated use of `typedef`. For example,

```
typedef struct
{
    int day;
    int month;
    int year;
}date;

typedef struct
{
    int roll_no;
    char name[30];
    char sex;
    float height;
    date date_of_birth;
} student;
```

Here `date` and `student` are user defined data type. The data type `date` is used to define the data type `student`.

11.8 Structures and Pointers

Like integer and other standard pointer variables, structure type pointer variables can also be declared.

If `var` is a structure type variable, then `&var` represents the starting address of that variable. A pointer for a structure type variable can be declared as

```
data_type *pv;
```

where `data_type` is the type of data. In this case, it is of type structure. `*pv` represents the name of the pointer variable.

To illustrate the structure type pointer variable, let us consider the following structure.

```
typedef struct
{
    int roll_no;
    char name[30];
    char sex;
    float height;
}student;
```

```
student cs_student, *ps;
```

Here cs_student is a variable of type student, but, ps is a pointer variable which points to student (structure data type).

It is obvious that when the variable cs_student is declared of type student, a space is allocated for this variable. For the variable cs_student, 37 bytes is allocated in computer memory.

Now, when the statement

```
pv=&cs_student;
```

is executed, then the beginning address of the allocated space for cs_student is assigned to pv.

The above declaration (the definition of structure as typedef and declaration of variable of type student) may be written as

```
struct
    {
        int roll_no;
        char name[30];
        char sex;
        float height;
    } cs_student, *pv;
```

Care has to be taken to access the individual structure member when a pointer is associated. An individual member is accessed with the help of the operator $->$ (composition of minus operator and greater than sign). If pv is a structure type pointer variable, then a member can be accessed by the expression

```
pv->member;
```

Note that $->$ is comparable to dot (.) operator and this expression is equivalent to

```
structure_variable.member;
```

Let us consider the following structure to illustrate the use of individual member.

```
typedef struct
    {
        int day;
        int month;
        int year;
    } date;
typedef struct
    {
        int roll_no;
        char name[30];
        char sex;
        float height;
```

```
                    date date_of_birth;
                } student;
```

Now, we consider

```
student cs_student, *pv;
```

and the address of cs_student is assigned to pv as

```
pv=&cs_student;
```

By this statement pv points to cs_student.

The roll_no of the cs_student can be accessed by any one of the following statements

```
cs_student.roll_no;   (here pointer is not used)
pv->roll_no;          (pointer pv is used)
(*pv).roll_no;
```

In the last expression parentheses are required as the precedence of dot is higher than parentheses. If parentheses are not used, then dot operator is applied first, i.e. the computer will try to determine the value of pv.roll_no, but it does not mean anything, so an error will occur.

The name of cs_student can be accessed by any one of the following expressions

```
cs_student.name      pv->name      (*pv).name
```

But, a particular character of name, say fifth character can be accessed by using any one of the following expressions

```
cs_student.name[4]       pv->name[4]         (*pv).name[4]
*(cs_student.name+4)     pv->(name+4)        *((*pv).name+4)
```

The last three expressions are more complicated than the first three.

The year of date_of_birth can be accessed by writing any one of the following

```
cs_student.date_of_birth.year       pv->date_of_birth.year
(*pv).date_of_birth.year
```

A pointer variable can also be included in a structure. If memberpt is a member of a structure and it is a pointer member and variable is a variable of the related structure, then *variable.memberpt gives the value associated to the member memberpt. Similarly, if pv is the pointer variable which points to a structure type variable, then *pv-> memberpt gives the value (content) of the pointer member memberpt.

Let us consider the following program to use the pointer variable as structure member.

Program 11.3

```
/* Use of pointer variable as structure member */
#include<stdio.h>
main()
  {
```

```
   int r=45;
   char nam[]="Aniket";
   char s='m';
   float h=48;
   int d=6,m=7,y=2001;
   typedef struct
      {
         int day;
         int month;
         int year;
      } date;
   typedef struct
      {
         int *roll_no;
         char *name;
         char *sex;
         float *height;
         date dob;
      } student;
   student *pv, cs_student;
   cs_student.roll_no=&r;
   cs_student.name=nam;
   cs_student.sex=&s;
   cs_student.height=&h;
   cs_student.dob.day=d;
   cs_student.dob.month=m;
   cs_student.dob.year=y;
   pv=&cs_student;          /* pv points to cs_student */
   printf("%d %s %c %f DOB=%d.%d.%d\n", *cs_student.roll_no,
      cs_student.name, *cs_student.sex,
      *cs_student.height,cs_student.dob.day,cs_student.dob.month,
      cs_student.dob.year);
   printf("%d %s %c %f DOB=%d.%d.%d\n", *pv.roll_no,
      pv.name, *pv.sex,*pv.height,pv.dob.day,pv.dob.month,pv.dob.year);
} /* main */
```

The output of this program is

```
45  Aniket  m   48  DOB=6.7.2001
45  Aniket  m   48  DOB=6.7.2001
```

Note that the assignment statement `roll_no` is a pointer variable, so `cs_student.roll_no` is a pointer variable and & operator is used to assign the value of r to `cs_student.roll_no`. In this case the address is assigned. `nam` is an array, so it points to a string and to assign it to `cs_student.name` no & operator is needed. `cs_student.dob.day`, `cs_student.dob.month` and `cs_student.dob.year` are ordinary variables, so & operator is not required for these assignment.

Again, since `cs_student.roll_no` is a pointer, therefore `*cs_student.roll_no` represents its content. Note that * is not required to print a string of characters. Again, since `cs_student.dob.day` is an ordinary variable, no * is required to print its value.

Observe that second print statement. `pr->roll_no, pv->sex, pv->height` represents pointer, to print their contents * is required. Note, that to access the content of `pv->roll_no`, we use the expression `*pv->roll_no` not `pv->*roll_no`. The latter one is incorrect. `dob.day, dob.month, dob.year` are ordinary variables. Therefore, no asterisk is required to print the values of these variables. But, the operator -> is used to indicate that `dob.day` is a member of `pv`.

Note that the precedence of the operator -> is high, i.e. the precedence of both the operator -> and . (dot) are same. Also, their associativity is left to right. Moreover, the precedence of the operator -> is higher than any unary operator, arithmetic, relational and logical or assignment operators. Thus, extreme care should be taken while using this operator.

Now, we will discuss about the arithmetic of a pointer variable. Since the precedence of -> is higher than the unary operator, say `++`, therefore the expressions `++pv->member` and `++pv->member.submember` are equivalent to `++(pv-member)` and `++(pv->member.submember)` respectively. Thus, if the value of `pv->member` is 40, then after execution of the expression `++pv->member` or `++(pv->member)` the value of `pv->member` will be 41. But, the expressions `(++pv)->member` and `++pv->member` are different. In the expression `++pv`, the increment operator is applied on the pointer variable `pv`. If at any instant the value of `pv` is `FFE6`, then after execution of the expression `++pv` the value will be `FFE6+size of (pv)`. If the size of the structure associate to `pv` is 49 bytes (31 in hex), then `FFE6+sizeof(pv)` will be `FFE6+31=10027`. Thus, `(++pv)` points to next structure type variable (this happens in case of array of structures) and `(++pv)->member` represents the value of the corresponding member's value.

11.9 Passing Structure to Function

Like ordinary variable, structure type variable can also be passed to a function. There are several ways to pass a structure type variable to a function or return a structure type result from a function. The simplest way to pass a structure type data is passing of individual member values (like ordinary variable), and the value of only one member can be returned through `return` statement. In other way a complete structure can be passed as argument.

Let us consider the following program to illustrate the transformation of individual arguments.

Program 11.4

```
/* Function call by individual structure member */
#include<stdio.h>
void main()
  {
    typedef struct
       {
         int roll_no;
         char name[30];
         int ph_mark,chem_mark,math_mark,total_mark;
       } student;
    student ankit;
    int total;
    int calculate_total(int,int,int);
    ankit.roll_no=100;
    ankit.name="Ankit Sarkar";
    ankit.ph_mark=50;
    ankit.chem_mark=60;
    ankit.math_mark=70;
    ankit.total_mark=calculate_total(ankit.ph_mark,
                      ankit.chem_mark,ankit.math_mark);
    printf("Total marks of %s is %d\n",ankit.name,ankit.total_mark);
  }
/* definition of function */
int calculate_total(int p, int c, int m)
  {
    return(p+c+m);
  }
```

In this program, a portion of structure (the fields `ph_mark`, `chem_mark` and `math_mark`) `ankit` is transferred to the function `calculate_total` and the single value, sum of these marks is returned to the main function.

An entire structure can be transferred to a function by passing a pointer argument, which points to a structure type variable. This logic is similar to passing an array to a function. This process (argument passed by pointer) is passed by **reference** rather by **value**.

Let us consider the following structure.

```
typedef struct
    {
        int roll_no;
        char name[30];
        char sex;
        float height;
```

```
                } student;
            student *pa,*pb,student1,student2;
```

Suppose the function add_height adds the heights of two students student1 and student2. The calling function will be of the form

```
add_height(&student1, &student2);
```

and the function definition is

```
float add_height(student *stud1, student *stud2)
  {
      float x;
      x=(*stud1).height+(*stud2).height;
      return x;
  }
```

Here the addresses of student1 and student2 are passed to the function. The individual member (height) of the pointer (structure type) stud1 is obtained from the expression (*stud1).height.

Example 11.9.1 (Arithmetic of complex number) Define a structure for complex number, which contains two parts real and imaginary. Then, define functions for addition, subtraction, multiplication and multiplication by scalar. Demonstrate these functions by evaluating the complex expression $z^2 - 2z + c$, where $c = 2 + 3i$ and z is a complex variable.

Solution. Six functions, viz. read, add, sub, mul, s_mul and print are defined here. The functions add, sub and mul adds, subtracts and multiplies two complex numbers. The function s_mul is used to multiply a complex number by a scalar. The functions read and print are used as input and output functions.

The expression $z^2 - 2z + c$ is evaluated as

$$\begin{aligned} z^2 - 2z + c &= z_1 - z_2 + c && \text{where } z_1 = \texttt{mul}(z, z), z_2 = \texttt{s\_mul}(2, z) \\ &= z_3 + c && z_3 = \texttt{sub}(z_1, z_2) \\ &= z_4 && z_4 = \texttt{add}(z_3, c). \end{aligned}$$

Thus, z_4 is the final value of the expression.

Program 11.5

```
/* Program to find the roots of a quadratic equation,
   using the concept of complex number  */
#include<stdio.h>
  typedef struct
    {
       float real, imag;
    } complex;
```

```
main()
  {
   complex c,z,z1,z2,z3,z4; /* note that complex is a new data type */
   complex read(); /* reading of a complex number */
   complex add(complex *,complex *); /* addition of complex numbers */
   complex sub(complex *,complex *); /* subtraction of complex numbers */
   complex mul(complex *,complex *); /* multiplication
                                     between two complex numbers */
   complex s_mul(float , complex *); /* multiplication by a scalar */
   void print(complex *); /* printing of a complex number */

   printf("Enter the value of z\n");
   z=read();
   /* c=(2,3) */
   c.real=2;
   c.imag=3;
   z1=mul(&z,&z); /* z1=z*z */
   z2=s_mul(2,&z); /* z2=2*z */
   z3=sub(&z1,&z2); /*z3=z1-z2 */
   z4=add(&z3,&c);  /*z4=z3+c=z1-z2+c=z^2-2*z+c */
   printf("The value of the expression =");
   print(&z4); /* value of the expression; returns a structure */
   return;
}
/* function for reading */
complex read()
  {
   complex a;
   printf("Enter real and imaginary parts\n");
   scanf("%f%f",&a.real,&a.imag);
   return a;
  }
/* function for printing */
void print(complex *a)
  {
   printf("(%f,%f)",(*a).real,(*a).imag);
  }
/* function addition */
complex add(complex *a, complex *b)
  {
    complex c;
```

```
    c.real=(*a).real+(*b).real;
    c.imag=(*a).imag+(*b).imag;
    return c;
  }
/* function for subtraction */
complex sub(complex *a, complex *b)
  {
    complex c;
    c.real=(*a).real-(*b).real;
    c.imag=(*a).imag-(*b).imag;
    return c;
  }
/* function for multiplication */
complex mul(complex *a, complex *b)
  {
    complex c;
    c.real=(*a).real*(*b).real-(*a).imag*(*b).imag;
    c.imag=(*a).real*(*b).imag+(*b).real*(*a).imag;
    return c;
  }
/* function for multiplication of a complex number by a scalar */
complex s_mul(float k, complex *a)
  {
    complex c;
    c.real=k*(*a).real;
    c.imag=k*(*a).imag;
    return c;
  }
```

A sample of input/output:

```
Enter the value of z
Enter real and imaginary parts
2.45 5.63
The value of the expression =(-28.594400,19.327002)
```

Now, we solve another problem involving a complex number.

Example 11.9.2 (Solution of quadratic equation) Write a program to find the roots of a quadratic equation.

Solution. Let the quadratic equation be $ax^2 + bx + c = 0$. The roots of this equation are

$$\frac{-b + \sqrt{b^2 - 4ac}}{2a} \text{ and } \frac{-b - \sqrt{b^2 - 4ac}}{2a}.$$

Let $d = b^2 - 4ac$. If $d < 0$, then $\sqrt{d}$ is a complex number, but $\sqrt{d}$ (for $d < 0$) cannot be calculated directly. Let $p = -b/(2a)$ and $q = \sqrt{|d|}/(2a)$. If $d \geq 0$, then the roots are $p + q$ and $p - q$ and if $d < 0$, then the roots are $p + iq$ and $p - iq$.

Program 11.6

```
/* Computation of roots of quadratic equation, using structure.
   This program also determines the complex roots */
#include<stdio.h>
#include<math.h>
  typedef struct
      {
         float real, imag;
      } complex;

main()
 {
   complex x1,x2;
   float a,b,c,p,q,d;
   complex cmplx(float , float ); /* converts real
                                          number to complex number */
   void print(complex *); /* printing of a complex number */
   printf("Enter the values of a,b,c\n");
   scanf("%f%f%f",&a,&b,&c);
   d=b*b-4*a*c; /* discriminant */
   p=-b/(a+a);
   q=sqrt(fabs(d))/(a+a);
   if(d<0)
     {
       x1=cmplx(p,q);   /* x1=p+iq */
       x2=cmplx(p,-q); /* x2=p-iq */
       printf("\nThe roots are complex and they are\n");
       print(&x1);
       print(&x2);
     }
    else if (d==0)
     {
       printf("\nRoots are real and equal and they are\n");
       printf("%f %f\n",p,p);
     }
    else
      {
       printf("\nRoots are real and unequal and they are\n");
```

```
    printf("%f %f\n",p+q,p-q);
   }
  return;
}

/* a pair of real numbers makes a complex number */
complex cmplx(float r, float i)
  {
   complex a;
   a.real=r;
   a.imag=i;
   return a; /* a=(r,i) */
  }
void print(complex *a)
  {
   printf("(%7.5f,%7.5f)",(*a).real,(*a).imag);
  }
```

A sample of input/output:

```
Enter the values of a,b,c
2.3 4.5 2.25
The roots are complex and they are (-0.9783,0.1458)(-0.9783,-0.1458)
```

Passing array of structures to function

The process to a passing an array to a function is used to pass an array of structures to function. The same syntax and properties are used to pass an array of structures.

Example 11.9.3 (Tabulation of student marks) Suppose a class of students studying three subjects `sub1`, `sub2` and `sub3`. The full marks of each subject is 100. The grade of the students are evaluated as follows.

Range of marks	Grade
$90 \leq$ percentage of marks ≤ 100	A
$80 \leq$ percentage of marks < 90	B
$70 \leq$ percentage of marks < 80	C
$60 \leq$ percentage of marks < 70	D
below 60 percent	F

Write a program to find the percentage of marks and grade of n students. Print the tabulation sheet containing roll numbers, names, marks of three subjects, total marks, percentage of marks and grades of students according to their merit.

Program 11.7

```
/* Preparation of merit list of a group of students, using structure */
#include<stdio.h>
  typedef struct
    {
      int roll;
      char name[15];
      int sub1,sub2,sub3,total;
      float p_mark;
      char grade;
    } student;
student s[50];   /* global declaration of student array */
main()
 {
   int i,n;
   void  grade_calculation(int);
   void sort(int);
   student read();
   printf("How many students ? ");
   scanf("%d",&n);
   for(i=0;i<n;i++) /* reading of records */
     {
      printf("Enter the record of %dth student\n",i+1);
      s[i]=read();
     }
   grade_calculation(n);
   sort(n);
   printf("The tabulation sheet of the students\n");
   printf("Roll \t\tName\tSub1\tSub2\tSub3\tTotal\tP_mark\tGrade\n");
   for(i=0;i<n;i++)
     {
      printf("%d\t%-15s\t%d\t%d",s[i].roll,s[i].name,s[i].sub1,
                                                      s[i].sub2);
      printf("\t%d\t%d\t%5.2f\t%c\n",s[i].sub3,s[i].total,
                                      s[i].p_mark,s[i].grade);
     }
return;
} / *end of main */

student read()
  {
    student t;
    printf("\nRoll No: ");
```

```
    scanf("%d",&t.roll);
    printf("\nName : ");
    scanf("%s",t.name);
    printf("\nMarks in three subjects: ");
    scanf("%d%d%d",&t.sub1,&t.sub2,&t.sub3);
    return t;
  }
/* calculation of total marks and percentage of marks */
  void grade_calculation(int n)
    {
      int i,k;
      float ave;
      for(i=0;i<n;i++)
        {
          s[i].total=s[i].sub1+s[i].sub2+s[i].sub3;
          s[i].p_mark=s[i].total/3;
          k=(int)(s[i].p_mark/10);
          /* 60<=p_mark<70  : k=6 : Grade=D
             70<=p_mark<80  : k=7 : Grade=C
             80<=p_mark<90  : k=8 : Grade=B
             90<=p_mark<100 : k=9 : Grade=A
             p_mark=100         : Grade=A */
  /* Calculation of grade */
          switch (k)
           {
           case 9:
             s[i].grade='A';
             break;
           case 8:
             s[i].grade='B';
             break;
           case 7:
             s[i].grade='C';
             break;
           case 6:
             s[i].grade='D';
             break;
           default:
             s[i].grade='F';
           }
         if(k==10) s[i].grade='A';
        }
```

```
 }
/* sorting of records according to decreasing order of total marks */
void sort(int n)
 {
   student temp;
   int i,j;
   for(i=0;i<=n-2;i++)
     for(j=i+1;j<=n-1;j++)
      {
        if(s[i].total<s[j].total)
         {
           temp=s[i];
           s[i]=s[j];
           s[j]=temp;
         }
      }
 }
```

A sample of input/output:

```
How many students ?
4
Enter the record of 1th student
Roll No: 11
Name : Aniket
Marks in three subjects: 56 78 90

Enter the record of 2th student
Roll No: 22
Name : Ranjan
Marks in three subjects: 61 72 34

Enter the record of 3th student
Roll No: 23
Name : Paru
Marks in three subjects: 45 67 89

Enter the record of 4th student
Roll No: 44
Name : Bulti
Marks in three subjects: 34 52 13

The tabulation sheet of the students
Roll Name          Sub1 Sub2 Sub3    Total P_mark  Grade
```

```
11   Aniket         56   78   90      224   74.00   C
23   Paru           45   67   89      201   67.00   D
22   Ranjan         61   72   34      167   55.00   F
44   Bulti          34   52   13      99    33.00   F
```

Here a structure `student` is defined, which contains the members `roll, name, sub1, sub2, sub3` (marks of three subjects), `total` (total mark), `p_mark` (percentage of mark) and `grade`.

The array `s` of type `student` is declared globally. The function `read()` is used to read the record of a student. This function returns a structure value. The function `grade_calculation()` calculates the total mark, percentage of mark and grade of each student, using `switch` statement. The function `sort()`, arrange the student records according to the decreasing order of the marks. The sorted tabulation sheet is then printed by this program.

11.10 Self-Referential Structures

In a structure, it is possible to include one member that is a pointer to the parent structure type. This type of structure is extensively used to define a data structure called *linked list*. Its general form is

```
struct tag{
  member1;
  member2;
  . . . .
  struct tag *ptr;
};
```

where `ptr` is the name of the pointer variables. That is, the structure of type `tag` contains a member that points to another structure of type `tag`. These types of structures are called **self-referential** structures.

Let us consider the following example.

```
struct node
  {
    int x;
    struct node *link;
  };
```

Here, the structure `node` is defined which has two members – an integer `x` and a pointer `link` to a structure of same type.

11.11 Linked Lists

Linked list is a list of some items. Each item in the list is called a **node** and contains two fields, a **data** field and a **link** field (address of the next node) (see Figure 11.3). The data field holds the actual element on the list. That is, a node is a structure element containing two elements – data (it may be an ordinary variable or an array or multiple values) and link. In C, it is defined with the help of self-referential pointers as shown below.

```
struct element
 {
     int data;
     struct element *link;
 };
```

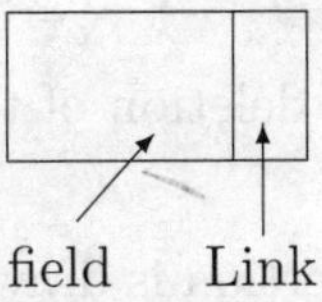

Figure 11.3: A node

The link field contains the address of the next node in the list. Such an address, which is used to access a particular node, is known as a **pointer**. The entire linked list is accessed from an external pointer called **head** node, which points to (contains the address of) the first node in the list. The link field of the last node in the list contains a special value, known as **null** or 0, which is not a valid address. This **null pointer** is used to signal the end of a list. The list with no nodes on it is called an **empty list** or the **null list**. The value of the external pointer **head** to such a list is the null pointer. Thus, a list can be initialized to the empty list by the operation `head=NULL`.

It is conventional to draw linked lists as an ordered sequence of nodes with links being represented by arrows (see Figure 11.4).

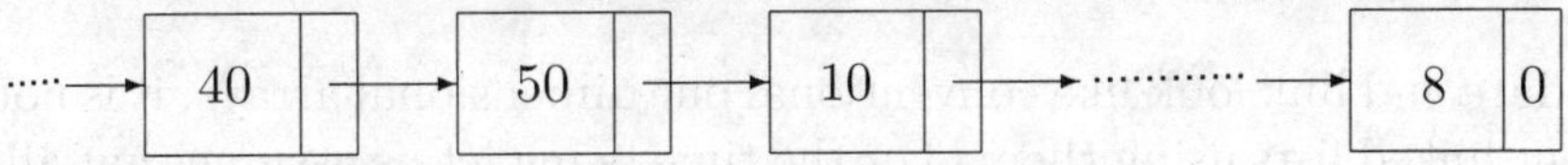

Figure 11.4: A portion of a list

Notice that we do not explicitly put in the values of the pointers but simply draw arrows to indicate that they are there. When a program is written which works with lists, we almost never look for a specific address except to test for `NULL` or 0.

Insertion and deletion of an item to the linked list are easy. To insert the data item 60 between 50 and 10 in the linked list of Figure 11.4, the following steps are to be performed.

(i) Get a node which is currently unused, let its address be X.

(ii) Set the data field of this node to 60.

(iii) Set the link field of X to point to the node after 50 which contains 10.

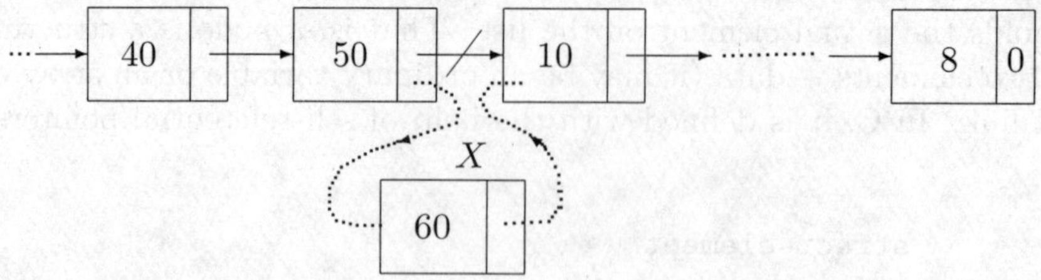

Figure 11.5: The list after insertion of the node X after the node containing 50.

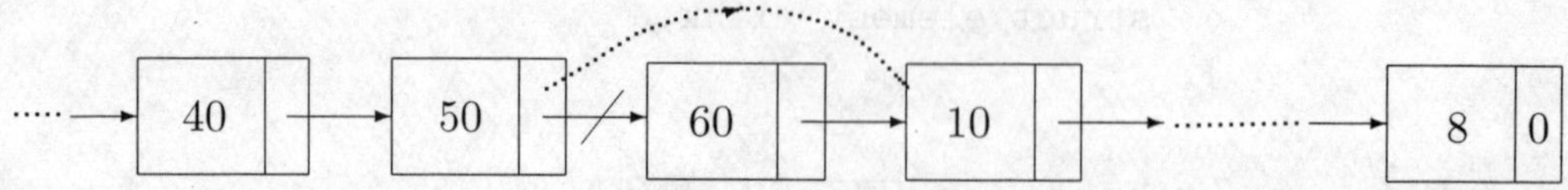

Figure 11.6: List after deletion of the node containing 60.

The Figure 11.5 shows how the insertion is drawn using our arrow notation. The new arrows are dashed. The important thing to notice is that when 60 is inserted in the list, no elements of the list have to move. We have overcome the need to move data at the expense of storage needed for the second field link.

Now, suppose we want to delete 60 from the list. For this purpose, it is required to find the element which immediately precedes 60, which is 50. Again, there is no need to move the data around. Even though the link field of 60 contains a pointer to 10, 60 is no longer in the list.

From this brief discussion of linked lists it is seen that the following capabilities are needed to make linked representations possible:

(i) A mechanism for dividing memory into nodes each having at least one link field.

(ii) A mechanism to determine which nodes are in use and which are free.

(iii) A mechanism to transfer nodes from the reserved pool to the free pool and vice-versa.

Though data and link look like conventional one dimensional arrays, it is not necessary to implement linked lists using them. For the time being let us assume that all free nodes are kept in a *black box* which is called the storage pool and that there exist subalgorithms:

(i) `X=getnode()` which provides in X a pointer to a free node but if no node is free, it prints an error message and stops;

(ii) `free(`X`)` which returns node X to the storage pool.

11.11.1 Use of linked lists

Example 11.11.1 (Evaluation of sum and maximum from list) Write an algorithm to create a linked list containing n elements $x_1, x_2, \ldots, x_n$. Find the sum of the elements of the list and the largest element among them.

Program 11.8

Program 11.8

```
/* Processing of linked list. This program creates a linked list,
   determines the sum of the elements in the list and also
   determines the largest element within the list */
#include<stdio.h>
#include<stdlib.h>
#include<ctype.h>
#define NULL 0

struct element { /* definition of a node */
  float data;             /* data item for a node */
  struct element *link; /* pointer to the next node */
 };
typedef struct element node;
node *getnode(); /* returns address of an empty node */
node *create();  /* returns address of the head node of the list */

void main()
  {
    node *head;
    float sum(node *);      /* function to find the sum of the
                               elements of the nodes */
    float largest(node *); /* finds the maximum among the
                               elements of the list */
    head=create();          /* creates a linked list. head stores the
                               address of the first node */
    /* computation of sum */
    printf("\nSum of the elements = %f",sum(head));
    /* computation of maximum value */
    printf("\nLargest element is %f",largest(head));
  }

/* Returns the address of a new node for use */
node *getnode()
  {
    return((node* )malloc(sizeof(node)));
  }

/* Function to create a new linked list */
node *create()
  {
    node *head,*prenode,*curnode; /* prenode and curnode are used to
                                     represent previous and current nodes */
```

```
    float x;
    int n,i=1;
    char ch;
    printf("\nHow many numbers ? ");
    scanf("%d",&n);
    printf("\nEnter first number ");
/* Creating head node */
    scanf("%f",&x);
    head=getnode();
    head->data=x;    /* set data filed as x */
    head->link=NULL; /* set link of the node */
    prenode=head;
    /* insertion of remaining members to the list */
    for(i=2;i<=n;i++)
     {
       printf("Enter %dth number ",i);
       scanf("%f",&x);
       curnode=getnode();
       curnode->data=x;
       curnode->link=NULL;
       prenode->link=curnode;
       prenode=curnode;
     }
    return(head);/* returns the address of the first node of list */
  }/* end of create */

/* Function to find the sum of the elements of the list */
float sum(node *h) /* h is the head node */
  {
    float s=0;
    do
      {
        s+=h->data;
        h=h->link; /* goto next node */
      }while(h!=NULL);
    return(s); /* returns a floating point value */
  } /* end of sum */

/* Function to find the largest element from the list */
float largest(node *h) /* h is the head node */
  {
    float max;
```

```
    max=h->data;
    h=h->link; /* goto second node */
    do
      {
        if(h->data>max) max=h->data;
        h=h->link;  /* goto next node */
      }while(h!=NULL);
    return(max); /* returns a floating point value */
  } /* end of largest */
```

A sample of input/output:

```
How many numbers ?
7
Enter first number
23
Enter 2th number
45
Enter 3th number
67.5
Enter 4th number
12.5
Enter 5th number
-23
Enter 6th number
34.6
Enter 7th number
20.25
Sum of the elements = 179.850006
Largest element is 67.500000
```

Example 11.11.2 (Insertion sort using linked list) Write an algorithm for insertion sort using linked list.

Solution. The basic step in this method is to insert a record R into a sequence of ordered records in such a way that the resulting sequence is also ordered. Here we sort the data in the ascending order.

In insertion sort a node is inserted to the list in such a way that the resulting list becomes a sorted sequence. Insertions are made in two ways. If the data of the head node is less than the input value x (at a particular instant), then a new node containing x is inserted before the head node and this new node becomes the head of the appended list, otherwise a search is initiated for the appropriate position for the input value and a new node is inserted containing this value.

Program 11.9

```
/* Insertion sort. Sorting of elements using linked list */
#include<stdio.h>
#include<stdlib.h>
#define NULL 0

struct element {
   float data;            /* data item for a node */
   struct element *link; /* pointer to the next node */
 };

typedef struct element node;
node *getnode();  /* returns address of an empty node */

void main()
  {
    node *head;
    node *insort(); /* declaration of function */
    void display(node*);
    head=insort(); /* sorting of elements */
    display(head); /* display the list */
  }

/* Returns a new node for use */
node *getnode()
  {
    return((node* )malloc(sizeof(node)));
  }

/* Insertion sort, sorting in ascending order */
node *insort()
  {
    node *head,*prenode,*curnode,*tempnode;
    float x;
    int n,i;

    printf("\nHow many numbers ? ");
    scanf("%d",&n);
    printf("\nEnter the numbers ");

    curnode=getnode(); /* node for the first element */
    scanf("%f",&x); /* x is the input data */
    head=curnode; /* head node of the list */
```

```
  curnode->data=x; /* assigns data to the node */
  curnode->link=NULL; /* assigns link to the node */
  prenode=curnode;
  for(i=2;i<=n;i++) /*insertion of remaining n-1 elements */
   {
    curnode=head;
    scanf("%f",&x);
    if(curnode->data>=x) /* insertion before head node */
      {
        curnode=getnode();
        curnode->data=x;
        curnode->link=head;
        head=curnode;
      }
    else
      { /* finds appropriate position for insertion */
        while((curnode->data<x) && (curnode!=NULL))
          {
            prenode=curnode; /* search appropriate position for x */
            curnode=curnode->link; /* goto next node */
          }
        /* insert a new node before curnode */
        tempnode=getnode();
        tempnode->data=x;
        prenode->link=tempnode;
        tempnode->link=curnode;
      }
   }/* end of for */
 return head;  /* returns head node of the sorted list*/
 } /* end of insort */

/* Displays all elements of the list */
void display(node *h) /* h is the head node */
 {
  printf("The sorted list is \n");
  do
    {
     printf("%0.3f  ",h->data);
     h=h->link; /* goto next node */
    }while(h!=NULL);
 } /* end of display */
```

A sample of input/output:

```
How many numbers ?
8
Enter the numbers
-34 56.7 89.3 -23 12 45.5 24.5
The sorted list is
-34.000 -23.000 12.000 24.500 45.500 56.700 89.300
```

For illustration, let us consider the data 15, 10, 25, 20.
At the initial stage the list is as follows:

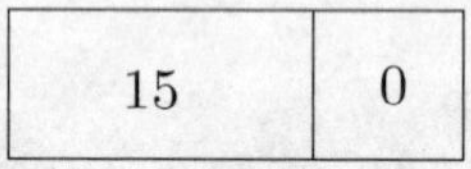

When $x = 10$, then a new node is inserted at the beginning of the list is as follows:

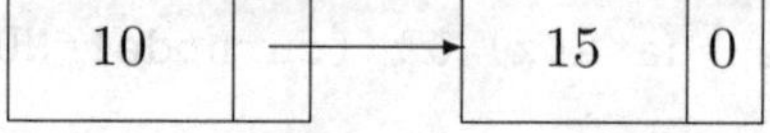

When $x = 25$, then a new node containing $x = 25$ is inserted at the end of the list.

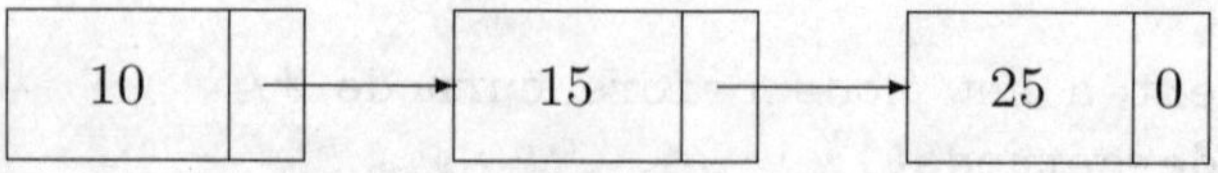

When $x = 20$, then a new node whose data field 20 is inserted between the nodes containing 15 and 25 is as follows:

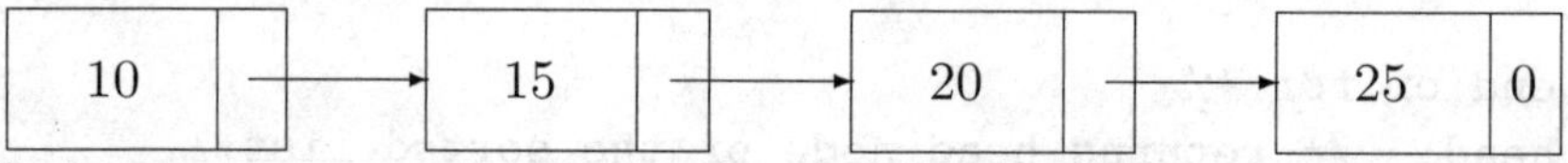

Observe that the list is sorted sequence at each instant.

Addition of two polynomials

The manipulation of symbolic polynomial has become a classical example of the use of list processing. In general, we want to represent the polynomial

$$P(x) = a_m x^{e_m} + a_{m-1} x^{e_{m-1}} + \cdots + a_1 x^{e_1}$$

where the a_i are non-zero coefficients with exponents e_i such that $e_m > e_{m-1} > \cdots > e_2 > e_1 \geq 0$. Each term will be represented by a node. A node will be of fixed size having three fields which represent the coefficient and exponent of a term plus a pointer to the next term as shown below:

coef	exp	link

For instance, the polynomial $P(x) = 3x^{150} - 4x^8 + 3$ would be stored as

Head node = P

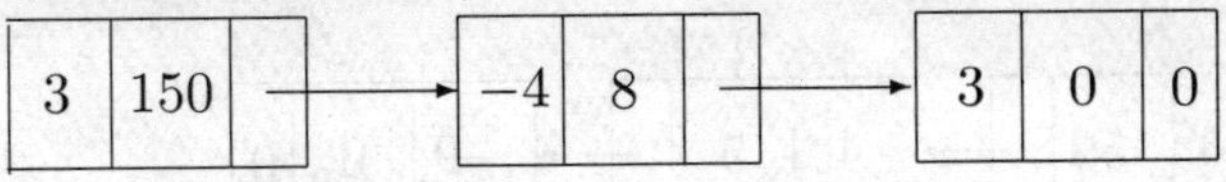

while $Q(x) = 21x^{200} - 3x^{150} + 4x^5 - 9$ would look like

Head node = Q

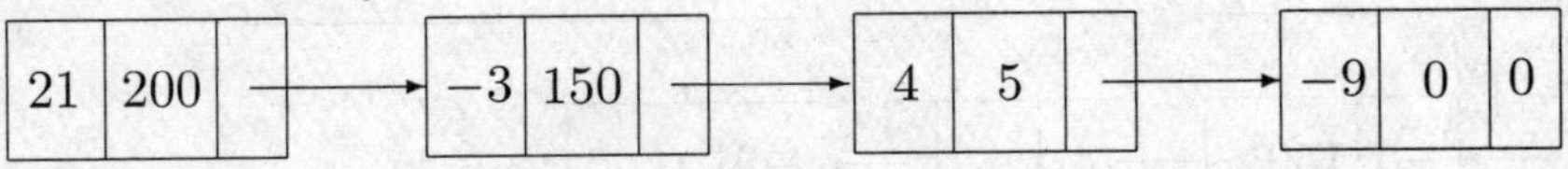

Here two polynomials P and Q are added and replace the value in the polynomial P.

In order to add two polynomials together, we examine their terms starting at the nodes after head nodes pointed by `P` and `Q`. Two pointers `X` and `Y` are used to move along the nodes of P and Q. If the exponents of two terms are equal, then the coefficients are added and replace it to the node of P and pointers `X` and `Y` are advanced to the next terms. If the exponent of the current term in P is less than the exponent of the current term of Q, then a duplicate term of Q is created and attached to P before the current term of P. The pointer `Y` is advanced to the current term of P. The pointer `Y` is advanced to the next term. If the exponent of the current term of P is greater than the exponent of the current term of Q, then advance the pointer `X` to the next term.

Step 1: (exp(`X`)<exp(`Y`)) (exp(`X`) is the exponent stored in the node `X`).

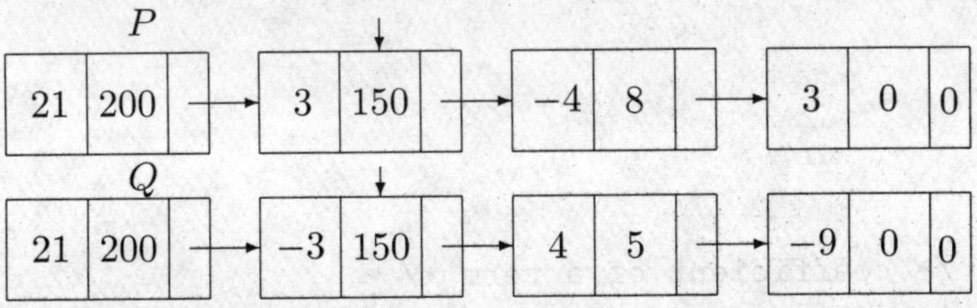

Step 2: (exp(`X`)=exp(`Y`))

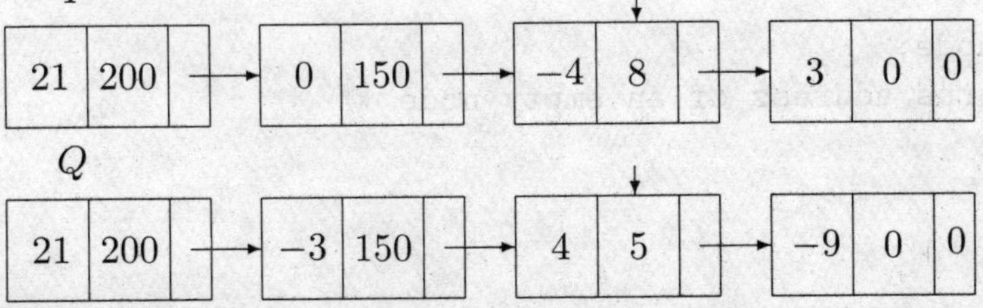

Step 3: (exp(`X`)>exp(`Y`))

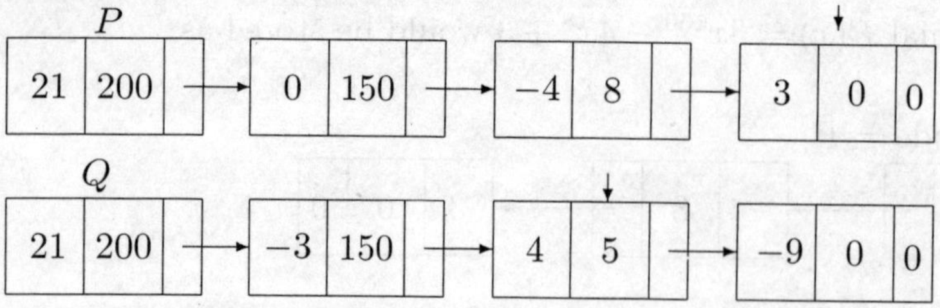

Step 4: (exp(X)<exp(Y))

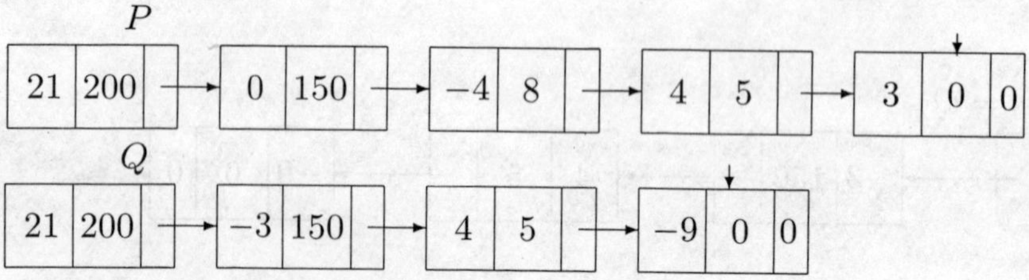

Step 5: (exp(X)=exp(Y))

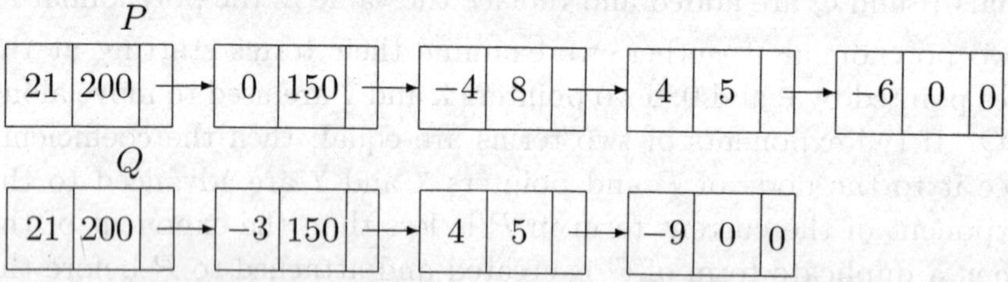

Program 11.10

```
/* Addition of two polynomials P and Q and stored it in P */
#include<stdio.h>
#include<stdlib.h>
#include<math.h>
#define NULL 0

struct element {
  float  coef;            /* coefficient of a term */
  int    exp;             /* exponent of a term */
  struct element *link; /* pointer to the next node */
 };
typedef struct element node;
node *getnode(); /* returns address of an empty node */
void display(node*);

void main()
  {
    node *S,*P,*Q;
```

```
    node *addpoly(node*,node*);
    node *create();

    printf("\nEnter first polynomial\n");
    P=create(); /* creates first polynomial */
    printf("\nEnter second polynomial\n");
    Q=create(); /* creates second polynomial */
    printf("The first polynomial is\n");
    display(P);
    printf("The second polynomial is\n");
    display(Q);
    S=addpoly(P,Q); /* adds polynomials */
    printf("The added polynomial is\n");
    display(S); /* display the result */
  }

/* Returns a new node for use */
node *getnode()
  {
    return((node* )malloc(sizeof(node)));
  }

/* Creates a new linked list */
node *create()
  {
    node *head,*prenode,*curnode;
    float x;
    int n,e,i=1;
    char ch;
    printf("How many terms ? ");
    scanf("%d",&n);
    printf("Exponents are in the descending order\n");
/* Creating head node */
    printf("Enter first term (coefficient and exponent) ");
    scanf("%f%d",&x,&e);
    head=getnode();
    head->coef=x;
    head->exp=e;
    head->link=NULL;
    prenode=head;
    for(i=2;i<=n;i++)
     {
```

```
        printf("Enter %dth term (coefficient and exponent) ",i);
        scanf("%f%d",&x,&e);
        curnode=getnode();
        curnode->coef=x;
        curnode->exp=e;
        curnode->link=NULL;
        prenode->link=curnode;
        prenode=curnode;
      }
    return(head);
  }/* end of create */

/* Addition of polynomials */
node *addpoly(node *P, node *Q)
   {
    node *X,*Y,*prex,*u;
    X=P;  prex=P;
    Y=Q;
    while(Y!=NULL)
     {
      if((X->exp)==(Y->exp))
        {
          X->coef=X->coef+Y->coef;
          if(X!=NULL){
             prex=X;
             X=X->link;
            }
           if(Y!=NULL) Y=Y->link;
        }
      else if((X->exp)<(Y->exp))
        {
          u=getnode();
          u->exp=Y->exp;
          u->coef=Y->coef;
          u->link=X;

          if(X==P) P=u; /* if insertion at the beginning */
             else
               prex->link=u;
          prex=u;
          if(Y!=NULL) Y=Y->link;
        }
```

```
      else //if(X->exp>Y->exp)
        {
          if(X!=NULL)
            {
              prex=X; X=X->link;
            }
          else /* add remaining terms of Q to P */
            {
              prex->link=Y;
              break;
             }
          }
      } /* while */
   return(P);
  }

/* Displays all elements of the list */
void display(node *h) /* h is the head node */
  {
   do
     {
    printf("%+.4fx^%-3d",h->coef,h->exp);
    h=h->link; /* goto next node */
      }while(h!=NULL);
   printf("\n");
  } /* end of display */
```

A sample of input/output:

```
Enter first polynomial
How many terms ?
5
Exponents are in the descending order
Enter first term (coefficient and exponent)
-2 10
Enter 2th term (coefficient and exponent)
3 7
Enter 3th term (coefficient and exponent)
4 5
Enter 4th term (coefficient and exponent)
2 4
Enter 5th term (coefficient and exponent)
-5.5 2
Enter second polynomial
```

```
How many terms ?
6
Exponents are in the descending order
Enter first term (coefficient and exponent)
3 12
Enter 2th term (coefficient and exponent)
4 8
Enter 3th term (coefficient and exponent)
4.5 5
Enter 4th term (coefficient and exponent)
5 4
Enter 5th term (coefficient and exponent)
5 2
Enter 6th term (coefficient and exponent)
23.5 0

The first polynomial is
-2.0000x^10 +3.0000x^7 +4.0000x^5 +2.0000x^4 -5.5000x^2
The second polynomial is
+3.0000x^12 +4.0000x^8 +4.5000x^5 +5.0000x^4 +5.0000x^2 +23.5000x^0
The added polynomial is
+3.0000x^12 -2.0000x^10 +4.0000x^8 +3.0000x^7 +8.5000x^5
  +7.0000x^4 -0.5000x^2 +23.5000x^0
```

11.12 Union

In a program all the variables occupies different memory locations to store their values. Also, the values of all the members of a structure are stored in different memory locations. But, sometimes we observe that a variable or an array is used for the first part (or a portion) of the program and another variable or array is used in the next part (other portion) of the program. To minimize the space, one can assign two or more variables or arrays into the same memory location. This can be done with the help of `union`. That is, the members within a union share the same storage area. This is useful when a program involves multiple data and the values need not be assigned to all of the members simultaneously. Only one memory of a union is active at a particular time instant. A mechanism is required to manage the space and to activate a particular member. All these are done by compiler automatically. However, the use must keep a track of what type of information is activated at any given time.

The declaration of a union is similar to the structure. The general form is

```
union union_name
  {
     data_type member1;
     data_type member2;
```

```
              . . . . . . . . .
              data_type membern;
         };
```

where union is the required keyword, data_type is the data type of each member member1, member2, ..., membern. union_name is the name of union, which is also called **tag**.

The variable of union type is declared as

```
storage_class union union_name variable1, variable2, ..., variablem
```

where variable1, variable2, ..., variablem are the variables of type union_name, storage_class is optional, it specifies storage class of union_name.

The above two declarations may also be combined as

```
         storage_class union union_name
         {
              data_type member1;
              data_type member2;
              . . . . . . . . .
              data_type membern;
         } variable1, variable2,. . ., variablem;
```

The union_name is optional for this type of declaration.

Since all the members of a union share same memory space, the compiler will allocate sufficient space for the variables of union to accommodate the largest member in the union. Other members also use the same space.

Define a union named emp with a variable var and a pointer *pu.

```
union emp
  {
     int emp_id;
     char name[30];
  };
union emp var, *pu;
```

The above declaration may be combined as

```
union emp
  {
     int emp_id;
     char name[30];
  } var, *pu;
```

Here, union is defined along with a variable var and a pointer variable *pu.

In this case, 30 bytes of memory space is allocated for the variable var.

The members of union can be accessed in similar way of structure, i.e. they can be accessed by either dot or $->$ operator.

Let us consider the above structure emp and the following declaration.

```
union emp e1, *e2;
e2=&e1;
```

The individual members can be accessed by the following statements

```
e1.emp_id;      /* access the emp_id */
e1.name;
e2->emp_id;
e2->name; /* access the name */
```

Assignments are also similar to assignment of structure.

11.12.1 Difference between structure and union

There is no difference in declaration of structure and union, only the keywords `struct` and `union` are used to declare them.

(i) The amount of space required to store a structure variable is the sum of the bytes needed to store all members of the structure. Whereas the space required to allocate a union type variable is equal to the bytes of largest members (the member needs maximum amount of computer memory).

For example, let

```
struct
   {
      int roll_no;
      char name[30];
      float height;
   } s_student;
union
   {
     int roll_no;
     char name[30];
     float height;
   } u_student;
```

The space occupied by the variable `s_student` and `u_student` can be determined by the operator `sizeof`. The value of `sizeof(s_student)` and `sizeof(u_student)` are respectively 36 bytes $(2+30+4$ bytes) and 30 bytes (the size of maximum member, i.e. `name`).

(ii) Again, all the members of a structure can be accessed at any instant simultaneously, but only one member of a union may be accessed at a time. The reason is, at any instant, only one member of a union carries a meaningful value. The member which is written at last, contains the correct value, and at this moment the other members contain garbage. Thus, the programmer should remember which member is active at a particular moment.

Let us consider the following example to illustrate the above concept.

Program 11.11

```
/* Illustration of union */
#include<stdio.h>
#include<string.h>
  union
    {
      int roll;
      char name[30];
      float height;
    } student;
void main()
 {
   student.roll=100;  /* roll is active now */
   printf("Roll No.: %d\n",student.roll);
   printf("Name    : %s\n",student.name);
   printf("Height  : %5.2f\n",student.height);
   strcpy(student.name,"Sachin");  /* name is active now */
   printf("Roll No.: %d\n",student.roll);
   printf("Name    : %s\n",student.name);
   printf("Height  : %5.2f\n",student.height);
   student.height=48.56;  /* height is active now */
   printf("Roll No.: %d\n",student.roll);
   printf("Name    : %s\n",student.name);
   printf("Height  : %5.2f\n",student.height);
 }
```

The output of this program is

```
Roll No.: 100                              /* correct value */
Name    : d                                /* incorrect value */
Height  :  0.00                            /* incorrect value */
Roll No.: 24915                            /* incorrect value */
Name    : Sachin                           /* correct value */
Height  : 4295090026267457750000000.00     /* incorrect value */
Roll No.: 15729                            /* incorrect value */
Name    : q=BBin                           /* incorrect value */
Height  : 48.56                            /* correct value */
```

It is observed that when a particular member is active, then the value of this active member is correct whereas the other values are garbage. Thus, the conclusion is that at any time only one member of a union variable carries correct value and other members contain meaningless values.

Important Points

1. A semicolon should be placed at the end of the definition of structure.
2. A structure variable can also be declared during definition of structure by placing it between closing brace and semicolon.
3. A structure variable cannot be declared at the time of creating a `typedef` definition. In this case, *new_data_type* is used to declare a variable in an independent statement. The *new_data_type* be placed in between closing brace and semicolon.
4. Assignment of a structure variable to another structure variable is possible only if they are of same type.
5. Two structure variables are same if all the members are equal.
6. When accessing a member with a pointer and dot notation, parentheses are required around the pointer, e.g. `(*pt).a`.
7. No space is allowed between − and > in the operator (− >). It is a single token.
8. Passing structures to functions by pointers is more efficient than passing by value.
9. A union variable can be assigned to another union variable, provided both the variables have the same composition.
10. The address of a union variable can be determined by the operator &.
11. A union variable can pass to a function as an argument.
12. A function can accept and return a union or a pointer to a union.
13. The arithmetic and logical operators on a union variable (as a whole) are not allowed.

Exercise XI

Review Questions

1. What is a structure? Define its members. How a structure is different from an array?
2. How structure variables are declared? Can a structure variable be defined as a member of another structure? Can an array be included as a member of a structure? Can an array have structures as elements?
3. Why a structure is called a heterogeneous data type? Explain the concept of self referential structure with an example.
4. How the members of a structure variable assign initial values? How is an array of structures initialized?
5. Write the rules for initializing structures.
6. Describe with examples, the different ways of assigning values to structure members.

7. How can an array of structure be initialized? What are the default values of the integer, float and character type members of a structure?
8. How can a member of a structure be accessed? What is the precedence of the operator . (period)?
9. Explain (i) nested structures, and (ii) array of structures.
10. How can the size of a structure be determined? What unit is used to measure the size of a structure?
11. What is the use of `typedef`? How can we define a special type of data?
12. Explain the meaning and the use of **`struct`**, **`typedef`** and **`sizeof`**.
13. How can a structure-type pointer variable be declared? How can an individual structure member be accessed in terms of its corresponding pointer variables? What is the precedence of the operator $->$? What is its associativity?
14. Suppose a member of a structure is a pointer variable. How can the object of the pointer be accessed in terms of structure variable name and the member name?
15. How one can pass a structure to a function? How can a structure be returned from a function?
16. Describe three different methods that can be used to pass structures as function arguments.
17. What is a union? How is a union different from a structure?
18. How is a union member accessed? How can a union member be processed? How is the member of a union variable assigned an initial value?
19. What is the difference between structure and union? Explain.

Problems

1. Define a structure `team` that contains the members (i) team name, (ii) number of matches won, (iii) number of matches lost, and (iv) percentage of matches won. Declare a variable `TT` of type `team`. Write the necessary statement(s) to initialize `TT` with the following values:
   Team name: Kolkata Knight Riders
   Won: 20
   Lost: 6
   Percentage: 76.92.
2. A structure `ABC` is defined as follows:

```
        int x;
        float y;
        char z[3];
```

Following statements are used to define the variables `a, b, c` of type `ABC`. Which of them is incorrect and why?

(a) `struct a, b, c;`
(b) `struct ABC a, b, c;`
(c) `ABC a, b, c;`
(d) `struct ABC a[];`
(e) `struct ABC a={ };`
(f) `struct ABC a={2,3,4};`
(g) `struct ABC a={2,4.5,"ROM"};`
(e) `struct ABC a=3, 5.6, "RED";`

3. Given the structure definitions and declarations

```
typedef struct AB          typedef struct XY
  {                          {
     int a;                     int x;
     float b;                   float y;
  };                         };
                           AB ab1,ab2;
                           XY xy1,xy2;
```

Find errors, if any, in the following statements.

(a) `ab1=ab2;`
(b) `ab1=xy1;`
(c) `ab1.a=100;`
(d) `ab2.a=10.45;`
(e) `printf("%d",a+x);`
(f) `printf("%d",ab1.a+xy1.x);`
(g) `printf("%d",ab1+xy1);`
(h) `if(ab1 != xy1) printf("%d",ab1.a);`

4. Find the errors in the following program segment.

```
typedef struct cost
  {
     char name[10];
     float price;
  }COST a[10];
cost b;
COST c;
```

5. Find the output of the following program segment.

```
main()
  {
     union
       {
```

```
            int i;
            float f;
            char c;
          }abc;
        printf("%d\n",sizeof(abc)):
        abc.i=345;
        printf("%d %f %c \n",abc.i,abc.f,abc.c);
        abc.f=34.55;
        printf("%d %f %c \n",abc.i,abc.f,abc.c);
        abc.c='R';
        printf("%d %f %c \n",abc.i,abc.f,abc.c);
    }
```

Programming Problems

1. Define a structure containing two floating point members, `real` and `imaginary`. Include the tag `complex` within the definition. Declare the variables `x1`, `x2` and `x3` as `complex`. Read the values of these variables and find their magnitudes ($\sqrt{real^2 + imaginary^2}$).
2. Consider the following structure declaration:

```
        struct comp{
            int x,y;
          };
        typedef struct comp complex;
```

   Write three functions called `sum`, `mult` and `show` that will add and multiply two complex numbers and display the complex number in $(x + iy)$ form respectively.
3. Define a structure `vector` with three members `xcomp`, `ycomp`, `zcomp` representing x-, y- and z- components of a vector respectively. Write a function which reads a `vector` and returns it to the main function. Write another function which receive two `vectors` and returns their sum. Write third function which receives a `vector` and returns its magnitude. Print all the values from the main function.
4. Define a structure `vector` with five members. Write a program to perform the following tasks:
   (a) Create a vector
   (b) Multiply by a scalar
   (c) Modify the value of a given element
   (d) Display its value in the form (10,-30,3.4,2.45,30).
5. Define a structure `tele` consisting two fields name and telephone number. Write a program to perform the following tasks.
   (a) Read 10 records
   (b) Modify the telephone number of a given person
   (c) Display the telephone number of a given person
   (d) Display the name of the person when a telephone number is given.

6. Define a structure consisting three members `roll`, `sex` and `name` and include the tag `student`. Declare an array `stud` of size 100 of type `student`. Write a program to read this array of size n ($<= 100$) and sort it with respect to the increasing order of `roll`.
7. Write a structure named 'student' with five members, viz. roll number (integer), name (string of length 20), sex (character), height (float) and mark (integer). Write a function which will read the records of 10 students and sort this data according to the decreasing order of the marks. Also find the average height of the students.
8. Define a structure that can describe a college. The members of this structure is the name of the college, address, grade, subjects offered along with the intake and number of teachers available for each subject. Write a program to perform the following tasks:
   (a) Print out the colleges of a given grade along with subjects offered
   (b) Print out the colleges with a specific subject along with intake
   (c) Print out the teachers of a particular subject of a specific college.
9. Define a structure `country` consisting name of a country, name of its capital and total population. Write a program to read the records of 10 countries and perform the following tasks.
   (a) Prepare a sorted list (sort according to the increasing order of country name) containing the name of the country, name of its capital and number of population
   (b) Prepare a sorted list (sort according to the decreasing order of population) containing the name of the country, name of the capital and number of population.
10. Define a structure called `cricket` containing the members player name, team name, total run, average run, number of centuries, number of games played and number of wickets taken. Declare an array `player` of type `cricket` of size 30. Write a program to read the information of 30 players and print out a team-wise list containing names, total run, average run, number of centuries.
11. Use the structure defined in Exercise 10 and declare an array `ODI` of type `cricket` which stores the information of the cricketers played who ODI. Write a program to read the information of 30 players and sort the array according to the decreasing order of the total run and print out a list of players containing names, team name and total run.
12. In a 2-dimensional Cartesian coordinates system, a point has two components namely (abscissa, ordinate). A line is an object connecting two such points. Using C structures how do you represent (i) a point, and (ii) a line. Write a function in C that accepts a line structure and returns
    (a) 1, if the line is horizontal,
    (b) 2, if the line is vertical, and
    (c) 3, if the line is oblique.

Chapter 12

File Processing

In the programs of previous chapters it is assumed that the input is supplied from the keyboard (the standard input device) and output is displayed on the monitor (the standard output device). But, when the size of input or output is large, then it is time consuming to enter data or to read output from the display terminal (monitor) at a time. Many business and scientific applications require large amount of data to be entered and saved for later use. Instead of reading (or writing) data from the keyboard (on monitor) one can read (or write) from (to) a unit called **data file** or simply **file**. The file primarily resides in primary memory and when it is saved it is stored in secondary memory. Thus, data files allow us to store information permanently and one can access and modify whenever necessary.

A data file is a collection of information. An individual information is called a **field**. Collection of fields form a **record** and collection of similar records form a **file**.

Depending on the storing technique, the data file are classified into two categories – **stream-oriented** (or **standard** or **ASCII** or **text**) files and **system-oriented** (or **low-level** or **binary**) files. The stream-oriented files are readable and opened in any text editor and it is so easy to work with these types of files. These files are commonly used. On the other hand, system-oriented (binary) files are not readable by any arbitrary text editor. To store information in ASCII file, it needs more space than a binary file.

The binary files are generally used to design and develop a complex database or to read and write a binary information. The binary file is more accurate because it stores the exact internal representation of data. There are no conversion errors or round off errors. Storing data in binary form takes less time as no conversion is required during storing data to a file. But, binary data file cannot be easily transferred from one computer to another due to variations in the internal representation of the data in the computer. On the other hand, the ASCII file or text file can easily be transferred from one computer to another.

12.1 File Pointer, Opening and Closing a File

A computer cannot read (or write) data directly from (or to) the file which resides in secondary storage. During reading from a data file, the information is transferred from data file to a special portion of primary memory called **buffer area**, and then it is used in a program. The use of buffer area speeds up the reading or writing to the data file.

To use a data file, at first we have to declare a special pointer of type `FILE` (all characters must be upper case) which points to the beginning of the buffer area. `FILE` is a structure defined in the header file `stdio.h`. A pointer of type `FILE` is declared as

```
FILE *fp;
```

The pointer `fp` is referred as a **stream pointer** or simply a **stream**. This pointer is very important during the use of data file.

After declaration of file pointer, the file must be opened for use (reading or writing or both for reading and writing). The function `fopen` is used to open a file. The general form is

```
fp=fopen(file_name, file_type);
```

where `file_name` and `file_type` are two strings (constants or variables) they represent the name of the data file and the manner in which it must be opened (reading, writing, both reading and writing, appending, overwriting, etc.). The `file_name` is a valid name of a file which is allowed by the operating system. For ASCII file, the `file_type` must be one of the strings as shown in Table 12.1.

file_type	Use
"r"	Open an existing file for reading only
"r+"	Open an existing file for both reading and writing
"w"	Open a new file for writing only. If a file with the file name `file_name` exists, it will be destroyed and then a new file will be created with name `file_name`.
"w+"	Open a new file for both reading and writing. If the file having name `file_name` exists, it will be destroyed and a new file will be created for both reading and writing.
"a"	Open an existing file for appending. That is, for adding new data at the end of file. If no such file exists, then a new file will be created.
"a+"	Open an existing file for both reading and appending. If no such file exists, then a new file will be created.

Table 12.1:

The `fopen` function returns a pointer which points to a buffer. If `fopen` returns a NULL pointer, then it indicates that the file associated in `fopen` function is not opened successfully.

The two statements

```
FILE *fp;
fp=fopen("sample.dat","r");
```

can be written as

```
FILE *fp=fopen("sample.dat","r");
```

In the first declaration, fp is declared as a file pointer and second statement opens a file named sample.dat for reading. While in the second declaration, the file pointer fp is declared as well as the function fopen is assigned to it.

If a file is opened, it must be closed. This can be done by the following statement

```
fclose(fp);
```

where fp is the file pointer associated to the file which is opened for use. When a file is closed, then the buffer created for it, will be destroyed and the memory allocated for buffer becomes free. If the file is not closed, the compiler will automatically close the file at the end of the program. Some times it may happen that if the data file is not properly closed, then the entire data is erased from the file. So it is a good practice to close a file explicitly using the function fclose.

12.2 File Handling Functions

Some functions are specially defined to access data files. These are discussed in the following.

(a) fopen

The general form of this function is

```
fopen(file_name,file_type);
```

This function returns a pointer, file_name is a character string representing the name of the file to be opened. If the file does not exist in the working folder, then the full path name is required. The double backslashes (for DOS) or a simple slash (for UNIX) are given in the path name. For example, if the data file test.dat resides in the folder cprog of d drive, then the file_name will be d:\\cprog\\test.dat (for DOS) or d:/cprog/test.dat (for UNIX).

The file_type represents the mode in which a file is to be opened. The possible values are r, w, r+, w+, a, a+. If the file is being opened or created as a text mode (ASCII), the character t (for text) may be written at the end of the above mentioned modes. For example, rt, wt, r+t, etc. The use of t is optional for text file. If the file is opened as a binary file, then the character b must be added at the end of above modes. For example, rb, wb, r+b, etc. If neither t nor b is used with the modes, then the file will open as text mode.

(b) fclose

The general form of this function is

```
fclose(file_pointer);
```

where file_pointer is a pointer of type FILE. This function releases the buffer associated with this pointer and closes the file. The standard file pointers stdin, stdout, etc. can also be closed using the function `fclose`. This function returns an integer 0 on success and `EOF` on error.

(c) `fgetc` or `getc`

These two functions have same utility. `fgetc` is the function version of `getc`. The general forms are

```
getc(file_pointer);
fgetc(file_pointer);
```

These functions read a character from the file which is associated to the pointer `file_pointer`. On success these functions return a character and on end-of-file or error return `EOF`.

(d) `fputc` or `putc`

These two functions also have the same use. `fputc` is the function version of `putc`. The general forms are

```
putc(ch, file_pointer);
fputc(ch, file_pointer);
```

These two functions write the character `ch` to the file associated to the file pointer `file_pointer`. On success these functions return the character `ch` and on error they return `EOF`.

(e) `getw` and `putw`

Similar to `fgetc` and `fputc` functions, the functions `getw` and `putw` are used to read and write integer values. The general form of these functions are

```
getw(file_pointer);
putw(x, file_pointer);
```

where `x` is an integer variable.

On success `getw` returns the next integer on the input stream and on error returns `EOF`. On success `putw` returns the integer `x` and on error returns `EOF`.

(f) `fscanf`

This function is similar to `scanf` function, except that the file pointer must be specified as first argument. Its general form is

```
fscanf(file_pointer, character_stream);
```

This function reads the values of the variables specified in `character_stream` from the file associated to the pointer `file_pointer`. The meaning of `character_stream` is same as that of `scanf` function.

(g) `fprintf`

This function is similar to `printf` function, except that the first argument must be the file pointer. Its general form is

```
fprintf(file_pointer, character_stream);
```

The `file_pointer` is the pointer which is associated to a file. The meaning of `character_stream` is same as that of `printf` function.

If `stdin, stdout`, etc. are used as file pointers and the effect will be the same as using `printf` and `scanf` functions. The `fscanf` and `fprintf` functions are used to read and write formatted data file (the file contains different types of data, viz. `int, float, char`, etc., in a particular order).

(h) `feof`

This function is used to test for an end of file condition. Its general form is

```
feof(file_pointer);
```

Here `file_pointer` is the only input of this function. This function returns a non-zero integer value if all the data from the file has been read successfully, and returns 0 otherwise. For example,

```
if(feof(fp))
    printf("We are at end-of-file!");
```

In this example, `fp` is a file pointer. If `feof(fp)` condition is true, then the message `We are at end-of-file!` is displayed on the screen.

12.3 Writing to a File

A data file can be created in two different ways. The first method is, one can create the file directly by using any text editor (for example, C editor). The process is same as creating a program file. The second method is, read the data from the keyboard using the functions `getchar, gets, scanf` and write them to a specified file using the functions `fputc, fputs` and `fprintf`. The last three functions are similar to `putchar, puts` and `printf`, except that the functions `fputc, fputs` and `fprintf` take a pointer to the `FILE` structure as the first parameter.

The following program reads the roll number, name and sex of five students and write them to a file named `student.dat`.

Program 12.1

```
/* Writing to a file */
#include<stdio.h>
main()
{
  int roll,i;
  char name[15];
```

```
  char sex;
  FILE *fp; /* declaration of file pointer */
  fp=fopen("student.dat","w"); /* opens the file student.dat
                                  as writing mode */
  for(i=0;i<5;i++)
    {
      printf("Enter record of student-%d",i+1);
      sex=getchar();
      scanf("%d",&roll);
      gets(name);
      /* writing to the file */
      fprintf(fp,"%d %s %c",roll,name,sex); /* fp is file pointer */
    }
  fclose(fp);
}
```

If the input for this program is

```
m 10 Rahul
m 20 Sachin
f 27 Sumita
m 27 Monojit
m 62 Nitu
```

then the content of the file `student.dat` is

```
10 Rahul   m
20 Sachin  m
27 Sumita  f
27 Monojit m
62 Nitu    m
```

The file `student.dat` can be viewed in many different ways. The file can be viewed by opening it by C editor or by other editors or by DOS command `type` or `print` or by UNIX command `cat`.

12.4 Reading From a File

The standard input functions are `getchar, gets, scanf`. To read data from a file, the functions `getc, fgets` and `fscanf` are used. The first argument of these functions is file pointer, otherwise these functions are similar to above functions.

Example 12.4.1 (Reading from a file) Suppose a file `triangle.in` contains three sides of some triangles, say n. The first line of the file `triangle.in` contains the value of n and next each line contains the value of three sides. Write a program to read the sides of the triangles and display three sides and corresponding area on the screen.

Program 12.2

```
/* This program reads n triplets and determines the area if
   a triplet forms a triangle, also displays the sides and area
   on the screen */
#include<stdio.h>
#include<math.h>
main()
{
  float a,b,c,s,t,area;
  int n,i;
  FILE *fp; /* file pointer */
  fp=fopen("triangle.in","r");
  /* checking for existence of a file */
  if(fp==NULL) /* if error, terminates the program */
    {
      printf("Error-opening file\n");
      exit(1);
    }
  fscanf("%d",&n);
  for(i=0;i<n;i++)
     {
       fscanf("%f%f%f",&a,&b,&c);
       s=(a+b+c)/2;
       t=s*(s-a)*(s-b)*(s-c);
       if(t>0)
         {
           area=sqrt(a);
           printf("%0.2f %0.2f %0.2f %f \n",a,b,c,area);
         }
       else
         printf("The sides do not form a triangle\n");
     }
   fclose(fp);
   return;
}
```

Let the content of the file triangle.in be

```
3
4 5 6
2 3 4
1 2 3
```

The output of this program is

```
4.00 5.00 6.00 9.921567
2.00 3.00 4.00 2.904737
The sides do not form a triangle
```

The `fprintf, fgets, getc, fgetc`, etc. functions are used to write the data to a file, but, in each execution of these functions the data is not transferred to the file directly. The data is stored into the buffer. When the buffer is full, then all the data stored in the buffer is transferred to the data file. After transferring the data from buffer to file, the buffer becomes empty, this process is called **flushing the buffer**.

In a program, more than one data file can be opened at a time, but there is a limit. Normally, it is 20, the actual value is obtained by the predefined constant `FOPEN-MAX`. Thus, if a file which is opened earlier, but is not required in the next part of the program, then it is better to close this file using the function `fclose`.

Predefined streams

Some predefine streams are automatically opened when the program is started. The following data streams (point to FILE structures) are available in C.

Name	Use
`stdin`	standard input device (for input) normally keyboard
`stdout`	standard output device (for output) normally monitor
`stderr`	standard error output device
`stdaux`	standard auxiliary device (both for input and output)
`stdprn`	standard printer (for output)

Table 12.2: Some predefined streams

Notice that these files are constants and not variables. Normally, `stdin` is connected to the keyboard, `stdout` and `stderr` are connected to the screen, `stdaux` is connected to the serial port `com1` and `stdprn` is connected to the parallel port `lpt1`. A list of predefined streams are given in Table 12.2.

The following program, segment reads an integer from the standard input device.

```
int x;
fscanf(stdin,"%d",&x);
```

Similarly, the following program segment prints an integer.

```
int x=55;
fprintf(stdout,"%d",&x);
```

If `stdout` is replaced by `stdprn`, then the integer will print on the printer connected to the computer.

Therefore, using the stream `stdprn` one can print an ASCII file to a printer.

Example 12.4.2 (Printing of a file) Write a program to read an ASCII file and print the entire file by printer.

Program 12.3

```
/* Program to read the content of an ASCII file and
   to print it by a printer */
#include<stdio.h>
main()
{
  char ch,fname[13];
  FILE *fp;
  printf("Enter file name to be printed\n");
  scanf("%s", fname); /* input file name */
  fp=fopen(fname,"r"); /* opening of file */
  /* reading a character from the file and printing it, while the
  file is not end */
  while(!feof(fp)) /* while not end of file fp */
    {
      fscanf(fp,"%c",&ch); /* reads a character from file */
      fprintf(stdprn,"%c",ch); /* prints the character to printer */
    }
  fclose(fp);
  return;
}
```

This program reads a file name whose content is to be printed. The file name is read as `fname`. This file is opened as `"r"` mode. In the `while` loop, the characters from the file are connected with the file pointer `fp` and are read one by one by the function `fscanf`. The character is stored to the variable `ch`. Then, the character `ch` sends to the printer by the function `fprintf` by taking file pointer as `stdprn`.

Example 12.4.3 Write a program to read a text file (ASCII) and display its content on the monitor.

Program 12.4

```
/* Program to read a file and display its content on the monitor */
#include<stdio.h>
main()
{
  char ch,fname[13];
  FILE *ifile;
  printf("Enter file name \n");
```

```
  scanf("%s", fname);
  ifile=fopen(fname,"r");
  /* checking the existence of the file */
  if(ifile==NULL)
    {
      printf("No such file exists!\n");
      exit(1);
    }
  /* reading a character from the file and printing it on the screen */
  while(!feof(ifile)) /* while not end of file ifile */
     {
       ch=fgetc(ifile); /* reads a character from ifile */
       putchar(ch);     /* prints on the screen */
     }
  fclose(ifile);
  return;
}
```

The above program reads all the characters from a file. The file name is supplied externally. The characters are displayed on the monitor screen.

The two lines

```
ch=fgetc(ifile);
putchar(ch);
```

can be written together as `putchar(fgetc(ifile));`

The above program reads a file and displays its content to the screen. Using this program (with a minor extension) one can save a file to another file. The details are given in the following program.

Example 12.4.4 (Copy of a file) Write a program which will save a text file to another file. The file names are to be supplied externally.

Program 12.5

```
/* Program to copy a file to another file */
#include<stdio.h>
#include<io.h>
main()
{
  char ch,ifname[13],ofname[13];
  FILE *ifile,*ofile;
  int count=0;
  /* source file */
```

```
printf("Enter source file name \n");
scanf("%s", ifname);
ifile=fopen(ifname,"r"); /* opens for reading */
/* checking the existence of the file */
if(ifile==NULL)
  {
    printf("Error - No such file exists!\n");
    exit(1);
  }
/* target file */
printf("Enter target file name \n");
scanf("%s", ofname);
ofile=fopen(ofname,"w"); /* opens for writing */
/* checking the existence of the file */
if(ofile==NULL) /* error checking */
  {
    printf("Error in file creation !\n");
    exit(0);
  }
/* reading a character from the file and writing it to another file */
while(!feof(ifile)) /* while not end of source file */
  {
    ch=fgetc(ifile); /* reads a character from ifile */
    count++;
    fputc(ch,ofile); /* writes to a file */
  }
fclose(ifile);
fclose(ofile);
printf("The number of characters in the source file is %d",count);
return;
}
```

This program reads two files - one is source (the file from which the data transferred) and other is target (the file to which the data is written).

A character is read out from the source file whose file pointer is `ifile` and it is written to the target file whose file pointer is `ofile`. This process is repeated until the source file reaches end-of-file condition. The variable `count` determines the number of characters in the source (also in target) file.

Example 12.4.5 (Merging of files) Write a program to merge two files into a single file.

Solution. Suppose `source1` and `source2` are the given files which are to be merged and the new\file `target` is created. At first `source1` is to be copied to `target` and then `source2` is appended to `target`. The program is shown below.

Program 12.6

```
/* Copying of two files into a third file */
#include<stdio.h>
void main()
{
  char ch,source1[13],source2[13],target[13];
  FILE *ifile,*ofile;
  printf("Enter first source file \n");
  scanf("%s", source1);
  printf("Enter second source file \n");
  scanf("%s", source2);
  printf("Enter target file name \n");
  scanf("%s", target);

  ifile=fopen(source1,"r"); /* open for reading */
  ofile=fopen(target,"w"); /* open for writing */
  while(!feof(ifile)) /* while not end of file ifile */
    fputc(fgetc(ifile),ofile); /* reading a character from source
                                  file and writing it to target */
  fclose(ifile); /* source1 is closed now */
  ifile=fopen(source2,"r"); /* open second file for reading */
  while(!feof(ifile)) /* while not end of file ifile */
    fputc(fgetc(ifile),ofile);
  fclose(ofile);
  fclose(ifile);
}
```

12.5 Operations on Data Files

12.5.1 Searching a file

Assume that the records (`roll_no` and `name`) of some students are stored in the file `stu.dat`. Let the key value of the record to be searched, be read as `s_roll` (the roll number). Now, a record from the file `stu.dat` is read and the key (`roll_no`) of the current record is compared with the search key (`s_roll`). If they are equal, then the record is printed and the search is terminated. If the search key `s_roll` does not match with any record, then a message 'Record does not exist' is printed and the program is halted there after.

Program 12.7

```
/* Searching in a file */
#include<stdio.h>
void main()
{
  char name[25],fname[13];
  int roll_no,s_roll;
  FILE *fp;
  printf("Enter file name \n");
  scanf("%s",fname);
  fp=fopen(fname,"r");
  printf("Enter roll number to be searched\n");
  scanf("%d",&s_roll);
  while(!feof(fp)) /* while not end of file */
     {
       fscanf(fp,"%d%[^\n]",&roll_no,name);
       if(roll_no==s_roll)
         {
           printf("Record found\n");
           printf("%d %s\n",roll_no,name);
           fclose(fp);
           exit(1);
         }
     }
  printf("Record does not exist\n");
}
```

Assume that the file stu.dat contains the following information.

```
125 ANITA PAL 333 ANIKET PAL 401 SUMITA BERA 504
PARTHA SAHA
```

The input/output of the above program is

```
Enter file name
stu.dat
Enter roll number to be searched
333
Record found
333   ANIKET PAL
```

12.5.2 Appending a file

Often it is required to add some records to an existing file. This addition can be done by opening the file in append (`"a"`) mode. A file `stu.dat` contains some records and each record has two fields `roll_no` and `name`. Any number of records may be appended to the file `stu.dat` using following program.

Program 12.8

```
/* Appending a file */
#include<stdio.h>
void main()
{
  char name[20],option='Y';
  int roll_no=0;
  FILE *fp=fopen("stu.dat","a");
  while(toupper(option)=='Y')
    {
      printf("\nEnter roll no. and name\n");
      scanf("%d%[^\n]",&roll_no,name);
      fprintf(fp,"\n%d %s",roll_no,name);
      printf("Do you want to enter another record (Y/N)?");
      option=getch();
    }
  fclose(fp);
}
```

Suppose the file stu.dat contains the following data.

```
125 ANITA PAL
333 ANIKET PAL
401 SUMITA BERA
504 PARTHA SAHA
```

A sample of input/output:

```
Enter roll no.  and name
432 MONOJIT BERA
Do you want to enter another record (Y/N)? y
Enter roll no.  and name
502 GANGA
Do you want to enter another record (Y/N)? n
```

The file stu.dat finally appended to

```
125 ANITA PAL
333 ANIKET PAL
401 SUMITA BERA
504 PARTHA SAHA
432 MONOJIT BERA
502 GANGA
```

12.5.3 Merging of two sequential files

Assume that the roll number, name and marks of some students of a college are stored in two files. Also, assume that the records are stored in ascending order of the roll numbers. The following program opens two files `stu1.dat` and `stu2.dat` and merge them into a new single file which will contain records of all students in ascending order of their roll numbers.

Let `roll1`, `name1` and `mark1` be the records retrieved from the file `stu1.dat` and `roll2`, `name2` and `mark2` from the file `stu2.dat`. These two files are to be merged and saved into the file `stu3.dat`. If `roll1<roll2`, then the record obtained from the file `stu1.dat` to be written to the file `stu3.dat` and the next record of the file `stu1.dat` to be read. If `roll1>roll2`, then the record obtained from the file `stu2.dat` is to be written to the file `stu3.dat` and next record of `stu2.dat` to be read. If `roll1=roll2`, then the record of the same student is available in two files. In this case, any one record is to be written to `stu3.dat` and then next record from both the files are to be read.

Program 12.9

```
/* Merging of two data files */
#include <stdio.h>
main()
{
 char name1[20],name2[20];
 int roll1,roll2,mark1,mark2;
 FILE *fp1=fopen("stu2.dat","r");
 FILE *fp2=fopen("stu1.dat","r");
 FILE *fp3=fopen("stu3.dat","w");
 /* reads first record from stu1.dat */
 fscanf(fp1,"%d%d%s",&roll1,&mark1,name1);
 /* reads first record from stu2.dat */
 fscanf(fp2,"%d%d%s",&roll2,&mark2,name2);
 clrscr();
 while ((!feof(fp1))&&(!feof(fp2))) /* either file becomes finished */
   {
     if(roll1<roll2)
       {
         fprintf(fp3,"%d %d %s\n",roll1,mark1,name1);
         /* reads next record from stu1.dat */
         fscanf(fp1,"%d%d%s",&roll1,&mark1,name1);
       }
     else if(roll1>roll2)
       {
         fprintf(fp3,"%d %d %s\n",roll2,mark2,name2);
```

```
          /* reads next record from stu2.dat */
          fscanf(fp2,"%d%d%s",&roll2,&mark2,name2);
        }
      else if(roll1==roll2)
        {
          printf("Duplicate record: Roll no. %d\n",roll1);
          fprintf(fp3,"%d %d %s\n",roll2,mark2,name2);
          fscanf(fp1,"%d%d%s",&roll1,&mark1,name1);
          fscanf(fp2,"%d%d%s",&roll2,&mark2,name2);
        }
    } /* end of while loop */
    if(feof(fp1)) /* when stu1.dat is finished */
      {
        /* printing of last scanned values*/
        fprintf(fp3,"%d %d %s\n",roll1,mark1,name1);
        fprintf(fp3,"%d %d %s\n",roll2,mark2,name2);
        while(!feof(fp2)) /* writing remaining data from stu2.dat*/
          {
            fscanf(fp2,"%d%d%s",&roll2,&mark2,name2);
            fprintf(fp3,"%d %d %s\n",roll2,mark2,name2);
          }
      }
    if(feof(fp2)) /* when stu2.dat is finished */
      {
        fprintf(fp3,"%d %d %s\n",roll2,mark2,name2);
        fprintf(fp3,"%d %d %s\n",roll1,mark1,name1);
        while(!feof(fp1)) /* writing remaining data from stu1.dat*/
          {
            fscanf(fp1,"%d%d%s",&roll1,&mark1,name1);
            fprintf(fp3,"%d %d %s\n",roll1,mark1,name1);
          }
      }
fclose(fp1);
fclose(fp2);
fclose(fp3);
return;
}
```

A sample of input/output:

Contents of the file stu1.dat

```
10 234 Aniket
20 231 Harun
```

```
22 324 Ajay
```

Contents of the file `stu2.dat`

```
15 345 Anu
20 231 Harun
30 321 Karan
40 123 Rana
45 332 Akul
```

The file `stu3.dat` after execution of the program.

```
10 234 Aniket
15 345 Anu
20 231 Harun
22 324 Ajay
30 321 Karan
40 123 Rana
45 332 Akul
```

12.5.4 Updating a file

Suppose `roll_no` and `name` of some students are stored in the file `stu.dat`. The following program will read `roll_no` and `name` of each student from the file `stu.dat` and marks of four subjects from keyboard. Then, the total marks, percentage of marks and class obtained are computed and the result is stored into a new file `stunew.dat`. The class is computed according to the following rule.

% of marks	Class
60 and above	I
45 to below 60	II
30 to below 45	III
below 30	FAIL

Finally, the name, roll_no, marks of four subjects, total marks, percentage of marks and the class of each student is printed.

Program 12.10

```
/* Updation of a file */
#include<stdio.h>
void main()
{
  char name[20],remark[4];
  int roll_no,mark1,mark2,mark3,mark4,total_mark;
  float percent;
```

```
  FILE *fpi,*fpo;
  fpi=fopen("stu.dat","r");
  fpo=fopen("stunew.dat","w");
  while(!feof(fpi))
    {
      fscanf(fpi,"%d%[^\n]",&roll_no,name);
      printf("Enter marks of four subjects of %d %s\n",roll_no,name);
      scanf("%d%d%d%d",&mark1,&mark2,&mark3,&mark4);
      total_mark=mark1+mark2+mark3+mark4;
      percent=total_mark/4.0;
      /* calculation of class */
      if(percent>=60)
         strcpy(remark,"I");
      else if((percent>=45) && (percent<60))
         strcpy(remark,"II");
      else if((percent>=30) && (percent<45))
         strcpy(remark,"III");
      else
         strcpy(remark,"FAIL");
      fprintf(fpo,"%d %s %d %d %d %d %d %0.2f %s\n",
              roll_no,name,mark1,mark2,mark3,mark4,
              total_mark,percent,remark);
    } /* end of while */
  fclose(fpi);
  fclose(fpo);
}
```

Suppose the data of the file `stu.dat` be

```
125  ANITA PAL
333  ANIKET PAL
401  SUMITA BERA
504  PARTHA SAHA
```

```
Enter marks of four subjects of 125 ANITA PAL
50 20 30 40
Enter marks of four subjects of 333 ANIKET PAL
40 60 90 87
Enter marks of four subjects of 401 SUMITA BERA
10 20 30 40
Enter marks of four subjects of 504 PARTHA SAHA
45 35 56 47
```

Finally, the file `stunew.dat` is updated as

```
125  ANITA PAL   50 20 30 40 140 35.00 III
333  ANIKET PAL  40 60 90 87 277 69.25 I
401  SUMITA BERA 10 20 30 40 100 25.00 FAIL
504  PARTHA SAHA 45 35 56 47 183 45.75 II
```

12.6 Binary Files

It is seen that structures, arrays are basically a group or a block of data. So, to store structures or arrays to the memory, we have to store blocks of data, where each block consists of a fixed amount of continuous bytes. In some applications, it may be required to read an entire block from the data file or write the entire block to the data file, rather than reading and writing of individual members. The functions `fread` and `fwrite` are used to read and write a block of data. These functions are sometimes referred as **unformatted** read and write functions.

(a) `fwrite` function

The general form of this function is

```
fwrite(var_pointer,record_size,n,file_pointer);
```

where `var_pointer` represents the pointer of the data to be written, `record_size` is the size of block to be written, `n` is the number of data items to be appended and `file_pointer` is the file pointer associated to a file in which the data is to be written.

For example,

```
fwrite(&cs_student,sizeof(cs_student),1,fp);
```

In this example, `cs_student` is a structure variable. `fp` is file pointer associated to a file which is opened for output and 1 indicates only one block of data being transferred.

(b) `fread` function

The `fread` function is reverse of `fwrite` function. Its general form is

```
fread(var_pointer,record_size,n,file_pointer);
```

where `var_pointer` is the pointer which points to a variable whose value is to be retrieved. `record_size` and `n` have same meaning as in `fwrite`. `file_pointer` is the pointer which points to a file buffer.

For example,

```
fread(&cs_student,sizeof(cs_student),1,fp);
```

reads one block of data of size `sizeof(student)` for the structure variable `cs_student`. The variable `cs_student` is a structure variable.

Example 12.6.1 Write a program which will read records (roll number, name and height) of some students from keyboard and write them to a binary file. Then open this binary file for reading. Read all the records from the newly created binary file and find the average height of the students.

Program 12.11

```
/* Processing of binary file */
#include<stdio.h>
main()
{
  typedef struct
     {
       int roll_no;
       int height;
       char name[20];
     }student;
   student s[20],temp;
   int n,i;
   float t_height=0;
   FILE *fp=fopen("sturec.dat","wb");  /* opened for writing */

   /* reading of students records from keyboard */
   clrscr();
   printf("How many students\n");
   scanf("%d",&n);
   for(i=0;i<n;i++)
      {
        printf("Enter the record of student-%d\n",i+1);
        printf("Enter roll number : ");
        scanf("%d",&s[i].roll_no);
        printf("Enter name : ");
        scanf("%s",s[i].name);
        printf("Enter height :  ");
        scanf("%d",&s[i].height);
        fwrite(&s[i],sizeof(s[i]),1,fp); /* writing to the file */
      }
   fclose(fp);  /* closed sturec.dat */

   fp=fopen("sturec.dat","rb"); /* reopen for reading */
   /* reading from the file sturec.dat and displaying on the screen*/
   i=0;
   /* while loop terminates when fread returns 0 */
   while(fread(&temp,sizeof(temp),1,fp))
      {
        s[i]=temp;  /* copy to the array s[i] */
        printf("%4d ",s[i].roll_no);
        printf("%-20s ",s[i].name);
        printf("%4d\n",s[i].height);
```

```
      t_height+=s[i].height;  /* total height */
      i++;
    }
   printf("Average height is %0.2f",t_height/i);
  return;
}
```

A sample of input/output:

```
How many students 4
Enter the record of student-1
Enter roll number : 12
Enter name : Aniket
Enter height : 120
Enter the record of student-2
Enter roll number : 33
Enter name : Suriya
Enter height : 130
Enter the record of student-3
Enter roll number: 55
Enter name : Raja
Enter height : 135
Enter the record of student-4
Enter roll number : 67
Enter name : Dev
Enter height : 124
Output

  12 Aniket               120
  33 Suriya               130
  55 Raja                 135
  67 Dev                  124
Average height is 127.25
```

12.7 File Positioning Functions

In a data file we can access a record directly. The position of a record in a data file is indicated by a pointer called **position pointer** which is always associated with a data file. Read and write of data are done at the position pointed by this pointer. The functions `fseek, ftell, fsetpos, fgetpos` and `rewind` are used to access a record randomly. These functions are discussed in the following.

(a) `fseek`

This function is used to move the file position to a desired location within the file.

The general form of this function is

```
fseek(file_pointer,offset,start_position);
```

This function sets a new position within the file which is opened with `file_pointer`. From this new position one can access the record. The value of `start_position` is one of the following three values.

Value	C constant	Use
0	SEEK_SET	Seeks from beginning of the file
1	SEEK_CUR	Seeks from current position
2	SEEK_END	Seeks from end of file

`offset` represents the number of bytes. The new position is determined by the `offset`. The current position will be the `start_position` plus `offset`. For example, if the value of `start_position` is `SEEK_CUR` and offset is 30, then the new position will be 30 bytes away (towards end of file) from the current position. The negative value of `offset` indicates that the position will be determined in the backward direction.

The function `rewind` can be used to reset the file position pointer at the beginning of the file. The general form is

```
rewind(fp);
```

On success, the function returns 0 otherwise it returns an error code.

Some typical examples of `fseek` function are listed below.

Function call	Meaning
`fseek(fp,0,0);`	Go to the beginning of the file
`rewind(fp);`	Go to the beginning of the file
`fseek(fp,0,1);`	Stay at the current position
`fseek(fp,0,2);`	Go to the end of the file
`fseek(fp,n,0);`	Go to $(n+1)$th byte in the file
`fseek(fp,n,1);`	Go forward by n bytes from current position
`fseek(fp,-n,1);`	Go backward by n bytes from current position
`fseek(fp,-n,2);`	Go backward by n bytes from the end

(b) `ftell`

The general form of this function is

```
ftell(file_pointer);
```

This function returns the pointer of the current position of the position pointer within the file which is associated with the file pointer `file_pointer`. For the binary file, the offset is measured in bytes from the beginning of the file. This value may be used to call `fseek` and other purpose.

(c) `fflush`

While writing data to the file, all the data is stored in the buffer and when buffer is full, then the data stored in the buffer is transferred to the file automatically. But, user can transfer the data stored in buffer to the file as desired.

Its general form is

```
fflush(file_pointer);
```

This function writes the values of buffer to the file associated to the `file_pointer`. The file remains open after the execution of this function.

(d) `setvbuf`

The user can also allocate a buffer for a specific file within a given size. Its general form is

```
setvbuf(file_pointer,buf,buffer_type,buffer_size);
```

This function set a buffer `buf` used for input/output for the file which is associated to the file pointer `file_pointer` of size `buffer_size` (amount of memory allocated for buffer). The `buffer_type` is one of the three predefined constants, viz. `-IOFBF`, `-IOLBF`, `-IONBF`. The limit for buffer size is 0 < buffer_size < 32767.

The meaning of different values of buffer type are given below.

Constant	Meaning
`-IOFBF`	In this case the file is fully buffered. For an empty buffer, the input operation will attempt to fill the entire buffer. On output, when the buffer is completely full, then the data will transfer to the file.
`-IOLBF`	In this case, the file is line buffered. For empty buffer, the input operation will attempt to fill the entire buffer. On output, the data will transfer to the file when a new line character occurs. In this case, the data is saved line by line.
`-IONBF`	In this case, the file is unbuffered. This means that the data is written directly to the file.

The size of a file can be determined using the functions `fseek` and `ftell`. The statements

```
fseek(fp,0,0);
n=ftell(fp);
```

give $n = 0$ because the file position has been set to the beginning of the file. Now, we consider the statement

```
fseek(fp,0,2);
n=ftell(fp);
```

The value of `n` is the number of bytes used by the file whose file pointer is `fp`. This is the size of the corresponding file in bytes.

Example 12.7.1 (Use of `fread` and `fwrite`) Suppose a file (`emprec.dat`) contains records of some employees of an organization. Each record contains an employee code (`code`), name (`name`) and age (`age`). Write a program to find the number of records stored in the file, file size and display the record of a specified employee, whose record number is given.

Program 12.12

```
/* Illustration of fread and fwrite functions */
#include<stdio.h>
void main()
{
  struct employee
    {
      int code;
      float age;
      char name[20];
    };
  struct employee emp;
  FILE *fp;
  int end_pos,cur_pos,n;
  fp=fopen("emprec.dat","rb");
  fseek(fp,0,2);
  end_pos=ftell(fp); /* size of file */
  n=end_pos/sizeof(emp); /* no. of records */
  printf("Size of the file emprec.dat is %d bytes\n",end_pos);
  printf("No. of records in the file is %d\n",n);
  printf("Enter record no. of the employee \n");
  scanf("%d",&n);
  cur_pos=(n-1)*sizeof(emp); /* starting position of the nth record */
  if(cur_pos>end_pos-sizeof(emp)) /* valid position of last record */
    {
      printf("No such record exists !!");
      exit(1);
    }
  fseek(fp,cur_pos,0);
  fread(&emp,sizeof(emp),1,fp); /* reads one record */
  printf("Details of %dth employee\n",n);
  printf("Emp code: %d Name: %s  Age: %0.2f\n",
                              emp.code,emp.name,emp.age);
}
```

A sample of input/output:

```
Size of the file emprec.dat is 260 bytes
No.  of records in the file is 10
Enter record no.  of the employee
5
Details of 5th employee
Emp code:  222 Name:  Anita Pal Age:  33.00
```

The data file used in the above program (`emprec.dat`) is created using the following program.

```
#include<stdio.h>
void main()
{
  struct employee
    {
      int code;
      float age;
      char name[20];
    };
  struct employee emp;
  char option='Y';
  FILE *fp;
  fp=fopen("emprec.dat","wb");
  while(toupper(option)=='Y')
  {
    printf("\nEnter employee code and name\n");
    scanf("%d%[^\n]",&emp.code,emp.name);
    printf("Enter employee age\n");
    scanf("%f",&emp.age);
    fwrite(&emp,sizeof(emp),1,fp);
    printf("Do you want to enter another record (Y/N)?");
    option=getch();
  }
fclose(fp);
}
```

Multiple choice test

Multiple choice test is one of the most popular method to prepare a merit list. In this test, we assume that each question has four answers (marked as a, b, c, d) and among them one is correct. An examinee should select the correct answer. If an examinee does not select any one of a, b, c, d, then a blank space is used against the corresponding question number.

Suppose each answer script contains the name, roll number and a sequence of answers (containing blank space, a, b, c, d). The following program reads the sequence of correct answer from the keyboard. The name, roll number and reply given by the examinees read from a file, say, 'MCT.DAT'.

The program counts the number of correct and incorrect replies. If the marks for correct and incorrect reply are respectively m_1 and m_2, then the total score of a candidate is

$$\text{score} = m_1 \times \text{ number of correct reply } + m_2 \times \text{ number of incorrect reply.}$$

The roll number, name, number of correct reply, number of incorrect reply and total score of each examinee are written to the file 'MCT.OUT'.

Program 12.13

```
/* Multiple choice test. mc, mn be the marks for correct
   and incorrect reply. assume roll is 3 digit number. name contains
   20 characters. cr,wr, nr represents number of correct, wrong and
   no reply.*/
#include<stdio.h>
#define MAX 50
main()
{
char name[20],ans[MAX],rep[MAX];
int cr,wr,nr,mc,mw,score,roll;
int i,n;
FILE *fp,*fpo;

clrscr();
printf("Enter number of questions\n");
scanf("%d",&n);
printf("Enter answer sequence\n");
scanf("%s",ans);
printf("Enter marks of correct and incorrect replies\n");
scanf("%d%d",&mc,&mw);
fp=fopen("mct.dat","r");
fpo=fopen("mct.out","w");
fprintf(fpo,"Correct anwers\n");
for(i=0;i<n;i++)
   putc(ans[i],fpo);
fprintf(fpo,"\nMarks of correct and incorrect reply are 1 -1\n");
fprintf(fpo,"Roll  Name      Correct Incorrect Score\n");
fprintf(fpo,"No.             Reply   Reply\n");
fprintf(fpo,"----------------------------------------------\n");

while(!feof(fp))
  {
    fscanf(fp,"%3d",&roll);
    fscanf(fp,"%20s",name);
    fscanf(fp,"%[abcd' ']",rep); /* reads only a, b, c, d and
                                    blank space */
    cr=0; wr=0; nr=0;
    for(i=0;i<n;i++)
```

```
        {
          if(ans[i]==rep[i]) cr++;
          else if (ans[i]==' ') nr++;
          else wr++;
        }
    score=cr*mc+wr*mw;
    fprintf(fpo,"%d %s\t %d \t%d\t %d\n",roll,name,cr,wr,score);
  }
fprintf(fpo,"-----------------------------------------------\n");
fclose(fp);
fclose(fpo);
return;
}
```

File name: MCT.DAT

```
111 Aniket abcdeabcda
222 Anita abcbcdebcc
400 Prativa abcabcdedc
500 Sonia dbcdeabcde
```

File name: MCT.out

```
Correct answers abcdeabcde
Marks of correct and incorrect replies are 1 -1
Roll  Name    Correct Incorrect  Score No.
              Reply   Reply
-------------------------------------------
111 Aniket       9      1          8
222 Anita        3      7         -4
400 Prativa      4      6         -2
500 Sonia        9      1          8
-------------------------------------------
```

Menu based program

The following is an interactive file oriented program that will maintain a list of roll numbers, names and marks obtained by the students. A menu is included that will allow the user to select any of the following features:

(i) Add a new record.
(ii) Delete a record.
(iii) Search a record.
(iv) Generate a complete list of records.
(v) End of execution.

Assume that the data (`rollno, name` and `marks`) of each student is stored in the file `stdrec.dat`.

At the beginning of the program, a menu (called main menu) will be displayed on the screen containing the following messages.

1. Add a new record.
2. Delete a record.
3. Search a record.
4. List of all records.
5. Stop.

Choose an option <1..5>

Read an option into `opt` whose value lies between 1 and 5 and if the value of `opt` does not lie between 1 and 5, then the program will ask to reenter the value of `opt`.

To add a new record, the function `addrec` is developed. In this function, the data file `stdrec.dat` is opened in `append` mode. A new record is append to the end of the data file. Any number of records can be entered through this routine and the routine will be terminated by entering 'N'. After completion of this routine the main manu will be displayed on the screen. The routine will also check the error of the input data.

The function `delrec` reads a roll number into `droll` which is to be deleted. All the records whose `rollno` is not equal to `droll` are stored into this temporary file. In other words, the temporary file will contain all the records except the record which is to be deleted. Then all the records from this temporary file are copied to `stdrec.dat` and the temporary file is automatically deleted.

In this program, a record is retrieved by using the subroutine `serrec`. The roll number of search record is read into `sroll` and the roll number of each record is compared with `sroll` and if `rollno` is equal to `sroll`, then the corresponding record is displayed on the screen, otherwise the message 'Record does not exist' is displayed.

The subroutine `list` will display `rollno, name` and `marks` of all the students.

Program 12.14

```
 /* A menu based program. Performs addition, deletion,
    searching, listing of records stored in a sequential file */
#include<stdio.h>
main()
{
int opt;
int addrec();
int delrec();
int serrec();
int list();

do
```

```
{
  clrscr();
  do{ /* repeats to read a valid option */
    printf("       1. Add a new record.\n");
    printf("       2. Delete a record.\n");
    printf("       3. Search a record.\n");
    printf("       4. List of all records.\n");
    printf("       5. Stop.\n");
    printf("       Choose an option <1..5>\n ");
    printf("       >>");
    scanf("%d",&opt);
   }while((opt<1) || (opt>5));
  switch (opt)
    {
      case 1: addrec();
          break;
      case 2: delrec();
          getch();
          break;
      case 3: serrec();
          getch();
          break;
      case 4: list();
          getch();
          break;
      case 5: exit(0);
    }
 }while(opt!=5); /* repeats until option=5 */
 return;
} /* end of main */

/*  Function to add a new record */
 int addrec()
  {
   int rollno,mark;
   char name[25],yn;
   FILE *fp=fopen("stdrec.dat","a"); /* opens in append mode */
   do{
     clrscr();
     printf("Enter rollno :\n");
     scanf("%d",&rollno);
     printf("Enter name :\n");
```

```
      scanf("%s",name);
      printf("Enter mark :\n");
      scanf("%d",&mark);
      fseek(fp,0,2);
      if(ftell(fp)!=0) fprintf(fp,"\n");
      fprintf(fp,"%3d%3d%-25s",rollno,mark,name);
      printf("Do you want to add more record (y/n) ?");
      yn=getche();
    }
   while(toupper(yn)=='Y');
   fclose(fp);
   return 0;
 } /* end of addrec() */

/* Subroutine to delete a particular record */
   int delrec()
    {
      char name[25];
      int rollno,droll,mark,flag=0;
      FILE *fp=fopen("stdrec.dat","r");
      FILE *fpt=fopen("temp.o","w");
      int temproll=0;
      printf("Enter roll number which to be deleted\n");
      scanf("%d",&droll);
      while(!feof(fp))
       {
         fscanf(fp,"%3d%3d%25s",&rollno,&mark,name);
         /* if rollno=droll then set
            flag=1 otherwise copy the record to the temporary
            file temp.o */
         if(rollno==droll)
            flag=1;
         else
           {
             fseek(fpt,0,2);
             if(ftell(fpt)!=0) fprintf(fpt,"\n");
             if(temproll!=rollno)
               {
                 temproll=rollno;
                 fprintf(fpt,"%3d%3d%-25s",rollno,mark,name);
               }
           }
```

```
      }
     fclose(fp);
     fclose(fpt);
     if(flag==0)
       printf("Record with roll no. %d is not in the file\n",droll);
    else
       printf("One record with roll no. %d has been deleted\n",droll);
    /*  copy of records from temporary file to stdrec.dat */
    fpt=fopen("temp.o","r");
    fp=fopen("stdrec.dat","w");
    temproll=0;
    while(!feof(fpt))
     {
      fscanf(fpt,"%3d%3d%25s",&rollno,&mark,name);
      fseek(fp,0,2);
      if(ftell(fp)!=0) fprintf(fp,"\n");
      if(temproll!=rollno)
        {
          temproll=rollno;
          fprintf(fp,"%3d%3d%-25s",rollno,mark,name);
        }
     }
    fclose(fp);
    fclose(fpt);
    return 0;
  } /* end of delrec */

 /* searching a record */
int serrec()
 {
     int rollno,sroll,mark;
     char name[25];
     FILE *fp=fopen("stdrec.dat","r");
     printf("Enter roll no. to be searched\n");
     scanf("%d",&sroll);
     while(!feof(fp))
       {
         fscanf(fp,"%3d%3d%25s",&rollno,&mark,name);
         if(rollno==sroll)
           {
             printf("%3d %-25s %3d\n",rollno, name, mark);
             fclose(fp);
```

```
        return 0;
      }
    }
  printf("Record does not exist !!");
  return 0;
} /* end of searching */

/* listing of all records */
  int list()
    {
      int rollno,mark,temproll=0;
      char name[25];
      FILE *fp=fopen("stdrec.dat","r");
      while(!feof(fp))
        {
          fscanf(fp,"%3d%3d%25s",&rollno,&mark,name);
          if (temproll==rollno) return 0; /* checking of
                                             duplicate record */
          temproll=rollno;
          printf("%d %d %-25s\n",rollno,mark,name);
        }
      fclose(fp);
      return 0;
    } /* end of list */
```

12.8 Error Handling

Sometimes it may happen that a file is opened by **fopen** function, but the specific file is not available. Without checking the existence of the file, if we try to read/write a data, the program terminates abnormally. Some other errors may also occur during input/output operations of file. The functions `ferror` and `feof` are used to detect errors in the files. The general form of `ferror` function is

```
ferror(file_pointer);
```

This function returns a non-zero integer, if an error is detected up to that point during processing. On success it returns 0. For example, the statements

```
if(ferror(fp)!=0)
printf("Error:  Check your code !\n");
```

will print an error message, if the reading is not successful.

It is already mentioned that whether a file is opened successfully or not can be checked by the following statements.

```
fp=fopen("test.dat","r");
if(fp==NULL)
    printf("File is not opened !\n);
```

The end-of-file can be checked by the statements

```
fp=fopen("test.dat","r");
if(feof(fp))
    printf("End of file !\n");
```

Important Points

1. A file must be opened before its use.
2. It is better to close all the files after use.
3. A file is accessed with its file pointer rather than its name.
4. If a file is opened as write mode, no data can be read from it and vice versa.
5. When an exiting file is opened as `w` mode, the contents of the file are deleted.
6. If a file is used for both reading and writing mode, it must be opened as `w+` mode.
7. It is better to check the existence of the file before reading from it.

Exercise XII

Review Questions

1. What are the advantages of using a data file?
2. Describe the different modes of usage of data file in C.
3. What is meant by opening a data file? Explain the use of the function `fopen`.
4. What is the purpose of the function `fclose`?
5. What do you mean by field, record and file? How many types of files are available in C?
6. Write short notes on : opening a file, closing a file, appending a file.
7. Explain the functions: `rewind, ftell, fseek, fread, fwrite`.
8. Describe two different approaches to update a data file. Which approach is better and why?
9. Describe the use and limitations of the functions `getc` and `putc`.
10. What are the uses of `feof` and `ferror`?
11. Distinguish between the following functions:
    (a) `getc` and `getchar`
    (b) `printf` and `fprintf`
    (c) `feof` and `ferror`
12. What is the difference between append mode and write mode?
13. What is the difference between `w` mode and `w+` mode?
14. What are the uses of `rewind` and `ftell`?
15. When the functions `free` and `rewind` are used?

16. Explain the function `fseek`. What is the difference between the statements `rewind(fp)` and `fseek(fp,0L,0)`?
17. Is it possible to read from a file and write to the same file without resetting the file pointer? Explain.
18. Explain the use of the following statement.

```
while( (c=getchar() !=eof())
    putc(c,fp);
```

19. What is meant by the following statement?
    `FILE(*fp) (void)`

Programming Problems

1. Suppose the file TRIANGLE.DAT contains three sides of some triangles. Write a program to read the sides of each triangle from the file TRIANGLE.DAT and calculate perimeter and area of the triangle and store them along with three sides, to the file TRIANGLE.OUT.
2. Suppose a file ABC.DAT has 1000 numbers, 10 numbers per line. Write a program to read these members, sort them and store the sorted numbers in the file XYZ.DAT.
3. Write a program to read a file and to display the contents of the file on the screen with line number.
4. Write a program to merge two files into one file.
5. Write a program to open a file named STD.DAT and read the roll number, name and total marks obtained by 100 students from keyboard and store them into the file STD.DAT.
6. Write a program to create a file EMP.DAT and read the empcode, name and salary of the employees of an organization from keyboard and store them in EMP.DAT. Also, introduce the scope of checking an error in the input. If there is an error on the input, then again read that record.
7. Suppose we have a file STD.DAT containing roll numbers, name and marks of some students. Write a program to read the name of a student and check whether the record of this student is available, in this file. If the record is available then print it with an appropriate message, otherwise print the message "Record does not exist".
8. A file STU.DAT contains roll numbers and name of some students. Write a program to read the roll numbers and name of each student from the file STU.DAT and display on the screen. Then, read the marks of four subjects obtained by the students from the keyboard and calculate the total marks and percentage of marks and store them in the file RESULT.

9. Two files FILE1 and FILE2 contain the telephone numbers and names of some people, according to the increasing order of their telephone numbers. Write a program to merge these two files according to the increasing order of telephone number and store them into a new file NFILE.
10. Write a program to open a direct access file named STDRAN.DAT and read roll number and name of certain students from the keyboard and store them in the file STDRAN.DAT, considering the roll numbers as key.
11. A random access file STDRAN.DAT contains the roll number and name of some students with roll numbers as key. Write a program to read a roll number into SROLL and print the record (roll number and name), if available, find out the student whose roll number is equal to SROLL.
12. Write a program to check whether a file TELREC.DAT is available in the current directory, if this file is available, then add some records (say, telephone number and name) to TELREC.DAT, otherwise create it and then add records of some people.
13. Suppose a file SEM1 contains roll numbers, names and total marks (out of 400) of some students of Semester-I Examination. Another file SEM2 contains the roll number, name of those students in the same order as in the file SEM1 with marks of four papers PAPER5, PAPER6, PAPER7, PAPER8 of Semester-II Examination. Write a program to prepare the result which is to be stored in the file RESULT of this examination containing roll number, name, marks in Semester-I, total percentage of marks and grade. The grade will be determined as

$$\begin{aligned} \text{\% of marks} \geq 90\% &\longrightarrow \text{Ex} \\ 80\% \leq \text{\% of marks} < 90\% &\longrightarrow \text{A} \\ 70\% \leq \text{\% of marks} < 80\% &\longrightarrow \text{B} \\ 60\% \leq \text{\% of marks} < 70\% &\longrightarrow \text{C} \\ 50\% \leq \text{\% of marks} < 60\% &\longrightarrow \text{D} \\ \text{\% of marks} < 50\% &\longrightarrow \text{FAIL.} \end{aligned}$$

14. A formatted file MASTER contains the employee code, name and basic pay of employees of an organization. Write a program to calculate the D.A., H.R.A. and gross income of each employee and store employee code, name, basic pay, D.A., H.R.A. and gross income to the file EMP.DAT, where D.A. is the 32% of basic pay, H.R.A. is 15% of basic pay but not more than Rs. 6000 and gross pay is the sum of basic pay, D.A. and H.R.A.
15. Write a program to prepare the results of the students of classes XI and XII indicating their (i) names, (ii) class, (iii) roll numbers and (iv) division. The data is available from two files CLASS11 and CALSS12 which is formatted and contains the name, age, class, roll number, address and marks obtained in English, Bengali, Mathematics, Physics and Chemistry of all the students of class XI and class XII respectively. The divisions are determined as follows:

Students with total marks 600 or above are placed in the first division, total marks 450 or above but less than 600 are placed in the second division, total marks 300 or more but less than 450 are placed in the P division, otherwise are placed in 'fail'. Full marks of each subject is 200 (100 in each class XI and XII).

16. Write a program to create a file which will contain total number of boys along with their average age and mark, total number of girls along with their average age and marks, taking data from an existing data file STDREC.DAT which contains name, sex, age and marks of all 100 students in a sequential order.
17. Write a program that reads x and y coordinates of some points from the input file 'XYVAL.IN'. Calculate the distance of each point from the point (0,0) and write the coordinates and distance in the file 'DIST.OUT'.
18. Write a program to create a file named STD.DAT containing roll numbers, names and total marks of 100 students. Sort these records according to decreasing order of marks and assign the rank to each student (rank of highest scorer is 1 and students securing equal marks should have same rank). Store these records to a new file STDREC.DAT containing roll numbers, names, total marks and rank.
19. Write an interactive file oriented program that will maintain a list of names, addresses and telephone numbers. Consider the information associated with each name as a separate record.

    Include a menu that will allow the user to select any one of the following facilities:
    (i) Add a new record
    (ii) Delete a record
    (iii) Modify an existing record
    (iv) Retrieve and display an entire record for a given name
    (v) Generate a complete list of all names, address and telephone numbers
    (vi) End of computation (Stop).
20. Write a program that creates a data file containing the list of countries and their corresponding capitals.
21. Write an interactive menu-driven program that will access the data file generated in Exercise 20 and then allow one of the following operations to be executed:
    (i) Search the capital of a specified country
    (ii) Search the country whose capital is specified.
22. Extend the program of Exercise 21 to include:
    (i) Add a new record
    (ii) Delete a record
    (iii) Generate a list of all the countries and their corresponding capitals
    (iv) End of execution (stop).

Chapter 13

Macro and Preprocessor

The C language provides some special features which are not available in any other high level programming languages. Here some more advanced features are presented. We have already used the **#define** statement. This statement is used to define (in earlier chapters) a symbolic constant within a program. The advantage to use this statement is that, before compilation of the program, all symbolic constants are replaced by their equivalent expressions. For example, let us consider the following statement

```
#define MAX 100
```

Now, if the constant MAX contains five places in the program, then before compilation MAX is replaced by 100 in such five places.

The **#define** statement can also be used for several purposes. It can be used to define **macros**, i.e. a single variable is used to define a constant, an expression, a complete statement or a group of statements. More precisely, using a single identifier one can define a function. Other than **#define** statement there are several similar statements. For example, **#if, #else, #elif, #endif, #ifdef**, etc. These are called preprocessors. The **preprocessor** is a program that processes the source code before passing it to the compiler. It is a collection of special statements called **directives** or **preprocessors command line**.

All the preprocessor directives are placed in the program before the main function. Before the source code passes through the compiler, it is examined by the preprocessor. After being examined by the preprocessor and their appropriate action, the source code is submitted for compilation.

13.1 Macros

It is mentioned that while using the concept of macro we define some constants by some symbolic names and the values of the symbolic names are replaced by the constants. The macro substitution is very important feature in C programming language and we can use a macro to define many things.

A macro is defined by the preprocessor directive **#define**. The general form is

```
#define identifier string
```

where `identifier` is a symbolic name (valid C variable) and `string` may be a constant, an expression of any type (`int, float, char`, etc). The three terms are separated by blank spaces. Note, that no semicolon is used at the end of this statement.

Some examples of macros are

```
#define PI 3.1415926
#define country "INDIA"
#define e-mail "mmaplvu@gmail.com"
#define NULL 0
#define begin {
#define EQ ==
```

Usually, in macro definition the identifiers are written in upper case alphabets to distinguish between symbolic name and other identifiers, but both upper case and lower case alphabets can be used.

Let us consider the following example

Program 13.1

```
/* Use of macro, without argument */
#include<stdio.h>
#define MAX 10
#define NAME "ARJUN"
main()
  {
    int a[MAX],i;
    printf("Name=%s",NAME);
    for(i=0;i<MAX;i++)
         scanf("%d",&a[i]);
  }
```

In this program two macros `MAX` and `NAME` are defined. During preprocessing the value of `NAME` and `MAX` are replaced by `ARJUN` and `10` respectively. The preprocessed program thus becomes

```
#include<stdio.h>
main()
  {
    int a[10],i;
    printf("Name=%s","ARJUN");
    for(i=0;i<10;i++)
         scanf("%d",&a[i]);
  }
```

Note that NAME outside the double quotations (in printf) mark is replaced by "ARJUN" and within quotations it is unaffected by macro substitution.

Macro definitions are placed at the beginning of the program, before any function declaration, even the main function. The scope of macro definition is over the whole program. It may be remembered that a macro defined in one file is not recognized within another file.

In the above program, some constants are defined as macros. But, a single statement, multiple statements, operators, function and any other valid string may be defined as macro.

The following are valid declarations.

```
#define BEGIN {
#define END }
#define AND &&
#define OR ||
#define SPACE
```

Let us consider the following program written in C.

```
/* Use of #define */
#include<stdio.h>
#define BEGIN {
#define END }
#define START main()
#define CHECK if(max>x)
#define THEN
#define PRINT printf("Max=%d",max);
/* beginning of the program */
  START BEGIN
  int x, max;
  x=10;
  max=15;
  CHECK THEN PRINT
END
```

This program is equivalent to

```
#include<stdio.h>
main()
 {
   int x, max;
   x=10;
   max=15;
   if(max>x) printf("Max=%d",max);
 }
```

Notice that the statement CHECK THEN PRINT is equivalent to

```
if(max>x)
    printf("Max=%d",max);
```

But, care should be taken to define macro. For example, macros X and Y are defined as

```
#define X a+b
#define Y c-d
```

and Z=X/Y is a statement in the program. When macros are substituted, the expression for Z becomes $a + b/c - d$ and obviously it is not a correct expression. The following definition resolves this drawback.

```
#define X (a+b)
#define Y (c-d)
```

Multiline macros can also be defined by placing a backward slash (\) at the end of each line except the last line. That means, a single macro can define a group of statements and other things.

This feature is explained by the following example.

Program 13.2

```
/* Use of multiline macros */
#include<stdio.h>
#define READ  scanf("%d",&n);          \
              for(i=0;i<n;i++){        \
                 scanf("%d",&a[i]);\
                 printf("%d ",a[i]);\
                }
#define SUM   sum=0;                   \
              for(i=0;i<n;i++)         \
                 sum+=a[i];

#define PRINT printf("Sum=%d\n",sum);

main()
 {
   int n, a[10],i,sum;
   READ
   SUM
   PRINT
 }
```

This program contains three multiline macros and using these macros the `main` function becomes shortened. Note, that no semicolon is needed at the end of three macros `READ`, `SUM` and `PRINT` (within main), because in these macros the semicolons are already given.

The preprocessed form of the above program is given below.

```
#include<stdio.h>
 main()
 {
   int n, a[10],i,sum;
   scanf("%d",&n);
   for(i=0;i<n;i++)
      {
        scanf("%d",&a[i]);
        printf("%d ",a[i]);
      }
   sum=0;
   for(i=0;i<n;i++)
      sum+=a[i];
   printf("Sum=%d\n",sum);
 }
```

13.1.1 Macros with arguments

Macros are also used in place of functions. A function needs some arguments, therefore the macro with arguments is also available. The general form of such macro is

`#define identifier(arg1,arg2,..,argn) string`

where `identifier` is a valid C variable which is also used as function name. `arg1, arg2, ..., argn` are the formal arguments without their data type and string is the expression for this function.

Let us consider the following simple example.

`#defin f(x) x*x+2*x+5.0`

Suppose the following statements are included in the program.

```
val1=f(2.5);
val2=f(2+3);
a=4;
val3=f(a++);
```

During preprocessing these three statements transferred to

$\texttt{val1} = 2.5 * 2.5 + 2 * 2.5 + 5.0 = 16.25$

$\texttt{val2} = 2 + 3 * 2 + 3 + 2 * 2 + 3 + 5.0 = 2 + 6 + 3 + 4 + 3 + 5.0 = 23.0$

$\texttt{val3} = (a++) * (a++) + 2 * (a++) + 5.0 = 4 * 5 + 2 * 6 + 5.0 = 37.0.$

Look at these three values `val1, val2` and `val3`. There is no problem in `val1`, this is absolutely correct. When `val2` is evaluated, x is replaced by the expression $2 + 3$ in straight forward way as shown in the expression of val2 and gives incorrect result. This error can be removed by defining the function $f(x)$ as

```
#define f(x) (x)*(x)+2*(x)+5.0
```

But, the third case is very serious. When f(a++) for a = 4 is called, the value of x is replaced by 4 (=a) and after replacement a is incremented to 5, this incremented value replaces x. Again, a is incremented to 6 and this is used in third place of x.

The use of macro in place of function reduces the running time of the program. Because, when macro is used, during preprocessing the function (defined in macro) is substituted in all places where it appears within the program and then it is compiled. That is, in this process no functions are called during program execution. Thus, if a macro is substituted in many places, then the object code becomes long. The use of macro becomes economic where there are relatively few function calls within a loop.

Example 13.1.1 (Evaluation of function using macros) Write a program to find the value of $f(x)$ and $g(x)$ for $x = 0, 0.2, 0.4, \ldots, 1.0$, where $f(x) = \sqrt{1+x}$ and $g(x) = \sin x$. Use macros for $f(x)$ and $g(x)$.

Program 13.3

```
/* Evaluation of function using macros, with argument */
#include<stdio.h>
#include<math.h>
#define f(x) sqrt(1+(x))
#define g(x) sin((x))
void main()
  {
    float x;
    printf(" f(x) \t g(x)\n");
    for(x=0.0;x<=1.0;x+=0.2)
       printf("%7.4f\t%7.4f\n",f(x),g(x));
  }
```

The output of the above program is shown below.

```
 f(x)    g(x)
 1.0000  0.0000
 1.0954  0.1987
 1.1832  0.3894
 1.2649  0.5646
 1.3416  0.7174
 1.4142  0.8415
```

13.1.2 Nesting macro

We can define a macro within another macro. This is called the nesting of macros. For example,

```
#define PI 3.14159
#define AREA(r) PI*r*r
```

In this example, the macro PI is defined at the first line and it is used in the second line for another macro AREA.

The other examples of such cases are given below.

```
#define MAX(a,b)     (((a)>(b)) ? (a):(b))
#define MAX(a,b,c)  ((c)>MAX((a),(b))) ? (c): MAX((a),(b))
#define SQR(x)       ((x)*(x))
#define CUBE(x)      (SQR(x)*(x))
#define FOUR(x)      (SQR(x)*SQR(x))
```

The parenthesis of a macro can be used to define another macro. Also, a macro which is defined can be undefined, using the following statement

```
#undef identifier
```

For this statement, the defined macro (with name identifier) becomes inactive.

13.2 The C Preprocessor

The statements `#include` and `#define` discussed earlier are preprocessor directives. The other preprocessor directives are `#if`, `#elif`, `#else`, `#endif`, `#ifdef`, `#ifndef`, `#line` and `#undef`. The more preprocessor directives are `#pragma`, `#error`, `#` and `##`. Among them the directives `#if`, `#elif`, `#else` and `#endif` are used frequently.

The preprocessor directives generally appear at the beginning of the program, but this is not mandatory. A preprocessor can be defined any where in the program. The directive will be active from the place of its appearance to the end of the program.

13.2.1 #ifdef, #ifndef preprocessors

These directives along with `#else`, `#elif` and `#endif` directives are frequently used as preprocessors. These are used in conditional compilation of the source program, depending on the value of test condition.

Let us consider the following example. A vector is a one-dimensional array and its number of rows and columns are denoted by 1 and COLUMNS (≥ 1). If number of rows becomes greater than one, then it is considered as a matrix. Thus, the number of rows and columns in a matrix are denoted by ROWS and COLUMNS, where ROWS (> 1) and COLUMNS (≥ 1). Also, assume that the objects (OBJECT) vector and matrix are denoted by VECTOR and MATRIX respectively. Now, we would like to define the size of vector or matrix by the preprocess directives.

```
#if defined (ROWS)
    #define COLUMNS 5
#endif
```

The preprocessor `#if defined()` is equivalent to `#ifdef`. Thus, the above statements are equivalent to

```
#ifdef ROWS
    #define COLUMNS 5
#endif
```

Thus, if `ROWS` is already defined, then 5 is assigned to the symbolic constant `COLUMNS`. The `#else` directive can also be used within `#ifdef` directive as illustrated below.

```
#ifdef ROWS                     /* if ROWS is defined */
    #define COLUMNS 5
#else
    #define ROWS    2
    #define COLUMNS 5
#endif
```

These statements check whether `ROWS` is defined or not. If `ROWS` is defined then `COLUMNS` is set to 5, otherwise the symbolic constants `ROWS` and `COLUMNS` are set to 2 and 5 respectively.

The above statements can also be rewritten using the directive `#ifndef` (if not defined) or `#if !defined()`.

```
#ifndef ROWS                    /* if ROWS is not defined */
    #define ROWS    2
    #define COLUMNS 5
#else
    #define ROWS 2
#endif
```

In the directives `#if`, `#ifdef`, `#ifndef` the last directive must be `#endif`. Thus, the general form of `#ifdef`, `#ifndef` and `#if` are

```
#if (or #ifdef or #ifndef) symbolic_constant
        .........
        .........
#else
        .........
        .........
#endif
```

If the `symbolic_constant` is true, then the statements between **#if** and **#else** are executed, otherwise the statements between **#else** and **#endif** are executed.

The following preprocessors directives illustrate the use of **#if**.

```
#if OBJECT==VECTOR
    #define ROWS    1
    #define COLUMNS 5
#else
    #define ROWS 2
    #define COLUMNS 5
#endif
```

It means, if the object is defined as vector, then the number of rows and columns are set to 1 and 5 respectively, otherwise (the object is matrix) the number of rows and columns are set to 2 and 5 respectively.

In C, the **#if** statement checks only one condition. But, if we have to check multi-conditions, then else if statement is used. Like C's control statement **else if** there is a similar preprocessor directive **#elif**. With **#if** directive, any number of **#elif** directives can be used, but only one **#else** directive is used. The **#else** directive is optional, depending on the program logic.

```
#if ROWS==1
    #define COLUMNS 5
#elif ROWS==2
    #define COLUMNS 10
#elif ROWS==3
    #define COLUMNS 12
#else
    #define COLUMNS 14
#endif
```

In the above examples we have use **#define** to define some symbolic constants within **#if, #elif** and **#endif** blocks. But, one can use any other C statements with these preprocessors directives as illustrated below.

```
#define ROWS 1
#define COLUMNS 10
#if (ROWS==1)
#define PRINT printf("The object is vector");    \
                 printf("Rows=%d Columns=%d",ROWS,COLUMNS);
#endif
```

13.2.2 #undef

The **#undef** directive is opposite to **#define** directive. The **#undef** directive undefines a symbolic constant. That is, if a macro is defined, then this macro negates the effect of the macro defined earlier.

Let us consider the following example.

```
/* Illustration of #define and #undef */
#include<stdio.h>
#define  ROWS 5    /* ROWS is defined now */
#define COLUMNS  10 /* COLUMNS is defined here */
main()
  {
    printf("ROWS=%d COLUMSN=%d",ROWS,COLUMNS);
    #undef ROWS /* ROWS is undefined here */
    printf("ROWS=%d COLUMSN=%d",ROWS,COLUMNS);
    #undef COLUMNS /* COLUMNS is undefined here */
    printf("ROWS=%d COLUMSN=%d",ROWS,COLUMNS);
  }
```

In this example, the first print statement gives the following output.

```
ROWS=5 COLUMNS=10
```

By the statement `#undef ROWS`, the symbolic constant `ROWS` becomes undefined, i.e. from this point `ROWS` is not a valid symbolic constant. Therefore, second print statement gives error to print the values of `ROWS`. Actually, this program is erroneous. After the execution of `#undef COLUMNS`, the `COLUMNS` becomes undefined and hence the third print statement is also erroneous.

13.2.3 #, ## directives

The preprocessor directive # is called **stringizing operator**. This operator converts a formal argument within a macro definition to a string. That is, if a formal argument is preceded by # operator, the corresponding actual argument will automatically be enclosed in double quotes, becomes a string. The white space characters and the special characters ' " and \ are replaced by a single blank space, and the escape sequences \' \" and \\ respectively. Also, the two consecutive strings combine to a single string automatically.

Consider the following example.

```
#define  mess(str) printf(#str,"\n");
main()
  {
    . . .
    . . .
    mess(This is use of "stringizing" operator);
  }
```

This macro is equivalent to

```
printf("This is use of \"stringizing\"operator\n");
```

Note that the double quotation mark `"` is automatically replaced by `\"` and two strings `"This is use of \" stringizing\" operator"` and `"\n"` combine together to make a single string.

The output of this program is

```
This is use of "stringizing" operator
```

The other directive `##` is called **token-pasting operator**. This operator concates two individual items into a single item within macro definition. The use of this operator is more complicated. Here a simple example is illustrated.

Suppose three variables $a1$, $a2$ and $a3$ are defined. A function `print` is defined which takes a constant input and displays the corresponding output.

```
/* Use of # and ## operators */
#include<stdio.h>
#define print(i) printf("a"#i"=%d\n",a##i)
main()
  {
    int a1=5,a2=10,a3=12;
    print(1);
    print(2);
    print(3);
  }
```

In `main`, the statement `print(1)` is replaced by `printf("a1=%d\n",a1)`

The output of the above program is

```
a1=5
a2=10
a3=12
```

In this example, both the operators `#` and `##` are used. Note that the argument of `print` must be a constant, it cannot be a variable.

13.2.4 `#error` directive

This preprocessor is used to generate messages (errors) during debugging. Its general form is

```
#error error_message
```

For example,

```
#ifndef OBJECT
#error No object is defined
#endif
```

When the `#error` directive is encountered, then the error message associated with `#error` is displayed and terminates the processing.

Two more directives, viz. #pragma and #line are available in C language. These are used by the advanced user.

Exercise XIII

Review Questions

1. What is a macro and how is it different from a C variable name?
2. Explain the role of the C preprocessor.
3. What are the advantages to use macro with arguments? What are the limitations of it?
4. What is the difference between function and macro with arguments?
5. What is the main advantage to use a macro rather than a function? What are its disadvantages?
6. How is multiline macro defined? What is its advantage?
7. What is the scope of a preprocessor directive within a program file?
8. When does a programmer use #include directives?
9. What is the difference between #ifdef and #if directives?
10. In #include directives, some file names are enclosed in angle brackets while others are enclosed in double quotation marks. Why?
11. Write a note on the preprocessor operators # and ##.
12. What is meant by conditional compilation? How does it help a programmer?
13. What do you mean by stringizing operator? Explain.
14. Explain the purpose of the following preprocessor directives.

```
(a) #if !defined(Flag)
        #define Flag 1
    #endif
```

```
(b) #ifdef CIRCLE
        #define area(r) 3.14159*r*r
    #else
        #define area(r) r*r
```

```
(c) #ifdef ERROR
        #define message(mess) printf(#mess)
    #endif
(d) #ifdef ERROR
        #define message(n) printf("%s\n",message##n)
    #endif
```

Programming Problems

1. Write a macro to find the maximum among three values. Demonstrate it by writing an appropriate program.
2. Define a macro for the constant π ($= 3.14159$). Write a program to find the surface area ($4\pi r^2$) and volume ($\frac{4}{3}\pi r^3$) of a sphere of radius r using macro.

3. Write a macro to find the sum of two numbers. Write a program to find the sum of n numbers using this macro.
4. Define a macro with two parameters to find the area of a rectangle. Write a program using this macro to compute the area of three rectangles whose sides are, (10.3, 23.2), (2.45,3.67) and (5.6, 4.5) respectively.
5. Write a macro with a single argument to define the function $f(t) = e^{-t} + t^2$. Write a program using this macro to find the values of $f(t)$ for the values of $t = -1$ to $t = 1$ with spacing 0.2.
6. Write a macro that receives an array and the number of elements in the array as arguments. Write a program using this macro to print out the elements of an array.
7. Define a macro to find the value of x^2. Use it to define the macros to find the values of x^3 and x^4. Write a program to find the value of the expression $y = 3x^5 - 10.4x^4 + 4x^3 - 20x + 2$ using these three macros.
8. Define a multiline macro to find the factorial of a positive integer. Write a program to find the factorials of 4, 5 and 8 using this macro.

Chapter 14

Miscellaneous Topics in C

In this chapter, three advanced topics in C are discussed. They are command line parameters, multifile programming and bitwise operations.

14.1 Command Line Parameters

In all the programs, as discussed earlier, the argument of the function `main` was void. But, the function `main` can take two arguments, they are generally denoted by `argc` and `argv`. The first argument `argc` is an integer variable and the second argument `argv` is an array of pointers of type characters. That is, `argv` is an array of strings and each string of this array is a parameter. All these strings are passed to the `main` function. The value of `argc` represents the number of parameters passed.

With arguments, the `main` function is of the following form:

```
main(int argc, char *argv[])
{
    . . .
    . . .
}
```

Suppose the above program is saved in the file `test.c`. After compilation, the compiler will generate the executable program `test.exe`. Now, this program can run in many different ways. Some compiler needs the program name at the *operating system level* for its execution. The program is then interpreted as an operating system command. The line where the file name is to be entered is called `command line`. In DOS, the standard/default command line is

`C:\>`

If the executable program `test.exe` resides in the folder `D:\TC>`, then to execute the program `test.exe`, we have to enter `test.exe` at this line. Suppose the command line be

`D:\TC>test aaa bbb ccc`

Then, the value of argc is 4 (because four arguments are entered in the command line) and the array argv is

```
argv[0]=D:\TC>test.exe or test.exe
argv[1]=aaa
argv[2]=bbb
argv[3]=ccc
```

The general form of command line is

```
program_name parameter1 parameter2 ... parametern
```

The parameters `parameter1, parameter2, ..., parametern` are separated by blank spaces or by tabs. These parameters are stored in the array `argv` and the number of arguments will automatically be stored in the argument `argc`.

If an argument contains blank space, then the argument must be entered within double quotations. For example, the following command line statement

```
D:\TC>test cow "Snow white" cat
```

will store the values of `argc` and `argv` as

```
argc=4
argv[0]=D:\TC>test.exe
argv[1]=cow
argv[2]=Snow white
argv[3]=cat
```

Example 14.1.1 Write a program to read an ASCII file. Converts all the characters of this file to upper case and write them to another file. The file names are supplied from command line.

Solution. To run this program exactly three arguments are needed. The first argument is the name of the executable program, second and third arguments are respectively source and target files.

Program 14.1

```
/* Program to convert all characters of a file to upper case.
   The file names are supplied from command line */
#include<stdio.h>
void main(int argc, char *argv[])
 {
   FILE *ofp, *ifp;
   char ch;
   if(argc<3) /* if number of arguments is less than 3 */
     {
      printf("Few parameters\n");
```

```
      exit(0);
    }
  ifp=fopen(argv[1],"r"); /* argv[1] is open as source file */
  ofp=fopen(argv[2],"w"); /* argv[2] is open as target file */
  if(ifp==NULL)
   { /* if source file does not exist */
    printf("File does not exist\n");
    exit(1);
   }
   /* converts the characters to upper case */
   while(!feof(ifp))
     {
      ch=getc(ifp); /* read a character from source */
      putc(toupper(ch),ofp); /* write it to target */
     }
   fclose(ifp);
   fclose(ofp);
}
```

The above program reads all the characters from the file which is supplied as `argv[1]`, one by one and converts it to upper case. Then this converted character is written in the file which is supplied as `argv[2]`.

Usually, `argc` and `argv` are used as arguments of `main`, however, one can change the name of the arguments. Different names are used in the following program.

Example 14.1.2 Write a program to merge some files to a single file, where the file names are to be passed through the command line.

Suppose n arguments are passed through command line including program name. Let the argument of main be n and `file_name`, i.e.

`main(int n, char *file_name[])`

Then, assume that `file_name[1]`, `file_name[2]`, ..., `file_name[n-2]` are source files (to be merged) and `file_name[n-1]` (last argument) be the target file. Source files are opened one by one. The content of a source file is copied to the target file and then closed it. Then, next file is opened as a source file and repeats the same process until the last source file is opened.

Program 14.2

```
/* Merging of several files */
#include<stdio.h>
void main(int n, char *file_name[])
 {
```

```
   FILE *fps, *fpt;
   char ch;
   int i;
   fpt=fopen(file_name[n-1],"w"); /* open as target file */
   for(i=1;i<n-1;i++) /* repeats for all source files */
     {
       fps=fopen(file_name[i],"r");/* opens ith source file */
       while(!feof(fps))
         {
           ch=getc(fps); /* reads a character from source */
           putc(ch,fpt); /* writes it to target */
         }
       fclose(fps); /* closes ith source file */
     }
     fclose(fpt); /* closes target file */
  }
```

Example 14.1.3 Write a program to find the sum of some integers which are supplied through the command line.

Solution. All the arguments are stored to the character-array a[]. The first element a[0] represents the program name and the remaining arguments represent the given integers.

Program 14.3

```
/* Program name sumcom.c. Sum of some integers
   supplied through command line */
#include<stdio.h>
void main(int n, char *a[])
 {
   int i, x, sum=0;
   for(i=1;i<n;i++)
     {
       x=atoi(a[i]); /* converts string to int */
       sum+=x;
     }
   printf("Sum=%d",sum);
 }
```

A sample of input/output:

```
D:\TC>sumcom 58 36 48 71
Sum=213
```

In this program, number of integers need not be supplied in advance. By supplying the integers only one can find the sum of all integers.

The parameters of command line can also be passed by running another program. Before discussing this feature, the function `system` is discussed below.

The function `system`, which is available in `stdlib.h` can execute any program or DOS commands. Also, this function can pass the command line parameters to other program.

The statement

```
system("dir");
```

will display the directory structure (folder) of the current directory (folder). If `test.exe` is an executable program, then this program can be run from the following program.

Program 14.4

```
/* Illustration of the function system */
/* Program name start.c */
#include<stdio.h>
#include<stdlib.h>
void main()
  {
    system("test.exe");
  }
```

Suppose the above code is stored in the program `start.c` and its executable program be `start.exe`. When the program `start` is executed, then this program calls the program `test.exe`.

On success this function returns an integer 0 and on failure it returns −1.

Let us consider the following program. This program will display the content of the file `"std.dat"`. The file name is supplied through a command line, but, the command parameters are called by the function `system`.

```
 /* Program std.c */
#include<stdio.h>
void main(int argc, char *argv[])
  {
    FILE *fp=fopen(argv[1],"r");
    char ch;
    while(!feof(fp))
      {
        ch=getc(fp);
        putchar(ch);
      }
    fclose(fp);
  }
```

This program is now compiled and the executable file be `std.exe`.

Now, consider the following program.

Program 14.5

```
/* Program name cal.c. Illustration of the
  function system with two arguments */
#include<stdio.h>
#include<stdlib.h>
void main()
  {
   int val;
   val=system("std.exe std.dat");
       /* std.dat is pass as parameter */
   if(val==0)
      printf("Execution successful\n");
   else
      printf("Unsuccessful execution\n");
  }
```

The executable program is `cal.exe`. When this program is executed, then the constant string `"std.exe std.dat"` is being passed as command line parameter. Computer will search for the file `std.exe`, if it is available in the working directory, then the execution of the program `std.exe` will start with command line parameter `std.dat`. This parameter is stored as `argv[1]`. Then, the content of `argv[1]` will be displayed on the monitor (done by the program `std.exe`).

14.2 Multifile Programs

Generally, beginners write their programs in a single file and compile it and then run it. But, if the source code is large, then it is difficult to find out a particular function or declaration within a large program. Thus, if we divide the whole program into some small program files, then it is better to identify the functions, variables, etc. That means, one can store some particular type of functions to a specific file, another particular type of function to another file, and so on. Now, the problem is how we can combine these files to get the solution of the problem. This approach allows greater flexibility in defining the scope of both functions and variables. But, the use of storage classes become more complicated. In a multifile program, a function definition is either external or static. A static function is recognized within the file in which it is defined, while external function is available within the entire program. The storage class static or external may be used whenever it is required. The default storage class for a function is external.

In a multifile program, when a function is defined in one file, it can be accessed from the same file and from the other files also.

The function declaration must be included in the file from where the function is accessed. This declaration informs that the function is defined some where else. Generally, the function declarations are placed at the beginning of the file and begins the declaration with storage class specifier `extern`. However, storage class specifier is not mandatory as the default storage class is external.

Like functions, in a multifile program, external variables can be defined in one file and can be accessed from other files. The storage class specifiers `extern` is not necessary to declare external (global) variable. One can initialize the external variable. The default values of external variables are zero.

The compilation of multifile program is not simple. Each individual file must be compiled. These files are linked together within a **project** (this facility is available in any C compiler). Now, compile this project to make an executable program. If a source file is modified, then compile it and also compile the project file. The re-compilation is not required for the other files (if they are not modified). If a new file is included to the project, compile the new file, add it to the project and re-compile the project file.

Now, to explain this feature let us consider the following three files.

First file: File name `p1.c`

```
#include<stdio.h>
extern void wc();
void display();
main()
  {
    wc();
    display();
  }
```

Second file: File name `p2.c`

```
extern void wc() /* function definition in a file */
  {
    printf("Welcome to multifile program\n");
    printf("Called from the file p2.c\n");
  }
```

Third file: File name `p3.c`

```
void display()
  {
    printf("Called from the file p3.c\n");
  }
```

Note that storage class specifier is not mentioned for the function `display`. Suppose the files `p1.c`, `p2.c` and `p3.c` are compiled. Select project menu option and click on open project/new project option (depends on compiler). Put a project name, add the files to the project by selecting appropriate option from project menu.

Suppose the project name is `ptest` (file extension depends on compiler). After adding all the source files, compile the project file `ptest` by compile/run option. The file `ptest.exe` is created. Now, one can run this executable file to get the desired result.

The output of the above program is shown below.

```
Welcome to multifile program
Called from the file p2.c
Called from the file p3.c
```

No header files are included into the files `p2.c` and `p3.c`. But, one can include the necessary header file to any program file where it is required.

There is another way to combine multifile in a program. Suppose, the three program files `p1.c`, `p2.c` and `p3.c` are available and the file `p1.c` is modified as

File name `p1.c`

```
#include<stdio.h>
#include "p2.c"
#include "p3.c"
extern void wc();
void display();
void main()
  {
    wc();
    display();
  }
```

The other files `p2.c` and `p3.c` remain unchanged. Now, compile the program file `p1.c`, the executable file `p1.exe` is created. By executing the file `p1.exe` one can get the output. The output will be same as the output of `ptest.exe`.

Note that the inclusion `#include "p2.c"`. By this inclusion, the entire contents of `p2.c` is included within the source code of the program `p1.c`. When a file is included within the double quotation marks, the search for the file is made first in the current folder and then in the standard folders. If we include `p2.c` by the statement `#include<p2.c>`, then the file `p2.c` is searched only in the standard folders. One file may also be included into another file.

The header file `stdio.h` is included in every C program. This file contains input/output, other functions, definition of symbolic constants and the information related to the use of the library functions. During compilation, the necessary functions (from header file) are merged with the source program. Without using the header file one can write a program by simply declaring the required library functions in the program. To explain this feature let us consider the following problem.

Example 14.2.1 Write a program to find the value of sin(x) for $x = 0.0, 5.0, 10.0,$ 15.0, 20.0, without using header file.

First we write the program using header file.

Program 14.6

```
#include<stdio.h>
#include<math.h>
void main()
 {
   float x;
   for(x=0.0;x<=20.0;x+=5.0)
      printf("x(%0.1f)=%6.4f\n",x,sin(x));
 }
```

This program uses two library functions `printf` and `sin`, they are defined in the files `stdio.h` and `math.h` respectively. Now, we rewrite the above program as follows.

Program 14.7

```
/* Program without using header files */
/* Note that no header files are included within the program */
extern int printf(); /* declaration of library function */
extern double sin(double); /* declaration of library function */
void main()
 {
   float x;
   for(x=0.0;x<=20.0;x+=5.0)
      printf("x(%0.1f)=%6.4f\n",x,sin(x));
 }
```

The compilation process of these programs are same. The output are also same. Note that the number of arguments and type are not mentioned in the function `printf` as the number of arguments may vary from one call to another. The draw back of the later technique is, the user should remember the return type and also the number and types of all arguments of the library functions. Also, each function is to be declared explicitly, obviously the source code will increase gradually.

User can define some of the library functions and can be used in a program. For example, the value of $\sin x$ can be obtained by executing the library function sin(x), which is available in `math.h`. However, we can write a function to evaluate $\sin x$.

There are two observations regarding the use of library function and user defined function. When the library function is used, the size of executable program becomes large, compared to the use of user defined function. The other observation is that the time to execute a program containing library function is less than the program containing user defined function.

14.3 Bitwise Operations

Sometimes it is required to manipulate individual bit within a word of memory. These types of operations are mainly used in assembly language or machine language programs. C provides several special operators for bitwise operations and these operations are divided into three categories - the 1's complement operator, the logical bitwise operators, and the shift operators. All these operations are applicable only for integer operands.

14.3.1 The 1's complement operator

This operator is denoted by ~ and always precedes its operand. This unary operator inverts (i.e. 1s become 0s and 0s become 1s) all the bits represented by its operand.

The operand must be an integer type, including character, octal and hexadecimal quantity.

To illustrate this operator, let us consider `a=1234` (decimal), `b=0x9248` (hexadecimal) and `c=0235` (octal). The values of `a, b, c` in binary form are `a=0000 0100 1101 0010, b=1001 0010 0100 1000, c=0000 0000 1001 1101.`

Then, the 1's complements of `a, b, c` are given below.

```
~a=1111 1011 0010 1101
~b=0110 1101 1011 0111
~c=1111 1111 0110 0010
```

14.3.2 Bitwise logical operators

C provides three bitwise logical operators, they are
(i) *bitwise AND* (&)
(ii) *bitwise OR* (|)
(iii) *bitwise exclusive OR* (∧)

Each of these binary operators require two integer operands. These operators are carried out bit by bit starting from least significant (i.e. the rightmost) bit. The result of bitwise operation of these operators are shown in Table 14.1.

Bitwise AND

The bitwise AND operator is denoted by a single ampersand (&). The result of AND operation is 1, if both the bits have a value 1, otherwise, the value is 0.

For illustration, let us consider

```
a=1101 1100 0000 1011
b=0100 1110 1110 1000
```

a	b	a&b	a|b	a∧b
0	0	0	0	0
0	1	0	1	1
1	0	0	1	1
1	1	1	1	0

Table 14.1: Result of bitwise logical operations

The value of the expression `a&b` is `0100 1100 0000 1000`.

The logical AND operation is often used to test whether a particular bit of an integer is 1 or 0.

The following program tests whether the sixth bit of a number is 1 or not.

Example 14.3.1 (Testing of 6th bit) Write a program which will read an unsigned integer and test whether the sixth bit of this integer (in binary form) is 1 or not.

Program 14.8

```
/* Testing of value of 6th bit of an integer */
#include<stdio.h>
void main()
 {
   int number;
   int testbit=32; /* 0000 0000 0010 0000 set 6th bit 1 */
   printf("Enter an integer\n");
   scanf("%d",&number);
   if((number & testbit) !=0) /* test 6th bit */
      printf("The 6th bit is 1\n");
   else
      printf("The 6th bit is 0\n");
 }
```

In this program, `testbit` is taken as 32, to set only the 6th bit to 1 and all other bits 0. When the logical AND operation is performed between `number` and `testbit`, all bits become 0, except 6th. If the 6th bit of `number` is 1, then the 6th bit of the expression `number & testbit` becomes 1, otherwise 0.

This technique may also be used to test whether an integer is odd or even. The least significant (rightmost) bit of an even integer is 0 and 1 for an odd integer.

By testing the least significant bit one can test whether an integer is odd or even.

Example 14.3.2 (Checking of even integer) Write a program to test whether an integer is even or odd using bitwise operation.

Program 14.9

```
/* Testing of odd or even integer using bitwise operation */
#include<stdio.h>
void main()
 {
  int a, mask=1; /* set first bit to 1 */
  printf("Enter an integer\n");
  scanf("%d",&a);
  if(a & mask) /* testing first bit position */
    printf("The number %d is odd\n",a);
  else
    printf("The number %d is even\n",a);
}
```

A sample of input/output:

```
Enter an integer
8656
The number 8656 is even
```

Note 14.3.1 The precedence of bitwise logical operators is lower than the relational operators.

Bitwise OR

The bitwise OR operator is denoted by single vertical bar (|). The result of OR operation is 1 if at least one bit is 1, otherwise it is 0.

Let us consider two binary numbers

`a=0000 0001 1101 1010`

`b=0100 1010 1110 1000`

Then, the result of `x|y` is `0100 1011 1111 1010`. Using this operation, a particular bit of an integer can be set to 1. Suppose we would like to set the 5th bit of `b` to 1. For this problem, let us consider the number `m=0000 0000 0001 0000` (= 16). When the statement `b=b|m` is executed, then the value of `b` becomes `0100 1010 1111 1000`.

Note that the 5th bit of `b` is now 1.

Example 14.3.3 Write a program to check whether a particular bit of an integer is 0 or not. If this bit is zero, replace it by 1.

Program 14.10

```
/* Testing of 0 at the nth position, and set to 1 if it is 0 */
#include<stdio.h>
#include<math.h>
```

```
void main()
 {
  int mask,a,n;
  printf("Enter an integer\n");
  scanf("%d",&a);
  printf("Enter position to be checked ");
  scanf("%d",&n);
  mask=pow(2,n-1); /* nth position 1 and other positions 0 */
  if(a & mask) /* testing nth bit position */
    printf("Bit of %dth position is 1\n",n);
  else
    {
      printf("Bit of %dth position is 0\n",n);
      a=a|mask; /* set nth position to 1 */
      printf("After setting of bit, a=%d\n",a);
    }
}
```

A sample of input/output:

```
Enter an integer
2048
Enter position to be checked 7
Bit of 7th position is 0
After setting of bit, a=2112
```

In this program, the nth bit of the integer a becomes 1, if this bit was 0. If the nth bit of a is changed to 1, the value of a will increase by 2^{n-1}.

Bitwise exclusive OR

This operator is denoted by the symbol $\wedge$. If both the bits are same, then the value of this operation is 0, otherwise it is 1. For example, if

a=1000 0010 0000 1101

b=0110 0010 1101 0101

then, $a \wedge b$=1110 0000 1101 1000.

The precedence of bitwise logical operators from highest to lowest is bitwise AND (&), bitwise exclusive OR ($\wedge$) and bitwise OR (|). Bitwise AND follows the equality operators (== and !=). Bitwise OR is followed by logical AND (&&). The associativity for each bitwise operator is left to right.

14.3.3 Bitwise shift operator

The shift operator is used to move bit patterns either to right or to left. Two shift operators are *shift left* (<<) and *shift right* (>>). These binary operators are applicable only for integer operands.

The general forms of these operators are

`a<<n` and `a>>n`

where `a` is an integer which represents the bit pattern to be shifted and n is an unsigned integer that indicates the number of bits to be shifted. The value of `n` must not exceed the number of bits associated with the word size of `a`.

When `a` is shifted to the left by `n` positions, then the `n` left most bits in the original bit pattern will be lost, and `n` right most positions become vacant. This vacant bits are filled by 0's.

For example, let `a=0110 1100 1010 1000` and `b=a<<5`.

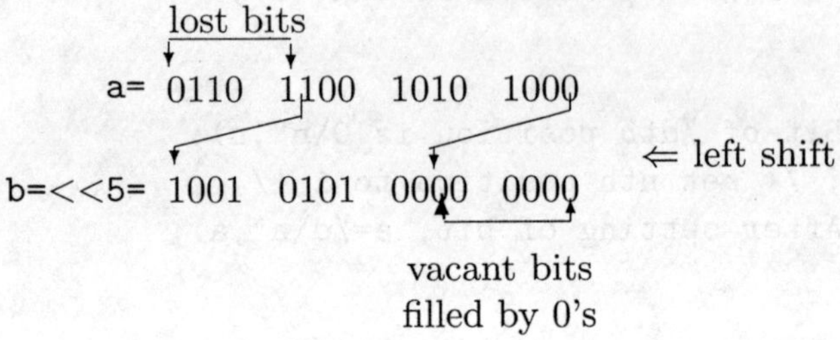

By this operation the left most 5 bits (01101) are lost and the right most 5 bits are filled by 00000.

The right shift operators are similar.

If `c=a>>5`, then 5 right most bits are lost, and left most 5 positions are filled by five 0's. That is,

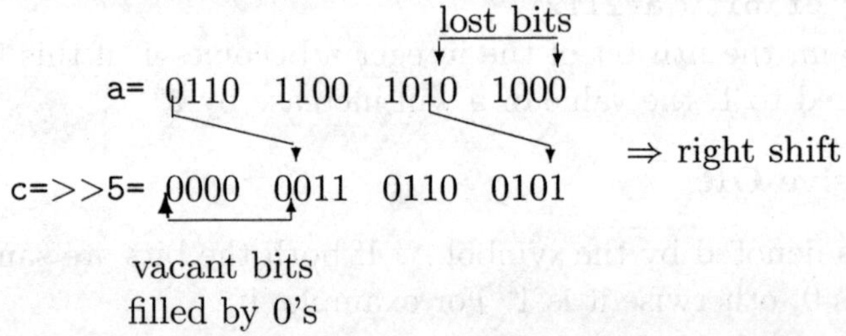

For the signed integer, the result of the shift operators may depend on the value of left most bits (the sign bit) and on the compiler.

The shift operators can also be used to multiply/divide an integer by 2 (or power of 2). For example, the statement

`a=b<<1;`

shifts one bit to the left in `b` and the result is stored in `a`. Then, the decimal value of `a` is equal to `2b`.

Similarly, the statement

`a=b>>1;`

shifts one bit to the right in `b` and the resulted value is stored in `a`. In this case, the value of `a` is equal to `b/2`.

Example 14.3.4 Write a program to multiply and divide an integer by 4 using bitwise operation.

Program 14.11

```
/* Multiply/divide an integer by 4 using bitwise operation */
#include<stdio.h>
void main()
 {
  unsigned int a,b,c;
  printf("Enter an integer\n");
  scanf("%d",&a);
  b=a<<1; /* multiply a by 2 */
  b=b<<1; /* multiply a by 4, b by 2 */
  c=a>>1; /* divide a by 2 */
  c=c>>1; /* divide a by 4, c by 2 */
  printf("a=%d 4a=%d a/4=%d\n",a,b,c);
}
```

A sample of input/output:

```
Enter an integer
3574
a=3574 4a=14296 a/4=893
```

Like arithmetic assignment operators, C also supports the following bitwise assignment operators.

`&=    ∧=    |=    <<=    >>=`

The expanded forms of these statements are given below.

```
a&=b    a=a&b
a∧=b    a=a∧b
a|=b    a=a|b
a<<=b   a=a<<b
a>>=b   a=a>>b
```

14.3.4 Masking

Masking is a process to transfer a given bit pattern into another bit pattern using logical bitwise operation. In this logical bitwise operation, one operand is the given integer of original bit pattern. The other operand, known as **mask**, is a specially selected bit pattern which helps to extract desired bit pattern.

The masking operations are used in different ways:

(i) A portion of a given bit pattern can be copied to a new variable, while the remaining bits of the new variable are filed by 0's. This can be done by bitwise AND operation.

(ii) A portion of a given bit pattern can be copied to a new variable, while the remaining bits of the new variable are filed by 1's. The bitwise OR operation is used in this purpose.

(iii) A portion of a given bit pattern can be copied to a new variable, while the remaining bits of the original bit pattern is inverted within the new word. This type of masking is performed by using bitwise exclusive OR.

To illustrate all these cases, let us consider the following examples.

Example 14.3.5 Let `a=0011 1000 1101 1001`. Extract left most 6 bits from `a` and assign them to `b` and fill all right most 10 bits of `b` by 0.

To solve this problem, selection of mask and bitwise operator is important.
For this problem, the appropriate mask is `mask= 1111 1100 0000 0000`.
Then

```
        a  =  0011  1000  1101  1001
     mask  =  1111  1100  0000  0000
--------------------------------------
 b=a&mask  =  0011  1000  0000  0000
```

Note that the left most 6 bits of `a` and `b` are same and remaining 10 right bits of `b` are filled by 0's.

Example 14.3.6 From the same `a` (of previous example), extract right most 10 bits of `a` and assign them to the variable `b`. Also, fill the left most 6 bits of `b` by 0.

In this case, the appropriate mask is `mask= 0000 0011 1111 1111`.
Now,

```
        a  =  0011  1000  1101  1001
     mask  =  0000  0011  1111  1111
--------------------------------------
 b=a&mask  =  0000  0000  1101  1001
```

Note that the right most 10 bits of `a` are copied to `b` and left most 6 bits of `b` are filled by 0's.

Example 14.3.7 Let `a=0011 1000 1101 1001`. Extract left most 6 bits from `a` and save it to `b` and fill right most 10 bits of `b` by 1.

Select the mask as `mask=0000 0011 1111 1111` and operator as bitwise OR. Then

```
        a  =  0011  1000  1101  1001
     mask  =  0000  0011  1111  1111
--------------------------------------
 b=a|mask  =  0011  1011  1111  1111
```

Note that the left most 6 bits of `a` and `b` are same and right most 10 bits of `b` are filled by 1.

The bitwise exclusive OR with appropriate mask is used to revert the desired bit pattern of the original integer.

Example 14.3.8 Revert the 5th to 10th bits (from left) of the number `a=0011 1000 1101 1001`.

Let the mask be `0000 1111 1100 0000`.

a	=	0011 1000 1101 1001
mask	=	0000 1111 1100 0000
b=a∧mask	=	0011 0111 0001 1001

Note that 5th and 10th bits in `b` have been changed and all other bits remain unchanged.

Again, we perform the operation `c=b∧mask`.

b	=	0011 0111 0001 1001
mask	=	0000 1111 1100 0000
c=b∧mask	=	0011 1000 1101 1001

Note that `c` and `a` are same. Thus, this operation is used as **toggle**.

Using the above bitwise operations, an integer (decimal, octal, hexadecimal) can be converted into its binary equivalent. The program is listed below.

Program 14.12

```
/* Convert an integer (decimal, octal or hexadecimal)
   into binary number and count number of 1's in
   the binary number using bitwise operations */
#include<stdio.h>
void main()
 {
  int a,i,count=0,bit,word;
  unsigned mask;
  printf("Enter an integer\n");
  scanf("%d",&a);
  mask=1;
  word=8*sizeof(int); /* set to word length */
  mask=mask<<(word-1); /* shift 1 to the leftmost position */
  printf("The binary equivalent is\n");
  for(i=1;i<=word;i++){
     bit=(a & mask)? 1: 0; /* identify bit 1 or 0 */
```

```
    printf("%d",bit);
    if(bit==1) count++; /* counting 1 */
    mask>>=1; /* Shift mask by 1 position to right */
  }
 printf("\nNumber of 1's is %d",count);
}
```

A sample of input/output:

```
Enter an integer
3565
The binary equivalent is
0000110111101101
Number of 1's is 9
```

14.3.5 Bit fields

Sometimes it may happen that the values of some variables are low. For example, the value of a boolean variable (whose value is either true or false) is either 1 or 0, the month of a date lies between 1 and 12, day of a date lies between 1 and 31, etc. In general, these values are stored using integer variables, but such data items can be packed into an individual word of memory. For this purpose, a word is divided into bit fields. These bit fields are defined as the members of a structure. Then each bit fields can be accessed as a member of structure.

The general form to define bit fields is

```
struct tag{
    unsigned field_name1 : bit_width1;
    unsigned field_name2 : bit_width2;
    . . . . . . . . . . . . . . . . .
    unsigned field_namen : bit_widthn;
  };
```

where `filed_name1, ..., filed_namen` are the individual field names as in structure and `bit_width1, ..., bit_widthn` are the unsigned integers representing the number of bits (field size) allocated for the variables `filed_name1, ..., filed_namen`.

The allocation of bit fields within a word may vary from a compiler to compiler. In some compilers, the bit fields are ordered from left to right and some other compilers may order from right to left. Here, we assume that *the bit fields are ordered from right to left.*

Let us consider the following example to illustrate the allocation of memory of bit fields.

```
struct XYZ{
    unsigned x : 2;
    unsigned y : 3;
```

```
        unsigned z : 1;
      }A;
```

In this definition three members `x, y, z` are defined within the same word. The widths of `x, y, z` are 2 bits, 3 bits and 1 bit respectively, in total 6 bits. The other bits within the allocated word remains unused. That is, one word is allocated for this purpose and only 6 bits are used to store three values.

Figure 14.1 illustrates the allocation of bit fields.

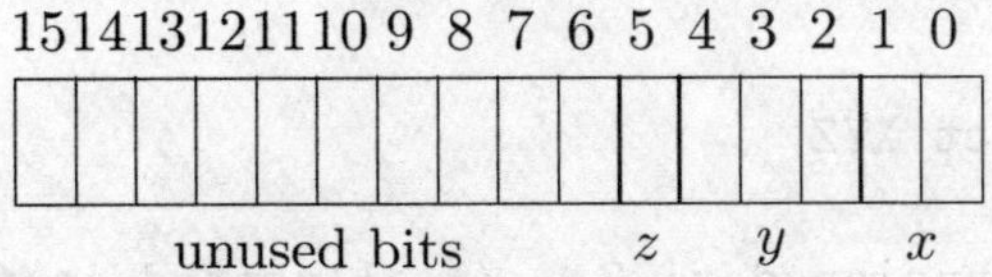

Figure 14.1: Bit fields within a 16-bit word

The variable `A` is declared as a structure variable of type `XYZ`, and the memory allocated for the variables `A.x, A.y, A.z` are 2 bits, 3 bits and 1 bit respectively. The range of values of these variables are 0 to 3, 0 to 7 and 0 to 1 respectively.

It must be remembered that the bit field can only be defined as a portion of an integer or an unsigned word. Some compilers may allow a bit field to be a portion of a character or a long word. But, the rules are same.

Normally, the bit fields are allocated within a single word, provided the sum of the bits used in the variables is less than or equal to the size of the word (i.e. 16 bits). If the sum of the bits is more than 16 bits, then another word will automatically be allocated to store the value. Thus, there is no scope for overlapping fields within a word. This situation is explained in the following example.

```
      struct XYZUV{
          unsigned x: 2; /* allocated in first word */
          unsigned y: 3; /* allocated in first word */
          unsigned z: 1; /* allocated in first word */
          unsigned u: 7; /* allocated in first word */
          unsigned v: 5; /* allocated in second word */
      }A;
```

Here the sum of the bits is 18. If the word length is 16 bits, then two words are required to store these fields. The sum of the bits of first four variables is 13. So the first four variables will be stored in the first word. Three bits (16-13=3) of first word remains unused, because the variable `v` (of size 5 bits) cannot be allocated within this space. To store the value of `v`, a second word is automatically allocated within the computer's memory. Thus, to store five variables only four bytes (two words) are used.

The allocation of bit fields are shown in Figure 14.2.

A bit field can also be declared without its name. The width of such field may be 0 or any unsigned integer. This facility is used to control the alignment of bit fields within

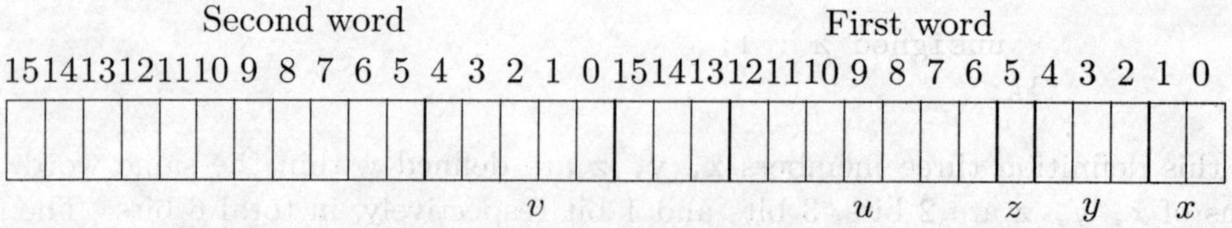

Figure 14.2: Five variables are allocated in two words

a word of memory. Such fields provide padding within the word. Look at the following example.

```
struct XYZ
  {
     unsigned x: 2;   /* allocated in first word */
     unsigned y: 3;   /* allocated in first word */
     unsigned z: 1;   /* allocated in first word */
     unsigned   : 10; /* fill out first word */
     unsigned u: 6;   /* allocated in second word */
  }A={2,5,1,10}; /* declaration and assignment */
```

To store the values of the structure variable A, two words are required. The values of first three fields x,y,z will be stored within the first word, along with the 10 vacant bits. The value of last field u will be stored at the beginning of the second word. In the above declaration the values of A.x, A.y, A.z and A.u are 2 (=10, in binary form), 5 (=101), 1 (=1) and 10 (=1010). (The numbers within brackets represent binary equivalent).

The above example is illustrated in Figure 14.3.

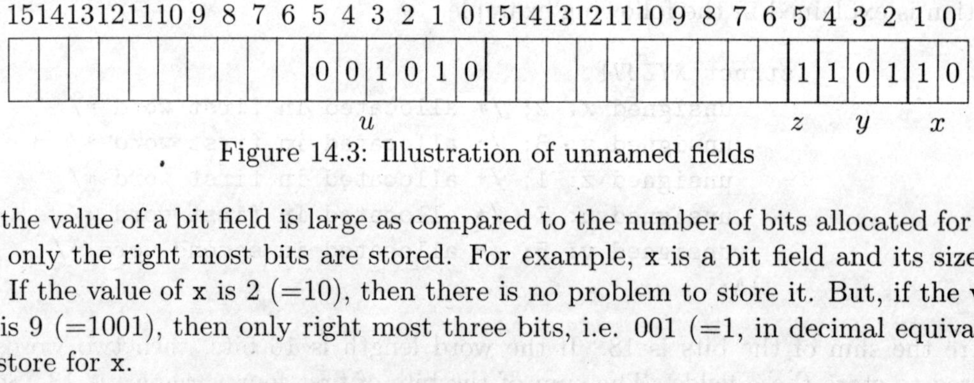

Figure 14.3: Illustration of unnamed fields

If the value of a bit field is large as compared to the number of bits allocated for this, then only the right most bits are stored. For example, x is a bit field and its size is 3 bits. If the value of x is 2 (=10), then there is no problem to store it. But, if the value of x is 9 (=1001), then only right most three bits, i.e. 001 (=1, in decimal equivalent) will store for x.

Another technique is also used to skip the bits of a particular word. This can be done with the help of an unnamed field whose width is zero. The action of the above and the following program segments are similar.

```
struct XYZ{
     unsigned x: 2;  /* allocated in first word */
     unsigned y: 3;  /* allocated in first word */
     unsigned z: 1;  /* allocated in first word */
```

```
        unsigned  : 0;  /* fill out first word */
        unsigned u: 6;  /* allocated in second word */
     }A={2,5,1,10}; /* declaration and assignment */
```

Note 14.3.2 The bit fields are used in the same way as the structure members. However, several restrictions are also imposed on their use. The arrays of bit fields are not allowed, the address operator (&) is not applicable to a bit field, a pointer cannot access a bit field and a function cannot return a bit field.

In the following, a complete program is written to illustrate the use of bit fields and also it is shown that how we can accommodate date using less memory space.

Example 14.3.9 Write a program to store name, age, height (in ft-in format) and sex of a group of students using bit fields. Then, compute the average height and average age of such students.

Solution. A structure `student` is defined whose field names are – `name` of 20 characters, `height` in ft-in format (4 bits for feet and 4 bits for inch), `sex` of 1 bit and `age` of 6 bits. That is, the memory needed to store the value of a variable of type `student` is 20 bytes (for name) + (4 bits + 4 bits) + 1 bit +6 bits = 20 bytes + 15 bits = 22 bytes.

Then, an array of `student s[10]` is declared. The values for the bit fields are read to the temporary variables of type integer. Then, these values are assigned to the bit fields.

Number of male students, average age and average height of the students are computed by using simple arithmetic operations on bit fields.

If the bit fields are not used to store the information of a single student, then (20 bytes (for name) + 2 bytes (for height) + 2 bytes (for age) + 1 byte (for sex) =) 25 bytes space is required for the purpose. Thus, 3 bytes space is saved for a single student.

The program is shown below.

Program 14.13

```
/* Use of bit fields. Calculates the average age, height and number
   of male students among a group of students */
#include<stdio.h>
#include<string.h>
void main()
 {
  struct student
    {
      char name[20];
      unsigned height_ft: 4; /* 4 bits for feet*/
      unsigned height_in: 4; /* 4 bits for in */
```

```
      unsigned sex     : 1; /* 1 bit for sex */
      unsigned age     : 6; /* 6 bits for age */
    };
  struct student s[10];
  int n,i,h_ft,h_in,agg,gender;
  int malecount=0,agesum=0;
  float heightsum=0;
  printf("Size of student struct =%d bytes\n",sizeof(struct student));
  printf("How many students ?\n");
  scanf("%d",&n);
  for(i=0;i<n;i++)
    {
      printf("\nEnter name \n");
      scanf("%s",s[i].name);
      printf("Enter height in ft (<=15) and in (<12)\n");
      scanf("%d%d",&h_ft,&h_in);
      printf("Enter age (<=63)\n"); /* 6 bits */
      scanf("%d",&agg);
      printf("Enter sex (1 for male 0 for female)\n");
      scanf("%d",&gender);
      s[i].height_ft=h_ft;
      s[i].height_in=h_in;
      s[i].age=agg;
      s[i].sex=gender;
    }
 for(i=0;i<n;i++)
   {
     printf("%s %d %d %d %d\n",s[i].name,s[i].sex,s[i].age,
                                  s[i].height_ft,s[i].height_in);
     if(s[i].sex==1) malecount++;
     agesum+=s[i].age;
     heightsum+=s[i].height_ft+(float)s[i].height_in/12.0;
   }
 printf("Number of male students : %d\n",malecount);
 printf("Average age              : %.2f yrs\n",(float)(agesum)/n);
 printf("Average height           : %.2f ft\n",(float)(heightsum)/n);
}
```

A sample of input/output:

```
Size of student struct =22 bytes
How many students ?
5
```

```
Enter name
Aniket
Enter height in ft (<=15) and in (<12)
4 5
Enter age (<=63)
10
Enter sex (1 for male 0 for female)
1

Enter name
Prapti
Enter height in ft (<=15) and in (<12)
5 1
Enter age (<=63)
12
Enter sex (1 for male 0 for female)
0

Enter name
Sebika
Enter height in ft (<=15) and in (<12)
5 5
Enter age (<=63)
18
Enter sex (1 for male 0 for female)
0

Enter name
Prithu
Enter height in ft (<=15) and in (<12)
4 2
Enter age (<=63)
8
Enter sex (1 for male 0 for female)
1

Enter name
Mimi
Enter height in ft (<=15) and in (<12)
3 1
Enter age (<=63)
5
```

```
Enter sex (1 for male 0 for female)
0

Aniket 1 10 4 5
Prapti 0 12 5 1
Sebika 0 18 5 5
Prithu 1  8 4 2
Mimi   0  5 3 1
Number of male students : 2
Average age             : 10.60 yrs
Average height          : 4.43 ft
```

Exercise XIV

Review Questions

1. The function `main()` have two formal arguments. What are they traditionally called? What are their respective data types?
2. Are the names of the formal arguments of `main()` fixed? Explain.
3. What information is represented by each formal argument in function `main()`? Is information passed explicitly to each argument?
4. When parameters are passed to a program from the command line, how is the program execution initiated? Where do the parameters appear?
5. Suppose `test.exe` is an executable program and can take data from command line. The following commands are supplied during the execution of the program.

   `test aaaa "Anjali Pal" 345`

   Determine the value of `argc` and that of `argv`.
6. What is the advantage to write a program into multifile?
7. In what situation is it desirable to write a program into multifile?
8. What is the purpose of a static function in a multifile program?
9. What is the purpose of a header file? Is the use of a header file absolutely necessary?
10. In a multifile program, what is the default storage class for a function if a storage class is not explicitly mentioned in the function definition?
11. Compare the use of function within a multifile program with the function within a single-file program. What additional options are available in the multifile program?
12. What is meant by bitwise operations?
13. Describe three logical bitwise operators. Also, explain the use of each of these operators.
14. What is the precedence and associativity of the logical bitwise operators?

15. What types of operands are required for the logical bitwise operators?
16. Describe two bitwise shift operators. What condition must be satisfied by the operands? What is the purpose of these operators?
17. What is the precedence and associativity of the bitwise shift operators?
18. Suppose four bits are shifted to the left. What value fills the rightmost bit positions that are vacated by the shifting bits? Does the type of operand being shifted affects this value? Explain.
19. List all the bitwise assignment operators and describe their purpose. Describe each of the operands used in a bitwise assignment operations.
20. What do you meant by masking? What is the purpose of the operands used in the masking?
21. Describe a masking operation in which a portion of a given bit pattern is copied, while the remaining bits are set to 0. Which logical bitwise operation is used for this operation? What is the procedure to select a mask?
22. Describe a masking operation in which a portion of a given bit pattern is copied, while the remaining bits are set to 1. Which logical bitwise operation is used for this operation? How is the mask defined?
23. How can a particular bit be toggled on and off repeatedly? Which logical bitwise operation is used for this purpose?
24. Suppose the fifth bit of a number is to be changed to 1, if it is 0. Describe a method to do this task.
25. What are bit fields? How bit fields are defined? How can individual bit fields be accessed? What is the advantage to use bit fields?
26. What are the rules to define bit fields?
27. What data type must be associated with each bit field?
28. What happens if a bit field overlaps a word within the memory?
29. Explain about the unnamed bit field and zero-width bit field.
30. In what order the bit fields are arranged within a word? Is this convention universal?
31. What types of operations are applicable for the bit fields and what types of operations are not useful for bit fields?
32. Suppose `x` and `y` are unsigned integers whose values are 0100 0101 1000 0011 and 0011 0001 0000 1100. Evaluate each of the following bitwise expressions. Use the original value of `x` and `y` in each case. Assume that `x` and `y` are stored in 16-bit words.

(a) `~ x` (b) `a>>3` (c) `a>>4`
(d) `x^y` (e) `x & y` (f) `x | y`
(g) `x^ ~x` (h) `x & ~x` (i) `x | ~x`
(j) `x & y<<4` (k) `x | y >> 3` (l) `(x | y) >>3`

33. Define a mask and write the appropriate masking operation for each of the following situations.

    (a) Copy the bits of odd positions (bits 1, 3, 5, ..., 15) and place zeros in the even bit positions (bits 0, 2, 4, ..., 14) of a 16-bit, unsigned integer quantity represented by the variable `x`. Assume that rightmost bit position is 0.

34. Toggle the values of the bits 2 and 10 of a 16-bit unsigned integer quantity represented by the variable `x`, while preserving all of the remaining bits. Assign a new bit pattern to `x`.
35. Assume a 16-bit integer word. Write a structure to define three bit fields `x`, `y` and `z` whose width are 6 bits, 5 bits and 3 bits respectively.
36. Write a structure to define three bit fields `x`, `y` and `z` whose width are 6 bits, 5 bits and 3 bits respectively. Force `y` to the beginning of a second word of storage. Also, separate `y` and `z` with 3 vacant bits.

Programming Problems

1. Write a complete C program to find the sum of certain floating point numbers. Enter the numbers from command line.
2. Write a program to find the maximum among some integers. The integers are supplied from command line.
3. Write a complete C program to find the nth term of the Fibonacci series. Enter the value of n from command line.
4. Write a program that will take the name of a text file from command line and will print all the words starting with a vowel into another file named `vowel.txt`.
5. Write a program to copy the content of the source file into the destination file. The file names are to be supplied through command line.
6. Write a C program to print the name of your program. That is, the name of the program that it is executing.
7. Write a program that reads an integer from standard input device and outputs the number of 1's in its binary representation to the standard output device. Note that if the integer read is negative, then the 2's complement will be considered as its binary representation.
8. Write a function that uses bitwise operators to print the binary representation of an integer number.
9. Write a program that reads an integer from the keyboard and check if it is odd. If the number is odd, then output the number of 1's in its binary representation, otherwise output of the integer is even. Use bitwise operation in this program.
10. Write a program that reads an integer and test whether a specific bit, say nth (≤ 16) bit of this integer (in binary form) is 1 or not.
11. Write a program to check whether a particular bit of an integer is 1 or not. If this bit is 1, replace it by 0.

12. Write a program to multiply and divide an integer by 8 using bitwise operation.
13. Write a program that will read a hexadecimal integer and convert it in its binary equivalent, using bitwise operation.
14. Write a program that reads an integer and revert a particular, say nth ($n \leq 16$), bit, using bitwise operation.
15. Write a program that returns x with the n bits that begin at position k inverted (i.e. 1 changed into 0 and vice versa), leaving the others unchanged.

Chapter 15

Numerical Methods

The solutions of mathematical problems are of two types – analytical and numerical. The analytical solution is error free. But for some classes of problems, it is very difficult to obtain analytical solution. For these types of problems, the numerical method is the only way to obtain a solution. But the solution obtained by the numerical method has some errors, which are negligible.

In this age of computers many complicated and large problems are solved in a significantly less time. But without using numerical methods one cannot solve any mathematical problem using a computer, as analytical methods are not applicable to solve a problem by computer.

Thus, the numerical methods are highly appreciated and extensively used by mathematicians, physicists, computer scientists, statisticians, engineers, etc.

15.1 Interpolation

Consider a function $f(x)$ which is not given in explicit form. The value of the function is given as a set of values for the different values of $x_0, x_1, \ldots, x_n$ of x. It is required to compute the value of $f(x)$ at a point different from the above list. To do this, we use a method known as **interpolation**.

So, the main objective of interpolation is to estimate the values of the function at non-tabular points. Based on the given tabulated values of $f(x)$ a polynomial $\phi(x)$, called the interpolation polynomial, of degree less than or equal to n (one less than the number of tabulated points) is constructed such that the values of the polynomial and that of the function are equal at the abscissa $x_0, x_1, \ldots, x_n$, i.e. a polynomial

$$\phi(x) = a_0 + a_1x + a_2x^2 + \cdots + a_nx^n$$

is formed such that $\phi(x_i) = f(x_i), i = 0, 1, 2, \ldots, n$. Many interpolation methods are available. In this section, the following interpolation methods are discussed.

- Lagrange interpolation for single variable
- Lagrange interpolation for two variables

- Newton-Gregory interpolation
- Cubic spline interpolation

15.1.1 Lagrange interpolation

Let $y = f(x)$ be a real valued function defined on an interval $[a, b]$. Let $a \leq x_0 < x_1 < \cdots < x_n \leq b$ be $n+1$ points at which the corresponding values $y_0, y_1, \ldots, y_n$ of $f(x)$ are tabulated. We construct a polynomial $\phi(x)$ of degree $\leq n$ such that $\phi(x_i) = y_i, i = 0, 1, 2, \ldots, n$.

The Lagrange interpolation polynomial $\phi(x)$ is of the form

$$\phi(x) = \sum_{i=0}^{n} l_i(x) y_i,$$

where,

$$l_i(x) = \frac{(x-x_0)(x-x_1)\cdots(x-x_{i-1})(x-x_{i+1})\cdots(x-x_n)}{(x_i-x_0)(x_i-x_1)\cdots(x_i-x_{i-1})(x_i-x_{i+1})\cdots(x_i-x_n)} = \prod_{j=0, j\neq i}^{n} \left(\frac{x-x_j}{x_i-x_j} \right)$$

is a polynomial of degree $\leq n$ in x, called Lagrange function. Therefore,

$$\phi(x) = \sum_{i=0}^{n} \prod_{j=0, j\neq i}^{n} \left(\frac{x-x_j}{x_i-x_j} \right) y_i.$$

This expression gives the approximate value of $f(x)$ for a given x.

Program 15.1

```
/* Program  to  interpolate a function  by Lagrange interpolation */
#include<stdio.h>
void main()
  {
    float x[20],y[20],term,value=0,X;
    int n,i,j;
    printf("Enter number of points\n");
    scanf("%d",&n);
    n--;
    printf("Enter x-and y-values\n");
    for(i=0;i<=n;i++) scanf("%f%f",&x[i],&y[i]);
    printf("Enter the value of x at which y is to be computed\n");
    scanf("%f",&X);
    for(i=0;i<=n;i++){
       term = y[i];
         for(j=0;j<=n;j++)
            if (i!=j) term *=(X-x[j])/(x[i]-x[j]);
```

```
        value+=term;
     }
   printf("X=%.4f  Value of Y=%.5f\n", X,value);
  }
```

A sample of input/output:

```
Enter number of points
5
Enter x-and y-values
2 5 4 9 5 11 6 13 7 15
Enter the value of x at which y is to be computed
3.5
X=3.5000 Value of Y=8.00000
```

Note 15.1.1 Lagrange interpolation formula can be used for unequal spaced points, and the function can be computed for any value of x.

15.1.2 Lagrange interpolation for two variables

Let $f(x, y)$ be a real valued function, defined at $(m+1).(n+1)$ distinct points $(x_i, y_j), i = 0, 1, \ldots, m; j = 0, 1, \ldots, n$. Let $f(x_i, y_j)$ be denoted by f_{ij}. We construct a polynomial $\phi(x, y)$ of at most degree $m + n$, where m is the at most degree of x and n of y, such that $\phi(x_i, y_j) = f_{ij}, i = 0, 1, \ldots, m; j = 0, 1, \ldots, n$. Using the Lagrange interpolation formula for a single variable, we can define

$$l_{x_i}(x) = \prod_{k=0,k\neq i}^{m} \left(\frac{x - x_k}{x_i - x_k}\right), l_{y_j}(y) = \prod_{k=0,k\neq j}^{n} \left(\frac{y - y_k}{y_j - y_k}\right), i = 0, 1, \ldots, m, j = 0, 1, \ldots, n.$$

The polynomial $l_{x_i}(x)$ and $l_{y_j}(y)$ are of degrees m and n respectively. The Lagrange's interpolation polynomial for two variables can then be expressed as

$$\phi(x, y) = \sum_{i=0}^{m}\sum_{j=0}^{n} l_{x_i}(x) l_{y_j}(y) f_{ij} = \sum_{i=0}^{m} l_{x_i}(x)\left(\sum_{j=0}^{n} l_{y_j}(y) f_{ij}\right).$$

Program 15.2

```
 /* Bivariate
Lagrange interpolation, m, n represent the number of
   intervals in x and y values and f(x,y) is the value of f at (x,y). */
#include<stdio.h>
void main()
  {
    float lx,ly,x[20],y[20],f[20][20],xg,yg,pxy=0,lyf;
    int m,n,i,j,k;
    printf("Enter number of x and y values\n");
```

```
    scanf("%d%d",&m,&n);
    m--; n--;
    printf("Enter values of x, y, f(x,y)\n");
    for(i=0;i<=m;i++) for(j=0;j<=n;j++)
       scanf("%f%f%f",&x[i],&y[j],&f[i][j]);
    printf("Given values of x,y,f(x,y)\n");
    for(i=0;i<=m;i++) for(j=0;j<=n;j++)
       printf("%.3f %.3f %.3f\n",x[i],y[j],f[i][j]);
    printf("Enter interpolate values of x,y\n");
    scanf("%f%f",&xg,&yg);
    printf("Value of x=%.3f  Value of y=%.3f\n",xg,yg);
    for(i=0;i<=m;i++){
        lyf=0; lx=1;
        for(k=0;k<=m;k++)
          if(i!=k) lx*=(xg-x[k])/(x[i]-x[k]);
        for(j=0;j<=n;j++){
            ly=1.;
            for(k=0;k<=n;k++)
            if(k!=j) ly*=(yg-y[k])/(y[j]-y[k]);
            lyf+=ly*f[i][j];
          }
        pxy+=lx*lyf;
      }
   printf("Value of the function = %.5f\n",pxy);
  }
```

A sample of input/output:

```
Enter number of x and y values
3 3
Enter values of x, y, f(x,y)
0 0 -1
0 1 0
0 2 3
1 0 0
1 1 1
1 2 4
2 0 3
2 1 4
2 2 7

Given values of x,y,f(x,y)
0   0   -1
0   1   0
```

```
0  2  3
1  0  0
1  1  1
1  2  4
2  0  3
2  1  4
2  2  7

Enter interpolate values of x,y
.5 1.5

Value of x=0.500  Value of y=1.500
Value of the function = 1.50000
```

15.1.3 Finite differences

Let $(x_i, y_i), i = 0, 1, \ldots, n$, be the tabulated values of a function $y = f(x)$, where values of x are equally spaced, that is, $x_i = x_0 + ih, i = 1, 2, \ldots, n$.

Forward differences

Let $y = f(x)$ be a function. The forward difference operator Δ is defined as $\Delta f(x) = f(x+h) - f(x)$, h being the spacing. Let $y_0, y_1, \ldots, y_n$ denote a set of values of $y = f(x)$, corresponding to $x = x_0, x_1, \ldots, x_n$ respectively. Then, $\Delta y_0 = y_1 - y_0, \Delta y_1 = y_2 - y_1, \Delta y_{n-1} = y_n - y_{n-1}$ are called first order forward differences of the function y. The second order forward differences are obtained from the first order differences as $\Delta^2 y_0 = \Delta y_1 - \Delta y_0 = y_2 - 2y_1 + y_0, \Delta^2 y_1 = \Delta y_2 - \Delta y_1 = y_3 - 2y_2 + y_1$, etc. In this way, the third, and the higher order forward differences can also be defined.

Backward differences

The backward difference of the function $y = f(x)$ is denoted by $\nabla f(x)$ and is defined by $\nabla f(x) = f(x) - f(x-h)$. The first order backward differences are given as $\nabla y_1 = y_1 - y_0, \nabla y_2 = y_2 - y_1, \ldots, \nabla y_n = y_n - y_{n-1}$. Similarly, backward differences of second, third and higher orders can be defined also. That is, $\nabla^2 y_2 = \nabla y_2 - \nabla y_1 = y_2 - 2y_1 + y_0, \nabla^3 y_3 = \nabla^2 y_3 - \nabla^2 y_2 = y_3 - 3y_2 + 3y_1 - y_0$, etc.

According to computation, there is no difference between forward and backward difference table. They have only different symbols. It may be noted that $\Delta^n y_i = \nabla^n y_{i+n}, i = 0, 1, 2, \ldots\ldots$.

The following program generates a forward difference table.

Program 15.3

```
/* Construction of a finite difference table */
#include<stdio.h>
void main()
  {
```

```
    float x[20],y[20][20];
    int n,i,j;
    printf("Enter number of points\n");
    scanf("%d",&n);
    printf("Enter the x-and y-values\n");
    for(i=1;i<=n;i++)
      scanf("%f%f",&x[i],&y[1][i]);
/* Computation of difference table */
    for(i=2;i<=n;i++)
      for(j=1;j<=n-i+1;j++)
        y[i][j] = y[i-1][j+1]-y[i-1][j];
/* Printing of difference table */
    printf("       X        Y        ");
    for(i=1;i<n;i++) printf("%2dDif.         ",i);
    printf("\n");
    for(i=1;i<=n;i++){
        printf("%8.2f ",x[i]);
        for(j=1;j<=n-i+1;j++) printf("%8.2f ",y[j][i]);
        printf("\n");
    }
  }
```

A sample of input/output:

```
Enter number of points
5
Enter the x-and y-values
1 56
3 89
4 76
7 89
9 110

     X        Y       1Dif.    2Dif.     3Dif.    4Dif.
   1.00    56.00    33.00   -46.00    81.00  -126.00
   3.00    89.00   -13.00    35.00    45.00
   4.00    76.00    22.00   -10.00
   7.00    98.00    12.00
   9.00   110.00
```

15.1.4 Newton-Gregory forward difference interpolation

For equally spaced values of the independent variable, $x_i = x_0 + ih, i = 0, 1, \ldots, n$, where h is the spacing, we have, $y_i = f(x_i), i = 1, 2, \ldots, n$.

The Newton-Gregory forward difference interpolation polynomial $\phi(x)$ is of degree not higher than n. It coincides with the values y_i at points x_i, that is, $\phi(x_i) = y_i, i = 0, 1, \ldots, n$. The expression for $\phi(x)$ is computed as

$$\begin{aligned}\phi(x) &= \phi(x_0 + uh) = y_0 + u\Delta y_0 + \frac{u(u-1)}{2!}\Delta^2 y_0 + \frac{u(u-1)(u-2)}{3!}\Delta^3 y_0 + \cdots \\ &+ \frac{u(u-1)\cdots(u-\overline{n-1})}{n!}\Delta^n y_0 = y_0 + \sum_{i=1}^{n}\left(\frac{u-i+1}{i}t_{i-1}\right)\Delta^i y_0\end{aligned}$$

where $u = \dfrac{x - x_0}{h}, x_i = x_0 + ih, i = 1, 2, \ldots, n$, and $t_i = \dfrac{u(u-1)(u-2)\cdots(u-i+1)}{i!}$, $i = 1, 2, \ldots, n$.

The program is listed below.

Program 15.4

```
/* Program for Newton Forward Interpolation. This program finds the
   value of y=f(x) at a given x when the function is supplied as
   (x[i],y[i]), i=0, 1, ..., n. Assumed that x's are equispaced.*/
#include<stdio.h>
#include<math.h>
void main()
{
  int i,j,n;
  float x[20],y[20],xg,sum,prod=1,u,dy[20],h;
  printf("Enter the number of subintervals ");
  scanf("%d",&n);
  printf("Enter x and y values ");
  for(i=0;i<=n;i++) scanf("%f %f",&x[i],&y[i]);
  printf("Enter interpolating point x ");
  scanf("%f",&xg);
  h=x[1]-x[0];
  u=(xg-x[0])/h;
  for(j=0;j<=n;j++) dy[j]=y[j];
  prod=1;  sum=y[0];  /* prod is ti */
  for(i=1;i<=n;i++){
      for(j=0;j<=n-i;j++) dy[j]=dy[j+1]-dy[j];
      prod*=(u-i+1)/i;
      sum+=prod*dy[0];
    }
  printf("The value of y at x=%f is %f ",xg,sum);
}
```

A sample of input/output:

```
Enter the number of subintervals 5
```

```
Enter x and y values
1 20
2 50
4 60
5 80
8 100
9 120
Enter interpolating point x 2.4
The value of y at x=2.400000 is 53.241600
```

Note 15.1.2 This formula is generally used for interpolating a function $y = f(x)$ in the neighbourhood of the initial value x_0. Otherwise, it will give an inaccurate result.

15.1.5 Spline interpolation

Spline interpolation method is found to be very useful for solving numerical differentiation, integration, solution of boundary value problem and many other problems. In spline interpolation, we interpolate a function between a given set of points by means of piecewise smooth polynomials.

A function $S(x)$ is called a piecewise cubic spline in $[x_0, x_n]$, if there exists a set of n cubic polynomials $p_1(x), p_2(x), \ldots, p_n(x)$, such that $S(x) = p_i(x)$ on $[x_{i-1}, x_i], i = 1, 2, \ldots, n$. For a cubic spline, the polynomials $p_i(x)$ have the same gradient and same curvature at the knots where they are joined, i.e. $p_i'(x_i) = p_{i+1}'(x_i)$ (same gradient) and $p_i''(x_i) = p_{i+1}''(x_i)$ (same curvature), $i = 1, 2, \ldots, n-1$. Also, $p_i(x_i) = y_i, p_i(x_{i+1}) = y_{i+1}, i = 0, 1, 2, \ldots, n-1$.

The continuity on derivative and on curvature are not specified at the end points x_0 and x_n.

Let $h_i = x_i - x_{i-1}, i = 1, 2, \ldots, n$, and $S''(x_i) = M_i, i = 0, 1, \ldots, n$. The polynomial $p_i(x)$, in $x_{i-1} \leq x \leq x_i$, is given as

$$p_i(x) = \frac{M_{i-1}}{h_i}\frac{(x_i - x)^3}{6} + \frac{M_i}{h_i}\frac{(x - x_{i-1})^3}{6} + E_{i-1}(x - x_{i-1}) + F_{i-1}(x_i - x),$$

$i = 1, 2, \ldots, n$, where $F_{i-1} = \frac{1}{h_i}(y_{i-1} - \frac{h_i^2}{6}M_{i-1}), E_{i-1} = \frac{1}{h_i}(y_i - \frac{h_i^2}{6}M_i)$, and

$$p_i'(x) = \frac{M_{i-1}}{h_i}\frac{(x_i - x)^2}{2} + \frac{M_i}{h_i}\frac{(x - x_{i-1})^2}{2} + E_{i-1} - F_{i-1},$$

$$p_i''(x) = M_{i-1}\frac{x - x_i}{x_{i-1} - x_i} + M_i\frac{x - x_{i-1}}{x_i - x_{i-1}},$$

$i = 1, 2, \ldots, n.$

Now, in $x_{i-1} \le x \le x_i$,

$$\begin{aligned}
p_i(x) &= \frac{M_{i-1}}{6h_i}(x_i - x)^3 + \frac{M_i}{6h_i}(x - x_{i-1})^3 + E_{i-1}(x - x_{i-1}) + F_{i-1}(x_i - x) \\
&= \frac{M_i - M_{i-1}}{6h_i}x^3 + \frac{x_i M_{i-1} - M_i x_{i-1}}{2h_i}x^2 \\
&+ \left\{E_{i-1} - F_{i-1} + \frac{(M_i x_{i-1}^2 - M_{i-1}x_i^2)}{2h_i}\right\} x \\
&+ \left\{F_{i-1}x_i - E_{i-1}x_{i-1} + \frac{M_{i-1}x_i^3 - M_i x_{i-1}^3}{6h_i}\right\} \\
&= T_{i1}x^3 + T_{i2}x^2 + T_{i3}x + T_{i4}
\end{aligned}$$

where $T_{i1} = \frac{M_i - M_{i-1}}{6h_i}$, $T_{i2} = \frac{x_i M_{i-1} - M_i x_{i-1}}{2h_i}$, $T_{i3} = E_{i-1} - F_{i-1} + \frac{M_i x_{i-1}^2 - M_{i-1}x_i^2}{2h_i}$, $T_{i4} = F_{i-1}x_i - E_{i-1}x_{i-1} + \frac{M_{i-1}x_i^3 - M_i x_{i-1}^3}{6h_i}$, for $i = 1, 2, \ldots, n$.

Note that all these T's are constants.

Here, the constants M's still remains unknown. They are computed from the following tri-diagonal system of equations.

$$h_i M_{i-1} + 2(h_i + h_{i+1})M_i + h_{i+1}M_{i+1} = 6\left\{\frac{y_{i+1} - y_i}{h_{i+1}} - \frac{y_i - y_{i-1}}{h_i}\right\},$$

or, $A_i M_{i-1} + B_i M_i + C_i M_{i+1} = D_i$,

where

$$\begin{aligned}
A_i &= h_i,\ B_i = 2(h_i + h_{i+1}),\ C_i = h_{i+1}, \\
D_i &= 6\left\{\frac{y_{i+1} - y_i}{h_{i+1}} - \frac{y_i - y_{i-1}}{h_i}\right\}, \\
& i = 1, 2, \ldots, n-1.
\end{aligned}$$

This is a system of $n-1$ linear equations with $n+1$ unknowns $M_0, M_1, \ldots, M_n$. Thus, to have a unique solution of the system two additional conditions are necessary. These conditions can be assumed to take one of the following forms:

1. $M_0 = M_n = 0$. If these conditions are satisfied, then the corresponding spline is called **natural spline**.
2. $S'(a) = y_0', S'(b) = y_n'$ or, $2M_0 + M_1 = \frac{6}{h_1}\left(\frac{y_1 - y_0}{h_1} - y_0'\right)$ and $M_{n-1} + 2M_n = \frac{6}{h_n}\left(y_n' - \frac{y_n - y_{n-1}}{h_n}\right)$. The corresponding spline satisfying the above conditions is called **non-periodic spline**.
3. If $M_0 = M_1 - \dfrac{h_1(M_2 - M_1)}{h_2}$ and $M_n = M_{n-1} + \dfrac{h_n(M_{n-1} - M_{n-2})}{h_{n-1}}$. The corresponding spline is called **extrapolated spline**.
4. If $M_0 = y_0''$ and $M_n = y_n''$ are specified. If a spline satisfy these conditions, then it is called **endpoint curvature-adjusted spline**.

The following program generates all cubic splines along with their corresponding intervals and also estimates the value y for a given x.

Program 15.5

```
/* Program for Cubic Spline.
   This program constructs cubic splines at each interval
   [x[i-1],x[i]], i=1, 2, ..., n and finds the value of
   y=f(x) at a given x when the function is supplied as
   (x[i],y[i]), i=0, 1, ..., n. */
#include<stdio.h>
#include<math.h>
#include<ctype.h>
#include<stdlib.h>
float M[21];
void main()
{
 int i,n;
 char opt,s[5];
 float x[20],y[20],h[20],A[20],B[20],C[20],D[20];
 float a[20],b[20],c[20],d[20],xg,yd0,ydn,temp,yc;
 void TriDiag(float a[],float b[],float c[],float d[],int n);
 printf("\nEnter number of subintervals ");
 scanf("%d",&n);
 printf("Enter x and y values ");
 for(i=0;i<=n;i++) scanf("%f %f",&x[i],&y[i]);
 printf("Enter interpolating point x ");
 scanf("%f",&xg);
 printf("The given values of x and y are\nx-value   y-value\n");
 for(i=0;i<=n;i++) printf("%f   %f\n",x[i],y[i]);
 for(i=1;i<=n;i++) h[i]=x[i]-x[i-1]; /* computation of h[i] */
 for(i=1;i<n;i++){ /* computation of A,B,C,D's */
      A[i]=h[i];
      B[i]=2*(h[i]+h[i+1]);
      C[i]=h[i+1];
      D[i]=6*((y[i+1]-y[i])/h[i+1]-(y[i]-y[i-1])/h[i]);
    }
 printf("\nN  Natural spline\n");
 printf("P  Non-Periodic spline\n");
 printf("E  Extrapolated spline\n");
 printf("C  End point Curvature adjusted spline\n");
 printf("   Enter your choice ");
 opt=getche();

 switch(toupper(opt))
   {
    case 'N': /* Natural spline */
```

```
            TriDiag(A,B,C,D,n-1);
            M[0]=0; M[n]=0;
            break;
   case 'P': /* Non-periodic spline */
            printf("\nEnter the values of y'[0] and y'[n] ");
            scanf("%f %f",&yd0,&ydn);
            D[0]=6*((y[1]-y[0])/h[1]-yd0)/h[1];
            D[n]=6*(ydn-(y[n]-y[n-1])/h[n])/h[n];
            for(i=n+1;i>=1;i--) D[i]=D[i-1];
            A[n+1]=1; B[n+1]=2;
            for(i=n;i>=2;i--){
               A[i]=A[i-1]; B[i]=B[i-1]; C[i]=C[i-1];}
            B[1]=2; C[1]=1;
            TriDiag(A,B,C,D,n+1);
            for(i=0;i<=n;i++) M[i]=M[i+1];
            break;
   case 'E': /* Extrapolated spline */
           B[1]=A[1]+B[1]+A[1]*h[1]/h[2];
           C[1]=C[1]-A[1]*h[1]/h[2];
           A[n-1]=A[n-1]-C[n-1]*h[n]/h[n-1];
           B[n-1]=B[n-1]+C[n-1]+C[n-1]*h[n]/h[n-1];
           TriDiag(A,B,C,D,n-1);
           M[0]=M[1]-h[1]*(M[2]-M[1])/h[2];
           M[n]=M[n-1]+h[n]*(M[n-1]-M[n-2])/h[n-1];
           break;
   case 'C': /* End point Curvature adjusted spline */
           printf("\nEnter the values of y''[0] and y''[n] ");
           scanf("%f %f",&yd0,&ydn);
           D[1]=D[1]-A[1]*yd0;
           D[n-1]=D[n-1]-C[n-1]*ydn;
           TriDiag(A,B,C,D,n-1);
           M[0]=yd0; M[n]=ydn;
           break;
  default : printf("\n No choice \n");
          exit(0);
} /* switch */
/* Computation of the coefficients of the splines */
for(i=0;i<=n-1;i++){
     a[i]=(M[i+1]-M[i])/(6*h[i+1]);
     b[i]=M[i]/2;
     c[i]=(y[i+1]-y[i])/h[i+1]-(2*h[i+1]*M[i]+h[i+1]*M[i+1])/6;
     d[i]=y[i];
```

```
    }
  /* printing of splines */
  printf("\nThe cubic splines are \n");
  for(i=0;i<n;i++){
    temp=x[i];
     printf("p%1d(x)=%7.4f(x%+7.4f)^3%+7.4f(x%+7.4f)^2%+7.4f
          (x%+7.4f)%+7.4f\n",i,a[i],-temp,b[i],
          -temp,c[i],-temp,d[i]);
     printf("      in [%7.4f,%7.4f]\n",x[i],x[i+1]);
   }
  /* computation of y at x=xg */
  if((xg<x[0]) || (xg>x[n])){
       printf("\nx outside the range ");
       exit(0);
     }
  for(i=0;i<=n-1;i++) /* determination of y */
     {
       if(xg<x[i+1]){
           temp=xg-x[i];
           yc=a[i]*temp*temp*temp+b[i]*temp*temp+c[i]*temp+d[i];
           printf("The value of y at x=%f is %f ",xg,yc);
           exit(0);
        }
     }
 } /* main */

void TriDiag(float a[20],float b[20],float c[20],float d[20],int n)
  {
  /* output M[i], i=1, 2,..., n, is a global array.*/
  int i;
  float gamma[10],z[10];
  gamma[1]=b[1];
  for(i=2;i<=n;i++){
      if(gamma[i-1]==0.0){
          printf("A minor is zero: Method fails ");
          exit(0);
        }
      gamma[i]=b[i]-a[i]*c[i-1]/gamma[i-1];
     }
  z[1]=d[1]/gamma[1];
  for(i=2;i<=n;i++)
      z[i]=(d[i]-a[i]*z[i-1])/gamma[i];
  /* Computation of M */
```

```
 M[n]=z[n];
 for(i=n-1;i>=1;i--)
     M[i]=z[i]-c[i]*M[i+1]/gamma[i];
} /*end of TriDiag */
```

A sample of input/output:

```
Enter number of subintervals 3
Enter x and y values
-1 1.0
1 0.5
2 3.5
3 5.0
Enter interpolating point x 1.2

The given values of x and y are
 x-value     y-value
 -1.000000    1.000000
 1.000000   0.500000
 2.000000   3.500000
 3.000000   5.000000

 N  Natural spline
 P  Non-Periodic spline
 E  Extrapolated spline
 C  End point Curvature adjusted spline
    Enter your choice n

 The cubic splines are
 p0(x)= 0.3152(x+ 1.0000)^3+ 0.0000(x+ 1.0000)^2- 1.5109(x+ 1.0000)
        + 1.0000 in [-1.0000, 1.0000]
 p1(x)=-1.1630(x- 1.0000)^3+ 1.8913(x- 1.0000)^2+ 2.2717(x- 1.0000)
        + 0.5000 in [ 1.0000, 2.0000]
 p2(x)= 0.5326(x- 2.0000)^3- 1.5978(x- 2.0000)^2+ 2.5652(x- 2.0000)
        + 3.5000 in [ 2.0000, 3.0000]
 The value of y at x=1.200000 is 1.020696
```

Another input/output:

```
Enter number of subintervals 3
Enter x and y values
-1 1.0
1 0.5
2 3.5
3 5.0
Enter interpolating point x 1.2
```

```
The given values of x and y are
x-value    y-value
-1.000000   1.000000
1.000000   0.500000
2.000000   3.500000
3.000000   5.000000

N  Natural spline
P  Non-Periodic spline
E  Extrapolated spline
C  End point Curvature adjusted spline
   Enter your choice p
Enter the values of y'[0] and y'[n] 0 1
The cubic splines are
p0(x)= 0.6250(x+ 1.0000)^3- 1.3750(x+ 1.0000)^2+ 0.0000(x+ 1.0000)
      + 1.0000 in [-1.0000, 1.0000]
p1(x)=-1.3750(x- 1.0000)^3+ 2.3750(x- 1.0000)^2+ 2.0000(x- 1.0000)
      + 0.5000 in [ 1.0000, 2.0000]
p2(x)= 0.6250(x- 2.0000)^3- 1.7500(x- 2.0000)^2+ 2.6250(x- 2.0000)
      + 3.5000 in [ 2.0000, 3.0000]
The value of y at x=1.200000 is 0.984000
```

15.2 Integration

The problem of numerical integration is to evaluate

$$I = \int_a^b f(x)\,dx.$$

There are three types of formulae for numerical integration or quadrature: (i) Newton-Cotes quadrature, (ii) Gaussian quadrature, and (iii) Monte-Carlo quadrature.

In this section, the following methods for integration are discussed.
For single variable function:

- Newton-Cotes quadrature
  - Trapezoidal rule
  - Simpson's 1/3 rule
- Gaussian quadrature
  - Gauss-Legendre rule
- Monte-Carlo quadrature

For two variables function

  - Simpson's 1/3 rule

Newton-Cotes Quadrature

15.2.1 Trapezoidal rule

The trapezoidal formula to evaluate the integration of $f(x)$ in the interval $[x_0, x_1]$ is

$$\int_{x_0}^{x_1} f(x)dx = \frac{h}{2}[y_0 + y_1]$$

where $y_0 = f(x_0)$, $y_1 = f(x_1)$ and $h = x_1 - x_0$ (length of the interval). The composite form of this formula is

$$\begin{aligned}\int_a^b f(x)\,dx &= \frac{h}{2}[y_0 + 2(y_1 + y_2 + \cdots + y_{n-1}) + y_n] \\ &= \frac{h}{2}[f(a) + 2\sum_{i=1}^{n-1} f(a+ih) + f(b)]\end{aligned}$$

where $h = \dfrac{b-a}{n}$ (length of the subintervals), $y_i = f(x_i)$, $x_0 = a, x_n = b, i = 0, 1, \ldots n$, n being the number of sub-intervals.

Applicability: Both a and b are finite, $f(x)$ is finite for all $x_i, i = 0, 1, \ldots, n$ (n being an integer).

Correctness: Error $= -\dfrac{h^3}{12} f''(\xi), a < \xi < b$. That is, if $f(x)$ is a polynomial of degree one, then this method gives the exact result. The degrees of freedom of this method is one. The error term indicates that if the value of h is sufficiently small (i.e. the value of n is large), then this rule gives more accurate result.

Algorithm to evaluate $\int_a^b f(x)\,dx$ by trapezoidal rule is presented below.

Step 1: Read a (lower limit), b (upper limit) and n (the number of subintervals).
Step 2: Compute $h = \dfrac{b-a}{n}$.
Step 3: For $i = 0$ to n do compute $y_i = f(a + ih)$.
Step 4: Set $sum = 0$.
Step 5: For $i = 1$ to $n - 1$ do
$sum = sum + y_i$.
Step 6: $result = \dfrac{h}{2}[y_0 + 2 \times sum + y_n]$.
Step 7: Print *result*.
Step 8: End.

The following program determines the values of two integrals by trapezoidal rule.

Example 15.2.1 (Evaluation of two integrals) Write a program to evaluate the integrals
$\int_{.5}^1 x^2\,dx$ and $\int_0^1 \dfrac{1}{1+x^2}\,dx$ using trapezoidal rule.

Program 15.6

```
/* Program to find the integration by trapezoidal rule.
   Taken 100 subintervals for two functions. Using the concept of
   external function. */
#include<stdio.h>
void main()
 {
   float Trap(), f1(), f2(),result;
   result=Trap(0.5,1.0,100,f1);
   printf("Value of first integral is %.5f\n",result);
   result=Trap(0.0,1.0,100,f2);
   printf("Value of second integral is %.5f\n",result);
 }
/* definition of function Trap */
float Trap(a,b,n,funct)
float (*funct)(); /* formal argument declaration
                     as a pointer to a function */
float a, b; int n;
  {
    float y[100],h,result,sum=0;
    int i;
    h=(b-a)/n;
    for(i=0;i<=n;i++)
      y[i]=(*funct)(a+i*h); /* the passing function is
                                  executed with argument a+ih */
    for(i=1;i<=n-1;i++)
      sum+=y[i];
    result=(y[0]+2.0*sum+y[n])*h/2.0;
    return(result);
  }
/* definition of the function f1 */
float f1(x)
float x;
  {
    return(x*x);
  }
/* definition of the function f2 */
float f2(x)
float x;
  {
    return(1.0/(1+x*x));
  }
```

The output of the above program is

```
Value of first integral is 0.29167
Value of second integral is 0.78539
```

15.2.2 Simpson's 1/3 rule

The Simpson's 1/3 formula to evaluate the integration of $f(x)$ in the interval $[x_0, x_2]$ is

$$\int_{x_0}^{x_2} f(x)dx = \frac{h}{3}[y_0 + 4y_1 + y_2]$$

where $y_0 = f(x_0)$, $y_1 = f(x_1)$, $y_2 = f(x_2)$ and $h = (x_2 - x_0)/2$ (length of the intervals).

The composite formula of this rule is

$$\begin{aligned}\int_a^b f(x)\,dx &= \frac{h}{3}[y_0 + 4(y_1 + y_3 + \cdots + y_{n-1}) + 2(y_2 + y_4 + \cdots + y_{n-2}) + y_n] \\ &= \frac{h}{3}[y_0 + 2\{(2y_1 + y_2) + (2y_3 + y_4) + \cdots + (2y_{n-1} + y_n)\} - y_n].\end{aligned}$$

where $x_0 = a, x_n = b, h = \dfrac{b-a}{n}, y_i = f(x_i), x_i = x_0 + ih, i = 0, 1, \ldots, n$, n being the number of sub-intervals.

Applicability: This method is applicable when a and b are both finite, $f(x)$ is finite for all $x_i, i = 0, 1, \ldots, n$, and n being an even integer.

Correctness: Error $= -\dfrac{h^5}{90} f^{iv}(\xi), a < \xi < b$. This shows that if $f(x)$ is a polynomial of degree three or less, then this method gives the exact value of the integration. So, the degrees of freedom of this method is three. Also the error term shows that when h is small, then the result is more accurate.

Simpson's 1/3 rule gives more accurate result than the trapezoidal rule.

Algorithm to evaluate $\int_a^b f(x)\,dx$ by Simpson's 1/3 rule is presented below.

Step 1: Read a (lower limit), b (upper limit) and n (the number of subintervals).
Step 2: Compute $h = \frac{b-a}{n}$.
Step 3: Set $sum = 0$.
Step 4: For $i = 0$ to n do
$y[i] = f(a + i * h)$.
Step 5: For $i = 1$ to $n - 1$ step 2 do
$sum = sum + 2y[i] + y[i+1]$.
Step 6: $result = \frac{h}{3}[y[0] + 2 \times sum - y[n]]$.
Step 7: Print $result$.
Step 8: End.

The following program computes the value of

$$\int_a^b \frac{e^x}{1+x^2}\,dx$$

for different values of a, b and n.

Program 15.7

```
/* Integration by Simpson's 1/3 rule, a,b,n are lower,
   upper limits and number of intervals, n should be an
   even integer. */
#include<stdio.h>
#include<math.h>
#define  f(x) exp((x))/(1.+(x)*(x))
void main()
  {
    float y[200],a,b,h,sum=0,result;
    int n,i;
    printf("Enter lower, upper limits and no. of subintervals\n");
    scanf("%f%f%d",&a,&b,&n);
    if(n%2 !=0){
         printf("No. of intervals is not even\n");
         exit(0);
      }
    h=(b-a)/n;
    for(i=0;i<=n;i++)
      y[i]=f(a+i*h);
    for(i=1;i<=n-1;i+=2)
       sum+=2*y[i]+y[i+1];
    result=h/3*(2*sum+y[0]-y[n]);
    printf("a=%.3f b=%.3f n=%3d\n",a,b,n);
    printf("Value of integration = %.5f\n",result);
  }
```

A sample of input/output:

```
0.00  1.00  100
a=0.000 b=1.000 n=100
Value of integration = 1.27072
```

Gauss-Quadrature

In Gaussian quadrature, the problem of integration is considered as

$$\int_{-1}^{1} \lambda(x) f(x)\,dx = \sum_{i=1}^{n} f(x_i)\omega_i$$

where $f(x)$ is the given integrand, $\lambda(x)$ is the weight function, ω_i is the weight at the abscissa x_i, to be chosen properly to hold the above equation.

For different choices of $\lambda(x)$, different quadrature formulae can be generated. Here we choose $\lambda(x) = 1$ (the Legendre's weight function). The corresponding quadrature formula is known as Gauss-Legendre rule.

15.2.3 Gaussian-Legendre rule

This method is also known as Gauss quadrature. When $\lambda(x) = 1$ then

$$\int_{-1}^{1} f(x)\,dx = \sum_{i=1}^{n} f(x_i)\omega_i$$

where the weight ω_i and the abscissa x_i are listed below for the different values of n.

n	Abscissa (x_i)	Weights (ω_i)
2	±0.5773502692	1.0000000000
3	0.00000000000	0.8888888889
	±0.7745966692	0.5555555556
4	±0.3399810436	0.6521451549
	±0.8611363116	0.3478548451
5	0.00000000000	0.5688888889
	±0.5384693101	0.4786286705
	±0.9061798459	0.2369268851
6	±0.2386191861	0.4679139346
	±0.6612093865	0.3607615730
	±0.9324695142	0.1713244924

Any finite interval $[a, b]$ can be transferred to the interval $[-1, 1]$ using the following transformation

$$x = \frac{b-a}{2}t + \frac{b+a}{2} = qt + p. \tag{15.1}$$

Then,

$$\int_{a}^{b} f(x)\,dx = \int_{-1}^{1} f(qt+p)\,q\,dt. \tag{15.2}$$

For $n = 2$ the quadrature is called two points, for $n = 4$ the quadrature is called four points, and so on.

The following algorithm finds the value of $\int_a^b f(x)\,dx$ using 6-point Gauss-Legendre's quadrature method.

Algorithm Gauss_Legendre
Input function $f(x)$;

Read a, b. //the lower and upper limits of the integral.//
Assign
$x_1 = 0.23861919$, $x_2 = -x_1$, $w_1 = w_2 = 0.46791393$,
$x_3 = 0.66120939$, $x_4 = -x_3$, $w_3 = w_4 = 0.36076157$,
$x_5 = 0.93246951$, $x_6 = -x_5$, $w_5 = w_6 = 0.17132449$,
Set $p = (a + b)/2, q = (b - a)/2$ //limits changed to –1, 1//
Initialize $Result = 0$;
for $i = 1$ to 6 do
    Compute $result = result + w_i * f(p + qx_i)$;
endfor;
Compute $result = result * q$;
Print *result*;
end Gauss_Legendre

Program 15.8

```
/* Program of 6-point Gauss-Legendre quadrature.
   Program to find the integration of a function by 6-point
   Gauss-Legendre method. Here f(x)=x^3+x+e^x. */
#include<stdio.h>
void main()
{
 float a,b,p,q,result=0,x[7],w[7]; int i;
 float f(float);
 printf("Enter the values of a, b ");
 scanf("%f %f",&a,&b);
 x[1]=0.23861919; x[2]=-x[1];
 x[3]=0.66120939; x[4]=-x[3];
 x[5]=0.93246951; x[6]=-x[5];
 w[1]=w[2]=0.46791393;
 w[3]=w[4]=0.36076157;
 w[5]=w[6]=0.17132449;
 p=(a+b)/2; q=(b-a)/2;
 for(i=1;i<=6;i++)
    result+=w[i]*f(p+q*x[i]);
 result*=q;
 printf("The value of the integration is %f ",result);
}

/* definition of the function f(x) */
float f(float x)
 {
   return(x*x*x+x+exp(x));
 }
```

A sample of input/output:

```
Enter the values of a, b 0 1
The value of the integration is 2.468282
```

Applicability: The above formula is applicable to any finite interval $[a,b]$. Even if a or b or both are infinite, then also, this formula is applicable. In this case, the interval $[a,b]$ is broken up at a non-zero finite point c, and replaces the variable x by $\frac{1}{x}$.

$$\text{e.g.} \int_0^\infty f(x)\,dx = \int_0^1 f(x)\,dx + \int_1^\infty f(x)\,dx$$
$$= \int_0^1 f(x)\,dx + \int_0^1 \frac{1}{x^2} f\Big(\frac{1}{x}\Big)\,dx = \int_0^1 \Big\{f(x) + \frac{1}{x^2} f\Big(\frac{1}{x}\Big)\Big\}\,dx.$$

It may be noted that the values of $f(a)$ and $f(b)$ are not included in the formula. So, if $f(x)$ is not finite at a and b, then also the formula is useful.

15.2.4 Double integration

Several formulae are available to calculate double integration of the form

$$\int_c^d \int_a^b f(x,y)\,dx\,dy.$$

Simpson's 1/3 rule is one of them.

For the rectangular region $[x_i, x_{i+2}; y_j, y_{j+2}]$ the integral is

$$\begin{aligned}
&\int_{y_j}^{y_{j+2}} \int_{x_i}^{x_{i+2}} f(x,y)\,dx\,dy \\
= \;& \frac{h_y}{3}\Big[\frac{h_x}{3}(f_{i+2,j+2} + 4f_{i+1,j+2} + f_{i,j+2}) + \frac{4h_x}{3}(f_{i+2,j+1} + 4f_{i+1,j+1} + f_{i,j+1}) \\
+ \;& \frac{h_x}{3}(f_{i+2,j} + 4f_{i+1,j} + f_{i,j})\Big] \\
= \;& \frac{h_x h_y}{9}\Big[(f_{i+2,j+2} + f_{i+2,j} + f_{i,j+2} + f_{i,j}) \\
+ \;& 4(f_{i+1,j+2} + f_{i+1,j} + f_{i+2,j+1} + f_{i,j+1}) + 16 f_{i+1,j+1}\Big]
\end{aligned}$$

where, $h_x = x_{i+1} - x_i$ and $h_y = y_{j+1} - y_j$, $i = 0, 1, 2 \ldots, n_x$; $j = 0, 1, 2, \ldots, n_y$; $x_0 = a, x_{n_x} = b; y_0 = c, y_{n_y} = d, n_x$ and n_y are the number of subintervals of the intervals of $[a,b]$ and $[c,d]$ respectively.

$$\begin{aligned}
\int_c^d \int_a^b f(x,y)\,dx\,dy \;=\; & \frac{h_x h_y}{9} \sum_{\substack{j=0 \\ \text{step } 2}}^{n_y} \sum_{\substack{i=0 \\ \text{step } 2}}^{n_x} \Big[(f_{i+2,j+2} + f_{i+2,j} + f_{i,j+2} + f_{i,j}) \\
& + 4(f_{i+1,j+2} + f_{i+1,j} + f_{i+2,j+1} + f_{i,j+1}) + 16 f_{i+1,j+1}\Big].
\end{aligned}$$

Program 15.9

```
/* Program to calculate double integration by Simpson's 1/3 rule,
   for 5 different subintervals. The function f(x,y) may be changed
   accordingly. ax,bx are the lower and upper limits of x and nx is
   the starting number of subintervals. Similarly ay,by,ny are that
   of y. */
#include<stdio.h>
#include<math.h>
#define f(x,y) exp((x)+(y))
void main()
  {
    float ax,ay,bx,by,sum,result,x,y,hx,hy;
    int nx,ny,i,j,k;
    printf("Enter lower \& upper limits of x \& no. of subintervals\n");
    scanf("%f%f%d",&ax,&bx,&nx);
    printf("Enter lower \& upper limits of y \& no. of subintervals\n");
    scanf("%f%f%d",&ay,&by,&ny);
    printf("ax=%.3f bx=%.3f ay=%.3f by=%.3f\n",ax,bx,ay,by);
    printf("  nx   ny      hx       hy        Result\n");
    for(k=1;k<=5;k++){
        nx=2*nx;
        ny=2*ny;
        hx=(bx-ax)/(2*nx);
        hy=(by-ay)/(2*ny);
        sum=0.;
        x=ax;
        for(i=1;i<=nx;i++){
            y=ay;
            for(j=1;j<=ny;j++){
                sum=sum+f(x,y)+f(x+2*hx,y)+f(x,y+2*hy)+f(x+2*hx,y+2*hy)
                   +4*(f(x,y+hy)+f(x+hx,y+2*hy)+f(x+hx,y)+f(x+2*hx,y+hy))
                   +16.*f(x+hx,y+hy);
                y=y+2*hy;
              }
            x=x+2*hx;
          }
        result=hx*hy/9.*sum;
        printf(" %3d  %3d  %8.5f %8.5f %11.7f\n",nx,ny,hx,hy,result);
    }
  }
```

A sample of input/output:

```
Enter lower & upper limits of X & no.  of subintervals
```

```
0 1 1
Enter lower & upper limits of Y & no.  of subintervals
0 1.5 2

 ax= 0.000 bx= 1.000 ay= 0.000 by= 1.500
  nx  ny       hx       hy          Result
   2   4    0.25000  0.18750      5.9826927
   4   8    0.12500  0.09375      5.9825330
   8  16    0.06250  0.04688      5.9825234
  16  32    0.03125  0.02344      5.9825253
  32  64    0.01563  0.01172      5.9825196
```

Applicability: The formula is applicable for any finite rectangular region. The values of n_x, n_y must be even.

15.3 Integration by Monte-Carlo Method

The Monte-Carlo method is used to solve a large number of problems. This method is invented by Stanislaw Ulam, a Polish mathematician in the year 1946.

This method depends on a random sample and it is not suitable for hand calculation, because it depends on a large number of random numbers. The algorithm of Monte-Carlo method is prepared to perform only one random trial. The trial is repeated for N times and the trials are independent. The final result is the average of all the results obtained in different trials.

Now, the Monte-Carlo method is introduced to find numerical integration of a single valued function. Suppose the definite integral be

$$I = \int_a^b g(x)\, dx, \tag{15.3}$$

where $g(x)$ is a real valued function defined on $[a, b]$. The idea is to manipulate the definite integral into a form that can be solved by Monte-Carlo method. To do this, we consider the uniform probability density function (pdf), which is defined on $[a, b]$ in the following.

$$f(x) = \begin{cases} \frac{1}{b-a}, & a < x < b \\ 0, & \text{otherwise.} \end{cases}$$

This function is inserted to the equation (15.3) to obtain the following expression for I.

$$I = (b-a) \int_a^b g(x) f(x)\, dx. \tag{15.4}$$

It is observed that the integral on the right hand side of the equation (15.4) is simply the expectation of $g(x)$ under uniform pdf. Thus,

$$I = (b-a) \int_a^b g(x) f(x)\, dx = (b-a)\overline{g}. \tag{15.5}$$

Now, a sample x_i is drawn from the pdf $f(x)$, and for each x_i the value of $g(x_i)$ is calculated. To get a good approximation, a large number of sample is considered and let G be the average of all the values of $g(x_i), i = 1, 2, \ldots, N$ (the sample size). Then

$$G = \frac{1}{N} \sum_{i=1}^{N} g(x_i). \tag{15.6}$$

It is easy to prove that the expectation of the average of N samples is the expectation of $g(x)$, i.e. $\overline{G} = \overline{g}$. Hence

$$I = (b - a)\overline{G} \simeq (b - a)\left(\frac{1}{N} \sum_{i=1}^{N} g(x_i)\right). \tag{15.7}$$

Figure 15.1 illustrates the Monte-Carlo method.

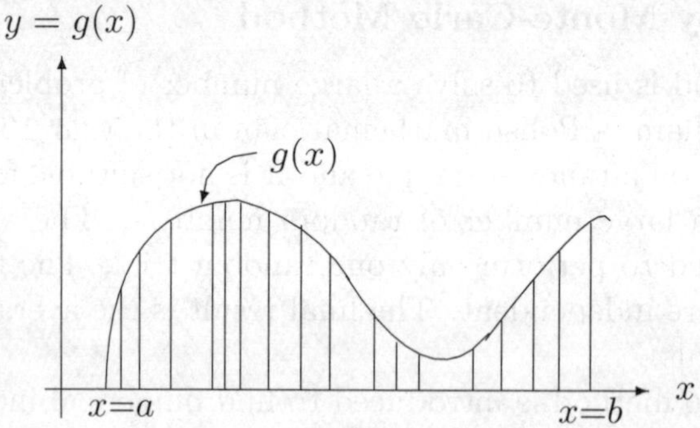

Figure 15.1: Random points are chosen in $[a, b]$. The value of $g(x)$ is evaluated at each random point (marked by straight lines in the figure).

Thus, the approximate value of the integral I on $[a, b]$ can be evaluated by taking the average of N observations of the integrand with the random variable x sampled uniformly over the interval $[a, b]$. This implies that the interval $[a, b]$ is finite, since an infinite interval cannot have a uniform pdf. The infinite limits of integration can be accommodated with more sophisticated techniques.

The following algorithm finds the value of the integral $\int_a^b f(x)\, dx$ using Monte-Carlo method based on a sample of size N.

Algorithm Monte_Carlo

Input function $g(x)$;

Step 1: Read sample size N and the lower and upper limits a, b, of the integral.

Step 2: For $i = 1$ to N do steps 2.1–2.3

Step 2.1: Generate a random number y_i between 0 and 1.

Step 2.2: Let $x_i = a + (b - a)y_i$. /* $a \le x_i \le b$. */

Step 2.3: Calculate $g(x_i)$ and compute $sum = sum + g(x_i)$.

/* Initially $sum = 0$ */

Step 3: Calculate $I = (sum/N) * (b - a)$.

Step 4: Print I.
end Monte_Carlo.

```
/* Program for Monte-Carlo method.
   Program to find the value of the integration of 1/(1+x^2)
   between 0 and 1 by Monte-Carlo method for different values of N. */
#include<stdio.h>
#include<stdlib.h>
void main()
{
 float g(float x);
 float x,y,I,sum=0.0,a=0.0,b=1.0;
 int i, N;
 srand(100); /* seed for random number */
 printf("Enter the sample size ");
 scanf("%d",&N);
 for(i=0;i<N;i++)
    {   /* rand() generates a random number between 0 and RAND_MAX */
      y=(float)rand()/RAND_MAX;
           /* generates a random number between 0 and 1*/
      x=a+(b-a)*y; /* x lies between a and b */
      sum+=g(x);
    }
I=sum*(b-a)/N;
printf("%f",I);
}
/* definition of function */
float g(float x) /* g(x) may be changed accordingly */
{
  return(1/(1+x*x));
}
```

The results obtained for different values of N are tabulated in the following.

N	Integration
500	0.790020
1000	0.789627
1500	0.786979
3000	0.786553
4000	0.784793
10000	0.784094
15000	0.782420

15.4 Solution of Algebraic and Transcendental Equations

In this section different methods are discussed to compute the roots of an equation of the form $f(x) = 0$. This equation may be algebraic or transcendental.

In order to use any of the numerical methods for finding real roots of an equation, it is necessary to find crude approximations or locations of the real roots of the equation.

A useful result, called the *intermediate value theorem*, stated below, is used to find the location of a real root.

Theorem: If $f(x)$ is continuous in the interval (a, b) and if $f(a)$ and $f(b)$ are of opposite in signs, then there exists at least one real root between a and b of the equation $f(x) = 0$.

The function $f(x)$ is tabulated for certain range of values of x in which a change in sign of the function is expected. The interval in which a change of sign occur contains a real root of $f(x) = 0$. In this section, the following methods are discussed to find a root of a transcendental equation.

- Bisection method
- Regula–Falsi method
- Iteration method
- Newton–Raphson method
- Bairstow method for polynomial equation
- Newton–Raphson method for two variables.

15.4.1 Bisection method

Let ξ be a root of the equation $f(x) = 0$ which lies in the interval $[a, b]$, i.e. $f(a).f(b) < 0$, and $(b-a)$ is not sufficiently small. The interval $[a, b]$ is divided into two equal intervals $[a, c]$ and $[c, b]$, each of length $\dfrac{b-a}{2}$, and $c = \dfrac{a+b}{2}$. If $f(c) = 0$, then c is an exact root.

If $f(c) \neq 0$, then the root lies either in the interval $[a, c]$ or in the interval $[c, b]$. If $f(a).f(c) < 0$, then the interval $[a, c]$ is taken as new interval, otherwise $[c, b]$ is taken as the next interval. Let the new interval be $[a_1, b_1]$ and use the same process to select the next new interval. In the next step, let the new interval be $[a_2, b_2]$. The process of bisection is continued until either the midpoint of the interval is a root, or the length $(b_n - a_n)$ of the interval $[a_n, b_n]$ (at nth step) is sufficiently small. The number a_n and b_n are the approximate roots of the equation $f(x) = 0$. Finally, $x_n = \dfrac{a_n + b_n}{2}$ is taken as the approximate value of the root ξ.

An algorithm of bisection method is presented below.

The following algorithm finds a real root of the equation $f(x) = 0$ which lies in $[a, b]$.

Algorithm Bisection
Input function $f(x)$;
/* Assume that $f(x)$ is continuous within $[a, b]$ and a root lies on $[a, b]$. */
Read ε; /* Tolerance for width of the interval */
Read a, b; /* Input of the interval */

Compute $fa = f(a)$; $fb = f(b)$; /* Compute the function values */
if $sign(fa) = sign(fb)$ then
/* $sign(fa)$ gives the sign of the value of fa. */
    Print '$f(a) \cdot f(b) > 0$, so there is no guarantee for a root within $[a, b]$';
    Stop;
endif;
do
    Compute $c = (a + b)/2$;
    Compute $fc = f(c)$;
    if $fc = 0$ or $|fc| < \varepsilon$ then
        $a = c$ and $b = c$;
    else if $sign(fb) = sign(fc)$ then
        $b = c$; $fb = fc$;
    else
        $a = c$; $fa = fc$;
    endif;
while ($|b - a| > \varepsilon$);
Print 'the desired root is' c;
end Bisection

The following program computes a real root of the equation $x^2 - \sin x - 9 = 0$ using bisection method.

Program 15.10

```
/* Program of Bisection method. Program to find a root of the equation
   x^2-sin x-9=0 by bisection method.
   Assume that a root lies between a and b. */
#include<stdio.h>
#include<math.h>
#include<stdlib.h>
#define f(x) (x)*(x)-sin(x)-9.0 /* definition of the function f(x) */
void main()
{
 float a,b,fa,fb,c,fc;
 float eps=1e-5; /* error tolerance */
 printf("\nEnter the value of a and b ");
 scanf("%f%f",&a,&b);
 fa=f(a);  fb=f(b);
 if(fa*fb>0){
     printf("There is no guarantee for a root within [a,b]");
     exit(0);
   }
 do{
```

```
    c=(a+b)/2.;
    fc=f(c);
    if((fc==0) || (fabs(fc)<eps)){
        a=c;b=c;
        }
    else if(fb*fc>0){
        b=c; fb=fc;
        }
    else{
        a=c; fa=fc;
        }
  }while(fabs(b-a)>eps);
  printf("\nThe desired root is %8.5f ",c);
} /* main */
```

A sample of input/output:

```
Enter the value of a and b 3 4
The desired root is 3.02013
```

Merits and Demerits: If the function is continuous, then, the method is applicable and the approximate root surely converges to the desired root. In this method no preprocessing is required, but the method is slow.

Note 15.4.1 If there is any problem in finding the initial interval for the root, then an obvious interval (−MAXFLOAT, MAXFLOAT), i.e. $(-3.37 \times 10^{38}, 3.37 \times 10^{38})$, equivalent to $(-\infty, \infty)$, may be taken as the initial interval.

15.4.2 Regula-Falsi method

This method is almost similar to the bisection method. The difference is that the new point c in (a, b) ((a, b) is the location of a root) is calculated by the following formula

$$c = a - \frac{f(a)}{f(b) - f(a)}(b - a) = \frac{af(b) - bf(a)}{f(b) - f(a)}.$$

The new point c is the intersection of the line joining the points (a, b) and $(f(a), f(b))$ and the c–axis.

Now, if $f(c) = 0$, then c is a root and if $f(a).f(c) < 0$, then the new interval is (a, c), otherwise, the new interval is (c, b). The process is repeated until a root is obtained with the required degree of accuracy.

Algorithm of Regula-Falsi method
Step 1: Read the initial interval (a, b) and error tolerance EPS.
Step 2: Set $fa = f(a)$ and $fb = f(b)$.
Step 3: If $fa.fb > 0$, then

Print, 'root does not lie within (a, b)'
stop.
endif.

Step 4: Compute $c = \dfrac{a \times fb - b \times fa}{fb - fa}$ and $fc = f(c)$.

Step 5: If $|fc|$ <EPS, then Print c as a root and Stop endif.

Step 6: If $fa.fc < 0$, then $b = c, fb = fc$ else $a = c, fa = fc$ endif.

Step 7: Goto Step 4.

Step 8: Stop.

The following program computes a real root of the equation $x^3 - 2x - 3 = 0$ using regula falsi method.

Program 15.11

```
/* Program of Regula-Falsi method.
   Program to find a root of the equation x*x*x-2x-3=0 by regula
   falsi method. Assumed that a root lies between x0 and x1. */
#include<stdio.h>
#include<math.h>
#include<stdlib.h>
#define f(x) (x)*(x)*(x)-2*(x)-3 /* definition of the function f(x) */
void main()
{
 float x0,x1,x2,fx0,fx1,fx2; /* here a,b,c are
                                represented by x0,x1 and x2 */
 float eps=1e-5; /* error tolerance */
 printf("\nEnter the value of x0 and x1 ");
 scanf("%f %f",&x0,&x1);
 fx0=f(x0);  fx1=f(x1);
 if(fx0*fx1>0){
   printf("There is no guarantee for a root within
           [%6.3f,%6.3f]",x0,x1);
   exit(0);
  }
 do{
    x2=(x0*fx1-x1*fx0)/(fx1-fx0);
    fx2=f(x2);
    if(fabs(fx2)<eps){
        printf("The root is %8.5f ",x2);
        exit(0);
      }
    if(fx2*fx0<0){
        x1=x2; fx1=fx2;
      }
```

```
        else{
            x0=x2; fx0=fx2;
        }
    }while(fabs(fx2)>eps);
  } /* main */
```

A sample of input/output:

```
Enter the value of x0 and x1 0 3
The root is 1.89329
```

Merits and Demerits: In this method, the evaluation of derivatives is not required. It is very simple to solve difficult problems and the sequence of roots is sure to converge. But the method is very slow for certain types of problems. If the root lies near any one of the extreme points a or b, then this method is faster as compared to bisection method.

15.4.3 Iteration method

In this method, we rewrite the equation $f(x) = 0$ in the form $x = \phi(x)$. Then, a sequence $\{x_n\}$ of approximate roots are obtained which converges to an exact root. The function $\phi(x)$ is known as the iteration function and this iteration is called **Picard iteration**. The convergence of $\{x_n\}$ depends on the suitable choice of $\phi(x)$. There are many ways to choose $\phi(x)$. We choose $\phi(x)$ in a such way that $|\phi'(x)| < 1$, for every $a < x < b$, (an exact root lies in the interval (a, b) is taken as assumption). This is the sufficient condition for the convergence of $\{x_n\}$. $x = x_0$ is considered as an initial approximation to the desired root. The first approximate root, $x_1 = \phi(x_0)$, can thus be obtained by substituting $x = x_0$ in $\phi(x)$. Similarly, the second approximate root, $x_2 = \phi(x_1)$, will be obtained by substituting x_1 for x in $\phi(x)$, and so on.

The successive approximations are given by

$$x_{n+1} = \phi(x_n), n = 0, 1, 2, \ldots$$

The process will terminate when $|x_{n+1} - x_n| < \varepsilon$, ε is the desired accuracy. Then the desired root is x_{n+1}.

Algorithm for iteration method

Step 1: Read x as approximate root and error tolerance EPS.
Step 2: Compute $x_{new} = \phi(x)$, $\phi(x)$ is obtained by rewriting $f(x) = 0$.
Step 3: If $|x_{new} - x|$ <EPS, then goto Step 4 else
set $x = x_{new}$; goto Step 2;
endif;
Step 4: Print x_{new} as a root.
Step 5: Stop.

The following program computes a real root of the equation $x^3 - 3x + 1 = 0$ by iteration method. The equation can be rewritten as $x = (3x - 1)/(x * x) = \phi(x)$ (say) and a root lies in the interval (1,2).

Program 15.12

```
/* Program for Fixed-Point iteration method.
   Program to find a root of the equation x*x*x-3x+1=0
   by fixed point iteration method. phi(x) is obtained
   by rewriting f(x)=0 as x=phi(x), which is to be supplied.*/
#include<stdio.h>
#include<math.h>
#include<stdlib.h>
#define phi(x) (3*(x)-1)/((x)*(x))
/* definition of the function phi(x) and it is to be
   changed accordingly */
void main()
{
 int k=0; /* counts number of iterations */
 float x1,x0;
 float eps=1e-5; /* error tolerance */
 printf("\nEnter the initial guess x0 ");
 scanf("%f",&x0);
 x1=x0;
 do{
    k++;
    x0=x1;
    x1=phi(x0);
 }while(fabs(x1-x0)>eps);
 printf("One root is %8.5f obtained at %d th iteration ",x1,k);
} /* main */
```

A sample of input/output:

```
Enter the initial guess x0 1
One root is 1.53209 obtained at 37th iteration
```

Merits and Demerits: The rate of convergence of this method is linear. If $|\phi'(x)| < 1$ for $x \in (a, b)$, then the sequence $\{x_n\}$ will surely converge to the desired root. But for some functions this condition is not required. The main disadvantage of this method is that one has to supply the function $\phi(x)$ instead of $f(x)$, which requires some pre-calculations.

15.4.4 Newton-Raphson method

This method is almost similar to the iteration method discussed above. Here, the sequence $\{x_n\}$ is computed from the relation

$$x_{n+1} = x_n - \frac{f(x_n)}{f'(x_n)}, \qquad n = 0, 1, 2, \ldots$$

where x_0 is the initial approximate to the root, which is to be supplied. From this relation the sequence of approximations to the root $\{x_n\}$ is computed and the process terminates when $|x_{n+1} - x_n| < \varepsilon$, where ε is the error tolerance.

Algorithm of Newton–Raphson method

Step 1: Read x as approximate root and error tolerance EPS.

Step 2: Compute $x_{new} = x - \dfrac{f(x)}{f'(x)}$, $f'(x)$ is the derivative of $f(x)$.

Step 3: If $|x_{new} - x|$ <EPS, then goto Step 4 else
set $x = x_{new}$; goto Step 2
endif;

Step 4: Print x_{new} as a root.

Step 5: Stop.

The following program computes a real root of the equation $x^3 - 3x + 1 = 0$ by Newton-Raphson method.

Program 15.13

```
/* Program for Newton-Raphson method.
   Program to find a root of the equation x*x*x-3x+1=0 by Newton-
   Raphson method. f(x) and its derivative fd(x) are to be supplied. */
#include<stdio.h>
#include<math.h>
#include<stdlib.h>
void main()
{
 int k=0; /* counts the number of iterations */
 float x1,x0; /* x0 is the initial guess */
 float eps=1e-5; /* error tolerance */
 float f(float x);
 float fd(float x); /* derivative of the function */
 printf("\nEnter the initial guess x0 ");
 scanf("%f",&x0);
 x1=x0;
 do{
     k++;
     x0=x1;
     x1=x0-f(x0)/fd(x0);
 }while(fabs(x1-x0)>eps);
 printf("One root is %8.5f obtained at %d th iteration ",x1,k);
} /* main */
/* definition of the function f(x) */
float f(float x)
 {
```

```
    return(x*x*x-3*x+1);
  }
/* definition of the function fd(x), the derivative of f(x) */
 float fd(float x)
  {
    return(3*x*x-3);
  }
```

A sample of input/output:

```
Enter the initial guess x0 1.1
One root is 1.53209 obtained at 7 th iteration
```

Merits and Demerits: If $f'(x)$ tends to be 0, then method fails to give the desired root. The rate of convergence is of second order, i.e. this method is faster as compared to other methods. But, the disadvantage is that one has to supply the derivative $f'(x)$ of $f(x)$. This method is also used to find complex root. In this case, the initial approximation x_0 is taken as a complex number.

Example 15.4.1 (Square root correct up to 15 decimals) Write a program to determine the square root of a given positive number.

Solution. Let a be the given positive number. Also let x be the value of $\sqrt{a}$, i.e. $x = \sqrt{a}$ or, $x^2 = a$.

Let $f(x) = x^2 - a$. Then the iteration scheme to compute x is

$$x_{n+1} = x_n - \frac{f(x_n)}{f'(x_n)} = x_n - \frac{x_n^2 - a}{2x_n} = \frac{x_n^2 + a}{2x_n}.$$

The following program computes the positive square root of a.

Program 15.14

```
/* Program to find the square root of a number correct up
   to 15 decimal places */
#include<stdio.h>
#include<math.h>
void main()
  {
    double a,x,xn;
    printf("Enter the number and initial guess\n");
    scanf("%lf%lf",&a,&x);
    xn=x;
    do{
       x=xn;
       xn=(x*x+a)/(2.*x);
     }while(fabs(xn-x)>1.0e-15);
    printf("The square root of %.3lf is %.15lf",a,x);
  }
```

A sample of input/output:

```
Enter the number and initial guess
17 4
The square root of 17.000 is 4.123105625617661
```

15.4.5 Roots of a polynomial equation

There are several methods available to compute the roots of a polynomial equation, out of which the **Bairstow** method is discussed here.

Bairstow Method

The roots of a polynomial equation can be determined by extracting a quadratic factor from the polynomial. The roots (real or complex) of a quadratic equation can determined using a known closed form formula. The **Bairstow method** is used to extract a quadratic factor.

Let the polynomial $P_n(x)$ of degree n be

$$x^n + a_1x^{n-1} + a_2x^{n-2} + \cdots + a_{n-1}x + a_n. \tag{15.8}$$

Let x^2+px+q be a factor of (15.8). If (15.8) is divided by the factor x^2+px+q, then we obtain a polynomial $Q_{n-2}(x)$ of degree $(n-2)$ and a remainder $Rx + S$ of degree one, where R and S are independent of x. Thus, the polynomial $P_n(x)$ can be written as

$$P_n(x) = (x^2 + px + q)Q_{n-2}(x) + Rx + S \tag{15.9}$$

where

$$Q_{n-2}(x) = x^{n-2} + b_1x^{n-3} + \cdots + b_{n-3}x + b_{n-2}. \tag{15.10}$$

The values of R and S depends on p and q.

These equations are two non-linear equations in p and q. The values of p and q can then, be determined by Newton-Raphson method for two variables.

Let (p_t, q_t) be the true values of p and q and Δp, Δq be the corrections to p and q. Then,

$$p_t = p + \Delta p \qquad \text{and} \qquad q_t = q + \Delta q.$$

The values of Δp and Δq are given by

$$\begin{aligned} \Delta p &= -\frac{b_n c_{n-3} - b_{n-1}c_{n-2}}{c_{n-2}^2 - c_{n-3}(c_{n-1} - b_{n-1})} \\ \Delta q &= -\frac{b_{n-1}(c_{n-1} - b_{n-1}) - b_n c_{n-2}}{c_{n-2}^2 - c_{n-3}(c_{n-1} - b_{n-1})}. \end{aligned} \tag{15.11}$$

The values of b_k's are calculated from the following recurrence relation.

$$b_k = a_k - pb_{k-1} - qb_{k-2}, \qquad k = 1, 2, \ldots, n \tag{15.12}$$

where $b_0 = 1, b_{-1} = 0$.

The recurrence relation to determine c_k using b_k is

$$c_k = b_k - pc_{k-1} - qc_{k-2}, k = 1, 2, \ldots, n-1 \text{ and } c_0 = 1, c_{-1} = 0. \qquad (15.13)$$

Thus, if p_0, q_0 be the initial values of p and q, then the improved values are

$$p_1 = p_0 + \Delta p \qquad \text{and} \qquad q_1 = q_0 + \Delta q. \qquad (15.14)$$

Once p_1 and q_1 are evaluated, the next improved values p_2, q_2 are determined from the relation

$$p_2 = p_1 + \Delta p, \qquad q_2 = q_1 + \Delta q.$$

In general,

$$p_{k+1} = p_k + \Delta p, \qquad q_{k+1} = q_k + \Delta q, \qquad (15.15)$$

the values of Δp and Δq are determined at $p = p_k$ and $q = q_k$.

The repetition terminates when p and q have been obtained to the desired accuracy.

The polynomial

$$Q_{n-2}(x) = P_n(x)/(x^2 + px + q) = x^{n-2} + b_1x^{n-3} + \cdots + b_{n-3}x + b_{n-2}$$

is called the **deflated polynomial**. The next quadratic polynomial can be obtained in similar process from the deflated polynomial.

The following algorithm extracts a quadratic factor from a polynomial of degree n and also determines the deflated polynomial, by Bairstow method.

Algorithm Bairstow

/* Extract a quadratic factor $x^2 + px + q$ from a polynomial $P_n(x) = x^n + a_1x^{n-1} + \cdots + a_{n-1}x + a_n$ of degree n and determines the deflated polynomial $Q_{n-2}(x) = x^{n-2} + b_1x^{n-3} + b_2x^{n-4} + \cdots + b_{n-2}$. */

Read $n, a_1, a_2, \ldots, a_n$; /* The degree and the coefficients of the polynomial. */

Read p, q, ε; /* The initial guess of p, q and error tolerance. */

Set $b_0 = 1, b_{-1} = 0, c_0 = 1, c_{-1} = 0$;

/* Compute b_k and c_k */

1. for $k = 1$ to n do

    Compute $b_k = a_k - pb_{k-1} - qb_{k-2}$;

endfor;

for $k = 1$ to $n - 1$ do

    Compute $c_k = b_k - pc_{k-1} - qc_{k-2}$;

endfor;

Compute $\Delta p = -\frac{b_n c_{n-3} - b_{n-1} c_{n-2}}{c_{n-2}^2 - c_{n-3}(c_{n-1} - b_{n-1})}$; $\quad \Delta q = -\frac{b_{n-1}(c_{n-1} - b_{n-1}) - b_n c_{n-2}}{c_{n-2}^2 - c_{n-3}(c_{n-1} - b_{n-1})}$;

Compute $p_{new} = p + \Delta p$, $q_{new} = q + \Delta q$;

if ($|p_{new} - p| < \varepsilon$) and ($|q_{new} - q| < \varepsilon$), then

    Print 'The values of p and q are', p_{new}, q_{new};

    Stop;

endif;
Set $p = p_{new}, q = q_{new}$;
go to 1.
Print 'The coefficients of deflated polynomial are',$b_1, b_2, \ldots, b_{n-2}$;
end Bairstow

Program 15.15

```
/* Program to find all roots of a polynomial equation by
   Bairstow method.
   Program to find all the roots of a polynomial equation by
   Bairstow method. Leading coefficient is 1. Assume that the
   initial guesses for all p and q are 0.5, 0.5.  */
 #include<stdio.h>
 #include<math.h>
 #include<stdlib.h>
 void main()
 {
  int n,i,k;
  float p,q,pnew,qnew,a[10],b[10],c[10],bm1,cm1,delp,delq;
  float epp=1e-5; /* error tolerance */
  void findroots(float p, float q);
  printf("\nEnter the degree of the polynomial ");
  scanf("%d",&n);
  printf("Enter the coefficients of the polynomial,
          except leading coeff.");
  for(i=1;i<=n;i++) scanf("%f",&a[i]);
  q=0.5;
  p=0.5;
  printf("The roots are \n");
  do
  {
     b[0]=1; bm1=0; c[0]=1; cm1=0;
     pnew=p; qnew=q;
     do{
        p=pnew; q=qnew;
        b[1]=a[1]-p*b[0]-q*bm1;
        c[1]=b[1]-p*c[0]-q*cm1;
        for(k=2;k<=n;k++) b[k]=a[k]-p*b[k-1]-q*b[k-2];
        for(k=2;k<=n;k++) c[k]=b[k]-p*c[k-1]-q*c[k-2];
        delp=-(b[n]*c[n-3]-b[n-1]*c[n-2])/
                (c[n-2]*c[n-2]-c[n-3]*(c[n-1]-b[n-1]));
        delq=-(b[n-1]*(c[n-1]-b[n-1])-b[n]*c[n-2])/
                (c[n-2]*c[n-2]-c[n-3]*(c[n-1]-b[n-1]));
```

```
        pnew=p+delp;
        qnew=q+delq;
      }while((fabs(pnew-p)>epp || fabs(qnew-q)>epp));
      findroots(p,q);
      n-=2;
      for(i=1;i<=n;i++) a[i]=b[i];
  }while(n>2);

/* Deflated polynomial is quadratic */
  if(n==2) findroots(b[1],b[2]);

/* Deflated polynomial is linear */
  if(n==1) printf("%f ",-b[1]);
 } /* main */

/* Find the roots of the quadratic x*x+px+q=0 */
 void findroots(float p, float q)
 {
  float dis;
  dis=p*p-4*q;
  if(dis>=0)
     {
       printf("%f  %f\n",(-p+sqrt(dis))/2,(-p-sqrt(dis))/2);
     }
  else
     {
       printf("(%f,%f), (%f,%f)\n",-p/2,sqrt(fabs(dis))/2,
         -p/2,-sqrt(fabs(dis))/2);
     }
 } /* findroots */
```

A sample of input/output:

```
Enter the degree of the polynomial 5
Enter the coefficients of the polynomial, except leading coeff.
3 4 -5 6 1
 The roots are
 (0.604068,0.729697), (0.604068,-0.729697)
 (-2.030660,1.861934), (-2.030660,-1.861934)
 -0.146816
```

15.4.6 Newton-Raphson method for two variables

Let $f(x, y) = 0$ and $g(x, y) = 0$ be two equations with two variables and (x_0, y_0) be an initial approximate root. Let h and k be the corrections to the approximate root x_0

and y_0. Then, $x_1 = x_0 + h$ and $y_1 = y_0 + k$ are the correct values of the roots. Here, h and k are given by

$$h = -\frac{1}{J}\begin{vmatrix} f(x_0, y_0) & f_y(x_0, y_0) \\ g(x_0, y_0) & g_y(x_0, y_0) \end{vmatrix} \quad \text{and} \quad k = +\frac{1}{J}\begin{vmatrix} f(x_0, y_0) & f_x(x_0, y_0) \\ g(x_0, y_0) & g_x(x_0, y_0) \end{vmatrix}$$

where

$$J = \begin{vmatrix} f_x(x_0, y_0) & f_y(x_0, y_0) \\ g_x(x_0, y_0) & g_y(x_0, y_0) \end{vmatrix}$$

and f_x, f_y, etc., are partial derivatives of $f(x, y)$ with respective to x and y respectively.

By successive approximation we get

$$x_{n+1} = x_n - \frac{1}{J}\begin{vmatrix} f(x_n, y_n) & f_y(x_n, y_n) \\ g(x_n, y_n) & g_y(x_n, y_n) \end{vmatrix}$$

$$y_{n+1} = y_n + \frac{1}{J}\begin{vmatrix} f(x_n, y_n) & f_x(x_n, y_n) \\ g(x_n, y_n) & g_x(x_n, y_n) \end{vmatrix}$$

$n = 0, 1, 2, \ldots$.

The process terminates when $|x_{n+1} - x_n| < \varepsilon$ and $|y_{n+1} - y_n| < \varepsilon$, where ε is the error tolerance.

The following program solves the simultaneous equations $f(x, y) \equiv 3x^2 - 2y^2 - 1 = 0$ and $g(x, y) \equiv x^2 - 2x + 2y - 8 = 0$, taking initial approximations $x_0 = 2.5$ and $y_0 = 3$.

Program 15.16

```
/* Newton-Raphson method (for a pair of non-linear equations).
   Program to find a root of a pair of non-linear equations
   by Newton-Raphson method. Partial derivative of f and g
   w.r.t. x and y are to be supplied.
   The equations are 3x*x-2y*y-1=0, x*x-2x+2y-8=0. */
#include<stdio.h>
#include<math.h>
#include<stdlib.h>
void main()
{
 int i,maxiteration;
 float eps=1e-5,x0,y0; /* initial guesses for x and y */
 float J,k,h,delfx,delfy,delgx,delgy,f0,g0;
 float f(float x, float y);
 float fx(float x, float y);
 float fy(float x, float y);
 float g(float x, float y);
 float gx(float x, float y);
 float gy(float x, float y);
```

```
 printf("Enter initial guesses for x and y ");
 scanf("%f %f",&x0,&y0);
 printf("Maximum iterations to be allowed ");
 scanf("%d",&maxiteration);

 for(i=1;i<=maxiteration;i++)
   {
    f0=f(x0,y0);
    g0=g(x0,y0);
    if(fabs(f0)<eps && fabs(g0)<eps){
       printf("One root is (%7.5f, %7.5f) obtained at %d iterations",
              x0,y0,i);
       exit(0);
     }
    delfx=fx(x0,y0); delfy=fy(x0,y0);
    delgx=gx(x0,y0); delgy=gy(x0,y0);
    J=delfx*delgy-delgx*delfy;
    h=(-f0*delgy+g0*delfy)/J;
    k=(-g0*delfx+f0*delgx)/J;
    x0+=h; y0+=k;
   }
 printf("Iteration does not converge in %d iterations",
        maxiteration);
 } /* main */

/* Definition of f(x,y) and its partial derivative w.r.t x and y
             fx(x,y) and fy(x,y) */
 float f(float x, float y)
 {
   return (3*x*x-2*y*y-1);
 }

 float fx(float x, float y)
 {
   return (6*x);
 }

 float fy(float x, float y)
 {
   return (-4*y);
 }
```

```
/* Definition of g(x,y) and its partial derivative w.r.t x and y
            gx(x,y) and gy(x,y) */
float g(float x, float y)
{
  return (x*x-2*x+2*y-8);
}

float gx(float x, float y)
{
  return (2*x-2);
}
float gy(float x, float y)
{
  return (2);
}
```

A sample of input/output:

```
Enter initial guesses for x and y 2.5 3
Maximum iterations to be allowed 50
One root is (2.64005, 3.15512) obtained at 4 iterations
```

15.5 Solution of System of Linear Equations

Let the system of linear equations be

$$\begin{aligned} a_{11}x_1 + a_{12}x_2 + \cdots + a_{1n}x_n &= b_1 \\ a_{21}x_1 + a_{22}x_2 + \cdots + a_{2n}x_n &= b_2 \\ \cdots\cdots\cdots\cdots\cdots\cdots\cdots &\cdots \cdots \\ a_{n1}x_1 + a_{n2}x_2 + \cdots + a_{nn}x_n &= b_n. \end{aligned} \tag{15.16}$$

This system of equations can be written as

$$A\mathbf{x} = \mathbf{b} \tag{15.17}$$

where

$$A = \begin{bmatrix} a_{11} & a_{12} & \cdots & a_{1n} \\ a_{21} & a_{22} & \cdots & a_{2n} \\ \cdots & \cdots & \cdots & \cdots \\ a_{n1} & a_{n2} & \cdots & a_{nn} \end{bmatrix}, \mathbf{x} = \begin{bmatrix} x_1 \\ x_2 \\ \vdots \\ x_n \end{bmatrix} \text{ and } \mathbf{b} = \begin{bmatrix} b_1 \\ b_2 \\ \vdots \\ b_n \end{bmatrix}. \tag{15.18}$$

There are two main techniques used to solve a system of linear equations: (i) direct method, and (ii) iteration method.

Direct Methods: There are several direct methods available to solve a system of linear equations. Some of them are Crammer's rule, matrix inversion, Gauss elimination, LU decomposition, etc.

Iteration Methods: Different iteration methods are also available to solve a system of linear equations. Two iteration methods that are mainly used are Jacobi's iteration, Gauss-Seidal iteration.

15.5.1 Evaluation of determinant

Triangularization, also known as **Gauss reduction** method, is the best way to evaluate a determinant. The basic principle of this method is to convert the given determinant into a lower or upper triangular form by using only elementary row operations. If the determinant is reduced to a triangular form (D'), then the value of D is obtained by multiplying the diagonal elements of D'.

Let $D = \begin{vmatrix} a_{11} & a_{12} & \cdots & a_{1n} \\ a_{21} & a_{22} & \cdots & a_{2n} \\ \cdots & \cdots & \cdots & \cdots \\ a_{n1} & a_{n2} & \cdots & a_{nn} \end{vmatrix}$ be a determinant of order n.

Using the elementary row operations, D can be reduced to the following form:

$$D' = \begin{vmatrix} a_{11} & a_{12} & a_{13} & \cdots & a_{1n} \\ 0 & a_{22}^{(1)} & a_{23}^{(1)} & \cdots & a_{2n}^{(1)} \\ 0 & 0 & a_{33}^{(2)} & \cdots & a_{3n}^{(2)} \\ \cdots & \cdots & \cdots & \cdots & \cdots \\ 0 & 0 & 0 & \cdots & a_{nn}^{(n-1)} \end{vmatrix},$$

where

$$a_{ij}^{(k)} = a_{ij}^{(k-1)} - \frac{a_{ik}^{(k-1)}}{a_{kk}^{(k-1)}} a_{kj}^{(k-1)}; \tag{15.19}$$

$i, j = k+1, \ldots, n;\ \ k = 1, 2, \ldots, n-1$ and $a_{ij}^{(0)} = a_{ij},\ \ i, j = 1, 2, \cdots, n.$

Then the value of D is equal to $a_{11}a_{22}^{(1)}a_{33}^{(2)} \cdots a_{nn}^{(n-1)}$.

To compute the value of $a_{ij}^{(k)}$ one division is required. If $a_{kk}^{(k-1)}$ is zero, then further reduction is not possible. If $a_{kk}^{(k-1)}$ is small, then the division leads to the loss of significant digits. To prevent the loss of significant digits, the pivoting techniques are used.

A **pivot** is the largest magnitude element in a row or a column or the principal diagonal or the leading or trailing sub-matrix of order i $(2 \le i \le n)$.

In the elementary row operation, if any one of the pivot element is zero or very small relative to other elements in that row, then we rearrange the remaining rows in such a way that the pivot becomes non-zero or not a very small number. The method is called pivoting. Pivoting are of two types – partial pivoting and complete pivoting. The partial pivoting is discussed in the following.

Partial pivoting

In the first stage, the first pivot is determined by finding the largest element in magnitude among the elements of first column and let it be a_{i1}. Then rows i and 1 are interchanged. In the second stage, the second pivot is determined by finding the largest element in magnitude among the elements of second column leaving first element. Let it be a_{j2}. The second and jth rows are interchanged. This process is repeated for $(n-1)$th times. In general, at ith stage, the smallest index j is chosen for which

$$|a_{ij}^{(k)}| = \max\{|a_{kk}^{(k)}|, |a_{k+1\,k}^{(k)}|, \ldots, |a_{nk}^{(k)}|\} = \max\{|a_{ik}^{(k)}|, i = k, k+1, \ldots, n\}$$

and the rows k and j are interchanged.

The algorithm for triangularization, i.e. to find the value of a determinant using partial pivoting is presented below.

The following algorithm finds the value of a determinant of order $n \times n$ using partial pivoting.

Algorithm Det_Partial_Pivoting.

/* The value of determinant using partial pivoting. */

Let $\mathbf{A} = [a_{ij}]$ be an $n \times n$ matrix.

Step 1. Read the matrix $\mathbf{A} = [a_{ij}], i, j = 1, 2, \ldots, n$.

Step 2. Set $k = 1$ and $sign = 1$ /* Sign indicates the sign of the determinant when interchanges two rows. */

Step 3. Find a pivot from the elements $a_{kk}, a_{k+1k}, \cdots, a_{nk}$ in the kth column of $\mathbf{A}$, and let a_{jk} be the pivot. That is, $|a_{jk}| = \max\{|a_{kk}|, |a_{k+1\,k}|, \ldots, |a_{nk}|\}$.

Step 4. If $a_{jk} = 0$, then $|\mathbf{A}| = 0$; print the value of $|\mathbf{A}|$ and Stop.

Step 5. If $j = k$, then go to Step 6.
Otherwise interchange the kth and jth rows and set $sign = -sign$.

Step 6. Subtract $\frac{a_{jk}}{a_{kk}}$ times the kth row from the jth row for $j = k+1, k+2, \ldots, n$, i.e. for $j = k+1, k+2, \ldots, n$, do the following $R_j' = R_j - \frac{a_{jk}}{a_{kk}}.R_k$, where R_j, R_j' are the old and new jth rows respectively.
/* This step makes $a_{k+1k}, a_{k+2k}, \cdots, a_{nk}$ zero. */

Step 7. Increment k by 1, i.e. set $k = k+1$. If $k < n$, then goto Step 3. Otherwise,
/* Triangularization is complete. */
Compute $|\mathbf{A}| = sign \times$ product of diagonal elements.
Print the value of $|\mathbf{A}|$ and Stop.

end Det_Partial_Pivoting.

Program 15.17

```
/* Program to find the value of a determinant using partial pivoting */
#include<stdio.h>
#include<stdlib.h>
#include<math.h>
```

```
void main()
{
 int n,k,i,j,sign=1;
 float a[10][10],b[10],prod,temp;
 int max1(float b[],int k, int n);
 printf("\nEnter the size of the determinant ");
 scanf("%d",&n);
 printf("Enter the elements row wise ");
 for(i=1;i<=n;i++) for(j=1;j<=n;j++)
    scanf("%f",&a[i][j]);
 for(k=1;k<=n;k++){
    for(i=k;i<=n;i++) b[i]=a[i][k];
       /* copy from a[k][k] to a[n][k] into b */
    j=max1(b,k,n); /* finds pivot position */
    if(a[j][k]==0){
         printf("The value of determinant is 0");
         exit(0);
       }
    if(j!=k){ /* interchange k and j rows */
         sign=-sign;
         for(i=1;i<=n;i++){
            temp=a[j][i]; a[j][i]=a[k][i]; a[k][i]=temp;
         }
       }
    for(j=k+1;j<=n;j++){ /* makes a[k+1][k] to a[n][k] zero */
           temp=a[j][k]/a[k][k];
           for(i=1;i<=n;i++)    a[j][i]-=temp*a[k][i];
         }
  } /* end of k loop */
 prod=sign;
 /* product of diagonal elements */
 for(i=1;i<=n;i++) prod*=a[i][i];
 printf("The value of the determinant is %f ",prod);
}/* main */
/* Finds position of maximum element among n numbers */
int max1(float b[],int k, int n)
  {
    float temp; int i,j;
    temp=fabs(b[k]);  j=k; /* initial maximum */
    for(i=k+1;i<=n;i++)
        if(temp<fabs(b[i])) {
           temp=fabs(b[i]); j=i;
```

```
        }
    return j;
}
```

A sample of input/output:

```
Enter the size of the determinant 3
Enter the elements row wise
0 2 5
1 3 -8
6 5 1
The value of the determinant is -163.000000
```

15.5.2 Inverse of a matrix

From the theory of matrices, it is well known that every square non-singular matrix has a unique inverse. The inverse of a matrix **A** can be determined from the relation

$$\mathbf{A}^{-1} = \frac{\textbf{adj A}}{|\mathbf{A}|}. \tag{15.20}$$

The matrix **adj A** is called adjoint of **A** and defined as

$$\textbf{adj A} = \begin{bmatrix} A_{11} & A_{21} & \cdots & A_{n1} \\ A_{12} & A_{22} & \cdots & A_{n2} \\ \cdots & \cdots & \cdots & \cdots \\ A_{1n} & A_{2n} & \cdots & A_{nn} \end{bmatrix},$$

where A_{ij} being the cofactor of a_{ij} in $|\mathbf{A}|$.

The main difficulty of this method is to compute the inverse of the matrix **A**. From the definition of **adj A**, it is easy to observe that to compute the matrix **adj A**, we have to determine n^2 determinants each of order $(n-1)$. So, it is very time consuming. Many efficient methods are available to find the inverse of a matrix, among them **Gauss-Jordan** is most popular. In the following, Gauss-Jordan method is discussed to find the inverse of a square non-singular matrix.

Gauss-Jordan Method

In this method, the given matrix **A** is augmented with a unit matrix of same size, i.e. if the order of **A** is $n \times n$, then the order of the augmented matrix $[\mathbf{A}\vdots\mathbf{I}]$ will be $n \times 2n$. The augmented matrix looks like

$$[\mathbf{A}\vdots\mathbf{I}] = \left[\begin{array}{cccc:cccc} a_{11} & a_{12} & \cdots & a_{1n} & 1 & 0 & \cdots & 0 \\ a_{21} & a_{22} & \cdots & a_{2n} & 0 & 1 & \cdots & 0 \\ \cdots & \cdots & \cdots & \cdots & \cdots & \cdots & \cdots & \cdots \\ a_{n1} & a_{n2} & \cdots & a_{nn} & 0 & 0 & \cdots & 1 \end{array}\right]. \tag{15.21}$$

Then the inverse of **A** is computed in two stages. In the first stage, **A** is converted into an upper triangular form, using only elementary row operations. In the second stage, the upper triangular matrix (obtained in first stage) is reduced to an identity matrix by row operations. All these operations are operated on the augmented matrix $[\mathbf{A}\vdots\mathbf{I}]$. After completion of these stages, the augmented matrix $[\mathbf{A}\vdots\mathbf{I}]$ is turned to $[\mathbf{I}\vdots\mathbf{A}^{-1}]$, i.e. the inverse of **A** is obtained from the right half of augmented matrix.

At the end of the operations, the matrix shown in (15.21) reduces to the following form:

$$\begin{bmatrix} 1 & 0 & \cdots & 0 & \vdots & a'_{11} & a'_{12} & \cdots & a'_{1n} \\ 0 & 1 & \cdots & 0 & \vdots & a'_{21} & a'_{22} & \cdots & a'_{2n} \\ \cdots & \cdots & \cdots & \cdots & \vdots & \cdots & \cdots & \cdots & \cdots \\ 0 & 0 & \cdots & 1 & \vdots & a'_{n1} & a'_{n2} & \cdots & a'_{nn} \end{bmatrix}. \tag{15.22}$$

The following algorithm computes the inverse of a non-singular square matrix of order $n \times n$ and if the matrix is singular, it prints the message 'the matrix is singular and hence not invertible'.

Algorithm Matrix_Inversion (using partial pivoting).
Let $\mathbf{A} = [a_{ij}]$ be an $n \times n$ matrix.

Step 1. Read the matrix $\mathbf{A} = [a_{ij}], i, j = 1, 2, \ldots, n$.

Step 2. /* Augment the matrix **A**. */
Augment the matrix **A** by a unit matrix of order $n \times n$. The resultant matrix **A** becomes of order $n \times 2n$.

i.e. $a_{i\,n+j} = \begin{cases} 0, & \text{for } i \neq j \\ 1, & \text{for } i = j \end{cases}$
for $i, j = 1, 2, \ldots, n$.

Stage I. *Make upper triangular form.*

Step 3. Set $k = 1$.

Step 4. Find a pivot from the elements $a_{kk}, a_{k+1\,k}, \ldots, a_{nk}$ in the kth column of **A** and let a_{jk} be the pivot.

Step 5. If $a_{jk} = 0$, then print 'the matrix is singular and hence not invertible' and Stop.

Step 6. If $j = k$, then goto Step 7.
Otherwise interchange the kth and jth rows.

Step 7. If $a_{kk} \neq 1$, then divide all the elements of kth row by a_{kk}.
Subtract a_{jk} times the kth row to the jth row for
$j = k+1, k+2, \cdots, 2n$;
i.e. $R'_j = R_j - a_{jk}R_k$.
//This step makes $a_{k+1\,k}, a_{k+2\,k}, \ldots, a_{nk}$ zero.//

Step 8. Increase k by 1, i.e. set $k = k + 1$.
If $k < n$, then goto Step 4. Otherwise goto Step 9.
/* Stage I is completed. */

Stage II. /* *Make the left half of* **A** *a unit matrix.* */
Step 9. Set $k = 2$.
Step 10. Subtract a_{jk} times the kth row to the jth row for $j = k - 1, k - 2, \ldots, 1$.
Step 11. Increase k by 1.
If $k < n$, then goto Step 10.
Otherwise, print the right half of **A** as inverse of **A** and Stop.

end Matrix_Inversion

Program 15.18

```
/* Program to find the inverse of a square matrix using
   partial pivoting */
 #include<stdio.h>
 #include<stdlib.h>
 #include<math.h>
 #define zero 0.00001
 void main()
 {
 int n,m,k,i,j;
 float a[10][20],temp;
 printf("\nEnter the size of the matrix ");
 scanf("%d",&n);
 printf("Enter the elements rowwise ");
 for(i=1;i<=n;i++) for(j=1;j<=n;j++) scanf("%f",&a[i][j]);
 /* augment the matrix A */
 for(i=1;i<=n;i++) for(j=1;j<=n;j++) a[i][n+j]=0;
 for(i=1;i<=n;i++) a[i][n+i]=1;
 m=2*n;
 for(k=1;k<=n;k++){
     /* finds pivot element and its position */
     temp=fabs(a[k][k]);  j=k; /* initial maximum */
     for(i=k+1;i<=n;i++)     /* determines maximum elements */
         if(temp<fabs(a[i][k])){
              temp=fabs(a[i][k]); j=i;
           }
     if(fabs(a[j][k])<=zero){ /* if a[j][k]=0 */
          printf("The matrix is singular and is not invertible");
          exit(0);
       }
```

```
    if(j!=k){ /* interchange k and j rows */
      for(i=1;i<=m;i++){
            temp=a[j][i]; a[j][i]=a[k][i]; a[k][i]=temp;
        }
      }
    if(a[k][k]!=1){
          temp=a[k][k];
          for(i=1;i<=m;i++) a[k][i]/=temp;
      }
    for(j=k+1;j<=n;j++){ /* makes a[k+1][k] to a[n][k] zero */
            temp=a[j][k];
            for(i=1;i<=m;i++)    a[j][i]-=temp*a[k][i];
        }
  } /* end of k loop */
  /* make left half of A to a unit matrix */
  for(k=2;k<=n;k++){
          for(j=k-1;j>=1;j--){
                temp=a[j][k];
                for(i=1;i<=m;i++) a[j][i]-=temp*a[k][i];
            }
      }
  printf("\nThe inverse matrix is \n");
  for(i=1;i<=n;i++){
       for(j=n+1;j<=m;j++)
          printf("%f ",a[i][j]); printf("\n");
    }
 }/* main */
```

A sample of input/output:

```
Enter the size of the matrix 3
Enter the elements rowwise
0 1 2
3 -2 1
4 3 2

 The inverse matrix is
 -0.218750  0.125000  0.156250
 -0.062500 -0.250000  0.187500
  0.531250  0.125000 -0.093750
```

Complexity of the algorithm

Step 4 determines the maximum among $n-k+1$ elements and takes $n-k+1$ comparisons. Step 6 takes $O(n)$ operations, if the kth and jth rows need to interchange. For a fixed

j, Step 7 needs $n-k$ additions and $n-k$ multiplications. Since j is running from $k+1$ to n, so the total time taken by Step 7 is $(n-k)^2$. Step 4 to Step 7 are repeated for n times ($k = 1, 2, \ldots, n$), therefore, Stage I takes $\sum_{k=1}^{n}(n-k)^2 + O(n) + n - k + 1 = O(n^3)$ operations.

Similarly, Stage II needs $O(n^3)$ operations. Hence, the time complexity to compute the inverse of a non-singular matrix is $O(n^3)$.

Since the Stage I is similar to the algorithm for finding the value of determinant using partial pivoting, so the time complexity to compute the determinant is $O(n^3)$.

15.5.3 Matrix inverse method

The system of equations (15.16) can be written in the matrix form (15.17) as

$$\mathbf{Ax} = \mathbf{b}$$

where $\mathbf{A}, \mathbf{b}$ and $\mathbf{x}$ are defined in (15.18).

The solution of $\mathbf{Ax} = \mathbf{b}$ is given by $\mathbf{x} = \mathbf{A}^{-1}\mathbf{b}$, where $\mathbf{A}^{-1}$ is the inverse of the matrix $\mathbf{A}$.

Once the inverse of $\mathbf{A}$ is known, then post multiplication of it with $\mathbf{b}$ gives the solution vector $\mathbf{x}$.

Program 15.19

```
/* Program for Matrix Inverse method. Program to find the solution
   of a system of linear equations by matrix inverse method. Partial
   pivoting is used to find matrix inverse. */
#include<stdio.h>
#include<stdlib.h>
#include<math.h>
#define zero 0.00001
float a[10][20],ai[10][10];
int n;
int matinv();
void main()
{
  int i,j;
  float b[10],x[10];
  printf("\nEnter the size of the coefficient matrix ");
  scanf("%d",&n);
  printf("Enter the elements rowwise ");
  for(i=1;i<=n;i++) for(j=1;j<=n;j++) scanf("%f",&a[i][j]);
  printf("Enter the right hand vector ");
  for(i=1;i<=n;i++) scanf("%f",&b[i]);
  i=matinv();
  if(i==0){
```

```
   printf("Coefficient matrix is singular: ");
   printf("The system has either no solution or many solutions");
   exit(0);
  }
 for(i=1;i<=n;i++){
    x[i]=0;
    for(j=1;j<=n;j++) x[i]+=ai[i][j]*b[j];
  }
 printf("Solution of the system is\n ");
 for(i=1;i<=n;i++) printf("%8.5f ",x[i]);
} /* main */
/* Function to find matrix inverse */
int matinv()
{
 int i,j,m,k; float temp;
/* augment the matrix A */
for(i=1;i<=n;i++) for(j=1;j<=n;j++) a[i][n+j]=0;
for(i=1;i<=n;i++) a[i][n+i]=1;
m=2*n;
for(k=1;k<=n;k++){
    /* Finds pivot element and its position */
    temp=fabs(a[k][k]);  j=k; /* initial maximum */
    for(i=k+1;i<=n;i++)
       if(temp<fabs(a[i][k])){
          temp=fabs(a[i][k]); j=i;
        }
    if(fabs(a[j][k])<=zero){ /* if a[j][k]=0 */
        printf("The matrix is singular and is not invertible");
        return(0);
       }
    if(j!=k){ /* interchange k and j rows */
       for(i=1;i<=m;i++){
            temp=a[j][i]; a[j][i]=a[k][i]; a[k][i]=temp;
         }
       }
    if(a[k][k]!=1){
        temp=a[k][k];
        for(i=1;i<=m;i++) a[k][i]/=temp;
       }
    for(j=k+1;j<=n;j++){ /* makes a[k+1][k] to a[n][k] zero */
          temp=a[j][k];
          for(i=1;i<=m;i++)   a[j][i]-=temp*a[k][i];
```

```
    }
  } /* end of k loop */
  /* make left half of A to a unit matrix */
  for(k=2;k<=n;k++)
     for(j=k-1;j>=1;j--){
         temp=a[j][k];
         for(i=1;i<=m;i++) a[j][i]-=temp*a[k][i];
        }
  for(i=1;i<=n;i++)
     for(j=n+1;j<=m;j++) ai[i][j-n]=a[i][j];
  return(1);
 }/* matinv */
```

A sample of input/output:

```
Enter the size of the matrix 3
Enter the elements rowwise
2 3 4
5 4 3
1 2 -9
Enter the right hand vector
3 4 5
Solution of the system is
-0.25000  1.50000  -0.25000
```

15.5.4 Gauss elimination method

In this method the variables are eliminated by a process of systematic elimination. Suppose we have n variables and n equations of the form (15.16). This procedure reduces the system of linear equations to an equivalent upper triangular system which can be solved by back-substitution. To convert an upper triangular system, x_1 is eliminated from second equation, x_1 and x_2 from the third equation, and so on.

To eliminate x_1 from second, third, $\cdots$, and nth equations, the first equation is multiplied by $-\frac{a_{21}}{a_{11}}, -\frac{a_{31}}{a_{11}}, \ldots, -\frac{a_{n1}}{a_{11}}$ respectively and successively added with the second, third, $\cdots$, nth equations (assuming that $a_{11} \neq 0$). This gives

$$\begin{aligned}
a_{11}x_1 + a_{12}x_2 + a_{13}x_3 + \cdots + a_{1n}x_n &= b_1 \\
a_{22}^{(1)}x_2 + a_{23}^{(1)}x_3 + \cdots + a_{2n}^{(1)}x_n &= b_2^{(1)} \\
a_{32}^{(1)}x_2 + a_{33}^{(1)}x_3 + \cdots + a_{3n}^{(1)}x_n &= b_3^{(1)} \\
\cdots\cdots\cdots\cdots\cdots\cdots\cdots\cdots & \cdots\ \cdots \\
a_{n2}^{(1)}x_2 + a_{n3}^{(1)}x_3 + \cdots + a_{nn}^{(1)}x_n &= b_n^{(1)}.
\end{aligned}$$

Again, to eliminate x_2 from the third, fourth, $\ldots$, and nth equations the second equation is multiplied by $-\dfrac{a_{32}^{(1)}}{a_{22}^{(1)}}, -\dfrac{a_{42}^{(1)}}{a_{22}^{(1)}}, \ldots, -\dfrac{a_{n2}^{(1)}}{a_{22}^{(1)}}$ respectively (assuming that $a_{22}^{(1)} \neq 0$), and successively added the third, fourth, ..., and nth equations to get the new system of equations as

$$\begin{aligned}
a_{11}x_1 + a_{12}x_2 + a_{13}x_3 + \cdots + a_{1n}x_n &= b_1 \\
a_{22}^{(1)}x_2 + a_{23}^{(1)}x_3 + \cdots + a_{2n}^{(1)}x_n &= b_2^{(1)} \\
a_{33}^{(2)}x_3 + \cdots + a_{3n}^{(2)}x_n &= b_3^{(2)} \\
\cdots\cdots\cdots\cdots\cdots\cdots\cdots &\cdots \;\cdots \\
a_{n3}^{(2)}x_3 + \cdots + a_{nn}^{(2)}x_n &= b_n^{(2)}
\end{aligned}$$

and so on.

Finally, after eliminating x_{n-1} the equations become

$$\begin{aligned}
a_{11}x_1 + a_{12}x_2 + a_{13}x_3 + \cdots + a_{1n}x_n &= b_1 \\
a_{22}^{(1)}x_2 + a_{23}^{(1)}x_3 + \cdots + a_{2n}^{(1)}x_n &= b_2^{(1)} \\
a_{33}^{(2)}x_3 + \cdots + a_{3n}^{(2)}x_n &= b_3^{(2)} \\
\cdots\cdots\cdots\cdots &\cdots \;\cdots \\
a_{nn}^{(n-1)}x_n &= b_n^{(n-1)}.
\end{aligned}$$

Now by back substitution, the values of the variables can be found out as follows:
From last equation, $x_n = \dfrac{b_n^{(n-1)}}{a_{nn}^{(n-1)}}$, from the last but one, i.e. $(n-1)$th equation, the value of x_{n-1} is determined and so on. Finally, from the first equation, the value of x_1 is obtained. The program to obtain the solution by Gauss elimination method is listed below.

Program 15.20

```
/* Program to find the solution of a system of linear equations by
   Gauss elimination method. Partial pivoting is used. */
 #include<stdio.h>
 #include<stdlib.h>
 #include<math.h>
 #define zero 0.00001 /* may be changed */
 void main()
 {
 int i,j,k,n,m;
 float a[10][10],b[10],x[10],temp;
 printf("\nEnter the size of the coefficient matrix ");
 scanf("%d",&n);
 printf("Enter the elements row wise ");
```

```
for(i=1;i<=n;i++) for(j=1;j<=n;j++) scanf("%f",&a[i][j]);
printf("Enter the right hand vector ");
for(i=1;i<=n;i++) scanf("%f",&b[i]);
/* Augment A with b[i], i.e. a[i][n+1]=b[i] */
m=n+1;
for(i=1;i<=n;i++) a[i][m]=b[i];
for(k=1;k<=n;k++){
 /* finds pivot element and its position */
 temp=fabs(a[k][k]);  j=k; /* initial maximum */
 for(i=k+1;i<=n;i++)
     if(temp<fabs(a[i][k])){
          temp=fabs(a[i][k]); j=i;
        }
  if(fabs(a[j][k])<=zero){ /* if a[j][k]=0 */
     printf("The matrix is singular:\n");
     printf("The system has either no solution or many solutions");
     exit(0);
    }
  if(j!=k){ /* interchange k and j rows */
      for(i=1;i<=m;i++){
          temp=a[j][i]; a[j][i]=a[k][i]; a[k][i]=temp;
      }
    }
  for(j=k+1;j<=n;j++){ /* makes a[k+1][k] to a[n][k] zero */
        temp=a[j][k]/a[k][k];
        for(i=1;i<=m;i++)   a[j][i]-=temp*a[k][i];
     }
  } /* end of k loop */
 /* forward substitution is over */
 /* backward substitution */
 x[n]=a[n][m]/a[n][n];
 for(i=n-1;i>=1;i--){
      x[i]=a[i][m];
      for(j=i+1;j<=n;j++) x[i]-=a[i][j]*x[j];
      x[i]/=a[i][i];
    }
 printf("Solution of the system is\n ");
 for(i=1;i<=n;i++) printf("%8.5f ",x[i]);
 } /* main */
```

Two sample input and output are given below.

```
Enter total number of variables
```

```
3
Enter coefficient matrix, row wise
1 2 3
2 3 4
3 4 5
Enter right hand vector
3 4 10
The matrix is singular:
The system has either no solution or many solutions
```

Second run:

```
Enter total number of variables
4
Enter coefficient matrix, row wise
2 3 -4 1
3 8 -7 4
2 0 2 1
2 8 3 4
Enter right hand vector
3 4 8 -3
Solution of the system is
2.85034   -2.49660   -0.41497 3.12925
```

Note 15.5.1 When any one of the pivots vanish, then the rows and columns are rearranged in such a way that all the pivots become non-zero. If this is not possible, then the system of equations has either no solutions or infinite many solutions.

15.5.5 LU-Decomposition method

This method is also known as **matrix factorization** or **Crout's reduction method**.

Let the system of linear equations be

$$\mathbf{Ax} = \mathbf{b} \tag{15.23}$$

where $\mathbf{A}, \mathbf{x}, \mathbf{b}$ are given by (15.18).

The matrix $\mathbf{A}$ can be factorized into the form $\mathbf{A} = \mathbf{LU}$, where $\mathbf{L}$ and $\mathbf{U}$ are the lower and upper triangular matrices respectively. *If the principal minors of* $\mathbf{A}$ *are non-singular,* i.e.

$$a_{11} \neq 0, \quad \begin{vmatrix} a_{11} & a_{12} \\ a_{21} & a_{22} \end{vmatrix} \neq 0, \quad \begin{vmatrix} a_{11} & a_{12} & a_{13} \\ a_{21} & a_{22} & a_{23} \\ a_{31} & a_{32} & a_{33} \end{vmatrix} \neq 0, \quad \cdots, \quad |\mathbf{A}| \neq 0 \tag{15.24}$$

then this factorization is possible and it is unique.

The matrices **L** and **U** are of the form

$$\mathbf{L} = \begin{bmatrix} l_{11} & 0 & 0 & \cdots & 0 \\ l_{21} & l_{22} & 0 & \cdots & 0 \\ l_{31} & l_{32} & l_{33} & \cdots & 0 \\ \vdots & \vdots & \vdots & \vdots & \vdots \\ l_{n1} & l_{n2} & l_{n3} & \cdots & l_{nn} \end{bmatrix} \text{ and } \mathbf{U} = \begin{bmatrix} u_{11} & u_{12} & u_{13} & \cdots & u_{1n} \\ 0 & u_{22} & u_{23} & \cdots & u_{2n} \\ 0 & 0 & u_{33} & \cdots & u_{3n} \\ \vdots & \vdots & \vdots & \vdots & \vdots \\ 0 & 0 & 0 & \cdots & u_{nn} \end{bmatrix}. \quad (15.25)$$

The equation $\mathbf{Ax} = \mathbf{b}$ becomes $\mathbf{LUx} = \mathbf{b}$. Let $\mathbf{Ux} = \mathbf{z}$, then $\mathbf{Lz} = \mathbf{b}$, where $\mathbf{z} = (z_1, z_2, \ldots, z_n)^t$ is an intermediate variable vector. The value of $\mathbf{z}$, i.e. $z_1, z_2, \ldots, z_n$ can be determined by forward substitution in the following equations.

$$\begin{array}{lcl} l_{11}z_1 & = & b_1 \\ l_{21}z_1 + l_{22}z_2 & = & b_2 \\ l_{31}z_1 + l_{32}z_2 + l_{33}z_3 & = & b_3 \\ \cdots\cdots\cdots\cdots\cdots\cdots\cdots\cdots & \cdots & \cdots \\ l_{n1}z_1 + l_{n2}z_2 + l_{n3}z_3 + \cdots + l_{nn}z_n & = & b_n. \end{array} \quad (15.26)$$

After determination of $\mathbf{z}$, one can compute the value of $\mathbf{x}$, i.e. $x_1, x_2, \ldots, x_n$ from the equation $\mathbf{Ux} = \mathbf{z}$, i.e. from the following equations by the backward substitution.

$$\begin{array}{rcl} u_{11}x_1 + u_{12}x_2 + u_{13}x_3 + \cdots + u_{1n}x_n & = & z_1 \\ u_{22}x_2 + u_{23}x_3 \cdots + z_{2n}x_n & = & z_2 \\ u_{33}x_3 + u_{23}x_3 \cdots + u_{3n}x_n & = & z_3 \\ \cdots\cdots\cdots\cdots\cdots\cdots & \cdots & \cdots \\ u_{n-1n-1}x_{n-1} + u_{n-1n}x_n & = & z_{n-1} \\ u_{nn}x_n & = & z_n. \end{array} \quad (15.27)$$

When $u_{ii} = 1$, for $i = 1, 2, \ldots, n$, then the method is known as **Crout's decomposition method**. When $l_{ii} = 1$, for $i = 1, 2, \ldots, n$ then the method is known as **Doolittle's method** for decomposition. In particular, when $l_{ii} = u_{ii}$ for $i = 1, 2, \ldots, n$ then the corresponding method is called **Cholesky's decomposition method**.

Procedure to compute L and U

Here, we assume that $u_{ii} = 1$ for $i = 1, 2, \ldots, n$. The values of l_{ij} and u_{ij} are given by $l_{i1} = a_{i1}$, $i = 1, 2, \ldots, n$ and $u_{1j} = \dfrac{a_{1j}}{l_{11}}$, $j = 2, 3, \ldots, n$ and l_{ij} and u_{ij} are given by

$$\begin{array}{rcl} l_{ij} & = & a_{ij} - \displaystyle\sum_{k=1}^{j-1} l_{ik}u_{kj}, \quad i \geq j, \qquad u_{ij} = \dfrac{a_{ij} - \sum_{k=1}^{i-1} l_{ik}u_{kj}}{l_{ii}}, \quad i < j \\ u_{ii} & = & 1, \quad l_{ij} = 0, \quad j > i \quad \text{and} \quad u_{ij} = 0, \quad i > j. \end{array}$$

The following algorithm finds the solution of a system of linear equations using LU-decomposition method. Assume that the principal minors of all order are non-zero.

Algorithm LU-decomposition

Let $\mathbf{Ax} = \mathbf{b}$ be the systems of equations and $\mathbf{A} = [a_{ij}]$, $\mathbf{b} = (b_1, b_2, \ldots, b_n)^t$, $\mathbf{x} = (x_1, x_2, \ldots, x_n)^t$.

/* Assume that the principal minors of all order are non-zero. */

/* Determine the matrices **L** and **U**. */

Step 1. Read the matrix $\mathbf{A} = [a_{ij}], i, j = 1, 2, \ldots, n$ and the right hand vector $\mathbf{b} = (b_1, b_2, \ldots, b_n)^t$.

Step 2. $l_{i1} = a_{i1}$ for $i = 1, 2, \ldots, n$; $u_{1j} = \frac{a_{1j}}{l_{11}}$ for $j = 2, 3, \ldots, n$; $u_{ii} = 1$ for $i = 1, 2, \ldots, n$.

Step 3. For $i, j = 2, 3, \ldots, n$ compute the following

$$l_{ij} = a_{ij} - \sum_{k=1}^{j-1} l_{ik} u_{kj}, \quad i \geq j$$

$$u_{ij} = \Big(a_{ij} - \sum_{k=1}^{i-1} l_{ik} u_{kj}\Big)/l_{ii}, \quad i < j.$$

Step 4. /* Solve the system $\mathbf{Lz} = \mathbf{b}$ by forward substitution. */

$$z_1 = \frac{b_1}{l_{11}}, \quad z_i = \frac{1}{l_{ii}}\Big(b_i - \sum_{j=1}^{i-1} l_{ij} z_j\Big) \text{ for } i = 2, 3, \ldots, n.$$

Step 5. /* Solve the system $\mathbf{Ux} = \mathbf{z}$ by backward substitution. */

Set $x_n = z_n$;

$$x_i = z_i - \sum_{j=i+1}^{n} u_{ij} x_j \text{ for } i = n-1, n-2, \ldots, 1.$$

Print $x_1, x_2, \ldots, x_n$ as solution.

end LU-decomposition

Program 15.21

```
/* Program for LU-decomposition method.
   Solution of a system of equations by LU-decomposition method.
   Assume that all order principal minors are non-zero. */
#include<stdio.h>
void main()
{
 float a[10][10],l[10][10],u[10][10],z[10],x[10],b[10];
 int i,j,k,n;
 printf("\nEnter the size of the coefficient matrix ");
 scanf("%d",&n);
 printf("Enter the elements rowwise ");
 for(i=1;i<=n;i++) for(j=1;j<=n;j++) scanf("%f",&a[i][j]);
 printf("Enter the right hand vector ");
 for(i=1;i<=n;i++) scanf("%f",&b[i]);
 /* computations of L and U matrices */
```

```
  for(i=1;i<=n;i++) l[i][1]=a[i][1];
  for(j=2;j<=n;j++) u[1][j]=a[1][j]/l[1][1];
  for(i=1;i<=n;i++) u[i][i]=1;
  for(i=2;i<=n;i++)
      for(j=2;j<=n;j++)
         if(i>=j){
            l[i][j]=a[i][j];
            for(k=1;k<=j-1;k++) l[i][j]-=l[i][k]*u[k][j];
           }
         else{
            u[i][j]=a[i][j];
            for(k=1;k<=i-1;k++) u[i][j]-=l[i][k]*u[k][j];
            u[i][j]/=l[i][i];
           }
  printf("\nThe lower triangular matrix L\n");
  for(i=1;i<=n;i++){
     for(j=1;j<=i;j++) printf("%f ",l[i][j]);
     printf("\n");
    }
  printf("\nThe upper triangular matrix U\n");
  for(i=1;i<=n;i++){
      for(j=1;j<i;j++) printf("          ");
      for(j=i;j<=n;j++) printf("%f ",u[i][j]);
      printf("\n");
     }
  /* solve Lz=b by forward substitution */
  z[1]=b[1]/l[1][1];
  for(i=2;i<=n;i++){
      z[i]=b[i];
      for(j=1;j<=i-1;j++) z[i]-=l[i][j]*z[j];
      z[i]/=l[i][i];
     }
/* solve Ux=z by backward substitution */
  x[n]=z[n];
  for(i=n-1;i>=1;i--){
     x[i]=z[i];
     for(j=i+1;j<=n;j++) x[i]-=u[i][j]*x[j];
    }
  printf("The solution is ");
  for(i=1;i<=n;i++) printf("%f ",x[i]);
 } /* main */
```

A sample of input/output:

```
Enter the size of the coefficient matrix 3
Enter the elements rowwise
4 2 1
2 5 -2
1 -2 7
Enter the right hand vector
3 4 5

 The lower triangular matrix L
 4.000000
 2.000000 4.000000
 1.000000 -2.500000 5.187500

 The upper triangular matrix U
 1.000000 0.500000 0.250000
          1.000000 -0.625000
                    1.000000
 The solution is -0.192771 1.325301 1.120482
```

15.5.6 Solution of tri-diagonal equations

When the coefficient matrix of a system of equations is of the form

$$\mathbf{A} = \begin{bmatrix} a_1 & b_1 & 0 & 0 & \cdots & 0 & 0 & 0 & 0 \\ c_2 & a_2 & b_2 & 0 & \cdots & 0 & 0 & 0 & 0 \\ 0 & c_3 & a_3 & b_3 & \cdots & 0 & 0 & 0 & 0 \\ \cdots & \cdots & \cdots & \cdots & \cdots & \cdots & \cdots & \cdots & \cdots \\ 0 & 0 & 0 & 0 & \cdots & 0 & c_{n-1} & a_{n-1} & b_{n-1} \\ 0 & 0 & 0 & 0 & \cdots & 0 & 0 & c_n & a_n \end{bmatrix}$$

that is, the main diagonal and the adjacent diagonals on the either side of it consists of only non-zero elements then, the system is called a **tri-diagonal system**. A tri-diagonal system can be solved using LU-decomposition method.

Let $\mathbf{A} = \mathbf{LU}$ where,

$$\mathbf{L} = \begin{bmatrix} \omega_1 & 0 & 0 & \cdots & 0 & 0 & 0 \\ \beta_2 & \omega_2 & 0 & \cdots & 0 & 0 & 0 \\ \cdots & \cdots & \cdots & \cdots & \cdots & \cdots & \cdots \\ 0 & 0 & 0 & \cdots & \beta_{n-1} & \omega_{n-1} & 0 \\ 0 & 0 & 0 & \cdots & 0 & \beta_n & \omega_n \end{bmatrix},$$

$$\mathbf{U} = \begin{bmatrix} 1 & \alpha_1 & 0 & \cdots & 0 & 0 & 0 \\ 0 & 1 & \alpha_2 & \cdots & 0 & 0 & 0 \\ \cdots & \cdots & \cdots & \cdots & \cdots & \cdots & \cdots \\ 0 & 0 & 0 & \cdots & 0 & 1 & \alpha_{n-1} \\ 0 & 0 & 0 & \cdots & 0 & 0 & 1 \end{bmatrix}.$$

By multiplying we get

$$\mathbf{LU} = \begin{bmatrix} \omega_1 & \omega_1\alpha_1 & 0 & \cdots & 0 & 0 & 0 \\ \beta_2 & \alpha_1\beta_2+\omega_2 & \alpha_2\omega_2 & \cdots & 0 & 0 & 0 \\ 0 & \beta_3 & \alpha_2\beta_3+\omega_3 & \cdots & 0 & 0 & 0 \\ \cdots & \cdots & \cdots & \cdots & \cdots & \cdots & \cdots \\ 0 & 0 & 0 & \cdots & 0 & \beta_n & \beta_n\alpha_{n-1}+\omega_n \end{bmatrix}.$$

Comparing the elements of the matrix **LU** with the matrix **A** we get the non-zero elements of **L** and **U** as

$\omega_1 = a_1,\ \alpha_1 = \dfrac{b_1}{\omega_1} = \dfrac{b_1}{a_1},$

$\beta_i = c_i,\ \omega_i = a_i - \alpha_{i-1}\beta_i,\ \alpha_i = \dfrac{b_i}{\omega_i}, i = 2, 3, \ldots, n-1,$

and $\beta_n = c_n,\ \omega_n = a_n - \alpha_{n-1}\beta_n$.

The solution of **Ax**=**b** can be obtained by first solving **Lz**=**b** and then solving **Ux**=**z** by back substitution. The solution of **Lz**=**b** is given by

$$\begin{aligned} z_1 &= \frac{b_1}{\omega_1}, z_i = \frac{b_i - \beta_i z_{i-1}}{\omega_i}, i = 2, 3, \ldots, n, \\ z_1 &= \frac{b_1}{a_1},\ \alpha_1 = \frac{b_1}{a_1},\ \alpha_i = \frac{b_i}{a_i - \alpha_{i-1}c_i},\ i = 2, 3, \ldots, n-1, \\ z_i &= \frac{b_i - c_i z_{i-1}}{a_i - \alpha_{i-1}c_i},\ i = 2, 3, \ldots, n-1 \end{aligned}$$

and the solution of **Ux**=**z** is

$$x_n = z_n,\ x_i = z_i - \alpha_i x_{i+1},\ i = n-1, n-2, \ldots, 1.$$

Therefore, computing α_i, z_i, x_i from above equations the tri-diagonal system of equations can be solved.

A C program to solve tri-diagonal system is given below.

Program 15.22

```
/* Solution of tri-diagonal system of equations */
float x[10]; /* Global declaration */
#include<stdio.h>
void main()
  {
     float a[10],b[10],c[10],d[10];
     int n,i;
     void tridia(float a[],float b[],float c[],float d[],int n);
     printf("Enter the order of the matrix\n");
     scanf("%d",&n);
```

```
    printf("Enter two elements of first row\n");
    scanf("%f%f",&a[1],&b[1]);
    printf("Enter three elements of other rows, line by line\n");
    for(i=2;i<=n-1;i++)
       scanf("%f%f%f",&c[i],&a[i],&b[i]);
    printf("Enter two elements of last row\n");
    scanf("%f%f",&c[n],&a[n]);
    printf("Enter right hand vector\n");
    for(i=1;i<=n;i++) scanf("%f",&d[i]);
    tridia(a,b,c,d,n);  /* function call */
    printf("Solution is\n");
    for(i=1;i<=n;i++) printf("x[%d]=%.3f ",i,x[i]);
  }
/* Function to solve tri-diagonal equations */
void tridia(float a[],float b[],float c[],float d[],int n)
  {
   float y[10],z[10];
   int i;
   z[1]=d[1]/a[1];
   y[1]=b[1]/a[1];
   for(i=2;i<=n-1;i++)
      y[i]=b[i]/(a[i]-y[i-1]*c[i]);
   for(i=2;i<=n;i++)
      z[i]=(d[i]-c[i]*z[i-1])/(a[i]-y[i-1]*c[i]);
   x[n]=z[n];
   for(i=n-1;i>=1;i--)
      x[i]=z[i]-y[i]*x[i+1];
  }
```

A sample of input/output:

```
Enter the order of the matrix
3
Enter two elements of first row
1 3
Enter three elements of other rows, line by line
2 3 9
Enter two elements of last row
1 8
Enter right hand vector
4 14 9
Solution is
x[1]=1.000 x[2]=1.000 x[3]=1.000
```

Complexity: The time complexity is of $O(n)$, where n is number of equations of the system.

15.5.7 Gauss-Seidal iteration method

Let us consider a system of n linear equations

$$\begin{aligned} a_{11}x_1 + a_{12}x_2 + a_{13}x_3 + \cdots + a_{1n}x_n &= b_1 \\ a_{21}x_1 + a_{22}x_2 + a_{23}x_3 + \cdots + a_{2n}x_n &= b_2 \\ \cdots\cdots\cdots\cdots\cdots\cdots\cdots\cdots\cdots & \cdots\ \cdots \\ a_{n1}x_1 + a_{n2}x_2 + a_{n3}x_3 + \cdots + a_{nn}x_n &= b_n \end{aligned}$$

where the diagonal coefficients a_{ii}, $i = 1, 2, \ldots, n$ are all non-zero. If this is not the case, then the above system of equations are rearranged in such a way that the above condition is held.

The ith equation of the above system can be written as $a_{i1}x_1 + a_{i2}x_2 + \cdots + a_{ii-1}x_{i-1} + a_{ii}x_i + a_{ii+1}x_{i+1} + \cdots + a_{in}x_n = b_i$, $i = 1, 2, \ldots, n$,
or

$$x_i = \frac{1}{a_{ii}}\left(b_i - \sum_{j=1}^{i-1} a_{ij}x_j - \sum_{j=i+1}^{n} a_{ij}x_j\right),\ i = 1, 2, \ldots, n.$$

To solve these equations an initial approximation $x_2^{(0)}, \ldots, x_n^{(0)}$ for the variables $x_2, \ldots, x_n$ respectively is considered. Substituting these values, we get the first approximate value of x_1, denoted by $x_1^{(1)}$. By substituting, $x_1^{(1)}$ for x_1 and $x_3^{(0)}, x_4^{(0)}, \ldots, x_n^{(0)}$ for $x_3, x_4, \ldots, x_n$ respectively, we get $x_2^{(1)}$, the first approximate value of x_2. By substituting $x_1^{(1)}, \ldots, x_{i-1}^{(1)}, x_{i+1}^{(0)}, \ldots, x_n^{(0)}$, for $x_1, \ldots, x_{i-1}, x_{i+1}, \ldots, x_n$ respectively, we get $x_i^{(1)}$, and so on.

If $x_i^{(k)}, i = 1, 2, \ldots, n$, be the kth approximate value of x_i, then the $(k+1)$th approximate value of x_i is given by

$$x_i^{(k+1)} = \frac{1}{a_{ii}}\left(b_i - \sum_{j=1}^{i-1} a_{ij}x_j^{(k+1)} - \sum_{j=i+1}^{n} a_{ij}x_j^{(k)}\right),\ k = 0, 1, 2, \ldots.$$

The iteration is repeated until $|x_i^{(k+1)} - x_i^{(k)}| < \varepsilon$ for all $i = 1, 2, \ldots, n$. The following program computes the roots of a system of linear equations by Gauss-Seidal iteration method, assuming that all diagonal elements are non-zero and diagonally dominated.

Program 15.23

```
/* Program for Gauss-Seidal iteration method.
   Solution of a system of linear equations by Gauss-Seidal's
   iteration method. Assume that the coefficient matrix satisfies
   the condition of convergence. Initial roots are taken as 0 for
```

```
   all variables */
#include<stdio.h>
#include<math.h>
void main()
{
 float a[10][10],b[10],x[10],xn[10],epp=0.00001,sum;
 int i,j,n,flag;
 printf("Enter number of variables ");
 scanf("%d",&n);
 printf("\nEnter the coefficients rowwise ");
 for(i=1;i<=n;i++)
    for(j=1;j<=n;j++) scanf("%f",&a[i][j]);
 printf("\nEnter right hand vector ");
 for(i=1;i<=n;i++)
     scanf("%f",&b[i]);
 for(i=1;i<=n;i++) x[i]=0; /* initialize */
 /* Testing of diagonal dominance may be included here
     from the program of Gauss-Seidal's method */
 for(i=1;i<=n;i++) printf("   x%d    ",i); printf("\n");
 do{
 for(i=1;i<=n;i++){
   sum=b[i];
   for(j=1;j<=n;j++){
       if(j<i)
         sum-=a[i][j]*xn[j];
       else if(j>i)
         sum-=a[i][j]*x[j];
       xn[i]=sum/a[i][i];
     }
   }
  for(i=1;i<=n;i++) printf("%8.5f ",xn[i]); printf("\n");
  flag=0; /* indicates |x[i]-xn[i]|<epp for all i */
  for(i=1;i<=n;i++)
     if(fabs(x[i]-xn[i])>epp) flag=1;
  if(flag==1) for(i=1;i<=n;i++) x[i]=xn[i]; /* reset x[i] */
  }while(flag==1);
  printf("Solution is \n");
  for(i=1;i<=n;i++) printf("%8.5f ",xn[i]);
 } /* main */
```

A sample of input/output:

```
Enter number of variables 5
Enter the coefficients rowwise
```

```
10 2 0 2 3
-2 13 4 5 2
0 2 15 6 2
2 3 -4 12 1
2 3 -1 2 14
Enter right hand vector
12 -8 13 14 15

   x1        x2        x3        x4        x5
 1.20000  -0.43077  0.92410  1.38239  0.86083
 0.75143  -1.44824  0.39203  1.46243  1.09350
 0.86911  -1.33301  0.31363  1.36848  1.05982
 0.87496  -1.26666  0.34685  1.36481  1.04767
 0.86607  -1.27497  0.35105  1.37078  1.05016
 0.86579  -1.27899  0.34887  1.37089  1.05089
 0.86635  -1.27838  0.34864  1.37051  1.05072
 0.86636  -1.27814  0.34879  1.37051  1.05068
 0.86632  -1.27818  0.34880  1.37054  1.05069
 0.86632  -1.27820  0.34879  1.37053  1.05069
 0.86633  -1.27820  0.34879  1.37053  1.05069

Solution is
0.86633 -1.27820 0.34879 1.37053 1.05069
```

Complexity: Time complexity is of $O(n^2k)$, where k is the number of iterations required to achieve the desired accuracy.

Conditions for convergent: The above method surely converges, if the coefficient matrix is diagonally dominant. The sufficient condition of convergence is either

$$\sum_{j=1,j\neq i}^{n} |a_{ij}| < |a_{ii}|, i = 1, 2, \ldots, n; \text{or}, \sum_{i=1,j\neq i}^{n} |a_{ij}| < |a_{jj}|, j = 1, 2, \ldots, n.$$

15.6 Ordinary Differential Equations

First order linear differential equations

15.6.1 Euler's method

Euler's method (or first order **Adams-Bashforth** method) is a simple but crude method to solve the differential equation of the form

$$\frac{dy}{dx} = f(x, y), \text{with } y(x_0) = y_0.$$

For a small increment h in x we have

$$\begin{aligned} y_1 = y(x_1) = y(x_0 + h) &= y(x_0) + h\left(\frac{dy}{dx}\right)_{(x_0,y_0)} + \cdots \\ &= y_0 + hf(x_0, y_0) \end{aligned}$$

(neglecting square and higher order terms of h).
Similarly,

$$\begin{aligned} y_2 &= y_1 + hf(x_1, y_1) \\ y_3 &= y_2 + hf(x_2, y_2) \\ &\vdots \\ y_{n+1} &= y_n + hf(x_n, y_n). \end{aligned}$$

For a given h, y_1 is computed using initial condition, then y_2 is computed using x_1 and y_1, and so on. This method is an **explicit method**, as by using y_i, h and $f(x_i, y_i)$, y_{i+1} can be calculated directly.

Merits and Demerits: It is a very slow method since h has to be very small to get the result of desired accuracy. A large h gives inaccurate result. But by using this method one can guess the value of y using fewer calculations.

Error: The local truncation error is $O(h^2)$.

The following program solves the differential equation $\frac{dy}{dx} = x^2 + y$ with the initial condition $x_0 = 0$ and $y_0 = 1$.

Program 15.24

```
/* Euler's method to solve a first order linear initial value
   problem. The equation is of the form dy/dx=f(x,y) with y(x0)=y0.
   f(x,y), x0, y0 to be changed accordingly. */
#include<stdio.h>
#include<math.h>
#define  f(x,y) (x)*(x)+(y)
void main()
  {
    float x,y,h,xlast,t;
    printf("Enter initial values of x and y\n");
    scanf("%f%f",&x,&y);
    printf("Enter the value of h and last value of x\n");
    scanf("%f%f",&h,&xlast);
    printf("    x           y\n");
    while(x<=xlast){
       printf(" %.3f   %.5f\n",x,y);
       t=f(x,y);
       y=y+h*t;
       x+=h;
    };
  }
```

A sample of input/output:

```
Enter initial values of x and y
0 1
Enter the value of h and last value of x
.1 1.0

   x         y
0.000    1.00000
0.100    1.10000
0.200    1.21100
0.300    1.33610
0.400    1.47871
0.500    1.64258
0.600    1.83184
0.700    2.05102
0.800    2.30513
0.900    2.59964
```

15.6.2 Modified Euler's method

Solution obtained from Euler's method can be modified to get more accurate value much quickly. Thus, starting from the crude approximation

$$y_{i+1}^{(0)} = y_i + hf(x_i, y_i)$$

the following iterative scheme is developed

$$y_{i+1}^{(k+1)} = y_i + \frac{h}{2}\Big[f(x_i, y_i) + f(x_{i+1}, y_{i+1}^{(k)})\Big], k = 0, 1, 2, \dots$$

The iterations will terminate when

$$|y_{i+1}^{(k+1)} - y_{i+1}^{(k)}| < \varepsilon,$$

where ε is the desired accuracy. Practically, the iterations converge quickly for a sufficiently small value of h.

This method is also known as Euler-Cauchy method.

Error: The local truncation error is $O(h^3)$.

Program 15.25

```
/* Program for Modified Euler method.
   Solution of a differential equation of the form y'=f(x,y),
   y(x0)=y0 by Modified Euler's method. */
#include<stdio.h>
#include<math.h>
```

```
void main()
{
 float x0,y0,xn,h,x,y;/* x0, xn are initial and final values of x*/
   /* y0 is initial value of y, h is the step length */
 float eps=1e-5; /* the error tolerance */
 float yc,yp,f1;
 float f(float x, float y);
 printf("Enter the initial (x0) and final (xn) values of x ");
 scanf("%f %f",&x0,&xn);
 printf("Enter initial value of y ");
 scanf("%f",&y0);
 printf("Enter step length h ");
 scanf("%f",&h);
 printf(" x-value         y-value\n");
 y=y0;
 for(x=x0;x<xn;x+=h){
      f1=f(x,y);
      yc=y+h*f1; /* evaluated by Euler's method */
      do{
        yp=yc;
        yc=y+h*(f1+f(x+h,yp))/2; /*modified Euler's method*/
      }while(fabs(yp-yc)>eps);
      y=yc;
      printf("%f    %f\n",x+h,y);
   }
} /* main */
/* Definition of the function f(x,y) */
float f(float x, float y)
 {
   return(x*x-2*y+1);
 }
```

A sample of input/output:

```
Enter the initial (x0) and final (xn) values of x
0 .5
Enter initial value of y 1
Enter step length h 0.1

 x-value    y-value
0.100000   0.909546
0.200000   0.837355
0.300000   0.781926
0.400000   0.742029
```

```
0.500000    0.716660
```

15.6.3 Fourth order Runge-Kutta method

This method is used to solve differential equations of the form $\frac{dy}{dx} = f(x, y)$, with $y(x_0) = y_0$. The value of y_{i+1}, for given x_i, y_i, is calculated from the formula.

$$y_{i+1} = y_i + \frac{k_1 + 2k_2 + 2k_3 + k_4}{6}$$

where
$k_1 = hf(x_i, y_i)$, $k_2 = hf(x_i + h/2, y_i + k_1/2)$,
$k_3 = hf(x_i + h/2, y_i + k_2/2)$, $k_4 = hf(x_i + h, y_i + k_3), i = 0, 1, 2, \ldots$.

Merits and Demerits: This method is time consuming because it requires several evaluations of first order derivatives, i.e. the value of the function f. But, the method is stable and self-starting.

This method can be used for solving a system of first order differential equations and equations of higher order by converting to first order equations.

Runge-Kutta methods is also used for finding the starting values of Predictor-Corrector methods.

Error: The local truncation error is $O(h^5)$.

Program 15.26

```
/* Program for fourth order Runge-Kutta method.
   Solution of a differential equation of the form y'=f(x,y),
   y(x0)=y0 by fourth order Runge-Kutta method. */
#include<stdio.h>
#include<math.h>
void main()
{
 float x0,y0,xn,h,x,y,k1,k2,k3,k4;
 float f(float x, float y);
 printf("Enter the initial values of x and y ");
 scanf("%f %f",&x0,&y0);
 printf("Enter last value of x ");
 scanf("%f",&xn);
 printf("Enter step length h ");
 scanf("%f",&h);
 y=y0;
 printf(" x-value    y-value\n");
 for(x=x0;x<xn;x+=h){
    k1=h*f(x,y);              k2=h*f(x+h/2,y+k1/2);
    k3=h*f(x+h/2,y+k2/2);  k4=h*f(x+h,y+k3);
```

```
    y=y+(k1+2*(k2+k3)+k4)/6;
    printf("%f   %f\n",x+h,y);
  }
} /* main */
/* Definition of the function f(x,y) */
float f(float x, float y)
 {
   return(x*x-y*y+y);
 }
```

A sample of input/output:

```
Enter the initial values of x and y 0 2
Enter last value of x 0.5
Enter step length h 0.1
 x-value     y-value
0.100000   1.826528
0.200000   1.695464
0.300000   1.595978
0.400000   1.521567
0.500000   1.468221
```

15.6.4 Fourth order Runge-Kutta method for a pair of equations

Let the pair of first order differential equations be $\frac{dy}{dx} = f(x, y, z)$ and $\frac{dz}{dx} = g(x, y, z)$ with $y(x_0) = y_0$ and $z(x_0) = z_0$.

For computing y_{i+1} and z_{i+1} from y_i and z_i the following formulae are used

$$y_{i+1} = y_i + \frac{k_1 + 2k_2 + 2k_3 + k_4}{6}, z_{i+1} = z_i + \frac{l_1 + 2l_2 + 2l_3 + l_4}{6}, i = 0, 1, 2, \ldots$$

where,

$$\begin{aligned}
k_1 &= hf(x_i, y_i, z_i), & l_1 &= hg(x_i, y_i, z_i),\\
k_2 &= hf(x_i + h/2, y_i + k_1/2, z_i + l_1/2), & l_2 &= hg(x_i + h/2, y_i + k_1/2, z_i + l_1/2),\\
k_3 &= hf(x_i + h/2, y_i + k_2/2, z_i + l_2/2), & l_3 &= hg(x_i + h/2, y_i + k_2/2, z_i + l_2/2),\\
k_4 &= hf(x_i + h, y_i + k_3, z_i + l_3), & l_4 &= hg(x_i + h, y_i + k_3, z_i + l_3),\\
x_{i+1} &= x_i + h.
\end{aligned}$$

Error: The local truncation error is $O(h^5)$.

Program 15.27

```
/* Program for Runge-Kutta method (for Pair of Equations).
   Solution of differential equations of the form y'=f(x,y,z),
   z'=g(x,y,z) with x=x0, y(x0)=y0 and z(x0)=z0 by fourth order
   Runge-Kutta method.
```

```
   Here the equations are taken as y'=y+2z, z'=3y+2z with
   y(0)=6, z(0)=4. */
#include<stdio.h>
#include<math.h>
void main()
{
 float x0,y0,z0,xn,h,x,y,z,k1,k2,k3,k4,l1,l2,l3,l4;
 float f(float x, float y, float z);
 float g(float x, float y, float z);
 printf("Enter the initial values of x, y and z ");
 scanf("%f %f %f",&x0,&y0,&z0);
 printf("Enter last value of x ");
 scanf("%f",&xn);
 printf("Enter step length h ");
 scanf("%f",&h);
 y=y0;
 z=z0;
 printf("x-value    y-value    z-value\n");
 for(x=x0;x<xn;x+=h){
     k1=h*f(x,y,z);
     l1=h*g(x,y,z);
     k2=h*f(x+h/2,y+k1/2,z+l1/2);
     l2=h*g(x+h/2,y+k1/2,z+l1/2);
     k3=h*f(x+h/2,y+k2/2,z+l2/2);
     l3=h*g(x+h/2,y+k2/2,z+l2/2);
     k4=h*f(x+h,y+k3,z+l3);
     l4=h*g(x+h,y+k3,z+l3);
     y=y+(k1+2*(k2+k3)+k4)/6;
     z=z+(l1+2*(l2+l3)+l4)/6;
     printf("%f   %f   %f\n",x+h,y,z);
   }
} /* main */
/* Definition of the function f(x,y,z) */
 float f(float x, float y, float z)
  {
   return(y+2*z);
  }
/* Definition of the function g(x,y,z) */
 float g(float x, float y, float z)
  {
   return(3*y+2*z);
  }
```

A sample of input/output:

```
Enter the initial values of x, y and z
0 6 4
Enter last value of x 0.4
Enter step length h 0.1
 x-value     y-value     z-value
 0.100000    7.776608    7.140725
 0.200000    10.538535    11.714149
 0.300000    14.759665    18.435406
 0.400000    21.147917    28.370275
```

15.6.5 Milne's predictor-corrector method

This method is used to solve the equations of the form $\frac{dy}{dx} = f(x, y)$, for given $y(x_0) = y_0, y(x_1) = y_1, y(x_2) = y_2$ and $y(x_3) = y_3$.

The initial values, y_0, y_1, y_2, y_3, of y, are obtained from self-starting method, e.g. Euler, Runge-Kutta or Taylor series method, etc.

The **predictor** formula

$$y_{i+4,p} = y_i + \frac{4h}{3}\Big(2f_{i+3} - f_{i+2} + 2f_{i+1}\Big)$$

is a multistep formula and the **corrector** formula

$$y_{i+4,c}^{(k+1)} = y_{i+2} + \frac{h}{3}\Big(f_{i+2} + 4f_{i+3} + f_{i+4,c}^{(k)}\Big)$$

where $f_i = f(x_i, y_i), f_{i,c}^{(k)} = f(x_i, y_{i,c}^{(k)})$ and $f_{i,c}^{(0)} = f(x_i, y_{i,p}), x_{i+1} = x_i + h, i = 0, 1, \ldots$.

If $\left|y_{i,c}^{(k+1)} - y_{i,c}^{(k)}\right| < \varepsilon$, then the final value of y_i is $y_{i,c}^{(k+1)}$, where ε is the error tolerance.

Error: The local truncation error is $O(h^5)$.

Program 15.28

```c
 /* Program for Milne Predictor-Corrector method.
    Solution of a differential equation of the form y'=f(x,y),
    y(x0)=y0 by Milne Predictor-Corrector method.
    Here Runge-Kutta 4th order method is used to find the values
    of y1, y2 and y3.
    Here the equation is taken as y'=x*y+y*y with y(0)=1.
 */
#include<stdio.h>
#include<math.h>
void main()
 {
  float x0,y0,xn,h,y1,y2,y3,yc,yp;
```

```
    /* x0, xn are initial and final values of x */
    /* y0,y1,y2,y3 are starting values of y,
       h is the step length */
  float eps=1e-5; /* the error tolerance */
  float x1,x2,x3,x4,f0,f1,f2,f3,yold;
  float f(float x, float y);
  float rk4(float x,float y,float h);
  printf("Enter the initial values of x and y ");
  scanf("%f %f",&x0,&y0);
  printf("Enter last value of x ");
  scanf("%f",&xn);
  printf("Enter step length h ");
  scanf("%f",&h);
  printf(" x-value   y-value\n");
 /* Initial values of y are computed using 4th order
                                     Runge-Kutta method */
  x1=x0+h;  x2=x1+h;  x3=x2+h;
  y1=rk4(x0,y0,h);  y2=rk4(x1,y1,h);  y3=rk4(x2,y2,h);
  f1=f(x1,y1); f2=f(x2,y2); f3=f(x3,y3);
  for(x4=x3+h;x4<=xn;x4+=h){
      yp=y0+4*h*(2*f1-f2+2*f3)/3;  /* predictor formula */
      yold=yp;
      yc=yp;
      do{
        yold=yc;
        yc=y2+h*(f2+4*f3+f(x4,yold))/3; /* corrector formula */
      }while((yc-yold)>eps);
      printf("%8.5f  %8.5f\n",x4,yc);
      y0=y1;  y1=y2;  y2=y3;  y3=yc;
      f1=f2;  f2=f3;  f3=f(x4,yc);
    }
 } /* main */
/* Definition of the function f(x,y) */
float f(float x, float y)
  {
    return(x*y+y*y);
  }
/* The fourth order Runge-Kutta method */
float rk4(float x,float y,float h)
  {
    float k1,k2,k3,k4;
    k1=h*f(x,y);             k2=h*f(x+h/2,y+k1/2);
```

```
    k3=h*f(x+h/2,y+k2/2);  k4=h*f(x+h,y+k3);
    y=y+(k1+2*(k2+k3)+k4)/6;
    return (y);
  }
```

A sample of input/output:

```
Enter the initial values of x and y 0 1
Enter last value of x 0.5
Enter step length h 0.05

  x-value    y-value
  0.20000    1.27740
  0.25000    1.38050
  0.30000    1.50414
  0.35000    1.65418
  0.40000    1.83901
  0.45000    2.07095
```

Merits and Demerits: This method is widely used. In this method, there is a scope to improve the value of y by repeated use of corrector formula. So, it gives more accurate results. But it requires the starting values y_0, y_1, y_2, y_3.

Second order linear differential equations

15.6.6 Fourth order Runge-Kutta method for IVPs

Consider a second order linear initial value problem (IVP) of the form

$$y'' + p(x)y' + q(x)y = r(x)$$

with initial conditions $y(x_0) = y_0$ and $y'(x_0) = z_0$. The basic idea of this method is to convert a given second order equation to a pair of first order equations by substituting $\frac{dy}{dx} = z$, where z is a new variable.

Let $\frac{dy}{dx} = z$. The given equation becomes

$$\frac{dz}{dx} + p(x)z + q(x)y = r(x)$$

$$\text{or,}\quad \frac{dz}{dx} = r(x) - p(x)z - q(x)y = g(x, y, z) \quad \text{(say).}$$

The initial values of x, y, z become x_0, y_0 and z_0 respectively. The values of y and z are calculated using the following formulae

$$y_{i+1} = y_i + \frac{yk_1 + 2(yk_2 + yk_3) + yk_4}{6}, \qquad z_{i+1} = z_i + \frac{zk_1 + 2(zk_2 + zk_3) + zk_4}{6},$$

where,

$yk_1 = hz_i, \quad zk_1 = hg(x_i, y_i, z_i),$
$yk_2 = h(z_i + zk_1/2), \quad zk_2 = hg(x_i + h/2, y_i + yk_1/2, z_i + zk_1/2),$
$yk_3 = h(z_i + zk_2/2), \quad zk_3 = hg(x_i + h/2, y_i + yk_2/2, z_i + zk_2/2),$
$yk_4 = h(z_i + zk_3), \quad zk_4 = hg(x_i + h, y_i + yk_3, z_i + zk_3)$
and $x_{i+1} = x_i + h, i = 0, 1, 2, \ldots.$

Consider the second order IVP, $y'' + \frac{1}{x}y' + y = 0$ with initial conditions $y(1) = 0.77$, $y'(1) = -0.44$. For this function $p(x) = 1/x$, $q(x) = 1, r(x) = 0$. Solution of this problem is obtained by the following program.

Program 15.29

```
/* Solution of second order linear differential equation of the
   form y''+p(x) y'+q(x) y=r(x) with initial condition
   x=x0, y=y0, y'=z0 by 4th order Runge-Kutta method.
   Values of p(x), q(x) and r(x) to be changed accordingly. */
#include<stdio.h>
#include<math.h>
void main()
  {
    float x,y,z,h,xl,yk1,zk1,yk2,zk2,yk3,zk3,yk4,zk4;
    float p(float );
    float q(float );
    float r(float );
    float g(float,float,float);
    printf("Enter the values of x,y,z,h, last value of x\n");
    scanf("%f%f%f%f%f",&x,&y,&z,&h,&xl);
    printf("   x           y                 z\n");
    do{
      yk1=h*z;           zk1=h*g(x,y,z);
      yk2=h*(z+zk1/2);   zk2=h*g(x+h/2,y+yk1/2,z+zk1/2);
      yk3=h*(z+zk2/2);   zk3=h*g(x+h/2,y+yk2/2,z+zk2/2);
      yk4=h*(x+h);       zk4=h*g(x+h,y+yk3,z+zk3);
      y+=(yk1+2*yk2+2*yk3+yk4)/6.;
      z+=(zk1+2*zk2+2*zk3+zk4)/6.;
      x+=h;
      printf(" %.3f      %.5f      %.5f\n",x,y,z);
    }while(x<=xl);
  }
/* Definition of the function p(x) */
float p(float x)
  {
    return(1.0/x); /* may be changed */
  }
```

```
/* Definition of the function q(x) */
float q(float x)
  {
    return(1.0); /* may be changed */
  }
/* Definition of the function r(x) */
float r(float x)
  {
    return(0.0); /* may be changed */
  }
/* Definition of the function g(x) */
float g(float x,float y,float z)
  {
    float g1;
    g1=r(x)-p(x)*z-q(x)*y;
    return(g1);
  }
```

A sample of input/output:

```
Enter the values of x,y,z,h, last value of x
1 .77 -.44 .1 1.5

   x          y           z
 1.100     0.75059    -0.47131
 1.200     0.73028    -0.50163
 1.300     0.70913    -0.53077
 1.400     0.68727    -0.55860
 1.500     0.66480    -0.58502
```

15.6.7 Finite difference method

Second order initial value problems (IVPs)

Consider the second order IVP of the form

$$y'' + p(x)y' + q(x)y = r(x)$$

with the preconditions $y(x_0) = y_0, y'(x_0) = y'_0$. We have

$$y'_i = \frac{y_{i+1} - y_{i-1}}{2h} - \frac{h^2}{6}y'''(\eta_i) \qquad \text{and} \qquad y''_i = \frac{y_{i+1} - 2y_i + y_{i-1}}{h^2} - \frac{h^2}{12}y^{iv}(\xi_i)$$

where $x_{i-1} < \eta_i, \xi_i < x_{i+1}$.

Using these values (neglecting higher powers of h), the given equation becomes

$$\frac{y_{i+1} - 2y_i + y_{i-1}}{h^2} + p(x_i)\frac{y_{i+1} - y_{i-1}}{2h} + q(x_i)y_i = r(x_i)$$

or, $y_{i-1}[2 - hp(x_i)] + y_i[2h^2 q(x_i) - 4] + y_{i+1}[2 + hp(x_i)] = 2h^2 r(x_i)$

$$\text{or,} \quad C_i y_{i-1} + A_i y_i + B_i y_{i+1} = D_i \tag{15.28}$$

where

$$C_i = 2 - hp(x_i), \qquad A_i = 2h^2 q(x_i) - 4,$$
$$B_i = 2 + hp(x_i) \quad \text{and} \quad D_i = 2h^2 r(x_i).$$

Again, $y'_0 = \dfrac{y_1 - y_{-1}}{2h}$ or,

$$y_{-1} = y_1 - 2hy'_0. \tag{15.29}$$

From (15.28),

$$C_0 y_{-1} + A_0 y_0 + B_0 y_1 = D_0. \tag{15.30}$$

Eliminating y_{-1} between (15.29) and (15.30) we get the value of y_1 as

$$y_1 = \frac{D_0 - A_0 y_0 + 2hC_0 y'_0}{C_0 + B_0}.$$

All other values of y are computed from the relation

$$y_{i+1} = \frac{D_i - C_i y_{i-1} - A_i y_i}{B_i}, x_{i+1} = x_i + h, i = 1, 2, \ldots$$

The following program solves the differential equation $y'' - y = 0$ with initial condition $x_0 = 0, y_0 = 0, y'_0 = 1$.

Program 15.30

```
/* Finite difference method to solve second order initial value
   problem of the form y''+p(x)y'+q(x)y=r(x) with y(x0)=y0 and
   y'(x0)=yd. The values of p, q, r are to be changed accordingly.*/
#include<stdio.h>
#include<math.h>
void main()
  {
    float x0,y0,yd,h,xl,xj,x1,yj,y1;
    float p(float);
    float q(float);
    float r(float);
    float a(float,float);
    float b(float,float);
    float c(float,float);
    float d(float,float);
    printf("Enter initial values x0,y0,yd and h, last value of x\n");
```

```
    scanf("%f%f%f%f%f",&x0,&y0,&yd,&h,&xl);
    x1=x0+h;
    y1=(d(x0,h)-a(x0,h)*y0+2*h*c(x0,h)*yd)/(c(x0,h)+b(x0,h));
    printf("   x         y\n");
    printf(" %6.3f  %9.6f\n",x1,y1);
    x1+=h;
    for(xj=x1;xj<=xl;xj+=h)
      {
        yj=(d(xj,h)-c(xj,h)*y0-a(xj,h)*y1)/b(xj,h);
        printf(" %6.3f  %9.6f\n",xj,yj);
        y0=y1;
        y1=yj;
      }
  } /* main */
/* Definition of the functions p,q,r,a,b,c,d */
float p(float x)
  {
    return (0.0);  /* may be changed */
  }
float q(float x)
  {
    return (-1.0);  /* may be changed */
  }
float r(float x)
  {
    return (0.0);  /* may be changed */
  }
float a(float x,float h)
  {
    float t;
    t=-4+2*q(x)*h*h;
    return (t);
  }
float b(float x,float h)
  {
    float t;
    t=2+p(x)*h;
    return (t);
  }
float c(float x,float h)
  {
    float t;
```

```
    t=2-p(x)*h;
    return (t);
  }
float d(float x,float h)
  {
    float t;
    t=2*r(x)*h*h;
    return (t);
  }
```

A sample of input/output:

```
Enter initial values x0,y0,yd and h, last value of x
0 0 1 .1 .8

     x        y
   0.100    0.100000
   0.200    0.201000
   0.300    0.304010
   0.400    0.410060
   0.500    0.520211
   0.600    0.635564
   0.700    0.757272
   0.800    0.886553
   0.900    1.024700
```

Error: Local truncation error is $O(h^4)$.

Second order boundary value problems (BVPs)

Consider the linear second order differential equation

$$y'' + p(x)y' + q(x)y = r(x), a < x < b$$

with boundary conditions $y(a) = \gamma_1$ and $y(b) = \gamma_2$. Let $y_i = y(x_i), x_i = x_{i-1} + h, i = 1, 2, \ldots, n$, where n represents the number of subintervals of $[a, b]$. The Taylor's series gives

$$y_i' = \frac{y_{i+1} - y_{i-1}}{2h} - \frac{h^2}{6}y'''(\eta_i) \qquad \text{and} \qquad y_i'' = \frac{y_{i+1} - 2y_i + y_{i-1}}{h^2} - \frac{h^2}{12}y^{iv}(\xi_i),$$

where $x_{i-1} < \eta_i, \xi_i < x_{i+1}$.

Neglecting $O(h^2)$ terms and substituting the values of y' and y'' in the given equation we obtain

$$\frac{y_{i+1} - 2y_i + y_{i-1}}{h^2} + p(x_i)\frac{y_{i+1} - y_{i-1}}{2h} + q(x_i)y_i = r(x_i)$$

or, $y_{i-1}[2 - hp(x_i)] + y_i[2h^2q(x_i) - 4] + y_{i+1}[2 + hp(x_i)] = 2h^2r(x_i)$

This equation can be written as

$$C_i y_{i-1} + A_i y_i + B_i y_{i+1} = D_i \tag{15.31}$$

where

$$C_i = 2 - hp(x_i), \qquad A_i = 2h^2 q(x_i) - 4,$$
$$B_i = 2 + hp(x_i) \quad \text{and} \quad D_i = 2h^2 r(x_i), \;\; i = 1, 2, \ldots, n.$$

The boundary conditions then are $y_0 = \gamma_1$ and $y_{n+1} = \gamma_2$.
For $i = 1$, (15.31) becomes $C_1 y_0 + A_1 y_1 + B_1 y_2 = D_1$,
or, $A_1 y_1 + B_1 y_2 = D_1 - C_1\gamma_1$ (as $y_0 = \gamma_1$) and
for $i = n$, $C_n y_{n-1} + A_n y_n + B_n y_{n+1} = D_n$,
or, $C_n y_{n-1} + A_n y_n = D_n - B_n \gamma_2$ (as $y_{n+1} = \gamma_2$).

Therefore, (15.31) becomes in matrix notation **Ay=b**, where **y**$= [y_1, y_2, \ldots, y_n]^T$, **b**$=2h^2[r(x_1) - C_1\gamma_1/2h^2, r(x_2), \ldots, r(x_{n-1}), r(x_n) - B_n\gamma_2/2h^2]^T$ and

$$\mathbf{A} = \begin{bmatrix} A_1 & B_1 & 0 & 0 & 0 & 0 \\ C_2 & A_2 & B_2 & 0 & 0 & 0 \\ \vdots & & \vdots & & & \vdots \\ 0 & 0 & 0 & C_{n-1} & A_{n-1} & B_{n-1} \\ 0 & 0 & 0 & 0 & C_n & A_n \end{bmatrix}.$$

This system of equations give the finite difference solution of the differential equation. It may be noted that the above system of equations is in tri-diagonal form and these equations can be solved by using the function `tridia`.

The following program solves the equation $y'' + y' - y = x$ with boundary condition $y(0) = 1$, $y(1) = 1$.

Program 15.31

```
/* Finite difference method to solve second order boundary
   value problem. The equation is of the form y''+p(x)y'+q(x)y=r(x)
   with y(xa)=ya and y(xb)=yb. p(x), q(x), r(x) may be changed. */
#include<stdio.h>
#include<math.h>
float u[10];
void main()
  {
    float a[10],b[10],c[10],d[10];
    float x,xa,ya,xb,yb,h;
    void tridia(float a[],float b[],float c[],float d[],int n);
    int i,n;
    float p(float);
    float q(float);
```

```
    float r(float);
    printf("Enter boundary values of x and y (xa,ya,xb,yb) and n\n");
    scanf("%f%f%f%f%d",&xa,&ya,&xb,&yb,&n);
    h=(xb-xa)/(n+1);
    x=xa;   u[0]=ya;
    for(i=1;i<=n;i++){
        x+=h;
        c[i]=2-h*p(x);    a[i]=-4+2*h*h*q(x);
        b[i]=2+h*p(x);   d[i]=2*h*h*r(x);
      }
    d[1]=d[1]-c[1]*ya; /* redefine d[1] and d[n] */
    d[n]=d[n]-b[n]*yb; /* solution of tri-diagonal system */
    tridia(a,b,c,d,n);
    x=xa;
    printf("   x          y\n");
    for(i=0;i<=n;i++)
        printf(" %6.3f  %8.4f\n",x,u[i]);
        x+=h;
      }
  }
/* Function to solve tri-diagonal equations */
void tridia(float a[],float b[],float c[],float d[],int n)
  {
    int i,j;
    float y[10],z[10];
    z[1]=d[1]/a[1];
    y[1]=b[1]/a[1];
    for(i=2;i<=n-1;i++)
      y[i]=b[i]/(a[i]-y[i-1]*c[i]);
    for(i=2;i<=n;i++)
      z[i]=(d[i]-c[i]*z[i-1])/(a[i]-y[i-1]*c[i]);
    u[n]=z[n];
    for(j=n-1;j>=1;j--)
      u[j]=z[j]-y[j]*u[j+1];
  }
/* Definition of p, q, r */
float p(float x)
  {
    return(1.0); /* may be changed */
  }
float q(float x)
  {
```

```
    return(-1.0);  /* may be changed */
  }
float r(float x)
  {
    return(x);  /* may be changed */
  }
```

A sample of input/output:

```
Enter boundary values of x and y (xa,ya,xb,yb) and n
0 1 1 1 4

     X        Y
   0.000    1.0000
   0.200    0.8884
   0.400    0.8367
   0.600    0.8393
   0.800    0.8938
```

Error: The local truncation error is $O(h^4)$.

15.7 Eigenvalue of a Matrix

The eigenvalues of a matrix **A** are the roots of the characteristic equation $det(\mathbf{A} - \lambda\mathbf{I}) = 0$, where λ is the variable. That is, the values of λ are the eigenvalues of **A**. The direct expansion of $det(\mathbf{A} - \lambda\mathbf{I})$ is very complicated, due to the presence of the variable λ. Second complicated step is the determination of roots of the characteristic equation. Several efficient methods are developed to find eigenvalues for different types of matrices.

Leverrier and Faddeev developed a method to construct the characteristic equation. This method generates all the coefficients of the characteristic equation.

15.7.1 Characteristic polynomial

Let $det(\mathbf{A} - \lambda\mathbf{I}) = \lambda^n + c_1\lambda^{n-1} + c_2\lambda^{n-2} + \cdots + c_n$ be the characteristic polynomial. The constants $c_1, c_2, \ldots, c_n$ are the coefficients of the polynomial.

The Leverrier method was modified by Faddeev by generating a sequence of matrices $\mathbf{B_1}, \mathbf{B_2}, \ldots, \mathbf{B_n}$ starting from **A** as shown below.

$$\begin{array}{lllll}
\mathbf{B_1} = \mathbf{A}, & d_1 = Tr.\,\mathbf{B_1}, & \mathbf{D_1} = \mathbf{B_1} - d_1\mathbf{I} \\
\mathbf{B_2} = \mathbf{AD_1}, & d_2 = \frac{1}{2}\,Tr.\,\mathbf{B_2}, & \mathbf{D_2} = \mathbf{B_2} - d_2\mathbf{I} \\
\mathbf{B_3} = \mathbf{AD_2}, & d_3 = \frac{1}{3}\,Tr.\,\mathbf{B_3}, & \mathbf{D_3} = \mathbf{B_3} - d_3\mathbf{I} \\
\cdots\ \cdots\ \cdots\cdots & \cdots\ \cdots\cdots & \cdots\cdots\ \cdots\cdots\cdots \\
\mathbf{B_{n-1}} = \mathbf{AD_{n-2}}, & d_{n-1} = \frac{1}{n-1}\,Tr.\,\mathbf{B_{n-1}}, & \mathbf{D_{n-1}} = \mathbf{B_{n-1}} - d_{n-1}\mathbf{I} \\
\mathbf{B_n} = \mathbf{AD_{n-1}}, & d_n = \frac{1}{n}\,Tr.\,\mathbf{B_n}, & \mathbf{D_n} = \mathbf{B_n} - d_n\mathbf{I}
\end{array} \tag{15.32}$$

The coefficients of the characteristic polynomial are given by

$$c_1 = -d_1, c_2 = -d_2, \ldots, c_n = -d_n.$$

It can be verified that $\mathbf{D_n} = \mathbf{0}$.

The following algorithm determines the characteristic equation $\lambda^n + c_1\lambda^{n-1} + \cdots + c_{n-1}\lambda + c_n = 0$ of a square matrix $\mathbf{A}$.

Algorithm Leverrier-Faddeev

Step 1: Read the matrix $\mathbf{A} = [a_{ij}], i, j = 1, 2, \ldots, n$.

Step 2: Set $\mathbf{B_1} = \mathbf{A}, d_1 = \sum_{i=1}^{n} a_{ii}$.

Step 3: for $i = 2, 3, \ldots, n$ do
Compute
(a) $\mathbf{B_i} = \mathbf{A}(\mathbf{B_{i-1}} - d_{i-1}\mathbf{I})$
(b) $d_i = \frac{1}{i}$ (sum of the diagonal elements of $\mathbf{B_i}$)

Step 4: Compute $c_i = -d_i$ for $i = 1, 2, \ldots, n$.
/* c_i's are the coefficients of the polynomial. */

end Leverrier-Faddeev.

Program 15.32

```
/* This program finds the characteristic polynomial of
   a square matrix, from which we can determine all the
   eigenvalues of the matrix. */
#include<stdio.h>
#include<math.h>
void main()
{
 int n,i,j,k,l;
 float a[10][10],b[10][10],c[10][10],d[11];
 printf("Enter the size of the matrix ");
 scanf("%d",&n);
 printf("Enter the elements row wise ");
 for(i=1;i<=n;i++) for(j=1;j<=n;j++) scanf("%f",&a[i][j]);
 printf("The given matrix is\n");
 for(i=1;i<=n;i++) /* printing of A */
     {
       for(j=1;j<=n;j++) printf("%f\t ",a[i][j]); printf("\n");
     }
   printf("\n");
 for(i=1;i<=n;i++) for(j=1;j<=n;j++) b[i][j]=a[i][j];
 d[1]=0;for(i=1;i<=n;i++) d[1]+=a[i][i];
 for(i=2;i<=n;i++)
    {
      /* construction of B[i-1]-d[i-1] I=C (say) */
      for(j=1;j<=n;j++) for(k=1;k<=n;k++) c[j][k]=b[j][k];
      for(j=1;j<=n;j++) c[j][j]=c[j][j]-d[i-1];
```

```
        /* product of A and B[i-1]-d[i-1]I */
        for(j=1;j<=n;j++) for(k=1;k<=n;k++)
            {
              b[j][k]=0;
              for(l=1;l<=n;l++) b[j][k]+=a[j][l]*c[l][k];
            }
        /* trace of B */
        d[i]=0;
        for(j=1;j<=n;j++)
                d[i]+=b[j][j];
        d[i]/=i;
    } /* end of i loop */
 printf("The coefficients of the characteristic polynomial are \n");
 printf("1.00000 ");
 for(i=1;i<=n;i++) printf("%8.5f ",-d[i]);
 }/* main */
```

A sample of input/output:

```
Enter the size of the matrix 5
Enter the elements row wise
2 3 0 1 2
3 5 6 2 1
2 3 0 1 0
0 0 2 3 8
1 2 3 0 2

 The given matrix is
 2.000000      3.000000     0.000000     1.000000     2.000000
 3.000000      5.000000     6.000000     2.000000     1.000000
 2.000000      3.000000     0.000000     1.000000     0.000000
 0.000000      0.000000     2.000000     3.000000     8.000000
 1.000000      2.000000     3.000000     0.000000     2.000000

 The coefficients of the characteristic polynomial are
 1.00000 -12.00000 18.00000 -29.00000 -142.00000 14.00000
```

15.7.2 Power method

Power method is generally used to find the eigenvalue, largest in magnitude, (sometimes called first eigenvalue) of a matrix **A**. Let, $\lambda_1, \lambda_2, \ldots, \lambda_n$ be all eigenvalues of the matrix **A**. We assume that

$$|\lambda_1| > |\lambda_2| > |\lambda_3| > \cdots > |\lambda_n|,$$

i.e. λ_1 is largest in the magnitude and $\mathbf{X_1}, \mathbf{X_2}, \ldots, \mathbf{X_n}$ be the eigenvectors corresponding to the eigenvalues $\lambda_1, \lambda_2, \ldots, \lambda_n$ respectively. The method is applicable, if the matrix **A** has n independent eigenvectors. Then, any vector $\mathbf{X}$ in the (vector) space of eigenvectors $\mathbf{X_1}, \mathbf{X_2}, \ldots, \mathbf{X_n}$ can be written as

$$\mathbf{X} = \mathbf{c_1 X_1} + \mathbf{c_2 X_2} + \cdots + \mathbf{c_n X_n}. \tag{15.33}$$

Multiplying this relation by $\mathbf{A}$ and using the results $\mathbf{AX_1} = \lambda_1 \mathbf{X_1}$, $\mathbf{AX_2} = \lambda_2 \mathbf{X_2}$, ..., $\mathbf{AX_n} = \lambda_\mathbf{n} \mathbf{X_n}$, we obtain

$$\begin{aligned} \mathbf{AX} &= c_1\lambda_1 \mathbf{X_1} + \mathbf{c_2}\lambda_\mathbf{2}\mathbf{X_2} + \cdots + \mathbf{c_n}\lambda_\mathbf{n}\mathbf{X_n} \\ &= \lambda_1\left[c_1\mathbf{X_1} + \mathbf{c_2}\left(\frac{\lambda_\mathbf{2}}{\lambda_\mathbf{1}}\right)\mathbf{X_2} + \cdots + \mathbf{c_n}\left(\frac{\lambda_\mathbf{n}}{\lambda_\mathbf{1}}\right)\mathbf{X_n}\right]. \end{aligned} \tag{15.34}$$

Again, multiplying this relation by $\mathbf{A}, \mathbf{A^2}, \ldots, \mathbf{A^k}$ successively and obtaining the relations

$$\mathbf{A^2X} = \lambda_1^2\left[c_1\mathbf{X}_1 + c_2\left(\frac{\lambda_2}{\lambda_1}\right)^2\mathbf{X}_2 + \cdots + c_n\left(\frac{\lambda_n}{\lambda_1}\right)^2\mathbf{X}_n\right]. \tag{15.35}$$

$$\vdots \qquad\qquad \vdots$$

$$\mathbf{A^kX} = \lambda_1^k\left[c_1\mathbf{X}_1 + c_2\left(\frac{\lambda_2}{\lambda_1}\right)^k\mathbf{X}_2 + \cdots + c_n\left(\frac{\lambda_n}{\lambda_1}\right)^k\mathbf{X}_n\right]. \tag{15.36}$$

$$\mathbf{A^{k+1}X} = \lambda_1^{k+1}\left[c_1\mathbf{X}_1 + c_2\left(\frac{\lambda_2}{\lambda_1}\right)^{k+1}\mathbf{X_2} + \cdots + \mathbf{c_n}\left(\frac{\lambda_\mathbf{n}}{\lambda_\mathbf{1}}\right)^{\mathbf{k+1}}\mathbf{X_n}\right]. \tag{15.37}$$

When $k \to \infty$, then right hand sides of (15.36) and (15.37) tend to be $\lambda_1^k c_1 \mathbf{X}_1$ and $\lambda_1^{k+1} c_1 \mathbf{X}_1$, since $\left|\frac{\lambda_i}{\lambda_1}\right| < 1$ for $i = 2, \ldots, n$. Thus for $k \to \infty$, $\mathbf{A^kX} = \lambda_1^k c_1 \mathbf{X}_1$ and $\mathbf{A^{k+1}X} = \lambda_1^{k+1} c_1 \mathbf{X}_1$. That is, for $k \to \infty$, $\lambda_1 \mathbf{A^k}\lambda = \mathbf{A^{k+1}X}$. It is well known that two vectors are equal, if their corresponding components are same. That is,

$$\lambda_1 = \lim_{k\to\infty} \frac{\left(\mathbf{A^{k+1}X}\right)_r}{\left(\mathbf{A^kX}\right)_r}, \quad r = 1, 2, \ldots, n. \tag{15.38}$$

The symbol $(\mathbf{A^kX})_r$ denotes the rth component of the vector $\mathbf{A^kX}$.

If $|\lambda_2| \ll |\lambda_1|$, then the term within square bracket of (15.37) tend faster to $c_1\mathbf{X}_1$, i.e. the rate of convergence is fast.

To reduce the round off error, the method is carried out by normalizing (reducing the largest element to unity) the eigenvector at each iteration. Let, $\mathbf{X}_0$ be a non-null initial (arbitrary) vector (non-orthogonal to $\mathbf{X}_1$) and we compute

$$\begin{aligned} \mathbf{Y}_{i+1} &= \mathbf{AX}_i \\ \mathbf{X}_{i+1} &= \frac{\mathbf{Y}_{i+1}}{\lambda^{(i+1)}}, \qquad \text{for } i = 0, 1, 2, \ldots. \end{aligned} \tag{15.39}$$

where $\lambda^{(i+1)}$ is the largest element in magnitude of $\mathbf{Y}_{i+1}$ and it is the $(i+1)$th approximate value of λ_1. Then

$$\lambda_1 = \lim_{k\to\infty} \frac{(\mathbf{Y}_{k+1})_r}{(\mathbf{X}_k)_r}, \quad r = 1, 2, \ldots, n. \tag{15.40}$$

and $\mathbf{X}_{k+1}$ is the eigenvector corresponding to the eigenvalue λ_1.

Note 15.7.1 The initial vector $\mathbf{X}_0$ is usually chosen as $\mathbf{X}_0 = (1, 1, \cdots, 1)^T$. But, if the initial vector $\mathbf{X}_0$ is poor, then the formula (15.40) does not give λ_1, i.e. the limit of the ratio $\frac{(\mathbf{Y}_{k+1})_r}{(\mathbf{X}_k)_r}$ may not exist. If this situation occurs, then the initial vector must be changed.

The following method determines the largest eigenvalue (in magnitude) and its corresponding eigenvector of a square matrix **A**.

Algorithm Power_Method

Step 1. Read the matrix $\mathbf{A} = [a_{ij}], i, j = 1, 2, \ldots, n$.
Step 2. Set initial vector $\mathbf{X_0} = (1, 1, 1, \ldots, 1)^T$ of n components.
Step 3. Find the product $\mathbf{Y} = \mathbf{AX_0}$.
Step 4. Find the largest element (in magnitude) of the vector **Y** and let it be λ.
Step 5. Divide all the elements of **Y** by λ and take it as $\mathbf{X_1}$, i.e. $\mathbf{X_1} = \mathbf{Y}/\lambda$.
Step 6. /* Let $\mathbf{X_0} = (x_{01}, x_{02}, \ldots, x_{0n})$ and $\mathbf{X_1} = (x_{11}, x_{12}, \ldots, x_{1n})$. */
If $|x_{oi} - x_{1i}| > \varepsilon$ for at least i, then
set $\mathbf{X_0} = \mathbf{X_1}$ and goto Step 3.
Step 7. Print λ as largest eigenvalue and corresponding eigenvector $\mathbf{X_1}$ of **A**.

end Power_Method

Program 15.33

```
/* Program for Power method.
   This program finds the largest eigenvalue (in magnitude)
   of any square matrix.*/
#include<stdio.h>
#include<math.h>
void main()
{
 int n,i,j,flag;
 float a[10][10],x0[10],x1[10],y[10],lambda,eps=1e-5;
 printf("Enter the size of the matrix ");
 scanf("%d",&n);
 printf("Enter the elements row wise ");
 for(i=1;i<=n;i++) for(j=1;j<=n;j++) scanf("%f",&a[i][j]);
 printf("The given matrix is\n");
 for(i=1;i<=n;i++){ /* printing of A */
      for(j=1;j<=n;j++) printf("%f ",a[i][j]); printf("\n");
```

```
    }
   printf("\n");
  for(i=1;i<=n;i++) {
      x0[i]=1; x1[i]=1; /* initialization */
    }
  do
  {
    flag=0;
    for(i=1;i<=n;i++) x0[i]=x1[i]; /* reset x0 */
    for(i=1;i<=n;i++) /* product of A and X0 */
        {
           y[i]=0;
           for(j=1;j<=n;j++) y[i]+=a[i][j]*x0[j];
        }
    lambda=y[1]; /* finds maximum among y[i] */
    for(i=2;i<=n;i++) if(lambda<y[i]) lambda=y[i];
    for(i=1;i<=n;i++) x1[i]=y[i]/lambda;
    for(i=1;i<=n;i++) if(fabs(x0[i]-x1[i])>eps) flag=1;
  }while(flag==1);
  printf("The largest eigenvalue is %8.5f \n",lambda);
  printf("The corresponding eigenvector is \n");
  for(i=1;i<=n;i++) printf("%8.5f ",x1[i]);
 }/* main */
```

A sample of input/output:

```
Enter the size of the matrix 5
Enter the elements row wise
3 4 5 6 7
0 0 2 1 3
3 4 5 -2 3
3 4 -2 3 4
0 1 2 0 0

 The given matrix is
 3.000000 4.000000 5.000000 6.000000 7.000000
 0.000000 0.000000 2.000000 1.000000 3.000000
 3.000000 4.000000 5.000000 -2.000000 3.000000
 3.000000 4.000000 -2.000000 3.000000 4.000000
 0.000000 1.000000 2.000000 0.000000 0.000000
 The largest eigenvalue is 10.41317
 The corresponding eigenvector is
  1.00000  0.20028  0.62435  0.41939  0.13915
```

Exercise XV

Programming Problems

1. Write a program for Lagrange interpolation and use it to solve the following problems:

   (a) Compute $(1.015)^{-49}$ from the given table of $u(x) = (1.015)^{-x}$.

x	48	50	52	54	56
$u(x)$	0.4893617	0.4750047	0.4610689	0.447519	0.4344118.

   (b) Estimate the population in the year 1936 by appropriate interpolation formula from the following data.

Year	1901	1911	1921	1931	1941	1951
Population (in crores)	12	15	20	27	39	52.

   (c) Find the value of $\sqrt{5.5}$, given that $\sqrt{5} = 2.236$, $\sqrt{6} = 2.449$, $\sqrt{7} = 2.646$, $\sqrt{8} = 2.828$.

   (d) From the following table find the value of y, when $x = 1.05$.

x	1.0	1.1	1.2	1.3	1.4	1.5
y	0.24197	0.21785	0.19419	0.17137	0.14973	0.12952.

2. Write a program for two variables Lagrange interpolation formula and use it to solve the following problem.

   (i) Find $f(1, 2)$ using the following table

x	0	0	1	1	2	2	3	3
y	1.5	2	2	8.5	8	3	1.5	2.5
$f(x,y)$	1.5	2	3	4.5	12	7	10.5	11.5

   (ii) The following table gives the values of $f(x, y)$ for given values of x and y. From this table find the value of $f(1.5, 0.5)$.

$y\backslash x$	0	1	2	3
-1	3.5	2	7	8
0	1.5	2	9	3
1	10	5	6	8

3. Write a program to prepare a forward difference table.
4. Write a program to prepare a divided difference table. (The first order divided difference is $f[x_i, x_{i+1}] = \frac{f(x_i)-f(x_{i+1})}{x_i-x_{i+1}}$, $i = 0, 1, 2, \ldots, n-1$; The second order divided difference is $f[x_i, x_{i+1}, x_{i+2}] = \frac{f[x_i,x_{i+1}]-f[x_{i+1},x_{i+2}]}{x_i-x_{i+2}}$, $i = 0, 1, 2, \ldots, n-2$, and so on).
5. Write a program for implementing Newton-Gregory interpolation and use it to solve the following problems:

   (a) Find the values of $\log_{10} 2.89$ and $\log_{10} 2.01$ from the following table.

x	3.0	2.8	2.6	2.4	2.2	2.0
$\log_{10} x$	0.47721	0.44716	0.41497	0.38041	0.34242	0.30103.

(b) Find from the following table the value of y, when $x = 1.11$

x	1.1	1.2	1.3	1.4	1.5	1.6
y	2.7183	3.3210	4.0552	4.9530	6.0496	7.3891.

(c) The following table gives the values of x and corresponding $f(x)$. Determine $f(0.31)$

x	0.20	0.22	0.24	0.26	0.28	0.30
$f(x)$	1.6596	1.6698	1.6804	1.6912	1.7024	1.7139.

(d) Find from the following table the value of y, when $x = 4.05$.

x	4.0	4.2	4.4	4.6	4.8	5.0	5.2
y	1.3863	1.4351	1.4861	1.5261	1.5686	1.6074	1.6487.

(e) Evaluate $f(x)$ at $x = 39^o10'40''$ from the following table

x	$39^o10'$	$39^o11'$	$39^o12'$	$39^o13'$
$f(x)$	9.8004272	9.8005823	9.8007372	9.8008921
x	$39^o14'$	$39^o15'$	$39^o16'$	$39^o17'$
$f(x)$	9.8104668	9.8012015	9.8013561	9.8015106.

6. Write a program to read the following data

$$x: \; x_0 \quad x_1 \quad \cdots \quad x_n$$
$$y: \; y_0 \quad y_1 \quad \cdots \quad y_n.$$

Then, construct and print the cubic splines for each of the intervals.

Also, determine the value of y for a given x.

(Write separate programs for natural spline, periodic spline and non-periodic spline.)

Using the above program (for natural spline), compute the values of $y(1.2)$ and $y(2.0)$, where the values of x and y are given below:

x	1	2	3	4
y	1.5	2.2	3.1	4.3.

7. Write programs to evaluate the integral $\int_a^b f(x)\,dx$ by (i) trapezoidal rule and (ii) Simpson's 1/3 rule.

8. Write programs to integrate a function using trapezoidal, Simpson's 1/3 and Simpson's 3/8 rules.

Use your programs to find the values of the following integrals.

(i) $\int_0^1 \frac{dx}{1+x^2}$, (ii) $\int_0^1 \frac{\ln(1+x)}{1+x^2}dx$, (iii) $\int_0^{1.2} \ln(1+x^2)dx$, (iv) $\int_{0.1}^{1.2} \frac{dx}{\sqrt{x}}$,
(v) $\int_0^1 \frac{\sqrt{x}}{1+x}dx$, (vi) $\int_0^1 \frac{dx}{(1+x^2)^{3/2}}$, (vii) $\int_0^1 \frac{dx}{1+\sqrt{x}}$, (viii) $\int_{.1}^{.5} \frac{dx}{\sqrt{x}+x}$,
(ix) $\int_0^1 \frac{x}{1+\sqrt{x}}dx$, (x) $\int_0^1 \sqrt{1+x+x^2}dx$, (xi) $\int_0^1 (\sqrt{x}+1)^{3/2}dx$,
(xii) $\int_0^1 \sin x^2 dx$, (xiii) $\int_0^{\pi/2} \sqrt{1-0.162\sin^2\phi}\, d\phi$, (xiv) $\int_0^1 \frac{\log(1+x^2)}{1+x^2}dx$,
(xv) $\int_0^{0.5} \frac{dx}{\sqrt{(1-x^2)(1-0.75x^2)}}$, (xvi) $\int_0^{\pi/2} \frac{\cos x}{1+x}dx$, (xvii) $\int_0^{.5} \sqrt{\frac{1-0.25x^2}{1-x^2}}dx$,
(xviii) $\int_2^3 \frac{dx}{1+\sqrt{\ln x}}$, (xix) $\int_0^{\pi/2} \frac{dx}{x+\sqrt{\cos x}}$, (xx) $\int_1^2 \frac{dx}{3+2x-x^2}$, (xxi) $\int_1^2 \frac{dx}{1+x^2+x^3}$,

(xxii) $\int_0^5 \log(1+x^2)dx$, (xxiii) $\int_{-3}^{3} \frac{1}{\sqrt{2\pi}} e^{-x^2/2} dx$, (xxiv) $\int_0^t \frac{1}{\sqrt{2\pi}} e^{-x^2/2} dx$, for a given t, (xxv) $\int_0^t e^{-x} x^{l-1} dx$, for given t and l, (xxvi) $\int_{1.0}^{1.5} (\log_e x)^2 dx$, (xxvii) $\int_{.4}^{1.6} \frac{x}{\sinh x} dx$, (xxix) $\int_0^{90^o} \sqrt{\sin x} dx$.

9. Write a program to evaluate the following integral by Gauss quadrature (using four points or six points formula).
(i) $\int_0^2 \log(1+x^2)dx$, (ii) $\int_{-1}^1 e^x \sin x \, dx$, (iii) $\int_1^\infty \frac{1}{x} e^{1/x} dx$, (iv) $\int_1^2 \frac{e^{-x}}{x} dx$,
(v) $\int_{0.5}^{1.5} \frac{2-2x+\sin(x-1)+x^2}{1+(x-1)^2} dx$, (vi) $\int_0^1 (1-x^2)^{-1/2} \cos 2x \, dx$, (vii) $\int_2^3 \frac{\cos 2x}{1+\sin x} dx$,
(viii) $\int_{-1}^1 (1-x^2)^{1/2} dx$,.
10. Integrate the integrals of Exercise 9 by Monte-Carlo method.
11. Write a program for evaluating the integral $\int_a^b f(x)dx$ by Simpson's 1/3rd rule taking N number of intervals where the expression of $f(x)$ is given. If there is any restriction on N, mention that.
12. Write a program to compute the integral $\int_0^2 \frac{dx}{\sqrt{1+x^2+x^4}} dx$ by taking 24 equal subintervals.
13. Write a program to evaluate $\int_1^2 f(x)\, dx$ using any method, where

$$f(x) = \begin{cases} x^2, & \text{if } x < 1.5 \\ 2x, & \text{if } x \geq 1.5. \end{cases}$$

14. Write a program to find the values of the following integrals.
(i) $\int_1^3 \int_1^2 (x^2+y^2) dy\, dx$, (ii) $\int\int_S e^{\frac{x-y}{x+y}} dy\, dx$, where S is the rectangular domain $1 \leq x \leq 2, 0 \leq y \leq 1.$, (iii) $\int_1^{.2} \int_0^{1.5} \frac{\sin xy}{1+xy} dx\, dy$, (taking steps of size 0.2),
(iv) $\int_1^5 \int_1^4 \frac{dx\, dy}{(x^2+y^2)^{1/2}}$, (v) $\int_0^{1.5} \int_1^3 \frac{2xy\, dx\, dy}{(1+x^2)(1+y^2)}$.
15. Write algorithms and draw flow charts to find a real root of the equation $f(x) = 0$ using (i) bisection, (ii) iteration, (iii) Newton-Rapson, and (iv) Regula-falsi methods.
16. Write programs to solve the following equations by (a) bisection, (b) iteration, (c) Newton-Rapson and (d) Regula-falsi methods.
(i) $\sin x - x + 1 = 0$, correct upto three decimal places.
(ii) $x^3 - 5.2x^2 + 3 = 0$, correct upto five significant digits.
(iii) $x^3 - 5 = 0$, correct upto five significant figures.
(iv) $x^3 - 8x - 4 = 0$, correct upto five significant figures.
(v) $x^3 + 2x - 1 = 0$, correct upto five significant figures.
(vi) $\tan x + x = 0$, correct upto five significant figures.
(vii) $x^3 - 5x + 4 = 0$, correct upto five significant figures.
(viii) $x^2 = \sin x$, (between 1/2 and 1) correct upto five significant figures.
(xi) $x = \tan x$, correct upto five significant figures.
(x) $xe^x - 1 = 0$, correct upto five significant figures.
(xi) $x^2 - 5 = 0$, correct upto five significant figures.
(xii) $\sin^2 x = x^2$, (xiii) $x^3 - x - 4 = 0$, (xiv) $x^3 + 2x - 1 = 0$,
(xv) $x^3 - 2x^2 - 0.2 = 0$, (xvi) $x^3 + 2x - 5 = 0$, (xvii) $2x - \log_{10} x - 7 = 0$,
(xviii) $\cos x = xe^x$.

17. The equation $f(x) = 0$, where $f(x) = 0.1 - x + \frac{x^2}{(2!)^2} - \frac{x^3}{(3!)^2} + \frac{x^4}{(4!)^2} - \cdots\cdots$ has one root in the interval (0,1). Write a program to find this root by bisection method.

18. Write a program to solve the equation $f(x) = c$ by Newton-Rapson's method, where c is real constant and $f(x)$ is defined as

$$f(x) = \begin{cases} \cos x, & \text{when } |x| \le 1 \\ \cos x + (x-1)^2, & \text{when } |x| \ge 1. \end{cases}$$

Take $c = (-1)^n$ at the nth iteration.

19. Write a program to find all the roots of the following polynomial equations: (i) $x^4 - 3x^3 + 3x^2 + 4x - 4 = 0$, (ii) $x^2 - 2x + 4 = 0$, (iii) $x^5 - 2x^4 + 4x^3 - x^2 - 7x + 5 = 0$, (iv) $x^3 - 3.7x^2 + 6.25x - 4.069 = 0$, (v) $x^3 + 3x^2 - 4 = 0$, (vi) $x^6 - 4.80x^4 + 3.30x^2 - 0.05 = 0$, (vii) $x^3 - 2x + 2 = 0$, (viii) $x^6 - x^4 - x^3 - 1 = 0$, (ix) $x^5 - 3x^4 + 2x^3 - x^2 + 3x - 2 = 0$, (x) $x^5 = 3x - 1$.

20. Write a program to solve the following equations by Newton-Rapson method
(i) $x^2 + y - 11 = 0, y^2 + x - 7 = 0$ near (3,-2).
(ii) $x^2 + y^2 = 1.12, xy = 0.25$, (iii) $\sin(xy) = y - x, y\cos(xy) + 1 = 0$, near (1,2),
(iv) $\sqrt{x}(1 + y\sqrt{x}) = 0, \log_e(x^2 + y) = 1 - y$, near (2.4,-0.6),
(v) $x^2 + y^2 - 3 = 0, xy = 1.5$, near (1,1).

21. Write a program to solve a system of linear equations by Crammer's rule. Find the solution of the following systems using this program:

(i) $x + 2y + z = 0, 2x + 2y + 3z = 3, -x - 3y = 2$.
(ii) $8x_1 + 2x_2 - 2x_3 = 8, x_1 - 8x_2 + 3x_3 = -4, 2x_1 + x_2 + 9x_3 = 12$.
(iii) $5x + 2y + z = 0, x + 7y - 3z = 1, 2x + 2y - 7z = 2$.
(iv) $x + 2y - 5z + 2w = -2, 3x - y + 2z + 4w = 19, 4x + y - 3z + 6w = 17, 2x - 3y + 7z + 2w = 21$.
(v) $x_1 - 2x_2 + x_3 - x_4 = 2, x_1 + x_2 - 2x_3 + 3x_4 = 5, 4x_1 + x_2 - 5x_3 + 8x_4 = 7, 5x_1 - 7x_2 + 2x_3 - x_4 = 2$.

22. Write programs to solve a system of linear equations by
(i) matrix inverse, (ii) Gauss elimination, and (iii) LU decomposition methods.

23. Write a program to solve a system of linear equations by Gauss-Seidal iteration method. Use it to solve the following problems.
(i) $8x_1 + 2x_2 - 2x_3 = 8,\ x_1 - 8x_2 + 3x_3 = -4,\ 2x_1 + x_2 + 9x_3 = 12$.
(ii) $5x + 2y + z = 0, x + 7y - 3z = 1, 2x + 2y - 7z = 2$.
(iii) $x + y + 5z = 1, 4x - y - z = 2, x - 6y + 2z = 3$.
(iv) $3x_1 + x_2 + x_3 = 3, 2x_1 + x_2 + 5x_3 = 5, x_1 + 4x_2 + x_3 = 2$.

24. Write a program to solve a linear tri-diagonal system of equations and use it to solve the following:

$$\begin{bmatrix} 2 & -1 & 0 & 0 & \cdots & 0 & 0 & 0 \\ -1 & 2 & -1 & 0 & \cdots & 0 & 0 & 0 \\ 0 & -1 & 2 & -1 & \cdots & 0 & 0 & 0 \\ \cdots & \cdots & \cdots & \cdots & \cdots & \cdots & \cdots & \cdots \\ \cdots & \cdots & \cdots & \cdots & \cdots & \cdots & \cdots & \cdots \\ 0 & 0 & 0 & 0 & \cdots & -1 & 2 & -1 \\ 0 & 0 & 0 & 0 & \cdots & 0 & -1 & 2 \end{bmatrix} \begin{bmatrix} x_1 \\ x_2 \\ x_3 \\ \vdots \\ \vdots \\ x_8 \\ x_9 \end{bmatrix} = \begin{bmatrix} 0.001 \\ 0.002 \\ 0.003 \\ \vdots \\ \vdots \\ 0.008 \\ 0.009 \end{bmatrix}.$$

25. Write programs to solve the differential equation of the form $\frac{dy}{dx} = f(x, y), y(x_0) = y_0$ by (i) Euler's method and (ii) Modified Euler's method.
Find the solution of the following differential equation by using the above programs.
(i) Find $y(1)$ taking $h = 0.2$, where $\frac{dy}{dx} = xy, y(0) = 1$.
(ii) Find y at $x = 0.01$, when y satisfies $\frac{dy}{dx} = x + y$, with initial condition $y_0 = 1$ at $x_0 = 1$ (choose $h = 0.01$).
(iii) Find $y(0.1)$, where $y' = x^2 + y^2, y(0) = 0$.
(iv) Evaluate $y(0.04)$, given $y' + y = 0, y(0) = 1$.
(v) Compute $y(0.02), y(0.04)$ and $y(0.06)$, given $y' - y = 0, y(0) = 1$.
(vi) Evaluate $y(4.4)$, given $5xy' = 2 - y^2, y(4) = 1$.
(vii) Find the values of $y(1.1), y(1.2)$ and $y(1.3)$, given $y' + \frac{y}{x} = \frac{1}{x^2}, y(1) = 0$.
(viii) Compute $y(2.5)$, given $y' = x^2 - y^2, y(0) = 5$.

26. Write programs to solve the problems of Exercise 25 by fourth order Runge-Kutta methods.
27. Write a program to solve the following system of differential equations by fourth order Runge-Kutta method.

$$\frac{dy}{dx} = f(x, y, z), \frac{dz}{dx} = g(x, y, z), y(x_0) = y_0, z(x_0) = z_0.$$

Find the solutions of the following problems
(i) $\frac{dy}{dx} = x + y + z, \frac{dz}{dx} = x + y/z, y(1) = 1/3, z(1) = 1$.
(ii) $y' = -2z, z' = 2y, y(0) = 1, z(0) = 1$
(iii) $y' = xy + z, z' = x^2 - y^2 + z, x(1) = 1, z(1) = 2$.
28. Write a program to solve the differential equation $\frac{dy}{dx} = f(x, y)$, $y(x_0) = y_0$ by Milne's Predictor-Corrector method.
29. Write a program to solve the second order initial value problem of the form $y'' + p(x)y' + q(x)y = r(x)$ with $y(x_0) = y_0, y'(x_0) = z_0$, using fourth order Runge-Kutta method.
Use this program to find the solutions of the following differential equations.
(i) Compute $y(1.1), y(1.2), y(1.3)$ and $y(1.4)$ by solving $y'' + y'/x + y = 0$ with $y(1) = 0.77, y'(1) = -0.44$.

(ii) Compute $y(0.5)$ and $y(0.7)$, given that $y'' = x^3(y+y')$ with $y(0) = 1, y'(0) = 1$.
(iii) Given $y'' - y = 0$ and $y(0) = 0, y'(0) = 1$, find $y(0.1), y(0.2)$ and $y(0.5)$.

30. Write a program to solve the second order boundary value problem by fourth order Runge-Kutta method.
Solve the following problems by using this program.
(i) $x^2y'' - 2y + x = 0$, with boundary condition $y(2) = y(3) = 0$, taking $h = 0.25$.
(ii) $(1 + x^2)y'' + (5x + 3/x)y' + \frac{4y}{3} + 1 = 0, y(-2) = y(2) = 0.6, h = 0.1$.
(iii) $\frac{d}{dx}[(1 + x^2)\frac{dy}{dx}] - y = x^2 + 1; y(-1) = y(1) = 0, h = .5$ and $h = 1$.
(iv) $y'' + 8(\sin^2 \pi x)y = 0; y(0) = y(1) = 1, h = 1/4$ and $1/6$.

31. Write a program to solve the second order IVP of the form
$$y'' + p(x)y' + q(x)y = r(x)$$
with initial condition $y(x_0) = y_0$, $y'(x_0) = y'_0$, by finite difference method.

32. Write a program to solve the second order BVP of the form
$$y'' + a(x)y' + b(x)y = c(x)$$
with boundary condition $y(x_0) = y_0$ and $y(x_n) = y_n$, by finite difference method.

33. Write a program to construct the characteristic polynomial of a matrix of order $n \times n$.
Use this program to find the characteristic equations of the following matrices.

$$\text{(i)} \begin{bmatrix} 2 & 3 \\ 0 & 1 \end{bmatrix} \text{(ii)} \begin{bmatrix} 1 & 1 & 0 \\ 2 & 3 & 1 \\ 2 & -1 & 0 \end{bmatrix} \text{(iii)} \begin{bmatrix} 1 & 2 & 3 \\ 2 & 3 & 4 \\ 3 & 4 & 5 \end{bmatrix} \text{(iv)} \begin{bmatrix} 3 & 0 & 1 & 2 \\ 3 & 4 & 2 & -2 \\ 3 & 0 & 1 & 1 \\ 4 & 1 & 0 & 2 \end{bmatrix}.$$

34. Write a program to find the characteristic equation of a matrix of order $n \times n$ and solve this polynomial by computing all eigenvalues of the matrix.
Using this program find all the eigenvalues of the following matrices:

$$\text{(i)} \begin{bmatrix} 1 & 3 & -1 \\ 3 & 2 & 4 \\ -1 & 4 & 1 \end{bmatrix} \text{(ii)} \begin{bmatrix} 2.5 & 3.1 & 1.6 \\ 3.1 & 8.9 & 7.2 \\ 1.6 & 7.2 & 3.8 \end{bmatrix}.$$

35. Write a program to find the largest eigenvalue with corresponding eigenvector of a matrix of order $n \times n$.

Find the largest eigenvalues and corresponding eigenvectors of the following matrices:

$$\text{(i)} \begin{bmatrix} 2 & 1 & 1 & 0 \\ 1 & 1 & 0 & 1 \\ 1 & 0 & 1 & 1 \\ 0 & 1 & 1 & 2 \end{bmatrix} \text{(ii)} \begin{bmatrix} 4 & 1 & 0 \\ 1 & 20 & 1 \\ 0 & 1 & 4 \end{bmatrix} \text{(iii)} \begin{bmatrix} 0 & 0 & 1 & 1 & 0 \\ 0 & 0 & 1 & 0 & 1 \\ 1 & 1 & 0 & 0 & 1 \\ 1 & 0 & 0 & 0 & 1 \\ 0 & 1 & 1 & 1 & 0 \end{bmatrix}.$$

Chapter 16

Statistical Methods

Statistics, at present, is not used as a device devoted solely for collecting numerical data. Its expanded usage can be found on sound techniques/ procedures developed for handling, analyzing and drawing valid inferences from the collected data. As such it is not confined to the affairs of the state but is intruding constantly into various diversified spheres of life be it social, economic, and political. It is now finding wide applications in almost all sciences, social as well as physical, such as, biology, psychology, education, economics, business, management, etc.

Here, we classify the input data into four categories, viz. (i) Simple distribution, (ii) Ungrouped frequency distribution, (iii) Grouped frequency distribution, (iv) Multivariate distribution.

In simple distribution, the sample i.e. data is stored into an array $x_1, x_2, x_3, \ldots, x_n$.

In ungrouped frequency distribution, the sample is stored into two arrays, given below:

$$\begin{array}{ll} \text{Value } (x_i): & x_1, x_2, \ldots, x_n \\ \text{Frequency}(f_i): & f_1, f_2, \ldots, f_n \end{array}$$

where n is the number of the observations and $N = \sum f_i$ is the total frequency.

In the grouped frequency distribution, the sample is stored into three arrays as follows:

$$\begin{array}{ll} \text{Lower limit/boundary } (l_i): & l_1, l_2, \ldots, l_n \\ \text{Upper limit/boundary } (u_i): & u_1, u_2, \ldots, u_n \\ \text{Frequency } (f_i): & f_1, f_2, \ldots, f_n. \end{array}$$

A sample of bivariate simple distribution is stored into two arrays as follows:

$$\begin{array}{ll} x\text{-value}: & x_1, x_2, \ldots, x_n \\ y\text{- value}: & y_1, y_2, \ldots, y_n. \end{array}$$

16.1 Frequency Distribution

When a sample (a set of observations) is available on a single characteristic of a large number of individuals, often it becomes necessary to condense the data as far as possible, without losing any information of interest. It is better to represent the data into classes and to determine the number of individuals in each class. This type of representation of the data (as above) is known as **frequency distribution**.

A table showing the distribution of the frequencies in the different classes is called a *frequency distribution table.* The manner in which the class frequencies are distributed over the class intervals is called the *grouped frequency distribution* of the variable.

The following program computes the maximum and minimum individuals and the range (= maximum − minimum) from a given sample $x_i, i = 1, 2, \ldots, n$, of size n. Then read the lower boundary of the first class interval (which should be less than or equal to the minimum value) and a suitable width of each class interval. The frequency of each class is computed as follows: Any individual falls in a particular class if its value is less than the upper limit and greater than or equal to the lower limit of the class.

The program also displays the class intervals together with the corresponding frequency, relative frequency (number of occurrence per unit size of sample) and cumulative frequency (less than type).

Program 16.1

```
/* Preparation of grouped frequency distribution table, x,l,f are sample,
   lower limit and frequency and cf is the cumulative frequency */
#include<stdio.h>
void main()
 {
   float max,min,width,l[50],x[50];
   int   f[50],cf,n,i,j,m;
   printf("Enter sample size and the sample \n");
   scanf("%d",&n);
   for(i=1;i<=n;i++) scanf("%f",&x[i]);
   printf("Sample size is %d and sample is \n ",n);
   for(i=1;i<=n;i++) printf("%.3f ",x[i]);
   max=x[1];    min=x[1];
   for(i=2;i<=n;i++){
      if(max<x[i]) max=x[i];
      if(min>x[i]) min=x[i];
     }
   printf("\nMinimum value= %0.3f\n",min);
   printf("Maximum value=%0.3f\n",max);
   printf("Range =%0.3f\n",max-min);
   printf("Enter lower limit of first interval\n");
   printf("and width\n");
```

```
   scanf("%f%f",&l[1],&width);
   m=1;
/*  Computation of lower boundary of all classes */
   f[1]=0;
   do{
     m++;
     l[m]=l[m-1]+width;
     f[m]=0;
   }while(l[m]<=max);
/* Computation of frequency */
   for(i=1;i<=n;i++)
     for(j=2;j<=n;j++){
         if(x[i]<l[j]){
            f[j-1]++;
            break;
           }
      }
   cf=0;
   printf("Class boundary  freq  relative cumula.\n");
   printf("                             freq.    freq.\n");
   printf("====================================\n");
   for(i=1;i<=m-1;i++){
      cf+=f[i];
      printf("%6.2f-%6.2f  %3d %10.5f %4d\n",l[i],l[i+1],
                                 f[i],f[i]/(float)n,cf);
    }
   printf("====================================\n");
 }
```

A sample of input/output:

```
Enter sample size and the sample
15
10 9 12 34 56 12 6 11 35 46 15 24 34 48 50
Sample size is 15 and sample is
10.000 9.000 12.000 34.000 56.000 12.000 6.000 11.000 35.000
46.000 15.000 24.000 34.000 48.000 50.000
Minimum value=6.000
Maximum value=56.000
Range =50.000
Enter lower limit of first interval and width
0 5

Class boundary  freq relative cumula.
```

```
                          freq.    freq.
=======================================
  0.00-  5.00    0     0.00000    0
  5.00- 10.00    2     0.13333    2
 10.00- 15.00    4     0.26667    6
 15.00- 20.00    1     0.06667    7
 20.00- 25.00    1     0.06667    8
 25.00- 30.00    0     0.00000    8
 30.00- 35.00    2     0.13333   10
 35.00- 40.00    1     0.06667   11
 40.00- 45.00    0     0.00000   11
 45.00- 50.00    2     0.13333   13
 50.00- 55.00    1     0.06667   14
 55.00- 60.00    1     0.06667   15
=======================================
```

16.1.1 Two common functions

To compute the statistical parameters, some basic functions have been designed, such as `sum`, `fsum`, `sorta`, which are frequently used in several programs.

Function `sum(n,x,i)`

This function takes an array x of size n and an integer i as input. The output of this function is $\sum_{j=1}^{n} x_j^i$. That is,

$$\texttt{sum(n, x, i)} = \sum_{j=1}^{n} x_j^i.$$

The C implementation is listed below.

```
/* math.h header file must be included while using this function */
  float sum(int n,float x[],int i)
    {
      float s=0;
      int j;
      for(j=1;j<=n;j++) s+=pow(x[j],i);
      return s;
    }
```

Function `fsum(n,x,f,i)`

This function takes two arrays x and f, each of size n and an integer i as input. The output of this function is $\sum_{j=1}^{n} x_j^p f_j$. That is,

$$\texttt{fsum(n, x, f, i)} = \sum_{j=1}^{n} x_j^i f_j.$$

The program for this function is listed below.

```
/* math.h header file must be included while using this function */
  float fsum(int n,float x[],int f[],int i)
    {
      float s=0;
      for(j=1;j<=n;j++)
        s+=pow(x[j],i)*f[j];
      return s;
    }
```

16.2 Measure of Central Tendency

Measure of central tendency is a single figure which describes the entire series of observations with their varying sizes.

There are four measures of central tendency, viz. mean, median, quartile, mode.

16.2.1 Mean

Arithmetic mean (A.M.) is generally denoted by $\overline{x}$, of a set of observations which is defined as their sum, divided by the number of observations. The mean for simple distribution is

$$\overline{x} = \frac{1}{n}\sum_{i=1}^{n} x_i = \texttt{sum}(n, x, 1)/n.$$

The mean for ungrouped frequency distribution is

$$(\bar{x}) = \frac{1}{N}\sum_{i=1}^{n} f_i x_i = \texttt{fsum}(n, x, f, 1)/N; \qquad \text{where } N = \sum_{i=1}^{n} f_i.$$

The mean of grouped frequency distribution with lower boundary (l_i), upper boundary (u_i) and corresponding frequency (f_i) is

$$(\bar{x}) = \frac{1}{N}\sum_{i=1}^{n} f_i x_i = \texttt{fsum}(n, x, f, 1)/N;$$

where $x_i = \dfrac{l_i + u_i}{2}$, $i = 1, 2, \ldots, n$, which is called the middle value of the class and $N = \sum\limits_{i=1}^{n} f_i$.

Program 16.2

```
/* Computation of mean of grouped frequency distribution */
#include<stdio.h>
void main()
  {
    float l[50],u[50],x,sum=0,xmean;
    int f[50],n,N=0,i;
    printf("Enter number of intervals n \n");
    scanf("%d",&n);
    printf("Enter lower limit, upper limit and frequency\n");
    for(i=1;i<=n;i++)
       scanf("%f%f%d",&l[i],&u[i],&f[i]);
    for(i=1;i<=n;i++){
        N+=f[i];
        x=(l[i]+u[i])/2;
        sum+=x*f[i];
      }
     xmean=sum/N;
     printf("The mean is %0.4f",xmean);
  }
```

```
Enter number of intervals n
5
Enter lower limit, upper limit and frequency
0 10 3
10 20 4
20 30 5
30 40 2
40 50 1
The mean is 21.0000
```

16.2.2 Median

The median of a set of observations is the value of the middle most item, when they are arranged in the order of magnitude.

Simple distribution

The median for the distribution 2, 5, 7, 8, 10 is 7 and that of 3, 8, 12, 14 is (8+12)/2 = 10. Thus, if $x_1, x_2, \ldots, x_n$ are ordered (i.e. either $x_i > x_{i+1}$ or $x_i < x_{i+1}$ for all i), then the median is $(x_{n+1})/2$, if n is odd, and $(x_{n/2} + x_{n/2+1})/2$, if n is even. The following program computes the median of a simple distribution.

Program 16.3

```
/* Computation of median for a simple distribution.
   Elements need not be sorted. */
```

```
#include<stdio.h>
#include<math.h>
float x[50]; /* x is global variable */
void main()
 {
   float me;
   int n,i;
   void sorta(int n);
   printf("Enter sample size and sample ");
   scanf("%d",&n);
   for(i=1;i<=n;i++) scanf("%f",&x[i]);
   printf("Given sample is\n");
   for(i=1;i<=n;i++)
     printf("%0.2f ",x[i]);
   sorta(n); /* sorting of input sample */
   if(fmod(n,2)==0)
     me=(x[n/2]+x[n/2+1])/2;
   else
      me=x[(n+1)/2];
   printf("\nThe median is %0.4f",me);
 }
/* Sorting of elements in ascending order */
void sorta(int n)
  {
   int i,j;
   float temp;
    for(i=1;i<=n-1;i++)
      for(j=i+1;j<=n;j++)
     if(x[i]>=x[j]) {
        temp=x[i];
        x[i]=x[j];
        x[j]=temp;
     }
  }
```

A sample of input/output:

```
Enter sample size and sample
8 12 34 56 23 14 78 10 24
Given sample is
12.00 34.00 56.00 23.00 14.00 78.00 10.00 24.00
The median is 23.5000
```

Grouped frequency distribution

The working formula for grouped frequency distribution is

$$Median = l_1 + \frac{\frac{N}{2} - F}{f_m} * c$$

where,
l_1=lower boundary of the median class;
N=total frequency;
F=cumulative frequency of preceding of median class;
f_m=frequency of the median class;
c=width of the median class.

In certain cases median is the real measure of central tendency, as it gives the value of the most central observation.

16.2.3 Quartiles

There are three types of quartiles, such as first, second and third quartiles. They are respectively denoted by Q_1, Q_2, Q_3. The kth quartile ($k = 1, 2, 3$), for grouped frequency distribution, is computed by the formula:

$$Q_k = l_1 + \frac{\frac{k*N}{4} - F}{f_k} * c$$

where,
l_1=lower boundary of the kth quartile class;
N=total frequency;
F=cumulative frequency of preceding of median class;
f_k=frequency of the kth quartile class;
c=width of the kth quartile class.

The second quartile (when $k = 2$) is called the median of the distribution. The working formula to compute the kth quartile is

$$Q_k = \texttt{quartl}(n, L, U, F, k) = L(m) + \frac{\frac{k \times N}{4} - \sum_{i=1}^{m} F(i)}{F(m)} \times (U(m) - L(m))$$

where m is the quartile class.

Example 16.2.1 (Computation of quartiles) Write a program to compute Q_1, Q_2 and Q_3 for a grouped frequency distribution.

Program 16.4

```
/* Computation of quartiles of grouped frequency distribution
   l[i], u[i] are the lower and upper limits of ith class with
   frequency f[i], i=1,2, ..., n; k (=1, 2, 3) for k-th quartile */
```

```
#include<stdio.h>
/* Function quartl which computes kth quartile */
float quartl(int n,float l[],float u[],int f[],int k)
  {
    int N=0,i,kn4,cf=0,m;
    float q;
    for(i=1;i<=n;i++)
       N+=f[i];
    kn4=k*N/4;
    for(i=1;i<=n;i++){/* finding quartile class */
        if(cf>=kn4) break;
        m=i;
        cf+=f[i];
     }
    cf-=f[m];
    if(cf<=0) cf=f[1];
    q=l[m]+(kn4-cf)*(u[m]-l[m])/f[m];
    return q;
 }
void main()
{
  float l[50],u[50],q1,q2,q3;
  int f[50],n,i;
  printf("Enter sample size and the\n ");
  printf("sample (lower, upper limits and frequency)\n");
  scanf("%d",&n);
  for(i=1;i<=n;i++)
    scanf("%f%f%d",&l[i],&u[i],&f[i]);
  q1=quartl(n,l,u,f,1);
  q2=quartl(n,l,u,f,2);
  q3=quartl(n,l,u,f,3);
  printf("The quartiles are \n");
  printf("Q1=%0.4f, Q2=%0.4f, Q3=%0.4f",q1,q2,q3);
}
```

A sample of input/output:

```
Enter sample size and the
sample (lower, upper limits and frequency)
6
0 10 2
10 20 4
20 30 7
30 40 5
40 50 3
```

```
50 60 1
The quartiles are
Q1=17.5000, Q2=27.1429, Q3=36.0000
```

16.2.4 Mode

Mode is a set of observations which occurs with the maximum frequency. It is a typical value, and it represents the true characteristic of the frequency distribution as a measure of its central tendency. If the frequencies of all observations are same, then the distribution has no mode.

Ungrouped frequency distribution

The program to compute mode of an ungrouped frequency distribution is listed below.

Program 16.5

```
/* Computation of the mode of a frequency distribution;
   f(i) is the frequency of x(i), i=1, 2,..., n; n is the
   number of observations. */
void modefd(int n, float x[], int f[])
  {
    short int flag;
    int max,i;
    max=f[1];
    for(i=2;i<=n;i++)  /* Computation of mode */
      if(f[i]>max) max=f[i];
    flag=0;
    /* flag=1 indicates that the frequencies of all
       observations are distinct */
    for(i=1;i<=n;i++)
      if (max !=f[i]) flag=1;
    if(flag==1) {
      printf("Mode of the distribution \n");
      for(i=1;i<=n;i++)
         if(max==f[i]) printf("%0.3f ", x[i]);
     }
     else
       printf("The distribution has no mode\n");
  }
void main()
  {
    float x[50];
    int f[50],n,i;
    printf("Enter n and x[i],f[i]\n");
    scanf("%d",&n);
```

```
    for(i=1;i<=n;i++) scanf("%f%d",&x[i],&f[i]);
    modefd(n,x,f);
  }
```

A sample of input/output:

```
Enter n and x[i],f[i]
6
6 10
7 12
10 10
8 12
15 9
16 6

 Mode of the distribution 7.000 8.000
```

Simple distribution

To compute the mode of a simple distribution, calculate the frequency of each sample value, and then, find the element whose frequency is maximum. The program is listed below.

Program 16.6

```
/* Computation of mode of a simple distribution */
#include<stdio.h>
float x[50],a[50]; /* global declaration */
int f[50];
void main()
  {
    int n,i,k;
    int freq(int);
    void modefd(int);
    printf("Enter the sample size\n");
    scanf("%d",&n);
    printf("Enter the sample \n");
    for(i=1;i<=n;i++) scanf("%f",&x[i]);
    k=freq(n); /* determines the frequency of each sample value */
    printf("The rearranged sample\n");
    for(i=1;i<=k;i++)
      printf("a[%d]=%0.3f f[%d]=%d\n",i,a[i],i,f[i]);
    modefd(k); /* computes mode */
  }
/* Computation of frequency of a simple distribution
   x is the given array of size n; a[i] is the output
```

```
   array of distinct elements with frequency f[i],
   i=1, 2,..., k(<=n), k is the number of distinct elements. */
int freq(int n)
  {
    void sorta(int);
    int k,i;
    float t;
    sorta(n); /* sorting of elements */
    t=x[1];
    k=1;
    f[1]=1;
    a[1]=t;
    for(i=2;i<=n;i++){
        if(t==x[i])
          f[k]++;
        else {
         t=x[i]; k++; f[k]=1;  a[k]=t;
        }
      }
    return k;
  }
/* Sorting of elements in ascending order */
void sorta(int n) /* Called by the function freq */
  {
   int i,j;
   float temp;
    for(i=1;i<=n-1;i++)
      for(j=i+1;j<=n;j++)
         if(x[i]>=x[j]) {
            temp=x[i];
            x[i]=x[j];
            x[j]=temp;
         }
  }
/* Computes the mode of a sample drawn from a frequency distribution */
void modefd(int n)
  {
    short int flag;
    int max,i;
    max=f[1];
    for(i=2;i<=n;i++)
       if(f[i]>max) max=f[i];
```

```
  flag=0;
  for(i=1;i<=n;i++)
     if (max !=f[i]) flag=1;
  if(flag==1) {
     printf("Mode of the distribution \n");
     for(i=1;i<=n;i++)
        if(max==f[i]) printf("%0.3f ", a[i]);
    }
   else
     printf("The distribution has no mode\n");
}
```

A sample of input/output:

```
Enter the sample size
10
Enter the sample
11 10 12 15 12 10 23 34 23 12
The rearranged sample
a[1]=10.000 f[1]=2
a[2]=11.000 f[2]=1
a[3]=12.000 f[3]=3
a[4]=15.000 f[4]=1
a[5]=23.000 f[5]=2
a[6]=34.000 f[6]=1
Mode of the distribution 12.000
```

Grouped frequency distribution

A class with the maximum frequency is called the modal class. This class is denoted by m.

The formula to calculate the mode for grouped frequency distribution is

$$Mode = l_1 + \frac{d_1}{d_1 + d_2} * c,$$

where,
l_1 = lower boundary of the modal class;
d_1 = difference in frequencies of the modal class and the preceding class
$= f_m - f_{m-1}$;
d_2 = difference in frequencies of the modal class and the following class
$= f_m - f_{m+1}$;
c = common width of classes, f_m being the frequency of the mth class.

The formula is applicable only when all the classes have the same width. When all the observations occur with equal frequency, mode does not exist. Again, there is more than one mode, if two or more values occur with the maximum frequency. The working formula for the mode is

$$\text{mode}(n, l, u, f) = l(m) + \frac{(f(m) - f(m-1))(u(m) - l(m))}{2f(m) - f(m-1) - f(m+1)}.$$

Program 16.7

```
/* Computation of mode of grouped frequency distribution
   l[i], u[i] be the lower and upper limits of the ith class with
   frequency f[i], i=1, 2,..., n; n is the number of classes; mc is
   the modal class. */
#include<stdio.h>
void main()
  {
   float l[50],u[50],mode;
   int f[50],max,mc,n,i;
   printf("Enter the number of classes and sample l[i],u[i],f[i]\n");
   scanf("%d",&n);
   for(i=1;i<=n;i++)
      scanf("%f%f%d",&l[i],&u[i],&f[i]);
   max=f[1];
   for(i=2;i<=n;i++)
     {
       if(max<=f[i]) {
          mc=i;
          max=f[i];
        }
     }
   mode=l[mc]+(f[mc]-f[mc-1])*(u[mc]-l[mc])/(2*f[mc]-f[mc-1]-f[mc+1]);
   printf("Mode is %.4f",mode);
  }
```

A sample of input/output:

```
Enter the number of classes and sample l[i],u[i],f[i]
6
0 10 7
10 20 8
20 30 9
30 40 12
40 50 7
50 60 2
Mode is 33.7500
```

16.3 Measures of Dispersion

A measure of dispersion is designed to state numerically the extent to which the individual observations vary on an average. There are several measures of dispersion. The commonly used parameters are range, quartile deviation, mean deviation, standard deviation, coefficient of variation, coefficient of quartile deviation, coefficient of mean deviation.

Range

Range is the difference between the largest and the smallest observations.

Range=Maximum value – Minimum value.

Quartile deviation

Quartile deviation is defined as half the difference between the lower and the upper quartiles.

$$\text{Quartile deviation (QD)} = \frac{Q_3 - Q_1}{2}.$$

Mean deviation

Mean deviation of a set of observations is the arithmetic mean of absolute deviations from mean or any other specified value.

$$\text{Mean deviation (MD) (about mean)} = \frac{1}{N}\sum_{i=1}^{n}|x_i - \bar{x}|f_i = \frac{1}{N}\sum_{i=1}^{n} y_i f_i, \text{ where } y_i = |x_i - \bar{x}|.$$

$$\text{Mean deviation (MDMe) (about median)} = \frac{1}{N}\sum_{i=1}^{n}|x_i - Me|f_i,$$

where Me is the median.

Standard deviation

Standard deviation of a set of observations is the positive square root of the arithmetic mean of squares of deviations from arithmetic mean.

$$\text{Standard deviation (SD)} = \sqrt{\frac{1}{N}\sum_{i=1}^{n}(x_i - \bar{x})^2 f_i} = \sqrt{\frac{1}{N}\sum_{i=1}^{n} y_i^2 f_i} = \sqrt{\texttt{fsum}(n, y, f, 2)/N},$$

where $y_i = x_i - \bar{x}$.

Program 16.8

```
/* Computation of standard deviation for a simple distribution */
#include<stdio.h>
#include<math.h>
void main()
 {
    float x[50],mean,y,sum=0,sd;
    int n,i;
    printf("Enter sample size and the sample\n");
    scanf("%d",&n);
    for(i=1;i<=n;i++) scanf("%f",&x[i]);
    for(i=1;i<=n;i++)
       sum+=x[i];
    mean=sum/n;
    sum=0.0;
    for(i=1;i<=n;i++){
         y=x[i]-mean;
         sum+=y*y;
       }
    sd=sqrt(sum/n);
    printf("Standard deviation is %.4f",sd);
 }
```

A sample of input/output:

```
Enter sample size and the sample
8
10 20 34 -10 25 30 22 12
Standard deviation is 13.0042
```

The following program computes the standard deviation for ungrouped frequencies.

Program 16.9

```
/* Computation of standard deviation of an ungrouped
   frequency distribution */
#include<stdio.h>
#include<math.h>
void main()
  {
    float x[50],mean,sum=0,y,sd;
    int f[50],n,N=0,i;
    printf("Enter sample size and the sample (x[i],f[i])\n");
    scanf("%d",&n);
    for(i=1;i<=n;i++){
        scanf("%f%d",&x[i],&f[i]);
        N+=f[i];
```

```
        sum+=x[i]*f[i];
    }
    mean=sum/N;
    sum=0.0;
    for(i=1;i<=n;i++){
        y=x[i]-mean;
        sum+=y*y*f[i];
    }
    sd=sqrt(sum/N);
    printf("Standard deviation is %0.4f",sd);
}
```

A sample of input/output:

```
Enter sample size and the sample (x[i],f[i])
6
10 8
12 9
15 6
17 5
19 4
20 3
Standard deviation is 3.4669
```

Coefficient of variation

$$\text{Coefficient of Variation (CV)} = \frac{\text{Standard Deviation}}{\text{Mean}} \times 100.$$

Coefficient of quartile deviation

$$\text{Coefficient of Quartile Deviation (CQD)} = \frac{\text{Quartile Deviation}}{\text{Mean}} \times 100.$$

Coefficient of mean deviation

Coefficient of Mean Deviation (about mean) (CMDM)

$$= \frac{\text{Deviation about mean}}{\text{mean}} \times 100.$$

Coefficient of Mean Deviation (about median) (CMDMe)

$$= \frac{\text{Deviation about median}}{\text{median}} \times 100.$$

Program 16.10

```
/* Computation of quartile deviation(qd), mead deviation(md)
   standard deviation(sd), coefficient of variation(cv),
   coeff. of quartile deviation(cqd), coeff. of mean deviation
   about mean(cmdm), coeff. of mean deviation about median (cmdme)
```

```
   for grouped frequency distribution. l[i], u[i] are the lower
   and upper limit of ith class (i=1,2,...,n) with frequency f[i];
   n is the number of classes. */
#include<stdio.h>
#include<math.h>
void main()
  {
    float l[50],u[50],x[50],md,mdme,cmdme,mean;
    float sd,cv,cmdm,q1,q2,q3,qd,cqd;
    int f[50],n,N=0,i;
    float fsum(int n,float x[],int f[],int k);
    float quartl(int n,float l[],float u[],int f[],int k);
    printf("Enter no. of observations and l,u,f line by line\n");
    scanf("%d",&n);
    for(i=1;i<=n;i++) {
        scanf("%f%f%d",&l[i],&u[i],&f[i]);
        N+=f[i];
        x[i]=(l[i]+u[i])/2;
      }
/* Computation of mean, md, sd, cv */
    mean=fsum(n,x,f,1)/N;
    for(i=1;i<=n;i++)
       x[i]=fabs(x[i]-mean);
    md=fsum(n,x,f,1)/N;
    sd=sqrt(fsum(n,x,f,2)/N);
    cv=sd*100/mean;
    cmdm=md*100/mean;
    printf("Mean deviation      = %0.4f\n",md);
    printf("Standard deviation = %0.4f\n",sd);
    printf("Coeff. of variation= %0.4f\n",cv);
    printf("Coeff. of mean dev.= %0.4f\n",cmdm);
/* Computation of q1,q2,q3,qd,cqd,cmd(about mean),cmd(about median) */
    q1=quartl(n,l,u,f,1);
    q2=quartl(n,l,u,f,2);
    q3=quartl(n,l,u,f,3);
    qd=(q3-q1)/2;
    cqd=qd*100/mean;
    for(i=1;i<=n;i++)
       x[i]=fabs((l[i]+u[i])/2-q2);
    mdme=fsum(n,x,f,1)/N;
    cmdme=mdme*100/q2;
    printf("Median                             = %0.4f\n",q2);
```

```
    printf("Quartile deviation                    = %0.4f\n",qd);
    printf("Mean deviation.(about mean)           = %0.4f\n",mdme);
    printf("Coeff. of quartile deviation          = %0.4f\n",cqd);
    printf("Coeff. of mean dev.(about median) = %0.4f\n",cmdme);
 }
/* Computation of quartiles of a grouped frequency distribution */
float quartl(int n,float l[],float u[],int f[], int k)
 {
   float q;
   int N=0,cf=0,i,kn4,m;
   for(i=1;i<=n;i++)
      N+=f[i];
   kn4=k*N/4;
   for(i=1;i<=n;i++) {
       if(cf>kn4) break;
       m=i;
       cf+=f[i];
     }
   cf-=f[m];
   if(cf<=0) cf=f[1];
   q=l[m]+(kn4-cf)*(u[m]-l[m])/f[m];
   return q;
 }
/* The function fsum */
float fsum(int n,float x[],int f[],int i)
  {
    float s=0;
    int j;
    for(j=1;j<=n;j++)
      s+=pow(x[j],i)*f[j];
    return s;
  }
```

<u>A sample of input/output:</u>

```
Enter no.  of observations and l,u,f line by line
5
10 20 5
20 30 8
30 40 10
40 50 7
50 60 5

Mean deviation      = 10.0735
```

```
Standard deviation = 12.5324
Coeff. of variation= 36.1016
Coeff. of mean dev.= 29.0182
Median                             = 34.0000
Quartile deviation                 = 10.2679
Mean deviation.(about mean)        = 10.2571
Coeff. of quartile deviation       = 29.5782
Coeff. of mean dev.(about median) = 30.1681
```

16.4 Moments, Skewness and Kurtosis

16.4.1 Moments

Given n observations $x_1, x_2, \ldots, x_n$ and an arbitrary constant A, the kth order moment about A is denoted by m_k and is defined as

$$m_k = \frac{1}{N}\sum_{i=1}^{n}(x_i - A)^k f_i.$$

The kth order central moment (μ_k) is defined as

$$\mu_k = \frac{1}{N}\sum_{i=1}^{n}(x_i - mean)^k f_i = \mathtt{fsum}(n, y, f, k)/N,$$

$y_i = x_i - mean,\ k = 1, 2, 3, 4.$

A measure of central tendency is given by the first moment about zero, which is the arithmetic mean. A measure of dispersion is given by the second central moment, which is the square of standard deviation. Measure of skewness and kurtosis are provided by the third and fourth central moments respectively.

Beta-coefficients and gamma-coefficients

Beta-coefficients are defined as:

$$\beta_1 = \frac{\mu_3^2}{\mu_2^3}; \qquad \beta_2 = \frac{\mu_4}{\mu_2^2}.$$

Gamma-coefficients are defined as:

$$\gamma_1 = \sqrt{\beta_1}; \qquad \gamma_2 = \beta_2 - 3.$$

Skewness

The word "skewness" is used to denote the 'extent of asymmetry' in the data. When the frequency distribution is not symmetrical, it is said to be skew. It may be positive or negative. It is measured by the following formula:

Bowley's measure:

$$\text{Skewness} = \frac{Q_3 - 2Q_2 - Q_1}{Q_3 - Q_1}$$

where Q_1, Q_2, Q_3 denote the first, second and third quartiles of the distribution. Moments measure:

$$\text{Skewness}(\gamma_1) = \sqrt{\beta_1} = \frac{\mu_3}{\sigma^3}, \text{ as } \mu_2 = \sigma^2.$$

Kurtosis

Kurtosis refers to the degree of "peakedness" of the frequency curve. Two distributions may have the same average, dispersion and skewness. Yet, in one, there may be high concentration of values near the mode, showing a sharper peak in the frequency curve than in the other. This characteristic of the frequency distribution is known as "kurtosis". The only measure of kurtosis is based on moments, and is given as

$$\text{Kurtosis}(\gamma_2) = \beta_2 - 3 = \frac{\mu_4}{\sigma^4} - 3.$$

Program 16.11

```
/* Computation of central moments, beta and gamma coefficients
   for ungrouped frequency distribution */
#include<stdio.h>
#include<math.h>
void main()
  {
    float x[50],mu1,mu2,mu3,mu4,mean,beta1,beta2,gamma1,gamma2;
    int f[50],N=0,n,i;
    float fsum(int,float [],int [],int);
    printf("Enter sample size and the sample \n");
    printf("(x[i],f[i]) line by line\n");
    scanf("%d",&n);
    for(i=1;i<=n;i++){
       scanf("%f%d",&x[i],&f[i]);
       N+=f[i];
     }
    printf("Given sample is \n");
    for(i=1;i<=n;i++)
       printf("%0.4f %d\n",x[i],f[i]);
    mean=fsum(n,x,f,1)/N;
    for(i=1;i<=n;i++)
       x[i]=x[i]-mean;
    mu1=fsum(n,x,f,1)/N;
    mu2=fsum(n,x,f,2)/N;
    mu3=fsum(n,x,f,3)/N;
```

```
    mu4=fsum(n,x,f,4)/N;
    beta1=mu3*mu3/(pow(mu2,3));
    beta2=mu4/(mu2*mu2);
    gamma1=sqrt(beta1);
    gamma2=beta2-3;
    printf("Mean                   = %0.4f\n",mean);
    printf("First central moments  = %0.4f\n",mu1);
    printf("Second central moments = %0.4f\n",mu2);
    printf("Third central moments  = %0.4f\n",mu3);
    printf("Fourth central moments = %0.4f\n",mu4);
    printf("Beta  coefficients: beta 1= %0.4f\n",beta1);
    printf("Beta 2                    = %0.4f\n",beta2);
    printf("Gamma coefficients:gamma 1= %0.4f\n",gamma1);
    printf("Gamma 2                   = %0.4f\n",gamma2);
 }
/* The function fsum */
float fsum(int n,float x[],int f[],int i)
[code of fsum to be included here]
```

A sample of input/output:

```
Enter sample size and the sample
(x[i],f[i]) line by line
5
5 7
8 9
11 6
15 7
18 9

Given sample is
5.0000 7
8.0000 9
11.0000 6
15.0000 7
18.0000 9
Mean                   = 11.5789
First central moments  = 0.0000
Second central moments = 22.9806
Third central moments  = 6.7344
Fourth central moments = 811.8133
Beta  coefficients: beta 1= 0.0037
Beta 2                    = 1.5372
Gamma coefficients:gamma 1= 0.0611
```

```
Gamma 2                    = -1.4628
```

16.5 Correlation and Regression

16.5.1 Correlation

The word "correlation" is used to denote the degree of association between variables. Two variables x and y be so related that, variations in the magnitude of one variable tends to be accompanied by variations in the magnitude of the other variable. Then these two variables are said to be correlated. Correlation may also be linear or non-linear.

Covariance:

Given a set of n pairs of observations $(x_1, y_1), (x_2, y_2), \ldots, (x_n, y_n)$, relating to two variables x and y, the covariance of x and y, represented by $\text{cov}(x, y)$, is defined as

$$cov(x,y) = \frac{1}{n}\sum_{i=1}^{n}(x_i - \bar{x})(y_i - \bar{y}) = \frac{1}{n}\sum_{i=1}^{n} x_i y_i - \bar{x}\bar{y}.$$

Correlation Coefficient(r):

The correlation coefficient between x and y is defined as

$$r = \frac{cov(x,y)}{\sigma_x . \sigma_y},$$

where

$$\sigma_x = \sqrt{\frac{1}{n}\sum_{i=1}^{n}(x_i - \bar{x})^2}, \ \sigma_y = \sqrt{\frac{1}{n}\sum_{i=1}^{n}(y_i - \bar{y})^2}$$

are the standard deviations of x and y respectively. Thus

$$r = \frac{\sum_{i=1}^{n}(x_i - \overline{x})(y_i - \overline{y})}{\sqrt{\sum_{i=1}^{n}(x_i - \overline{x})^2(y_i - \overline{y})^2}}.$$

It is used as a measure of linear correlation between x and y. The value of covariance lies between $-\infty$ and ∞, but, the value of correlation coefficient lies between -1 and 1.

Program 16.12

```
/* Computation of covariance and correlation coefficient
   of a bivariate distribution */
#include<stdio.h>
#include<math.h>
```

```
void main()
  {
    float x[50],y[50],xbar,ybar,sigmax,sigmay,cov=0,cc;
    int n,i;
    float sum(int,float [], int);
    printf("Enter the sample size and the sample (x[i],y[i])\n");
    scanf("%d",&n);
    for(i=1;i<=n;i++)
       scanf("%f%f",&x[i],&y[i]);
    printf("The given sample is\n");
    for(i=1;i<=n;i++)
       printf("%0.4f %0.4f\n",x[i],y[i]);
    xbar=sum(n,x,1)/n; /* mean of x */
    ybar=sum(n,y,1)/n; /* mean of y */
    for(i=1;i<=n;i++){
       x[i]=x[i]-xbar; /* x[i]=x[i]-mean */
       y[i]=y[i]-ybar;
       cov+=x[i]*y[i];
      }
    cov=cov/n;
    sigmax=sqrt(sum(n,x,2)/n);
    sigmay=sqrt(sum(n,y,2)/n);
    cc=cov/(sigmax*sigmay);
    printf("Mean(x)              = %0.4f\n",xbar);
    printf("Mean(y)              = %0.4f\n",ybar);
    printf("s.d(x)               = %0.4f\n",sigmax);
    printf("s.d(y)               = %0.4f\n",sigmay);
    printf("Covariance           = %0.4f\n",cov);
    printf("Correlation coeff.= %0.4f\n",cc);
  }
/* Function to compute the sum of n elements */
float sum(int n,float x[], int p)
[code of sum to be included here]
```

A sample of input/output:

```
Enter the sample size and the sample (x[i],y[i])
6
6 7
10 12
11 14
15 9
16 10
17 12
```

```
The given sample is
10.0000 12.0000
12.0000 15.0000
14.0000 19.0000
16.0000 18.0000
18.0000 14.0000
20.0000 10.0000
Mean(x)            = 15.0000
Mean(y)            = 14.6667
s.d(x)             = 3.4157
s.d(y)             = 3.1447
Covariance         = -2.3333
Correlation coeff.= -0.2172
```

16.5.2 Regression

The word "regression" is used to denote estimation or prediction of the average value of one variable for a specified value of another variable. The estimation is done by the means of suitable equations, derived on the basis of available data. Such an equation is known as **regression equation**.

The estimate of y is obtained from an equation of the form

$$y - \bar{y} = b_{yx}(x - \bar{x}) \quad \text{or} \quad y = b_{yx}.x + (\bar{y} - b_{yx}.\bar{x}) = b_{yx}.x + c_1 \tag{16.1}$$

where $c_1 = \bar{y} - b_{yx}.\bar{x}$, and that of x from an equation of the form

$$x - \bar{x} = b_{xy}(y - \bar{y}) \quad \text{or} \quad x = b_{xy}.y + (\bar{x} - b_{xy}.\bar{y}) = b_{yx}.x + c_2, \tag{16.2}$$

where $c_2 = \bar{x} - b_{xy}.\bar{y}$.

Equation (16.1) is known as regression equation of y on x, and equation (16.2) as regression equation of x on y. The coefficient b_{yx} is known as the regression coefficient of y on x and b_{xy} is the regression coefficient of x on y, where

$$b_{xy} = r\frac{\sigma_x}{\sigma_y} = \frac{cov(x,y)}{\sigma_x\sigma_y}\frac{\sigma_x}{\sigma_y} = \frac{cov(x,y)}{\sigma_y^2} = \frac{\sum(x_i - \bar{x})(y_i - \bar{y})}{\sum(y_i - \bar{y})^2} = \frac{\sum X_iY_i}{\sum Y_i^2}$$

and

$$b_{yx} = r\frac{\sigma_y}{\sigma_x} = \frac{\sum(x_i - \bar{x})(y_i - \bar{y})}{\sum(x_i - \bar{x})^2} = \frac{\sum X_iY_i}{\sum X_i^2}, \text{ where } X_i = x_i - \bar{x}, Y_i = y_i - \bar{y}.$$

Program 16.13

```
/* Computation of regression coefficients and regression lines */
#include<stdio.h>
#include<math.h>
void main()
 {
   float x[50],y[50],xbar=0,ybar=0,xy=0,x2=0,y2=0,bxy,byx,c1,c2;
   int n,i;
   printf("Enter sample size and the sample (x[i],y[i])\n");
   scanf("%d",&n);
   for(i=1;i<=n;i++)
     {
       scanf("%f%f",&x[i],&y[i]);
       xbar+=x[i];  /* sum of x[i] */
       ybar+=y[i];  /* sum of y[i] */
     }
   printf("Given sample is\n");
   for(i=1;i<=n;i++)
      printf("%0.4f %0.4f\n",x[i],y[i]);
   xbar/=n;  /* mean of x */
   ybar/=n;  /* mean of y */
   for(i=1;i<=n;i++){
      x[i]-=xbar;  /* x[i]=x[i]-mean */
      y[i]-=ybar;  /* y[i]=y[i]-mean */
      xy+=x[i]*y[i];
      x2+=x[i]*x[i];
      y2+=y[i]*y[i];
    }
   bxy=xy/y2;
   byx=xy/x2;
   printf("Regression coeff. of x on y is %.4f:\n",bxy);
   printf("Regression coeff. of y on x is %.4f:\n",byx);
   c1=ybar-byx*xbar;
   printf("Regression line of y on x is:\n");
   printf("y=%8.3f x %-+8.3f\n",byx,c1); /* -,+ flags are used together*/
   c2=xbar-bxy*ybar;
   printf("Regression line of x on y is:\n");
   printf("x=%8.3f y %-+8.3f\n",bxy,c2);
 }
```

A sample of input/output:

```
Enter sample size and the sample (x[i],y[i])
5
2 9
```

```
4 10
6 16
7 20
9 22

Given sample is
2.0000 9.0000
4.0000 10.0000
6.0000 16.0000
7.0000 20.0000
9.0000 22.0000
Regression coeff. of x on y is 0.4497:
Regression coeff. of y on x is 2.0822:
Regression line of y on x is:
y=   2.082 x +3.740
Regression line of x on y is:
x=   0.450 y -1.325
```

16.6 Bivariate Curve Fitting

In this section some programs are presented to fit (i) linear, (ii) parabolic, and (iii) geometric curves by the method of least square.

Linear curve

Let

$$y = a + bx \tag{16.3}$$

be the equation of a linear curve (i.e. a straight line). Let $(x_i, y_i), i = 1, 2, \ldots, n$, be a bivariate sample of size n. To fit (16.3), we have to find the values of the parameters a and b in terms of sample values.

Let Y_i be the value of y obtained from (16.3), when $x = x_i$. That is,

$$Y_i = a + bx_i. \tag{16.4}$$

The error at the ith observation is $y_i - Y_i$. The sum of square of errors is $S = \sum_i (y_i - Y_i)^2 = \sum_i (y_i - a - bx_i)^2$. In the method of least square we have to choose a and b in such a way that S is minimum. That is, $\frac{\partial S}{\partial a} = \frac{\partial S}{\partial b} = 0$. Therefore,

$$\sum y_i = na + b \sum x_i. \tag{16.5}$$

$$\sum x_i y_i = a \sum x_i + b \sum x_i^2. \tag{16.6}$$

These equations are known as **normal equations**. Solving these equations, we get

$$b = \frac{n\sum x_i y_i - \sum x_i \sum y_i}{n\sum x_i^2 - (\sum x_i)^2} = \frac{n \times SXY - SX1 \times SY1}{n \times SX2 - (SX1)^2}$$

where $SX1 = \sum x_i, SY1 = \sum y_i, SXY = \sum x_i y_i, SX2 = \sum x_i^2$ and

$$a = \frac{1}{n}\sum y_i - \frac{b}{n}\sum x_i = \frac{SY1}{n} - b * \frac{SX1}{n}.$$

The fitted curve is obtained after estimating a and b.

The sum of square of errors is evaluated as $S = \sum_{i=1}^{n} (Y_i - y_i)^2$.

Program 16.14

```
/* Fitting a straight line y=a+bx by least square method,
   using bivariate sample (xi,yi) of size n. */
#include<stdio.h>
#include<math.h>
void main()
 {
   float x[50],y[50],sx1=0,sy1=0,sx2=0,sxy=0,b,a,s=0,t;
   int n,i;
   printf("Enter sample size and sample\n");
   scanf("%d",&n);
   for(i=1;i<=n;i++) scanf("%f%f",&x[i],&y[i]);
   for(i=1;i<=n;i++){
      sx1+=x[i];
      sx2+=x[i]*x[i];
      sy1+=y[i];
      sxy+=x[i]*y[i];
    }
   b=(n*sxy-sx1*sy1)/(n*sx2-sx1*sx1);
   a=sy1/n-b*sx1/n;
   printf("The fitted line is:\n");
   printf("y=%8.3f %+8.3f x\n",a,b);
/* Estimation of the error, sum of square of errors */
   for(i=1;i<=n;i++){
       t=a+b*x[i];
       s+=pow((t-y[i]),2);
     }
   printf("The sum of square of errors: %0.5f\n", s);
 }
```

A sample of input/output:

```
Enter sample size and sample
5
0 3 2 7 4 10 6 16 8 22

 The fitted line is:
y=    2.200    +2.350 x
The sum of square of errors: 4.30000
```

Parabolic curve fitting

Let the second degree parabolic curve be

$$y = a + bx + cx^2. \tag{16.7}$$

As above, the normal equations are

$$\begin{aligned}\sum y_i &= na + b\sum x_i + c\sum x_i^2\\ \sum x_i y_i &= a\sum x_i + b\sum x_i^2 + c\sum x_i^3\\ \sum x_i^2 y_i &= a\sum x_i^2 + b\sum x_i^3 + c\sum x_i^4.\end{aligned}$$

Let $\sum x_i = SX1, \sum x_i^2 = SX2, \sum x_i^3 = SX3, \sum x_i^4 = SX4, \sum y_i = SY0$, $\sum x_i y_i = SY1$ and $\sum x_i^2 y_i = SY2$.

The above equations become
$SY0 = na + b \times SX1 + c \times SX2$
$SY1 = a \times SX1 + b \times SX2 + c \times SX3$
$SY2 = a \times SX2 + b \times SX3 + c \times SX4.$

Using Crammer's rule (or any other similar method) we can solve this system of equations for the unknown a, b, c. If a^*, b^*, c^* be the solution of the above system of equations, then the fitted curve is

$$y = a^* + b^* x + c^* x^2.$$

The values of a, b, c obtained by Crammer's rule are given by

$$den = \begin{vmatrix} n & sx1 & sx2 \\ sx1 & sx2 & sx3 \\ sx2 & sx3 & sx4 \end{vmatrix}, \quad a = \frac{1}{den}\begin{vmatrix} sy0 & sx1 & sx2 \\ sy1 & sx2 & sx3 \\ sy2 & sx3 & sx4 \end{vmatrix},$$

$$b = \frac{1}{den}\begin{vmatrix} n & sy0 & sx2 \\ sx1 & sy1 & sx3 \\ sx2 & sy2 & sx4 \end{vmatrix}, \quad c = \frac{1}{den}\begin{vmatrix} n & sx1 & sy0 \\ sx1 & sx2 & sy1 \\ sx2 & sx3 & sy2 \end{vmatrix}.$$

Program 16.15

```
/* Fitting a parabolic curve y=a+bx+cx^2 by least square method.
   using bivariate sample (xi,yi) of size n. */
#include<stdio.h>
#include<math.h>
void main()
  {
    float x[50],y[50],sx1=0,sx2=0,sx3=0,sx4=0;
    float sy0=0,sy1=0,sy2=0,x2,den,a,b,c,s=0,t;
    float det3(float,float,float,float,float,float,float,float,float);
    int n,i;
    printf("Enter sample size and sample\n");
    scanf("%d",&n);
    for(i=1;i<=n;i++) scanf("%f%f",&x[i],&y[i]);
    printf("The given sample is\n");
    for(i=1;i<=n;i++) printf("%0.3f \t %0.3f\n",x[i],y[i]);
    for(i=1;i<=n;i++){
        sx1+=x[i];
        x2=x[i]*x[i];
        sx2+=x2;
        sx3+=x[i]*x2;
        sx4+=x2*x2;
        sy0+=y[i];
        sy1+=x[i]*y[i];
        sy2+=x2*y[i];
      }
/* Solution of normal equations */
    den=det3((float)n,sx1,sx2,sx1,sx2,sx3,sx2,sx3,sx4);
    a=det3(sy0,sx1,sx2,sy1,sx2,sx3,sy2,sx3,sx4)/den;
    b=det3((float)n,sy0,sx2,sx1,sy1,sx3,sx2,sy2,sx4)/den;
    c=det3((float)n,sx1,sy0,sx1,sx2,sy1,sx2,sx3,sy2)/den;
    printf("The fitted curve is:\n");
    printf("y=%8.3f %+8.3f x %+8.3f x*x",a,b,c);
/* Estimation of error, sum of square of errors */
    for(i=1;i<=n;i++) {
        t=a+b*x[i]+c*x[i]*x[i];
        s+=pow((t-y[i]),2);
      }
    printf("\nThe sum of square of errors: %0.4f", s);
}
/* Computation of determinant of order 3x3 */
float det3(float a1,float a2,float a3,float b1,float b2,float b3,
float c1,float c2,float c3)
```

```
{
  float val;
  val=a1*(b2*c3-b3*c2)-a2*(c3*b1-c1*b3)+a3*(b1*c2-c1*b2);
  return val;
}
```

A sample of input/output:

```
Enter sample size and sample
7
-3 16
-2 12
-1 9
0 3
1 5
2 8
3 18

The given sample is
-3.000      16.000
-2.000      12.000
-1.000      9.000
0.000       3.000
1.000       5.000
2.000       8.000
3.000       18.000
The fitted curve is:
y=   4.619   -0.214 x    +1.381 x*x
The sum of square of errors: 21.3809
```

Geometric curve fitting

Let the curve be given as $y = ab^x$. Taking logarithm of both sides we get

$$\log y = \log a + x \log b, \text{ or } Y = A + Bx$$

where $Y = \log y, A = \log a$, and $B = \log b$, which represents a straight line. Note that the values of y_i must be positive. This straight line may be fitted by the method as described earlier. The values of A and B are computed as

$$B = \frac{n \sum x_i Y_i - \sum x_i \sum Y_i}{n \sum x_i^2 - (\sum x_i)^2}, A = \frac{1}{n} \sum Y_i - \frac{b}{n} \sum x_i,$$

and finally, the parameters of the curve are given by $a = e^A$ and $b = e^B$. Therefore, the fitted curve is

$$y = a^*(b^*)^x$$

where a^* and b^* are the estimated values of a and b respectively.

Program 16.16

```
/* Fitting a curve of type  y=ab^x by least
   square method, using bivariate sample (xi,yi) of size n. */
#include<stdio.h>
#include<math.h>
void main()
  {
    float x[50],y[50],sx1=0,sx2=0,sy1=0,sxy=0,s=0,a,b,t;
    int n,i;
    printf("Enter sample size and sample\n");
    scanf("%d",&n);
    for(i=1;i<=n;i++) scanf("%f%f",&x[i],&y[i]);
    for(i=1;i<=n;i++)
      {
        y[i]=log(y[i]);
        sx1+=x[i];
        sx2+=x[i]*x[i];
        sy1+=y[i];
        sxy+=x[i]*y[i];
      }
    b=(n*sxy-sx1*sy1)/(n*sx2-sx1*sx1);
    a=sy1/n-b*sx1/n;
    a=exp(a);
    b=exp(b);
    printf("The fitted curve is:\n");
    printf("y=%6.3f(%6.3f)^x\n",a,b); /* ^ represents power */

/* Estimation of error, sum of square of errors */
    for(i=1;i<=n;i++)
      {
        t=a*pow(b,x[i]);
        s+=pow((t-exp(y[i])),2);
      }
    printf("The sum of square of errors: %.4f", s);
  }
```

A sample of input/output:

```
Enter sample size and sample
6
-1 1.5 0 3.25 1 5.75 2 11.80 3 24.50 4 48.15
The fitted curve is:
y= 3.040( 1.992)^x
The sum of square of errors: 0.4933
```

16.7 Multiple Correlation and Regression

In many cases, however, it becomes necessary to consider the effect of more than one independent variable on a dependent variable. In multiple regression, consider more than one independent variable. The best, (i.e. the most possible relationship of the dependent variable with these independent variables) is found out. Here, only two independent variables are considered.

Let x_1 be the dependent variable and x_2, x_3 be two independent variables. Let us assume that the relationship between them is approximately given by

$$X_1 = a + b_{12.3}x_2 + b_{13.2}x_3 \tag{16.8}$$

Denoting the variance of x_i by S_i^2 and the correlation coefficient between x_i and x_j by r_{ij}. The values of $b_{12.3}$ and $b_{13.2}$ are given by

$$b_{12.3} = \frac{S_1}{S_2}\frac{r_{21}r_{33} - r_{31}r_{23}}{r_{22}r_{33} - r_{32}r_{23}} = \frac{S_1}{S_2}\frac{r_{12} - r_{13}r_{23}}{1 - r_{23}^2} \tag{16.9}$$

$$b_{13.2} = \frac{S_1}{S_3}\frac{r_{22}r_{31} - r_{32}r_{21}}{r_{22}r_{33} - r_{32}r_{23}} = \frac{S_1}{S_3}\frac{r_{13} - r_{12}r_{23}}{1 - r_{23}^2}. \tag{16.10}$$

[As $r_{22} = r_{33} = 1, r_{13} = r_{31}, r_{12} = r_{21}$, etc.]

The value of a is

$$a = \bar{x_1} - b_{12.3}\bar{x_2} - b_{13.2}\bar{x_3}. \tag{16.11}$$

Thus, the regression line of x_1 on x_2 and x_3 is

$$X_1 = a + b_{12.3}x_2 + b_{13.2}x_3,$$

where $a, b_{12.3}$ and $b_{13.2}$ are computed from (16.9), (16.10) and (16.11) respectively.

Multiple correlation

The multiple correlation coefficient of x_1 on x_2 and x_3 is

$$r_{1.23} = \left[\frac{r_{12}^2 + r_{13}^2 - 2r_{12}r_{13}r_{23}}{1 - r_{23}^2}\right]^{1/2}.$$

Partial correlation

The partial correlation coefficient $r_{12.3}$ between the variables x_1 and x_2 is given by

$$r_{12.3} = \frac{r_{12} - r_{13}r_{23}}{\sqrt{1 - r_{13}^2}\sqrt{1 - r_{23}^2}}.$$

Program 16.17

```
/* Computation of multiple regression, multiple correlation,
   partial correlation */
#include<stdio.h>
#include<math.h>
#define M 50
void main()
 {
    float x1[M],x2[M],x3[M],r12,r13,r23,s1,s2,s3,b123,b132,a,r123,rp123;
    int n,i;
    float mean(float x[], int n);
    float sigma(float x[], int n);
    float r(float x[],float y[],int n);
    printf("Enter the size of the sample\n");
    scanf("%d",&n);
    printf("Enter the values of (x1,x2,x3)\n");
    for(i=1;i<=n;i++)
     scanf("%f%f%f", &x1[i],&x2[i],&x3[i]);
/* Computation of regression coefficients */
    r12=r(x1,x2,n);
    r13=r(x1,x3,n);
    r23=r(x2,x3,n);
    s1=sigma(x1,n);
    s2=sigma(x2,n);
    s3=sigma(x3,n);
    b123=((r12-r13*r23)*s1)/((1-r23*r23)*s2);
    b132=((r13-r12*r23)*s1)/((1-r23*r23)*s3);
    a=mean(x1,n)-b123*mean(x2,n)-b132*mean(x3,n);
    printf("mean(x1)=%.4f mean(x2)=%.4f mean(x3)=%.4f \n",
                mean(x1,n),mean(x2,n),mean(x3,n));
    printf("sd(x1)=%.4f sd(x2)=%.4f sd(x3)=%.4f \n",
                sigma(x1,n),sigma(x2,n),sigma(x3,n));
    printf("r12=%0.4f r13=%.4f r23=%.4f \n",
                r(x1,x2,n),r(x1,x3,n),r(x2,x3,n));
    printf("\nCoefficients of regression equation are \n");
    printf("a=%0.5f b1.23=%0.5f b1.32=%0.5f\n",a,b123,b132);
    r123=sqrt((r12*r12+r13*r13-2*r12*r13*r23)/(1-r23*r23));
    printf("\nMultiple correlation coefficient r1.23=%.4f\n",r123);
    rp123=(r12-r13*r23)/sqrt((1-r13*r13)*(1-r23*r23));
    printf("Partial correlation coefficient r12.3=%0.4f",rp123);
 }
/* Function to compute mean */
```

```
float mean(float x[], int n)
  {
    float s=0;
    int i;
    for(i=1;i<=n;i++)  s+=x[i];
    return (s/n);
  }
/* Function to compute standard deviation (sigma) */
float sigma(float x[], int n)
  {
    float xbar,s=0,y;
    int i;
    float mean(float x[], int n);
    xbar=mean(x,n);
    for(i=1;i<=n;i++){
       y=x[i]-xbar;
       s+=y*y;
      }
    return (sqrt(s/n));
  }
/* Function to compute covariance between x and y */
float cov(float x[],float y[],int n)
  {
    float  s=0,xbar,ybar;
    int i;
    float mean(float x[], int n);
    xbar=mean(x,n);
    ybar=mean(y,n);
    for(i=1;i<=n;i++)
       s+=(x[i]-xbar)*(y[i]-ybar);
    return (s/n);
  }
/* Function to compute correlation coefficient */
float r(float x[],float y[],int n)
  {
    float r;
    float sigma(float x[], int n);
    float cov(float x[],float y[],int n);
    r=cov(x,y,n)/(sigma(x,n)*sigma(y,n));
    return r;
  }
```

A sample of input/output:

```
Enter the size of the sample
18
Enter the values of (x1,x2,x3) line by line
19 8 4 51 15 5
30 11 3 42 21 3
25 7 2 18 5 1
44 10 4 56 13 6
38 12 3 32 13 4
25 5 2 10 6 3
20 4 4 27 8 4
13 7 3 49 12 5
27 6 3 55 16 7

mean(x1)=32.2778 mean(x2)=9.9444 mean(x3)=3.6667
sd(x1)=14.0230 sd(x2)=4.4281 sd(x3)=1.4142
r12=0.7679 r13=0.7190 r23=0.5205

Coefficients of regression equation are
a=-0.65073 b1.23=1.70983 b1.32=4.34324

Multiple correlation coefficient r1.23=0.8541
Partial correlation coefficient r12.3=0.6634
```

16.8 Fitting a Theoretical Distribution to Observed Distribution

To fit a theoretical distribution into a given observed distribution, the aim is to test whether the observed distribution can be regarded as the distribution of a random variable X, which is drawn from the population characterized by the theoretical distribution. The first step to fit a theoretical distribution is to estimate the parameters of the theoretical distribution from the observed one, unless the values of the parameters are not known previously.

Several methods are available to estimate the parameters. Among them the most simple is the method of moments. Suppose, the theoretical distribution has k parameters to be estimated. The method estimates the parameters by performing the following steps.

(i) The first k moments of the theoretical distribution are found out in terms of the parameters, which is of the observed distribution.

(ii) The first k moments of the theoretical and observed distribution are equated.

(iii) The k resulting equations are solved in order to determine the k parameters.

The first k moments are taken because the error in a higher order moment will increase due to sampling.

Fitting a binomial distribution

The probability mass function of binomial distribution is $f_i = {}^nC_i p^i(1-p)^{n-i}, i = 0, 1, \ldots, n$, where n (a positive integer) and p $(0 < p < 1)$ are the two parameters. For this distribution, the first moment about zero is np, and the first moment about zero of the observed distribution is $\bar{x}$.

Therefore, $np = \bar{x}$, and finally the estimated value of p is $p^* = \bar{x}/n$.

The estimated frequency will be

$$N \times f_i = N \times {}^nC_i(p^*)^i(1-p^*)^{n-i}$$

for $i = 0, 1, 2, \ldots, n$, where N is the total frequency, that is, the total number of sets of n trials. It may be observed that

$$\frac{f_i}{f_{i-1}} = \frac{n-i+1}{i}\frac{p}{1-p} \text{ or } f_i = \left(\frac{n-i+1}{i}\frac{p}{1-p}\right)f_{i-1}$$

for $i = 1, 2, \ldots, n$ and $f_0 = (1-p)^n$.

Program 16.18

```
/* Fitting a binomial distribution to an observed distribution.
   Reads a univariate sample (xi,fi) of size n and fits into
   binomial distribution */
#include<stdio.h>
#include<math.h>
void main()
  {
    float x[50],s=0,xbar,p,fi,exfreq,error=0;
    int f[50],N=0,n,i;
    printf("Enter no. of observations \n");
    scanf("%d",&n);
    n--;
    printf("Enter the distribution (xi,fi)\n");
    for(i=0;i<=n;i++)
       scanf("%f%d",&x[i],&f[i]);
    for(i=0;i<=n;i++){
         N+=f[i];
         s+=x[i]*f[i];
      }
    xbar=s/N;
    p=xbar/n;
    fi=pow((1-p),n);
    s=N*fi;
    printf("  i    fi      expected  observed\n");
```

```
   printf("                  freq.      freq.\n");
   printf("-----------------------------------\n");
   printf("  0   %6.4f   %6.2f %6d\n",fi,N*fi,f[0]);
   for(i=1;i<=n;i++){
      fi=((n-i+1)*p)/(i*(1-p))*fi;
      exfreq=N*fi;
      s+=exfreq;
      error+=fabs(exfreq-f[i]);
      printf(" %2d   %6.4f    %6.2f %6d\n",i,fi,exfreq,f[i]);
    }
   printf("-----------------------------------\n");
   printf(" Total         %8.2f %6d\n",s,N);
   printf("Total error = %0.4f\n",error);
 }
```

A sample of input/output:

```
Enter no.  of observations
8
Enter the distribution (xi,fi)
0 2 1 4 2 8 3 10 4 7 5 3 6 2 7 1
  i     fi      expected observed
                freq.     freq.
---------------------------------
  0   0.0190      0.70      2
  1   0.1012      3.74      4
  2   0.2313      8.56      8
  3   0.2937     10.87     10
  4   0.2238      8.28      7
  5   0.1023      3.78      3
  6   0.0260      0.96      2
  7   0.0028      0.10      1
---------------------------------
 Total           37.00     37
Total error = 5.6785
```

Preparation of standard normal probability table

The standard normal probability integral is

$$\Phi(x) = \frac{1}{\sqrt{2\pi}} \int_{-\infty}^{x} e^{-t^2/2}\, dt.$$

Its power series expansion is

$$\Phi(x) = \frac{1}{2} + \frac{1}{\sqrt{2\pi}} \sum_{n=0}^{\infty} \frac{(-1)^n x^{2n+1}}{n!\, 2^n\, (2n+1)} \quad \text{for } x \geq 0.$$

Due to symmetry of standard normal probability density curve,
$\Phi(-x) = 1 - \Phi(x)$ and $\Phi(0) = 0.5$.

Let $t_n = \dfrac{(-1)^n\, x^{2n+1}}{n!\, 2^n\, (2n+1)}$. Then $\Phi(x) = \dfrac{1}{2} + \dfrac{S}{\sqrt{2\pi}}$ where $S = \sum_{n=0}^{\infty} t_n$.

Now, $t_{n+1} = \dfrac{(-1)^{n+1}\, x^{2n+3}}{(n+1)!\, 2^{n+1}\, (2n+3)}$, $t_0 = x$.

Thus $\dfrac{t_{n+1}}{t_n} = -\dfrac{x^2\,(2n+1)}{2(n+1)(2n+3)}$

or, $t_{n+1} = -\dfrac{2n+1}{(2n+2)(2n+3)} x^2\, t_n$.

The following function PHI(x) computes the sum of the series $\Phi(x)$ for a given x by direct summation up to the terms whose magnitude is greater than 10^{-6}.

Program 16.19

```
/* Preparation of normal probability integral table */
#include<stdio.h>
#include<math.h>
#define PI 3.141592618
void main()
 {
   float p[10],x;
   int i,j;
   float PHI(float);
   FILE *fp=fopen("normal.out","w");
   for(i=1;i<=5;i++) fprintf(fp," ");
   for(i=0;i<=9;i++) fprintf(fp,"%3.2f    ",i*0.01);
   fprintf(fp,"\n");
   for(x=0;x<=3.0;x+=0.1)
    {
      for(i=0;i<=9;i++) p[i]=PHI(x+i/100.0);
      fprintf(fp,"%3.1f ",x);
      for(j=0;j<=9;j++) fprintf(fp,"%7.4f",p[j]);
      fprintf(fp,"\n");
    }
 }
/* Following function compute PHI(x) at a given x
  correct up to six significant figures */
float PHI(float x)
 {
    float eps=1.0e-6,t,s;
    int n=0;
    t=x;
```

```
    s=x;
    while(fabs(t)>eps)
      {
        t=-(2*n+1.)*x*x*t/((2*n+2.)*(2*n+3.));
        s+=t;
        n++;
      }
    return(0.5+s/sqrt(2.0*PI));
 }
```

Output file name: normal.out

	0.00	0.01	0.02	0.03	0.04	0.05	0.06	0.07	0.08	0.09
0.0	0.5000	0.5040	0.5080	0.5120	0.5160	0.5199	0.5239	0.5279	0.5319	0.5359
0.1	0.5398	0.5438	0.5478	0.5517	0.5557	0.5596	0.5636	0.5675	0.5714	0.5753
0.2	0.5793	0.5832	0.5871	0.5910	0.5948	0.5987	0.6026	0.6064	0.6103	0.6141
0.3	0.6179	0.6217	0.6255	0.6293	0.6331	0.6368	0.6406	0.6443	0.6480	0.6517
0.4	0.6554	0.6591	0.6628	0.6664	0.6700	0.6736	0.6772	0.6808	0.6844	0.6879
0.5	0.6915	0.6950	0.6985	0.7019	0.7054	0.7088	0.7123	0.7157	0.7190	0.7224
0.6	0.7257	0.7291	0.7324	0.7357	0.7389	0.7422	0.7454	0.7486	0.7517	0.7549
0.7	0.7580	0.7611	0.7642	0.7673	0.7704	0.7734	0.7764	0.7794	0.7823	0.7852
0.8	0.7881	0.7910	0.7939	0.7967	0.7995	0.8023	0.8051	0.8078	0.8106	0.8133
0.9	0.8159	0.8186	0.8212	0.8238	0.8264	0.8289	0.8315	0.8340	0.8365	0.8389
1.0	0.8413	0.8438	0.8461	0.8485	0.8508	0.8531	0.8554	0.8577	0.8599	0.8621
1.1	0.8643	0.8665	0.8686	0.8708	0.8729	0.8749	0.8770	0.8790	0.8810	0.8830
1.2	0.8849	0.8869	0.8888	0.8907	0.8925	0.8944	0.8962	0.8980	0.8997	0.9015
1.3	0.9032	0.9049	0.9066	0.9082	0.9099	0.9115	0.9131	0.9147	0.9162	0.9177
1.4	0.9192	0.9207	0.9222	0.9236	0.9251	0.9265	0.9279	0.9292	0.9306	0.9319
1.5	0.9332	0.9345	0.9357	0.9370	0.9382	0.9394	0.9406	0.9418	0.9429	0.9441
1.6	0.9452	0.9463	0.9474	0.9484	0.9495	0.9505	0.9515	0.9525	0.9535	0.9545
1.7	0.9554	0.9564	0.9573	0.9582	0.9591	0.9599	0.9608	0.9616	0.9625	0.9633
1.8	0.9641	0.9649	0.9656	0.9664	0.9671	0.9678	0.9686	0.9693	0.9699	0.9706
1.9	0.9713	0.9719	0.9726	0.9732	0.9738	0.9744	0.9750	0.9756	0.9761	0.9767
2.0	0.9772	0.9778	0.9783	0.9788	0.9793	0.9798	0.9803	0.9808	0.9812	0.9817
2.1	0.9821	0.9826	0.9830	0.9834	0.9838	0.9842	0.9846	0.9850	0.9854	0.9857
2.2	0.9861	0.9864	0.9868	0.9871	0.9875	0.9878	0.9881	0.9884	0.9887	0.9890
2.3	0.9893	0.9896	0.9898	0.9901	0.9904	0.9906	0.9909	0.9911	0.9913	0.9916
2.4	0.9918	0.9920	0.9922	0.9925	0.9927	0.9929	0.9931	0.9932	0.9934	0.9936
2.5	0.9938	0.9940	0.9941	0.9943	0.9945	0.9946	0.9948	0.9949	0.9951	0.9952
2.6	0.9953	0.9955	0.9956	0.9957	0.9959	0.9960	0.9961	0.9962	0.9963	0.9964
2.7	0.9965	0.9966	0.9967	0.9968	0.9969	0.9970	0.9971	0.9972	0.9973	0.9974
2.8	0.9974	0.9975	0.9976	0.9977	0.9977	0.9978	0.9979	0.9979	0.9980	0.9981
2.9	0.9981	0.9982	0.9982	0.9983	0.9984	0.9984	0.9985	0.9985	0.9986	0.9986
3.0	0.9986	0.9987	0.9987	0.9988	0.9988	0.9989	0.9989	0.9989	0.9990	0.9990

16.9 Generation of Random Numbers and its Applications

The random numbers are generated by a random process and these numbers are the values of a random variable. Several methods are available to generate random numbers. Practically, these methods do not generate ideal random numbers, because these methods follow some algorithms. So, the available methods generate *pseudo random numbers.*

The commonly used simplest method to generate random numbers is the *power residue method.* A sequence of non-negative integers $x_1, x_2, \ldots$ is generated from the following relation

$$x_{n+1} = (a\,x_n)\,(\text{mod } m)$$

where x_0 is a starting value called the seed, a and m are two positive integers ($a < m$). The expression (ax_n) (mod m) gives the remainder when ax_n is divided by m. The possible values of x_{n+1} are $0, 1, 2, \ldots, m-1$, i.e. the number of different random numbers is m. The period of random number depends on the values of a, x_0 and m. Appropriate choice of a, x_0 and m gives a long period random numbers.

Suppose, the computer which will generate the random numbers have a word-length of b bits. Let $m = 2^{b-1} - 1$, a = an odd integer of the form $8k \pm 3$ and closed to $2^{b/2}$, x_0 = an odd integer between 0 and m. Now, ax_0 is a $2b$ bits integer. The least b significant bits form the random number x_1. The process is repeated for a desired number of times.

For a 32-bit computer, $m = 2^{31} - 1 = 2147483647, a = 2^{16} + 3 = 65539, x_0 = 1267835015$, $(0 < x_0 < m)$.

To obtain the random numbers between $[0, 1]$, all numbers are to be divided by $m-1$. These numbers are uniformly distributed over $[0, 1]$.

Fortunately, C provides a function `rand` which will generate a random number between 0 and `RAND_MAX` (=3276746) with period 232. This function is available in the header file `stdlib.h`. To generate a random number between 0 and a specified value, say 50, divide the random number by $50 + 1 = 51$. The remainder will be the required random number.

The following program generates 40 random numbers between 0 and 50.

Program 16.20

```
/* Generation of random numbers between 0 and 50 */
#include <stdlib.h>
#include <stdio.h>
void main(void)
 {
   int i;
   printf("Forty random numbers between 0 and 50\n");
   for(i=0; i<40; i++)
      printf("%02d ", rand() % 51);
}
```

Output:

```
Forty random numbers between 0 and 50
40 28 17 19 28 28 00 40 49 16 28 23 01 31 30 34 06 48 23 06
38 25 50 11 02 20 09 00 40 28 06 16 43 31 11 50 01 14 06 27
```

Modifying the above program one can generate a random number between 0 and 1. To get a random number between 0 and 1, divide the random number obtained from the function `rand` by `RAND_MAX`, since the function `rand` generates a random number between 0 and `RAND_MAX`.

The following program generates 40 random numbers between 0 and 1.

Program 16.21

```
/* Generation of random numbers between 0 and 1 */
#include <stdlib.h>
#include <stdio.h>
void main(void)
 {
   int i;
   float x;
   printf("Forty random numbers between 0 and 1\n");
   for(i=0; i<40; i++){
      x=(float)rand()/RAND_MAX;
      printf("%.4f ", x);
   }
 }
```

Output:

```
Forty random numbers between 0 and 1
0.0106 0.0040 0.3352 0.0333 0.3557 0.2172 0.5370 0.1958 0.7003 0.9499
0.2748 0.4443 0.1090 0.6982 0.5643 0.0415 0.1652 0.8155 0.6855 0.7644
0.8276 0.9595 0.2194 0.4268 0.9526 0.8395 0.9232 0.8109 0.4510 0.6048
0.6617 0.5997 0.5492 0.7200 0.1140 0.4062 0.1214 0.6713 0.4749 0.4911
```

The above two programs generate same set of random numbers in its every execution. To generate different sets of random numbers, we have to change the value of x_0 (called seed). This can be done by calling a C function `randomize`. The function `randomize` initializes the random number generator with a *random value.* The general form of this function is `void randomize()`. Since `randomize` is implemented as a macro that calls the time function prototype in `time.h`, therefore, the header file `time.h` should be included in the program. This function does not return any value.

The following program illustrates the use of the function `randomize`.

```
/* Use of the function randomize */
#include <stdlib.h>
#include <stdio.h>
#include <time.h>
void main(void)
{
```

```
    int i;
    randomize(); /* generates a random seed */
    printf("Twenty random numbers between 0 and 99\n");
    for(i=0; i<20; i++)
        printf("%d ", rand() % 100);
}
```

Output: From first run

```
Twenty random numbers between 0 and 99
26 26 53 85 13 69 70 63 94 89 22 20 75 76 68 35 55 89 31 36
```

Output: From second run

```
Twenty random numbers between 0 and 99
91 79 75 29 30 12 14 41 63 87 67 79 85 11 41 47 34 7 61 71
```

Observe that the same program generates different sets of random numbers in different runs. Thus, to generate a random number, inclusion of the function `randomize` is highly recommended.

The user can also initialize a seed as per requirement, using the function `srand`. The random number generator is reinitialized by calling `srand` with an argument. The general form of this function is `void srand(unsigned int)`. The generator can be set to a new starting point by calling `srand` with a given seed number.

16.9.1 Evaluation of π by Monte-Carlo method

Let $x^2 + y^2 = 1$ be the equation of a circle whose centre is $(0, 0)$ and radius 1. An approximate area of the circle can be found by counting the random points in a square of side 1 unit into which a circle of radius 1 is inscribed. Consider the first quadrant of the circle.

Now generate a pair of random numbers x and y between 0 and 1. If these random numbers satisfy the inequation $x^2 + y^2 \leq 1$, then the point (x, y) lies within the first quadrant of the circle. The area of the square is 1 unit and that of the circle in first quadrant is $\pi/4$. Now, generate a large number of random pairs and count the number of points within the first quadrant of the circle. If n_1 be the number of points within the first quadrant of the circle and n be the total number of points generated, then the required value of $\frac{\pi}{4}$ is $\frac{n_1}{n}$.

The following program computes the value of π using Monte-Carlo method.

Program 16.22

```
/* Evaluation of pi by Monte-Carlo method */
#include<stdio.h>
#include<stdlib.h>
```

```
#include<time.h>
void main()
 {
   int n,n1=0,i;
   float x,y,approxpi;
   printf("Enter number of points to be generated\n");
   scanf("%d",&n);
   randomize();
   for(i=1;i<=n;i++){
       x=(float)rand()/RAND_MAX;
       y=(float)rand()/RAND_MAX;
       if(x*x+y*y<=1.) n1++;    /* within first quadrant */
     }
   approxpi=4.0*(float)n1/n;
   printf("n=%d, n1=%d\n",n,n1);
   printf("The approximate value of Pie is %.7f\n",approxpi);
 }
```

A sample of input/output:

```
Enter number of points to be generated
32000
n=32000, n1=25165
The approximate value of Pie is 3.1456251
```

16.9.2 Simulation of coin tossing

By generating the random numbers 0 and 1, the probability of getting 'head' or 'tail' in a single toss can be determined. Suppose 0 and 1 represent the head and tail respectively. Generate a large number of random numbers, say n, and count the occurrence of 0, let it be n_1, then the probability of occurrence of head in a single trial is $\frac{n_1}{n}$ and similarly the probability of tail is $\frac{n-n_1}{n}$. The following program finds the probability of occurrence of head in a single trial.

Program 16.23

```
/* Simulation of coin tossing. 0 and 1 respectively
   represent head and tail. */
#include<stdio.h>
#include<math.h>
#include<stdlib.h>
#include<time.h>
void main()
 {
   int n,n1=0,i,m;
```

```
float p;
printf("Enter number of points to be generated\n");
scanf("%d",&n);
randomize();
for(i=1;i<=n;i++){
    m=rand() % 2; /* random numbers 0 and 1 */
    if(m==0) n1++;
   }
p=(float)n1/n;
printf("Favourable points=%d Total points=%d
                   Probability=%0.4f\n",n1,n,p);
}
```

A sample of input/output:

```
Enter number of points to be generated
700
Favourable points=353 Total points=700 Probability=0.5043
```

Exercise XVI

Programming Problems

1. Write a function `fsum` to compute the sum of n numbers and use it to read n numbers and print their sum.
2. Use the function `fsum` from the previous example, and compute the mean of a simple sample.
3. Write a program to compute the mean of the sample $(x_i, f_i), i = 1, 2, \ldots, n$, where f_i is the frequency of an item x_i.
4. Write a program to read a sample of size n and compute the range of the sample.
5. Write programs to read n numbers and prepare a frequency distribution table when (i) the length of the intervals is given, and (ii) the number of intervals is given.
6. Write a program to find the median of a simple distribution.
7. Write a program to find the median of a sample taken from grouped frequency distribution. Write a function to compute the kth ($k = 1, 2, 3$) quartile Q_k, and use it to compute Q_1, Q_2 and Q_3, for a sample of grouped frequency distribution.
8. Write a program to compute the first (Q_1), second (Q_2) and third (Q_3) quartiles of a simple distribution.
9. Write a program to compute the mode of a (i) simple distribution, (ii) frequency distribution, and (iii) grouped frequency distribution.
10. Write a program to read a simple sample of size n and compute the frequency of each element.

11. Write a program to read n numbers and compute its standard deviation.
12. Write a program to read a sample $(x_i, f_i), i = 1, 2, \ldots, n$, from a frequency distribution and compute (i) the standard deviation, (ii) the mean deviation (about mean), (iii) the mean deviation (about median), and (iv) quartile deviation.
13. Write a program to read a sample of size n and compute (i) the coefficient of variation, (ii) the coefficient of quartile deviation, and (iii) the coefficient of mean deviation (about mean and median).
14. Write a program to compute the first four moments of a sample about a specified number.
15. Write a program to compute first four central moments of a sample and hence, calculate the beta and gamma coefficients.
16. Write a program to compute the first (Q_1), second (Q_2) and third (Q_3) quartiles and use them to compute skewness and kurtosis.
17. Write a program to read a bivariate sample (x_i, y_i), $i = 1, 2, \ldots, n$, of size n. Calculate (i) covariance, (ii) standard deviations of x and y, and (iii) correlation coefficient.
18. Write a program to read a bivariate sample and calculate (i) the regression coefficients and (ii) the regression lines of y on x, and x on y.
19. Write a program to read a bivariate sample (x_i, y_i) of size n and fit it to
    (i) the straight line $y = a + bx$.
    (ii) the parabolic curve $y = a + bx + cx^2$.
    (ii) the geometric curve $y = ab^x$.
20. Write a program to read a multivariate sample $(x_{1\alpha}, x_{2\alpha}, x_{3\alpha})$ of size n and find a multivariate regression line of x_1 on x_2 and x_3.
21. Write a program to find multiple and partial correlation coefficients.
22. Write a function CC to compute correlation coefficient between two sets of data. Now, write a main program to read a multivariate sample $(x_{1\alpha}, x_{2\alpha}, x_{3\alpha})$ of size n and by using the function CC, compute the correlation coefficient between (i) x_1 and x_2, (ii) x_1 and x_3, and (iii) x_2 and x_3.
23. Write a program to read a univariate sample and check whether it fits to binomial distribution or not.
24. Write a program to read a univariate sample and fit it to a Poisson distribution. Calculate an absolute error.
25. Write a program to fit the straight line $x = a + by$ for a bivariate sample. Estimate the sum of the square of the errors.
26. Write a program to fit the rectangular parabola $y = \frac{1}{a+bx}$ for a bivariate sample.
27. Write a program to read a bivariate sample and fit it in the curve $y = ae^{bx}$. Also, estimate the sum of the square of errors.

28. Write an interactive menu based program to fit a bivariate sample to one of the following curves:
(i) linear curve ($y = a + bx$)
(ii) parabolic curve ($y = a + bx + cx^2$)
(iii) geometric curve ($y = ab^x$)
(iv) exponent curve ($y = ae^{bx}$).

Estimate the sum of square of errors.

29. Write a program to read a bivariate sample and test which of the following curves is more appropriate for this given sample.
(i) linear curve
(ii) parabolic curve
(iii) geometric curve
(iv) exponent curve.

[If the sum of the square of errors is minimum for a curve, then we say that this curve is more appropriate for this sample.]

30. Write a program to integrate a function using Monte-Carlo method.

Chapter 17

Quick References

17.1 Escape Sequences

Escape sequence	Character/use	ASCII value
`\a`	bell (alert)	007
`\b`	backspace	008
`\t`	horizontal tab	009
`\n`	newline (line feed)	010
`\v`	vertical tab	011
`\f`	form feed (new page)	012
`\r`	carriage return	013
`\"`	double quotation	034
`\'`	single quotation	039
`\?`	question mark	063
`\\`	backslash	092
`\0`	null	000

17.2 Key Words

auto	break	case	char	const	continue	default
do	double	else	enum	extern	float	for
goto	if	int	long	registrar	return	short
signed	sizeof	static	struct	switch	typedef	union
unsigned	void	volatile	while			

Some compilers may also support the following keywords.

`ada` `far` `near` `asm` `fortran` `pascal` `entry` `huge`

17.3 Operator Summary

Precedence Group	Operators	Associativity
function	( )	$L \rightarrow R$
array	[ ]	$L \rightarrow R$
structure member	.	$L \rightarrow R$
pointer to structure member	− >	$L \rightarrow R$
unary operators	−, ++, −−, !, , ∗, & ∼, `sizeof`, `(type)`	$R \rightarrow L$
arithmetic multiply, divide, remainder	*, /, %	$L \rightarrow R$
arithmetic add and subtract	+, −	$L \rightarrow R$
bitwise shift operators	<<, >>	$L \rightarrow R$
relational operators	<, <=, >, >=	$L \rightarrow R$
equality operators	==, ! =	$L \rightarrow R$
bitwise AND	&	$L \rightarrow R$
bitwise OR	|	$L \rightarrow R$
bitwise exclusive OR	^	$L \rightarrow R$
logical AND	&&	$L \rightarrow R$
logical OR	‖	$L \rightarrow R$
conditional operator	? :	$L \rightarrow R$
assignment operators	=, +=, − =, *=, /=, %= &=, ^=, | =, <<=, >>=	$R \rightarrow L$
comma operator		$L \rightarrow R$

17.4 Data Types

Data type	Description	Typical memory requirements
`char`	Single character	1 byte
`signed char`	Single character with numerical values from −128 to 127	1 byte
`unsigned char`	Single character with numerical values from 0 to 255	1 byte
`int`	Integer quantity	2 bytes or 1 word (varies from computer to computer)
`short int`	Short integer quantity	2 bytes or 1 word (varies from computer to computer)
`long int`	Long integer quantity	1 or 2 words (varies from computer to computer)
`unsigned int`	Unsigned (positive) integer quantity	2 bytes or 1 word (varies from computer to computer)
`float`	Floating-point number	1 word
`double`	Double-precision floating-point number	2 words
`long double`	Double-precision floating-point number	2 or more words
`void`	Special data type for function that do not return any value	no memory required
`enum`	Enumeration constant (special type of `int`)	2 bytes or 1 word

17.5 ASCII Character Set

ASCII value	Character	ASCII value	Character	ASCII value	Character	ASCII value	Character
000	NUL	032	blank	064	@	096	`
001	SOH	033	!	065	A	097	a
002	STX	034	”	066	B	098	b
003	ETX	035	#	067	C	099	c
004	EOT	036	$	068	D	100	d
005	ENQ	037	%	069	E	101	e
006	ACK	038	&	070	F	102	f
007	BEL	039	′	071	G	103	g
008	BS	040	(	072	H	104	h
009	HT	041	)	073	I	105	i
010	LF	042	*	074	J	106	j
011	VT	043	+	075	K	107	k
012	FF	044	’	076	L	108	l
013	CR	045	-	077	M	109	m
014	SO	046	.	078	N	110	n
015	SI	047	/	079	O	111	o
016	DLE	048	0	080	P	112	p
017	DC1	049	1	081	Q	113	q
018	DC2	050	2	082	R	114	r
019	DC3	051	3	083	S	115	s
020	DC4	052	4	084	T	116	t
021	NAK	053	5	085	U	117	u
022	SYN	054	6	086	V	118	v
023	ETB	055	7	087	W	119	w
024	CAN	056	8	088	X	120	x
025	EM	057	9	089	Y	121	y
026	SUB	058	:	090	Z	122	z
027	ESC	059	;	091	[	123	{
028	FS	060	<	092	\	124	|
029	GS	061	=	093	]	125	}
030	RS	062	>	094	↑	126	~
031	US	063	?	095	–	127	DEL

The ASCII Symbols

NUL	-	Null character	DLE	-	Data Link Escape
SOH	-	Start of Heading	DC	-	Device Control
STX	-	Start of Text	NAK	-	Negative Acknowledge
ETX	-	End of Text	SYN	-	Synchronous Idle
EOT	-	End of Transmission	ETB	-	End of Transmission Block
EQN	-	Enquiry	CAN	-	Cancel
ACK	-	Acknowledge	EM	-	End of Medium
BEL	-	Bell	SUB	-	Substitute
BS	-	Backspace	ESC	-	Escape
HT	-	Horizontal Tabulation	FS	-	File Separator
LF	-	Line Feed	GS	-	Groups Separator
VT	-	Vertical Tabulator	RS	-	Record Separator
FF	-	Form Feed	US	-	Unit Separator
CR	-	Carriage Return	SP	-	Space (Blank)
SO	-	Shift Out	DEL	-	Delete
SI	-	Shift In			

17.6 Control Statement Summary

Statement	General form	Example

break	`break;`	`do{`
		`    scanf("%d",&a);`
		`    if(a<0) break;`
		`    sum+=a;`
		`}while (++n<10);`

continue	`continue;`	`do{`
		`    scanf("%d",&a);`
		`    if(a==0) continue;`
		`    sum+=a;`
		`}while (++n<10);`

do-while	`do{`
	`    statements;`
	`}while(expression);`
		`do{`
		`    scanf("%d",&x);`
		`    count++;`
		`}while (count<=100);`

for	`for(exp1; exp2; exp3)`
	`    {`
	`    statements;`
	`    }`
		`for(i=1;i<=10;i++){`
		`    scanf("%d",&a);`
		`    sum+=a;`
		`    }`

goto	`goto label;`
	`...`
	`label:  statement`
		`if (d<=0)`
		`goto case3;`
		`...`
		`case3:  printf("Roots are`
		`complex");`

if	`if (expression)` `statement`	`if(d>=0)` `printf("Roots are real");`

if-else	`if (expression)`
	`    statement1`
	`else`
	`    statement2`
		`if(d>=0)`
		`    printf("Roots are real");`
		`else`
		`    printf("Roots are imaginary");`

return	`return (expression);`	`return (a+n);`

Statement	General form	Example

switch	`switch(expression) {`
	`case expression1:`
	`    statement1;`
	`    ......`
	`    break;`
	`case expression2:`
	`    statement1;`
	`    ......`
	`    break;`
	`......`
	`case default:`
	`    statement1;`
	`    ......`
	`}`
		`switch(k) {`
		`case 1:`
		`    p=x*x-5*x;`
		`    break;`
		`case 2:`
		`    p=2*x+2;`
		`    break;`
		`case 3:`
		`    p=x+1;`
		`    break;`
		`default:`
		`    p=0;`
		`}`

while	`while(expression){`
	`    statements`
	`}`
		`while(sum<100){`
		`    scanf("%d",&x);`
		`    sum+=x;`
		`}`

17.7 scanf and printf Conversion Characters

scanf conversion characters

Conversion character	Meaning
c	Data item is a single character
d	Data item is a decimal integer
f, g, G	Data item is a floating-point number
e, E	Data item is a floating-point number in exponent form
i	Data item is a decimal, octal or hexadecimal integer
o	Data item is an octal integer
x, X	Data item is a hexadecimal integer
u	Data item is an unsigned decimal integer
s	Data item is a string followed by the null character '\0'
[···]	Data item is a string which may include whitespace characters

The prefixes `h, l, L` are also used for short integer or short unsigned integer, long integer or long unsigned integer or double, and long double respectively.

For example, `hd, ld, Lf` are used to read short integer, long integer and long double respectively.

printf conversion characters

Conversion character	Meaning
c	Value is displayed as a single character
d	Value is displayed as a signed decimal integer
f	Value is displayed as a floating-point number without an exponent
e, E	Value is displayed as a floating-point number with an exponent
g, G	Value is displayed as a floating-point number using either e-type or f-type conversion, depending on the value
i	Value is displayed as a signed decimal integer
o	Value is displayed as an octal integer, without a leading zero
x, X	Value is displayed as a hexadecimal integer, without a leading ox
u	Value is displayed as an unsigned decimal integer
s	Value is displayed as a string

Here the prefixes `h, l, L` are used for short integer or short unsigned integer, long integer or long unsigned integer or double, and long double respectively.

Flags used in printf

Flag	Meaning
−	Value is displayed with left justified within the filed (blank spaces are used to fill the remaining positions of the field)
+	A sign (either + or −) will displays precede each signed numerical value.
0	Displays leading zeros instead of leading blanks. Applicable only to data items which are right justified within a field whose minimum size is larger than the data item.
#	Displays `0` and `0x` at the beginning of octal and hexadecimal data items, respectively. With `o` and `x` type conversion.
#	Displays a decimal point in all floating-point numbers, even if the data item is a whole number. With `e`, `f` and `g` type conversion.

17.8 Header Files

Header file	Description
alloc.h	Declares memory management functions (allocation, deallocation, etc.).
bios.h	Declares various functions used in calling IBM-PC ROM BIOS routines.
conio.h	Declares various functions used in calling the DOS console I/O routines.
ctype.h	Contains information used by the character classification and character conversion macros.
dir.h	Contains structures, macros, and functions for working with directories and path names.
dos.h	Defines various constants and gives declarations needed for DOS and 8086-specific calls.
float.h	Contains parameters for floating-point routines.
graphics.h	Declares prototypes for the graphics functions.
io.h	Contains structures and declarations for low-level input/output routines.
limits.h	Contains environmental parameters, information about compile-time limitations, and ranges of integral quantities.
malloc.h	Memory management functions and variables.
math.h	Declares prototypes for the math functions, defines the macro HUGE_VAL, and declares the exception structure used by matherr.
stdio.h	Define types and macros needed for the Standard I/O Package defined in Kernighan and Ritchie and extended under UNIX System V. Defines the standard I/O predefined streams stdin, stdout, stdprn, and stderr, and declares stream-level I/O routines.
stdlib.h	Declares several commonly used routines: conversion routines, search/sort routines, and others.
string.h	Declares several string- and memory-manipulation routines.
time.h	Defines a structure filled in by the time-conversion routines, and a type used by other time routines; also provides prototypes for these routines.
values.h	Defines important constants, including machine dependencies; provided for UNIX System V compatibility.

17.9 Some C Constants

The following constants are available in the header file `limits.h`. These are related to the integer type data.

Name	Meaning	
CHAR_BIT	8	Number of bits in a `char`
CHAR_MAX	255	Maximum value of `char`
CHAR_MIN	0	Minimum value of `char`
INT_MAX	+32767	Maximum value of `int`
INT_MIN	−32767	Minimum value of `int`
LONG_MAX	+2147483647	Maximum value of `long`
LONG_MIN	−2147483647	Minimum value of `long`
SCHAR_MAX	+127	Maximum value of `signed char`
SCHAR_MIN	−127	Minimum value of `signed char`
SHRT_MAX	+32767	Maximum value of `short`
SHRT_MIN	−32767	Minimum value of `short`
UCHAR_MAX	255	Maximum value of `unsigned char`
UINT_MAX	65535	Maximum value of `unsigned int`
ULONG_MAX	4294967295	Maximum value of `unsigned long`
USHRT_MAX	65535	Maximum value of `unsigned short`

The constants related to the floating-point arithmetic are available in `float.h` as listed below.

Name	Meaning	
FLT_RADIX	2	Radix of exponent representation
FLT_ROUNDS		Floating-point rounding mode for addition
FLT_DIG	6	Decimal digits of precision
FLT_EPSILON	1E−5	Smallest number x such that 1.0+x is not equal to 1.0
FLT_MANT_DIG		Number of base `FLT_RADIX` digits in mantissa
FLT_MAX	1E+37	Maximum floating-point number
FLT_MAX_EXP		Maximum n such that `FLT_RADIX`^{n}`-1` is representable
FLT_MIN	1E−37	Minimum normalized floating-point number
FLT_MIN_EXP		Minimum n such that 10^n is a normalized number
DBL_DIG	10	Decimal digits of precision
DBL_EPSILON	1E−9	Smallest number x such that 1.0+x is not equal to 1.0
DBL_MANT_DIG		Number of base `FLT_RADIX` digits in mantissa
DBL_MAX	1E+37	Maximum double floating-point number
DBL_MAX_EXP		Maximum n such that `FLT_RADIX`^{n}`-1` is representable
DBL_MIN	1E−37	Minimum normalized double floating-point number
DBL_MIN_EXP		Minimum n such that 10^n is a normalized number

17.10 Library Functions

The arguments of the functions are denoted as follows:

c	character-type argument	d	double-precision argument
i	integer argument	f	file argument
l	long integer argument	p	pointer argument
s	string argument	u	unsigned integer argument
*	pointer argument		

Function	Type	Purpose	Header file
abs(i)	int	Return the absolute value of i	stdlib.h
acos(d)	double	Return the value of $\cos^{-1} d$	math.h
asctime(l)	char*	Convert date and time to ASCII	time.h
asin(d)	double	Return the value of $\sin^{-1} d$	math.h
atan(d)	double	Return the value of $\tan^{-1} d$	math.h
atan2(d1,d2)	double	Return the value of $\tan^{-1}(d1/d2)$	math.h
atof(s)	double	Convert the string s to a double-precession quantity	stdlib.h
atoi(s)	int	Convert the string s to an integer	stdlib.h
atol(s)	long	Convert the string s to a long integer	stdlib.h
calloc(u1,u2)	void*	Allocate memory for an array containing u1 elements, each of length u2 bytes	malloc.h or stdlib.h
ceil(d)	double	Return a value rounded up to the next higher integer	math.h
clock()	long int	Return the processor time elapsed since the beginning of the program invocation	time.h
cos(d)	double	Return the value of $\cos d$	math.h
cosh(d)	double	Return the value of $\cosh d$	math.h
ctime(l)	char*	Convert date and time to string	time.h
difftime(l1,l2)	double	Return the time difference l1-l2, where l1 and l2 represent elapsed time beyond a designated base time	time.h
exit(u)	void	Close all files and buffers, and terminate the program	stdlib.h

Function	Type	Purpose	Header file
exp(d)	double	Return the value of e^d	math.h
fabs(d)	double	Return the absolute value of d	math.h
fclose(f)	int	Close the file f. Return 0, if the file is successfully closed.	stdio.h
feof(f)	int	Return a non-zero value, if the end-of-condition has been reached, otherwise return 0.	stdio.h
ferror(f)	int	Return a non-zero integer if an error is detected in the named stream, 0 otherwise	stdio.h
fgetc(f)	int	Enter a single character from the file f.	stdio.h
fgetpos(f)	int	Get the current file pointer	stdio.h
fgets(s,i,f)	char*	Enter string s, containing i characters, from the file f.	stdio.h
floor(d)	double	Return a value rounded down to the next lower integer.	math.h
fmod(d1,d2)	double	Return the remainder of $d1/d2$.	math.h
fopen(s1,s2)	file*	Open a file named s1 of type s2 and return a pointer to the file.	stdio.h
fprintf(f,...)	int	Send the values of the variables to the file f.	stdio.h
fputc(c,f)	int	Send a single character c to the file f.	stdio.h
fputs(s,f)	int	Send a string s to the file f.	stdio.h
fread(s,i1,i2,f)	int	Read i2 data item each of size i1 from file f to the string s.	stdio.h
free(p)	void	Free a block of memory whose initial address is p.	malloc.h or stdlib.h
frexp(d,i)	double	Split a double number into its mantissa and exponent	math.h
fscanf(f,...)	int	Read data item from the file f.	stdio.h
fseek(f,l,i)	int	Move the pointer for the file f at a distance l byte from the position i, (i represents the beginning, current position or end of the file).	stdio.h
fstat(i,l)	int	Return file statistics	sys\stat.h
ftell(f)	long int	Return the current pointer position within the file f.	stdio.h

Function	Type	Purpose	Header file
fwrite(s,i1,i2,f)	int	Send i2 data item each of size i1 bytes from the string s to file f.	stdio.h
getc(f)	int	Enter a single character from file f	stdio.h
getchar()	int	Enter a single character from the keyboard	stdio.h
gets(s)	char*	Enter string s from the standard input device	stdio.h
isalnum(c)	int	Return a non-zero value, if c is alphanumeric, 0 otherwise	ctype.h
isalpha(c)	int	Return a non-zero value, if c is alphabet, 0 otherwise	ctype.h
isascii(c)	int	Return a non-zero value, if c is ASCII character, 0 otherwise	ctype.h
iscntrl(c)	int	Return a non-zero value, if c is ASCII control character, 0 otherwise	ctype.h
isdigit(c)	int	Return a non-zero value, if c is a decimal digit, 0 otherwise	ctype.h
isgraph(c)	int	Return a non-zero value, if c is a graphic ASCII character, 0 otherwise	ctype.h
islower(c)	int	Return a non-zero value, if c is a lower case alphabet, 0 otherwise	ctype.h
isodigit(c)	int	Return a non-zero value, if c is an octal digit, 0 otherwise	ctype.h
isprint(c)	int	Return a non-zero value, if c is a printing ASCII character, 0 otherwise	ctype.h
ispunct(c)	int	Return a non-zero value, if c is a punctuation character, 0 otherwise	ctype.h
isspace(c)	int	Return a non-zero value, if c is a white space character, 0 otherwise	ctype.h
isupper(c)	int	Return a non-zero value, if c is an upper case alphabet, 0 otherwise	ctype.h
isxdigit(c)	int	Return a non-zero value, if c is a hexadecimal digit, 0 otherwise	ctype.h
labs(l)	long int	Return the absolute value, of l	math.h
ldexp(d,i)	double	Return the value of $d * 2^i$	math.h

Function	Type	Purpose	Header file
`log(d)`	`double`	Return the natural logarithm of `d`	`math.h`
`log10(d)`	`double`	Return the logarithm (base 10) of `d`	`math.h`
`malloc(u)`	`void*`	Allocate `u` bytes of memory and return a pointer to the beginning of the allocated space	`stdlib.h` or `malloc.hq`
`pow(d1,d2)`	`double`	Return the value of $d1^{d2}$	`math.h`
`printf(...)`	`int`	Send data item to the video screen	`stdio.h`
`putc(c,f)`	`int`	Send a single character `c` to the file `f`	`stdio.h`
`putchar(c)`	`int`	Send a single character `c` to the video screen	`stdio.h`
`puts(s)`	`int`	Send the string `s` to the video screen	`stdio.h`
`rand()`	`int`	Return a random number (a positive integer)	`stdlib.h`
`realloc(i)`	`void`	Attempt to shrink or expand the previously allocated block	`stdlib.h`
`remove(s)`	`int`	Delete the file specified by `s`	`stdlib.h`
`rename(s1,s2)`	`int`	Change the name of a file from `s1` to `s2`	`stdlib.h`
`rewind(f)`	`void`	Move the file pointer to the beginning of file `f`	`stdio.h`
`rmdir(s)`	`int`	Return 0, if the directory `s` is successfully deleted	`stdlib.h`
`scanf(...)`	`int`	Enter data item from keyboard	`stdio.h`
`sin(d)`	`double`	Return the value of $\sin d$	`math.h`
`sinh(d)`	`double`	Return the value of $\sinh d$	`math.h`
`sprintf(...)`	`int`	Write the formatted output to a string	`stdio.h`
`sqrt(d)`	`double`	Return the square root of d	`math.h`
`srand(u)`	`void`	Initialize the random number generator	`stdlib.h`
`sscanf(...)`	`int`	Scan and format input from a string	`stdio.h`
`strcat(s1,s2)`	`char*`	Append the string `s2` to the end of the string `s1`	`string.h`
`strchr(s,c)`	`char*`	Return a pointer to the first occurrence of the character `c` in `s`	`string.h`
`strcmp(s1,s2)`	`int`	Compare two strings `s1` and `s2`. Return 0, if `s1==s2`, negative value, if `s1<s2` and positive value, if `s1>s2`	`string.h`

Function	Type	Purpose	Header file
strcpy(s1,s2)	char*	Copy s2 to the string s1	string.h
strlen(s)	int	Return the number of characters in the string s	string.h
strncat(s1,s2,i)	char*	Append at most i characters of the string s2 to the end of the string s1	string.h
strncmp(s1,s2,i)	int	Compare i characters of the string s1 with the string s2	string.h
strncpy(s1,s2,i)	char*	Copy at most i characters from s2 to the string s1	string.h
strrchr(s,i)	char*	Return a pointer to the last occurrence of the character c	string.h
strspn(s1,s2)	double	Return the length of the initial segment of s1, which consists entirely the characters from s2	string.h
strset(s,c)	char*	Set all characters within s to c except null character	string.h
strstr(s1,s2)	char*	Return a pointer to the element in s1 where s2 begins	string.h
strtod(s)	double	Return the value of s as a double	string.h
system(s)	int	Pass command s to the operating system. Return 0, if the command is successfully executed, otherwise return a non-zero value	stdlib.h
tan(d)	double	Return the value of tan d	math.h
tanh(d)	double	Return the value of tanh d	math.h
time(p)	long int	Return the number of second elapsed	time.h
toascii(c)	int	Return the ASCII value of the character c	ctype.h
tolower(c)	int	Convert the character c to lower case character	ctype.h or stdlib.h
toupper(c)	int	Convert the character c to upper case character	ctype.h or stdlib.h

Bibliography

[1] Balagurusamy, E., *Programming in ANSI C, 4ed*, Tata McGraw-Hill, 2009.

[2] Barkakati, N., *Microsoft C Bible*, SAMS, 1990.

[3] Barker, L., *C Tools for Scientists and Engineers*, McGraw-Hill, 1989.

[4] Borland International, *Turbo C/C++ User's Guide.*

[5] Gottfried, B., *Programming with C, 2ed*, Tata McGraw-Hill Edition, 2001.

[6] Hancock, L. and Krieger, M., *The C Primer*, McGraw-Hill, 1987.

[7] Hunt, W.J., *The C Toolbox*, Addison-Wesley, 1985.

[8] Hunter, B.H., *Understanding C*, Sybex, 1985.

[9] Kernighan, B.W. and Ritchie, D.M., *The C Programming Language*, Prentice-Hall, 1977.

[10] Kochan, S.G., *Programming in C*, Hyden, 1983.

[11] Miller, L.H. and Quilici, E.A., *C Programming Language: An Applied Perspective*, John Wiley & Sons, 1987.

[12] Pal, M., *Numerical Analysis for Scientists and Engineers*, Narosa Publishing House and Alpha Science, 2006.

[13] Pal, M., *Fortran 77 with Numerical and Statistical Analysis, 2ed*, Asian Books Pvt. Ltd. 2002.

[14] Radcliffe, R.A. *C Encyclopedia*, Sybex, 1990.

[15] Schildt, H, *C Made Easy*, Osborne McGraw-Hill, 1987.

[16] Schildt, H, *Advanced C*, Osborne McGraw-Hill, 1988.

[17] Schildt, H, *C: The Complete Reference*, McGraw-Hill, 2000.

[18] Tim Grady, M., *Turbo C Programming Principles and Practices*, MsGraw-Hill, 1989.

[19] Venugopal, K.R., and Prasad, S.R., *Programming with C*, Tata McGraw-Hill, 2005.

[20] WSI Staff, *C User's Handbook*, Addison-Wesley, 1984.

[21] Wortman, L.A., and Sidebottom, T.O., *The C Programming Tutor*, Prentice-Hall, 1984.

[22] Wikipedia, the free encyclopedia.

[23] http://mathworld.wolfram.com

Index